D1197115

Marxism
and Totality

Marxism
and Totality

*The Adventures of a Concept
from Lukács to Habermas*

Martin Jay

UNIVERSITY OF CALIFORNIA PRESS
Berkeley · Los Angeles

An earlier version of Chapter 7 appeared in *Theory and Society* 11 (January 1982).

University of California Press
Berkeley and Los Angeles, California

Library of Congress Cataloging in Publication Data
Jay, Martin, 1944–
    Marxism and totality.

    Bibliography: p.
    Includes index.
    1. Communism and philosophy—History.   2. Whole and
parts (Philosophy)   3. Holism.   4. Marx, Karl, 1818–1883.
I. Title.
HX533.J39   1984   335.4'11   83-17950
ISBN 0-520-05096-7

For Cathy

Contents

Acknowledgments   ix

Introduction: The Topography of
    Western Marxism   1

1. The Discourse of Totality Before
    Western Marxism   21
2. Georg Lukács and the Origins of the Western
    Marxist Paradigm   81
3. The Revolutionary Historicism of Karl Korsch   128
4. The Two Holisms of Antonio Gramsci   150
5. Ernst Bloch and the Extension of Marxist Holism
    to Nature   174
6. Max Horkheimer and the Retreat from
    Hegelian Marxism   196
7. Anamnestic Totalization: Memory in the
    Thought of Herbert Marcuse   220
8. Theodor W. Adorno and the Collapse of the
    Lukácsian Concept of Totality   241
9. Henri Lefebvre, the Surrealists and the Reception
    of Hegelian Marxism in France   276
10. Totality and Marxist Aesthetics: The Case of
    Lucien Goldmann   300

11. From Totality to Totalization: The Existentialist
      Marxism of Jean-Paul Sartre   331
12. Phenomenological Marxism: The Ambiguities of
      Maurice Merleau-Ponty's Holism   361
13. Louis Althusser and the Structuralist Reading
      of Marx   385
14. Scientific Marxism in Postwar Italy: Galvano
      Della Volpe and Lucio Colletti   423
15. Jürgen Habermas and the Reconstruction of
      Marxist Holism   462

      Epilogue: The Challenge of Post-Structuralism   510

      Selected Bibliography   539

      Index   547

Acknowledgments

It is never easy to pinpoint the moment when a book is conceived, but if one could be singled out for *Marxism and Totality*, it would have to be the day in September, 1969, when *Barron's*, the Dow Jones weekly newspaper, emblazoned its front page with the headline "Total Break with America." These defiant words were quoted from a talk at the fifth annual Social Scholars Conference held earlier that month at Hofstra University. The full quotation, which was repeated several times in the article and placed in a special box alongside equally inflammatory remarks by Ralph Schoenman and Robin Blackburn, read: "Our movement is a movement which, in effect, is a total break with America." Sentiments of this kind were, to be sure, not very unusual in the late 1960s, but what made them catch my eye was the fact that they were attributed to "Socialist Scholar Martin Jay."

To be featured so prominently in *Barron's* pathetic attempt to depict the handful of leftist academics at the conference as a serious threat to the American way of life was something of an honor. But, alas, it was an undeserved one. For although the words "total break with America" had indeed passed my lips, they were uttered in reference to an earlier remark by one of my predecessors on a panel devoted to the work of Herbert Marcuse. Rather than boasting that "our movement" was a "total break with America," I was in fact voicing my concern with the counter-productive rhetorical excess I saw in so global and sweeping a repudiation of everything that the word "America" suggested. The befuddled reporter from *Barron's* had thus credited me with upholding precisely the view I was trying to challenge.

The upshot of this episode was relatively harmless: unearned praise from my more radical friends and a few tense moments with one of my professors at Harvard, whose confidence in my scholarly promise had to be gradually restored. But in retrospect, *Barron's* blunder does seem to have had a long-term impact on my intellectual career. For in evoking the apocalyptic power of the image of a "total break," both for the radicals who espoused it and the conservatives it so frightened, the misquotation alerted me to the importance of totality in Marxist (and anti-Marxist) discourse. Thus, my first acknowledgment of gratitude must be extended to the stalwarts of responsible journalism at the Dow Jones weekly.

In the years since that headline appeared, I have incurred considerably more substantial debts that require a far less whimsical word of thanks. To begin where Marxist analyses traditionally do, with my material base of support, I have received generous financial assistance from the John Simon Guggenheim Foundation, the National Endowment for the Humanities, and the University of California Committee on Research. St. Antony's College, Oxford, graciously provided me a physical and collegial home when I was doing my initial research in 1974–75, and the University of Denver History Department was no less hospitable when I began to write in 1979–1980. The staff of the Institute of International Relations at Berkeley, most notably Peggy Nelson, cheerfully and competently typed the manuscript when the writing was done.

My personal debts are even more extensive and pleasing to record. Over the years, excellent research assistance has been provided by Herrick Chapman, Steven Light, Stephen Treuer, Michael Bess, and Lois Pryor. My colleagues in the Berkeley History Department have been unfailingly supportive of my work in a wide variety of ways. The shifting cast of characters in the Berkeley *Telos* group has helped me sharpen my ideas about many of the issues raised in the book. And I have benefited from my association with *Theory and Society*, whose founding editor, the late Alvin Gouldner, would have discovered many of his ideas scattered through my pages.

Several of the figures about whom I have written, Lucio Colletti, Michel Foucault, and Jürgen Habermas, kindly answered my questions either by mail or in person, as did Annie Goldmann, the widow of another. Friends who are themselves among the leading scholars of Western Marxism have read either part of or, in several especially hardy cases, the entire manuscript. In the former group are Alison Brown, Jean Cohen, Fred Dallmayr, Andrew Feenberg, Mary Evans, Maurice Finnochiaro, David Gross, Wayne Hudson, Barry Kātz, Paul Rabinow, Robert Resch, Gian

Enrico Rusconi, Gershon Schafir, Paul Piccone, Trent Schroyer, and Richard Wolin. The latter include Eugene Lunn, Mark Poster, and Paul Thomas. Their keen analytic scrutiny and remarkable knowledge of the material helped spare me many embarrassments. A special acknowledgment, however, must go to a deeply valued friend who read the entire manuscript not only with the eye of a scholar, but also with the passionate interest of someone who had participated in the intellectual events it recorded. What Herbert Marcuse wrote in the acknowledgments of his last book, *The Aesthetic Dimension*, can be repeated here without any emendation: "Leo Lowenthal has again proved his reputation as a fierce reader and critic."

I also would like to thank Alain Hénon of the University of California Press for his enthusiasm and encouragement from the moment I contacted him about the project. Not the least of his contributions was his assigning the manuscript to two extremely helpful readers, Walter Adamson and Paul Breines, whose astute comments helped refine my argument in important ways. No less helpful was the U.C. Press copyeditor, Kate Gross. I am also deeply grateful to Michael Bess and Lawrence Frohman for the arduous task of preparing the book's index.

Far less intellectual or professional in nature, but no less essential, is the debt I have incurred over the long gestation period of this book to members of my family. My parents, Edward and Sari Jay, and sister, Beth Jay, were consistently supportive in the ways that fortunate sons and brothers know so well. Although my father did not live to see the book's completion, I think he knew that I count myself in that company. My stepdaughter Shana, who was present when the research began, and daughter Rebecca, who arrived halfway through its completion, found other means of lightening my load, if on occasion they may have seemed to be doing the opposite. I hope they will come to forgive me for all the times totality prevented me from responding to their particular needs.

Finally, I have to record a unique debt that is at once material, intellectual and deeply personal. Catherine Gallagher, to whom this book is lovingly dedicated, has been its companion as well as my own ever since it began. Those who know her will see many of her strengths reflected in its pages.

Introduction:
The Topography of Western Marxism

There are no easy ways to map the rugged and shifting terrain of the intellectual territory known as Western Marxism. Indeed, its very boundaries and most prominent features have themselves been the source of heated dispute.[1] Most commentators have followed the lead of Maurice Merleau-Ponty, who in his 1955 study *Adventures of the Dialectic* popularized the term to designate the body of thought generated thirty-two years earlier by Georg Lukács' heterodox masterpiece, *History and Class Consciousness.*[2] For Merleau-Ponty and those who adopted his usage, Western

1. Much of the controversy was sparked by Perry Anderson's *Considerations on Western Marxism* (London, 1976). See, for example, the critical reviews by Jeffrey Herf in *Socialist Revolution* 7:5 (September–October 1977); Richard D. Wolff in *Monthly Review* 30:4 (September 1978); and Paul Piccone in *Telos* 30 (Winter 1976–77). See also my response to Piccone in *Telos* 32 (Summer 1977) and the rebuttal by Piccone and Andrew Arato in the same issue. With all of the confusion over its meaning, it is not surprising to find Stanley Aronowitz conclude in his recent book, *The Crisis in Historical Materialism: Class, Politics and Culture in Marxist Theory* (New York, 1981):

The term "Western" Marxism is a signifier that connotes no particular body of doctrine. Its historical function has been linked to the anti-Leninist movements of this century both as the object of accusation and, less often, a self-description of a melange of dissenters. Its theoretical status is not only ambiguous, it is problematic. (p. xiii)

An even clearer expression of uncertainty over the term's meaning appears in an article by Tom Long, "Marx and Western Marxism in the 1970s," *Berkeley Journal of Sociology* 24 (1980), where the author uses "Western Marxism" to include figures like Michel Foucault and Jacques Derrida with the explanation:

I shall use "Western Marxism" to refer to certain self-proclaimed Marxists as well as certain self-proclaimed non-Marxists since Lukács who have in some important way taken up the challenge of Marx by probing the strengths and weaknesses of his theory from the perspective of the possibility of human emancipation. (p. 57)

2. Maurice Merleau-Ponty, *Adventures of the Dialectic,* trans. Joseph Bien (Evanston, 1973). The term's first use can be traced back to the polemical attack on Lukács and Korsch in 1923 by the Comintern. See the reference in Karl Korsch, *Marxism and Philosophy,* trans.

Marxism was thus identified solely with a subterranean tradition of humanist, subjectivist and undogmatic Marxism that was the negation of its official Soviet (or Eastern) counterpart. The latter had been turned into a doctrinaire ideology of legitimation by a tyrannical regime, whereas Western Marxism, nowhere in power, had retained the libertarian, emancipatory hopes of the socialist tradition.

In its Merleau-Pontyan version, the reason Western Marxism had preserved those hopes lay in its challenge to the scientific self-understanding of its orthodox rivals. Rather than trying to ape the methods of bourgeois science, Western Marxism recognized its true origins in the tradition of philosophical critique that began with Kant and German Idealism.[3] In the vivid language of one of its most celebrated founders, Antonio Gramsci, Western Marxism demanded a revolution "against *Capital*,"[4] that is, against the false belief that objective economic laws would automatically bring about the collapse of capitalism and the victory of the proletariat. Philosophical critique showed instead that radical change could come only when human action overthrew the man-made structures oppressing mankind.

Western Marxism, in this reading, was therefore opposed not only to the fatalistic economism of the Second International, but also to the voluntarist vanguardism of the Third. In contrast to both, it insisted that true praxis was a collective expression of self-emancipation involving all of mankind. The reawakening of the potential for such a collective subject was thus a central preoccupation of the Western Marxists who represented what another early exponent, Ernst Bloch, liked to call the "warm" rather than "cold" current of socialism.

Because Lukács, Gramsci, Bloch and others in the Western Marxist camp insisted on the importance of Marx's debt to Hegel, Western Marx-

---

with intro. Fred Halliday (New York and London, 1970), pp. 119–20. But it was not until Merleau-Ponty's work that the term became widely used. Here, too, there was some controversy over its meaning. See, for example, Raymond Aron, *Marxism and the Existentialists*, trans. Helen Weaver et al. (New York, 1969), p. 64, where it is claimed that "Western Marxism was in fact the Marxism of the Second International."

3. For an identification of Western Marxism exclusively with Critical rather than Scientific Marxism, see Alvin W. Gouldner, *The Two Marxisms: Contradictions and Anomalies in the Development of Theory* (New York, 1980); for a critique of some of the problems with this identification, see Martin Jay, "For Gouldner: Reflections on an Outlaw Marxist," *Theory and Society* 11:6 (November 1982).

4. Antonio Gramsci, "The Revolution Against *Capital*" in *History, Philosophy and Culture in the Young Gramsci*, eds. Pedro Cavalcanti and Paul Piccone (St. Louis, 1975). Gramsci, it should be noted, was not contrasting "Western" and "Eastern" Marxism in this essay, which in fact is about the Bolshevik Revolution. His real target was the political quietism of the Second International.

ism in this view has often been equated with Hegelian Marxism. The recovery of Marx's early writings in the late 1920s and the subsequent publication of the *Grundrisse* a generation later helped strengthen this
equation, as they demonstrated for many that Marx had indeed been
what Lukács and the others had said he was: a radical Hegelian. Accordingly, such terms as alienation, mediation, objectification, and reification
were understood to have a special place in the lexicon of Western Marxism. Culture, defined both widely as the realm of everyday life and narrowly as man's most noble artistic and intellectual achievements, was also
a central concern of the tradition, which tended as a result to neglect the
economy and, at times, politics. Western Marxism, therefore, meant a
Marxism that was far more dialectical than materialist, at least as those
terms were traditionally understood.

Defined in this way, Western Marxism was created by a loose circle of
theorists who took their cue from Lukács and the other founding fathers
of the immediate post–World War I era, Antonio Gramsci, Karl Korsch
and Ernst Bloch. Included in their number were the members of the
Frankfurt School, notably Max Horkheimer, Theodor W. Adorno, Herbert Marcuse, Leo Lowenthal and Walter Benjamin; the French Hegelian
Marxists Henri Lefebvre and Lucien Goldmann; and the existentialist
Marxists, Jean-Paul Sartre and Maurice Merleau-Ponty. Certain other
figures were frequently admitted to their ranks, in particular Bertolt
Brecht, Wilhelm Reich, Erich Fromm, the Council Communists in Holland, the *Arguments* group in France, and second-generation Frankfurt
School members like Jürgen Habermas and Alfred Schmidt. And still others like Alfred Sohn-Rethel, Leo Kofler, Franz Jakubowsky, Claude Lefort
and Cornelius Castoriadis were sometimes candidates for inclusion.

This traditional conception of Western Marxism has generally been held
by both its friends and enemies.[5] Or at least it was until the publication of
Perry Anderson's *Considerations on Western Marxism* in 1976.[6] For An-
derson, who writes from an Anglo-Trotskyist perspective outside the tradi-
tion, Western Marxism should also include the anti-Hegelian critics of
Marxist Humanism who came to prominence in Italy and France after
World War II, the schools of Galvano Della Volpe and Louis Althusser.
Rather than contending that critical and scientific Marxists are two sepa-

5. For examples of its enemies who use it in this way, see Lucio Colletti, *Marxism and
Hegel*, trans. Lawrence Garner (London, 1973), p. 189; and Neil McInnes, *The Western
Marxists* (London, 1972), which twists many of Colletti's arguments in a crudely anti-
Marxist direction, thus anticipating Colletti's own later use of them.

6. See note 1. Anderson's book was intended as the opening essay for a collection of
articles on Western Marxism, which the *New Left Review* then published independently as
Western Marxism: A Critical Reader (London, 1977).

rate breeds, one calling for a revolution against *Capital* and the other defending its continued relevance, Anderson argues that certain shared characteristics allow them to be placed roughly in a common camp.

Although one might justifiably question Anderson's choice of precisely who belongs to this enlarged camp—he ignores, for example, Bloch, Reich and Habermas, as well as all English Marxists[7]—his general point does seem to be well taken. Far too much has occurred both in theory and in practice since 1955 to permit us to remain content with Merleau-Ponty's initial definition. To help us decide who should be included under the rubric now, Wittgenstein's notion of "family resemblances" tells us that no perfectly uniform set of characteristics need be found to identify members of a collective entity. Insofar as both neo-Hegelians and anti-Hegelians share certain other traits that cut across their antagonism over Marx's debt to German Idealism, they can be understood as cousins, if not brothers, in an extended family. When compared with other Marxist traditions, such as Social Democracy, Austro-Marxism, Stalinism, Trotskyism or Maoism, these commonalities become more obvious. In acknowledging them, we can discern certain unexpected alliances that cut across the boundary determined solely by their attitudes toward Hegel or humanism. We will also avoid the petty sectarianism of those who jealously guard the purity of their version of the tradition against all the rest.

The most obvious common denominator among Western Marxists is that all were born or came of intellectual age in continental Western Europe. This sets them apart from the generation of Marxist intellectuals maturing directly before World War I, typified by Lenin, Luxemburg, Hilferding, Bukharin, Trotsky, and Bauer, who had less direct contact with Western European intellectual traditions. Apparent exceptions, such as Lukács, born in Hungary, and Goldmann, originally from Rumania,

---

7. The exclusion of English Marxists like Maurice Dobb, Christopher Caudwell, Maurice Cornforth, Eric Hobsbawm, Christopher Hill and Raymond Williams is a source of particular chagrin to Richard Wolff in his review of Anderson in *Monthly Review* 30:4 (p. 56). Insofar as the introduction of continental thought to England by Anderson and his *New Left Review* colleagues was intended as, and understood by its targets to be, a corrective to the insularity of British Marxism, it is appropriate to distinguish Western from Anglo-Marxism, at least until the 1970s. The ongoing polemic between Anderson and E. P. Thompson demonstrates many of the tensions between the two traditions. See E. P. Thompson, *The Poverty of Theory and Other Essays* (New York, 1978) and Perry Anderson, *Arguments Within English Marxism* (London, 1980).

One very important distinction between continental and English Marxism was, in fact, the far greater importance accorded by the former to the concept of totality. Aside from several suggestive references to culture as a "whole way of life" in the early work of Williams, totality did not really enter the English debate until the Althusserian wave of the 1970s. Many English Marxists were historians with that discipline's characteristic distaste for generalizing concepts.

can be included by virtue of the German and French contexts in which they matured intellectually. Although the influence of Hungarian intellectuals, such as the poet Endre Ady and the syndicalist Ervin Szabó, can be detected on the early Lukács, his most formative philosophical experiences occurred in Heidelberg in the 1910s. And even though he spent most of his later life in Budapest and Moscow, the impact of his work was felt far more keenly in Western than in Eastern Europe. As for Goldmann, his most significant intellectual training took place in Paris and Geneva, not the Bucharest which he left when he was only twenty. A third possible exception to the rule, Louis Althusser, was born in Algeria, but he was schooled in Marseilles and Paris. The other major Western Marxists, both Hegelian and anti-Hegelian, were born and intellectually nurtured in France, Italy, and Germany, although a number came to spend several years in American exile during the fascist era. (Significantly, of those forced to emigrate only Lukács went eastward.)

The impact of that period combined with subsequent translations of major works meant that American outposts of Western Marxism had developed by the 1960s. But on the whole, their occupants merely absorbed and adapted ideas that had been developed in Europe over the previous half century. A similar situation prevailed in England, where the *New Left Review* was the major conduit of continental ideas. The same derivative status may be accorded the reception of Western Marxist ideas in the countries under Soviet control after the Second World War. Although such thinkers as the Polish philosopher Leszek Kolakowski (during this Marxist Humanist phase) and the Czech philosopher Karel Kosík were certainly important in their own right, their work was nonetheless built upon the earlier thought of Western Marxists, as was that of the Yugoslav theoreticians published in the journal *Praxis*.[8]

Western Marxism also earned its name through the doggedly consistent Eurocentrism of most of its adherents, both Hegelian and anti-Hegelian. Walter Benjamin's suicide on the brink of his departure from Europe for America in 1940 may be seen as an idiosyncratically extreme expression of that inclination. But many of those who did emigrate

8. The concept of totality was particularly important in the work of Kosík. See especially Karel Kosík, *Dialectics of the Concrete: A Study on Problems of Man and World,* trans. Karel Kovanda with James Schmidt (Dordrecht, 1976). It was also frequently used by contributors to *Praxis*. See the discussion in Gerson S. Sher, *Praxis: Marxist Criticism and Dissent in Socialist Yugoslavia* (London, 1977), p. 84f. One should also mention the so-called Budapest School that developed around Lukács in his later years, the members of which, in most cases, were forced into exile after his death. Its most notable figures are Agnes Heller, Ferenc Feher, György Márkus, Maria Márkus, Mihály Vajda and Andras Hegedüs. As would be expected, the concept of totality often played a key role in their work.

to America—Horkheimer, Adorno, Bloch, Brecht—returned home at the first opportunity.

Although impressed and troubled by the example of the Russian Revolution, whose implications they heatedly debated for decades, the Western Marxists remained true to Marx's expectation that a genuine socialist revolution could succeed only in the most advanced capitalist societies. If occasionally finding something to praise in the Chinese Revolution, they rarely derived anything of real theoretical substance from the thoughts of its revered leader.[9] And even though they staunchly supported the process of decolonization, few believed global revolution could be led by the emerging Third World.

Geographically, then, Western Marxism can be located in continental Western Europe, even though certain of its members spent considerable amounts of time elsewhere. Temporally, the pattern is somewhat more complicated. Anderson suggests that it may be divided into two or possibly three generations: those born in the fifteen years before the turn of the century, who were radicalized by the First World War and its aftermath— Lukács (b. 1885), Bloch (b. 1885), Korsch (b. 1886), Gramsci (b. 1891), Benjamin (b. 1892), Horkheimer (b. 1895), Reich (b. 1897), Brecht (b. 1898) and Marcuse (b. 1898); those born after 1900 and radicalized in the interwar period or during the Second World War—Lowenthal (b. 1900), Lefebvre (b. 1901), Adorno (b. 1903), Sartre (b. 1905), Merleau-Ponty (b. 1908), Goldmann (b. 1913), and Althusser (b. 1918); and those born after the First World War and whose political education came after the Second—Colletti (b. 1924) and Habermas (b. 1929). The only major exception to this pattern is Della Volpe, who was born in 1897 but became a Marxist only near the end of World War II. As might be expected, each generation tended to concentrate on the different issues central to their life histories, such as the Bolshevik Revolution, the rise of Fascism, or the political significance of the Resistance. Similarly, each was open to influences from non-Marxist schools of thought such as psychoanalysis, existentialism, and structuralism, according to the coincidence of those competing systems with their own intellectual development.

One of the generalizations Anderson attempts to make about generational uniformity is that the earliest group tended to find a closer link between its theory and political practice than the later ones. From the eleventh Thesis on Feuerbach onwards Marxism has, of course, been preoccupied with the necessity of forging that link. During the era of the Second Interna-

---

9. The only exception to this generalization was Althusser. See *For Marx*, trans. Ben Brewster (New York, 1970).

tional, many Marxists thought they had discovered the means to do so, although of course there were serious clashes over the organizational and tactical form which theoretically directed practice was to take. Western Marxism, like Leninism, grew out of a disillusionment with the results of the Second International's theory-practice nexus. But whereas Leninism tended to change its practice without seriously questioning the theory it had inherited, Western Marxism understood the need to revise both. For while recognizing that there had indeed been a connection between theory and practice before 1914, the Western Marxists argued that it was a most unfortunate one. The scientistic, determinist economistic theory of Engels, Kautsky, Plekhanov et al. had contributed to the bureaucratic, non-revolutionary, and ultimately impotent politics of the Second International's mass parties, most notably the Social Democratic Party of Germany (SPD). In fact, if there is anything on which Western Marxists, neo-Hegelian and anti-Hegelian alike, completely agreed, it is the utter repudiation of the legacy of the Second International. Only towards the work of Rosa Luxemburg, whose political radicalism seemed more attractive than her theoretical orthodoxy, did they make an exception.

Less uniform was their response to the new attempts to unify theory and practice after World War I, when the bureaucratic model of the Second International was discredited. Schematically put, these attempts were reducible to the Bolshevik model of small, disciplined vanguard parties and the alternative, more "leftist" council-communist model of soviets or *Räte*. Initially, it seemed to some in the first generation that there was no real contradiction between the two, but ultimately a choice had to be made. A few like Lukács and, somewhat less decisively, Gramsci chose the party; others like Korsch opted for the councils, even though they realized the impracticality of their choice in the short run.[10] In the subsequent generations, fewer were drawn to the Leninist alternative, although at times Althusser, Della Volpe, Lefebvre and Colletti found it enticing. The majority were attracted to more libertarian modes of political activism like the councils out of a sober realization that the Soviet Union's sorry history had compromised Leninism irreparably. In some cases, this insistence on a Marxism that would not surrender its theoretical purity and

10. For a discussion of the importance of the councils in the origins of Western Marxism, see Russell Jacoby, *Dialectic of Defeat: Contours of Western Marxism* (Cambridge, 1981). Although the main theoretician of Council Communism, Anton Pannekoek, seems to have derived much of his inspiration from the vulgar Marxist philosophy of Joseph Dietzgen, he was nonetheless hostile to crude materialism in ways that have earned him a tentative comparison with the early Western Marxists. See the discussions in Serge Bricianer, *Pannekoek and the Workers' Councils,* intro. John Gerber, trans. Malachy Carroll (St. Louis, 1978); and D. A. Smart, ed., *Pannekoek and Gorter's Marxism* (London, 1978).

high aspirations meant a tenacious, even desperate search for historical "subjects" who would regain the momentum lost when the councils were defeated after the First World War. The so-called "existentialist Marxists" in France and Marcuse in America thought they found a possible surrogate in the counter-cultural student movement of the late 1960s, but they came to recognize the prematurity of their optimism. Others such as Goldmann sought an alternative in the "new working class" of technicians and white collar workers defined by Serge Mallet and André Gorz in France and Victor Foa and Bruno Trentin in Italy. Still others, primarily Adorno and Horkheimer, retreated from the hope that such a subject could be discovered in the near future and fell back on a nuanced defense of theory as itself a form of non-resigned practice.

However they may have "resolved" their dilemma, Western Marxists rarely, if ever, deluded themselves into believing that theirs was a time in which the unity of theory and practice was easily achieved. In fact, after the early 1920s Western Marxism was marked by a growing pessimism. Although moments of renewed hope appeared during the Resistance era and in the late 1960s, by and large Western Marxism never regained the confidence characteristic of its most utopian period, after the end of World War I. It experienced instead what one recent commentator has called a "dialectic of defeat."[11]

None of its major figures, however, underwent the kind of extreme "God that failed" disillusionment so frequent among more orthodox Communist defectors. Except for the former Althusserians who became leaders of the "New Philosophy" in France after 1975, and perhaps the later Horkheimer, Western Marxists did not move radically to the right. Instead, they directed a great deal of their intellectual energy towards investigating the means by which advanced capitalism prevented the unity of theory and practice from being achieved. The critical role of culture in this process was affirmed as it could not have been during the era of the Second International, when the primacy of the economy was an unchallenged article of faith. Having originally come to Marxism in the hope that it would address the crisis in bourgeois culture, many Western Marxists continued to be preoccupied with cultural questions.

Marxist aesthetics, in fact, came of age during the Western Marxist era in the writings of Lukács, Brecht, Bloch, the Frankfurt School, Benjamin, Sartre, Goldmann, Della Volpe, and Althusser. Their work went well be-

11. Jacoby, *Dialectic of Defeat*, which sets out to challenge "the ethos of success that has drained off the critical impulse of Marxism" and to "salvage a Western Marxism that rarely knew victory" (p. 4).

yond the scattered observations of Marx and Engels[12] on cultural questions, and was a major advance over the reductionist theories of Plekhanov, Mehring and others in the Second International. If one adds the name of Raymond Williams,[13] perhaps the only English Marxist able to hold his own with his continental peers, it can be plausibly argued that Western Marxism has enriched cultural theory more than economic or political theory. Hegelian and non-Hegelian Marxists alike have recognized that the problem of "cultural hegemony," as Gramsci called it, was key to understanding the staying power of capitalism. Furthermore, many understood that a purely "scientific" theory gives little indication of the potential advantages of socialism beyond the abolition of economic exploitation.

In its efforts to understand the resilience of capitalism, Western Marxism was also generally open to psychological explanations of the unexpected turns taken by advanced capitalist society, in particular the advent of Fascism in the interwar period. Although a few of the older generation, most notably Lukács and Korsch, remained absolutely anti-psychological, Western Marxists tended to take the challenge of Freud and his successors very seriously. Some added forms of psychological estrangement to the other expressions of alienation in the experience of everyday life. Others argued that emancipatory praxis had to include a form of collective, and perhaps even individual, radical therapy. Still others, who were less impressed by the direct therapeutic benefits of psychology, claimed that psychoanalysis could be used on a purely theoretical level to enrich Marxism's sensitivity to the subtle nature of human needs and gratification. Yet another group teased out the linguistic implications of Freudian theory to bring to life an entire dimension of Marxism hitherto underdeveloped; even anti-subjectivist theorists such as Althusser were able to find in Freud an inspiration for their work. Those who felt Freud was insufficient in certain ways found Gestalt psychology or Piaget's genetic structuralism useful instead.

Western Marxism's openness to psychology in general and psychoanalysis in particular was, in fact, only one manifestation of its essential readiness to draw on non-Marxist intellectual currents to make up de-

12. For a selection of their thoughts on aesthetics, see *Marx and Engels on Literature and Art,* ed. Lee Baxandall and Stefan Morawski, intro. Lee Baxandall (St. Louis, 1973).

13. For a recent retrospective analysis of Williams' remarkable career, see the interviews he gave the *New Left Review* in *Politics and Letters* (London, 1979). One of his former students and a frequent critic, Terry Eagleton, might also be included in the list of major Western Marxist aestheticians. Or at least so Eagleton confidently tells us. See his *Walter Benjamin: Or Towards a Revolutionary Criticism* (London, 1981), p. 96. For an analysis of some of the problems in both Williams and Eagleton, see Catherine Gallagher, "The New Materialism in Marxist Aesthetics," *Theory and Society* 9:4 (July 1980).

ficiencies (or develop incipient leads) in the inheritance from the nine-teenth century. This process, to be sure, had already begun during the Second International with the Revisionists' attempt to link Marx and Kant, and with Plekhanov's interest in Spinoza and Kautsky's in Darwin, but only after 1918 did the practice become widespread. The result was a series of adjectival Marxisms—existentialist, phenomenological, struc-turalist, Hegelian, even Schopenhauerian—which parallelled on a theo-retical level the proliferation of parties and sects on a practical one. Those engaged in one or another of these cross-fertilizations defended their posi-tion as a synthetic enrichment which helped Marxism to adjust to the changed circumstances of the modern world. To their opponents, how-ever, the results were a feeble eclecticism that defiled the essential validity of Marx's teaching.[14] As early as Lukács' reproach to Bloch in *History and Class Consciousness*, that Marxism did not need the supplement of religious utopianism,[15] some Western Marxists looked askance at the syn-thesizing efforts of their peers. Indeed, in general Western Marxists have been uncharitable towards their fellows, if they deigned to notice them at all. Displaying in classic form what Freud once called the narcissism of small differences, Western Marxists frequently maligned and deprecated each other, often after misrepresenting the positions they attacked.[16] Po-tential allies were thus lost in the eagerness for theoretical correctness, a failing that is still manifest in the assertion of absolute opposition be-tween Critical and Scientific Marxism.

The reverse side of this internecine quarreling has been the enormous creative fecundity of the tradition, which sharply sets it apart from its orthodox Marxist or Marxist–Leninist opponents. Western Marxism has been open and experimental in a way that is not comparable with any-thing in this century except perhaps aesthetic modernism, which also ex-ploded in a whirl of movements and counter-movements. Lacking the means to impose intellectual conformity, the various subcurrents of West-ern Marxism have had to coexist uneasily and engage, if often indirectly, in a critical dialogue that has been sadly absent in the institutionalized socialist world.

To compare Western Marxism with aesthetic modernism is to draw attention to yet another characteristic of its adherents. All were members

14. This charge was hurled, for example, by the Althusserian Göran Therborn against Habermas. See his "Jürgen Habermas: A New Eclecticism" in *New Left Review* 67 (May–June 1971).

15. Georg Lukács, *History and Class Consciousness: Studies in Marxist Dialectics*, trans. Rodney Livingstone (Cambridge, Mass., 1971), p. 193.

16. A prime example of this tendency can be found in Colletti's diatribes against the Frankfurt School, which will be discussed in Chapter 14.

of an intellectual avant-garde with highly ambivalent relations to the majority of their fellow men, for whom they nonetheless often claimed to speak. Marcuse's description of Goldmann could easily be extended to others in the tradition: "a radical intellectual who was proud to be an intellectual—without the slightest inferiority complex, so widespread among the New Left, of being a revolutionary and not being a worker. To him, intellect was by its nature revolutionary."[17] Here they were set apart not only from the more anti-intellectual elements in the New Left, but also from the organized socialist parties whose characteristic attitude towards intellectuals was one of suspicion and mistrust.[18] Whatever their political position, Western Marxists were united in their distaste for "vulgar Marxism," the crude ideology of uneducated spokesmen for the oppressed. Here Lenin's assessment of the trade-union, or "economistic," consciousness of the majority of the working class was tacitly accepted, although his solution of bringing revolutionary class consciousness from without, which had been foreshadowed by Kautsky, often was not. Indeed, one might say that the example of a tightly disciplined vanguard party, in which intellectuals were compelled to curb their independence, haunted Western Marxists to the extent that many came to equate any party allegiance with the sacrifice of critical power.

And yet, the elitist character of the Leninist party was unwittingly duplicated in the often elitist nature of their work. Rather than attempt to present their theories in a manner easily accessible to uneducated minds, they almost invariably wrote in a style whose complexity defied popular comprehension. There could be no easy "ABC of Marxism" for the Western Marxists, as there had been for Soviet ideologues like Bukharin, because popularization risked the dilution, if not perversion, of meaning,[19]

17. Herbert Marcuse, "Some General Comments on Lucien Goldmann" in Goldmann, *Cultural Creation in Modern Society*, trans. Bart Grahl, intro. William Mayrl, (St. Louis, 1976), p. 129.

18. The tension between workers and intellectuals in the socialist movement can be seen as early as the 1840s and Marx's battles with the tailor, Wilhelm Weitling. Marx's frustrations at his anti-intellectual opponents led him to exclaim impatiently: "Ignorance never yet helped anybody!" For a description of the clash, see David McLellan, *Karl Marx: His Life and Thought* (London, 1973), p. 155, where Paul Annenkov's reminiscences are quoted at length. The tension between intellectuals and workers in the socialist movement has been thematically developed in the work of Alvin Gouldner, most notably in *The Two Marxisms* where he argues that behind "the unity of theory and practice" lies the putative alliance of theorists and the masses.

19. Perhaps the only major Western Marxist to attempt a popular introduction to Marxism was Karl Korsch, whose *Karl Marx*, 2nd ed. (New York, 1963) was designed to spell out the tenets of Marxism in a reasonably accessible form. Ironically, at the same time as the book first appeared in 1938, Korsch was voicing reservations about the validity of many of the same principles he presented without qualification for his popular audience. See the discussion in *Karl Korsch: Revolutionary Theory*, ed. with intro. by Douglas Kellner (Austin, 1977), p. 169.

as well as the danger of premature co-optation. In general they spoke to a relatively circumscribed audience of intellectuals, or to a mass public yet to be created. Theirs was a democracy of the future, not the present. As a result, they were often pilloried for their elitism, an accusation leveled as early as the Comintern's denunciation of the "professorial" Marxism of Lukács and Korsch in 1924. On occasion this reproach led to bouts of self-criticism, such as Lukács' condemnation of his *History and Class Consciousness* and Althusser's repudiation of his early "theoreticist deviation,"[20] or somewhat less frequently to attempts at direct communication with the masses, most notably in Brecht's *Lehrstücke* (didactic plays) and Reich's Sex-Pol clinics. But by and large, Western Marxists were content to point out that defiance of the status quo could be expressed only in terms not easily absorbed and neutralized by current popular discourse.

Although Gramsci had called for a class of "organic intellectuals" growing out of the working class, the Western Marxists, with the sole exception of Gramsci himself, came from educated, relatively comfortable middle-class families. Despite Benjamin's insight into the economic proletarianization of the writer under capitalism,[21] they never truly merged into the class for whom they spoke. Although they scorned such concepts as Karl Mannheim's "free-floating intelligentsia," they often came to resemble the model despite themselves. For all their efforts to find the proper role for the radical intellectual—party militant, fellow-traveller, critical outsider, etc.—the results were often deeply unsatisfactory. Indeed, if one had to select one major characteristic that set Western Marxists apart from their rivals, it would have to be their increasing isolation from mass politics.

Their "inorganic" relation to those for whom they spoke was reflected not only in the hermeticism of the way in which they spoke, but also and perhaps more fundamentally in one of the major terms of their discourse. That term, "totality," had a special place in the lexicon of all Western Marxists. In privileging it as they did, they betrayed their unmistakable status as intellectuals: throughout modern history, only "men of ideas" have combined the time (and economic support) to reflect on matters beyond their immediate material concerns with the hubris to believe they might know the whole of reality. Often only marginally related to their

20. Louis Althusser, *Essays in Self-Criticism,* trans. with intro. Grahame Lock (London, 1976), p. 105.
21. Walter Benjamin, "The Author as Producer," in *Reflections: Essays, Aphorisms, Autobiographical Writings,* trans. Edmund Jephcott, ed. with intro. Peter Demetz (New York and London, 1978). Benjamin, however, notes that because of his special education, "even the proletarianization of an intellectual hardly ever makes a proletarian" (p. 268).

class of social origin, frequently tending to be cosmopolitan rather than provincial in their loyalties, intellectuals have rarely been reluctant to impute to themselves a universal function in society. Along with this self-image has gone a willingness to assume a totalistic perspective and speak for all members of the relevant whole, whether it be local, national, or global. In fact, as Alvin Gouldner has remarked,

It is not only that intellectuals *can* take the standpoint of the social "whole," by reason of their structural position or special culture; intellectuals often occupy social roles and have had educations that induce them to define themselves as "representatives" of the larger society or nation, or of the historical or native tradition of the group. Teachers and clerks are often educated to define themselves as having a responsibility to their group as a whole. However "false" such a consciousness may be, it is often real in its consequences, inducing some intellectuals to accept responsibility for and obligation to cultural symbols and social structures that *unite* the group as a whole.[22]

From the seventeenth-century "Revolution of the Saints" in England through the eighteenth-century Jacobins to the modern intellectual elites who led the Russian Revolution and subsequent upheavals in the Third World, revolutionary intellectuals in particular have been motivated by a totalistic imagination normally absent among more self-interested and short-sighted men. In Nietzsche's pungent phrase, they have been the "knights of totality,"[23] arrogating to themselves a teleological mission to speak for the whole. Even Marx and Engels justified themselves in these terms when they wrote in *The Communist Manifesto* that "a portion of the bourgeoisie goes over to the proletariat; and in particular a portion of the bourgeois ideologists, who have raised themselves to the level of comprehending theoretically the historical movement as a whole."[24]

A totalistic stance has not, of course, had only revolutionary political implications. Before modern times, religious elites were spokesmen for a holism that had profoundly conservative implications. More recently, there have been mandarinates whose claim to speak for their society also affirmed its present status, a salient example being the bureaucratically entrenched *Bildungsbürgertum* (cultural bourgeoisie) in Germany whose

22. Alvin Gouldner, "Prologue to a Theory of Revolutionary Intellectuals," *Telos* 26 (Winter 1975–76), p. 12. Gouldner develops his general theory of intellectuals as a "flawed universal class" in *The Future of Intellectuals and the Rise of the New Class* (New York, 1980). For similar observations on the intellectuals in Eastern Europe, see George Konrád and Ivan Szelényi, *The Intellectuals on the Road to Class Power: A Sociological Study of the Role of the Intelligentsia in Socialism*, trans. Andrew Arato and Richard E. Allen (New York and London, 1979).
23. Quoted in Konrád and Szelényi without a specific citation, p. 134.
24. Marx and Engels, *Manifesto of the Communist Party* in *The Marx-Engels Reader*, ed. Robert C. Tucker (New York, 1972), p. 343.

fortunes have been traced by Fritz Ringer.[25] In our century, holistic perspectives of a non-radical kind have been developed by a wide range of thinkers including Karl Mannheim, Othmar Spann, Talcott Parsons, and the adherents of such movements as structuralism, Gestalt psychology, and systems theory. The celebrated claim made by Lukács in *History and Class Consciousness*,[26] that Marxism is differentiated from bourgeois thought by its adoption of the point of view of totality, is thus on the face of it untrue.

But by and large it is correct to say that the issue of totality has been at the center of the Marxist, or at least Western Marxist, debate as it has not been with bourgeois thought, especially in its positivist, neo-Kantian or existentialist guises. Possibly because of their marginal relation both to the class of their origin and the class to which they gravitated, the intellectuals in the Western Marxist tradition were particularly prone to think holistically. But if collectively drawn to the concept of totality, they were by no means unified in their understanding of its meaning or in their evaluation of its merits. Indeed, it might be said that the major subterranean quarrel of this subterranean tradition has been waged over this concept's implications. By forcing that quarrel to surface, through examining representative figures in the tradition, we can discern certain patterns that would otherwise be obscured if, for example, we remained tied to obvious dichotomies such as those between Hegelian and anti-Hegelian or Scientific and Critical Western Marxisms. Indeed, we might argue that by spelling out the various meanings of totality and investigating their implications for other aspects of Marxist theory, we can fruitfully make sense of the tradition in new and revealing ways. Or, to put it in the terms of our initial metaphor, it is to the concept of totality that we can look for a compass to help us traverse the vast and uncharted intellectual territory that is Western Marxism.

It is, to be sure, not the only compass that we might use, for although totality has been of enormous importance for Western Marxists, the totality of their work cannot be reduced to it alone. Other key concepts such as praxis, subjectivity, or dialectics might also be explored profitably by historians of the tradition. But again, each of these taken in isolation would not be sufficient to give us a complete view of its topography. And even if we could somehow work our way through complicated analyses of how all of these key terms were used by the major Western Marxists, it is by no means certain that they would then come together in a grand, coherent synthesis.

25. Fritz K. Ringer, *The Decline of the German Mandarins: The German Academic Community, 1890–1933* (Cambridge, Mass., 1969).
26. Lukács, *History and Class Consciousness*, p. 27.

Moreover, we are still too close to the tradition, which is by no means at its end, to attempt such a conclusive totalization. As will become evident later in the text, one of the most frequent points of contention among holistic thinkers is whether or not epistemological totalization can occur solely in retrospect. For those who so argue, the dusk of Western Marxism has by no means yet fallen, and thus Minerva's omniscient owl must remain in its nest. *Pace* Perry Anderson, it is too early to offer a "historical balance sheet"[27] of the movement as a whole. In Imre Lakatos' terms, Western Marxism is still a progressive rather than degenerating research program.

Consequently, it would be inappropriate for the structure of this study to assume a totalistic form of the kind, say, employed by M. H. Abrams in his *Natural Supernaturalism,*[28] a history of an earlier period in which totality was a central issue. Abrams' narrative ends where it begins, and thus mimics the unity –disunity –unity pattern whose development in the Romantic era he traces. Besides prematurely terminating the still open-ended history of Western Marxism, employing such an approach here would also mean subtly accepting one of the major holistic schemes of the Western Marxists, but by no means the only one.

Inevitably, any work of scholarship begins somewhere and ends somewhere and thus presents a sense of closure and completion. But as we have recently come to appreciate, no text is isolated from its intertextual context, a context which differs for the writer and each of his readers, however much overlapping may occur. If this is true for works of art, to which the quality of totality has been often ascribed, it is even more so for works of scholarship, especially those that enter into an ongoing theoretical dialogue. Although written by a historian, this study does not aspire to the status of a "definitive" work on a past phenomenon, foreclosing all further discussion of the issues it treats; it is aimed instead at making a contribution to the still-lively debate on those issues.

Although that debate is taking place primarily among Marxists, the contributions of non-Marxist thinkers to our understanding of holism cannot be dismissed. As has been argued, Western Marxism derived much of its strength from its non-doctrinaire openness to stimuli from without. Accordingly, this study will not presume that Marxism is itself

27. Anderson, *Considerations on Western Marxism,* p. vii.
28. M. H. Abrams, *Natural Supernaturalism: Tradition and Revolution in Romantic Literature* (New York, 1971). Claiming that both Romantic poetry and classical idealist philosophy follow the same pattern of initial unmediated unity, necessary alienation and ultimate reconciliation on a higher level, Abrams ends the book where it begins, with a discussion of Wordsworth's prospectus for *The Recluse.* Not surprisingly, this book was the target of a critical polemic by the American deconstructionist, J. Hillis Miller. See his review in *Diacritics* 2 (Winter 1972).

an impermeable theoretical totality with nothing to gain from dialogue with its competitors. This presumption would be particularly inappropriate where the concept of totality is concerned because, as we have noted, holism has also been frequently discussed by non-Marxist theorists. It would be possible to write an entire book on the ways in which holism has been treated in debates between Marxists and their opponents, using such examples as the dialogue with Christians in post-war France, the Positivism Dispute in Germany, or the more recent polemic with systems theorists. But considerations of length preclude going much beyond the discourse of Western Marxism *per se.* The only case we will examine closely is the critique of holism by recent post-structuralists, for their work has directly entered into the Western Marxist debate itself.

One final methodological word is necessary before plunging into the material. Although unravelling the history of a concept may recall the approach of Arthur Lovejoy and his controversial History of Ideas school, it would do violence to the history of Marxist thought were a restricted methodology adopted. Western Marxism may seem a body of thought sufficient unto itself, but the Western Marxists were intellectuals, often deeply engaged intellectuals, whose work responded to the events of their day. To understand the development of the concept of totality in their work is to probe that response. Although it cannot be demonstrated that immediate and direct parallels exist between their ideas and, say, their political histories or the national traditions which nurtured them—indeed, to presume so is to accept a version of totality that most of them would have questioned—certain mediated and indirect relations often can be discerned. Without trying to determine non-intellectual causes for every variation in their positions, when relations or links do seem present they will be explored. It would be tempting to try to forge those links individually for all of the figures included in this study, as I have tried to do elsewhere on a modest scale for Siegfried Kracauer,[29] but the number of relevant characters is simply too large and the available data too uneven to permit such an approach. Here again final totalizations, should they ever be possible, will require more time and perspective. They may be delayed until either Western Marxism's fondest hopes or its worst fears are realized. As long as neither is a likely prospect, studies such as this can speak of totality without pretending to embody it.

If such a defense of the limited intentions of this study still seems to some readers a violation of the stern Marxist imperative always to ground

29. Martin Jay, "The Extraterritorial Life of Siegfried Kracauer," *Salmagundi* 31–32 (Fall 1975–Winter 1976).

thought in its social context, let them examine the frequent practice of Marxists themselves in reflecting on their own tradition. Although the occasional Karl Korsch has attempted to turn the critical tools of Marxism on Marxism itself and write a radical sociology of radical knowledge, most Marxists, rightly or wrongly, have applied such a technique only to the currents within the tradition that they have found objectionable. In fact, as George Steiner has recently reminded us,

The scheme of origins, authority and continuum in force in the Marxist world derives its sense of identity and its daily practices of validation and exclusion from a canon of texts. It is the reading of those texts—exegetic, Talmudic, disputative to an almost pathological degree of semantic scruple and interpretative nicety—which constitutes the presiding dynamic in Marxist education and in the attempts, inherently ambiguous as are all attempts to 'move forward' from sacred texts, to make of Marxism an unfolding, predictive reality-principle.[30]

Although it is far from my intention to treat any of the texts I will examine as "sacred," and it is certainly my hope that the attention I will pay to them stops short of pathology, I nonetheless want to respect the arguments they contain rather than treat them as mere symptoms of external circumstances. Insofar as intellectual historians have come to recognize contexts as themselves texts requiring hermeneutic decipherment, we can no longer expect answers by referring to an unproblematic social reality fully external to the works we examine. Nonetheless, I do think we can discern a pattern of argumentation among the texts of Western Marxism that goes beyond the self-comprehension of their authors and yet does as little violence as possible to the arguments' place in the general *oeuvre* of those authors. In part, this will require attention both to the authors' life histories and to the general history of European Marxism in this century. I will therefore try to reconstruct the discourse on totality in Western Marxism without losing sight of the fact that living individuals have been the participants in that discourse.

But it is nonetheless important to acknowledge that the pattern I have "discerned" will to a certain degree be one I have created. In the terms of a hermeneutic distinction recently emphasized by Timothy Bahti,[31] this pattern can be called a *Nachkonstruktion* rather than a simple *Rekonstruktion*. That is, instead of being a neutral recording of history "as it actually happened," to cite the familiar phrase from Ranke, it will be a rhetorical reenactment shaped by my own concerns and experiences.

30. George Steiner, *On Difficulty and Other Essays* (Oxford, 1978), p. 5.
31. Timothy Bahti, "Vico, Auerbach and Literary History," in *Vico: Past and Present*, ed. Giorgio Tagliacozzo (Atlantic Highlands, N.J., 1981), vol. 2, p. 113.

The inevitability of such a (re)constructive role in the shaping of historical accounts has recently been emphasized by a wide variety of theorists, ranging from Hans-Georg Gadamer and Paul Ricoeur in the hermeneutic camp to Michel Foucault in the post-structuralist. Hayden White's widely discussed *Metahistory* and the Derridean arguments of Dominick LaCapra have helped stimulate a debate in the English-speaking world on similar issues.[32] Without addressing all of their complexity,[33] I would like to register my general agreement with their common premise: that although the historian does not construct his or her narrative out of whole cloth, he or she nonetheless creates a coherence that the participants in the account may well have failed to perceive. Like "secondary elaboration" in Freud's dream work, historical narrative tends to fill in the gaps and smooth out the inconsistencies in the raw (or better put, partly cooked) materials left by the past. And it inevitably does so from the finite perspective of the historian's present. There is thus what Gadamer calls a "fusion of horizons" between past and present that makes historical thinking a never-completed, infinitely interpretative process.

To try to characterize my own horizon in an adequate way would be impossibly demanding and not likely to engage the interest of many readers. But some indication of where this account of Western Marxism originates may be of use to those it is designed to persuade and enlighten. From an initial interest in the Frankfurt School's Critical Theory, which grew in part out of a tempered sympathy for the New Left of the 1960s, my focus has widened to include the general tradition of Western Marxism as it has been revealed in the past decade or so of scholarship, partisan and otherwise. For better or worse, this process has been largely a scholarly rather than a more broadly political one, at least in the United States, where the Left has been increasingly ghettoized in smaller and smaller academic enclaves. As a university professor with no sectarian political allegiances, I have been inevitably part of what some would disdainfully call the "academization of Marxism." The tradition of Western Marxism has come alive to me not through its concrete embodiments in movements, mass or otherwise, for radical social change, but rather through a dispersed cultural community of radical (and now sometimes formerly radical) intellectuals. Composing learned commentaries and critiques in books and

---

32. Hayden White, *Metahistory: The Historical Imagination in Nineteenth-Century Europe* (Baltimore and London, 1973); Dominick LaCapra, *A Preface to Sartre: A Critical Introduction to Sartre's Literary and Philosophical Writings* (Ithaca, 1978).

33. I have tried to discuss some of the issues in greater detail in "Should Intellectual History Take a Linguistic Turn?" in *Modern European Intellectual History: Reappraisals and New Perspectives*, eds. Dominick LaCapra and Steven L. Kaplan (Ithaca, 1982).

journals like *Telos, New Left Review, Theory and Society, New German Critique* and *Marxist Perspectives*, its members have contributed to a burgeoning awareness of the richness as well as the inadequacies of a tradition of thought that as recently as 1972 could be called Marxism's "unknown dimension."[34] For many in this group, its recovery provided an alternative to the discredited orthodoxies of its Eastern competitor, which had long since proved their irrelevancy to the American scene.

What can now be seen as a distinct generation of non-dogmatically leftist intellectuals has defined itself largely by reference to the absorption of themes from Western Marxism, itself basically the creation of comparably unaffiliated men of ideas rather than action. To mention only a few of their number, and with apologies to those excluded by chance or ignorance, this generation includes Walter Adamson, Frank Adler, John Alt, Andrew Arato, Stanley Aronowitz, Ronald Aronson, David Bathrick, Jessica Benjamin, Russell Berman, Seyla Benhabib, Carl Boggs, Samuel Bowles, Paul Breines, Stephen Bronner, Susan Buck-Morss, Jean Cohen, Fred Dallmayr, Robert D'Amico, Andrew Feenberg, Todd Gitlin, Herb Gintis, David Gross, Jeffrey Herf, Dick Howard, Andreas Huyssen, Russell Jacoby, Fredric Jameson, Douglas Kellner, Karl Klare, Joel Kovel, William Leiss, Eugene Lunn, Thomas McCarthy, James Miller, Paul Piccone, Mark Poster, Moishe Postone, Anson Rabinbach, James Schmidt, Morton Schoolman, Trent Schroyer, Jeremy Shapiro, Paul Thomas, Shierry Weber, Joel Whitebook, Richard Wolin, Erik Olin Wright, Jack Zipes and Sharon Zukin.

Although it should be left to some future Robert Wohl to chart the history of this "generation of 1968," as it might be called, one general observation is necessary. Whereas the initial interest in Western Marxism was sparked by the excitement of the late 1960s, its full reception was played out against the disheartening events of the 1970s. Not surprisingly, some who were originally convinced that one variant or another of Western Marxism had all the answers to questions both theoretical and practical began to lose their confidence.[35] Although nothing as widely remarked as the defection of the New Philosophers in France occurred in America, here too what might be called a "dialectic of defeat" accompanied the critical absorption of Western Marxist ideas, in some ways echo-

34. Dick Howard and Karl Klare, eds., *The Unknown Dimension: European Marxism Since Lenin* (New York, 1972).
35. The loss of confidence is evident in Dick Howard's *The Marxian Legacy* (New York, 1977); it is also apparent in the recent writings of Andrew Arato, Mark Poster, William Leiss, James Schmidt, James Miller and Paul Piccone. The internal polemics in *Telos*, beginning with issue 31 (Spring 1977), document the change. For a useful overview of the journal's history, see John Fekete, "*Telos* at 50," *Telos* 50 (Winter 1981–82).

ing the original dialectic that had accompanied their creation. In certain cases the alternative proved to be one or another version of post-structuralism,[36] but for most of the members of this generation, a final resting place has yet to be found. No one, for example, has yet come to espouse a kind of dogmatic anti–New Leftism comparable to the "God that failed" anti-Communism that so often was the result of earlier disillusionments.

Having myself never been certain that Marxism, Western or otherwise, offered all the answers, I have experienced less disenchantment than those who seem to be repeating the familiar pattern of deradicalization which succeeds every period of revolutionary enthusiasm. The narrative I have constructed may seem to some a bleak tale of dashed expectations emplotted in a tragic or satiric mode, but I do not want to leave the impression that I believe the story is over and these are its only narrative forms. Totality is a concept whose adventures are not yet at an end.

What follows is not meant as an explicit exposé of the delusions of the Western Marxists or their recent American devotees, nor as an implicit confession of its author's benighted youth. Although it will be readily apparent that I feel the initial Western Marxist attempts at a viable concept of totality miscarried, that effort, I argue, helped clarify a large number of important questions. Nor do I feel, as my concluding chapter on Habermas will demonstrate, that new attempts to reconstruct Marxist holism have shown themselves to be equally unworkable. If, in fact, this book both contributes to the progress of the debate over those attempts and provides a usable account of their origins, its purposes will be served. For if the study of intellectual history is to have any ultimate justification, it is its capacity to rescue the legacy of the past in order to allow us to realize the potential of the future.

36. Poster, for example, has turned increasingly to Foucault. Another alternative has been Lacan. See, for example, Rainer Nägele, "The Provocation of Jacques Lacan: Attempt at a Theoretical Topography apropos a Book about Lacan," *New German Critique* 16 (Winter 1979). The book in question is Samuel Weber, *Rückkehr zu Freud. Jacques Lacans Entstellung der Psychoanalyse* (Frankfurt, Berlin and Vienna, 1978). Weber, it should be noted, began his intellectual career as a supporter of the Frankfurt School; in 1967 he helped translate Adorno's *Prisms*.

CHAPTER ONE

The Discourse of Totality
Before Western Marxism

The whole is a riddle, an enigma, an inexplicable mystery. Doubt, uncertainty, suspense of judgment appear the only result of our most accurate scrutiny, concerning this subject. But such is the frailty of human reason, and such the irresistible contagion of opinion, that even this deliberate doubt could scarcely be upheld.

DAVID HUME

"There is no single tendency in the history of modern social thought," the political theorist Roberto Mangabeira Unger has written, "more remarkable in its persistence or more far-reaching in its influence than the struggle to formulate a plausible version of the idea of totality."[1] "Totality" has indeed enjoyed a privileged place in the discourse of Western culture. Resonating with affirmative connotations, it has generally been associated with other positively charged words, such as coherence, order, fulfillment, harmony, plenitude, meaningfulness, consensus and community. And concomitantly, it has been contrasted with such negatively valenced concepts as alienation, fragmentation, disorder, conflict, contradiction, serialization, atomization and estrangement. Although it has not entirely escaped censure—Albert Camus' linkage of it with totalitarianism in *The Rebel*[2] is a striking example—it has normally been imbued with what Lovejoy called "metaphysical pathos,"[3] the power to arouse a positive mood on the part of its users by the congeniality of its subtle associations.

Clearly, the concept's widespread and perennial appeal cannot be attributed solely to its intellectual content. An early explanation for its pop-

1. Roberto Mangabeira Unger, *Knowledge and Politics* (New York and London, 1975), p. 125.
2. Albert Camus, *The Rebel: An Essay on Man in Revolt*, trans. Anthony Bower (New York, 1956). Camus contrasts unity with totality, arguing: "Rebellion's demand is unity; historical revolution's demand is totality. The former starts from a negative supported by an affirmative, the latter from an absolute negation and is condemned to every aspect of slavery in order to fabricate an affirmative that is dismissed until the end of time. One is creative, the other nihilist" (p. 251).
3. Arthur Lovejoy, *The Great Chain of Being: A Study of the History of an Idea* (New York, 1936), p. 11.

ularity was advanced by Durkheim,[4] who speculated that the idea of totality reflected the group nature of society itself, and like other concepts of
this kind absorbed the sacred aura of society. More recently, psychological
interpretations have prevailed. In 1930, the celebrated linguist Edward
Sapir broke down its affective power into two categories. The first, which
he called the "all feeling," was "the feeling of rest or of inability to proceed
after a count, formal or informal, has been made of a set or series or aggregation of objects." The second, which he dubbed the "whole feeling," grew
out of the "feeling of inability or unwillingness to break up an object into
smaller objects."[5] At approximately the same time, Freud speculated on
the source of religious sentiment in "the oceanic feeling,"[6] an infantile
state of oneness with the mother. Although he confined his discussion to
religion, Freud's hypothesis could as easily be applied to other forms of
nostalgia for primal unity, including those expressed in certain forms of
totalistic thinking. Somewhat later, Erik Erikson attributed the desire for
totality to the rigid need for absolute boundaries aroused by psychic disorientation, which he claimed followed from the loss of a healthier, more
open unity he called "wholeness."[7] In a very different psychoanalytic tradition Jacques Lacan posited a "mirror stage" through which all children
pass, a stage before language when the self is falsely perceived as a coherent and unified whole.[8] Later searches for wholeness, he suggested, are re-
gressions to this early and illusory phase of development.

Most of these psychological explanations of totality's appeal are, to be
sure, reductive and debunking in intention, but they nonetheless point to

4. Emile Durkheim, *The Elementary Forms of the Religious Life*, trans. Joseph Ward
Swain (New York, 1965), pp. 489–90.

5. Edward Sapir, "Totality," *Language Monographs* 6 (September 1930), p. 7.

6. Sigmund Freud, *Civilization and Its Discontents*, trans. James Strachey (New York,
1961). p. 11f.

7. Erik Erikson, "Wholeness and Totality: A Psychiatric Contribution" in *Totalitarianism*, ed. Carl J. Friedrich (New York, 1964), p. 161:

Wholeness seems to connote an assembly of parts, even quite diversified parts, that enter into a fruitful
association and organization. This concept is most strikingly expressed in such terms as wholeharted-
ness, wholemindedness, wholesomeness, and the like. As a *Gestalt*, then, wholeness emphasizes a sound,
organic, progressive mutuality between diversified functions and parts within an entirety, the boundaries
of which are open and fluent. Totality, on the contrary, evokes a *Gestalt* in which an absolute boundary is
emphasized: given a certain arbitrary delineation, nothing that belongs inside must be left outside, nothing that must be outside can be tolerated inside. . . . When the human being, because of accidental or
developmental shifts, loses an essential wholeness, he restructures himself and the world by taking recourse to what we may call *totalism*.

8. Jacques Lacan, *The Language of the Self: The Function of Language in Psychoanalysis*, trans., with notes and commentary, Anthony Wilden (New York, 1968), p. 173f. Lacan
writes that he must "object to any reference to totality in the individual, since it is the subject
who introduces division into the individual, as well as into the collectivity which is his equivalent. Psychoanalysis is properly that which reveals both the one and the other to be simply
mirages" (p. 56).

possible sources of its uncommon power. Whether or not these sources can be determined with certainty, it is still important to acknowledge the highly charged nature of the term itself. It is also crucial to recognize that many systems of thought have drawn on its appeal. In fact, as Hayden White and Alvin Gouldner have recently observed in their analyses of the rhetorical and paleo-symbolic levels of Marxist theory,[9] the stubborn attractiveness of that theory in many different contexts owes much to its implicit reliance on totalistic associations. Perhaps nowhere in the history of Marxism has that reliance been as explicitly articulated and self-consciously defended as in the body of thought that is the subject of this study. Thus, to take a series of examples from the writings of Western Marxists, Lukács contended that "what is crucial is that there should be an aspiration towards totality,"[10] Goldmann claimed a "fundamental need for *coherence and totality* which characterizes all human, social life,"[11] and Lefebvre spoke of "the need for totality (i.e., for fulfillment, plenitude in the exercise of all activities, gratification of all desires)."[12]

For analytic purposes, the concept in these statements can be called normative because it equates totality with a desirable goal that is yet to be achieved. Western Marxists have been unwilling to spell out in any detail precisely what an accomplished totality would look like under Communism, but they all agree that present conditions under capitalism or state socialism fail to embody it. Yet in their work they also use the concept of totality to analyze present and past societies. This second general use is non-normative; it stems from a methodological insistence that adequate understanding of complex phenomena can follow only from an apprecia-

9. Hayden White, *Metahistory: The Historical Imagination in Nineteenth-Century Europe* (Baltimore and London, 1973). White argues that the underlying rhetorical strategy of Marx's work is comic, rather than tragic or ironic, because of his faith in the resolution of conflict at the end of the historical process. Because of his faith, Marx's writing was dominated by the figure of speech known as synecdoche in which "the parts merged into a whole which is qualitatively superior to any of the entities that comprise it" (p. 282). In "The Metaphoricality of Marxism and the Context-Freeing Grammar of Socialism," *Theory and Society 1*, (1974), Alvin W. Gouldner posits a number of paleo-symbolic levels of meaning in Marxism that account for its appeal in different settings. The most basic he calls the struggle of the Subject to overcome the domination of the Object, and concludes that "Marxist socialism is the political economy of the 'identical subject-object'" (p. 406). Although this formula may owe too much to Lukács' version of Marxism, it expresses one of the fundamental appeals of Marxism to the intellectuals we will be examining in this study.

10. Georg Lukács, *History and Class Consciousness*, trans. Rodney Livingstone (Cambridge, Mass., 1971), p. 198.

11. Lucien Goldmann, "Interdependencies between Industrial Society and New Forms of Literary Creation" in *Cultural Creation and Modern Society*, trans. Bart Grahl (St. Louis, 1976), p. 77 (italics in original).

12. Henri Lefebvre, *The Sociology of Marx*, trans. Norbert Guterman (New York, 1968), p. 41.

tion of their relational integrity. When, for example, Western Marxists talk of the "totality of bourgeois society," they obviously do not mean that this society has achieved the harmonious order of a true whole. Instead, they suggest that the various component parts of bourgeois society, as disparate and unconnected as they appear, are inextricable elements in a larger complex whole. How that whole is itself to be conceived is, to be sure, a bone of considerable contention. What its internal structure may be, how one is to understand its boundaries, what its relation to human agency may be, how it may be connected with other totalities, how its objective existence is captured in human thought, all of these were and still are questions very much in dispute. But that Marxism must be a holistic rather than individualist theory has been and remains an article of common faith among Western Marxists. As a result, whether normative or descriptive, totality must be recognized as what Whitehead would have called one of the "God-terms" of this discourse.

Totality has, of course, functioned for non-Marxist schools of thought in a similar way. In fact, to introduce the world "holism," itself a coinage of the South African politician and scientist Jan Smuts in his 1926 study *Holism and Evolution*,[13] is to remind us that the Marxist adoption of totality must be placed in the larger tradition of holistic thought. Indeed, many of the issues fought over by Western Marxists were introduced by earlier theorists, if in significantly different contexts. It would be wrong, therefore, to isolate Marxist from non-Marxist holisms, although it would be equally dangerous to equate them indiscriminately. Changed historical circumstances, which account for the development of the discussion within Marxism itself, make such an equation clearly erroneous. And although there are significant parallels between other twentieth-century holisms and those of Western Marxism, here too no simple equivalence can be posited. From the perspective of analytic or individualist thought, all holisms may seem alike, but from within the discourse the differences are extremely important. To enter the Western Marxist debate over totality, it is thus imperative to make some sense of its background without, however, reducing the dynamics of the Marxist debate to a mere repetition of that of its predecessors.

The background of the debate is crucial enough for us to linger with it for some time. Yet it would be unwise to attempt anything like an exhaus-

13. Jan C. Smuts, *Holism and Evolution* (New York, 1926). For a discussion of Smuts' contribution to the holism debate, see H. L. Anspacher, "On the Origin of Holism," *Journal of Individual Psychology* 17:2 (1961).

tive history of the concept of totality in Western thought; not only would such an account try the reader's patience, but it would also convey the misleading impression that a unified and coherent history of holism could be written with Western Marxism as its telos. Rather than constructing such a teleological narrative, which would itself be true to only one of the versions of totality we will encounter in this study, it is preferable to suggest the variety of holistic speculations that were available for different Western Marxists to claim as their own. For as we will see, defending their interpretation of Marxism by reference to its debt to or compatibility with certain of the great traditions of Western thought was a strategy common to all.

Although one might begin with primitive religion, where Mircea Eliade and others have pointed to the importance of totality,[14] the proper place to start an investigation of its philosophical roots is with the ancient Greeks. As early as Parmenides' attempt to dissociate the One as an indivisible unity from the concept of wholeness, which included the presence of parts, Greek philosophy was concerned with the nature of the *hólon*.[15] In addition to descriptive analyses of the whole or the One, Greek thought entertained normative ideas of totality as well, which culminated in the elaborate neo-Platonic attempts to overcome the contingency of man's finite existence through recovering his lost unity with the universe.[16] The Greeks were also holistically inclined in much of their thinking about more mundane matters such as politics. Both Plato and Aristotle focused on the state, rather than on what a later age would call society, as the significant totality of human life. To Aristotle in particular, the state was like an organism that was differentiated into complementary parts subordinate to the whole. "The state," he contended in the *Politics*, "is by nature clearly prior to the individual, since the whole is prior to the parts."[17] In an argument that would be repeated many times, he wrote, "The proof that the state is a creation of nature and prior to the individual is that the individual, when isolated, is not self-sufficing; and therefore he is like a part in relation to the whole."[18]

14. Mircea Eliade, *Occult, Witchcraft and Cultural Fashions* (Chicago, 1976), p. 89. Leszek Kolakowski, *Main Currents of Marxism*, trans. P. S. Falla (Oxford, 1978), vol. 1, p. 11.

15. For a discussion of the various uses of *hólon* in Greek thought, see F. E. Peters, *Greek Philosophical Terms: A Historical Lexicon* (New York, 1967), p. 84f. See also the discussions in Stanley Rosen, *G. W. F. Hegel: An Introduction to the Science of Wisdom* (New Haven, 1974), chap. 4; G. N. Giordano Orsini, "The Ancient Roots of a Modern Idea" in G. S. Rousseau, ed., *Organic Form: The Life of an Idea* (London, 1972).

16. Kolakowski, vol. 1, pp. 12–23. The crucial difference between the neo-Platonic and Marxist normative totalities lay in the former's belief in an undifferentiated whole.

17. Aristotle, *Politics*, trans. B. Jowett (Oxford, 1920), 1253a.

18. Ibid.

What Greek thought lacked, however, was a belief that history could be understood as a progressively meaningful whole with a beginning, middle and end. Preferring to see time as repeating itself in infinite cycles without any progress or, in the case of Hesiod and others, stressing decline, the Greeks failed to develop what might be called an optimistic, "longitudinal" concept of totality. Here Jewish and, more importantly, Christian thought provided a corrective. Although St. Augustine limited the progress he posited to the spiritual realm of the City of God and denied it to the mundane City of Man, more heterodox Christian thinkers, most notably the twelfth-century mystic Joachim of Fiore, introduced a full-fledged doctrine of historical fulfillment.[19] Joachim's prophecy of a Third Kingdom on earth, ushering in the reign of the Holy Ghost, was anathema to the official Church but won converts among millenarian movements, whose hope for a realm of perfect grace prefigured later utopian and, some like Ernst Bloch would argue, Marxist notions of normative wholeness as well.

However lacking in this historical dimension, Aristotle's argument from nature still had a profound impact on late medieval thought after the translation of his *Politics* c. 1260 and its assimilation into Scholasticism. Even before that time, an organic view of the state had been posited in such non-Aristotelian works as John of Salisbury's *Policraticus* (1150s) in which the metaphor of the body politic was exploited to justify the hierarchy of the medieval polity. Not coincidentally, this occurred at roughly the same time as the centralization of royal power in the hands of the Angevins, Capetians and Hohenstaufens. Medieval organicism perhaps reached its peak in the work of the Florentine Dominican Remigio di Girolemi (1235–1319), Aquinas' pupil and Dante's teacher, who wrote: "If you are not a citizen you are not a man, because a man is naturally a civil animal" and added that "the whole is more fully united to the part than the part is to itself."[20]

Whether or not all medieval political and social thought was as organic as that of John or Remigio is an issue that has exercised scholars since the debate over Otto von Gierke's *Das deutsche Genossenschaftsrecht*[21] in the

19. For a discussion of pagan and Christian notions of historical time see Frank E. Manuel, *Shapes of Philosophical History* (Stanford, 1965). For a more nuanced view of the varieties within each tradition, see *History and the Concept of Time, History and Theory, Beiheft* 6 (1966).

20. Cited in John B. Morrall, *Political Thought in Medieval Times* (New York, 1958), p. 29.

21. Gierke's major work, *Das deutsche Genossenschaftsrecht*, was written from 1868 to 1913. Its major argument was directed both against the bureaucratic state and against abstract individualism. In contrast to both, von Gierke favored intermediate corporate bodies, which he claimed dominated medieval, especially German, society. For a brief discussion of

late nineteenth century, and it need not concern us now. It suffices to note that organic theory based on the analogy between the state and a living organism provided one vital source of later holistic thought. Although the so-called "social physics" of Hobbes and his successors presented a serious challenge to it, theorists such as Hooker, Pascal, and Shaftesbury, each in different ways, kept it alive. And of course it reemerged during the Romantic era in the early nineteenth century, often for conservative purposes. No less indebted to organicism was the new science of sociology, which set out to restore a sense of order after the initial traumas of the French and Industrial revolutions.[22] Although Saint-Simon and Comte were important figures in the rise of positivism, they nonetheless combined their allegiance to the scientific method, as they understood it, with an organic and holistic vision of the social realm.

It has sometimes been argued that Marxism, because of its links to Romantic conservatism through Hegel and to the early positivists through French socialism, shared an essentially organic vision of the social whole.[23] And insofar as all these movements did have a common dislike for the fragmentation and atomization caused by the emergence of bourgeois society there is some truth to this contention. But in crucial ways Marx's use of totality clashed with that of the organicists, even though at times Marx labeled his position naturalist and even evoked the organic metaphor.[24] Organic naturalism was generally used to legitimate social differentiation and hierarchy,[25] a function it served as early as Aris-

his work, see Georg G. Iggers, *The German Conception of History: The National Tradition of Historical Thought from Herder to the Present* (Middletown, Conn., 1968), pp. 131–33.

22. For a history of sociology that stresses its conservative response to the twin revolutions, see Robert A. Nisbet, *The Sociological Tradition* (New York, 1966). For a critique of his interpretation, see Norman Birnbaum, *Toward a Critical Sociology* (New York, 1971). For an older, but still important, account of the links between Marx and conservatism, see Karl Mannheim, "On Conservative Thought" in *From Karl Mannheim*, ed. Kurt H. Wolff (New York, 1971).

23. For interpretations of Marx that stress the organic nature of his thought, see Werner Stark, *The Fundamental Forms of Social Thought* (New York, 1963); Maurice Mandelbaum, *History, Man and Reason: A Study in Nineteenth-Century Thought* (Baltimore and London, 1971), and Melvin Rader, *Marx's Interpretation of History* (New York, 1979). Mandelbaum undercuts his argument when he admits that organicism stresses "the passivity of man" (p. 144), which is hard to reconcile with Marx's emphasis on *praxis*. For a good analysis of Marx's relation to the Saint-Simonian tradition, see Maximilien Rubel, *Marx Critique du Marxisme* (Paris, 1974), pp. 252–71.

24. For example, in the first preface to *Capital*, he writes, "The present society is no solid crystal, but an organism capable of change, and is constantly changing" ([New York, 1906], p. 16). And in the *Grundrisse*, he finishes a discussion of exchange and circulation with the remarks: "Mutual interaction takes place between the different moments. This is the case with every organic whole" (trans. Martin Nicolaus [New York, 1973], p. 100).

25. Rader (pp. 75–81) argues that Marx's organicism was also hierarchic because of its awareness of structural levels within the whole. Lukács, however, points out that

totle's defense of slavery. In this way it helped reconcile men to the status
quo by naturalizing it. The sense of wholeness and community underlying
the normative use of totality could be achieved by surrender to the current
reality and recognition of one's proper place in it. The priority of the
whole over the parts generally meant little, if any, acknowledgement of the
claims of the individual against the whole. Through a kind of transfigura-
tion of the existing order, true wholeness in the normative sense was assumed to be already in existence. Other naturalist metaphors, such as that
later used by the Social Darwinists, posited a whole that was more competitive than harmonious, but they also tended to valorize the status quo.
Marx's own holism was clearly more critical in intention and less naturalistic in substance than that of his organicist predecessors, even if at times
he adopted their terminology.

To clarify his differences with organicist holisms, it is useful to pause
for a moment and examine his relation to the greatest naturalist and holist
philosopher of the early modern period, Baruch Spinoza. Marx, to be
sure, read Spinoza with enthusiasm in 1841, was attracted to his liberal
critiques of religion and censorship, and initially saw him as a corrective
to Hegel's authoritarian statism.[26] But when it came to deriving the lineage of his materialism, he preferred French *philosophes* like Diderot,
Holbach and Helvétius to Spinoza.[27] Although one of the major Western
Marxists, Louis Althusser, credited Spinoza with anticipating Marx's
anti-inductivist epistemology and his alleged anti-subjectivism,[28] there
are nonetheless clear differences between their concepts of totality.

Spinoza's identification of God and nature and his monistic denial of
the separate existence of thought and extension, which he considered
mere attributes of the one divine/natural substance, did anticipate Marx's

---

A hierarchic system is not only something that exists for all time, it also has to render its categories
homogeneous, in order to arrange them in a definitive connection (even at the cost of impoverishing or
violating their content), and reduce them as far as possible to a single dimension of their relationship.
Those thinkers who have had a genuine ontological sense for the rich and varied character of the dynamic
structure of reality have precisely come to focus their interest on those kinds of relationships which cannot
be adequately brought into any kind of system.

(Georg Lukács, *The Ontology of Social Being: Marx's Basic Ontological Principles*, trans.
David Fernbach [London, 1978], pp. 18–19.)

    Although it is true that Marx often saw social relations in terms of superordination and
subordination, he was nonetheless wary about eternalizing the elements involved. Thus, for
example, contrary to certain vulgar Marxists, he never made the economy the determining
factor in all societies, however much it may have served this function under capitalism.

    26. Rubel, *Marx Critique du Marxisme*, pp. 172–73.
    27. David McLellan, *Karl Marx, His Life and Thought* (London, 1973), p. 135.
    28. Louis Althusser, *Essays in Self-Criticism*, trans. Grahame Lock (London, 1976), pp.
132–41. There are also many favorable references to Spinoza in *Reading Capital*, with
Etienne Balibar, trans. Ben Brewster (London, 1970).

critique of transcendental philosophies with their dualism of mind and external reality. But for Spinoza, the intelligible order of reality was understood as eternal and without development. Viewed *sub specie aeternitatis*, reality thus lacked any historical dimension, which for Marx was crucial. Spinoza's totality was in permanent existence, whereas for Marx, it was in the process of becoming, at least as a normative goal. Along with his denial of a Divine Creator in the Judeo-Christian sense, Spinoza also dismissed the possibility of creative human agency to change the world. Rather than a reciprocity between the whole and the parts, Spinoza's whole dominated the parts entirely. Despite his liberal stress on the value of free thought, there was no place in his system for human agency; indeed free will itself was an illusion which an understanding of the logical necessity of reality would dispel.[29]

Accordingly, like other naturalist and organic holisms, Spinoza's tended to legitimate surrender to the status quo. As Stuart Hampshire writes,

Real happiness (*beatitudo*) consists [for Spinoza] in this contemplation of the whole machinery and system of Nature, and in reflecting within his own mind the whole common order of things. . . . We shall bear with equanimity those things which happen to us and which are contrary to what our interest demands, if we are conscious that we have done our duty and cannot extend our actual power to such an extent as to avoid these things, and further that we are a part of Nature as a whole, and we follow its order.[30]

Finally, as even Althusser admits,[31] Spinoza's celebrated belief that "all determination is a negation" did not lead to an appreciation of the dialectical role of contradiction in reality, which Marx had to get from Hegel.

Although Spinoza was wisely admired by the Romantics, many of whom shared Goethe's excitement over his nature-worship, his star had been very much on the wane during the eighteenth century. Pierre Bayle's scathing (and often misguided) attack in his *Dictionary* of 1697 set the tone for the Enlightenment's dismissal of Spinoza's philosophy, even though it grudgingly admitted his importance as an earlier historical critic of the Bible.[32] Until Lessing, who himself qualified a generally positive appraisal of Spinoza with a Leibnizian appreciation of the importance of

---

29. Among certain Second International theorists, Spinoza's determinism made him an honored forerunner of Marxism. The most prominent of their number was Plekhanov. See the discussion in Lucio Colletti, *From Rousseau to Lenin: Studies in Ideology and Society*, trans. John Merrington and Judith White (London, 1972), pp. 71–72.

30. Stuart Hampshire, *Spinoza* (London, 1976), pp. 166–67.

31. Althusser, *Essays in Self-Criticism*, p. 141.

32. On Bayle and the Enlightenment's attitude towards Spinoza, see Ira O. Wade, *The Intellectual Origins of the French Enlightenment* (Princeton, 1971), pp. 606–12.

particularity,[33] Spinoza was roundly condemned by his anti-systematic and anti-metaphysical successors.

As Marx's materialism was derived less from Spinoza's than from that of the radical *philosophes*, so too was his concept of totality. At first glance, the Enlightenment seems an unlikely source for an idea of totality, Marxist or otherwise. The traditional image of the Enlightenment, despite countless revisions and reevaluations, is of a movement whose major intellectual impulses were critical, analytic, scientific, mechanistic and anti-metaphysical. Epistemologically, the Enlightenment is normally seen as sensationalist and associationist, with a straight line running from Locke to the outright skepticism of Hume. The deductive reasoning characteristic of seventeenth-century metaphysicians like Spinoza and Leibniz was replaced by empiricist induction. Politically, the Enlightenment is usually associated with social contract theory, individualism, natural right theory, and the pursuit of self-interest, rather than the search for community or the justification of hierarchy. Although Aristotle was important for the Enlightenment in a number of ways, his view of man as a political animal subordinate to the whole was not. Even Peter Gay, who stresses the links with the Greeks, admits that "when the philosophes turned to the ancients for inspiration, they looked for philosophical rather than political models."[34] And finally, the psychology of the Enlightenment has been identified with egoism and intellectualism, and not with that affective attachment to entities beyond the self which is the source of much holistic thinking.

These generalizations can, of course, be modified and nuanced, but by and large they do hold for most figures identified with Enlightenment thought. And yet the concept of totality, which seems on the surface foreign to the Enlightenment, can be said to have emerged in its interstices. In fact, it is possible to isolate many different Enlightenment sources for later concepts of totality in Western Marxism. Among these perhaps the most obvious is the *philosophes*' essential confidence in the capacity of mankind to know the world. Despite its scorn for the hollow deductive systems of the seventeenth century, the Enlightenment did not hold a modest view of the power of rationality. In Ernst Cassirer's words, for the Enlightenment, "Reason cannot stop with the dispersed parts, it has to build from them a new structure, a true whole. But since Reason creates this whole and fits the parts together according to its own rule, it gains

33. Ernst Cassirer, *The Philosophy of the Enlightenment*, trans. Fritz C. A. Koelln and James P. Pettegrove (Boston, 1964), p. 191.
34. Peter Gay, *The Enlightenment: An Interpretation; The Rise of Modern Paganism* (New York, 1968), p. 45.

complete knowledge of the structure of its product. Reason understands this structure because it can reproduce it in its totality and in the ordered sequence of its individual elements."[35]

Although one might question Cassirer's overly Kantian vision of the Enlightenment expressed in these remarks, it is nonetheless true that the *philosophes* had a fundamental faith in the human potential to know reality whole. No better monument to this belief exists than the great *Encyclopedia* of Diderot and D'Alembert, which paid tribute to what Cassirer calls the Enlightenment's *libido sciendi*, its lust for knowledge. Although Marxism was to emphasize practice more than knowledge, an emphasis by no means foreign to the Enlightenment itself, there is more than a trace of the *philosophes*' hubris in the claims of Marxist intellectuals to know the whole.

The confidence behind this claim was grounded in part in the Enlightenment belief in the essential unity of mankind. The concept of progress held by Turgot, Condorcet and others was predicated on the assumption that the course of human history was a unified whole with a common destiny. Jettisoning Augustinian divisions between cities of God and of man, they conceived of "History" as a unified process, the story of a single subject, "Mankind" or "Humanity." To speak of progress at all necessitated a faith in a universal standard by which to measure advance or decline. Although Marxism would later challenge the ahistorical homogenization of mankind implicit in the Enlightenment view of progress, there would be enough of an evolutionary bias left in its own assumptions to warrant a comparison.[36]

A genuinely "longitudinal" use of the concept of totality, with an optimistic bias, can thus be discerned both in the Enlightenment and in Marxism. Perhaps the one aspect of the Enlightenment view that renders the comparison imperfect is its assumption that the process of growth, the continual resolution of new problems, is open-ended and infinite. This refusal to round off the future, which was clearly articulated in Kant, anticipated those Western Marxists who spoke of open-ended totalization rather than closed totality. But as we will see, for those Marxists who stressed the latter, a solution derived from Hegel proved effective.

Another contribution of the *philosophes* to the holistic tradition can be noted in their expansion of the scope of historical inquiry. Although generally maligned by nineteenth-century critics, the Enlightenment clearly possessed an historical sense much in advance of its predecessors. Instead of merely chronicling the deeds of kings and popes, Voltaire, Gibbon and some of their peers investigated the cultural life of the entire society of the period they studied. The belief that cultures were, in fact, coherent unities whose common features were expressed in their art, religion, institutions, social mores and political constitutions animated the work of Herder, Hamann and others who fed directly into nineteenth-century historicism. Indeed, the very notion of a *Zeitgeist* or "Spirit of the Times," with its implication that each era was a coherent whole, can be traced back beyond the Romantics to the eighteenth century.[37] Although the Enlightenment thinkers tended to simplify the unity of the cultures they isolated, a "latitudinal" use of totality can be found in their interest in whole cultures. Marxism, in fact, can be said to have more closely approximated the Enlightenment's balance between a universal homogenization of mankind and an interest in specific cultures than the later Romantics' overemphasis on the latter.

More specifically, the Enlightenment produced several thinkers whose ideas would later find echoes in Marxist holism. Most important among them were Montesquieu, Rousseau, Kant and Vico (who is sometimes omitted from the Enlightenment when it is narrowly defined). One might add as well Quesnay and the Physiocrats, who were the first to isolate the economy as a system capable of holistic analysis, although the very isolation of the economy from the rest of society was a target of Marx's holism properly understood. Vico and Montesquieu were the earliest of their number and can be said to have inaugurated, or at least anticipated, traditions which produced very different Marxist concepts of totality. It is thus necessary to pause with each of them before examining the other Enlightenment thinkers whose links to Marxism have been more frequently traced.

Once neglected and all but forgotten outside of his native Naples, Giambattista Vico has now become the focus of a remarkable amount of scholarly attention.[38] His most influential work, *The New Science*, whose first edition was completed in 1725, has been celebrated as the source or prefiguration of virtually every major intellectual advance of the past two centuries. As Jules Michelet, who did the most to popularize Vico's ideas

37. Mandelbaum, *History, Man and Reason*, p. 429, fn. 3.
38. For a full bibliography of the scholarship on Vico in English, see Molly Black Verene, "Critical Writings on Vico in English" in *Giambattista Vico's Science of Humanity*, ed. Giorgio Tagliacozzo and Donald Phillip Verene (Baltimore, 1976) and "Critical Writings on Vico in English: A Supplement," *Social Research* 43:4 (Winter 1976).

in the nineteenth century, put it, "All the giants of criticism are already contained, with room to spare, in the little pandemonium of *The New Science*."[39] Because *The New Science* was indeed a pandemonium and many of its insights cryptically or only embryonically expressed, the precise nature of Vico's influence has never been easy to gauge.

Vico's impact on Marx and Marxism has been especially hard to measure. In the nineteenth century, Marxists like Lafargue, Labriola, and Sorel all claimed Vico as an important forerunner of a number of Marx's ideas; more recently, figures as diverse as Trotsky, Horkheimer, Max Adler and Edmund Wilson have echoed their argument.[40] Non-Marxist scholars like Vico's English translators, Fisch and Bergin, and Isaiah Berlin, have done so as well.[41] Although there has been considerable difference of opinion over the precise nature of the debt, the linkage of Vico and Marx has been widely accepted.

Recently, however, Eugene Kamenka has attempted to minimize Vico's importance for Marx's own work and, with the exception of Gramsci, for that of the Western Marxists.[42] Except for allusions in private letters written in 1862 and one footnote in *Capital*, there are no direct references to Vico in all of Marx's voluminous work. For Kamenka, "the reason is probably simple. As a philosopher of history Vico would have seemed to Marx . . . to have been absorbed and transcended by Hegel; as a social scientist or materialist, Vico would have seemed to him a herald rather than a performer."[43] Later Marxists, Kamenka suggests, had only a superficial knowledge of Vico's actual work and introduced his name for little more than ornamental purposes.

Although Kamenka's argument is persuasive in terms of Vico's direct influence on Marx, there can be little doubt that he anticipated Marx's stress on totality (even if all Marxists did not interpret the concept in a Vichian sense). Most obviously, Vico's recognition of the importance of his-

39. Quoted in Intro. to *The Autobiography of Giambattista Vico*, trans. Max Harold Fisch and Thomas Goddard Bergin (Ithaca and London, 1975), p. 78.

40. For a discussion of all of these figures in relation to Vico, see Fisch and Bergin, pp. 104–107. The two examples they neglect are Adler, "Die Bedeutung Vicos fur die Entwicklung des soziologischen Denken," *Grünbergs Archiv*, 14 (1929), and Horkheimer, *Anfänge der bürgerlichen Geschichtsphilosophie* (Stuttgart, 1930). For the Austro-Marxist Adler, Vico was important because his insight into the "ideal eternal history" of mankind was an anticipation of the social laws of development perceived by Marx. For a similar view of Vico as the first modern sociologist, see Leo Kofler, *Die Wissenschaft von der Gesellschaft* (Cologne, 1971), p. 24.

41. Fisch and Bergin, op. cit. and Isaiah Berlin, *Vico and Herder: Two Studies in the History of Ideas* (New York, 1977), pp. 161, 120.

42. Eugene Kamenka, "Vico and Marxism" in *Giambattista Vico: an International Symposium*, ed. Giorgio Tagliacozzo, co-ed. Hayden V. White (Baltimore, 1969).

43. Ibid., p. 139.

tory, at a time when the dominant thought was Cartesian and thus anti-historical, opened up the possibility of totality as an historical category, thus adding an element absent from the naturalistic and Spinozist traditions. Beyond merely defending the validity of historical thought, Vico's *New Science* attempted to plot the "ideal eternal history traversed in time by the history of every nation in its ri :e, development, maturity, decline and fall,"[44] with the exception of the Hebrews. In so doing, Vico assumed that history made sense as a whole, an anticipation of similar assumptions in Hegel and, to a certain extent, Marx. Where Vico differed from both, however, was in his cyclical view of the course of that history, which went through a succession of *corsi* and *ricorsi* from barbarism to culture and back again. His was thus not a fully "comic" vision of a universal history with a positive outcome, in the sense that Hayden White has argued Marxism is, even though Vico did believe in the role of Providence in guiding the whole. The idea of linear progress in history was absent in this system, although, as J.B. Bury remarked, "it is obvious how readily his doctrine could be adapted to the conception of Progress as a spiral movement."[45]

Descending from the level of universally traversed "ideal eternal history" to that of specific societies, Vico clearly anticipated Marx's idea that the components of those societies could be understood only in relation to each other, that is, as part of a coherent whole. Furthermore, he recognized that pure thought was not the dominant element in the totality; "The order of ideas," he contended, "must follow the order of institutions."[46] To Vico, these institutions were not the product of conscious and deliberate contrivance, as social contract theorists from Locke to Rousseau argued; they arose instead in the course of an historical process ruled more by imagination and passion than by reason. The true creators of history were the same as the poets of ancient times; in fact, the Greek word for "poet," he claimed, was the same as that for "creator."[47]

But even if he stressed the poetic and irrational side of creation, Vico still insisted that human creativity was at the root of social and cultural institutions. This stress on *making* was, as many commentators have observed, Vico's seminal contribution to historical thinking, and by extension to Marxism and, in particular, Western Marxism (at least in its Hegelian guise). In his quarrel with Descartes and Spinoza, he advanced his most revolutionary epistemological principle, *verum et factum conver-*

44. *The New Science of Giambattista Vico*, trans. from 3rd ed., Thomas Goddard Bergin and Max Harold Fisch (New York, 1961), p. 62.
45. J.B. Bury, *The Idea of Progress: An Inquiry into its Growth and Origin* (New York, 1955), p. 269.
46. *The New Science*, p. 36.
47. Ibid., p. 75.

tuntur: the true and the made are interchangeable. Therefore, Vico argued, men can know history, which they have made, better than they can know nature, whose cause is God alone.

It was to this principle that Marx alluded in his famous footnote in *Capital*:

Since as Vico says, the essence of the distinction between human history and natural history is that the former is made by man and the latter is not, would not the history of human technology be easier to write than the history of natural technology? By disclosing man's dealings with nature, the productive activities by which his life is sustained, technology lays bare his social relations and the mental concepts that flow from them.[48]

Marx's reduction of Vico's theory of human history to a comment on technology perhaps buttresses Kamenka's argument that Vico's influence was indirect. For technology, as Berlin has pointed out,[49] involves an interaction between man and nature, which cannot be reduced to creation *ex nihilo*, and therefore cannot be the source of perfect knowledge. Whether or not other aspects of human history can be so reduced is itself problematic, as some of the Western Marxists came to appreciate, but the argument is on firmer ground if the dialectic between man and nature that is technology is left aside. Vico's belief in the human origins of history and the concomitant superiority of historical over natural knowledge might then seem compelling, as indeed it was for Lukács and other Western Marxists.

Or at least it might if several other difficulties in the argument are resolved. First, as noted above, Vico denied an intellectually rational interpretation of the word "made" in his thesis; the poet–creators of culture were not Cartesian thinking machines. Nor did Vico, who included the "barbarism of reflection" in his *corsi* and *ricorsi*, hold out any hope for a future determination of history by rational intentionality. Although Marx agreed about deliberate creation in the past—he too had no use for social contract theory or the myth of the wise law-giver—he clearly thought otherwise about the future. Indeed, he talked about true history beginning only when men gained conscious control over the social process. Unreflective making would then give way to reflective creation. The implications for knowing the totality of history, especially before the onset of Communism, were thus clouded, for, in the famous words from *The Eighteenth Brumaire,* "Men make history, but they do not make it just as they please; they do not make it under circumstances chosen by themselves, but under

48. Marx, *Capital*, p. 406.
49. Berlin, *Vico and Herder*, p. 110.

circumstances directly encountered, given and transmitted from the past. The tradition of all the dead generations weighs like a nightmare on the brain of the living."[50] Until they awaken from that nightmare, Marx implied, men will not fully "make" their own history. This suggests, as Horkheimer was perhaps the first to point out,[51] that Vico's formula about knowing what we have made cannot be unequivocally applied to all previous history. And thus the perfect symmetry between cognition and production posited by Vico must await some future state when true history can be said to have begun.

The second difficulty with Vico's *verum–factum* principle for Marxism concerns the object of inquiry which can be known by men. Although his positing of an "ideal eternal history" for all societies suggests prediction as well as retrospection, the linkage of making with knowing has other epistemological implications. It suggests that the object of historical knowledge is entirely in the past: what men have made, not what they are making or will make, is *verum*: the truth. The well-known implication that Hegel drew from this premise, that the owl of Minerva flies only at dusk when the story is already over, could not be adopted by a future-oriented Marxism, which stressed theoretically directed *praxis* over interpretation or recognition. Vico's holism was thus better suited to a retrospective theory of knowledge than to one with a practical orientation. In fact, as Perry Anderson has recently admitted,[52] historical materialism as a theory based on such a view of the past was inherently passive and thus problematically related to the activist dimension in the Marxist tradition. Although certain Western Marxists, Lukács in particular, thought otherwise, this conclusion was drawn by many who came to see Vico's legacy as more ambiguous than was originally perceived.[53]

That legacy was indeed mixed. Although Vico freed the idea of totality from naturalism and tied it to human artifice, certainly a critical step in the development of Marxist holism, he left unresolved a number of problems. In addition to those mentioned above, the real identity of the true maker of history and the proper relationship between that making and the domination of nature were also to trouble many Western Marxists. So too was the secularized version of his notion of Providence, which had appeared in the Second International era as the so-called laws of historical

50. *Karl Marx: Selected Writings,* ed. David McLellan (Oxford, 1977), p. 300.

51. Max Horkheimer, "Zum Problem der Voraussage in den Sozialwissenschaften," *Zeitschrift für Sozialforschung* 2:3 (1933).

52. Perry Anderson, *Considerations on Western Marxism* (London, 1976), p. 110.

53. Martin Jay, "Vico and Western Marxism" in *Giambattista Vico: New Studies and Recent Interpretations,* ed. Giorgio Tagliacozzo, vol. 2 (New York, 1981).

development, laws which most Western Marxists thought were honored more in the breach than the observance. Nor finally did his faith in that "ideal eternal history" followed by all gentile peoples, which in orthodox Marxism became the evolutionary development from slavery to feudalism, capitalism and then socialism, survive the scrutiny of Western Marxists aware of the vagaries of historical development. The rediscovery of Vico by certain Western Marxists, in fact, thus posed almost as many questions as it resolved.

The lessons to be derived from the work of Montesquieu, the other early Enlightenment progenitor of the concept of totality, were equally ambiguous. Although Montesquieu was a contemporary of Vico's and learned of *The New Science* on a visit to Venice, there is no evidence to indicate he read it or borrowed anything directly from it.[54] His contributions to holistic thinking were close to Vico's in certain respects, but significantly different in others. The two men shared an interest in history and believed that it possessed an intelligible order. Like Vico, Montesquieu had no use for social contract theory and rejected the then fashionable notion of a natural man antecedent to society. And finally, Montesquieu joined with Vico in holding that societies could be understood as coherent wholes whose elements were meaningfully interrelated. In *The Spirit of the Laws* of 1748, he presented his celebrated typology of governmental forms, each ruled by a specific principle: a republic by virtue, a monarchy by honor, and a despotism by fear. What might be called the totalizing impulse behind his typology was Montesquieu's correlation of specific social organizations with those principles, e.g., republican virtue implied social equality whereas aristocratic honor involved hierarchy. In so linking governmental form, social organization and ruling principle, Montesquieu acknowledged, as had Vico, the necessity of viewing man's collective life in holistic terms.

Where he differed from his Neapolitan contemporary was in his conception of the origin of the totalities he described. To Montesquieu they represented natural, not man-made, relations. In fact, one of the primary goals of *The Spirit of the Laws* was to establish the primacy of natural over human laws. And, as has been often remarked, he defended a version of natural law very different from that entailed in the notion of God's com-

54. Berlin, p. 90. For a new and heterodox interpretation of Montesquieu, see Mark Hulliung, *Montesquieu and the Old Regime* (Berkeley, 1976), which emphasizes his radical rather than reactionary side.

mandments. To Montesquieu, law was discovered, not created, a tradi-
tionalist view that he turned against the traditions of the ancien régime. Far
closer to Descartes than Vico in his epistemology, Montesquieu represented a new variation of the naturalist and organic version of totality.
Accordingly, he laid great emphasis on the climate and terrain of a country in explaining the governmental type best suited to it.

From a humanist or idealist perspective, it is clear that Montesquieu's
ideas on totality can be seen as more a reversion to Spinoza than an advance over Vico. Not all Western Marxists, however, were comfortable
with such a perspective, and so, not surprisingly, Montesquieu has been
hailed as the true forerunner of Marx by the anti-Hegelian Althusser.
In his first work, *Montesquieu: Politics and History*, written in 1959,[55]
Althusser praised him for having discovered that states were coherent totalities, which were pure, if their principle and nature were unified, and
impure or contradictory, if they were not. To Althusser, whose "scientific"
reading of Marx will be examined later, Montesquieu was the founder of a
true political science because of the banishment of intentionality and teleology from his analysis:

*Montesquieu was probably the first person before Marx who undertook to think
history without attributing to it an end*, i.e., without projecting the consciousness
of men and their hopes onto the time of history. This criticism is entirely to his
credit. *He was the first to propose a positive principle of universal explanation for
history*; a principle which is not just *static*: the totality explaining the diversity of
the laws and institutions of a given government; but also *dynamic*: the law of the
unity of nature and principle, a law making it possible to think the development of
institutions and their transformations in real history, too.[56]

Going beyond this claim, Althusser attempted to find in Montesquieu a
correlate to his own notion of one determining factor in the totality, which
he claimed set Marx apart from Hegel and the Hegelian Marxists. In
Montesquieu, Althusser argued, the determining element was the principle (virtue, honor, or fear); this was comparable to Marx's notion of the
economy as determinant "in the last instant." Later, however, after he
developed a less monocausal notion of totality and came to stress overdetermination, Althusser modified his appraisal of Montesquieu:

Borrowing from Montesquieu the idea that in a historical totality all concrete
determinations, whether economic, political, moral or even military, express one
single principle, Hegel conceives history in terms of the category of the expressive totality.[57]

55. This work is translated in Louis Althusser, *Politics and History: Montesquieu, Rousseau, Hegel and Marx*, trans. Ben Brewster (London, 1972).
56. Ibid., p. 50.
57. Althusser, *Essays in Self-Criticism*, p. 182.

Expressive totality, as will become clearer later, was seen by Althusser as profoundly non-Marxist, and thus for him the mantle of Marx's true predecessor on the question of totality was shifted to Spinoza's shoulders. For many other Western Marxists, however, neither Montesquieu nor Spinoza was the proper figure to honor in this fashion. Instead, they tended to trace their lineage back to Vico by way of Hegel, Fichte, Schiller, Kant and Rousseau.[58] In other words, they came to appreciate the importance of German Idealism as the crucial source of Marxist holism, although of course recognizing to varying degrees the extent to which Marx's materialist critique of that tradition meant a new departure. Accordingly, our account of the pre-Marxist development of holism must probe the contribution of Idealism to that concept in some detail.

Rousseau's stimulus to German Idealism has often been noted, perhaps most influentially in Cassirer's classic studies of his relation to Kant.[59] Here questions of will, morality, virtue, community and political organization were key issues, as we will see shortly. But before investigating Rousseau's contribution to Idealism, one other important innovation of this most innovative thinker must be pursued, especially because it was perhaps the starting point for yet another strain of holistic thinking which found its way into the Western Marxist debate.

In the years immediately prior to the French Revolution, Rousseau's ideas about politics and community were far less widely known or discussed than his novel, autobiography, and various treatises on cultural or educational issues. As we have known since the work of Mornet,[60] *The Social Contract* had practically no direct influence on the Revolution until after it began, whereas *Emile*, the *Confessions*, the two *Discourses*, and *La Nouvelle Héloise* enjoyed enormous popularity. Their cumulative effect was to make Rousseau into the apostle of pre-Romanticism, the scourge of the rationalist Enlightenment, and the guiding spirit of the rebellious generation of the 1770s and '80s in Germany known as the "Sturm und Drang." This was the Rousseau of sentiment, sensibility, emo-

58. For a recent summary of this tradition, see Kolakowski, *Main Currents of Marxism*, vol 1. Although hostile to Marxism, Kolakowski closely follows Lukács' interpretation of its origins. For a more extensive discussion of the tradition before Marx, see the excellent study by George Armstrong Kelly, *Idealism, Politics and History: Sources of Hegelian Thought* (Cambridge, 1969).

59. Ernst Cassirer, *The Question of Jean-Jacques Rousseau*, trans. and intro., Peter Gay (Bloomington, 1963); idem., *Rousseau, Kant, Goethe* (Princeton, 1947). For a more recent treatment of the Rousseau–Kant relationship, see William A. Galston, *Kant and the Problem of History* (Chicago, 1975), p. 93f.

60. Daniel Mornet, *Origines intellectuelles de la Révolution française* (Paris, 1933).

tion, and imagination, who seems far more the progenitor of a kind of Romantic anarchist individualism than holism in any form.

If Rousseau had not chosen to write *The Social Contract*, this judgment may have had arguable validity. Even so, there was one vital way in which the non-political Rousseau made his contribution to the tradition of thinking about totality that merits our attention. For perhaps no one in the eighteenth century posed the question of individual or personal totality as acutely as did Rousseau,[61] who suffered a particularly devastating loss of his own sense of personal wholeness. Although one can find similar insights in Diderot's remarkable *Rameau's Nephew*,[62] or even possibly in Montesquieu's *Persian Letters*,[63] no one did more than Rousseau to dramatize the agony of personal fragmentation or searched as frantically for ways to end it. His constant goal, pursued by a series of changing means, was to find a framework—an order—in which, as he put it in *Emile*, "I shall be me without contradiction, without division."[64] Although dimly echoing the ideal of the universal man in classical and Renaissance thought, Rousseau's understanding of that ideal had a proto-existentialist dimension, an awareness of the virtual impossibility of attaining it, that marked him a clearly modern figure. Indeed, inasmuch as he perceived the integrity of the individual to be fragile he was set apart from most other *philosophes*, who saw more confidently what a later age would call "ego integration," fostered by the growing power of reason. Their confidence is not surprising, for, after all, the "individual" had only recently emerged as a discrete entity during the Renaissance and Reformation; in Rousseau's time the dissemination of the bourgeois notion of self-interest, that "possessive individualism" discussed by C. B. Macpherson,[65] was only beginning and thus not yet prominent enough for critical scrutiny.

But for reasons that cannot be explored here, Rousseau was able to comprehend the delicate and brittle quality of the new individualism. Drawing on the same Protestant conscience, albeit in its Calvinist rather than Pietist form, that would inspire Kant and the German Idealists, he

61. To be sure, there were earlier thinkers in the Christian tradition, like Augustine, who anticipated Rousseau. See William J. Bouwsma, "Christian Adulthood," *Daedalus* 105:2 (Spring 1976).

62. For a discussion of *Rameau's Nephew* that treats this issue, see Lionel Trilling, *Sincerity and Authenticity* (Cambridge, 1974), p. 27f. Trilling, however, overemphasizes the agony in Diderot's depiction of the splits in the nephew's personality.

63. For a discussion of Montesquieu that makes this claim, see Marshall Berman, *The Politics of Authenticity: Radical Individualism and the Emergence of Modern Society* (New York, 1972).

64. *Emile*, 4, quoted in Kelly, *Idealism*, p. 65.

65. C. B. Macpherson, *The Political Theory of Possessive Individualism: Hobbes to Locke* (Oxford, 1962).

denounced the shallowness implicit in the rationalist definition of personality. Just as bitterly, he called into question the compromises demanded of personal integrity by the modern, urbane society of his day. To live in the civilized world of the Enlightenment, the world of fashionable salons and literary politics, meant to live inauthentically and thus estranged from one's deeper self. To break free from that estrangement meant ending one's dependence on external values, which fed what he called *amour-propre*, the desire for status in the eyes of others. Instead, one should express and follow only one's inner demands, an injunction which nurtured that culture of expressivity out of which German Idealism grew,[66] and to which the "expressive" concept of totality can in part be traced.

By so insistently vilifying the society of his day, Rousseau gave the impression that he placed no faith in social answers to personal fragmentation, whence his popular reputation as a primitivist extolling the noble savage.[67] To those who interpreted him in this way, among them the poets of the "Sturm und Drang," personal totality could only be regained through individual rebellion against society or escape from it into art. But the Rousseau who had a more immediate impact on Marxist notions of totality offered a very different remedy, which can best be understood as non-individualist. In *The Social Contract* of 1762, Rousseau's solution to personal dissociation was clearly holistic and collectivist. Here he turned his back on "natural man" and embraced the artificial citizen as the answer to his dilemma. The road to personal wholeness, he argued, could only come through the transcendence of the empirical self with all its petty needs and desires, and the achievement of a new moral personality through allegiance to a higher moral community.[68] As he put it in *Emile*, written in the same year as *The Social Contract*,

Civil man is only a fraction of a whole, his value lying in his relation to the whole, which is the social body. Good institutions are those which best strip man of his nature, taking away his absolute existence to give him a relative one, and transfer-

66. For an illuminating discussion of the expressive tradition, see Charles Taylor, *Hegel* (Cambridge, 1975), chapter 1.

67. Arthur Lovejoy, "The Supposed Primitivism of Rousseau's *Discourse on Inequality*" in *Essays in the History of Ideas* (New York, 1960).

68. In the words of *The Social Contract*, "He who dares to undertake the making of a people's institutions, ought to feel himself capable, so to speak, of changing human nature, of transforming each individual, who is by himself a complete and solitary whole, into part of a greater whole from which he in a manner receives his life and being." ([London, 1955], p. 32). Normally, the transformation is understood to be essentially moral, although there are other interpretations. See, for example, Althusser, *Politics and History*, p. 143, where self-interest rather than morality is stressed as the motivation behind the alienation of the self from the community.

ring his *Self* into a common unity; so that each individual no longer believes himself to be one, but part of a unit, and is no longer aware except in the whole.[69]

In the General Will, as opposed to the Will of All, the unity of this new whole would be concretely expressed. Because each gives himself to all, he gives himself to nobody in particular, and thus avoids new forms of external dependence. Whereas earlier Rousseau had nostalgically looked back to a semi-primitive lost age, before the corruption of civilization, for his model of wholeness, now his reference point was a political–moral community reminiscent of classical Sparta.

Ungenerously interpreted, this model has persuaded some conservative commentators to condemn Rousseau as the progenitor of "totalitarian democracy."[70] But like Montesquieu, from whom Rousseau seems to have obtained the insight that each society should be understood as a unique whole, Rousseau realized that the social contract made sense only in small communities where public life between equals was a real possibility. The democratic principle of virtue could operate in states the size of the classical Greek *polis*, where an identity of rulers and ruled—an isonomy—was possible. He thus held out no hope for the realization of his political solution to personal fragmentation in the modern world of giant nation-states, and recognized the dangers in trying to achieve it. Like his other answers, the social contract remained only a thought-experiment which lacked any means of implementation. Having no faith in progress, or indeed in history itself, Rousseau was a moralist without the hope that his utopia might be realized.[71]

His successors, however, were far less pessimistic. Rousseau died in 1778, eleven years before the revolution that would try to make individual men into citizens of a moral collectivity. Although Robespierre's virtuous republic was short-lived, the French Revolution gave the lie to Rousseau's disdain for history. Meaningful transformation was now understood to be a possibility, and new totalities in the normative sense might be hoped for, indeed fought for. The means to heal the fractured personality need no longer be seen as solely individual, but could be envisaged in collective terms as well. Actual mass political mobilization meant that the dream of a new meta-subjective totalizer, a collective subject of history, was no longer a utopian fantasy.

69. Quoted in Colletti, *From Rousseau to Lenin: Studies in Ideology and Society*, p. 173.
70. J. L. Talmon, *The Origins of Totalitarian Democracy* (New York, 1961).
71. Judith N. Shklar, *Men and Citizens: A Study of Rousseau's Social Theory* (Cambridge, 1969).

The true history of *The Social Contract* thus begins after the Revolution with its absorption into German Idealism and, through it, the thought of Karl Marx. Rousseau's expressive vision of the self was developed by Herder and the historicist tradition, and later fed both Hegel's and Marx's analyses of alienation.[72] His model of an artificial moral community based on popular sovereignty and the general will, with its open hostility to liberal, pluralistic, representative parliamentary institutions, was the major source of Marx's critique of bourgeois democracy. As Della Volpe and Colletti in particular among the Western Marxists came to recognize,[73] there was a direct line from *The Social Contract* to Marx's "On the Jewish Question" with its impatient critique of political emancipation and the continued split between man and citizen. For Rousseau as for Marx, this split was a form of alienation, which could be overcome by the further dissolution of the individual self into the collective moral community.

Instead of surrender to that natural totality which organicist theorists had assumed to be already in existence, Rousseau here proposed surrender to an artificial totality of man's own collective creation, one which would express the authentic, higher self potentially within him. Unlike Vico, whose cultural wholes were unconsciously created by poets, Rousseau stressed the deliberate, conscious decision involved in their origins, even if he concentrated that decision in the person of the wise legislator. The implication of all this was that the solution to fragmentation lay less in a return to nature than in the creation of a new "second nature," which would transcend the limitations of the first. Although, much later, Marxists such as Lukács were to use the concept "second nature" in a more pejorative sense to mean the ahistorical naturalization of capitalist institutions, German Idealism came to draw heavily on the notion that such a second nature might be fashioned to realize the wholeness which Rousseau had only posited as an unreachable dream. The personal education he had described in *Emile* was broadened to become a kind of collective cultural *Bildung* of mankind in which totality in its normative sense might be realized.

The most direct vehicle of Rousseau's influence on German Idealism was, of course, Immanuel Kant, whose admiration for *The Social Contract*

72. For an analysis of Rousseau's contribution to the later use of alienation, see Richard Schacht, *Alienation* (Garden City, New York, 1971), p. 18f.
73. Galvano Della Volpe, *Rousseau and Marx, and Other Writings,* trans. with intro. John Fraser (London, 1978); and Colletti, *From Rousseau to Lenin.*

and *Emile* in particular was considerable. In the history of the concept of totality, no figure has played as ambiguous and uncertain a role as Kant. For Lukács in *History and Class Consciousness*, Kant's work epitomized the bourgeoisie's inability to transcend the dualism of its concrete existence and achieve a totalistic grasp of reality. Kant's scornful rejection of dialectics as a legitimate mode of cognition seemed to Lukács an ahistorical transformation of the specific contradictions of bourgeois society into eternal categories. Western Marxism thus began with an attack on the legacy of Kant's thought as it affected both bourgeois and socialist theory in the years before the Russian Revolution. It quickly distanced itself from Austro-Marxism, which still drew on Kant's principles. To Lukács, Kantianism in philosophy was the equivalent of Revisionism in politics, an equation made all the more plausible by Eduard Bernstein's confused embrace of Kant.[74] In later years, the neo-Hegelian wing of the Western Marxist tradition, as such works as Marcuse's *Reason and Revolution* demonstrate,[75] tended to adopt Lukács' critique of Kant.

But the hostility was by no means universal. Aside from the anti-Hegelian Colletti, whose dualistic inclinations made him sympathetic to Kant's philosophy, surprising resistance to Lukács' condemnation came from one of his most prominent disciples, Lucien Goldmann. In his doctoral dissertation for the University of Zurich, published in 1945 as *Mensch, Gemeinschaft und Welt in der Philosophie Immanuel Kants*,[76] Goldmann attempted to identify tendencies in Kant's work that demonstrated his grasp of the concept of totality and its relation to the achievement of social community. Implicitly arguing against Lukács, for whom he nonetheless had only praise throughout the book, Goldmann contended that Kant was "the first modern thinker to recognize anew the importance of the *Totality* as a fundamental category of existence, or at least to recognize its problematic character."[77] For Goldmann, Kant was prevented from achieving a full-blown philosophy of totality by two factors: his desire to

74. On Bernstein's Kantianism, see Peter Gay, *The Dilemma of Democratic Socialism: Eduard Bernstein's Challenge to Marx* (New York, 1962), p. 151f.

75. Herbert Marcuse, *Reason and Revolution: Hegel and the Rise of Social Theory* (Boston, 1960). This view of Kant was not confined to Western Marxists. Karl Jaspers, for example, wrote that "Kant's philosophy goes counter to the totalizations that began with the systems of German idealism and led by way of Marxism to the practice of total knowledge and total planning" (*The Great Philosophers*, trans. Hannah Arendt and Ralph Manheim [New York, 1962], vol. 1, p. 346).

76. A slightly revised edition is the basis for the translation into English: Lucien Goldmann, *Immanuel Kant*, trans. Robert Black (London, 1971). George Lichtheim contended that Goldmann was actually following Lukács' interpretation of Kant (*The Concept of Ideology and other Essays* [New York, 1967], p. 279), but I see no evidence to support this view. For a recent critique of Goldmann's interpretation, see Galston, *Kant*, pp. 177, 186, 256.

77. Goldmann, *Kant*, p. 36. Later, Goldmann would grant Pascal this honor.

avoid the immanent pantheism of Spinoza, which contradicted his Christian belief in a transcendent God, and the underdeveloped condition of eighteenth-century Germany, which rendered social community too remote and utopian a possibility to support a totalistic philosophy.

In addition, Goldmann acknowledged the impact of Hume's empiricism, which had convinced Kant that no theoretical or practical totality existed as a given fact. Goldmann insisted, however, that hope for the future was a dominant motif in Kant's thought:

> But for all this, empiricism had not carried the day. For the totality retained all its reality and all its importance. Kant had merely been seeking it in the wrong direction. It is not external to man, but *in him*; it is not *given* and existing, but an ultimate *goal* which gives man his human dignity. It is a transcendental ideal, a practical postulate.[78]

In other words, Rousseau's nostalgia for the past totality that cannot be recaptured was replaced in Kant by a belief that future totalization, in the normative sense of the term, was a human possibility. By thus linking the concept of progress, absent in both Vico and Rousseau, with the ideal of normative totality, Kant, according to Goldmann, justified his reputation as *the* philosopher of the French Revolution.

A thorough investigation of Kant's thought would be necessary to arbitrate between the two opposing interpretations of Kant in Lukács and Goldmann, an investigation clearly beyond the scope of these cursory remarks. Suffice it to say that depending on which aspects of Kant's philosophy are emphasized, he can be read as an opponent or proponent of the concept of totality. If one looks solely at his critical epistemology, as it was developed primarily in the *Critique of Pure Reason* with its stress on the limits of cognition, its separation of the phenomenal and noumenal realms, its denigration of dialectics in the name of analytics, its positing of formal mental categories indifferent to content, and its general stress on scientific as opposed to historical thinking, it is easy to depict Kant as the enemy of holism in philosophy. In the first *Critique*, totality, along with unity and plurality, is included as a category of quantity and is correlated with singular judgments, but, beyond that, it plays no significant role in Kant's system at all.

This impression is further strengthened by Kant's second major work, the *Critique of Practical Reason*, in which Rousseau's concern for a moral community to be created by the general will was transformed into an internal and private moral sense instilled in man by his Creator. Here the

78. Ibid., p. 105.

more individualist lessons of *Emile* were taken to heart. Kant's celebrated concluding evocation of the starry heaven above him and the moral law within him, the first enclosing man in his animal-like, empirical being, the second linking his intelligible self to a higher reality beyond all sense experience, perfectly expresses the duality of the human condition Kant accepted as an unalterable given. Significantly, when Lukács sought a poetic way to express his yearning to go beyond the duality in *The Theory of the Novel*, he pointedly referred to a "starry sky" which would be the "map of all possible paths" for a happy age "complete in meaning—in *sense*—and complete for the senses."[79] The normative totality sought by Lukács meant a reconciliation of Kant's two types of reason and the overcoming of man's bifurcated state as a natural and moral being who is at once bound by external causality and internally free.

That Kant may himself have harbored a similar hope is evident elsewhere in his work, most centrally in his last major effort, the *Critique of Judgment* (1790), devoted to an analysis of organic nature and aesthetics, and in his shorter work on history, the *Idea for a Universal History with Cosmopolitan Intent* (1784). In the earlier essay Kant outlined and commented on nine propositions which dealt with the manifestations of the will in action; the narrative of these actions was human history. Optimistically, he argued that underlying the apparent chaos of that narrative was a coherence determined by universal natural laws. The nature to which he referred was not, however, that of Newton's mechanically caused universe knowable to man through the a priori synthetic judgments of his pure, theoretical reason. The nature of which Kant spoke was teleological instead; it implanted in men capacities which were to be developed over time. The chief capacity distinguishing man, Kant claimed, was his reason, which would be completely developed through the collective work of the species, rather than that of the isolated individual. The self-cultivation, or *Bildung*, of the species meant the progressive transcendence of man's purely animal existence and the increased perfection of his rational faculty, which implied practical or moral reason. From a state of heteronomous subservience to nature, man would achieve autonomous self-determination; to temporalize the ahistorical language of the first two critiques, his phenomenal self would be progressively transcended by his noumenal self.

The means nature employed to effect this progress was the mutual antagonism of men, which Kant called their "unsocial sociability." In finding

---

79. Georg Lukács, *The Theory of the Novel*, trans. Anna Bostock (Cambridge, Mass., 1971), p. 29.

a virtue in that *amour-propre* which Rousseau had only been able to condemn, Kant echoed the theodicies of the early Enlightenment, rephrasing
them in temporal terms.[80] From this justification of struggle as a means to
the ultimate totalization of mankind it was only a short step, as many
commentators have noted, to Hegel's idea of dialectical contradiction and
Marx's notion of class struggle as the motors of history. Kant, however,
did not view the process in socio-economic terms; he envisaged it instead
politically as the creation of a world federation of nations in which each
state would have a perfected constitution. Although experience discloses
this ideal course of history only dimly, a priori reasoning, Kant tells us,
allows the possibility of its achievement. To be sure, the possibility is not a
likely one because man is no angel and "one cannot fashion something
absolutely straight from wood which is as crooked as that of which man is
made."[81] But as a goal, a regulative principle drawing man on, totality is a
potent heuristic concept.

Even from this abbreviated account of Kant's thoughts on history, it is
apparent that his contribution to the tradition of holistic thinking was an
important one. History, he contended, must be conceptualized as an endless process of totalization in which the telos of rationality—the practical
rationality that meant above all moral intelligibility—determined the
random movements of the whole. In other words, history was what we
have called a "longitudinal totality": possessing coherence and structure as a whole. And it was as well a normative totality whose end was
an international community of civil societies "which administers law
(*Recht*) generally."[82] Moreover, the instrument of totalization was mankind itself, not the workings of providential intervention, for "nature has
intended that man develop everything which transcends the mechanical
ordering of his animal existence, entirely by himself and that he does not
partake of any other happiness or perfection except that which he has
secured himself by his own reason and free of instinct."[83] Here was an
anticipation of the humanist "expressive totality" notion found in Hegel,
the early Marx and several Western Marxists, most notably Lukács.

The familiar linkage of Kant with the French Revolution is thus perhaps
justified not only because the anti-dogmatic "terrorism" of his critical
method may have surpassed that of Robespierre, as Heine once observed,[84]

80. Lovejoy, *The Great Chain of Being*, p. 265.
81. "Idea for a Universal History with Cosmopolitan Intent" in *The Philosophy of Kant*,
ed. with intro. Carl J. Friedrich (New York, 1949), p. 123.
82. Ibid., p. 121.
83. Ibid., p. 119.
84. Heinrich Heine, *Concerning the History of Religion and Philosophy in Germany* in
Selected Works, trans. and ed., Helen M. Mustard (New York, 1973), p. 369.

but also because Kant shared many of the hopes that fed the Revolution. Unlike Rousseau with his nostalgia for Sparta, or Winckelmann and the generations of Germans inspired by his reverence for Athens, or the Romantics with their threnodies to the Middle Ages, Kant placed his normative totality firmly in the future. Although he recognized his as only an age of enlightenment and not yet an enlightened age, he believed that the collective subject that was mankind, working through its "unsocial sociability," would ever more closely approximate that state. That it would never quite reach it, however, Kant did not deny, anticipating those Western Marxists who spoke of totalization rather than totalities.

Mentioning classical models of totality brings us to the other strain in Kant's work that contributed to the holistic tradition we are examining. In his *Critique of Judgment*, Kant linked the teleological view of nature he had developed in his *Idea of a Universal History* with a consideration of aesthetics. What might be called the aesthetization of totality, in which society is likened to a work of art, has its origins here. To explicate his argument in its entirety is impossible in this space, but certain points must be noted. The teleological concept of nature, Kant explained, should be understood epistemologically rather than ontologically. It belongs to what in his vocabulary are reflective rather than determinant judgments, that is, ones which are ultimately subjective, unlike those of pure theoretical reason, which are objective. We use reflective judgments to guide our investigations of the world, but we cannot assume they are true expressions of objective reality. In short, we view nature teleologically when we see it *as if* it were a work of art.

It is heuristically useful to view nature as if it were formed purposively in the way an art work is formed, even though we can never know this to be true. For Kant, art works are themselves purposive wholes from which human desire, a function of man's animal nature, is excluded. Despite art's sensuous appeal, it is best understood as "purposiveness without purpose"; that is, works of art are unified totalities shaped teleologically, but they do not have ends extrinsic to themselves. Because of their disinterested character, they suggest a non-hierarchical, non-exploitative relationship between subject and object. Moreover, because the aesthetic subject is without personal interest in the work of art, his appreciation suggests that the universality of reason can be reconciled with the natural or sensuous realm of existence. This last connection, however, Kant left underdeveloped, so that the relationship between his writings on history and on aesthetics remains only imperfectly realized.

Kant's work on aesthetics also made a more specific contribution to the idealist discourse on totality. Following conventional eighteenth-century practice, he discriminated between the beautiful and the sublime as sources of aesthetic pleasure. The former derived from the form of an object which consisted in limitation, the latter from formlessness and lack of limitation. Whereas beautiful objects correspond to the human capacity to imagine in a pleasing way, sublime ones cannot be encompassed by our imaginative powers. Seriously deficient in that sense of purposiveness that Kant ascribed to all works of art, sublime objects nonetheless give pleasure (as well as repel us) because of their ability to evoke indeterminate "Ideas of Reason." In his first critique, Kant had attacked such ideas as the source of illusion, based as they were on speculative, dialectical reasoning rather than on synthetic a priori judgments. Accordingly, he granted the beautiful greater philosophical significance than the sublime, a ranking that was strengthened still further by his claim that moral and beautiful experiences had something in common. All of this is important because when Kant's aesthetic arguments were incorporated into the ensuing discussion of totality in German Idealism, it was his description of beauty with its emphasis on form, limitation and purposiveness without purpose that struck the most respondent chord. Indeed, many years later, one of the leading Western Marxists, Jürgen Habermas, would be accused by a post-structuralist critic of still upholding the idea of beauty against the sublime![85]

Although anticipated in the earlier work of Kant and Alexander Baumgarten, the aestheticization of totality was nowhere as brilliantly expounded as in the letters Friedrich Schiller wrote between 1793 and 1795 to the Danish Prince Friedrich Christian of Schleswig-Holstein and Augustenburg. In these celebrated letters, which have come down to us under the title *On the Aesthetic Education of Man*,[86] Schiller integrated many of Kant's ideas on art and history with that vision of Greek culture as "noble simplicity and quiet greatness"[87] introduced by Winckelmann into Germany in the mid-eighteenth century. Although drawing heavily on the *Critique of Judgment*, Schiller minimized the stern moral element in Kant's view of normative totality and in its place raised to prominence an undeveloped remark Kant had made about art as a kind of play. In the

85. Jean-François Lyotard, "Reponse à la question: qu'est-ce que le post-moderne?," *Critique* 419 (April 1982), p. 365.

86. Friedrich Schiller, *On the Aesthetic Education of Man in a Series of Letters*, trans. with intro. Reginald Snell (New York, 1965).

87. J.J. Winckelmann, *Gedanken über die Nachahmung der Griecheschen Werke, etc.* (Stuttgart, 1885), p. 24.

so-called "aesthetic state," which Schiller posited as the telos of that process of species totalization Kant outlined in his *Idea of a Universal History*,[88] mankind would leave behind the fragmentation and alienation that characterize its painful but necessary emergence from the state of pure naturalness. Like Kant with his notion of "unsocial sociability," Schiller argued that discord was a necessary means to ultimate harmony: "The antagonism of powers is the great instrument of culture, but it is only the instrument; for as long as it persists we are only on our way towards culture."[89] Also like Kant, he had a basic faith in the natural tendency of mankind to overcome disharmony:

Should Nature be able, by her designs, to rob us of a completeness which Reason prescribes to us by hers? It must be false that the cultivation of individual powers necessitates the sacrifice of their totality, or however much the law of Nature did have that tendency, we must be at liberty to restore by means of a higher Art this wholeness in our nature which Art has destroyed.[90]

But unlike Kant, Schiller contended that reason and the drive for form in art were matched by an equally urgent drive for sensuous, material gratification, the two drives merging in play. Left to itself reason tended to dominate nature, whereas Schiller wanted a harmonious relationship between man and the objective world. In his fourteenth letter, he spelled out the means by which this reconciliation was to occur:

The sense impulse requires variation, requires time to have a content; the form impulse requires the extinction of time, and no variation. Therefore the impulse in which both are combined (allow me to call it provisionally the *play impulse*, until I have justified the term), this play impulse would aim at the extinction of time *in time* and the reconciliation of becoming with absolute being, of variation with identity.[91]

Beauty, Schiller explains, is the unification of the object of the sense impulse, which is life, with the form impulse, which is shape. Combining the two, the aesthetic condition relates "to the totality of our various powers, without being a specific object for any single one of them."[92] Its characteristic expression is play, which is seen as man's quintessentially human activity. Through play, time is itself tamed and mastered, which allows us to

88. Schiller was, in fact, somewhat ambiguous about the aesthetic state as the ultimate stage of development or merely the preliminary stage before the achievement of moral culture, but the emotional energy of the letters seems to be behind the first alternative.
89. Schiller, p. 43. As M. H. Abrams points out in *Natural Supernaturalism: Tradition and Revolution in Romantic Literature* (New York, 1971), Schiller shared a secularized version of the Christian myth of the fortunate fall with many in his generation.
90. Schiller, p. 45.
91. Ibid., p. 74.
92. Ibid., p. 99.

achieve a sense of totality. Art is thus a contrivance for the suspension of time, a way to avoid the open-ended boundlessness of the infinite.

Perhaps even more important from the point of view of the general tradition we are examining, beauty for Schiller is a socially constructive principle:

> Though need may drive Man into society, and Reason implant social principles in him, Beauty alone can confer on him a *social character*. Taste alone brings harmony into society, because it establishes harmony in the individual. All other forms of perception divide a man, because they are exclusively based either on the sensuous or on the intellectual part of his being; only the perception of the Beautiful makes something whole of him, because both his natures must accord with it.[93]

But is this socialization to be achieved outside the realm of art itself? Can all human society be placed within the kingdom of Beauty, the "aesthetic state"? Here Schiller remains a faithful Kantian and is unsure: "This equilibrium," he writes, "always remains only an idea, which never can be wholly attained by actuality."[94] Like the perfect civil constitution in Kant's *Idea for a Universal History*, Schiller's aesthetic state is no more than a regulative ideal whose complete fulfillment is tantalizingly out of reach. "As a need, it exists in every finely tuned soul; as an achievement we might perhaps find it, like the pure Church, or the pure Republic, only in a few select circles."[95]

Schiller's vision of an aesthetic totalization always to be sought, but never fully realized, was a foundation of much Romantic thinking on the subject.[96] Goethe's *Faust* and Hölderlin's *Hyperion* are often seen as classic examples of its power. Although the desire for totality was a pronounced feature of Friedrich Schlegel's aesthetic theory,[97] the Romantics were generally frustrated in their attempt to achieve it. The disillusionment which resulted was very much at the root of that ironic world-view so characteristic of German Romanticism in particular. The pervasive Romantic *Streben nach dem Unendlichen* (striving for the infinite) was clearly the mark of a culture which had yet to achieve a sense of its own wholeness, a failure not surprising in the light of German conditions in

93. Ibid., p. 138.
94. Ibid., p. 81.
95. Ibid., p. 140.
96. Arthur Lovejoy, "Schiller and the Genesis of German Romanticism," *Essays in the History of Ideas*.
97. "Like Schiller," Oskar Walzel writes, "Friedrich Schlegel, in his early 'objective' days, had designated the Greeks as representatives of a harmony which dissolved all antitheses completely. Then there occurred to him as the ideal of human totality the idea of protean mobility, of the ability to spring from one antithesis to another and to combine the most contradictory situations into unity. This ideal was at the basis of romantic poetry" (*German Romanticism*, trans. Alma Elise Lussky [New York, 1966], p. 101).

the early nineteenth century. Only imperfectly extricated from the abstract cosmopolitanism of the *Aufklärung* and deeply confused about its attitude toward the French Revolution, German culture had not yet gained that blustery confidence in its national genius that Meinecke[98] and others were later to celebrate as the central legacy of the period.

The aesthetic image of totality evoked by Schiller came to play a crucial role in that cultural development. As George Mosse has recently demonstrated,[99] an aestheticized politics in which the classical legacy of Winckelmann was monumentalized and vulgarized helped to nationalize the German masses. By and large cultic, irrational and mythic in tenor, this aestheticized politics tended to feed the *völkisch* anti-liberalism that culminated in the Third Reich. On the Left, however, a similar if less successful adaptation of aethetic motifs can be traced in the politics of the socialist movement.[100] Its effects can also be observed in the more strictly theoretical tradition we are examining, perhaps most notably in the work of Herbert Marcuse. What Marcuse was to call "the aesthetic dimension"[101] was a vital aspect of his image of totality. In *Eros and Civilization*, he in fact explicitly acknowledged the importance of Schiller's "play drive" for his own thought.[102]

Although less enthusiastic about Schiller's stress on play than was Marcuse, Lukács also paid tribute to the importance of his aesthetic attempt to overcome dissonance and fragmentation.[103] He interpreted that attempt as a response to the capitalist division of labor, and he claimed it was derived more from the Enlightenment's moral tradition, in particular the work of Adam Ferguson, than from that of the Romantics. While Lukács claimed to prefer Hegel's more explicitly political notion of totality to what he saw as Schiller's too exclusively aesthetic alternative, it is clear

98. Friedrich Meinecke, *Cosmopolitanism and the National State*, trans. Robert B. Kimber, intro. Felix Gilbert (Princeton, 1970).

99. George L. Mosse, *The Nationalization of the Masses: Political Symbolism and Mass Movements in Germany From the Napoleonic Wars Through the Third Reich* (New York, 1975).

100. Ibid., Chapter 7. For a discussion of the aestheticization of politics within certain segments of the New Left, see Martin Jay, "The Politics of Terror," *Partisan Review*, 38:1 (1971).

101. Herbert Marcuse, *The Aesthetic Dimension: Toward a Critique of Marxist Aesthetics* (Boston, 1978). For a discussion of Marcuse's debt to Schiller, see Fredric Jameson, *Marxism and Form* (Princeton, 1971). Adorno, on the other hand, was far less positively inclined to Schiller's "play drive." See his critique in *Aesthetische Theorie, Gesammelte Schriften*, 7 (Frankfurt, 1970), p. 469f.

102. Herbert Marcuse, *Eros and Civilization: A Philosophical Inquiry Into Freud* (Boston, 1955), p. 169f.

103. Georg Lukács, "Schiller's Theory of Modern Literature" in *Goethe and His Age*, trans. R. Anchor (London, 1968); and Lukács, *The Young Hegel: Studies in the Relations Between Dialectics and Economics*, trans. Rodney Livingstone (London, 1975), pp. 40–41.

that in his own thought a strong aesthetic impulse was at work. As we will see later in examining the debate over Marxist aesthetics, there is more than one way to aestheticize politics.

But one relatively firm dividing line separated the rightist from the leftist inheritors of Schiller's mingling of the two realms. Unlike the *völkisch* purveyors of aesthetic politics, their leftist counterparts never abandoned Schiller's belief that reason and art were ultimately reconcilable. To understand the development of Marxist holism, it is thus necessary to return to the Idealist tradition where reason played a central role. Indeed, as has often been pointed out, Kant's successors abandoned his critical philosophy precisely because of their impatience with the limitations he had placed on the power of speculative reason. Fichte and Schelling were the first representatives of this yearning to go beyond Kant, if one excepts Jacobi whose desire for metaphysical certainty led him beyond reason altogether to intuition and faith. Their direct impact on Marxism, however, was mediated through the thinker whose system presented the most elaborate version of holism in the history of philosophy.[104] The thinker in question is, of course, George Wilhelm Friedrich Hegel, whose importance for the Western Marxist tradition was second only to that of Marx himself.

In the preface to his *Philosophy of Fine Art*, Hegel generously acknowledged Schiller's particular genius, his "artistic sense of a profound, and at the same time philosophic, mind which demanded and proclaimed the

104. The only real competitor for this title is Schelling, but his *System of Transcendental Idealism* too hastily suppressed differentiation in the name of absolute identity in a way that rendered it less fruitful than Hegel's system, which was also far more rationalist. For a discussion of the differences between the two, see Kelly, *Idealism*, p. 299 and Taylor, *Hegel*, pp. 532–33.

The other figure in Hegel's era who powerfully expressed a sense of wholeness was, of course, Goethe, but he did so in a less systematic rationalist way. Moreover, as Karl Löwith points out,

The difference in their ways of mediation resides in the fact that Goethe sees the unity from the point of view of nature as it is perceived, but Hegel from the point of view of the *historical spirit*. This corresponds to the fact that Hegel recognizes a "cunning of reason," and Goethe a cunning of nature. In each case, it lies in the fact that the affairs of men are subordinated to the service of the whole.

(*From Hegel to Nietzsche: the Revolution in the Nineteenth-Century Thought*, trans. David E. Green [Garden City, New York, 1967], pp. 7–8.)

Although Marx was to list Goethe, along with Aeschylus and Shakespeare, among his favorite poets, it is clear that he could find no real solace in Goethe's Olympian affirmation of the natural order. Later Marxists like Lukács have made much of the social side of *Faust*, Part II, but its implications are not all positive. For a recent discussion of the play as a "tragedy of development" see Marshall Berman, *All That is Solid Melts into Air: The Experience of Modernity* (New York, 1982).

principle of totality and reconciliation as against that abstract infinity of thought, that duty for duty's sake, that formless intelligence"[105] which were the failings of Kant's earlier system. For Hegel, Kantianism was marked by abstract and ahistorical antinomies that only dialectical thought, with its appreciation of the importance of totality, could overcome. Schiller had understood the necessity to overcome but had lacked insight into the power of reason to bring it about. His over-reliance on art and still Kantian uncertainty about the realization of the aesthetic state held Schiller back from a rigorous and all-encompassing philosophical system that would demonstrate, as Hegel put it in the preface to *The Phenomenology of the Spirit*, that "the true is the whole."[106] This truth appeared in all facets of that system, epistemological, ontological, political and ethical.

Kant had condemned dialectical thinking and speculative reason (*Vernunft*) in general as the source of illusion; Hegel responded that only by employing such thinking and reasoning could the illusory dualisms posited by the understanding (*Verstand*) be reconciled. Among these were the distinctions between knowledge of the world of appearances (phenomena) and of the world of essences or things-in-themselves (noumena), between the sensible and the intelligible, between the moral "ought" and the empirical "is," and between finite historical time and the suprahistorical infinite. An appreciation of the central role of totality was necessary to overcome these dichotomies.

Hegel's epistemological confidence was rooted in a basic ontological assumption that harkened back to Vico's *verum–factum* principle. For Hegel, the subject of knowledge and the object of knowledge were inherently identical because the latter was produced out of and constituted by the former. Thus nature, which for Kant was opposed to spirit, was at its most basic level the spirit's emanation. Hegel called the meta-subject, both creator and created, the Absolute Spirit, a combination of the Greek *Logos* and the Christian divinity, who served as the unifying ground of all being. Although in some ways reminiscent of Spinoza's equation of God and nature and his all-encompassing vision of the totality of being, Hegel's philosophy rejected the static and objective bias of his Dutch predecessor. For him, the Absolute Spirit was dynamic and subjective, the pro-

105. Quoted in Snell's intro. to Schiller, *On the Aesthetic Education of Man*, p. 11. For a discussion of Hegel's relation to Schiller, see George Armstrong Kelly, *Hegel's Retreat from Eleusis: Studies in Political Thought* (Princeton, 1978), chap. 3.

106. G. W. F. Hegel, *Phenomenology of Spirit*, trans. A. V. Miller, foreword by J. N. Findlay (Oxford, 1979), p. 11. For general studies of Hegel's concept of totality, see W. Van Dooren, *Het Totaliteitsbegrip Bij Hegel en Zijn Voorgangers* (Assen, 1965), with a summary in German of the main argument, and Stanley Rosen, *G. W. F. Hegel: An Introduction to the Science of Wisdom*.

tagonist in a kind of cosmic drama of its own making. The Absolute Spirit might be called an expressive subject, whose ultimate function was to differentiate its primal immediacy into a richly articulated universe of mediated particulars, then recognize itself in that plenitude. Indeed, only after differentiation and recognition was the Absolute Spirit truly itself, for "of the Absolute it must be said that it is essentially a result, that only at the end is it what it is in very truth."[107] Because of the importance of the dynamic nature of reality for Hegel, history, which Kant discussed only in his relatively minor writings, was given central importance. In a sense, it was the record of the Subject's formation, a kind of *Bildungsroman* of the Absolute. The historical totality was thus a self-reflexive one: the subjective totality at the beginning of the process recognized as itself the objective totality at the end.

To Hegel, the apparent dualisms naturalized by Kant were merely way-stations on the journey of self-recognition and reconciliation that was the progress of the Absolute Spirit through time. Contradiction, fragmentation, estrangement, alienation were real and necessary aspects of that progress; appearances were as "real" as essences, which was why Hegel wrote a "phenomenology" and not a "noumenology." To dismiss these appearances was to commit the mistake of Schelling who in his haste to reach the Absolute had stumbled into "a night in which, as the saying goes, all cows are black."[108] For Hegel, the very motor of history was contradiction and determinate negation. To ignore this motor was to return to a static and empty notion of the Absolute comparable to Spinoza's immobile God/Nature. When the journey was completed, the contradictions and dualisms which had manifested themselves along the way would be reconciled, but the type of reconciliation achieved would also include their preservation. In the well-known Hegelian pun, their *Aufhebung* would mean that they were retained as well as cancelled and transcended. Thus the final identity that would be reached would be "between identity and non-identity."[109] One implication of this system was a theodicy in which apparent evil could be ultimately seen as part of a larger good, as had been the case with Kant's "unsocial sociability" in his *Idea for a Universal History.*

Another implication was that the journey itself was a cyclical rather than

107. Hegel, *The Phenomenology of Spirit,* quoted in Lukács, *The Ontology of Social Being: Hegel's False and His Genuine Ontology,* trans. David Fernbach (London, 1978), p. 68.
108. Hegel, *Phenomenology of Spirit,* p. 9.
109. Hegel, *Differenz des Fichteschen und Schellingschen Systems* in *Werke* (Frankfurt, 1970), vol. 2, p. 96.

simply linear progress, for the origin, the Absolute Spirit, was also the goal. Time for Hegel thus had a dual aspect. Historical time was a uni-directional, if dialectically uneven, flow in which the Absolute Spirit expressed its potential dimensions and objectified its subjectivity. At its end, the reconciliation of contradictions, most notably between subject and object, would be accomplished; reality, in other words, would be adequate to its concept. But at any one instant of that process, all of the elements of the whole were present, as the Absolute Spirit was immanent in each of its moments. Thus time was both continuous and coinstantaneous. This latter quality meant the overcoming of that yearning and frustration which marked the open-ended temporality of Kant, Fichte, Schiller and the Romantics for whom full reconciliation was an unattainable goal. Hegel characterized their version of time as a "bad infinity" because it was boundless and thus without form and order. In contrast, he posited a "good infinity" which was less an endless aggregate of moments than a circular totality, a coherent and formed whole containing finitude rather than being opposed to it.[110] The boundary of the "good infinity" was not external, because by definition nothing was beyond infinity, but rather its internal structure, which was the articulated expression of the Absolute Spirit. In this sense, totality was an anti-transcendental concept, as it had been for Spinoza, but now it included time in a way that his totality had not. Like Schiller's "play drive," Hegel's concept of totality was a means to suppress the open-ended limitlessness of historical time commonly understood. Not surprisingly, the conservative reading of Hegel's thought drew in large measure from this stifling of yearning and desire, as it did from his reassurance that reason was "the rose in the cross of the present."[111]

Crucial to Hegel's system was the corollary assumption that the ontological process was ultimately knowable by the human subject, whose rationality partakes of the general rationality permeating the whole. Thus, the method of *Wissenschaft*, or science, was comparably holistic, circular and dialectical:

Each of the parts of philosophy is a philosophical whole, a circle rounded and complete in itself. In each of these parts, however, the philosophical Idea is found in a particular specificality or medium. The single circle, because it is a real total-

110. For good discussions of time and infinity in Hegel, see Ivan Soll, *An Introduction to Hegel's Metaphysics* (Chicago and London, 1969), pp. 116–18, Taylor, *Hegel*, p. 114, and Kelly, *Idealism* p. 319. Kelly's treatment is indebted to that of Althusser in *Reading Capital*.
111. G. W. F. Hegel, *The Philosophy of Right and Law* in *The Philosophy of Hegel*, ed. Carl Friedrich (New York, 1954), p. 226. Interestingly, Lenin thought that Hegel's view of time was also profoundly conservative and attacked it in his *Philosophical Notebooks* (*Collected Works* [Moscow, 1946–67], vol. 48, p. 228).

ity, bursts through the limits imposed by its special medium, and gives rise to a wider circle. The whole of philosophy in this way resembles a circle of circles.[112]

Unlike Vico, Hegel did not posit an ultimate subordination of man the maker to God the maker in terms of their relative ability to know what they had made. Man was himself a moment in the Absolute Spirit; its self-recognition was also his own. All subsequent humanizations of Hegel's system entered through the door opened by this identification, although in Hegel himself the supra-human vision of the Absolute Spirit clearly prevailed.[113]

When applied to the more concrete historical development of mankind, Hegel's holism permeated his judgments about past, present and future cultures and societies. Inspired by Winckelmann's image of Greece, he admired the *polis* for its achievement of community and Hellenic art for its harmony and formal beauty.[114] But his nostalgia was tempered by a recognition that Greek society was too immediate in its unity and not sufficiently self-conscious and that Greek art was too irrational and naturalistic in its indifference to the higher value of truth. These same qualms informed his attitude towards Greek ethics, which

> though extremely beautiful, attractive and interesting in its manifestations, is not the highest point of spiritual self-consciousness. It lacks the form of infinity, the reflection of thought within itself. It lacks emancipation from the natural element, the sensuous that is involved in the very nature of beauty and divinity, and from the immediacy of Greek ethics. Infinity of self-consciousness and self-comprehension on the part of thought is wanting.[115]

The simple, naive unity of the Hellenic totality had to be destroyed for reasons that were similar to those invoked in the Christian myth of the fortunate fall.[116] Only through the development of inwardness, individu-

112. Hegel, *The Logic*, quoted in Abrams, *Natural Supernaturalism*, p. 226.
113. There has been a long-standing debate over the extent of Hegel's religiosity. Lukács, in *The Young Hegel*, argued for Hegel's radical humanism as did Walter Kaufmann in *Hegel: A Reinterpretation* (New York, 1966). Both Kelly and Taylor, on the other hand, have tried to restore the religious component of his philosophy, as has Emil Fackenheim, *The Religious Dimension in Hegel's Thought* (Boston, 1967). Ironically, Hegel's first detractors were convinced that he was a dangerous enemy of religion. See the discussion in Shlomo Avineri, "Hegel Revisited," in *Hegel: A Collection of Critical Essays*, ed. Alasdair MacIntyre (Garden City, New York, 1972), p. 339.
114. The standard work on the impact of Winckelmann is still E. M. Butler, *The Tyranny of Greece Over Germany* (Boston, 1958), although she treats only the aesthetic and cultural dimensions of German Hellenism, neglecting the philosophical and political. For a discussion of Hegel's debt to the Greeks, see Judith N. Shklar, "Hegel's *Phenomenology*: an Elegy for Hellas" in *Hegel's Political Philosophy: Problems and Perspectives*, ed. Z. A. Pelczynski (Cambridge, 1971).
115. Hegel, *The Philosophy of History* in *Philosophy of Hegel*, p. 72–73.
116. Abrams, *Natural Supernaturalism*.

ality and self-consciousness could a higher, more mediated totality be achieved. Broadly speaking, Hegel saw the role of Christianity as fostering these values, even though in certain of its manifestations, such as the medieval Church, they appeared in distorted and alienated forms. This intermediate stage of estrangement, which Hegel identified in *The Phenomenology of Spirit* with the "unhappy consciousness," was necessary, but temporary. It was followed by successively closer approximations to the concrete totality that Hegel equated with the embodied truth.

For Hegel, the concrete was complexly mediated and richly articulated, the very opposite of the more familiar, empirical notion of concreteness, which equated it with unmediated and simple facticity. Hegel chose to call the empiricist idea of the concrete the "abstract," as he did the opposite mode of thought expressed in general, empty and formal universals. The failure to mediate between these two abstractions—discrete facts and empty universal categories—was a version of "bad infinity." The web of relations among seemingly bounded and discrete entities was the proper focus of a philosophy that would be adequate to reality, rather than the isolated entities themselves or the general categories under which they might be subsumed.

In political terms, a version of "bad infinity" had appeared in Rousseau's *Social Contract*, where totality meant the liquidation of all intermediate articulations between the individual and the General Will. Hegel, for all his early and sustained enthusiasm for the French Revolution, recognized its indebtedness to this abstract holism which contributed to the leveling egalitarianism of the Jacobin Terror. In contrast, his vision of the truly concrete in political and social terms involved the creative interplay of various levels of social reality—family, civil society, and the state— rather than the suppression of some in the name of the universality of one of the others. Although the state played a critical role in rationally expressing the interests of the whole, Hegel never intended it to cancel out the other, more particular components of the totality. Unlike Rousseau, Hegel was content with a series of countervailing social and political institutions that resisted abstract homogenization. The separation of man into bourgeois and citizen, private and public, was not a source of chagrin for him, as it had been for Rousseau and was to be for Marx. Nor did the persistence of war between the separate totalities that were sovereign states seem an impediment to the rationality of the whole, at least in the present.[117] Nor was the maintenance of a sphere of personal, private sub-

117. For a discussion of Hegel on war, see Shlomo Avineri, *Hegel's Theory of the Modern State* (Cambridge, 1972), p. 194f., and D. P. Verene, "Hegel's Account of War," in Pelczynski, ed. *Hegel's Political Philosophy.*

jectivity seen as a danger to the integrity of the whole; unlike previous holistic philosophers such as Plato and Rousseau, Hegel did not subordinate negative to positive freedom, although he strongly applauded the virtues of the latter.[118]

In summation, then, it is obvious that Hegel's contribution to the holistic tradition was profound and multi-dimensional. First, by his bold identification of "good infinity" with totality, he made plausible the "longitudinal" notion of closed yet dynamic totality that incorporated all of history into the whole. A circular image of time meant that the difficult problem of origin and end need not be raised. The romantic striving for the infinite, with all its agonizing frustrations, was thus tamed. Universal history included the past and future to their farthest reaches because they were ultimately identical. Nothing exists outside of the totality of history, which has no external boundary. Hegel's totality was thus both temporally and spatially immanent.

Second, by employing the term "totality" to refer to all coherent entities within the cosmic whole, Hegel encouraged the vision that lesser or partial totalities existed on all levels of the meta-totality. This acceptance of what we have called "latitudinal totalities" meant that any part in a larger whole might itself be considered an organized whole from the perspective of its internal dynamics. Thus reality for Hegel was populated by multitudes of hierarchically linked or horizontally juxtaposed totalities, which defied comprehension through reduction to their component parts. Indeed, the concreteness of the meta-totality depended on the existence of these internally related but differentiated sub-totalities. Human society was thus not to be understood as a homogeneous aggregate in the manner of what later would be called mass society. Its movement was generated through the interaction of the various sub-totalities, whose relations became more intense and complicated as the process pressed forward.

Third, Hegel's identification of totality with its creator subject, his argument that substance and subject were ultimately one, meant that his totality was an "expressive" or "genetic" one. All the particular articulations of the meta-totality were united in their common source as emanations of the Absolute Spirit. From the point of view of the isolated human individual, this meant that personal totalization was impossible outside of the context of global totalization. Hegel, in fact, mocked Diderot's "I"

---

118. For a good discussion of Hegel's views on this issue, see Richard L. Schacht, "Hegel on Freedom," in MacIntyre, ed., *Hegel*. The position that Hegel was an unabashed proponent of positive freedom is best developed in the classic essay by Isaiah Berlin, "Two Concepts of Liberty," in *Four Essays on Liberty* (Oxford, 1969). For a critique, see C. B. Macpherson, *Democratic Theory: Essays in Retrieval* (Oxford, 1973).

character in *Rameau's Nephew* for presenting himself as an "honest soul" whose personality was allegedly whole and sincere. He preferred instead the disintegrated consciousness of the nephew who more faithfully expressed the still unreconciled contradictions of his day (a judgment with which Marx was fully to concur).[119] Similarly, Hegel scorned the Romantics' attempt to achieve personal wholeness by escaping from the world, for which he sarcastically used Goethe's term "beautiful soul," anticipating Sartre's defense of "dirty hands" against "clean hands" in his famous dispute with Camus a century later. Read in a humanistic fashion, the expressive notion of totality meant the existence of a collective subject of history—whose objectifications were the sole source of the social whole—as well as the denial of personal totalization outside the larger supra-individual process.

Finally, Hegel's insistence that ontology and epistemology were ultimately aspects of a single reality, his refusal to countenance the agnosticism and dualism at the heart of Kant's more modest system, meant that the relationship between totalistic knowledge and the "real" totality in the objective world was for him an uncomplicated one. Like Spinoza, although without his ahistorical bias, Hegel defused the highly volatile question of how one could verify the correspondence between holistic thought and the totality of existence. The reason for his optimism was Vico's *verum–factum* principle, with the Absolute Spirit cast in the role of both subject and object of knowledge, the maker of reality and the made reality itself. Identify theory was thus the basis for his belief that he had overcome the antinomies of previous idealist systems and passed beyond a critical philosophy to an affirmative one.

Western Marxism would question the affirmative moment in Hegel's legacy and seek to recapture its negative and subversive impulse. The process of salvaging the critical dimensions of Hegel's thought, to be sure, had begun long before. In the Second International, it was fashionable to distinguish between Hegel's method, which was valuable and worth emulating, and his system, which was not.[120] Although this precise distinction

119. Hegel's remarks on *Rameau's Nephew* are in *The Phenomenology of Spirit*, pp. 318, 332. Marx's comments on Hegel's reading are found in a letter to Engels, April 15, 1869, quoted in *Diderot, Interpreter of Nature: Selected Writings*, ed. with intro. Jonathan Kemp (New York, 1963) pp. 354–55.

120. This distinction can be found as early as Engels' *Anti-Dühring* (1878) and was included in the sections of that work published in pamphlet form two years later as *Socialism: Utopian and Scientific*. For all his hostility to Engels, Lukács maintained the same

now seems overly schematic, Marxism from its inception was attracted less to the content of Hegel's system than to the dialectical process by which he claimed to have derived that content. At the center of dialectics was an emphasis on holistic as opposed to atomistic thinking. And clearly, Marx's own holism emerged in critical confrontation with and partial assimilation of Hegel's thought. Along with his critique of classical political economy, Marx's critique of Hegelianism was the cornerstone of his own thought. To spell out that critique and present a detailed account of Marx's own views on totality at this stage of our narrative would be premature, because to do so would take us to the very heart of the debate among Western Marxists that will occupy us for the remainder of the book. Still, certain points can be made which were generally accepted by all participants in the discussion.

To begin with the most obvious, all Western Marxists (although not all Marxologists)[121] have agreed that Marx was indeed a holistic thinker. The word "totality" or synonyms such as "the whole" appear frequently and affirmatively in his writings. Even before his exposure to Hegel's dialectical holism, he passed through a Romantic phase whose effects never fully left him.[122] As early as his days as a student of law, he wrote to his father:

---

distinction in *History and Class Consciousness*, extending it even to Marxism for which he argued orthodoxy "refers exclusively to *method*" (p. 1). In his 1967 preface to the book, Lukács shifted his ground somewhat:

> The problem with Marx is precisely to take his method and his system *as we find them* and to demonstrate that they *form a coherent unity that must be preserved*. The opposite is true of Hegel. The task he imposes is to separate out from the complex web of ideas with its sometimes glaring contradictions all the *seminal elements* of thought and rescue them *as a vital intellectual force for the present*. (p. xiv, italics in original)

121. For arguments that Marx was in fact a methodological individualist, see Joachim Israel, "The Principle of Methodological Individualism and Marxian Epistemology," *Acta Sociologica* 14:3 (1971); Laird Addis, *The Logic of Society: A Philosophical Study* (Minneapolis, 1975), p. 187f; and Louis Dumont, *From Mandeville to Marx: The Genesis and Triumph of Economic Ideology* (Chicago and London, 1977). The passages in Marx's work that are most often adduced to support this claim are the following: (1) "It is not 'history' which uses men as a means of achieving—as if it were an individual person—*its* own ends. History is *nothing* but the activity of men in pursuit of their own ends" (*The Holy Family* in Marx and Engels, *Collected Works* [New York, 1975], p. 93). (2) "It is above all necessary to avoid restoring society once more as a fixed abstraction opposed to the individual" (*Economic and Philosophic Manuscripts* in *Karl Marx: Selected Writings*, p. 91).

Although these statements clearly show Marx's hostility to an idealist holism in which the whole is hypostatized as prior to and independent of the parts, they do not mean that no other types of holism inform his thought.

122. For a recent study of Marx's indebtedness to the Romantic tradition, see Leonard P. Wessell, *Karl Marx, Romantic Irony, and the Proletariat: Studies in the Mythopoetic Origins of Marxism* (Baton Rouge, 1979). See also Michael Lewin, "Marxism and Romanticism: Marx's Debt to German Conservatism," *Political Studies* 22:4 (December 1974) and Alvin W. Gouldner, "Romanticism and Classicism: Deep Structure in Social Science" in *For Sociology: Renewal and Critique in Sociology Today* (New York, 1973).

In the concrete expression of a living world of ideas, as exemplified by law, the
state, nature and philosophy as a whole, the object itself must be studied in its
development; arbitrary divisions must not be introduced, the rational character of
the object itself must develop as something imbued with contradictions in itself
and find unity in itself.[123]

Shortly thereafter, in the 1844 work entitled "Critical Notes on the Article,
'The King of Prussia and Social Reform', by a Prussian [Arnold Ruge]," he
insisted that

A *social* revolution involves the standpoint of the *whole* because it is a protest of
man against dehumanized life even if it occurs in only *one* factory district, because
it proceeds from the standpoint of the *single actual individual* because the *community* against whose separation from himself the individual reacts is the *true*
community of man, *human* existence.[124]

Marx's chastisement of political revolutionaries like Ruge for lacking an
understanding of the partial nature of political emancipation, which was
given its classic formulation amidst the noxious anti-semitic phrases of
"On the Jewish Question," was parallelled by a similar scorn for those
political economists who isolated economics from the social whole. As he
wrote in the *Economic and Philosophical Manuscripts of 1844*:

Society as it appears to the political economist is *civil society*, in which every
individual is a totality of needs and only exists for the other person, as the other
exists for him, in so far as each becomes a means for the other. The political
economist reduces everything (just as does politics in its *Rights of Man*) to man,
i.e., to the individual whom he strips of all determinateness so as to class him as
capitalist or worker.[125]

The political economists fail to understand that behind the seemingly immutable laws of their theory lies a world of historically changing human
relations, the totality of "actual life." In these and in a wealth of other
polemics, Marx frequently castigated his opponents for their inability to
grasp the total context of meaningful relations.

Secondly, it is clear that Marx believed grasping that totality meant
understanding it historically. In *The German Ideology*, he stated:

Our conception of history depends on our ability to expound the real process of
production, starting out from the simple material production of life, and to com-

123. Marx to Heinrich Marx, November 10, 1837, quoted in Donald R. Kelley, "The
Metaphysics of Law: An Essay on the Very Young Marx," *American Historical Review* 83:2
(April 1978), p. 355.
124. *Writings of the Young Marx on Philosophy and Society*, ed. L. Easton and K. Gud-
datt (New York, 1967), pp. 356–57.
125. Karl Marx, *The Economic and Philosophic Manuscripts of 1844*, ed. with intro.
Dirk J. Struik (New York, 1964), p. 159.

prehend the form of intercourse connected with this and created by this (i.e. civil society in its various stages), as the basis of all history; further, to show it in its action as State; and so, from this starting-point, to explain the whole mass of different theoretical products and forms of consciousness, religion, philosophy, ethics, etc., etc., and trace their origins and growth, by which means, of course, the whole thing can be shown in its totality (and therefore, too, the reciprocal action of these various sides on one another).[126]

Furthermore, like Hegel he had no use for those theorists, usually Romantic, who despaired of history ever reaching a new normative totalization and pined instead for the restoration of a lost wholeness. In contrast, he recognized that alienation and estrangement were necessary stages on the road to a higher level of fulfillment. In the *Grundrisse*, he made this optimism clear:

In earlier stages of development the single individual seems to be developed more fully, because he has not yet worked out his relationships in their fullness, or erected them as independent social powers as relations opposite himself. It is as ridiculous to yearn for a return to that original fullness as it is to believe that with this complete emptiness history has come to a standstill.[127]

In other words, for Marx, history was to be understood descriptively as a totality and normatively as promising a new totalization in the future.

In many ways, these aspects of Marx's holism link him clearly with Hegel, but it is no less certain, and this is the third indisputable point, that Marx's holism was not simply equivalent to that of his philosophical mentor. But precisely how different their two positions actually were became a bone of vigorous contention among Western Marxists.[128] All, of course, agreed that Marx rejected the idealist premises of Hegel's holism. As he made clear in the sentence following that quoted above from *The German Ideology*:

[Our conception of history] has not, like the idealistic view of history, in every period to look for a category, but remains constantly on the real ground of history; it does not explain practice from the idea but explains the formation of ideas from material practice. . . .[129]

All also concurred that Marx challenged the social implications of Hegel's

126. Karl Marx, *The German Ideology*, ed. with intro. R. Pascal (New York, 1968), p. 28.

127. Marx, *Grundrisse*, p. 162.

128. And not only among them. See, for example, Melvin Rader's critique of the conflation of the Marxist and Hegelian concepts of totality in Bertell Ollmann's *Alienation: Marx's Conception of Man in Capitalist Society*, 2nd ed. (Cambridge, 1976). Rader argues that Marx did not extend his notion of totality to the cosmos as Hegel did (*Marx's Interpretation of History*, p. 71f).

129. *Op. cit.*

valorization of the current totality. As he stressed in "On the Jewish Question" and elsewhere, the split between man as bourgeois and man as citizen, the continued distinction between civil society and the state, meant that a truly human totality in the normative sense had not yet been achieved. Although never advocating a return to the leveling "terrorism" implicit in Rousseau's *Social Contract* with its obliteration of intermediate bodies, Marx clearly felt that the present mediations, most notably social classes, were not conducive to human freedom. Hegel's idealist *Aufhebung* of the present contradictions of society left them firmly in place. And finally, all Western Marxists agreed that Marx rejected the contemplative attitude towards totality registered in Hegel's famous remark about Minerva's owl and perpetuated in the work of the Young Hegelians such as Bruno and Edgar Bauer, whose still idealist "Critical Criticism" Marx excoriated in *The Holy Family*:

By investigating the "whole as such" to find the conditions for its existence, Critical Criticism is searching in the genuine theological manner, outside the whole, for the conditions for its existence. . . . Critical Criticism dispenses with the study of this real movement which forms the whole in order to be able to declare that it, Critical Criticism as the calm of knowledge, is above both extremes of the contradiction, and that its activity, which has made the "whole as such", is now alone in a position to abolish the abstraction of which it is the maker.[130]

In other words, Marx challenged the contemplative and non-practical epistemology of Hegel and the Young Hegelians, which was based on the belief that the whole could be understood only from without and retrospectively. For Hegel, those who acted in history were not the same as those who made it—or more precisely put, the people who acted and the people who understood were different, even if the Absolute Spirit encompassed both. Marx, however, saw knowledge as active rather than passive; instead of waiting for dusk to fall, the owl of Minerva accompanied the creators of history as they made it. The Western Marxists generally endorsed this position, which emerged in their activist stress on praxis and/or production.

But beyond these very general areas of agreement, Western Marxists found little common ground on which to reach consensus regarding the concept of totality. To what extent did Marx endorse the "longitudinal" notion of totality in which all of history, including the future, had intelligible coherence? Did he base such a notion on Hegel's identification of a "good infinity" with totality, or was there some other way in which he avoided the obvious objection that the future was still unknowable? Did he

130. *Karl Marx: Selected Writings*, p. 134.

include nature in the "latitudinal" totalities he saw as part of the historical process? What was the genesis of these totalities? Were they expressions of the creativity of a meta-subject, a humanist's version of Hegel's Absolute Spirit? Or was the question of ultimate origin unanswerable and thus unimportant? What were the internal structures of the totalities? Were their elements related in a morphologically homogenous way or were they decentered and irreducible to a formally regular pattern? How did specific totalities relate to each other structurally, functionally, historically? Did Marx share with the organic tradition a belief in the ontological priority of the whole over the parts, or was his holism merely methodological and without ontological intent? Was he always convinced that social reality was holistically organized, or did he at times recognize that something escaped organization and remained irreducibly incoherent?[131]

These questions concerned the descriptive use of totality in Marx's work, but there was no more of a consensus when its normative use was considered. Did Marx share with the Romantics a vision of the whole man whose fragmented consciousness and divided existence would be healed under Communism?[132] If so, would this healing take the Hegelian form of man's existence becoming fully identical with his essence or "species being"? Or were more materialist aspects of the process of reconciliation, such as the aesthetic cultivation of the senses, more important? How far did Marx hope the de-alienation of man could go in reuniting him with the natural world? Was his normative image of the whole equal to that pacified, Arcadian utopia favored by critics of the driven, unfulfilled Faustian man of Western civilization, or did Marx's own strong identification with the figure of Prometheus[133] mean that striving and yearning would still be a source of redemption in the society of the future? If the latter, was man's holistic integrity to be purchased at the cost of the continuing subjugation of nature, or could nature be acknowledged as a subject of its own in an advanced form of the dialectic of recognition? Was Communism, moreover, to be understood as a new, non-contradictory form of Becoming or the final achievement of authentic Being? Were all contradictions resolved under Communism, or merely antagonistic ones?

131. For a recent attempt to demonstrate an occasional anti-totalizing impulse in Marx, see Jeffrey Mehlman, *Revolution and Repetition: Marx/Hugo/Balzac* (Berkeley, 1977). For Mehlman, "*The Eighteenth Brumaire* is above all the site where that heterogeneity, in its unassimilability to every dialectical totalization, is *affirmed*" (p. 13; italics in original).

132. A full collection of quotations on this issue can be found in the chapter entitled "The Dream of the Whole Man" in Ernst Fischer, in collaboration with Franz Marek, *Marx in His Own Words*, trans. Anna Bostock (London, 1970).

133. For a discussion of Marx's fascination with Prometheus, see Lewis S. Feuer, *Marx and the Intellectuals* (Garden City, New York, 1969).

Or was it simply foolish to speculate from the "realm of necessity" about the future "realm of freedom"?

These and other questions about Marx's views were still open and unresolved by the advent of the Western Marxist tradition in the 1920s. Either the writings in which Marx had given possible answers were still unpublished or forgotten, or if clues were present in the available works they were too ambiguous and underdeveloped to provide clear guidance. Moreover, the Marxism that emerged in the work of Marx's immediate successors in the era of the Second International (1889–1914) did not dwell with any sustained interest on the issue of totality. There was, to be sure, some residual Hegelianism—in particular the dialectics of nature and such logical categories as the integration of opposites and the negation of the negation—in the Dialectical Materialism fashioned by Engels, Kautsky, Plekhanov and their followers.[134] But aside from vague statements about the "interconnection which binds all these natural processes into one great whole,"[135] the concept of totality was not rigorously employed. Imprecise evocations of cosmic unity appeared in the work of such heterodox figures as Jean Jaurès[136] but without any serious philosophical reflection on their significance. By transforming Marx's historical materialism into a full-fledged metaphysics of matter and by reducing consciousness to an epiphenomenal status,[137] Dialectical Materialism avoided dealing with the troublesome question of the role of subjectivity in the totality. Exuding a misplaced confidence in the scientific working-out of historical laws, "orthodox" Marxists unquestioningly included the future in their implicit longitudinal totality. And by equating Marx's method to that of the natural sciences, they failed to examine the premises of their epistemology and to justify their knowledge of the social whole.

Moreover, within the German Social Democratic Party (SPD), the dominant party of the International, was a subterranean residue of the Lassallean identification of the whole with the state, a right-wing Hege-

134. Z. A. Jordan, *The Evolution of Dialectical Materialism* (New York, 1967); Lucio Colletti, *Marxism and Hegel*, trans. Lawrence Garner (London, 1973); and Samuel H. Baron, *Plekhanov: The Father of Russian Marxism* (Stanford, 1963), p. 288f.

135. Engels, *Ludwig Feuerbach and the End of Classical German Philosophy* in Karl Marx and Friedrich Engels, *Selected Works* (Moscow, 1968), p. 621. It can, however, be argued that Engels' systemic understanding of society was ambiguous enough to anticipate both Scientific and Critical Marxism. For an argument to this effect, see Alvin W. Gouldner, *The Two Marxisms: Contradictions and Anomalies in the Development of Theory* (New York, 1980), p. 241. Perhaps the most obvious inheritor of this ambiguity was Rosa Luxemburg, whose legacy was claimed by both Eastern and Western Marxism.

136. Kolakowski, *Main Currents of Marxism*, vol 2: *The Golden Age*, p. 121.

137. In private correspondence, most notably his celebrated letter of September 21–22, 1890, to Josef Bloch, Engels protested against this reductionism, but the majority of Second International theory was economic-determinist.

lian premise that was exorcised only imperfectly with Marx's apparent triumph over Lassalle at Gotha in 1875 and Erfurt in 1891. This statist bias contributed to a growing reliance on capturing state power through the ballot box with the expectation that social revolution would follow, a belief held explicitly by Bernstein and the Revisionists and implicitly by many of their centrist opponents. Cultural issues and the role of subjectivity were concomitantly underplayed.

If it were not for the disastrous political consequences of Second International theory, which led to the "negative integration"[138] of the socialist movement and a strategy of "revolutionary *attentismus*"[139] whose most unfortunate effect was the debacle of internationalism in 1914, the issue of totality might never have emerged so insistently after the war. It was revived politically because the anti-subjectivist materialism and over-reliance on economic determinism of the orthodox theorists had been discredited by the success of Lenin's very different perspective. Although not until after his death in 1924 was it revealed that Lenin had been re-reading Hegel during the war,[140] his revolutionary success could be interpreted, and was by Lukács and others, as resulting precisely from his dialectical grasp of the totality of social relations in all their concrete complexity. In fact, however much the Western Marxists of subsequent generations moved away from Lenin and his legacy, the founding fathers—Lukács, Korsch and Gramsci—all were avid Leninists in the early 1920s; only Korsch later repudiated his allegiance. The restoration of the concept of totality to its central role in Marxist theory must, therefore, be understood in relation to Lenin's repudiation of economism and determinism and his sensitivity to the interplay of social forces in the Russia of his day.

But of perhaps even greater significance was the fact that Lenin's example was filtered through the theoretical presuppositions of the early Western Marxists, whose intellectual training was firmly grounded in bourgeois philosophy. Indeed, it is arguable that without their schooling in these traditions, the recovery of totality might have been ultimately

138. Guenther Roth, *The Social Democrats in Imperial Germany: A Study in Working-Class Isolation and Negative Integration* (Totowa, New Jersey, 1963).
139. Dieter Groh, *Negative Integration und Revolutionärer Attentismus: Die Deutsche Sozialdemokratie am Vorabend des Ersten Weltkrieges* (Frankfurt, 1973). The term "*attentismus*" refers to the attitude of patient waiting for the revolution to come that characterized the fatalism of the SPD. For another account of this phenomenon, see J. P. Nettl, "The German Social-Democratic Party 1890–1914 as a Political Model," *Past and Present* 30 (1965).
140. For an appreciative discussion of Lenin's discovery of Hegel, see Raya Dunayevskaya, *Philosophy and Revolution: From Hegel to Sartre and from Marx to Mao* (New York, 1973), p. 95f. For a critical comment, see Kolakowski, *Main Currents in Marxism*, vol. 2: *The Golden Age*, p. 461f.

thwarted. For in the years when Dialectical Materialism was dominant in the official socialist movement, it was non-Marxist thought that kept the concept of totality alive and developed it in fruitful ways. To understand Western Marxism, it is thus necessary to make a brief detour through the bourgeois thought of the late nineteenth century, a period of both intellectual crisis and creativity.[141]

From the perspective of the Western Marxist tradition itself, it has often seemed as if bourgeois culture were completely dominated by individualistic, analytic, detotalizing modes of thought. Lukács' rigid dichotomy between Marxist and non-Marxist intellectuals, based on the latter's inability to think holistically, has already been mentioned. Goldmann echoed this judgment when he claimed that the period before the 1910s could be called the era of "liberal capitalism" because it was "the individualist period in which the idea of the ensemble as totality (*l'idée d'ensemble de totalité*) tends to disappear from consciousness."[142] To the extent that the more analytic variants of positivism and neo-Kantianism flourished in Western Europe during much of the nineteenth century, this broad generalization retains some plausibility. But at no time did these more analytic intellectual styles sweep holism entirely from the field. Although it is true that the highly innovative generation of the 1890s reacted against what was felt to be a positivist stranglehold on European thought,[143] its members did so in part by recovering and reworking the contrary impulses that had never really been lost.

Even in England, which, for most continental thinkers and Marxists in particular, was the bastion of individualism in thought and politics, a counter-trend can be observed. From Burke and Coleridge through Pugin and Arnold up to Green, Bosanquet and Bradley,[144] atomizing and analytic ways of thought were firmly rejected. The tradition of seeking solace for the disintegrative effects of industrialism in the realm of culture, which

141. Although a generation old now and not very concerned with the origins of Western Marxism, H. Stuart Hughes, *Consciousness and Society* (New York, 1958) is still the best general survey of the crisis in European thought of this era.
142. Goldmann, *Cultural Creation in Modern Society*, p. 52.
143. This is the main thesis of Hughes' book. For a discussion of the enduring power of variants of idealism in the nineteenth century, see Mandelbaum, *History, Man and Reason*. Even among positivists, certain holistic motifs can be observed. See, for example, the impact of Gestaltism on Alexius Meinong discussed in David R. Lindenfeld, *The Transformation of Positivism: Alexius Meinong and European Thought, 1880–1920* (Berkeley, 1980).
144. For discussions of the late nineteenth-century English idealists, see A. J. M. Milne, *The Social Philosophy of English Idealism* (London, 1962) and Melvin Richter, *The Politics of Conscience: T. H. Green and His Age* (London, 1964). The literature on Burke, Coleridge, Pugin and Arnold is, of course, too vast to need citation.

Raymond Williams trenchantly followed in *Culture and Society*,[145] was often the repository of more holistic hopes. Even a figure like John Stuart Mill, so closely identified with Benthamism, was attracted at times to its Coleridgian competitor and flirted with Comtean organic positivism.[146] On a more popular level, the desire for community was a powerful element in British working-class culture, where spokesmen like Cobbett infused their critique of capitalist social relations with nostalgia for medieval organicism.

England, to be sure, remained generally resistant to Marxist theory. Native advocates like William Morris grafted it onto Cobbett's anti-modernism and prepared the way for a guild socialism that smacked more of Ruskin than of Marx. The development of British social science in the years from 1870 to 1914, in direct contrast to the continent, was virtually unaffected by the need to answer the challenge of Marxism.[147] By the early twentieth century, Fabianism, with its pragmatic scorn for dialectical thinking,[148] came to dominate the Left intelligentsia, which rejected the calls for total revolution by more isolated figures like the syndicalist Tom Mann. At about the same time, the neo-idealism of Green and his associates collapsed under the onslaught of Moore, Russell and Whitehead. In social science, a pragmatic, ethically charged empiricism came to dominate economics and the less-well-developed field of sociology. The holistic interpretation of culture failed to make significant contact with the working-class movement and its supporters and became instead the preserve of more conservative ideologues like T. S. Eliot. Those few social psychologists like William McDougall who tried to go beyond individualism did so out of a disillusionment with democratic politics and the possibility of rational collective action. By the 1960s, Perry Anderson, the young editor of the *New Left Review*, was bemoaning the virtual elimination of the concept of totality from social and political thought in Britain.[149] The only exceptions he noted were literary criticism, where the idea of culture still hovered above that of society, and anthropology, where totality could be safely projected onto exotic peoples far away from home.

145. Raymond Williams, *Culture and Society, 1780–1950* (London, 1958).

146. For a discussion of Mill's complicated relationship to Comte, see Iris W. Mueller, *John Stuart Mill and French Thought* (Urbana, Ill., 1956).

147. For a recent discussion of British social science in this era, see Reba N. Soffer, *Ethics and Society in England: The Revolution in the Social Sciences, 1870–1914* (Berkeley, 1978). Significantly, there is not a single reference to Marx or Marxism in her narrative.

148. For a good treatment of the theoretical inclinations of the Fabians, see A. M. McBriar, *Fabian Socialism and English Politics, 1884–1918* (Cambridge, 1966).

149. Perry Anderson, "Components of the National Culture," *New Left Review* 50 (July–August 1968).

On the continent, however, nineteenth-century holistic thought had a more direct and profound impact on several theories in general and on Marxist theory in particular. In France, the positivist tradition itself was the locus of a certain kind of holistic thought, which reacted to the corrosive effects of the democratic and industrial revolutions. "Society," Saint-Simon wrote, "is, above all, a veritable organized machine, all of whose component parts contribute in a different way to the working of the whole."[150] August Comte even more thoroughly integrated organic motifs into his elaborate system; "The social organism," he wrote, "is single whole just as, and even more than, the individual organism."[151] Comte's insistence on the irreducibility of sociology to psychology, his scorn for social contract theory, and his belief that biology provided a rough model for understanding society, excluded any individualist tendencies from his thought. Comte's Enlightenment faith in the collective progress of humanity led him to posit a longitudinal view of totality no less complete than Hegel's. His fear of the corrosive and atomizing effects of the French and Industrial revolutions aroused in him a yearning for a normative totality scarcely less avid than that expressed by the counter-revolutionaries de Maistre and de Bonald. In short, Comtean positivism shared the general distaste for l'individualisme that permeated French society throughout the nineteenth century.[152]

Although, to be sure, Comte's successors included figures like Emile Littré, who adopted his inductive method while rejecting his organic system, they were balanced by other, more eclectic followers such as Taine and Renan, who found ways to combine Comte with Hegel.[153] The holistic impulse in French positivism emerged even more clearly in the sociological theory of Durkheim, who, according to his most eminent biographer, "had a strong tendency always to conceive of 'society' as a whole, rather than in terms, say, of a plurality or conflict between different social groups and forces."[154] Transmitted through his nephew, Marcel Mauss,[155] to the later structuralist movement, the holistic impulse in French positivism surfaced ultimately in the Marxist structuralism of Althusser. In For Marx, Althus-

150. Quoted in Z. A. Jordan, *Dialectical Materialism*, p. 148.
151. *Auguste Comte and Positivism: The Essential Writings*, ed. with intro. Gertrud Lenzer (New York, 1975), p. 427. For a good discussion of Comte's organicism, see Mandelbaum, p. 171f.
152. Steven Lukes, *Individualism* (New York, 1973), pp. 3–16.
153. D. G. Charlton, *Positivist Thought in France During the Second Empire, 1852–1870* (Oxford, 1959).
154. Steven Lukes, *Emile Durkheim: His Life and Work: A Historical and Critical Study* (London, 1973), p. 21.
155. For a discussion of Mauss's use of totality, see Chito Guala, "Uso e Significato del Concetto di Totalita' Nel Pensiero e Nell'Opera di Marcel Mauss," *Sociologia* 8:1 (January 1973).

ser pointedly praised Comte as "the only mind worthy of interest produced by French thought in the 130 years after 1789,"[156] and in a later work included Durkheim with him as one of the "few great minds"[157] worth salvaging from the disastrous history of French philosophy.

Holism in France, however, was also nurtured by another intellectual tradition that extended as far back as Pascal, whose tragic vision Goldmann saw as "the great turning point in Western thought, the moment at which it began to abandon the atomistic approach of rationalism and empiricism, and to move towards a dialectical reasoning."[158] In opposition to the analytic proclivities of the dominant Cartesian intellectual climate, this mode of thought relied on the power of intuition to grasp entities in their irreducible wholeness. Through later figures like Maine de Birain and Bergson, intuitionist thought presented a challenge both to idealist rationalism and analytic positivism. It achieved its most potent social formulation in the work of Georges Sorel, who defended irrational myths as modes of global consciousness capable of arousing the masses to political action.[159] Sorel moved fitfully from movement to movement before the war, attempting to find an audience for his advocacy of apocalyptic violence. After 1918, his arguments were more readily heeded both on the Right, where Mussolini acknowledged their persuasiveness, and on the Left, where Lukács, through the Hungarian anarcho-syndicalist Ervin Szabó, absorbed Sorel's stress on praxis and subjective consciousness. Although Colletti surely exaggerated in tracing a direct line from Bergson through Sorel to Lukács,[160] the influence of what might be called the Pascalian current in French thought cannot be entirely discounted in probing the prehistory of Western Marxism.

The more explosive impact of Hegelian thought did not, however, really begin to affect French Marxism until the 1930s and the important lectures of Kojève and Hyppolite.[161] In Italy and Germany, on the other

156. Louis Althusser, *For Marx*, trans. Ben Brewster (New York, 1970), p. 25.

157. Louis Althusser, *Lenin and Philosophy and Other Essays*, trans. Ben Brewster (New York, 1971), p. 28.

158. Lucien Goldmann, *The Hidden God: A Study of Tragic Vision in the Pensées of Pascal and the Tragedies of Racine*, trans. Philip Thody (New York, 1964), p. 5.

159. It should be noted that in his social scientific moods, Sorel was wary of holism. See the discussion of his *diremptions* as anti-holistic in John L. Stanley's intro. to *From Georges Sorel: Essays in Socialism and Philosophy*, trans. John and Charlotte Stanley (New York, 1976), p. 36f.

160. Colletti, *Marxism and Hegel*, chapter 10.

161. For a discussion of the impact of Hegel in France during this period, see Mark Poster, *Existential Marxism in Postwar France: From Sartre to Althusser* (Princeton, 1975), chapter 1. For a corrective to Poster's claim that Hegel was virtually ignored in France before that time, see Michael Kelly, "Hegel in France to 1940: A Bibliographical Essay," *Journal of European Studies* 11:1 (March 1981).

hand, Hegel became a central figure at an earlier date. In both of those countries, holistic thought in general flourished at a time when the struggle for national unification was being waged. In that struggle, intellectuals often assumed a pivotal role, despite setbacks such as that experienced by the Frankfurt Parliament of 1848. The close link between bureaucratic and cultural life, especially in Germany, meant that intellectuals often assumed responsibility for the welfare of the society as a whole. As members of an educated *Bildungsbürgertum* with allegedly purer and more disinterested motives than either the old aristocracy or the new commercial *Besitzbürgertum*, they claimed immunity from the petty squabbles of interest-oriented politicians. Hegel's ideology of the bureaucracy as the universal class was an early expression of this self-image. Although in the Italy of the *Risorgimento* the Church prevented intellectuals from consolidating their position to the same extent as in Germany,[162] there too they often attempted to speak for the whole. In fact, at a time when Hegelianism was on the wane in Germany, it began to attract supporters among Italian intellectuals, many of them in the liberal camp.

Whenever liberalism was identified solely with its laissez-faire, utilitarian, individualistic traditions, holism was an anti-liberal phenomenon. But where the task of political unification loomed much larger than the maintenance of a capitalist economy, liberalism could take on more holistic forms. With the globalizing and anti-analytic impulses of the Renaissance still potent and the memory of Vico not entirely obliterated, Italian culture in the period of the *Risorgimento* was able to absorb holistic assumptions and turn them in a progressive direction. Dialectical thought gained a foothold in Italy as early as the 1840s, with the first translations of Hegel by Augusto Vera and Giambattista Paserini.[163] The Neopolitan philosopher Bertrando Spaventa was most influential in linking neo-Hegelianism with the struggle for Italian unification. Attributing to intellectuals a leading role in that process, Spaventa argued for what a modern observer has called "a bourgeois *ethical* state which, unlike the *liberal* variety based on *abstract* individualism, had as its fundamental task the creation of conditions leading to the genesis of social individuality."[164] Unlike his major competitor Vera, whose

---

162. Gramsci's analysis focused on the anti-national effects of the clerical intellectuals' role in Italian life: "As far as Italy was concerned the central fact is precisely the international or cosmopolitan function of its intellectuals, which is both cause and effect of the state of disintegration in which the peninsula remained from the fall of the Roman Empire up to 1870." *Selections from the Prison Notebooks*, ed. and trans. Quintin Hoare and Geoffrey Nowell Smith (New York, 1978), pp. 17–18.

163. For a good treatment of Hegelian thought in nineteenth-century Italy, see Paul Piccone, "From Spaventa to Gramsci," *Telos* 31 (Spring 1977).

164. Ibid, p. 57.

more conservative reading of Hegel's system paralleled that of the German Right Hegelians, Spaventa argued that reason still had to be realized in the world, a postulate later resurrected by Herbert Marcuse and other neo-Hegelian Western Marxists.

Following Spaventa's death in 1883, a more ethically neutral positivism came to dominate Italian philosophical life. Its ascendency can perhaps be best understood in terms of the anti-ideological "*trasformismo*" that characterized post-unification Italian politics, although the general European intellectual climate cannot be ignored. The holistic impulse of Spaventa's thought was not, however, entirely extirpated. It reemerged full-blown in Benedetto Croce's "philosophy of liberty," which dominated twentieth-century Italian culture for two generations, as well as in the liberal statism of later figures such as Guido de Ruggiero and the non-liberal statism of others like Giovanni Gentile.[165] And more important for our purposes, it surfaced in the Marxist theory of Antonio Labriola[166] and, even more significantly, of Antonio Gramsci. Personal links were part of the reason for this reemergence—Labriola had been a student of Spaventa's in the 1860s, and Croce grew up in the household of Spaventa's brother, Silvio, and studied with Labriola—but the major explanation must be sought in the failure of *trasformismo* to realize the promise of the *Risorgimento*. When national unification failed to create the sense of community its early advocates had promised, holistic yearnings reemerged in the radical movements of both the Left and Right that ended the era of liberalism in 1922.

In Germany, a similar disillusionment can be discerned. As noted earlier, the aesthetic notion of totality played a pivotal role in the nationalization of the German masses. Initially enthusiastic about Bismarck's Second Reich, many nationalists came increasingly to yearn for something more authentically holistic. The *völkisch* movement and accompanying "politics of cultural despair,"[167] which historians have argued helped prepare the way for the Third Reich, often voiced demands for a new totality. In fact, German bourgeois culture in general during much of the nineteenth century tended to favor holistic modes of thought. Despite certain counter-examples, such as the mechanical materialism of Büchner, Vogt

165. H. S. Harris, *The Social Philosophy of Giovanni Gentile* (Urbana, 1966).
166. For discussions of Labriola, see Edmund E. Jacobitti, "Labriola, Croce and Italian Marxism (1895–1910)," *Journal of the History of Ideas* 36:2 (April–June 1975); Paul Piccone, "Labriola and the Roots of Eurocommunism," *Berkeley Journal of Sociology* 22 (1977–1978); Kolakowski, *Main Currents of Marxism* vol. 2: *The Golden Age*; and Serge Hughes, *The Fall and Rise of Modern Italy* (New York, 1967), chapters 2 and 3.
167. Fritz Stern, *The Politics of Cultural Despair* (Berkeley, 1964).

and Moleschott, influential in the 1850s and 1860s, and the radical individualism of Max Stirner and the later Nietzsche, most German intellectuals were attracted with varying fervency to the concept of totality.

Perhaps the most obvious example of this predilection can be found in
the historiographical tradition known as historicism.[168] Historicism saw
history in holistic terms, either as a universal process with a coherent
meaning or as a series of discrete totalities that were the separate nation-
states of world history. From Humboldt through Ranke, Droysen, Dilthey
and up to Troeltsch and Meinecke, they accepted the assertion, expressed
by Ranke, that:

The whole (*Totale*) is as certain as its every outward expression at every moment.
We must dedicate our full attention to it. . . . (If we are studying) a people, we are
not interested in all the individual details through which it expresses itself as a
living thing. Rather its idea speaks to us through its development as a whole, its
deed, its institutions, its literature.[169]

Holism was so much a part of the historicist world-view that when its
exponents talked of the individuals of history they generally meant those
collective entities known as nations or states, a bias that emerges in their
well-known insistence on the primacy of foreign policy. Although the historicist tradition underwent a severe crisis in the 1890s, when its underlying religious assumptions were called into question, its holistic bias was
rarely challenged. Writing in 1910, Dilthey argued that the historical
world should be understood as a

system of interactions centered on itself; each individual system of interactions
contained in it has, through the positing of values and their realization, its center
within itself; but all are structurally linked into a whole in which, from the
significance of the individual parts, the meaning of the social-historical world
arises: thus every value judgment and every purpose projected into the future,
must be based exclusively on this structural context.[170]

And as late as 1924, Karl Mannheim could write: "Whereas in Western
Science, the 'atomizing' and causally connecting approach gradually be-

168. There is a widespread literature concerning historicism with little consensus over
its precise meaning. The idiosyncratic usage in Karl Popper's *The Poverty of Historicism*
(New York, 1960), where the term is employed to criticize those who try to discern historical
laws in order to predict the future, is generally condemned as untrue to the nineteenth-
century movement meant here. Friedrich Meinecke's *Die Entstehung des Historismus*, 2
vols. (Munich, 1936) provides a looser definition that stresses the ideas of development and
individuality as the key elements in the tradition, individuality used, of course, to describe
the individual wholes of history unconstrained by universal law. For more recent treatments
of the tradition, see the studies cited above by Iggers and Mandelbaum.
169. Quoted in Iggers, *The German Conception of History*, p. 79.
170. Wilhelm Dilthey, *Pattern and Meaning in History: Thoughts on History and Society*, ed. with intro. H. P. Rickman (New York, 1961), p. 82.

came paramount in the historical and sociological disciplines also, German philosophy of history is dominated by the categories of 'individual totality' and 'evolution,' understood in a dialectical sense."[171]

A comparable holistic impulse was manifest in other areas of German cultural life, especially after the turn of the century. In biology, the vitalism of Hans Driesch postulated a unifying entelechy controlling the living organism as a coherent whole.[172] In economics, the so-called "historical school" led by Gustav Schmoller and Adolph Wagner scorned the analytic methods of classical economics, engaged in a spirited *Methodenstreit* with such latter-day defenders of these methods as Carl Menger, and defined the role of the state as the servant of the general interest in a way consonant with the cameralist traditions of German economic history.[173] Even in psychology, which had long been criticized for its submission to the canons of an atomizing natural science, a holistic counter-trend developed in the Gestaltist School, whose origins can be traced to Max Wertheimer's celebrated paper of 1912 on "Perception of Apparent Movement."[174]

Perhaps most important of all among the social sciences in its impact on Western Marxism, sociology also evinced a keen awareness of the need to treat societies as coherent wholes and expressed a heightened longing for wholeness in normative terms. Although certain figures such as Max Weber were cautious in their adoption of holistic assumptions,[175] other German sociologists rivaled the historicists in their stress on the need to

171. Karl Mannheim, "Historicism" in *Essays on Sociology of Knowledge*, ed. Paul Kecskemeti (New York, 1952), p. 100.

172. Hans Driesch, *The Science and Philosophy of the Organism* (London, 1908).

173. See Kenneth D. Barkin, *The Controversy Over German Industrialization, 1890–1902* (Chicago, 1970) for a discussion of the ways in which the Historical School influenced German politics in the late nineteenth century. For a discussion of the methods controversy, see David Frisby, intro. to English trans. of Theodor W. Adorno et al., *The Positivist Dispute in German Sociology* (London, 1976), p. xvi.

174. For a brief discussion of the origins of Gestalt psychology, see D. C. Phillips, *Holistic Thought in Social Science* (Stanford, 1976), chapter 7. For a discussion of the proto-Gestaltist work of Christian von Ehrenfels, see Lindenfeld, p. 115 f.

175. Weber is normally understood as a social action theorist who was individualist in his methodology. As W. G. Runciman puts it, "If there is one basic assumption, or set of assumptions, underlying Weber's thought which distinguishes it from that of Marx—or, for that matter, of Comte or Durkheim—it is the assumption deriving from the joint influence of Kant and Nietzsche that reality cannot be objectively grasped by the human mind as a whole" (*Max Weber: Selections in Translation*, ed. W. G. Runciman, trans. E. Matthews [Cambridge, 1978], p. 4). From the point of view of the Althusserian Nicos Poulantzas, however, Weber is still within the expressivist holistic camp:

Here we should not forget the direct descent of Lukács from Weber, for it is this filiation which allows us to elucidate the relationship between Lukács' Hegelian "totality" and the *functionalist* totality which in large part predominates in contemporary social science. What links Weber's theories to contemporary functionalism, as Parsons has noted, is that the global social structure is, in the last analysis, considered as the *product* of a society-subject which creates in its teleological development certain social *values* or *ends*.

"Marxist Political Theory in Great Britain," *New Left Review* 43 [May–June 1967], p. 61.)

know the whole. The concern for community, which one recent observer has called "the most fundamental and far-reaching of sociology's unit-ideas,"[176] was given its classic formulation in Ferdinand Tönnies' cele-brated work of 1887, *Community and Society*.[177] Building on the recent rediscovery of medieval communitarianism by von Gierke, Maine and Fustel de Coulanges, Tönnies turned his own personal nostalgia for the simpler life of his youthful *Heimat* in rural Schleswig into a critique of the alienating effects of modern society.[178] Without that nationalist faith in the power of the new Prussianized, bureaucratized *Reich* to restore com-munitarian values, which comforted more orthodox social theorists such as Schmoller or Wagner, Tönnies foreshadowed both right- and left-wing attempts to go beyond the state in search of a new *Gemeinschaft*. Lukács, for example, knew him in Heidelberg from 1912 to 1917, and as late as 1925 evoked his name as a corrective to the scientism of Karl August Wittfogel.[179] Tönnies' sharply etched distinction between naturally har-monious communities and artificially discordant societies appealed to both right- and left-wing critics of liberalism.

In German philosophy, the movement most closely identified with lib-eralism, and thus the frequent target of holists' abuse, was neo-Kantian-ism.[180] Yet a brief glance at its history will show that it too was unable to resist the lure of totalistic thinking. The "Back to Kant" movement emerged in the 1850s and 1860s in opposition to both Hegelian specula-tive reasoning and mechanical materialism. The Kant to whom Lotze, Zeller, Kuno Fischer, Lange and their successors returned was not the author of the *Idea of a Universal History* or even the *Critique of Judg-ment,* those works which, as we have seen, opened the door to post-critical Idealism. Instead, "Back to Kant" meant a revival of the first two Critiques with their scepticism about dialectical reason, dualistic episte-mology and radical separation of facts from values. Initially interested more in Kant's philosophy of science, a concern that still animated the Marburg School in the late nineteenth century, the neo-Kantians came

176. Nisbet, *The Sociological Tradition,* p. 47.
177. Ferdinand Tönnies, *Community and Society,* trans and ed. Charles Loomis (East Lansing, Michigan, 1957).
178. See Arthur Mitzman, *Sociology and Estrangement: Three Sociologists of Imperial Germany* (New York, 1973), for a discussion of Tönnies' background.
179. Lukács, *Political Writings, 1919–29,* trans. Michael M. Colgan, ed. Rodney Livingstone (London, 1972), p. 144.
180. For a recent history of neo-Kantianism, see Thomas E. Willey, *Back to Kant: The Revival of Kantianism in German Social and Historical Thought, 1860–1914* (Detroit, 1978). See also Fritz K. Ringer, *The Decline of the German Mandarins: The German Aca-demic Community, 1890–1933* (Cambridge, 1969), and Andrew Arato, "The Neo-Idealist Defense of Subjectivity," *Telos* 21 (Fall 1974).

increasingly to focus on Kant's moral teachings, his *Critique of Practical Reason*. In the Southwest German School of Heinrich Rickert and Wilhelm Windelband, strenuous but ultimately vain efforts were made to avoid the relativism implied by the breakdown of historicism's religious supports. By searching for a realm of transcendent values above the flux of history, they opened themselves up to the charge of abstract formalism. Although their investigations of the differences between the natural and cultural sciences were of seminal importance, their attempt to find absolutes amidst the rapidly changing circumstances of European culture failed. What Lukács was to identify as a "craving for the concrete"[181] could find no satisfaction in their abstract notions of human reason grounded in a universal transcendental apperception.

The acuteness of their failure was registered perhaps nowhere as keenly as in the thought of Georg Simmel,[182] the philosopher and sociologist whose indebtedness to neo-Kantianism was balanced by a strong attraction to the *Lebensphilosophie* of Nietzsche and Dilthey. Simmel believed that the unity of life and form, of existence and meaning, was a human impossibility. Totality, he claimed, was a function of man's capacity to unify inchoate matter into formal patterns, but something irreducible always remained untotalized. Objective Spirit,[183] the cumulative residue of men in their form-giving capacity, likewise resisted reappropriation on the part of those who came at a later stage of the objectification process. The resulting conflict between submission to received forms and the desire to create anew, or between the intersubjective legacy of the cultural past and the subjective need to break free from it, produced what Simmel called the tragedy of culture. In short, the alienation that both Hegel and Marx thought could be overcome was for Simmel a permanent part of the human condition.

Moreover, in several classic studies of modern life, which focussed on such themes as the psychological effects of the city and the alienating function of money,[184] he argued that the situation was worsening. Like

181. Georg Lukács, "Emil Lask; Ein Nachruf," *Kant Studien* 22 (Berlin, 1918), p. 350.

182. For a general discussion of Simmel, see Rudolph H. Weingartner, *Experience and Culture: The Philosophy of Georg Simmel* (Middletown, Conn. 1962). See also the intro. by Donald N. Levine to *Georg Simmel on Individuality and Social Form: Selected Writings* (Chicago, 1971), and Arato, "The Neo-Idealist Defense of Subjectivity."

183. Objective Spirit was originally a Hegelian term that had been reappropriated by Dilthey in an irrationalist sense to signify the cultural context confronting the individual subject. Both Hegel and Dilthey saw no irreconcilable gap between objective and subjective spirit, but Simmel clearly did. See the discussion of Dilthey's use of the term in Rudolf A. Makkreel, *Dilthey: Philosopher of the Human Studies* (Princeton, 1975), p. 306f.

184. Georg Simmel, *The Philosophy of Money*, trans. Tom Bottomore and David Frisby (London and Boston, 1978) and "The Metropolis and Mental Life" in *The Sociology of Georg Simmel*, trans. and ed. with intro. Kurt H. Wolff (New York, 1964).

Max Weber, he saw no way out of the "iron cage" of modernization, no way back from *Gesellschaft* to *Gemeinschaft*. Similarly, he was skeptical about philosophy's pretension to know the whole, arguing instead that "the very image of the *whole*, which seems to imply the fullest and purest objectivity, reflects the peculiarity of its possessor much more than the objective image of any particular thing usually reflects it."[185] The result, as a recent defender of Lukács has put it, was that

> Simmel's *Lebensphilosophie* only confirmed the cultural world as the naturalizing positivists implicitly saw it: as an alienated second nature. Or rather, it "surpassed" the dualism of an increasingly fragmented subject and the alienated second nature only in terms of an irrationalist theory of life as attained by immediate intuition. Simmel's re-conceptualization of alienation as the "self-alienation" of life left everything as it was.[186]

Simmel, however, was generally considered an outsider by his contemporaries, a thinker whose corrosive insights were attributed as often to his Jewish background as to the validity of his perception. For those anxious not to leave "everything as it was," the possibility of achieving a new totality and ending the tragedy of culture was still a very live one. In fact, by the turn of the century, defections from within the ranks of the neo-Kantians began to grow. Some were attracted to what they saw as the more vitalistic *Lebensphilosophie* of Dilthey, who promised to replace the diluted "lymph of reason"[187] that had flowed through the veins of neo-Kantian man with the blood of real life. Although Dilthey shared with Hegel a retrospective view of totality—the meaning of a culture, like that of a life, he claimed,[188] could only be known at the moment of death—he argued that the whole must include the irrational as well as the rational.

Other disillusioned neo-Kantians, for whom the early Dilthey was too psychologistic, began exploring the path back to the concrete blazed by Edmund Husserl that would lead to the movements of Phenomenology and *Existenzphilosophie*, which came into their own during the 1920s. Still others, such as the young Heidelberg philosopher Emil Lask, turned to an ahistorical neo-Platonism in their search for absolute, yet concrete, values beyond the temporal flow. And at first tentatively and then more

185. Quoted in Weingartner, p. 166.
186. Arato, p. 161. Although Arato's later view of Lukács was less favorable, this essay is written from a clearly Lukácsian perspective. For a discussion of Simmel's importance for Lukács himself, see James Schmidt, "The Concrete Totality and Lukács Concept of Bildung," *Telos* 24 (Summer 1974).
187. Quoted in Hajo Holborn, "Wilhelm Dilthey and the Critique of Historical Reason," in *European Intellectual History Since Darwin and Marx*, ed. W. Warren Wagar (New York, 1966), p. 65.
188. Dilthey, *Pattern and Meaning in History*, p. 106.

vigorously, there occurred a renaissance of interest in the philosopher the neo-Kantians had buried two generations earlier: Hegel.[189] In 1905, Dilthey wrote a highly influential history of Hegel's early theological writings, which redirected attention toward the period before his mature philosophy was formalized.[190] By 1910 even Windelband was noting, with some discomfort, a "hunger for world-views, which has seized our younger generation and which finds satisfaction in Hegel."[191] Although Windelband, still loyal to Kant's critical method, identified this hunger with mystical, religious and irrational longings, seeing it as a revival of the Romantic revulsion against the Enlightenment,[192] the Hegel renaissance inevitably sought a way to transform (or transfigure) the concreteness of lived experience into rational terms. The first generation of Western Marxists was inspired by the same impulse, although later figures in the tradition such as Lucio Colletti came to have serious second thoughts.[193]

The desire to rationalize lived experience was, to be sure, part of that larger insistence on action, rational or otherwise, that was voiced by so many European intellectuals before the war. In a second lecture in 1910, entitled "On the Mysticism of Our Time," Windelband spoke of a new demand for a philosophy of "the deed and of will."[194] Sometimes this yearning could lead in a right-wing direction as was the case with the *Action française* in France, Gentile's "Philosophy of the Act" in Italy, and the nationalist embrace of the "Ideas of 1914" on the part of such neo-Kantians as Paul Natorp and Emil Lask[195] in Germany. The coming of the war seemed for many to provide an answer to their craving for normative totality. Even Simmel, who normally remained an aloof observer, "found his absolute," as Ernst Bloch put it, "in the trenches."[196]

But for others, to whom the internationalism of the Marxist tradition still appealed, the answer could not be found in the short-lived German *Burgfrieden* or the French *union sacrée*. The politics of their cultural

189. Heinrich Levy, *Die Hegel-Renaissance in der deutschen Philosophie* (Charlottenberg, 1927).

190. Dilthey, *Die Jugendgeschichte Hegels und andere Abhandlungen zur Geschichte des deutschen Idealismus,* ed. Hermann Nohl, 2nd ed. (Stuttgart, 1959).

191. Windelband, "Die Erneuerung des Hegelianismus," *Präludien: Aufsätze und Reden zur Philosophie and ihrer Geschichte,* 5th ed. (Tübingen, 1915), vol. 1, p. 278.

192. Windelband, "Von der Mystik unserer Zeit," *Präludien,* p. 291.

193. Colletti, *Marxism and Hegel.*

194. Windelband, "Die Erneuerung des Hegelianismus," p. 288.

195. On Natorp, see Willey, *Back to Kant,* p. 116f. On Lask, see Heinrich Rickert, *Geleitwort* to vol. 1 of Emil Lask, *Gesammelte Schriften* (Tübingen, 1923).

196. Quoted in Kurt Gassen and Michael Landmann, eds., *Buch des Dankes an Georg Simmel* (Berlin, 1958), p. 13. For a general analysis of the impact of the war, see Robert Wohl, *The Generation of 1914* (Cambridge, Mass., 1979).

despair did not lead in the same direction as did those of their contemporaries who found holistic answers in the nation-state. Some became imperialists or pan-nationalists. Others, like the anarchist Gustav Landauer,[197] sought a solution in left-wing communitarianism, which tried to remedy the failings of orthodox Marxism through a benign rendering of the *völkisch* tradition. Still others were less willing to equate Marxism with its "orthodox" incarnation, and thus abandon it entirely. Accepting that description of the modern predicament most keenly rendered by Simmel, but scornful of his pessimism; impatient with the mechanistic assumptions of Second International Marxism, but still inspired by Marx's general analysis; aware of the inadequacies of bourgeois holism, but sharing its desire for a new totality—they sought an answer in the radical rethinking of Marxist theory that became known as Western Marxism. The exemplary figures in this new departure were Lukács, Korsch and Gramsci. Of the three, Lukács was most insistent on the importance of totality as the critical category that would restore Marxism's theoretical vigor, enabling it to match the practical achievements of Lenin and the Bolshevik Revolution. And so, it is to Lukács that we must turn first to perceive the intimate relation of the concept of totality with the birth of Western Marxism.

197. The best recent treatment of Landauer is Eugene Lunn, *Prophet of Community: The Romantic Socialism of Gustav Landauer* (Berkeley, 1973). See also Charles B. Maurer, *Call to Revolution: The Mystical Anarchism of Gustav Landauer* (Detroit, 1971) and Ruth Link-Salinger (Hyman), *Gustav Landauer: Philosopher of Utopia* (Indianapolis, 1977).

CHAPTER TWO

Georg Lukács and the Origins of the Western Marxist Paradigm

Had Georg Lukács ceased writing in 1917, the year of the Russian Revolution, he would be remembered solely as a particularly intense contributor to the creative ferment of pre-war bourgeois culture.[1] Among his earliest

1. The literature on Lukács' early career has grown to substantial proportions in recent years. Among the more noteworthy contributions are Lucien Goldmann, "The Early Writings of Georg Lukács," *Triquarterly* 9 (Spring 1967); Andrew Arato, "Lukács' Path to Marxism (1910–1923)," *Telos* 7 (Spring 1971); David Kettler, "Culture and Revolution: Lukács in the Hungarian Revolution," *Telos* 7 (Spring 1971); Gareth Stedman Jones, "The Marxism of the Early Lukács," *New Left Review* 70 (November–December 1971), reprinted in *Western Marxism: A Critical Reader*, ed. *New Left Review* (London, 1977), from which the following citations come; Paul Breines, "Lukács, Revolution and Marxism: 1885–1918," *The Philosophical Forum* 3, 3–4 (Spring, Summer 1972); Andrew Arato, "Georg Lukács: The Search for a Revolutionary Subject" in *The Unknown Dimension: European Marxism Since Lenin*, ed. Dick Howard and Karl E. Klare (New York and London, 1972); Jörg Kammler, "Ästhetizistische Lebensphilosophie," *Text + Kritik*, 39/40 (October 1973); Silvie Rücker, "Totalität als ethisches und ästhetisches Problem," *Text + Kritik*, 39/40 (October 1973); Lee Congdon, "The Unexpected Revolutionary: Lukács' Road to Marx," *Survey*, 10, 2–3 (Spring–Summer 1974); James Schmidt, "The Concrete Totality and Lukács' Concept of Proletarian *Bildung*," *Telos* 24 (Summer 1975); György Markus, "The Young Lukács and the Problem of Culture," *Telos* 32 (Summer 1977); Ferenc Feher, "The Last Phase of Romantic Anti-Capitalism: Lukács' Response to the War," *New German Critique* 10 (Winter 1977); Dennis Crow, "Form and the Unifications of Aesthetics and Ethics in Lukács' *Soul and Form*," *New German Critique* 15 (Fall 1978); and Paul Breines, "Young Lukács, Old Lukács, New Lukács," *Journal of Modern History* 513 (September 1979). There are also valuable discussions of Lukács' pre-Marxist phase in G. H. R. Parkinson, ed. *Georg Lukács: The Man, His Work and His Ideas* (New York, 1970); István Mészáros, *Lukács' Concept of Dialectic* (London, 1972); Fredric Jameson, *Marxism and Forms Twentieth-Century Dialectical Theories of Literature* (Princeton, 1971); Lucio Colletti, *Marxism and Hegel*, trans. Lawrence Garner (London, 1973); Michael Löwy, *Georg Lukács: From Romanticism to Bolshevism*, trans. Patrick Camiller (London, 1979); Andrew Arato and Paul Breines, *The Young Lukács and the Origins of Western Marxism* (New York, 1979); and Lee Congdon, *The Young Lukács* (Chapel Hill, 1983).

These works supplement and correct parts of Lukács own somewhat tendentious reminiscences in his new prefaces to *The Theory of the Novel* (1962) and *History and Class*

works, many written under the aristocratic name von Lukács,[2] were several short essays on drama, a spirited appreciation of the Magyar poet Endre Ady, and an unfinished treatise on aesthetics.[3] All of these, however, were composed in his native Hungarian, and it was only with the collection of essays, *Soul and Form,* translated into German in 1911, and *The Theory of the Novel,* published in a German journal in 1916, that he reached a Europe-wide audience.[4] Although a concern for social and political issues appeared in the Hungarian writings, it was almost entirely absent from those that were available to that larger public. As a result, Lukács was known as a thinker for whom cultural, ethical and philosophical problems were far more central than social, political or economic ones. There were few, if any, indications in his published work of anything but scorn for the theory and practice of the Second International.

Methodologically as well, Lukács before the Revolution was firmly, if uneasily, within the confines of bourgeois culture, specifically the neo-Kantianism of the Heidelberg to which he had moved in 1912. His primary theoretical mentors were Dilthey, Simmel, Weber and Lask, his approach to cultural questions largely that of the *Geisteswissenschaften,* and his general prognosis for the future similar to that of the normally right-wing purveyors of cultural despair. He counted among his friends such conservative figures as the dramatist Paul Ernst,[5] as well as more radical ones such as Ernst Bloch. While interested in political questions, he nonetheless enthusiastically supported the writings of that great "un-

---

Consciousness (1967) and his earlier essay, "Mein Weg zu Marx," (1933), reprinted in *Georg Lukács, Schriften zur Ideologie und Politik,* ed. Peter Ludz (Neuwied and Berlin, 1967). They also avoid many of the weaknesses of Victor Zitta's *ad hominem* and reductive attack on Lukács in his *Georg Lukács' Marxism: Alienation, Dialectics, Revolution: A Study in Utopia and Ideology* (The Hague, 1964), and the hurried judgments of George Lichtheim in his *George Lukács* (New York, 1970).

2. Lukács' father, a prominent Budapest banker, had been ennobled in 1899. Lukács continued to use the German form "von Lukács" for some of his writings until 1918. For a discussion of the complicated history of ennobled Hungarian Jews, see William O. McCagg, Jr., *Jewish Nobles and Geniuses in Modern Hungary* (New York, 1972), which tries to explain the extraordinary frequency of gifted thinkers among this group.

3. For a complete bibliography of Lukács' early works in Hungarian, see Mészáros, p. 153f. For a discussion of his work on Hungarian literature, see Peter Nagy, "Lukács and Hungarian Literature," *New Hungarian Quarterly* 60 (Winter 1975). Löwy's treatment of the Hungarian revolutionary intelligentsia, at once Jacobin and anti-bourgeois, is invaluable for understanding Lukács' debt to Ady and other Hungarian radicals.

4. Georg Lukács, *Soul and Form,* trans. Anna Bostock (Cambridge, Mass., 1974); Lukács, *The Theory of the Novel,* trans. Anna Bostock (Cambridge, Mass., 1971). The latter was first published in the *Zeitschrift für Aesthetik und Allgemeine Kunstwissenschaft* in 1916, and as a book four years later.

5. Their correspondence has been published in *Paul Ernst und Georg Lukács: Dokumente einer Freundschaft,* ed. Karl August Kutzbach (Düsseldorf, 1974). For a discussion of the friendship, see Feher.

political" defender of German *Kultur*, Thomas Mann, who returned his praise in kind.[6]

Unlike many of his contemporaries within the Hungarian Jewish upper middle-class, whose intellectual organs were significantly called *Nyugat* (*The West*) and *Huszadik Szagad* (*The Twentieth Century*), Lukács held out little hope for the "westernization" of central and eastern Europe. Although drawn to religious figures like Kierkegaard, he had no use for either traditional or heterodox spiritual consolations. Nor did he find very attractive the chauvinist "Ideas of 1914," which seduced others of similar outlook, including men he admired such as Lask, Mann and Ernst. When the war came, he was later to recall, Marianne Weber challenged his despair with little success:

My only reply was: "The better the worse!" When I tried at this time to put my emotional attitude into conscious terms, I arrived at more or less the following formulation: the Central Powers would probably defeat Russia; this might lead to the downfall of Tsarism; I had no objection to that. There was also some probability that the West would defeat Germany; if this led to the downfall of the Hohenzollerns and the Hapsburgs, I was once again in favor. But then the question arose: who was to save us from Western civilization?[7]

The only herald of a possible new age Lukács could acknowledge was the ambiguous figure of Dostoevsky,[8] whose writings seemed to prefigure a new cultural configuration, although one whose outlines were not yet clearly visible.

Had Lukács' voice then been stilled during the war, he would be known today as one of a large number of radical critics of bourgeois culture, whose radicalism was still incoherent in political terms. But, of course, Lukács lived and wrote well beyond the war, indeed up until his

6. Lukács first wrote on Mann in 1909 for *Nyugat*, where he praised his work for its ability to grasp the objective connectedness of all things. (Quoted in Mészáros, p. 42). He continued to praise Mann throughout his life; see his *Essays on Thomas Mann*, trans. Stanley Mitchell (London, 1964). Mann, for his part, was generally positive towards Lukács as a culture critic, although he had no use for his politics. He signed the 1919 appeal to prevent the Austrian government from extraditing Lukács to Horthy's Hungary, but portrayed Lukács in a very ambivalent light as the character Naphta in *The Magic Mountain* a few years later. For more on the Mann–Lukács relationship, see Judith Marcus Tar, "Thomas Mann und Georg Lukács" (Ph.D. diss., U. of Kansas, 1976). For an extensive discussion of the Naphta–Lukács link, see Löwy, p. 56f.

7. Preface to *The Theory of the Novel*, p. 11; for more on Lukács' attitude towards war, see Feher.

8. Notes for Lukács' projected book on Dostoevsky were recovered after his death in a suitcase in Heidelberg containing much unpublished material. See the discussion in Feher, "Lukács' Response to the War," p. 104f. For an analysis of the general interest in Dostoevsky during these years, see Leo Lowenthal, "Die Auffassung Dostojewskis in Vorkriegsdeutschland," *Zeitschrift für Sozialforschung* 3, 3 (1934). See also Zoltan Feher, "Lukács and Dostoevsky," (Ph.D. diss., U.C.L.A., 1977).

death in 1971 at the age of 86. And having found in 1918 an answer to his despondency in the Communism he championed for the rest of his long life, he is best remembered as a Marxist theoretician of uncommon breadth and power. More significant for our purposes, he is of central importance as the founding father of Western Marxism, the theoretician who placed the category of totality at its heart. His work of 1923, *History and Class Consciousness*, has been generally acknowledged as the charter document of Hegelian Marxism, the highly controversial inspiration of a loyal (and sometimes not so loyal) opposition to institutional Marxism in this century.

That *History and Class Consciousness* was a milestone in Marxist theory is undisputed; what is far less certain is its status as a purely Marxist exercise. Schematically put, the main question is whether or not it represents a recapitulation of Lukács' bourgeois preoccupations in Marxist guise or a recapturing of Marx's own most fundamental arguments in an original and explosive form. For those who hold the former position, *History and Class Consciousness* was little more than a kind of irrationalist Marxist version of *Lebensphilosophie*, "the first major irruption of the romantic anti-scientific tradition of bourgeois thought into Marxist theory."[9] For those favoring the latter view, the book was an extraordinarily prescient recovery of those humanist elements in Marx's early work whose existence would be confirmed with the publication of his *Economic and Philosophic Manuscripts* a decade later.[10] For those defending the former position, Lukács' subsequent repudiation of *History and Class Consciousness* was a mark of his theoretical maturation, which accompanied his abandonment of the messianic sectarianism of the immediate

9. Jones, "The Marxism of the Early Lukács," p. 33. This contention is challenged in Alvin Gouldner, *For Sociology: Renewal and Critique in Sociology Today* (New York, 1973), p. 365, where Marx's own indebtedness to Romanticism is stressed. For an extension of this argument, see Paul Breines, "Marxism, Romanticism and the Case of Georg Lukács: Notes on Some Recent Sources and Situations," *Studies in Romanticism* 16, 4 (Fall 1977).

10. For a debate over how prescient Lukács really was, see Henry G. Shue, "Lukács: Notes on His Originality," and George Lichtheim, "Reply to Professor Shue," *Journal of the History of Ideas* 34, 4 (October–December 1973). For an excellent discussion of the similarities and differences between Lukács and the young Marx, see Andrew Feenberg, *Lukács, Marx and the Sources of Critical Theory* (Totowa, New Jersey, 1981).

The literature on *History and Class Consciousness* is even more extensive than on the pre-Marxist Lukács. For a bibliography until 1972, see Mészáros, *Lukács' Concept of Dialectic*. Among the works not included there that I have found particularly useful are Andrew Arato, "Lukács' Theory of Reification," *Telos* 11 (Spring 1972); Paul Piccone, "Dialectic and Materialism in Lukács," *Telos* 11 (Spring 1972); Andrew Feenberg, "Lukács and the Critique of 'Orthodox' Marxism," *The Philosophical Forum* 3, 3–4 (Spring–Summer 1972); Andrew Arato, "Notes on History and Class Consciousness," *The Philosophical Forum* 3, 3–4 (Spring–Summer, 1972); István Mészáros, ed., *Aspects of History and Class Consciousness* (London, 1971). Several of the works cited in note 1 also deal insightfully with *History and Class Consciousness*.

post-war period. For their opponents, his later career was marred by an ambiguous reconciliation with the very theory and practice denounced by *History and Class Consciousness;* his rejection of that book is thus an indication of a "devil's pact"[11] with power and authority.

Lukács' own attitude hovered between these extremes. In a 1967 preface to a long-delayed republication of the book, he expressed his thoughts more honestly than was possible during his earlier, more ritualized denunciation in 1933. While acknowledging a number of irretrievable errors, most of them centering on the idealist residue in his argument, and regretting that "it is precisely those parts of the book that I regard as theoretically false that have been most influential,"[12] he nonetheless defended those other parts that he felt were still valid. Prime among these was the argument that defines the importance of the book for the present study:

It is undoubtedly one of the great achievements of *History and Class Consciousness* to have reinstated the category of totality in the central position it had occupied throughout Marx's works and from which it had been ousted by the "scientism" of the social-democratic opportunists.[13]

Lukács then went on to contrast his own use of totality unfavorably to Lenin's in the latter's *Philosophical Notebooks,* admitting that he had erroneously placed "totality in the center of the system, overriding the priority of economics."[14] But he clearly resisted the imputation that a stress on totality *per se* was evidence of non-scientific "romantic anti-capitalism."[15] And indeed in all of his later work, totality remained an absolutely central category.

But did the same word mean different things at various stages of his career? Was there a shift from an essentially bourgeois use to a more authentically Marxist one? Or if the phrase "more authentically Marxist" begs too many of the questions this study will try to answer, can one discern a shift from one Marxist use of totality to another? To answer these questions and place *History and Class Consciousness* properly in both Lukács' own intellectual development and the history of Western Marxism, it is necessary to explore the ways in which the concept of totality entered Lukács' work in its pre-Marxist phase, most notably in *Soul and*

11. The term is George Steiner's from *Language and Silence: Essays on Language, Literature and the Inhuman* (New York, 1967).
12. Preface to *History and Class Consciousness,* trans. Rodney Livingstone (Cambridge, Mass., 1971), p. xxvii.
13. Ibid., p. xx.
14. Ibid.
15. This phrase was Lukács' own; see ibid., p. x. It has been used by commentators to characterize his entire pre-Marxist period.

Form and *The Theory of the Novel.*[16] For only by doing so can one recognize both the continuities and discontinuities in his remarkable career, as well as understand the subtle relationship between Western Marxism and bourgeois culture.

As has often been remarked, *Soul and Form* is a work permeated by the atmosphere of bourgeois culture in crisis. Its eleven essays, written between 1907 and 1910, were composed in a lyrical and frequently over-wrought mood. Although engendered in part by Lukács' troubled love affair with Irma Seidler, the agony expressed in the work had a far more universal source. The choice of the essay form itself, as Lukács explained in the open letter to his friend Leo Popper that began the collection, was the appropriate means of expressing the problematic nature of contemporary culture. Reflecting the subjective vision of the writer, the essay, Lukács argued, is a precursor form, anticipating an objective truth that has yet to become manifest. In the meantime, its tentative and fragmentary nature captures the painful reality that Simmel characterized as the "tragedy of culture," the inability of subjective and objective meaning to coincide.

In *Soul and Form*, Lukács explicitly described this dilemma in terms close to Simmel's *Lebensphilosophie*:

Life is an anarchy of light and dark: nothing is ever completely fulfilled in life, nothing ever quite ends; new, confusing voices always mingle with the chorus of those that have been heard before. Everything flows, everything merges into another thing, and the mixture is uncontrolled and impure; everything is destroyed, everything is smashed, nothing ever flowers into real life. To live is to live something through to its end: but *life* means that nothing is ever fully and completely lived through to the end.[17]

All of the essays express this basic insight: the chaotic richness of life struggles to achieve coherent form, but it can do so only at the cost of what makes it alive. System and life, form and fullness, conventional ethics and authentic existence (or "soul"), all of these are antinomies whose resolution can only be sought, but never achieved. When, for example, Kierkegaard tried to give his life coherent form through the public gesture of spurning his fiancée, he merely created a new series of ambiguities that

16. Markus points to places in Lukács' unpublished Heidelberg manuscripts on aesthetics where totality also played a critical role (Markus, "The Young Lukács," p. 96).

17. Lukács, *Soul and Form*, pp. 152–153. Lukács confirmed the importance of Simmel for his early work in his 1918 obituary, "Georg Simmel" in *Buch des Dankes an Georg Simmel: Briefe, Erinnerungen, Bibliographie*, ed. K. Gassen and M. Landmann (Berlin, 1918). Much later in the far cruder polemic of *Die Zerstörung der Vernunft* (Berlin, 1954), Lukács castigated Simmel as an irrationalist in the tradition that culminated in Nazism.

mocked his attempt at closure. Similarly, when modern writers try to compose true tragedies, they must fail, because tragedy seeks to detemporalize the rush of life and to give it an essential meaning, whereas neither goal can be accomplished short of death. Normative totalization can, in fact, come only at the cost of life, never in accord with it.

Because of this pessimistic appraisal of the antinomies of culture, Lukács had little patience with those who claim to have found an underlying meaning in life. Echoing Kierkegaard's critique of Hegel's theodicy, he refused to acknowledge a hidden rationality behind the incoherence of experience.[18] Nor did he sympathize with those who attempt to escape from that incoherence into an alternate reality in which normative totality allegedly can be found. In his essay on Novalis, Lukács singled out the Romantics for special criticism in this regard:

> They looked for order, but for an order that comprised everything, an order for the sake of which no renunciation was needed; they tried to embrace the whole world in such a way that out of the unison of all dissonances might come a symphony. To combine this unity and this universality is possible only in poetry, and that is why poetry for the Romantics became the center of the world. . . . The actual reality of life vanished before their eyes and was replaced by another reality, the reality of poetry, of pure psyche. They created a homogenous, organic world unified within itself and identified it with the real world. . . . The tremendous tension that exists between poetry and life and gives both their real, value-creating powers was lost as a result.[19]

Although recognizing that art could create a simulacrum of wholeness through perfect form, Lukács rejected the pan-poetic aestheticization of reality as an illusion.

Nor did he have any tolerance for the claim that totality could be achieved on an individual or personal level. Unlike most mainstream vitalists, he held to the Idealist assumption that the objectification of subjectivity, the entrance into Objective Spirit, was necessary to achieve authentic wholeness. In his essay on Richard Beer-Hofmann, he pondered the meaning of a friend's death and concluded that it painfully brought home the interconnectedness of all men: "The sense that I can do nothing without striking a thousand resonances everywhere, most of which I do not and cannot know, so that each action of mine—whether I am aware of it or not—is the consequence of many thousands of waves which have met in

18. Lukács was, in fact, absorbed in Kierkegaard's writings during this period. In 1913, he began a work on Kierkegaard and Hegel that was never completed.

19. Lukács, *Soul and Form*, pp. 48–50. In *History and Class Consciousness*, Lukács returned to the same issue, this time with Schiller as the major exponent of the aesthetic totalization of reality (pp. 137–140).

me and will flow from me to others."[20] In short, as James Schmidt has noted,[21] the traditional German ideal of *Bildung*, of self-formation through entrance into the world of intersubjectivity, was a guiding ideal of Lukács in *Soul and Form* and beyond.

Lukács' rejection of individual solutions to fragmentation extended as well to the assumption that personal wholeness or its absence could be understood in psychological terms.[22] Lukács' life-long antipathy to psychology, particularly to its philosophical misuse, expressed itself in *Soul and Form* in a distinction between monumental deeds and gestures, which perfectly reveal their essential meaning, and psychological explanations of those deeds and gestures, which are infinitely regressive in their search for hidden motives:

Where psychology begins, monumentality ends: perfect clarity is only a modest expression of a striving for monumentality. Where psychology begins, there are no more deeds but only motives for deeds; and whatever requires explanation, whatever can bear explanation, has already ceased to be solid and clear. . . . Life dominated by motives is a continual alternation of the kingdoms of Lilliput and Brobdingnag; and the most insubstantial, the most abysmal of all kingdoms is that of the soul's reason, the kingdom of psychology. Once psychology has entered into a life, then it is all up with unambiguous honesty and monumentality.[23]

Tied to his distaste for psychologism, which he shared with the later Dilthey,[24] Husserl,[25] and most of the defenders of the *Geisteswissenschaf-*

20. Ibid., p. 112.
21. Schmidt, "The Concrete Totality."
22. Remarking on Lukács' aesthetic conservatism of the 1930s, Ferenc Feher notes, "In its proclamation of the unquestionable and unproblematic supremacy of reason over our whole personality structure, Lukács' classicism revealed a naiveté reminiscent of the most over-confident periods of the Enlightenment. In this sense Lukács may be called the Anti-Freud: the theoretician of the 'pure' Ego for whom the whole problematic of the Id ('psychological character' as opposed to moral character) is dismissed with a single gesture. A constant character trait of Lukács since his youth recurs here, namely the hatred of psychology as an empirical branch of learning incapable of adequately explaining the 'soul' (later the substantial personality)" ("Lukács in Weimar," *Telos* 39 [Spring 1979], p. 124). That this trait of his youth was preserved into Lukács' old age is shown in his remarks in his interview in *New Left Review* 68 (July–August 1971), where he claimed:

I must say that I am perhaps not a very contemporary man. I can say that I have never felt frustration or any kind of complex in my life. I know what these mean, of course, from having read Freud. But I have not experienced them myself. (p. 58)

The only time Lukács dealt with Freud at some length was a review in 1921 of *Group Psychology and the Analysis of the Ego* reprinted in György Lukács, *Littérature, philosophie, marxisme, 1922–1923*, ed. Michael Löwy, (Paris, 1978).
23. Lukács, *Soul and Form*, p. 39.
24. The early Dilthey, however, had hoped that psychology might be integrated into the historical sciences. Lukács criticized this position in his obituary of Dilthey in 1911 in *Szellem*. See Markus, "The Young Lukács," p. 102.
25. For a discussion of his general relation to Husserl, see Mihály Vajda, "Lukács' and Husserl's Critique of Science," *Telos* 38 (Winter 1978–79).

ten, was an equally strong hostility to the principles of natural science assumed to underlie it. Lukács leveled the same charge of infinite formlessness against science in general as he had against psychology in particular and significantly juxtaposed the work of art to both:

The crucial difference between a work of art and a scientific work is perhaps this: the one is finite, the other infinite; the one closed in upon itself, the other open; the one is purpose, the other is a means. The one—we are judging now by consequences—is incomparable, a first and a last, the other is rendered superfluous by a better achievement. To put it briefly, the one has form and the other has not.[26]

In discussing the "new solitude" expressed in Stefan George's poetry, Lukács remarked, "Our knowledge of humanity is a psychological nihilism: we see a thousand relationships, yet never grasp any real connection."[27]

That such connections might ever be perceived and psychological nihilism overcome, *Soul and Form* seemed to deny; not surprisingly Lucien Goldmann and others saw it as an anticipation of the bleak perspectives of a later existentialism.[28] But in at least three places in the text, Lukács did hint at the possibility of change. His proto-existentialist metaphysics of tragedy was subtly challenged by a still inchoate sense of historical mutability.[29] In the essay on Beer-Hofmann, he mused:

There have been times—at least, we believe there have been—when the thing we call form today, the thing we look for so feverishly, the thing we try to snatch from the continual movement of life in the cold ecstasy of artistic creation, was simply the natural language of revelation—an unstifled scream, the untramelled energy of a convulsive movement. In those times, no one asked questions about the nature of form, no one separated form from matter or from life, no one knew that form is something different from either of these; form was just the simplest way, the shortest path to understand between two similar souls, the poet's and the public's.[30]

In his appreciative discussion of Theodor Storm, he talked of his own generation's "impotent nostalgia"[31] for the days of Storm's bourgeois so-

26. Lukács, *Soul and Form*, pp. 73–74.
27. Ibid., p. 87.
28. Goldmann, "Early Writings of Georg Lukács" and Alberto Asor Rosa, "Der junge Lukács: Theoretiker der bürgerlichen Kunst," *Alternative* 12 (1969). One expression of his proto-existentialism was his obsession with the importance of death, especially clear in his 1911 essay "On the Poverty of Spirit." The suicide of his former lover, Irma Seidler, was its inspiration. See the discussion in Arato and Breines, *The Young Lukács*, p. 43f; and Congdon, *The Young Lukács*, p. 66f.
29. This shift in emphasis has also been detected by Feher and Markus in the unpublished manuscript, "Zur Aesthetik der 'Romance'," written in 1911, which they claim presents a more optimistic counterpoint to the bleakness of "The Metaphysics of Tragedy" essay in *Soul and Form*.
30. Lukács, *Soul and Form*, p. 114.
31. Ibid., p. 55.

lidity; like Thomas Mann's character Tonio Kröger,[32] he longed for the seemingly "healthy and unproblematic"[33] life of Storm and his kind.

And if the past contained such totalities, perhaps the future might as well; history may seem chaotic,

yet there *is* an order concealed in the world of history, a composition in the confusion of its irregular lines. It is the undefinable order of a carpet or a dance; to interpret its meaning seems impossible, but it is still less possible to give up trying to interpret it. It is as though the whole fabric of fanciful lines were waiting for a single word that is always at the tip of our tongues, yet one which has never yet been spoken by anyone.[34]

In *Soul and Form*, Lukács refused to venture beyond this vague intimation of a possible new totality. He knew himself incapable of uttering that single word which would reveal the figure in the carpet, the design in the dance.

In his next work *The Theory of the Novel*, Lukács' reluctance grew only marginally less firm, but now he was ready to probe with greater specificity the historical ground of the gap between form and life. The terrain on which he operated was the novel, which he recognized in *Soul and Form* as providing what the short story or the drama could not: "the totality of life by its very contents, by inserting its hero and his destiny in the full richness of an entire world."[35] Moving beyond his neo-Kantian indifference to history as the mediator of antinomies, he now adopted Hegel's aesthetic outlook in which the truth of art was its expression of objective historical ideas. Kant's formalist aesthetics, which still dominated his unfinished treatise on aesthetics of the war years,[36] was replaced by a new stress on content. Kant's emphasis on subjective judgment, which was preserved without its universal dimension in Lukács' earlier defense of the essay form, was now shunted aside in favor of an essentially mimetic theory of culture. Indeed, as Lukács later recognized, his reliance on mimesis went beyond even that of Hegel, who had contrasted problematic art with non-problematic reality:

The idea put forward in *The Theory of the Novel*, although formally similar, is in fact the complete opposite of this: the problems of the novel form are here the mirror-image of a world gone out of joint.[37]

32. Mann, in fact, was to single this essay out for special praise in *Betrachtungen eines Unpolitischen* (Berlin, 1918), p. 149.
33. Lukács, *Soul and Form*, p. 59.
34. Ibid., p. 167.
35. Ibid., p. 73.
36. Markus, "The Young Lukács," p. 104.
37. Preface to *The Theory of the Novel*, p. 17. The mimetic bias of the book has been challenged by Paul de Man, who points to Lukács' emphasis on irony as the dominant principle of the novel:

Accordingly, he chose a phrase from Fichte's *Characteristics of the Present Age*, "the epoch of absolute sinfulness,"[38] to describe present reality, rather than anything more affirmative from Hegel.

In making his case for the congruence of problematic art and problematic reality, Lukács divided the history of the West into four loosely demarcated eras: the era of the Homeric epic, that of the transition from the epic to the novel identified with Dante, that of the bourgeois novel, and finally, the post-novel era, only dimly anticipated in the works of Dostoevsky. The era of the novel Lukács further subdivided into several subcategories: the novel of abstract idealism, epitomized by *Don Quixote*; the novel of disillusionment, whose most characteristic exemplar was *The Sentimental Education*; the *Bildungsroman*, best seen in *Wilhelm Meister's Apprenticeship*; and the novel that "attempts to go beyond the social forms of life," quintessentially those of Tolstoy. In his 1962 preface to the work, Lukács admitted that these categories were generated by the imprecise methods of the *Geisteswissenschaften* elaborated in such works as Dilthey's *Lived Experience and Literary Creation* of 1905:

> It became the fashion to form general synthetic concepts on the basis of only a few characteristics—in most cases only intuitively grasped—of a school, period, etc., then to proceed by deduction from these generalizations to the analysis of individual phenomena, and in that way to arrive at what we claimed to be a comprehensive overall view.[39]

But unlike the other members of the *Geisteswissenschaften* school, Lukács had turned from Kant to Hegel and thus closed the gap between allegedly timeless aesthetic values and the flow of history. The often quoted opening sentences of the first chapter of *The Theory of the Novel*, "Integrated Civilizations," expressed with lyric poignancy Lukács' very anti-Kantian belief that normative totalities in which pure and practical reason had been united were in fact an historical reality:

> Happy are those ages when the starry sky is the map of all possible paths—ages whose paths are illuminated by the light of the stars. Everything in such ages is

---

If irony is the determining and organizing principle of the novel's form, then Lukács is indeed freeing himself from preconceived notions about the novel as an imitation of reality. Irony steadily undermines this claim at imitation and substitutes for it a conscious, interpreted awareness of the distance that separates an actual experience from the understanding of this experience. The ironic language of the novel mediates between experience and desire, and unites ideal and real within the complex paradox of the form. This form can have nothing in common with the homogeneous, organic form of nature; it is founded on an act of consciousness, not on the imitation of the natural object. (*Blindness and Insight: Essays in the Rhetoric of Contemporary Criticism* [New York, 1971], p. 56)

What de Man fails to understand is that for Lukács the novel imitates a heterogeneous, inorganic form of society, not a "homogeneous, organic form of nature." Its irony is an appropriate expression of the irreconcilable antinomies of that society.

38. Lukács, *The Theory of the Novel*, p. 152.
39. Ibid., p. 13.

new and yet familiar, full of adventure and yet their own. The world is wide and yet is like a home, for the fire that burns in the soul is of the same essential nature as the stars; the world and the self, the light and the fire, are sharply distinct, yet they never become permanent strangers to one another, for fire is the soul of all light and all fire clothes itself in light. Thus each action of the soul becomes meaningful and rounded in this duality: complete in meaning—in *sense*—and complete for the senses; rounded because the soul rests within itself even while it acts; rounded because its action separates itself from it and, having become itself, finds a center of its own and draws a closed circumference round itself.[40]

Lukács concluded this paragraph with Novalis' remark that "Philosophy is really homesickness; it is the urge to be at home everywhere,"[41] by which he suggested that truly integrated civilizations knew no philosophy. Like Nietzsche in *The Birth of Tragedy*, to which he did not however refer, Lukács saw philosophy as a mark of degradation, a falling off from the wholeness of pre-philosophical times. And like Nietzsche, he found those times in the classical era before Socrates and Plato. Whereas in his earlier work on the theater he had contrasted the Greek tragedy favorably to its modern counterpart,[42] now he moved back beyond the age of Aeschylus and Sophocles to that of Homer, contending, this time unlike Nietzsche, that "great epic writing gives form to the extensive totality of life, drama to the intensive totality of essence."[43] Contrasting it to the epic, Lukács claimed the drama reflected a period in which human relations had already grown problematic; indeed the very distinction between essence and appearance suggested a lack in existence as it was experienced:

The concept of essence leads to transcendence simply by being posited, and then, in the transcendent, crystallizes into a new and higher essence expressing through its form an essence that *should be*—an essence which, because it is born of form, remains independent of the given content of what merely *exists*. The concept of life, on the other hand, has no need of any such transcendence captured and held immobile as an object.[44]

The epic provided a narrative complete and meaningful in itself, without the tension between what was and what should be that the drama evinced.

Whereas in *Soul and Form*, Lukács had pitted the chaos of life against the yearning for coherent form, he now contended that the two had been

40. Ibid., p. 29.
41. Ibid. By denigrating philosophy as inherently less capable than epic narrative of expressing a fulfilled totality, Lukács showed how non-Hegelian he still was, even in this, his most Hegelian work.
42. Markus, p. 110.
43. Lukács, *The Theory of the Novel*, p. 46. In *Soul and Form*, Lukács argued a similar position: "The inner style of the drama is realistic within the medieval, scholastic meaning of the work [universal essences were most real], but this excludes all modern realism" (p. 159).
44. Lukács, *The Theory of the Novel*, p. 47.

fused in the lives of the Homeric Greeks, which was in turn reflected in their epics. This conclusion, however, was based far more on the image of the Greeks in German culture, for example in the writings of Hegel and Friedrich Theodor Fischer,[45] than on any legitimate historical analysis of the Homeric period. In fact, for all his belief that art expressed the lived experience of an era, Lukács derived that presumed experience solely from the evidence of the art itself. The material basis of the Homeric normative totality was completely ignored; the class analysis he had previously used in certain of his Hungarian writings was nowhere to be seen. The mimesis he invoked—and in this sense he was close to Hegel—was of the idea of an integrated civilization, rather than of its material foundation. The Greeks were thus as romantically depicted as in any of the earlier fantasies of Winckelmann and his followers.

Lukács also neglected to do what that other great commentator on the realism of the Homeric epic, Erich Auerbach, was later to do in the brilliant first chapter of his *Mimesis*.[46] That is, he confined classical civilization to the Greeks and failed to examine another seminal ancient text, the Hebrew Bible. If he had, he might have noted that some of the same characteristics that he had attributed to the modern novel, and which he saw as reflections of the "epoch of absolute sinfulness," were present in the great document of an age of absolute faith, albeit faith in a transcendent rather than immanent God.

Be that as it may, Lukács' idealized characterization of the Homeric era nonetheless provided him, as István Mészáros has put it, with "an abstract regulative principle"[47] by which to measure later periods. And it provides us with an invaluable series of clues to his image of normative totality during this period of his intellectual development. First of all, for the Lukács of *The Theory of the Novel*, normative totality lacked any ontological differentiations; the Homeric world was "a homogeneous world, and even the separation between man and world, between 'I' and 'You' cannot disturb its homogeneity."[48] In this homogeneous world, there are no Kantian distinctions between morality and inclination, duty and desire, form and life:

Totality of being is possible only where everything is already homogenous before it has been contained by forms; where forms are not a constraint but only the becoming conscious, the coming to the surface of everything that had been lying

45. For a discussion of the links between Fischer and Lukács, see Horst Althaus, *Georg Lukács oder Bürgerlichkeit als Vorschule einer marxistischen Aesthetik* (Bern, 1962), p. 7.
46. Erich Auerbach, *Mimesis: The Representation of Reality in Western Literature*, trans. Willard R. Trask (Princeton, 1953).
47. Mészáros, *Lukács' Concept of Dialectic*, p. 61.
48. Lukács, *The Theory of the Novel*, p. 32.

dormant as a vague longing in the innermost depths of that which had to be given form; where knowledge is virtue and virtue is happiness, where beauty is the meaning of the world made visible.[49]

The Homeric world is so homogeneous that the very distinction between transcendence and immanence is overcome; it is "empirical and meta-physical, combining transcendence and immanence inseparably within itself."[50]

Second, the Homeric world is without any historical change; in the narrative of the *Iliad*, there is "no beginning and no end."[51] In fact, in both the drama and the epic, "the past either does not exist or is completely present. Because these forms know nothing of the passage of time, they allow of no qualitative difference between the experiencing of past and present."[52] The later introduction of temporality into art mirrors the decay of the integrated civilization that spawned the epic. Where the Homeric Greeks had only answers, their successors posed troubling questions, which could only be resolved at some future date. The very existence of an ethical imperative, the "ought," "in whose desperate intensity the essence seeks refuge because it has become an outlaw on earth,"[53] means that the present needs the future to complete it. In short, time is a form of corruption and normative totality requires its suspension.

Third, the Homeric Greeks knew no real individuality. Epic heroes were eponymous, standing for all men. In the world of the epic, "an individual structure and physiognomy is simply the product of a balance between the part and the whole, mutually determining one another; it is never the product of polemical self-contemplation by the lost and lonely personality."[54] Moreover, the "I" of the epic was empirical rather than what Lukács called intelligible, as it was in the drama. That is, the epic subject lived in an immediate and fulfilled manner; he was never equivalent to a principle that transcended and was in tension with his existence. Accordingly, the role of subjectivity in the epic was minimized. The subject was receptive and passive, the beneficiary of divine grace. "In the epic," Lukács contended, "totality can only truly manifest itself in the contents of the object; it is meta-subjective, transcendent, it is a revelation and grace."[55] In fact, once the subject becomes active and dominant, the epic is lost: "The subject's form-giving, structuring, delimiting act, his sovereign dominance over the created object, is the lyricism of those epic forms which are without totality."[56]

49. Ibid., p. 34.   50. Ibid., p. 49.   51. Ibid., p. 55.   52. Ibid., p. 126.
53. Ibid., p. 48.   54. Ibid., pp. 66–67.   55. Ibid., p. 50.
56. Ibid., p. 51. This extremely passive view of subjectivity makes it difficult to accept Arato's characterization of Lukács' pre-Marxist period as a "search for a revolutionary subject."

Finally, the epic reveals a world in which man and nature are at one. There is no meaningful split between the social or historical and the natural. Thus, totality in the epic must be understood organically. The community underlying it is "an organic—and therefore intrinsically meaningful— concrete totality."[57] In fact, the very distinction between nature and society, or a first and "second nature,"[58] is a mark of detotalization. "The first nature," he wrote, "nature as a set of laws for pure cognition, nature as the bringer of comfort to pure feeling, is nothing other than the historico-philosophical objectivation of man's alienation from his own constructs."[59]

With this highly idealized image of the Homeric Greeks as his standard, Lukács then proceeded to mark the process of decay that followed it. In his account, there is none of that complicated dialectical awareness of the necessity of alienation that can be found in Schiller, Hegel and Marx, with their secularized versions of the Christian myth of the fortunate fall. Although Lukács uses the same metaphor as Marx did in assigning the epic to the childhood of man and the novel to the age of "virile maturity,"[60] he shared none of Marx's unsentimental preference for maturation. Instead, the modern era is a period of "transcendental homelessness;"[61] men live in a world that had been "abandoned by God."[62] In that world, the first and second nature, the latter experienced as a "charnel-house of long-dead interiorities,"[63] are irrevocably split; men perceive their "self-made environment as a prison instead of a parental home."[64] As Lukács himself later admitted,[65] this attitude was far closer to Kierkegaard's than to Hegel's or Marx's, even though on the descriptive level it echoed Marx's distinction between "living" and "dead" labor and anticipated his own later discussion of capitalist reification.

The art work that best expressed this dismal reality was the novel, "the epic of an age in which the extensive totality of life is no longer directly given, in which the immanence of meaning in life has become a problem,

57. Ibid., p. 67.
58. Ibid., p. 64.
59. Ibid.
60. Ibid., p. 71. Marx's well-known comparison between the Greeks and the childhood of mankind appeared in the *Grundrisse* (1857–8).
61. Lukács, *The Theory of the Novel*, p. 41.
62. Ibid., p. 88.
63. Ibid., p. 64.
64. Ibid. If any evidence is needed to demonstrate Lukács' indebtedness to the Romantic tradition, these images clearly provide it. Compare, for example, this description of Teufelsdröckh's vision of wholeness in "The Everlasting Yes" chapter of Thomas Carlyle's *Sartor Resartus*: "The Universe is not dead and demoniacal, a charnel-house with spectres; but godlike and my Father's" (*Sartor Resartus* [London, 1881], p. 130).
65. Lukács, *The Theory of the Novel*, p. 18. For a critique of this work from a position close to Lukács' own later beliefs, see Ferenc Feher, "Is the Novel Problematic? A Contribution to the Theory of the Novel," *Telos* 15 (Spring 1973).

yet which still thinks in terms of totality."[66] After passing quickly over the transitional phenomenon of Dante's *Divine Comedy*, in which religion, even in its transcendent form, provided certain features of the Homeric era, Lukács began his highly schematic analysis of the novel with *Don Quixote*, the novel of abstract idealism. He then proceeded through the other types mentioned above, and concluded with the ambitious, but ultimately unsuccessful, attempts of Goethe and Tolstoy to transcend the limitations of the form. It would take us too far afield to recapitulate his typology and examine its specific implications, but certain aspects of his general discussion of the novel per se merit our attention.

In virtually all of its respects, the novel, as Lukács presented it, is the antithesis of the epic. Its formal properties manifest the fragmentation and dissonance of the world that it reflects. Nostalgia for lost unity or longing for a new one animates the novel; as a result, it lacks the perfect stillness of the epic: "Only the novel, the literary form of the transcendent homelessness of the idea, includes real time—Bergson's *durée*—among its constitutive principles."[67] The subject of the novel, untouched by grace, at odds with his world, driven by an ethical imperative that transcends his existence, is necessarily impelled on a quest for immanent meaning, but one that is doomed to frustration. The novel's attempt to grasp life whole leads to a limitless aggregation of disparate elements, very much like Hegel's notion of a "bad infinity," "whereas the infinity of purely epic matter is an inner, organic one."[68] Because the novel seeks totality, but cannot achieve it, its characteristic posture is self-referential and reflective, "sentimental" in Schiller's well-known distinction, rather than "naive." In fact, "the need for reflection is the deepest melancholy of every great and genuine novel."[69] The novelist himself cannot transcend the ironic implications of this situation. "Irony, the self-surmounting of a subjectivity that has gone as far as it was possible to go," Lukács contended, "is the highest freedom that can be achieved in a world without God."[70]

---

66. Lukács, *The Theory of the Novel*, p. 56. For a recent and arresting analysis of the novel's inability to achieve totalizing closure that reformulates and particularizes this argument in deconstructionist terms, see D. A. Miller, *Narratability and Its Discontents: Problems of Closure in the Traditional Novel* (Princeton, 1981). Miller, to be sure, remains solely within the texts themselves whereas Lukács sought his answers outside them.

67. Lukács, *The Theory of the Novel*, p. 121. The only way the corrosive power of time is overcome in the novel is through memory, which Lukács sees as injecting an epic quality into certain novels. In his very stimulating chapter on *The Theory of the Novel* in *The Subject in Question: The Languages of Theory and the Strategies of Fiction* (Chicago, 1982), David Carroll shows how Flaubert's *Sentimental Education* typifies this process. But he then assigns it the role of leading Lukács out of his pessimism, an honor that more properly belongs to Dostoevsky's works.

68. Lukács, *The Theory of the Novel*, p. 181.

69. Ibid., p. 85.   70. Ibid., p. 93.

In *The Theory of the Novel*, Lukács held out only a very tentative hope that anything better might be achieved. His final chapter, "Tolstoy and the Attempts to Go Beyond the Social Forms of Life," examined the great Russian novels of the nineteenth century. His wife at this time, to whom he dedicated the book, was Yelena Andreyevna Grabenko, a Russian "social revolutionary." He seems to have been captivated by the possibility that Russia might "save us from Western Civilization," although precisely how he did not know. Because of the "greater closeness of nineteenth century Russian literature to certain organic natural conditions,"[71] he speculated, it expressed the normative totality present in the Homeric epic better than any other novels. Although his work was in one sense the "final expression of European Romanticism,"[72] Tolstoy was able at certain moments to explode the limitations of the novel to show a "clearly differentiated, concrete and existent world, which, if it could be spread out into a totality, would be completely inaccessible to the categories of the novel and would require a new form of artistic creation: the form of the renewed epic."[73] The major flaw in Tolstoy's vision derived from his over-reliance on nature as the arena of totalization, whereas "a totality of men and events is possible only on the basis of culture."[74]

Intimations of a new normative totality capable of sustaining a renewed epic were more clearly present, Lukács concluded, in the messianic antinomian world of Dostoevsky, for a critique of whom *The Theory of the Novel* had originally been intended as a preface. In fact, "it is in the words of Dostoevsky that this new world, remote from any struggle against what actually exists, is drawn for the first time simply as a seen reality. That is why he, and the form he created, lie outside the scope of this book."[75] But whether or not the vision of a new normative totality present in Dostoevsky really foreshadowed a radical change, Lukács chose not to say. *The Theory of the Novel* ended on a note only marginally more hopeful than that sounded in *Soul and Form*; Lukács was still mired in the problematic of bourgeois culture in disarray and could see no easy and immediate way out.

He does seem to have felt certain, however, that the answer lay within the realm of culture. His chastisement of Tolstoy for failing to see that totality was an affair of culture rather than nature was characteristic of his intense preoccupation with the idea of culture during the years immediately preceding and following his sudden embrace of Marxism. His concomitant hostility to socio-economic categories was evinced as well in his

71. Ibid., p. 145.   72. Ibid., p. 151.
73. Ibid., p. 152.   74. Ibid., p. 147.
75. Ibid., p. 152.

depiction of the new world foreshadowed by the Russian novelists: "This world is the sphere of pure soul-reality in which man exists as man, neither as a social being nor as an isolated, unique, pure and therefore abstract interiority."[76] For Lukács, social was equivalent to what Tönnies had called *gesellschaftlich*, connoting a world of alienation and disharmony. *Gemeinschaft* (community) was a cultural, not social phenomenon. It was the realm of those direct and immediate confrontations between pure souls prefigured in Dostoevsky's fictional world.

In the period after *The Theory of the Novel* was published, Lukács shed his pessimistic evaluation of the possibilities of change, but his preference for cultural rather than socio-economic solutions continued. An essay he published in December, 1918, the very month of his "conversion"[77] to Marxism, was entitled "Bolshevism as a Moral Problem."[78] In it, he pondered the dilemma presented by the Leninist adoption of evil means to achieve good ends, "or as Razumikhin says in Dostoevsky's *Crime and Punishment,* that it is possible to lie our way through to the truth."[79] With a concern for the ethical authenticity that had motivated much of his earlier work, Lukács refused to adopt Razumikhin's logic, and specifically rejected the Bolsheviks' "credo quia absurdum est—that no new class struggle will emerge out of this class struggle."[80] Although in a second essay published two months later entitled "Tactics and Ethics"[81] Lukács did justify that leap of faith by accepting the sacrifice of individual ethical purity in the name of "an imperative of the world-historical situation, an historico-philosophical mission,"[82] he nonetheless continued to focus on cultural and moral issues, if now with a revolutionary intent.

76. Ibid.
77. Most commentators follow the lead of Lukács' friends from this period, such as Arnold Hauser and Anna Lesznai, who saw his change as sudden and unexpected; in Lesznai's words, "from Saul became Paul" (quoted in Kettler, "Culture and Revolution," p. 69). Goldmann's later stress on the irrational Pascalian "wager" at the heart of Marxism was possibly stimulated by Lukács' example. Jameson, however, argues that the notion of a semi-religious conversion experience mystifies the essential continuities in Lukács' position, which he sees as "a continuous and lifelong meditation on narrative, on its basic structures, its relationship to the reality it expresses, and its epistemological modes of understanding" (p. 163). As this chapter attempts to show by focusing on the continuities and discontinuities between Lukács' uses of totality, neither extreme captures the nuances of his development.
78. Appearing first in December, 1918 in *Szabadgondolat* (*Free Thought*), the official journal of a group of Hungarian radical intellectuals known as the "Galileo Circle," the article has been translated with an introduction by Judith Marcus Tar in *Social Research* 44, 3 (Autumn, 1977).
79. Ibid., p. 424.
80. Ibid., p. 423.
81. English translation in *Political Writings, 1919–1929*, trans. Michael McColgan, ed. Rodney Livingstone (London, 1972).
82. Ibid., p. 10. Here too, Lukács relies on a Russian example to make his point. But instead of a character from Dostoevsky, he chose the real-life terrorist, Ropischin (Boris Savinkov), who justified terror by defining "the ultimate moral basis of the terrorist's act as

In fact, before committing himself entirely to Marxism, he went through a period that David Kettler has aptly called "revolutionary culturalism."[83] His stance was shared in varying degrees by other members of the Budapest "Sunday Circle,"[84] such as Karl Mannheim, Arnold Hauser, Béla Balázs, Frigyes Antal and Béla Forgarasi, to which Lukács had belonged since returning to Hungary during the war. It combined elements of extreme left-wing and extreme right-wing critiques of bourgeois society and culture. With leftists like Ervin Szabó,[85] the Hungarian anarcho-syndicalist from whom Lukács learned of Sorel, the revolutionary culturalists expressed contempt for parliamentary politics, indeed all politics, and believed instead in apocalyptic and total change. With conservatives such as Thomas Mann, they endorsed Alfred Weber's distinction between culture and civilization, equating the latter with the prosaic achievements of mechanistic technology characteristic of the Western industrial democracies. And like both, the revolutionary culturalists stressed the special role of intellectuals, with their ability to know the whole, in leading society out of its current dilemma.[86]

---

the sacrifice for his brethren, not only of his life, but also of his purity, his morals, his very soul. In other words, only he who acknowledges unflinchingly and without any reservations that murder is under no circumstances to be sanctioned can commit the murderous deed that is truly—and tragically—moral" (p. 11). Lukács' ascetic and self-agnegating streak, which appeared again in his remarks on party discipline in *History and Class Consciousness* as well as in his actions after its denunciation, can perhaps be traced back to this earlier identification with the higher morality of justifiable terrorism.

83. Kettler, "Culture and Revolution," p. 36. It derives, he claims, "intrinsic interest from striving to advance the distinctly humanist values without succumbing to the ethical callousness, if not inhumanity, which normally mars the aristocratic culturist view." For a recent defense of the cultural emphasis throughout Lukács' work, see Feenberg, *Marx, Lukács and the Sources of Critical Theory*, Chapters 5 and 6.

84. This extraordinary group of intellectuals met every Sunday from 1915 to 1918 in the home of Béla Balázs. In 1917, they organized a series of lectures given under the auspices of a "Free School for Studies of the Human Spirit." The Hungarian word for spirit (*szellem*) became an informal way of referring to the circle, which was colloquially called "The Sprites" (*Szellemkék*). The best account of them in English can be found in Congdon, *The Young Lukács*, Chapter 2.

85. See György Litván, "A Moralist Revolutionary's Dilemma: In Memory of Ervin Szabó," *Radical History Review* 24 (Fall, 1980).

86. After his embrace of Marxism, Lukács continued to wrestle with the role of intellectual leadership. In a 1919 essay entitled "Intellectual Workers and the Problem of Intellectual Leadership," he argued against the claim that socialism disparaged the intellect. Linking Marx very closely to Hegel, he concluded: "We Marxists not only believe that the development of society is directed by the so-often-disparaged Spirit, but we also know that it was only in Marx's work that this spirit became conscious and assumed the mission of leadership." But then, as if anticipating his friend Mannheim's celebration of the free-floating intelligentsia, he added: "But this mission cannot be the privilege of any 'intellectual class' or the product of 'supra-class' thinking. The salvation of society is a mission which only the proletariat, by virtue of its world-historical role, can achieve" (*Political Writings, 1919–1929*, p. 18).

Lukács' revolutionary culturism was most clearly expressed in his essay "The Old Culture and the New Culture," first published in Hungarian in *Internationale* on June 15, 1919, and then in German in the ultra-left journal *Kommunismus* on November 7, 1920.[87] Written when Lukács was Minister of Education in Béla Kun's revolutionary government and sponsoring moralistic (and counterproductive) policies such as the prohibition of alcohol,[88] the essay expresses many of the ambiguities of his transitional period. Here, unlike in *The Theory of the Novel*, a specific link between the crisis of capitalism and crisis of culture was an explicit theme. But the characterization of capitalism was couched in terms closer to the right-wing critique of civilization than to the traditional Marxist language of economic exploitation. "Civilization, and its most developed form, capitalism," Lukács wrote, "has brought to its peak man's slavery to social production, to the economy. *And the sociological precondition of culture is man as an end in himself.*"[89]

Like Gramsci, with his contention that the Russian Revolution was a revolt "against *Capital*,"[90] although without Gramsci's more complicated mediation of politics and culture, Lukács interpreted the economic determinism of orthodox Marxism as a mistaken universalization of the unique, and regrettable, situation of capitalism. In fact, he went so far as to challenge the priority of economics during the pre-revolutionary period as well, arguing that "*the culture of the capitalist epoch had collapsed in itself and prior to the occurrence of economic and political breakdown.*"[91] And he claimed that with the onset of the revolution, the importance of culture increased even more dramatically: "During capitalism every ideological movement was only the 'superstructure' of the revolutionary process which ultimately led to the collapse of capitalism. Now in the proletarian dictatorship, this relationship is reversed."[92] The new culture that is now being created will end the rule of civilization, the division of labor, and the primacy of the economy over man. It will restore the conditions that had generated "the greatness of old cultures (Greek, Re-

---

87. Lukács, "The Old and the New Culture," *Telos* 5 (Spring 1970) with an excellent introduction by Paul Breines, and in Georg Lukács, *Marxism and Human Liberation*, ed. with intro. E. San Juan, Jr. (New York, 1973). The following quotations are from the latter.

88. Rudolf L. Tökés, *Béla Kun and the Hungarian Soviet Republic: The Origins and Role of the Communist Party of Hungary in the Revolutions of 1918–1919* (New York, 1967), p. 153.

89. Lukács, "The Old and the New Culture," p. 15.

90. "The Revolution Against *Capital*," first published in the Milan edition of *Avanti* (November 1917); in English in *History, Philosophy and Culture in the Young Gramsci*, ed. Pedro Cavalcanti and Paul Piccone (St. Louis, 1975).

91. Lukács, "The Old Culture and the New Culture," p. 4.

92. Ibid., p. 13.

naissance)," which "consisted in the fact that ideology and production were in harmony; the products of culture could organically develop out of the soil of social being."[93] When Communism ends anarchic individualism, Lukács concluded, "human society will form an organic whole."[94]

Understood in terms of the later debate over whether Marx thought freedom lay in the realm of de-alienated labor, a position expressed in the *1844 Manuscripts*, or beyond labor altogether, as claimed in the third volume of *Capital*, Lukács (who, of course, had not yet seen the *1844 Manuscripts*) can be placed clearly in the latter camp. He in fact defined culture as "the ensemble of valuable products and abilities which are dispensible in relation to the immediate maintenance of life,"[95] and argued that it was accessible only when strenuous labor ended and "free energies are at the disposal of culture."[96] Such opportunities may have been open only to an elite in earlier times, but Communism would universalize them. In fact, one of Lukács' primary goals in the Kun government was the democratization of culture, which, to be sure, did not mean toleration for all varieties of cultural expression.[97]

Revolutionary culturalism thus suggested a continuity with Lukács' "romantic anti-capitalist" phase because of his stress on culture over economics and politics, but it also suggested a movement away from it in his linking of a "new culture" with the triumph of the proletariat. That movement grew more pronounced in the years following the publication of "The Old Culture and the New Culture," years in which Lukács was able to reflect on the failure of the Kun government and his own messianic ultra-leftism. Although Lukács' concern for culture, *Bildung,* and ethics was by no means left behind, his new emphasis on proletarian class consciousness and reification signified a firmer grasp of Marx's method and intentions. For the first time in his thinking, political as well as cultural transformation came to play a central theoretical role. The lessons of Lenin, as he understood them, directed his attention to issues of praxis and organization. The result of these changes was a book whose stress on the methodological importance of totality was given credence by its author's ability to link cultural, political, social, and (albeit to a lesser ex-

93. Ibid., pp. 10–11.
94. Ibid., p. 17.
95. Ibid., p. 4.
96. Ibid.
97. For more on Lukács' role in the cultural politics of the Kun regime, see Béla Köpeczi, "Lukacs in 1919," *New Hungarian Quarterly* 20, 75 (Autumn 1979). Kopeczi discusses accusations of dictatorial intolerance leveled at Lukács by some of his Party comrades, most notably Commissar for Public Education Zsigmond Kunfi, but generally defends Lukács against them.

tent) economic issues in one powerful argument. *History and Class Consciousness* put the relationship between theory and practice at the center of the Marxist debate in a way that transcended the limitations of both revolutionary culturalism and the orthodoxy of the Second International. It is to that extraordinary work, the seminal text of Western Marxism, that we may now finally turn.

Because the general tenor of what follows will be critical of Lukács' argument in *History and Class Consciousness,* it must be stressed at the outset how remarkable an achievement the work really was. At a time when Marxist theory still lagged behind many of its bourgeois counterparts in reflective sophistication, Lukács almost single-handedly succeeded in raising it to a respectable place in European intellectual life. The widespread dismissal of Marxism in the 1890s as another variant of scientism or positivism was now no longer tenable, at least in German-speaking countries where Lukács' book could be read at first hand. As one of his staunchest critics, Lucio Colletti, later acknowledged, it was "the first Marxist book after Marx (Labriola was too isolated a phenomenon) which deals with Hegel and German classical philosophy at a European level and with a thorough knowledge of the subject; it is the first book in which philosophical Marxism ceases to be a cosmological romance and thus, a surrogate 'religion' for the 'lower' classes."[98] Indeed, along with Korsch's *Marxism and Philosophy,* it reestablished the possibility of exploring Marxism's philosophical dimension, rather than seeing it as a science that had overcome the need for philosophical reflection.[99] Although, to be sure, it remained largely just a possibility for many years, the fuse had been lit which ultimately ignited Marxism's critical potential. Moreover, *History and Class Consciousness* anticipated in several fundamental ways the philosophical implications of Marx's *1844 Manuscripts,* whose publication it antedated by almost a decade. It was also the first work by a Marxist of European-wide stature to develop the insight, anticipated in the writings of Mondolfo, Brzozowski, Koigen, Plenge and Helander,[100] that Marx and Engels should not always be conflated into advo-

98. Colletti, *Marxism and Hegel,* p. 178.

99. Ironically, among the Soviet critics of Lukács and Korsch were a group of philosophers around Abram Deborin, who were shortly thereafter themselves attacked for overemphasizing the philosophical nature of Marx's thought. See the informative discussion in Russell Jacoby, "Toward a Critique of Automatic Marxism: The Politics of Philosophy from Lukács to the Frankfurt School," *Telos* 10 (Winter 1971), p. 134f.

100. Rodolfo Mondolfo, *Il Materialismo storico in Federico Engels* (Genoa, 1912); Stanislaw Brzozowski, *Idee (Ideas)* (Lemberg, 1910)—see the discussion in Leszek Kolakowski, *Main Currents of Marxism,* vol. 2: *The Golden Age,* trans. P. S. Falla (Oxford,

cates of an identical position. And finally, it offered a brilliant, if ultimately false, explanation of and justification for the success of the Bolshevik Revolution at a time when Lenin and his followers were too busy or too confused to provide an adequate one themselves. As such, *History and Class Consciousness* can be seen as the most articulate expression on a theoretical level of the world-historical events of 1917, sharing in fact all of their fateful ambiguities. It thus presented a twentieth-century parallel to Kant's *Critiques* and their relation to the French Revolution. In fact, as we will see, the high-water mark of Hegelian Marxism came with the cresting of the revolutionary wave; its decline, which can already be discerned in the last sections of Lukács' book, followed swiftly the postwar revolutions' reversal of fortune. Its partial revival had to await an apparently comparable revolutionary wave in the 1960s.

In short, *History and Class Consciousness* has to be regarded as one of those rare synthetic visions that launch a new paradigm or problematic in thought, in this case Western Marxism. In fact, it was so synthetic in harnessing Hegelian Marxism for Bolshevik purposes that a distinctive Western Marxism did not really emerge until *after* the book was condemned by the Soviet authorities in 1924 at the fifth World Congress of the Comintern. For Lukács, like Korsch and Gramsci, saw himself as a loyal follower of Lenin, so much so, in fact, that when the condemnation came, Lukács chose the Party over the complete integrity of his own ideas.

But those ideas, of course, came very quickly to have a life of their own, despite their author's second thoughts. In what follows, we will concentrate on only one of them (although, to be sure, a central one). Indeed, for Lukács, it was so central that he insisted:

It is not the primacy of economic motives in historical explanation that constitutes the decisive difference between Marxism and bourgeois thought, but the point of view of totality. The category of totality, the all-pervasive supremacy of the whole over the parts, is the essence of the method which Marx took over from Hegel and brilliantly transformed into the foundations of a wholly new science. . . . Proletarian science is revolutionary not just by virtue of its revolutionary ideas which it opposes to bourgeois society, but above all because of its method. *The primacy of the category of totality is the bearer of the principle of revolution in science.*[101]

1978); David Koigen, *Ideen zur Philosophie der Kultur* (Munich and Leipzig, 1910); Johann Plenge, *Hegel und Marx* (Tübingen, 1911); Sven Helander, *Marx und Hegel* (Jena, 1922), first published in Swedish in 1922. For a recent study making this same point, see Norman Levine, *The Tragic Deception: Marx Contra Engels* (Santa Barbara, 1975). For a powerful critique of this argument in Levine and elsewhere, see Alvin W. Gouldner, *The Two Marxisms: Contradictions and Anomalies in the Development of Theory* (New York, 1980).
101. Lukács, *History and Class Consciousness*, p. 27.

As this paragraph reveals, Lukács' concern for totality was part of his even more fundamental assumption that methodology was the critical determinant of a revolutionary intellectual posture. In fact, the essay which opened with this statement posed the question "What is Orthodox Marxism?" and answered it by claiming that orthodoxy lay not in the acceptance of Marxist doctrine, but rather in the use of the correct method. Lukács carried this argument to the dubious extreme of saying that even if all of the conclusions to which the method led were shown to be false, the method would nonetheless still be valid. This position, it might be noted in passing, was one he never repudiated.[102]

The main targets of this contention were Eduard Bernstein and the Revisionists, who believed Marx's alleged predictions had been invalidated by contrary factual evidence. In an earlier version of "What is Orthodox Marxism?" Lukács had ridiculed the fetish of facts in particularly vehement terms, arguing in a way reminiscent of Sorel that "decisions, real decisions, precede the facts. To understand reality in the Marxist sense is to be master and not the slave of the imminent facts."[103] He finished this earlier draft by flinging the provocative challenge of Fichte at the vulgar Marxists: "So much the worse for the facts."[104] In the version of the essay printed in *History and Class Consciousness,* Fichte's words were deleted, but the same argument against the passive fetishism of facts remained. Lukács linked action and knowledge, contending that the inert immediacy of facts had to be overcome by mediating them through a dynamic understanding of the whole:

Only in this context, which sees the isolated facts of social life as aspects of the historical process and integrates them in a *totality*, can knowledge of the facts hope to become knowledge of *reality*. This knowledge starts from the simple and (to the capitalist world) pure, immediate, natural determinants described above. It progresses from them to the knowledge of the concrete totality, i.e., to the conceptual reproduction of reality.[105]

What from a positivist point of view would seem oxymoronic, linking concreteness with totality, was accepted by Lukács because of his Hegelian notion of the concrete. Instead of equating it with discrete entities or individual facts, he followed Marx's Hegelian usage: "The concrete is concrete because it is a synthesis of many particular determinants, i.e.

102. Ibid., p. xxvi.
103. Lukács, *Political Writings, 1919–1929*, p. 26.
104. Ibid., p. 27. Much later, in his 1963 piece "Reflections on the Sino-Soviet Dispute," reprinted in *Marxism and Human Liberation*, Lukács singled out this Fichtean phrase (p. 79) as the epitome of the left sectarianism he had abandoned after Lenin's rebuke.
105. Lukács, *History and Class Consciousness*, p. 8.

a unity of diverse elements."[106] The totality could be concrete precisely because it included all of the mediations that linked the seemingly isolated facts.

What is perhaps most striking in these arguments is Lukács' new confidence in his ability, using the right method, to achieve a "conceptual reproduction of reality." The change was due to a number of revisions of his attitude towards the historical process, as well as a more complex use of the concept of totality itself. It is these changes that warn us against seeing *History and Class Consciousness* as merely a transposition of Lukács' earlier viewpoint into a Marxist key.

Whereas in *The Theory of the Novel* Lukács had rejected Hegel's optimistic vision of the historical process as a whole, agreeing with Fichte instead that the modern age was one of absolute sinfulness, he now saw history as a coherent and meaningful unity, what we have called a progressive longitudinal totality. Instead of viewing time as an agent of corruption and equating normative totality with the stillness of the epic, he now saw dynamism as an integral part of the whole. In the earlier draft of "What is Orthodox Marxism?" he wrote, "Like the classical German philosophers, particularly Hegel, Marx perceived world history as a homogeneous process, as an uninterrupted, revolutionary process of liberation."[107] In the revised version, he asserted in a similar vein that Marx "concretely revealed the real substratum of historical evolution and developed a seminal method in the process."[108] Later, in the central essay of the collection, "Reification and the Consciousness of the Proletariat," Lukács referred the reader back to this earlier contention:

As we have shown, the question of universal history is a problem of methodology that necessarily emerges in every account of even the smallest segment of history. For history as a totality (universal history) is neither the mechanical aggregate of individual events, nor is it a transcendent heuristic principle opposed to the events of history, a principle that could only become effective with the aid of a special discipline, the philosophy of history. The totality of history is itself a real historical power—even though one that has not hitherto become conscious and has therefore gone unrecognized—a power which is not to be separated from the reality (and hence the knowledge) of the individual facts without at the same time annulling their reality and their factual existence. It is the real, ultimate ground of their reality and their factual existence and hence also of this knowability even as individual facts.[109]

106. Ibid., p. 9. The quotation is from Marx's *Contribution to the Critique of Political Economy*, trans. N. I. Stone (London, 1904), p. 293.
107. Lukács, *Political Writings, 1919–1929*, pp. 24–25.
108. Lukács, *History and Class Consciousness*, p. 17.
109. Ibid., pp. 151–152.

In short, for Lukács, the past, present and future were all to be understood as moments in a coherent and meaningful process of emancipation, an argument which, as we will see, later Western Marxists were to question as a theodicy.

In *The Theory of the Novel*, to point to another contrast, Lukács had argued that certain novels were able to approach the epic's cessation of temporal corruption through memory: "The genuinely epic quality of such memory is the affirmative experience of the life process. The duality of interiority and the outside world can be abolished for the subject if he (the subject) glimpses the organic unity of his whole life through the process by which his living present has grown from the stream of his past life dammed up within his memory."[110] This vision of a retrospective totalization, with its echo of Hegel's Owl of Minerva flying only at dusk and Dilthey's idea of death as the sole moment of personal totalization, was absent from *History and Class Consciousness*. Lukács' stress on deeds, action and praxis meant that those who make history were no longer separated from those who came later to understand it. Although, as we will see when looking at Marcuse's notion of totality, the redemptive power of memory was not entirely abandoned by all Western Marxists, it was clearly subordinate in *History and Class Consciousness* to a stress on the convergence between acting and knowing.

This revision necessarily entailed a radical rethinking of the subject for Lukács. No longer did he talk of a passive, receptive subject who achieves totality through some kind of grace. From what in Dilthey's well-known lexicon might be called the "objective idealism" of *The Theory of the Novel*, Lukács now turned to Dilthey's "idealism of freedom," an attitude bringing him in some ways closer to Fichte than to Hegel. Fichte, in fact, had held a fascination for Lukács for some time, possibly because of Lask's extensive exploration of his ideas.[111] In one of his pre-Marxist works, "Towards a Sociology of Drama," Lukács had claimed that "in its basic essentials . . . Marx's whole philosophy sprang from one source— Fichte."[112] Although he no longer held this drastic estimation of Fichte's sole influence, the notion of the subject in *History and Class Consciousness* bore unmistakable traces of Fichte's subjective activism. In fact, Lukács specifically praised Fichte's impatient dismissal of the impenetrability of the Kantian noumenon and his belief that the subject was the creator

110. Lukács, *The Theory of the Novel*, p. 127.
111. Lask's doctoral dissertation was entitled "Fichtes Idealismus und die Geschichte" (1902); reprinted in *Gesammelte Schriften*, 3 vols. (Tübingen, 1923, 1923 and 1924).
112. Quoted in Breines, "Lukács, Revolution and Marxism: 1885–1918," p. 414. See also the discussion in Arato and Breines, p. 26f.

of the object, and not merely its passive observer: "In the most general terms we see here the origin of the philosophical tendency to press forward to a conception of the subject which can be thought of as a creator of the totality of content."[113] Although elsewhere in the text Lukács lapsed into the more orthodox notion that "history" controlled men,[114] his quasi-Fichtean emphasis on subjectivity lent itself to a humanist interpretation of the historical process.

In fact, he criticized Fichte and Idealism in general for their transcendental and ahistorical notion of the subject. And like Marx, he chastised Feuerbach for correcting this fallacy only to the point of substituting an equally abstract anthropological notion of man for the Idealists' Spirit. To grasp the subject of history, he insisted, was to recognize which social groups, which classes, were practically active and which were not.

Throughout all previous history, Lukács contended, no social group could legitimately lay claim to the role of universal subject, although some had attempted to do so. Only now, Lukács thought, with the rise of the proletariat to power an imminent prospect, could such a claim be justly entertained. The implications of this new universal subject for Lukács were profound. Whereas in the past, Simmel's "tragedy of culture" accurately described the gap between a particular subject and the residues of other subjects' objectifications, now the situation had changed drastically. The assumptions underlying Lukács' belief in that change were ultimately traceable to a strictly humanist reading of Vico's *verum—factum* principle. Although Fredric Jameson has discerned traces of it in the last chapter of *The Theory of the Novel*,[115] it was not really until *History and Class Consciousness* that Lukács' new view of the subject allowed him to

113. Lukács, *History and Class Consciousness*, pp. 122–123.
114. "The totality of history is itself a real historical power—even though one that has not hitherto become conscious and has therefore gone unrecognized—a power which is not to be separated from the reality (and hence the knowledge) of the individual facts without at the same time annulling their reality and their factual existence. It is the real, ultimate ground of their reality and their factual existence and hence also of their knowability even as individual facts" (p. 152). "The active and practical side of class consciousness, its true essence, can only become visible in its authentic form when the historical process imperiously requires it to come into force, i.e. when an acute crisis in the economy drives it to action" (p. 40). Statements like these prepare the observer of Lukács' career for his later *modus vivendi* with orthodox dialectical materialism. They also give some credence to the somewhat exaggerated accusation of Mihály Vadja that "Lukács' concept of history in general is purely an economistic-deterministic one" ("The State and Socialism" in *Political Essays* [London, 1981], p. 49). Ironically, passages like that also allow Andrew Feenberg to argue that Lukács' concept of totality was never completely expressive, because they show that he believed "the proletariat is not a free will expressing itself in history, but is still bound in an order of objective constraints" ("Culture and Practice in the Early Marxist Work of Lukács," *Berkeley Journal of Sociology* 26 [1981], p. 34).
115. Jameson, *Marxism and Form*, p. 181.

see Vico's argument as central. Quoting Marx's own citation of Vico in *Capital*,[116] Lukács built his refutation of Simmel's acceptance of the tragedy of culture, which Lukács now called "the antinomies of bourgeois thought," on the belief that man knows history better than nature because he can know what he has made better than what is made outside of him.

Vico, as we have seen, did not worry about distinguishing man in general from specific historical subjects. Nor did he confine the process of making to intentional, conscious and rational action. Lukács, like Hegel before him, contended that the *verum–factum* principle applied only when a universal totalizer made history in a deliberate and rational manner. To know the whole was thus dependent on the existence of a collective historical subject who could recognize itself in its objectifications:

Only when a historical situation has arisen in which a class must understand society if it is to assert itself; only when the fact that a class understands itself means that it understands society as a whole and when, in consequence, the class becomes both the subject and the object of knowledge; in short, only when these conditions are all satisfied will the unity of theory and practice, the precondition of the revolutionary function of the theory, become possible.

Such a situation has in fact arisen with the entry of the proletariat into history.[117]

Capitalism, to be sure, had laid the groundwork for the proletariat's entrance by its relentless socialization of the world, its incorporation of more and more of the globe into its economic system. But knowledge of the whole was denied to the capitalists themselves because they were not the true makers of history, however much they may have parasitically benefited from the labor of those who unconsciously were. Accordingly, although there were a few bourgeois thinkers who tried to think holistically—Lukács mentioned the psychologist Wundt in this regard[118]—mainstream bourgeois thought could not transcend its individualist, analytic and formalist biases. An adequate theory had to be understood as "essentially the intellectual expression of the revolutionary process itself,"[119] and clearly bourgeois theory could only be in opposition to that process.

Because of Lukács' reliance on the *verum–factum* principle and his contention that theory expressed the revolutionary process, the view of totality he was advocating has justly been called "expressive" by his more recent structuralist critics.[120] According to this notion, the whole expresses the intentionality and praxis of a creator–subject, who recognizes

116. Lukács, *History and Class Consciousness*, p. 112.
117. Ibid., pp. 2–3.   118. Ibid., p. 110.   119. Ibid., p. 3.
120. Jones, "The Marxism of the Early Lukács," p. 39. For an analysis challenging the applicability of the expressive totality category to Lukács, see Feenberg, "Culture and Practice in the Early Marxist Work of Lukács." Arguing against the existence of a strong Fichtean influence in *History and Class Consciousness*, he claims that Lukács believed "subjectivity is

itself in the objective world around it. Other ways of making the same point are to call it a "genetic" or "reflective" or "self-activating" view of totality, because the whole is understood as a reflection of its own genesis, the product of its own praxis. For Lukács, at least in certain moments in *History and Class Consciousness*, the subject of history and the object of history are ultimately one. The Western Marxist use of totality can be said to have begun with this expressive view of totality although, as we will soon see, it certainly did not end with it.

In adopting an expressive notion of the whole, Lukács was able to achieve seemingly valid resolutions of the antinomies of bourgeois thought and culture that had been plaguing him since he began to write. The source of these intellectual and spiritual contradictions, he claimed, lay in the contradictory nature of bourgeois existence. Extrapolating from Marx's discussion of the "fetishism of commodities" in *Capital,* and applying insights from Bergson, Simmel and Weber, he introduced the notion of reification to characterize the fundamental experience of bourgeois life. This term, one not in fact found in Marx himself, meant the petrification of living processes into dead things, which appeared as an alien "second nature." Weber's "iron cage" of bureaucratic rationalization, Simmel's "tragedy of culture" and Bergson's spatialization of *durée* were thus all part of a more general process. Lukács was able to move beyond the stoic pessimism of

---

situated in a *decentered* totality of which it is not so much the source as the *decentered* mediation" (p. 28). Rather than holding on to a constitutive concept of subjectivity, Lukács, according to Feenberg, agreed with Hegel's doctrine of essence in the *Logic,* which posited a relational immanence that did not annihilate the specificity of the entities bound together in the relation. As a consequence, Lukács argued that the proletariat could never create the social world out of itself and recognize itself in its objectifications. Instead, Feenberg contends, he argued only that the proletariat "alters the social signification and function of its objects" (p. 34). Accordingly, "Lukács argues that under socialism society could become increasingly subject to conscious control, but not that the tension between man and society would disappear" (p. 37).

This reading of Lukács seems to me truer to Lucien Goldmann's revision of his work than to Lukács himself. Feenberg, who was a student of Goldmann, is more generous than the texts allow. Indeed, as he himself concedes, "The critique of Lukács is by no means entirely misplaced. Unfortunately, Lukács' constant use of the language of productive subjectivity suggests that even though he defines this concept in a Hegelian manner, he wants it to bear the burden of solving the sort of problems Kant first posed, and Fichte later resolved with the undialectical concept of expressive totality" (p. 38). Perhaps the most telling piece of evidence against Feenberg's reading is that a subjective mediation of objective reality that merely "altered" its social signification and function would not really overcome the Kantian thing-in-itself problem, which Lukács clearly set out to resolve. It seems therefore correct to conclude with Arato and Breines that "Lukács' consideration of Hegel's discovery of the historical dialectic does not amount to an abrogation of the Fichtean roots of his concept of 'subject'" (p. 128). For yet another discussion of those roots, see Gillian Rose, *Hegel Contra Sociology* (London, 1981), p. 31. In his book, Feenberg comes close to recognizing this point when he acknowledges that there are two competing models of practice in Lukács' work, practice as production (basically Fichtean) and practice as mediation (essentially Hegelian). He prefers, of course, to emphasize the latter. See the discussion on p. 126f.

Weber and Simmel by linking their intellectual dilemmas to the reified nature of bourgeois life, an explanation that grounded them historically. And he was able to offer a similar explanation for the infection of Second International socialist thought by the same antinomies; the Revisionists with their neo-Kantian split between facts and values and the orthodox with their economic fatalism and failure to consider subjective praxis were both ideological expressions of a still non-revolutionary age, an age before the collective totalizer achieved self-consciousness.

The central antinomies Lukács identified as characteristic of the bourgeois era were the separation of facts and values; the distinction between phenomena, or appearances, and noumena, or essential things-in-themselves; and the oppositions between free will and necessity, form and content, and subject and object. For Lukács, as we have seen in examining his pre-Marxist writings, the gap between "is" and "ought" was a source of particular distress. The epic was distinguished from the drama and novel by its incorporation of morality into immediate life. To regain this unity was possible only if a transcendental and ahistorical morality in the Kantian sense was replaced by the more Hegelian notion of ethical life (*Sittlichkeit*) as the concrete customs (*Sitte*) of a specific historical totality. The answer to the moral relativism haunting bourgeois thought was thus not a flight into an imagined world of transcendental values, as attempted by Rickert and other neo-Kantians. It was instead an acceptance of the partial relativism of the historical process in which collective values were posited by specific historical subjects.[121] To Lukács the "is" and the "ought" would merge once the subject of history, the proletariat, objectified its ethical principles in the concrete mores of Communist society. Recognizing itself in the world it had created, it would no longer be subjected to the moral alienation plaguing bourgeois culture. As part of a collective subject, the individual would no longer be troubled by the types of doubts Lukács himself had voiced in "Bolshevism as a Moral Problem."

121. In his seminal study of Lukács in the "'Western' Marxism" chapter of *Adventures of the Dialectic*, trans. Joseph Bien (Evanston, 1973), Merleau-Ponty recognized the importance of this answer, which he says was directed at Lukács' "teacher," Weber:

He does not reproach him for having been too relativistic but rather for not having been relativistic enough for not having gone so far as to "relativize the notions of subject and object." For, by so doing, one regains a sort of totality. Certainly nothing can change the fact that our knowledge is partial in both senses of the word. It will never be confused with the historical in-itself (if this word has a meaning). We are never able to refer to completed totality, to universal history, as if we were not within it, as if it were spread out in front of us. The totality of which Lukács speaks is, in his own terms, "the totality of observed facts," not of all possible and actual beings but of our coherent arrangement of all the known facts. When the subject recognizes himself in history and history in himself, he does not dominate the whole, as the Hegelian philosopher does, but at least he is engaged in a work of totalization. (p. 31)

Although Merleau-Ponty reads Lukács through the lenses of an existentialist Marxist for whom open-ended totalization has priority over finished totality, he nonetheless perceives with considerable acuity the answer Lukács tried to give to neo-Kantian transcendentalism.

A comparable resolution of the antinomy between phenomena and noumena would follow from the same coming-to-consciousness of the universal totalizer, the proletariat; for from the point of view of totality:

The two main strands of the irrationality of the thing-in-itself and the concreteness of the individual content and of totality are given a positive turn and appear as a unity. This signals a change in the relation between theory and practice and between freedom and necessity. The idea that we have made reality loses its more or less fictitious character: we have—in the prophetic words of Vico already cited—made our own history and if we are able to regard the whole of reality as history (i.e. as *our* history, for there is no other), we shall have raised ourselves in fact to the position from which reality can be understood as our 'action.'[122]

In other words, the mysterious impenetrability of the thing-in-itself will be revealed as no more than the illusion of a reified consciousness incapable of recognizing itself in its products.

In addition, the felt distance between will and fate, freedom and necessity, would also narrow once the external world were no longer perceived as ruled by alien forces experienced as if they were a "second nature." The very opposition, popular among vulgar materialists and neo-Kantians alike, between a world of objective matter and subjective consciousness would end as men adopted a practical attitude towards the objective world. Being would then be understood as Becoming, things would dissolve into processes, and most important of all, the subjective origin of those processes would become apparent to the identical subject-object of history.

Freedom was reconcilable with necessity because it was equivalent to collective action, action which constituted the world out of itself. For bourgeois notions of "negative freedom," the freedom from interference in individual affairs, Lukács had nothing but contempt: "Above all one thing must be made clear: freedom here does *not* mean the freedom of the individual."[123] The very notion of the individual isolated from the social context was a mark of reification. The antinomy between form and content, which had bothered Lukács so much in his earlier writings, was itself a reflection of the reified individual's sense of his own unique life in opposition to the alien forms of social interaction. Once he recognized himself as part of the collective source of those very forms, their foreignness would dissolve. As in the Homeric world, men would live lives of immediate formal and substantive wholeness. The normative totality to which men had so long aspired would be finally achieved.

122. Lukács, *History and Class Consciousness*, p. 145.
123. Ibid., p. 315.

Lukács' solutions to the antinomies of bourgeois culture were enormously powerful taken on their own terms. But it soon became apparent
that their elegant simplicity could not bear close scrutiny. There are, in fact,
indications in *History and Class Consciousness* itself that Lukács had
sensed the difficulties even before his critics began to detail them. Perhaps
the most obvious instance was Lukács' highly controversial notion of "ascribed" or "imputed" class consciousness, which was the philosophical correlate of Lenin's insistence in *What is to Be Done?* that, left to itself, the
proletariat could only develop reformist "trade-union consciousness." By
introducing this notion, Lukács admitted the gap between his ideal construction of the proletariat as the subject-object of history and the reality of
its current status. In rejecting the Revisionists' fetishism of facts, Lukács
invoked, as we have seen, the Hegelian distinction between essence and
appearance, both of which had to be understood as mediated elements in a
concrete totality. In discussing the level of awareness of the proletariat in the
contemporary world of revolutionary transition, a world still ruled by capitalist reification, it was necessary to distinguish between empirical and essential class consciousness. To make his point, Lukács borrowed Weber's
notion of "objective possibility,"[124] but gave it an ontological dimension
absent from Weber's more neo-Kantian usage. Instead of a fictional construct produced by the observer's educated imagination, objective possibility for Lukács was rooted in the actual conditions of society. It was logically
appropriate to the reality it described because that reality was ultimately
the practical objectification of the collective subject of which the individual
observer was a part. But because this equation was only true in an ultimate
sense, it was still necessary to theorize ahead of the empirical consciousness
of the proletariat. Presumably, of course, once the process of "dereification"
proceeded, the gap between empirical and imputed class consciousness
would narrow and finally vanish; objective possibility would become subjective actuality.

But in the transitional period, which Lukács thought would not last
indefinitely, an intermediary was necessary. Here Lenin's example was
crucial for Lukács, because he still believed that Lenin's professed faith in
the combined power of party and soviets conformed to Bolshevik practice.
The intermediary was the organizational embodiment of the theoretical
self-consciousness of the proletariat's objective possibility. In the early es-

124. For excellent discussions of Lukács' use of Weber's term, see Iring Fetscher, "Zum
Begriff der 'Objektiven Möglichkeit' bei Max Weber und Georg Lukács," *Revue Internatio-
nale de Philosophie* 106 (1973); Arato, "Lukács' Theory of Reification," p. 62f; and Francis
Hearn, "The Dialectical Use of Ideal Types," *Theory and Society* 2, 4 (Winter 1975).

says of *History and Class Consciousness,* with their frequent expressions of respect for Rosa Luxemburg, Lukács favored an organizational mix in which the soviets played a key role in mediating between the masses and the leadership of the revolution. By the collection's last essays, "Critical Observations on Rosa Luxemburg's 'Critique of the Russian Revolution'" (January 1922) and "Toward a Methodology of the Problem of Organization" (September 1922), the balance had shifted clearly in favor of the highly disciplined vanguard party. Criticizing Luxemburg's "illusion of an 'organic,' *purely proletarian* revolution,"[125] Lukács recognized that the party must lead various revolutionary elements of society, while at the same time articulating the imputed class consciousness of the one element that could ultimately become a universal subject of history. Although protesting that the party ought not to "function as a stand-in for the proletariat even in theory,"[126] the logic of his argument, with its recognition that the revolution was an inorganic phenomenon, and the more fateful logic of events in the Soviet Union, soon made this protestation sound hollow. By the time *History and Class Consciousness* was published, the links between masses, soviets and party were virtually dissolved. The soviets remained meaningful in name only and the power of the party grew beyond all expectations. The process of substitution, against which critics of Bolshevism (including the young Trotsky) had long warned, now began in earnest.

Whether this sad course of events was produced by the exigencies of civil war and the failure of revolution elsewhere or followed inexorably from pre-revolutionary Bolshevik political assumptions, it was soon clear that the gap between empirical and imputed class consciousness had widened rather than narrowed. The workers' uprising in Kronstadt in March of 1921, ruthlessly crushed by the Soviet leadership, gave an indication of things to come. Lukács' choice was for the leadership over the workers, for imputed over empirical class consciousness. His only reference to Kronstadt in *History and Class Consciousness* was a contemptuous linking of it with the reactionary General Kornilov:

Their "critique" of the dictatorship of the proletariat is not a self-criticism performed by the proletariat—the possibility of which must be kept open institutionally even under the dictatorship. It is a corrosive tendency in the service of the bourgeoisie.[127]

125. Lukács, *History and Class Consciousness,* p. 303. For a defense of Luxemburg against this charge, see Norman Geras, *The Legacy of Rosa Luxemburg* (London, 1976), p. 175f.

126. *History and Class Consciousness,* p. 327.

127. Ibid., p. 293.

With this attitude towards the widening chasm between workers and party, Lukács inevitably had to modify the expressive use of totality that was at the heart of his "solution" to the antinomies of bourgeois thought, as we will see momentarily.

But the solution itself contained a number of fundamental theoretical difficulties. As Lukács himself came to understand after reading Marx's *1844 Manuscripts* a decade later,[128] he had erroneously conflated the processes of objectification and reification in an essentially idealist way. By equating praxis with the objectification of subjectivity, instead of seeing it as an interaction of a subject with a pre-given object, Lukács had missed the importance of the dialectic of labor in constituting the social world. Thus, although stressing activity as opposed to contemplation and arguing that the abolition of contradictions "cannot simply be the result of thought alone, it must also amount to their *practical* abolition as the *actual forms of social life*,"[129] he nonetheless underestimated the material resistance of those forms. In the essay of 1919, "Tactics and Ethics," he had spoken of blind forces being awakened to consciousness, and added in a footnote:

"Consciousness" refers to that particular stage of knowledge where the subject and object of knowledge are substantively homogeneous, i.e. where knowledge takes place *from within* and not *from without*. ... *The chief significance of this type of knowledge is that the mere fact of knowledge produces an essential modification in the object known: thanks to the act of consciousness, of knowledge, the tendency inherent in it hitherto now becomes more assured and vigorous than it was or could have been before.*[130]

In *History and Class Consciousness*, the same basic argument remained:

The coercive measures taken by society in individual cases are often hard and brutally materialistic, but *the strength of every society is in the last resort a spiritual strength.* And from this we can only be liberated by knowledge. This knowledge cannot be of the abstract kind that remains in one's head—many "socialists" have possessed that sort of knowledge. It must be knowledge that has become flesh of one's flesh and blood; to use Marx's phrase, it must be "practical critical activity."[131]

128. Ibid., p. xxxvi, where Lukács writes:

I can still remember even today the overwhelming effect produced in me by Marx's statement that objectivity was the primary material attribute of all things and relations. This links up with the idea already mentioned that objectification is a natural means by which man masters the world and as such it can be either a positive or negative fact. By contrast, alienation is a special variant of that activity that becomes operative in definite social conditions. This completely shattered the theoretical foundations of what had been the particular achievement of *History and Class Consciousness*.

129. Ibid., p. 177.
130. Lukács, *Political Writings, 1919–1929*, p. 15.
131. Lukács, *History and Class Consciousness*, p. 262.

It is somewhat exaggerated to contend, as one of Lukács' structuralist critics has, that

The exact analogy of this procedure with the movement of Hegel's Spirit needs no emphasis. All that it omits is the brute material struggle for power—strikes, demonstrations, lock-outs, riots, insurrections or civil wars—that is the stuff of terrestrial revolutions.[132]

But it is true that, as Lukács himself later admitted, "The proletariat seen as the identical subject-object of the real history of mankind is no materialist consummation that overcomes the constructions of idealism. It is rather an attempt to out-Hegel Hegel."[133] Nor, as Andrew Arato has argued,[134] was there an acknowledgement of the dialectic of concrete human needs in *History and Class Consciousness* that might have tempered the reduction of subjectivity to consciousness implicit in Lukács' position. Equally lacking, as a disillusioned former student of Lukács, Mihály Vajda, has pointed out,[135] was an awareness that the collective interest of the proletariat was based on an abstract notion of a fully unifiable class. Here Lukács' hostility to sociology, which he considered an inappropriate misuse of natural scientific methods, like psychology, had its costs. The result was a normative totality, a goal of complete constitutive subjectivity, that was little more than an "abstract negation of a totally reified world."[136]

Lukács' inability to move beyond idealism was even more blatantly obvious in his treatment of nature. Here his indebtedness to Fichte, Dilthey and the *Geisteswissenschaften* tradition was particularly strong.[137] Ironically, it was because of his zeal in trying to free Marxism from another variant of idealism, one in which nature was seen as the objectification of a meta-subject, that he fell prey to an idealism of a less global kind. In his opening essay, Lukács remarked in an important footnote:

It is of the first importance to recognize that the method [of Marxism] is limited here to the realm of history and society. The misunderstandings that arise from Engels' account of dialectics can in the main be put down to the fact that Engels—following Hegel's mistaken lead—extended the method to apply also to nature. However, the crucial determinants of dialectics—the interaction of subject and

132. Jones, "The Marxism of the Early Lukács," p. 45.
133. Lukács, *History and Class Consciousness*, p. xxiii.
134. Arato, "Lukács' Theory of Reification," p. 65.
135. Vajda, *The State and Socialism*, p. 19. His position reflects the Budapest Circle's conceptualization of the difference between needs and interests. See Agnes Heller, *The Theory of Need in Marx* (London, 1976).
136. Breines, "Praxis and its Theorists: The Impact of Lukács and Korsch in the 1920s," *Telos* 11 (Spring 1972), p. 102.
137. For a discussion of this debt, see Arato, "Lukács' Theory of Reification," pp. 39–40.

object, the unity of theory and practice, the historical changes in thought, etc.—
are absent from our knowledge of nature.[138]

Lukács was, to be sure, correct in protesting Engels' naive assimilation of
history to nature, but he himself erred in the opposite direction by separating them too categorically.

Restricting dialectics to history and society was, however, essential for
his argument: only by doing so could Vico's *verum–factum* principle be
invoked as the answer to the antinomies of bourgeois thought. Otherwise,
Lukács would have been forced to confront the fact that Kant's distinction
between noumena and phenomena had referred to objects in the natural
world, which could not be construed as objectifications of a creator–subject. Hegel had been able to assume that they were such objectifications
because of his pantheistic objective idealism. Lukács, contrary to some
interpretations,[139] could not, with the result that nature outside of man
was reduced to a kind of residual status in his system and one that was
abandoned to a positivist methodology. When nature did affect man, Lukács could only see it filtered through the same methodology that applied
to the study of society and history. In his 1925 review of Wittfogel's *The
Science of Bourgeois Society,* Lukács sternly repeated this point:

> For the Marxist as an historical dialectician both *nature* and all the forms in which
> it is mastered in theory and practice are *social categories*; and to believe that one
> can detect anything supra-historical or supra-social in this context is to disqualify
> oneself as a Marxist.[140]

That man might be construed as being rooted in a natural reality, as well as
capable of transcending it through history, Lukács chose to ignore. Focussing solely on the "second nature" that was reified history, he neglected to
probe the role of the "first nature" in human life, a mistake for which Western Marxists of very different persuasions were to take him to task.[141] With

138. Lukács, *History and Class Consciousness*, p. 24.
139. Alfred Schmidt, *The Concept of Nature in Marx*, trans. B. Fowkes (London, 1971),
pp. 69–70. Schmidt takes Lukács ambiguous remark that "nature is a social category" to
mean that the subject of history actually creates nature. For a defense of Lukács against this
charge, see Arato, "Lukács' Theory of Reification," p. 41, and Feenberg, *Lukács, Marx and
the Sources of Critical Theory*, p. 205. Feenberg offers a suggestive improvement of Lukács
weak position on nature in the last two chapters of his book. It is similar to that offered in
another recent consideration of the problem: Fred P. Dallmayr, *Twilight of Subjectivity:
Contributions to a Post-Individualist Theory of Politics* (Amherst, Mass., 1981), chapter 3.
140. Lukács, *Political Writings, 1919–1929*, p. 144. Wittfogel's position seems to have
been more subtle than Lukács had understood. See G.L. Ulmen, *The Science of Society:
Toward an Understanding of the Life and Work of Karl August Wittfogel* (The Hague,
1978), p. 48f.
141. The realization among Western Marxists that Lukács had handled the question of
nature inadequately began immediately in the work of Gramsci and Korsch. See Gramsci,
"Critical Notes on an Attempt at Popular Sociology," in *Selections from the Prison Note-*

the exception of Ernst Bloch, who adopted the neo-Hegelian belief that nature could itself ultimately be seen as a subject, they generally chose to emphasize the non-identical dialectic of subject and object that encompassed both history and nature. The consequences of this shift for their concepts of totality will be discussed later in our narrative.

Lukács' hostility to the dialectics of nature and his inability to mediate nature and history in a non-idealistic way reflected in part that critical attitude towards science evident in his pre-Marxist works. As we have seen, in *Soul and Form* he had denigrated works of science in comparison with works of art for being infinite, open, instrumental and formless. In criticizing scientific psychology, he had attacked its positing of an infinitely regressive series of motivations rather than understanding the immanent meaningfulness of a monumental gesture. He was no less hostile to bourgeois sociology for the same reasons. Science, in short, was incapable of grasping reality as a totality. In *History and Class Consciousness*, Lukács added the further reproach that science was an inherently contemplative enterprise, the witnessing by a detached observer of a process outside of his control. Once again Engels was singled out for special criticism in this regard:

Engels' deepest misunderstanding consists in his belief that the behavior of industry and scientific experiment constitutes praxis in the dialectical, philosophical sense. In fact, scientific experiment is contemplation at its purest. The experimenter creates an artificial, abstract milieu in order to be able to *observe* undisturbed the untrammelled workings of the laws under examination, eliminating all irrational factors both of the subject and the object.[142]

For Lukács, to view society through the eyes of the scientist was thus to be complicitous in its reification; for such an allegedly neutral point of view was incompatible with the engaged practice that would overthrow the dualism of subject and object and create a normative totality.

In his 1967 preface, Lukács specifically retracted the equation of science with contemplation,[143] but he still insisted that Marxism was irreducible to the methodology of the natural sciences. In his posthumously published *The Ontology of Social Being*, Lukács conceded that

---

books, trans. and ed., Quinton Hoare and Geoffrey Nowell Smith (New York, 1971), p. 448. The editors try in an unpersuasive footnote to rescue Lukács from Gramsci's charge. See Korsch, "The Present State of the Problem of 'Marxism and Philosophy': An Anti-Critique" in *Marxism and Philosophy*, trans. with intro. Fred Halliday (New York and London, 1970), p. 122.

142. Lukács, *History and Class Consciousness*, p. 132.

143. Ibid., p. xx.

Above, all, social being presupposes in general and in all specific processes the existence of inorganic and organic nature. Social being cannot be conceived as independent from natural being and as its exclusive opposite, as a great number of bourgeois philosophers do with respect to the so-called "spiritual sphere."[144]

But he then added immediately thereafter that

Marx's ontology of social being just as sharply rules out a simple, vulgar material-ist transfer of natural laws to society, as was fashionable for example in the era of "social Darwinism." The objective forms of social being grow out of natural being in the course of the rise and development of social practice, and become ever more expressly social. This growth is certainly a dialectical process, which begins with a leap, with the teleological project in labor, for which there is no analogy in nature. ... With the act of teleological projection in labor, social being itself is now there.[145]

This leap out of nature into social being, the "retreat of the natural bound-ary," as Marx put it,[146] remained for Lukács the crucial step for mankind. It justified his continued stress on the applicability of the dialectical method, with its mediation of subject and object, primarily to history alone.

Lukács' privileging of history over nature, his emphasis on subjective consciousness over objective matter, his premature confidence that the proletariat would emulate its most radical wing, and his reliance on an expressive view of totality to resolve the antinomies of bourgeois culture were all obvious indications of the euphoric mood engendered by the events of 1917 and their immediate aftermath. To some, and Lukács seems to have been among them, the end of the realm of necessity was close at hand and the beginning of the realm of freedom not far behind. When the euphoria ended, by 1923 or 1924, theoretical revisions were inevitable. The later essays in *History and Class Consciousness,* with their shift to a more "realistic" appraisal of the role of the vanguard party and their critique of "organic" theories of revolution, already registered a sub-tle transformation of Lukács' position. By 1926, he had left behind virtu-ally all residues of his "infantile leftism."[147] In the intervening three years, Lenin had died, the German revolution shared the unsuccessful fate of the Hungarian, all attempts to establish workers' councils had miscarried, the Comintern had concluded that capitalism had entered a period of

144. Lukács, *The Ontology of Social Being: Marx's Basic Principles,* trans. David Fern-bach (London, 1978), p. 7.
    145. Ibid.
    146. Quoted in ibid., p. 9.
    147. For good discussions of Lukács' development in the mid-twenties, see Michael Löwy and Ferenc Feher, "Lukács in Weimar." Arato and Breines agree with Löwy's general argument, but want to push the date of reconciliation back before 1926. See their discussion, p. 199.

"relative stability," and Stalin's doctrine of "socialism in one country" had displaced any thoughts of a "permanent revolution." Lukács himself had completed his move away from the adventurist Béla Kun, whom he accused of fostering bureaucratic degeneration within the Hungarian Party,[148] to the more moderate Jenö Landler. His defense of the German Party's ill-fated "March Action" of 1921 was his last major expression of support for a radical, maximalist policy on the international scene.[149]

In direct political terms, Lukács' move rightward was most explicitly demonstrated in the so-called "Blum Theses" of 1928—Blum was his Party name—which were a draft program for the Hungarian Party.[150] Following the lead of Landler, who had recently died, Lukács argued for a democratic dictatorship of workers and peasants based on the moderate slogan of "the republic." Unfortunately, his timing was inopportune as the Comintern, stung by its defeats in China and England, suddenly shifted leftward in the following year. All united-front policies, whether from above or below, were denounced, and the Social Democrats were branded "social fascists." Although Lukács had no use for this new maximalist turn, he accepted the rebuke of the Executive Committee of the Hungarian Communist Party and gave up active politics for what proved to be almost three decades. He would later cite the example of Korsch's ostracism from the KPD and his own (very dubious) belief that staying within the Communist movement was the only way to fight Fascism to explain his self-criticism.[151] But unlike his earlier turn away from Left sectarianism, this new shift, he contended, had been for tactical reasons alone. The basic impulses of the Blum Theses were continued in the literary criticism that occupied him during the remainder of the Stalinist period.[152] To

148. Lukács' movement away from Kun's position began as early as 1919 with his implicit criticism of bureaucratization in his essay "Party and Class," reprinted in *Political Writings, 1919–1929*. Here his criticism may be seen as still leftist in origin. By 1922, in the essay "The Politics of Illusion—Yet Again" reprinted in *Political Writings, 1919–1929*, Lukács had added the rightist epithet "adventurist" to his denunciation of Kun's policies. Lukács was not alone in shifting from an extreme left position to a more moderate one. According to Tökés, other "survivors of the Szamuely-led left opposition" (p. 215) were among the members of the Landler faction.

149. See his essay of 1921, "Spontaneity of the Masses, Activity of the Party," reprinted in *Political Writings, 1919–1929*.

150. Lukács, *Political Writings, 1919–1929*, p. 227f.

151. Lukács, *History and Class Consciousness*, p. xxx. What makes this argument less than compelling is the fact that the left turn of the Comintern during these years meant that Communists were more hostile to the Social Democrats than to the Fascists. The disastrous policy of "after Hitler, us" meant that they were far more interested in undermining the Weimar Republic than in preventing a Nazi takeover.

152. Löwy, *Georg Lukács*, p. 201. For a modification of this argument, see Russell Berman, "Lukács' Critique of Bredel and Ottwalt: A Political Account of an Aesthetic Debate of 1931–1932," *New German Critique* 10 (Winter 1977). Berman argues that Lukács' up-

what extent he compromised with Stalin solely out of tactical considerations has been debated ever since, although as Löwy has argued,[153] he
felt most comfortable when Stalin followed a popular front strategy close
to his own inclinations.

Theoretically, Lukács' movement away from *History and Class Consciousness* can be traced in four short works written in the aftermath of its
controversial reception: *Lenin, A Study in the Unity of His Thought*, a
review of Bukharin's *Historical Materialism*, a longer review of a new
edition of Lassalle's letters, and an extended essay entitled "Moses Hess
and the Problems of Idealist Dialectics."[154] In these works, the expressive
use of totality so central to the argument of *History and Class Consciousness* and, accordingly, to the origins of Western Marxism, was quietly set
aside in favor of a more complicated, but ultimately less coherent, alternative. Although it is arguable that Lukács returned to certain of the attitudes expressed in *History and Class Consciousness* shortly before his
death,[155] the revised position he had formulated by 1926 remained more
or less a permanent part of his mature work.

Lenin was hastily written in February, 1924, to commemorate the loss
of "the greatest thinker to have been produced by the working-class movement since Marx."[156] It was also probably designed to head off the accusations of heresy stimulated by *History and Class Consciousness* that Lukács saw coming. Virtually all residues of his ultra-leftist sectarianism
were purged from the argument; instead, Lenin's "Realpolitik" (a term, to
be sure, Lukács had approvingly used as early as 1920)[157] was invoked as
an antidote to the utopian musings of the Left sectarians. Instead of "revolutionary culturalism," which reduces politics to a means, Lukács firmly
asserted the primacy of the political. The role of the state, he argued, was
far more important than any ideological agitation in the class struggle. He
praised Lenin's theory of the vanguard party with few of those Luxemburgist qualifications evident in at least the early essays of *History and
Class Consciousness*. Although the soviets were still lauded as the locus of
dual power under a bourgeois regime and the means by which the split

---

holding of the party's dictatorial role in aesthetic matters in the 1930s can be traced back
before the Blum Theses to his earlier Left sectarianism.
    153. Löwy, p. 202.
    154. Georg Lukács, *Lenin, A Study in the Unity of His Thought*, trans. Nicholas Jacobs
(Cambridge, Mass., 1971); the three essays are all reprinted in *Political Writings, 1919–
1929*.
    155. Löwy, p. 205f.
    156. Lukács, *Lenin*, p. 9.
    157. See the essay "Opportunism and Putschism" reprinted in *Political Writings, 1919–
1929*, p. 76.

between economics and politics was overcome, they were severed entirely from any notion of majoritarian democracy, for "it must always be remembered that the great majority of the population belongs to neither of the two classes which play a decisive part in the class struggle, to neither the proletariat nor the bourgeoisie."[158] This generalization, clearly based on the Russian experience but not entirely wrong for Germany either, may have been a subtle acknowledgement of the fact that the soviets were themselves only an expression of an "aristocracy of labor," the skilled workers who were to be swamped by the mass of unskilled labor brought into the factories by the changes in capitalist production introduced in the 1920s.[159] But it was clearly at odds with the theoretical basis of *History and Class Consciousness* with its premise of the proletariat as an imminently universal class. In the long run, so Lukács expected, it would achieve that status, but for the present, its class consciousness was still too inchoate to allow it to realize the role of subject and object of history.

Lenin, however, was by no means a clean break with *History and Class Consciousness.* Lukács, for example, chose to ignore entirely Lenin's çrude reflection theory of consciousness in his *Materialism and Empirio-Criticism* and interpreted Leninism instead as a "hitherto unprecedented degree of concrete, unschematic, unmechanistic purely-praxis-oriented thought."[160] He further argued, as he had in "What is Orthodox Marxism?," that "Historical materialism is the theory of the proletarian revolution. It is so because its essence is an intellectual synthesis of the social existence which produces and fundamentally determines the proletariat; and because the proletariat struggling for liberation finds its clear self-consciousness in it."[161] And most importantly for our purposes, he praised Lenin for grasping the concrete totality of social relations; without having known of Lenin's wartime reading of Hegel, Lukács sensed a strong Hegelian element in his political practice.

But Lukács' view of Hegel and the notion of totality had undergone a subtle revision. In *Lenin,* he did, to be sure, retain his earlier belief in a longitudinal totality:

158. Lukács, *Lenin,* p. 66.
159. Piccone, p. 115. It should be noted here that the term "aristocracy of labor" was first used by Lenin to describe those elements of the working class bought off by the benefits of selective capitalist amelioration. In fact, in the revolution of the immediate post-war era, it was this group that tended to be most radical. See E. J. Hobsbawm, "Lenin and the 'Aristocracy of Labor'" in *Revolutionaries: Contemporary Essays* (New York, 1973) for a discussion of Lenin's usage.
160. Lukács, *Lenin,* p. 88.
161. Ibid., p. 9. In his 1967 Postscript to *Lenin,* Lukács singled out this belief as demonstrating "the prejudices of the time" (p. 90).

For every genuine Marxist there is always a reality more real and therefore more important than *isolated* facts and tendencies—namely, *the reality of the total process*, the totality of social development.[162]

But no longer did he try to equate that totality with the objectifications of a creator–subject. Perhaps anticipating Josef Revai's pointed observation in his 1924 review of *History and Class Consciousness* that if only the proletariat was the subject and object of history, there could not have been an original creator–subject of the historical process,[163] Lukács disentangled his longitudinal view of totality from his earlier expressive one. In accepting Lenin's realistic assessment of the need to forge alliances between oppressed groups, an assessment that led to the success of the Russian Revolution in contrast to its Hungarian counterpart, Lukács moved to what might be best called a modified "decentered" or non-genetic view of totality. No longer was the proletariat the meta-subjective totalizer of history.

Not surprisingly, his recent structuralist critics would find in *Lenin* a significant advance over *History and Class Consciousness*.[164] That this new concept of totality with its implicit jettisoning of Vico's *verum–factum* principle cast into doubt Lukács' resolution of the antinomies of bourgeois culture, neither he nor his later structuralist opponents remarked. Nor did Lukács himself immediately recognize the tension between his assertion that "historical materialism is the theory of the proletarian revolution" and his admission that the revolution was not a purely proletarian one. In his later work, as his 1967 postscript to *Lenin* made clear, Lukács did recognize that a choice had to be made, and he made it in a way very different from those who, like Korsch or the Council Communists, remained wedded to the belief that theory reflected practice:

Without orientation towards totality there can be no historically true practice. But knowledge of the totality is never spontaneous; it must always be brought into activity 'from the outside,' that is theoretically.

162. Ibid., p. 18.
163. Revai's important review has been translated with an introduction by Ben Brewster in *Theoretical Practice* 1 (January, 1971). Merleau-Ponty recognized the significance of Revai's objection in *Adventures of the Dialectic*:

The proletariat "projects" a subject into the past which totalizes the experience of the past and undoubtedly projects into the empty future a subject which concentrates the meaning of the future. This is a well-founded "conceptual mythology," but a mythology, since the proletariat is not truly able to enter into a precapitalist past or a postcapitalist future. The proletariat does not realize the identification of subject or history. It is nothing but the "carrier" of a myth which presents this identification as desirable. This extension offered by Revai reduces Lukács' philosophical effort to nothing because, if the proletariat is only the carrier of a myth, the philosopher, even if he judges this myth to be well-founded, decides this in his profound wisdom or unlimited audacity, which becomes a court of last appeal. (p. 54)

164. Jones, "The Marxism of the Early Lukács," p. 50f. See also Robin Blackburn and Gareth Stedman Jones, "Louis Althusser and the Struggle for Marxism," in Howard and Klare, eds. *The Unknown Dimension*, p. 281.

The predominance of practice is therefore only realizable on the basis of a theory which aims to be all-embracing. But, as Lenin well knew, the totality of being as it unfolds objectively is infinite, and therefore can never be adequately grasped.[165]

These admissions were a far cry from the optimistic assumptions underlying *History and Class Consciousness*. Even the notion of "imputed class consciousness," which salvaged the theoretical consistency of that book, was replaced by a more realistic confession that theory did not express practice, even on the level of "objective possibility," but led it instead. As we will see, the Western Marxists were sharply divided over the implications of this position, implications which Lukács himself had not yet fully grasped in 1924.

Lenin was written at a time when Lukács still thought Bolshevism and a variant of Hegelian Marxism were compatible. In his critique of Bukharin's *Theory of Historical Materialism*, which appeared in the *Grünberg Archiv* in 1925, Lukács expressed his continued adherence to a philosophically informed Marxism on essentially Hegelian lines. Like the review of Wittfogel that was published in the same issue of the *Archiv*,[166] the essay was directed against a scientific Marxism that naturalized the dialectic and overemphasized the autonomy of technological factors in the historical process:

The closeness of Bukharin's theory to bourgeois, natural-scientific materialism derives from his use of "science" (in the French sense) as a model. In its concrete application to society and history it therefore frequently obscures the specific feature of Marxism: that all *economic or "sociological" phenomena derive from the social relations of men to one another.* Emphasis on false 'objectivity' in theory leads to fetishism.[167]

The political implications of this position, Lukács hinted, were passive and fatalistic: "Bukharin's basic philosophy is completely in harmony with a contemplative materialism."[168] Lukács did not notice that *The Theory of Historical Materialism* was in fact written in the fall of 1921 when, as Stephen Cohen points out,[169] Bukharin was advocating radically activist "war communism" programs. And oddly enough, by 1925, Bukharin was identified with the more gradualist wing of the Soviet lead-

165. Lukács, *Lenin*, p. 99.
166. Reprinted in *Political Writings, 1919–1929.*
167. Lukács, *Political Writings, 1919–1929*, p. 136. For a defense of Bukharin against Lukács (and Gramsci), see Maurice A. Finocchiaro, "Philosophical Theory and Scientific Practice," *Studies in Soviet Thought* 21, 2 (May, 1980).
168. Lukács, *Political Writings, 1919–1929*, p. 142.
169. Stephen F. Cohen, *Bukharin and the Bolshevik Revolution: A Political Biography, 1888–1938* (New York, 1973), p. 109.

ership, advocating a coalition with the peasants in a manner very similar to Lukács' own argument in his later "Blum Theses." What makes Lukács' review of Bukharin particularly important for our purposes is its critique of Bukharin's attempt to interpret Marxism as a general sociology:

As a necessary consequence of his natural-scientific approach, sociology cannot be restricted to a pure method, but develops into an independent science with its own substantive goals. The dialectic can do without such independent substantive achievements; its realm is that of the historical process as a whole, whose individual, concrete, unrepeatable moments reveal its dialectical essence precisely in the qualitative differences between them and in the continuous transformation of their objective structure. The *totality* is the territory of the dialectic.[170]

What Lukács was asserting here was the distinction between historical and philosophical versions of Marxism, which were based on the idea of totality, and sociological ones, which substituted the notion of system, often understood as an analogue of a biological organism. Bukharin's book had, in fact, developed an equilibrium theory of society that saw social systems tending towards stability in a manner similar to biological adaptation.[171] Outside of the Bolshevik movement, other Marxists, most notably the neo-Kantian Austro-Marxists around Max Adler,[172] had contended that Marxism was a sociology. In this review, Lukács began a long tradition of Western Marxist attacks on the sociologization of Marxism, a tradition to which Korsch, Gramsci, the Frankfurt School, and Lefebvre made perhaps the most notable contributions.[173] All later attempts to find parallels between Marxist notions of totality and such sociological positions as the functionalism of Talcott Parsons were ignorant of the critique Lukács and other Western Marxists had made of Bukharin and his successors.[174]

In 1925 Lukács also reviewed for the *Grünberg Archiv* Gustav Mayer's new edition of Ferdinand Lassalle's letters. The concept of totality played only a very marginal role in Lukács' argument, which was aimed primarily at discrediting Lassalle as "*the* theoretician of the bourgeois revolu-

170. Lukács *Political Writings, 1919–1929*, pp. 139–140.
171. Cohen, p. 116.
172. See, for example, Adler's essay "The Sociological Meaning of Marx's Thought" in *Austro–Marxism*, trans. and ed. Tom Bottomore and Patrick Goode (Oxford, 1978).
173. Korsch, *Marxism and Philosophy, passim*; Gramsci, *Selections from the Prison Notebooks*, pp. 243–45, 425–430; Max Horkheimer, *Critical Theory: Selected Essays*, trans. Matthew J. O'Connell and others (New York, 1972), p. 190f; Henri Lefebvre, *The Sociology of Marx*, trans. Norbert Guterman (New York, 1968), pp. 3–24.
174. For a discussion of this issue, see Alan Swingewood, *Marx and Modern Social Theory* (New York, 1975), chapter 8. Swingewood rejects the identification of Marxism with functionalism, but tries to salvage its non-philosophical, scientific status. For an attempt to rescue sociology from the contention that it is inherently anti-dialectical, see Alvin W. Gouldner, *For Sociology*.

tion."[175] The reason for this judgment, Lukács contended, was the extent of Fichte's influence on Lassalle's philosophical development. Rather than emphasizing the progressive moments in Fichte's activist philosophy, as he had done in *History and Class Consciousness*, Lukács now attacked him for being naively utopian and believing that the Idea was active in history. In contrast, Hegel was praised for being far more aware of the concrete relations of his own epoch:

> The Hegelian notion of "reconciliation," the culmination of the philosophy of history in the present, implies—for all that it is politically reactionary and ends up philosophically and methodically in pure contemplation—a more profound connection between the logical categories and the structural forms of bourgeois life.[176]

Here for the first time Lukács emphasized the idea of "reconciliation" with reality, which was to be a frequent theme in much of his later work. Although he always maintained that this idea should be understood as contradictory, he nonetheless insisted, as he put it in *The Young Hegel*, that "the dialectical core of this view is always the recognition of social reality as it actually is."[177] No longer stressing the subjective dimension of totalization in Fichte's sense, he now emphasized Hegel's objective totality of existing reality. Accordingly, when he invoked the category of totality in the essay on Lassalle, he did so only to debunk the primacy of subjective consciousness:

> The collective fate of a class is only the *expression* in terms of consciousness of its socio-economic situation and is conditioned *simultaneously* by its correct totality-relationship to the whole society and to the historical process both really and cognitively.[178]

Lukács' move away from Fichtean activism towards the Hegelian notion of "reconciliation" was given its classic formulation in his major essay of 1926, "Moses Hess and the Problem of Idealist Dialectics." Here the Young Hegelians, most notably Hess, Cieszkowski, and Bauer, are described as regressing to Fichtean idealism and Feuerbachian moralism, while Marx is credited with grasping the concrete, mediated totality of existing relations through his own reading of Hegel. Lukács' attribution of a direct relationship between Marx and Hegel was helped by his insistence that Hegel's thought was already deeply imbued with the economic

175. Lukács, *Political Writings, 1919–1929*, p. 177.
176. Ibid., p. 153.
177. Georg Lukács, *The Young Hegel: Studies in the Relations Between Dialectics and Economics*, trans. Rodney Livingstone (London, 1975), p. 70.
178. Lukács, *Political Writings, 1919–1929*, p. 163.

categories of the classical economists, an argument he was to make even more extensively in *The Young Hegel.* Thus, whereas the Young Hegelians were mesmerized by the idealist elements in Hegel's philosophy, Marx was able to recover its materialist dimensions.

Curiously, Lukács blamed Hess's deficiencies in this regard on his non-proletarian background:

Hess philosophizes from the standpoint of the revolutionary *intelligentsia* sympathetic to the coming social revolution. The sufferings of the proletariat form the starting-point of his philosophizing, the proletariat is the *object* of his concern and his struggle.[179]

Anticipating the later Marxist critique of his friend Karl Mannheim's notion of a "free-floating intelligentsia," Lukács added the explanation:

The fond belief that he inhabits a sphere above all class antagonisms and all egotistical interests of his fellow-men is typical of the intellectual who does not participate—directly—in the process of production and whose existential basis, both material and intellectual, seems to be the "whole" of society, regardless of class differences.[180]

How Marx, or Lukács himself for that matter, had avoided this situation and come to "participate—directly—in the process of production," Lukács did not choose to explain. Insofar as virtually all of the Western Marxists were like Hess in this regard, this omission was an important one. What it indicated was a certain willingness on Lukács' part to subordinate the autonomy of the intellect to the allegedly superior wisdom of those who participated in the production process. This "workerist" attitude, as it became known, was, however, counterbalanced by his belief that in non-revolutionary times theory had to be in advance of practice. The compromise he reached to reconcile these extremes was to subordinate his personal intellectual autonomy to the wisdom of the party, which supposedly was rooted in the working class, if in advance of it theoretically. Few other Western Marxists would find this a very satisfactory solution.

In any event, what was clear in "Moses Hess and the Problems of Idealist Dialectics" was the distance Lukács had travelled since the days when he wrote *History and Class Consciousness.* The only real residue from that period in the essay was the argument that for Hegel, alienation and reification "cannot be overcome either epistemologically or in ethical-utopian fashion; only by self-sublation in the identical subject-object of history can they attain their resolution."[181] But Lukács significantly did not use this formula to describe Marx's method as well, which he claimed was

179. Ibid., pp. 196–7.   180. Ibid., p. 197.   181. Ibid., p. 214.

a "theory of a completely different kind (albeit profoundly connected with the Hegelian dialectic): *the critique of political economy.*"[182] And although Lukács then went on to refer the reader in a footnote to the essay, "Reification and the Consciousness of the Proletariat," he carefully avoided any reference to the subjectivist emphasis of that work.

In short, by 1926 Lukács' use of the concept of totality had altered in essential ways, most importantly through the weakening of its expressive and Fichtean dimensions. Although Lukács still continued to stress praxis, subjectivity and consciousness, these emphases were countered by a new appreciation of the inertial force of the objective elements in the totality. It is inaccurate to argue then, as one commentator has, that "the Lassalle and Hess essays, like the criticism of Bukharin, indicate that on the theoretical plane he did not retreat a step from his earlier anathematized position."[183] Michael Löwy's conclusion that the essay on Hess "provided the methodological basis for his support for the Soviet 'Thermidor'" is closer to the truth.[184] And, as we will see in the chapter on Goldmann and Marxist aesthetics, it also provided the philosophical foundation for Lukács' highly influential writings of the 1930s on culture and literature, writings in which the concept of totality continued to play a critical—but changed—role.

Lukács' tortured later history is as much a part of "Eastern" as Western Marxism, if not more so. To detail it at any length would thus be beyond the scope of this study. What will interest us instead is the subterranean influence of *History and Class Consciousness,* which, despite all of its author's second thoughts, launched the problematic we are examining in this study. Lukács had not, to be sure, been alone in challenging the philosophical and political assumptions of the orthodox dialectical materialists. Accordingly, his concept of totality was not the only one the Western Marxists were able to adopt. Karl Korsch, Antonio Gramsci, and to a lesser extent Ernst Bloch were the other members of the first generation of Western Marxists who contributed to the debate about holism. It is to their work that we now must turn.

182. Ibid., p. 218.
183. Breines, "Praxis and its Theorists: The Impact of Lukács and Korsch in the 1920s," p. 88.
184. Löwy, *Georg Lukács,* p. 196.

CHAPTER THREE

The Revolutionary Historicism
of Karl Korsch

Among the founders of Western Marxism, no one insisted on the centrality of the concept of totality as fervently as Georg Lukács. But for all those
of his generation who sought to restore the philosophical—that is, Hegelian—dimension of Marxist theory, totality was of vital importance. If
less thoroughly articulated than in Lukács' work, the concept nonetheless
permeated the thinking of three figures in particular: Karl Korsch, Antonio Gramsci and Ernst Bloch. From the point of view of more scientific or
structuralist variants of Marxism, these thinkers have often been closely
identified with Lukács as defenders of a common Hegelian or humanist
version of holism. And, in fact, they were generally united on a number of
crucial issues, such as the importance of subjective praxis and the inadequacy of economistic determinism. Yet they also introduced subtle variations on the theme of totality in their work in the 1920s, variations that
would become more marked in some of their later writings. Indeed, if it
can be said that Lukács' own theorizing in that turbulent decade was by
no means fully consistent, the speculations of Korsch, Gramsci and Bloch
made it certain that Western Marxism would begin with at least tendentially disparate concepts of totality. The process of recognizing those variations has nowhere been as striking as in the reception of Korsch's legacy,
to which we will turn first.

The history of Korsch's early and persistent identification with Lukács
has often been told.[1] Its major source was the virtually simultaneous pub-

---

1. The best discussion of their identification appears in Paul Breines, "Praxis and Its
Theorists: The Impact of Lukács and Korsch in the 1920s," *Telos* 2 (Spring 1972), which is
summarized in part in Andrew Arato and Paul Breines, *The Young Lukács and the Origins of
Western Marxism* (New York, 1979). Other general treatments of Korsch that deal with this

lication in 1923 of their most explosive works: Lukács' *History and Class Consciousness* and Korsch's *Marxism and Philosophy*.[2] The two men independently reached similar conclusions in the early 1920s about the necessity of recovering the practical impulse in Marxism. They also concurred that its loss was attributable in large measure to the repression of Hegel by the Second International's orthodox theorists. As early enthusiasts of the Bolshevik Revolution, they both claimed to be expressing the philosophical correlate of its practical achievement by showing that Marxism, properly understood, unified critical theory with revolutionary praxis. More important still for the ultimate identification of Lukács and Korsch, their provocative books were immediately perceived by the guardians of both Bolshevik and Social Democratic orthodoxy as presenting a common threat.[3] The former in particular launched a campaign of defamation that came to a head at the fifth congress of the Comintern in June, 1924. No less a figure than Zinoviev, then one of the Soviet Union's ruling triumverate and the leader of the Third International, singled out Lukács and Korsch (along with a third culprit, the Italian Antonio Graziadei)[4] for special criticism. Linking theoretical revisionism with the ultra-left deviation Lenin had previously denounced as an "infantile disorder," Zinoviev lashed out with characteristic bureaucratic suspicion at the

---

issue are Douglas Kellner, intro. to *Karl Korsch: Revolutionary Theory* (Austin, 1977) and the articles in the special issue of the *Jahrbuch Arbeiterbewegung*, vol. 1: "Über Karl Korsch," ed. Claudio Pozzoli (Frankfurt, 1973), especially the essay by Michael Buckmiller. Several of the other contributions have been translated into English in the special Korsch issue of *Telos* 26 (Winter 1975–76). "Über Karl Korsch" contains a useful bibliography of his works and an extensive chronology of his life. See also the interview with his widow Hedda Korsch, "Memories of Karl Korsch," *New Left Review* 76 (November–December 1972); the essays in Michael Buckmiller, ed., *Zur Aktualität von Karl Korsch* (Frankfurt, 1981); and Patrick Goode, *Karl Korsch: A Study in Western Marxism* (London, 1979).

2. Karl Korsch, *Marxismus und Philosophie* (Leipzig, 1923), first published in the *Grünberg Archiv*, vol. 2; English trans., with intro. by Fred Halliday (New York and London, 1970). All citations are from the latter. This work is now included as the third volume of the ten-volume *Gesamtausgabe* of Korsch's writings edited by Michael Buckmiller for the Europäische Verlagsanstalt, a project still in progress.

3. The Social Democratic attack was led by Kautsky, who reviewed *Marxism and Philosophy* in *Die Gesellschaft* 1 (June 1924). In the same issue, another Social Democrat, the neo-Kantian Siegfried Marck, explicitly identified Lukács and Korsch as "new Communists" with ties to the young Marx. The orthodox Marxist-Leninist critics included Jan Sten, Hermann Duncker, Abram Deborin, G. K. Bammel and I. K. Luppol. See the discussions in Breines, "Praxis and Its Theorists;" Goode, Chapter 5; and the earlier treatment in Iring Fetscher, *Marx and Marxism*, trans. John Hargreaves (New York, 1971), p. 94f.

4. Graziadei, who shared little with Korsch and Lukács beyond the status of an intellectual, had written a book questioning Marx's theory of surplus value, which consisted of essays he wrote when, in Zinoviev's words, he was a "Social Democratic revisionist." For the full text of Zinoviev's speech, see Peter Ludz, ed., *Georg Lukács: Schriften zur Ideologie und Politik* (Neuwied and Berlin, 1967), pp. 719–726. They key paragraph is translated in Arato and Breines, *The Young Lukács*, p. 180.

impudence of "professors" who dared spin out theories undermining working class solidarity. His assimilation of Korsch to Lukács was then reinforced by other Soviet critics, such as the philosopher Abram Deborin,[5] in more extended attacks. Thus, it is understandable that when Korsch's work was initially recovered after his death in 1961, following a long eclipse, he was seen as Lukács' virtual double.[6]

In the interim, however, the two men had gone very different ways. Inevitably, the subtle and not-so-subtle differences in their political and intellectual developments began to attract serious attention. Korsch's political choice after his denunciation by the Comintern had led him away from mainstream Communist politics into the labyrinth of sectarian factions to the left of the party. His affinities on the international scene were with Left opposition figures like Amadeo Bordiga and T. W. Sapronow. Refusing to compromise his intellectual independence, he defended *Marxism and Philosophy* in a 1930 "Anti-Critique" that emphasized the common ground on which both his Social Democratic and Bolshevik critics stood.[7] Lukács, as we have seen, accepted the Comintern's rebuke and remained a Party stalwart, despite whatever private misgivings he may have had about the wisdom of certain of the Third International's policies. In later years, he came to justify his decision by reference to Korsch's isolation and impotence in the fight against Fascism.[8] By the 1930s, the former allies were deeply at odds, Lukács (in exile in the U.S.S.R.) defending Stalinism, and Korsch (then in the West) equating it with Nazism as counter-revolutionary.

Not surprisingly, those in the 1960s who came to link Western Marxism with the purism of the ultra-Left, and thus found Lukács' later development an embarrassment, judged Korsch's path the more honorable one. His decision to favor the workers' councils over the Party as the appropriate form of proletarian organization also endeared him to critics of the

5. Deborin went so far as to characterize Korsch as Lukács' "disciple," a description he extended with only marginally more cause to Béla Fogarasi and Josef Revai as well. See Arato and Breines, p. 171.

6. The process of recovery first started, in fact, shortly before Korsch's death with the brief mention of his work in the "Western Marxism" chapter of Maurice Merleau-Ponty's *Adventures of the Dialectic* (1955) and Iring Fetscher's essay of 1956, "From the Philosophy of the Proletariat to Proletarian *Weltanschauung*," translated in Fetscher, *Marx and Marxism*. In both cases, Lukács and Korsch were closely linked, as happened as well in such later discussions as those of Mario Spinella and Lucio Colletti in Italy. For a treatment of the latter, see Giacomo Marramao, "Korsch in Italy," *Telos* 26 (Winter 1975–76). A general account of the reception of Korsch's work can be found in Michael Buckmiller, "Aspekte der internationalen Korsch-Rezeption," in Buckmiller, ed., *Zur Aktualität von Karl Korsch*.

7. "The Present State of the Problem of 'Marxism and Philosophy'—An Anti-Critique," included in the English translation of *Marxism and Philosophy*.

8. Lukács, 1967 "Preface" to *History and Class Consciousness*, trans. Rodney Livingstone (Cambridge, Mass., 1971), p. xxx. Hedda Korsch remembers, however, that they remained on friendly personal terms until the emigration (pp. 41–2).

bureaucratized party system of the Soviet Union.[9] And his deep distrust of statist forms of Marxism attracted the New Left's more anarchistic adherents. In short, although precisely when Korsch abandoned his early support of Leninism has been debated,[10] he universally came to be seen as far more of an embodiment of the libertarian, anti-authoritarian, activist impulse in Marxism than did Lukács.

Ironically, at the same time as Korsch's political continuity was earning praise in certain quarters, his theoretical transformations were being celebrated in others. After the high water mark of his neo-Hegelianism in *Marxism and Philosophy*, Korsch returned to the more scientific and empiricist inclinations of his earlier years. In 1938, after his emigration to America, he published a general defense of Marxism entitled *Karl Marx*, in which he contended that Marx had abandoned Hegel's method entirely in favor of a "strictly empirical"[11] analysis of society. To those like the followers of the anti-Hegelian Della Volpe in Italy,[12] Korsch's later thought was a considerable advance over his earlier. Lukács *and* Korsch became, in the title of a 1968 study by Giuseppe Vacca, *Lukács or Korsch*,[13] with the latter

9. This judgment was not, however, shared by all those on the New Left who were critical of Stalinism. In Italy, the followers of Mario Tronti claimed that Korsch's thoughts on the councils were reactionary because they were grounded in a positive attitude towards a "worker aristocracy." See the discussion in Marramao, "Korsch in Italy," p. 180.

10. The traditional view, defended by such commentators as Erich Gerlach and E. H. Carr, that Korsch had been hostile to Leninism from his entry into the Communist movement has been branded a legend by Kellner, who claims Korsch was a staunch Leninist until 1925. Kellner's revision of the conventional wisdom has, in turn, been challenged by Henry Pachter, writing under the pseudonym Henri Rabasseire, "Kellner on Korsch," *Telos* 28 (Summer 1976); by Arato and Breines, pp. 244–45, and by Russell Jacoby, "The Inception of Western Marxism: Karl Korsch and the Politics of Philosophy," *Canadian Journal of Political and Social Theory* (Fall 1979), pp. 20, 31. Although this is not the place to go into the intricacies of the debate, it seems fair to conclude that, as during other phases of his career, Korsch had difficulty in interpreting political realities. He held on to an idealized vision of Leninism that blinded him to the consequences of Bolshevik policy for some time, although he grew increasingly skeptical about its implications. Paradoxically, one of the reasons that Korsch cannot be simply grouped with the ultra-Left was his insistence that theory should follow practice. As he put it in an unpublished manuscript in 1935, "*One cannot protest against a reality simply in the name of an abstract principle*" (Kellner, ed., *Karl Korsch*, p. 165). Because at times Leninism seemed like the only show in town, Korsch, despite his severe misgivings, was prone to accept it. In the manuscript just cited, he concluded:

It is unavoidable that up until the rise of a new, independent movement of the international proletariat, even the working class itself and precisely its more revolutionary components can look at today's Soviet Russia as the *real* and thence revolutionary-*rational* implementation of the posited goals that are today still not implemented in their own countries. (p. 166)

He chose not to make these sentiments public, but they help to show why he kept his earlier doubts about Leninism under control until he was forced to leave the movement in 1925–26. On Korsch's general attitude towards the Bolshevik Revolution, see Claude Orsini, "Karl Korsch und die Russische Revolution," in Buckmiller, ed., *Zur Aktualität von Karl Korsch*.

11. Karl Korsch, *Karl Marx*, 2nd ed. (New York, 1963), p. 65.

12. Marramao, "Korsch in Italy," p. 176.

13. Giuseppe Vacca, *Lukács o Korsch?* (Bari, 1969); see the discussion in Marramao, p. 177, and the review by Paul Breines in *Telos* 5 (Spring 1970).

being clearly preferred. Korsch was thus paradoxically seen as a model for both the Hegelian and anti-Hegelian wings of Western Marxism.

His differences with Lukács were given added emphasis by the realization that Bertolt Brecht, Lukács' major adversary among Marxist aestheticians, had acknowledged Korsch as his teacher in Marxist theory.[14] Although Korsch had written virtually nothing on artistic questions, his emphasis on the practical imperative of Marxism and his stress on historical specificity were understood to have influenced Brecht's "epic theater," which sought to transform the spectator's consciousness through exposing the productive underpinnings of theatrical illusion. Thus, in addition to the contrast between Korsch's and Lukács' political development and their conflicting attitudes toward the scientific nature of Marxism, the implications of their theories for Marxist aesthetics also drew wide comment.

Once these differences between the authors of *History and Class Consciousness* and *Marxism and Philosophy* were understood, the tensions between the two books themselves also came under close scrutiny. By the 1970s, commentators like Furio Cerutti, Mihály Vajda and Paul Breines were detailing the nuances separating Lukács and Korsch even at the moment of their greatest apparent unanimity.[15] Korsch himself, to be sure, had briefly alluded to several of these in his 1930 "Anti-Critique," but he had left it to others to spell out their full implications. In what follows, this task will be pursued with specific reference to the theme of totality, whose full ramifications have yet to be considered in the comparisons between the two figures.

Although a contemporary of Lukács—he was born in 1886 in the north German town of Todstedt, the son of a moderately prosperous banker—Korsch seems to have been relatively untouched by the crisis in bourgeois culture to which Lukács so passionately responded. Although his father had strong philosophical interests and he himself did not neglect philosophy when at the universities of Munich, Geneva, Berlin and

14. Heinz Brüggemann, "Bert Brecht und Karl Korsch: Fragen nach Lebendigem und Totem im Marxismus," in Claudio Pozzoli, ed., "Über Karl Korsch." See also Brüggemann's "Überlegungen zur Diskussion über das Verhältnis von Brecht und Korsch: Eine Auseinandersetzung mit Werner Mittenzwei" in Buckmiller, ed., *Zur Aktualität von Karl Korsch.*
15. Furio Cerutti, "Hegel, Lukács and Korsch: On the Emancipatory Significance of the Dialectic in Critical Marxism," *Telos* 26 (Winter 1975–76), originally in Oskar Negt, ed., *Aktualität und Folgen der Philosophie Hegels* (Frankfurt, 1970); Mihály Vajda, "Karl Korsch's Marxism and Philosophy'" in Dick Howard and Karl Klare, eds., *The Unknown Dimension: European Marxism Since Lenin* (New York, 1972); Paul Breines, "Korsch's 'Road to Marx,'" *Telos* 26 (Winter 1975–76).

Jena, Korsch chose the more practical subject of the law for his major concentration. In 1911, he earned his doctorate in jurisprudence at Jena, and left shortly thereafter for England with Hedda Gagliardi, the woman he was soon to marry, in order to translate and comment on a text by the legal theorist, Sir Ernest Schuster. During his three-year stay in London, Korsch was drawn into the circle of the Fabian Society, whose common-sensical attitude toward the tasks of socialist implementation he found attractive.[16] Like Eduard Bernstein a generation earlier, Korsch admired the Fabians' impatience with the fatalistic determinism of orthodox Marxism and their recognition of the role of will in achieving change. In fact, even after his transformation into an ultra-leftist critic of all manifestations of reformism, Korsch still admired certain aspects of Revisionism more than the theories of its orthodox critics.[17]

With the outbreak of the war, Korsch was compelled to return to Germany, where he enlisted but refused to bear arms. Like many others, Korsch was further radicalized by the war and grew more receptive to urgent calls for total change, such as those emanating from the circle of politicized Expressionists around Kurt Hiller. "The Activists," as they were called, combined a neo-Kantian emphasis on subjectivity with a pacifist abhorrence of war that appealed to intellectuals anxious to escape the fatalism of more orthodox variants of Marxism. For a while, Korsch was even associated with the politically ambiguous cultural radicals around Eugen Diederichs' *Die Tat*, although he never appears to have absorbed their neo-Romantic critique of bourgeois culture. Instead, he espoused what he called "practical socialism," and spelled out carefully considered plans for the transition from capitalism to its socialist successor. By 1920, he moved beyond neo-Kantianism of any kind to embrace dialectical materialism wholeheartedly as a theory grounded in Hegel's supersession of Kant. In that same year, he joined with the Independent Socialist Party faction that agreed to enter the Third International and thus chose membership in the German Communist Party. He became the editor of one of its major journals, *Internationale,* generally supported the Bolshevization of the Party, and was justice minister in the coalition gov-

16. As Breines suggests, Korsch may also have been attracted to the managerial dimension of Fabianism, which possibly accounts for his sympathy for the same impulse in Leninism. See Breines, "Korsch's 'Road to Marx,'" pp. 52–53.
17. See, for example, his essay, "The Passing of Marxian Orthodoxy: Bernstein—Kautsky—Luxemburg—Lenin," of 1932 in which he called Bernstein's theory "nothing more than a truthful expression of the actual character of [SPD] practice" (Kellner, ed., *Karl Korsch,* p. 179). It might be noted in passing that this positive attitude towards the veracity of Bernstein's position was shared by another radical theorist, Georges Sorel, who praised it in *Reflections on Violence,* trans. T. E. Hulme and J. Roth (London, 1950), p. 214.

ernment of Thuringia in 1923–24. For a while at least, he seems to have seen no difficulty in linking Leninism with Hegelian Marxism.[18]

His discovery of dialectics led, among other things, to a new emphasis on the concept of totality in his work. Its first appearance seems to have come in his 1919 essay, "What is Socialization?,"[19] where Korsch attempted to find a formula combining nationalization with workers' councils. In reacting to one-sided interpretations of socialization favoring one or the other of these alternatives, Korsch argued: "The goal of socialization in the spirit of socialism, however, is neither consumer-capitalism nor producer-capitalism, but rather true community property for the totality of producers and consumers."[20] He later continued, "Internal transformation of the concept of property is needed, a total subordination of every special property to the viewpoint of the common interest of the totality."[21] In this essay, however, the term was introduced as a vague synonym for the common good and carried little theoretical weight.

Korsch's next treatment of the theme of socialist transition, "Fundamentals of Socialization" published in 1920,[22] used the term with somewhat greater precision. In this work, which has been called Korsch's first really Marxist essay,[23] he singled out Kautsky's timidity in proposing plans for the transition, calling instead for "concepts of realization" that would spell out concrete proposals for change. These concepts, he claimed, "arise out of a full knowledge of the economic and psychological

18. One of the points at issue between Kellner and his critics is the extent to which Hegelian Marxism is ultimately inconsistent with Leninism. Kellner writes, "There was supposed to be some kind of profound connection between 'idealist deviations' and 'ultra-leftism': Hegel would have smiled" (p. 46). Jacoby responds, "If Hegel would have smiled, it would have been a knowing smile; at least most recent scholarship has put to rest the equation of Hegel's idealism and reactionary politics" (p. 31). Hegel, indeed, is no longer simply seen as a conservative supporter of the Prussian state, but this is a far cry from equating the political implications of his philosophy with ultra-leftism. It would be more correct to say that certain aspects of his work could be turned in a radical direction, but by no means all of them. Lukács, after all, discovered the Hegelian notion of "reconciliation" at the same time as he made his peace with Stalinism, whereas Korsch remained a Left-oppositionist throughout the period of his growing estrangement from Hegelianism. Jacoby's insistence on the inherent links between neo-Hegelianism and ultra-leftism is historically problematic, as is his parallel assertion that "throughout his life, Korsch stitched together the politics and philosophy of Western Marxism" (p. 22).

It has also been argued by such commentators as Iring Fetscher, Raya Dunayevskaya, and Neil McInnes, with varying degrees of approbation, that Lenin himself was significantly influenced by Hegel during the war, but this is an issue that cannot be resolved here.

19. "What Is Socialization? A Program of Practical Socialism," New German Critique 6 (Fall 1975), with intro. by Gian Enrico Rusconi.

20. Ibid., p. 68.

21. Ibid., p. 74.

22. "Fundamentals of Socialization," in Kellner, ed., Karl Korsch: Revolutionary Theory.

23. Kellner, p. 120.

totality (*Gesamtlage*) and its perceivable tendencies of development."[24] Kautsky was particularly deficient in his ability to see the future latent in the present: "From the fact that Kautsky and all of those who stand close to him do not possess such creative, faithful revolutionary fantasy we can explain their all too long denial of practical future-oriented thoughts."[25] This last passage is of particular interest because it is one of the few places in Korsch's writing that the anticipatory moment in the totality is stressed.[26] But the main importance of the essay as a whole for our purposes is its demonstration of Korsch's clearly post-Kantian faith in the possibility of "full knowledge of the economic and psychological totality."

The basis for that confidence was made manifest in the more philosophically informed work that followed, culminating in *Marxism and Philosophy* itself. In "The Marxist Dialectic" of 1923, Korsch spelled out his epistemological premises:

The immense significance of Marx's theoretical achievement for the practice of proletarian class struggle is that he concisely fused together for the first time the total content of those new viewpoints transgressing bourgeois horizons, and that he also formally conceptualized them into a solid unity, into the living totality of a scientific system. These new ideas arose by necessity in the consciousness of the proletarian class from its social conditions. ... [Marx] created the theoretical-scientific expression adequate to the new content of consciousness of the proletarian class, and thereby at the same time elevated this proletarian class consciousness to a higher level of its being.[27]

Two implications of this passage are especially noteworthy. The first is Korsch's faith in the scientificity of Marx's theory, a faith that would later grow even stronger in such works as *Karl Marx*. Unlike Lukács, Korsch refused to emphasize the tension between science and philosophy. While stressing the importance of Hegel for Marx's development, he had no sense of the possible difficulties in transforming dialectics into a science based on empirical verification. Indeed, he claimed that

Only by taking the form of a strict "science" could this complex of proletarian class views, contained in "modern socialism," radically purify itself from the bourgeois views with which from its origin it was inextricably connected. And only by becoming a "science" could socialism actually fulfill the task which Karl Marx

24. "Fundamentals of Socialization," p. 127.
25. Ibid.
26. For criticisms of Korsch on this point, see Cerutti, p. 173, Kellner, p. 74, and Nick Xenos, "Introduction to Korsch," *Telos* 26 (Winter 1975–76), p. 39. For a partial defense of Korsch, see Stephen Eric Bronner, review of Kellner, *Telos* 34 (Winter 1977–78), p. 229.
27. "The Marxist Dialectic," in Kellner, pp. 135–360.

and Frederick Engels had set for it: to be the "theoretical expression" of revolutionary class action.[28]

Korsch did not, to be sure, mean that Marxism was scientific in the anti-philosophical manner of a Bukharin; in fact, he shared Lukács' disdain for the sociologism of *The Theory of Historical Materialism*.[29] As he emphasized in *Marxism and Philosophy*, Marxism was the realization of Hegelian philosophy, not its simple negation. But he felt that this realization could come through the unification of a critically inclined science of society with revolutionary proletarian practice. Whether or not this unity was possible became a bone of very heated contention among subsequent Western Marxists.

The second and perhaps even more significant implication of Korsch's argument in "The Marxist Dialectic" derived from his contention that Marxist science "arose by necessity in the consciousness of the proletarian class from its social conditions," and was the "'theoretical expression' of revolutionary class action." In other words, Korsch claimed that theory followed or expressed practice, or more specifically, that Marxist theory arose out of the praxis of the working class "by necessity." The unity of theory and practice that all early Western Marxists stressed thus meant for Korsch the priority of practice over theory. That practical emphasis so evident in his Fabian and Activist periods (if the latter can be called a real "period" in his development) now reemerged in Hegelian-Marxist guise. As he put it in *Marxism and Philosophy*,

Hegel formulated this principle in a more general way, when he wrote that every philosophy can be nothing but "*its own epoch comprehended in thought*." Essential in any event for a real understanding of the development of philosophical thought, this axiom becomes even more relevant for a revolutionary period of social evolution.[30]

This fundamental premise of Korsch's thought has aptly been called "revolutionary historicism"[31] by Douglas Kellner because it was grounded in a radically historicist disdain for transcendental theory. Kellner sees it as one of the enduring earmarks of Korsch's thought, if at times uneasily

28. Ibid., p. 136.
29. See his remarks in *Marxism and Philosophy*, 63, and in "On Materialist Dialectic" in Kellner, p. 141.
30. Korsch, *Marxism and Philosophy*, p. 43.
31. Kellner, p. 33f. Korsch, it should be recognized, had cause for attributing this view to Marx himself. In the *Communist Manifesto*, Marx and Engels had written that Communist arguments "merely express, in general terms, actual relations springing from an existing class struggle, from a historical movement going on under our very eyes" (*Communist Manifesto*, trans. S. Moore [New York, 1964], p. 81). Elsewhere, to be sure, Marx's epistemology was very different, as the *Grundrisse* clearly demonstrates.

married to an objectivist view of science that denied the link between knowledge and class status.

In any event, it is clear that *Marxism and Philosophy* was fundamentally historicist, so much so in fact that Korsch boldly attempted to explain the development of Marxist theory itself as a reflection of proletarian practice. He divided the history of historical materialism into three basic eras. The first of these he identified with the revolutionary ferment of the years from 1843 to 1848, which he saw theoretically expressed in Marx's works from the *Critique of Hegel's Philosophy of Right* to the *Manifesto*. The second phase, Korsch claimed, began in the bloody aftermath of the June Days and lasted until the turn of the century; less revolutionary in practical terms, its theory also stressed objective and determinist laws of development rather than subjective action. Although in the works of Marx and Engels themselves the revolutionary moment was still preserved, it was lost in the hands of their less dialectical followers. The fatalistic "scientific socialism" of the Second International was an expression of the quietistic politics of its adherents. The third period, beginning around 1900, saw an upsurge of socialist activism and a concomitant growth in radical, subjectivist theory. Such apparently irreconcilable currents as trade union reformism, revolutionary syndicalism and Bolshevism all expressed this third phase, which Korsch saw culminating in the revolutionary dynamism of the postwar era. Its proper theoretical expression was the recovery of the Hegelian dimension of Marxist theory.

Unconventionally candid about the links between theory and practice, Korsch's argument was fresh and original; it was to be often repeated by later Western Marxists such as Lucien Goldmann.[32] But a number of questions come immediately to mind. Was the pre-1848 era really one of *proletarian* revolutionary action? Or were the discontents leading to the explosions of that year attributable to a complex of factors, including the defensive anti-capitalism of artisans and bourgeois nationalism? If the latter, was it correct to say, as Korsch did in a later essay, that "the *materialist view of history* grew out of a revolutionary period prior to 1850 as an integral part of the *subjective action* of a revolutionary class"?[33] Was it also plausible to say that in the second period Marx and Engels somehow failed to register the theoretical implications of the waning of revolution-

---

32. Lucien Goldmann, *The Human Sciences and Philosophy*, trans. H. V. White and R. Anchor (London, 1969), pp. 80–81. According to Paul Piccone, Korsch's general argument was itself anticipated by Labriola, but it is unlikely that Korsch was directly in his debt. See Piccone, "Labriola and the Roots of Eurocommunism," *Berkeley Journal of Sociology* 22 (1977–78).

33. "The Crisis of Marxism" (1927) in Kellner, p. 173.

ary practice? In his "Anti-Critique" of 1930, Korsch lamely defended the "anachronistic" character of Marx's theory by claiming that "two processes unfolded side by side in relative independence of each other. One was the *development under novel conditions of the old theory which had arisen in a previous historical epoch.* The other was the *new practice of the workers' movement.*"[34] But if Marx and Engels were somehow exempted from the primacy of practice over theory, what was left of the notion that every philosophy can be nothing but "its own epoch comprehended in thought"?

Moreover, how was one to distinguish between a scientific theory and an ideological one, if science was the expression of the class struggle at any moment in history? Why was the fatalistic "scientific socialism" of the Second International more of an ideology than any other available theory during that period, if the proletariat was relatively docile? To confuse the matter even more, in his "Anti-Critique," where Korsch admitted that the characterization of the second period as uniformly quietistic was oversimplified, he acknowledged that "at the time when the practice of the movement was most revolutionary, its theory was essentially 'populist' and democratic (under the influence of Lassalle and Dühring) and only sporadically 'Marxist'."[35] This description may well be valid, but it wreaks havoc with the contention that Marxist science is the necessary expression of revolutionary activism. Finally, was there not something highly ominous about the implication that the quantitative increase in Marxist adherents meant a qualitative decline in the purity of their theory? What did this suggest for the democratic pretensions of Marxism?

In addition to these difficulties, Korsch's revolutionary historicism also complicated his notion of totality, as a brief comparison with Lukács' use of the term will demonstrate. In certain respects, Korsch and Lukács were in agreement. Both, for example, assumed a longitudinal view of totality in which all of history was a meaningful whole. As Korsch wrote in *Marxism and Philosophy*,

There is one unified historical process of historical development in which an "autonomous" proletarian class movement emerges from the revolutionary movement of the third estate, and the new materialist theory of Marxism "autonomously" confronts bourgeois idealist philosophy. All these processes affect each other reciprocally. The emergence of Marxist theory is, in Hegelian-Marxist terms, only the "other side" of the emergence of the real proletarian

34. Korsch, *Marxism and Philosophy*, p. 117.
35. Ibid., p. 111.

movement; it is both sides together that comprise the concrete totality of the historical process.[36]

And both shared, at least for a while, a radically expressive notion of totality, although Korsch never specifically adopted the Hegelian concept of an identical subject-object history or flirted with Fichte's absolute subject creating the objective world as a field for its practical action.

In fact, one of the difficulties in Korsch's use of totality was the unexamined ambiguity marking his expressivism. Against the Second International's economic version of expressivism, in which the base was assumed to determine the superstructure, Korsch employed several terms to describe the genetic center of the whole. At one point in his argument, he wrote that the transformations of Marxist theory were determined "by the totality of the historical-social process of which they are a general expression."[37] Elsewhere, he claimed that "scientific socialism is the theoretical expression of a revolutionary process."[38] In yet another place, he wrote of the "historical *subject* which accomplishes the real development of society with either a true or false consciousness."[39] And a year later, in his essay on "Lenin and the Comintern," he described Marxism as "essentially the concrete comprehension of the proletarian revolution as historical process and as a historical action of the proletarian class."[40]

This last formulation betrays the fatal ambiguity of his position most clearly. For was the historical *process* precisely the same as the historical *action* of the proletariat? In the apparently revolutionary days of the early 1920s, Korsch seemed to think it was. In his 1920 essay "Fundamentals of Socialization," he described the Marxist concept of socialization as the "identity of the historical process of development and revolutionary hu-

36. Ibid., p. 45. This formulation calls into some question the comparison between Lukács and Korsch made by Nick Xenos in his "Introduction to Korsch":

Whereas Lukács introduced a concept of totality which comprises the whole of history and is mediated in both time and space, and which has the proletariat as both the subject and object of that historical totality, an identity which allows for the emergence of the party as the bearer of historical truth, Korsch's concept of totality is open-ended because it is immediate. Truth, for Korsch, rests solely in actuality; theory and practice form an inseparable unity, and any theory which is not an expression of that reality is ideology and hence "false." (p. 38)

Although Xenos does point here to a tendential difference between the two figures, Korsch did at times violate his own principles and posit a totality that transcended the current practice of the working class. The passage from *Marxism and Philosophy* quoted here was just such a moment. Later, as we will see, Korsch lost his confidence in the coherence of the longitudinal totality.

37. Korsch, *Marxism and Philosophy*, p. 56.
38. Ibid., p. 69.
39. Ibid., p. 77.
40. "Lenin and the Comintern," in Kellner, p. 155.

man activity."[41] Thus, for Korsch, the expressive center of the totality was the unity of revolutionary process and proletarian praxis, which was then expressed in theoretical terms in Marxist science.

But what was the expressive center during non-revolutionary periods when the proletariat failed to act radically? By introducing the term "process," Korsch risked reducing theoretical consciousness to an epiphenomenal status, despite his intentions. Indeed, as Leonardo Ceppa pointed out, "Korsch's self-historicization of Marxism appears to fall back on an equivocal conception of consciousness as a 'reflection' of real external processes."[42] That Korsch was indeed vulnerable to this regression is demonstrated in his description of Marx's method in his 1932 introduction to *Capital*, where he wrote:

Marx grasps and portrays the *totality* of the capitalist mode of production, and the bourgeois society that emerges from it. He describes and connects all its economic features, together with its legal, political, religious, artistic, and philosophical—in short, *ideological*—manifestations.[43]

In *Marxism and Philosophy*, Korsch, to be sure, resisted the reduction of consciousness to a "manifestation" of the mode of production. And in fact, the book was praised by an early reviewer, Lazlo Radvanyi, for showing that "the entire Marxist world view is based on the assumption that the world of consciousness and the material world are not two separate realms. These worlds are rather two parts of a unified totality where nothing exists by itself but develops in continual interaction and mutual penetration. The parts of this whole are not isolated but are drawn to each other and reciprocally conditioned."[44] But the tension between process and praxis could not be indefinitely contained.

Korsch was able to avoid choosing between them for a long time, however, because of an unexamined assumption he held about the harmonious nature of the totality. In describing Marx's method during the revolutionary era before 1848, for example, Korsch wrote:

It is a theory of *social development* seen and comprehended as a living totality; or, more precisely, it is a theory of *social revolution* comprehended and practised as a living totality. At this stage there is no question whatever of dividing the economic,

41. "Fundamentals of Socialization," in Kellner, p. 133.
42. Leonardo Ceppa, "Korsch's Marxism," *Telos* 26 (Winter 1975–76), p. 97.
43. "Introduction to *Capital*" in *Three Essays on Marxism*, intro. Paul Breines (New York, 1972), p. 45.
44. Lazlo Radvanyi, review of *Marxism and Philosophy*, in *Archiv für Sozialwissenschaft und Sozialpolitik* 52, 2 (February 1925); reprinted in *Telos* 8 (Summer 1971), p. 136. Korsch referred to this review in his 1930 "Anti-Critique" as "thorough and penetrating" (p. 99).

political and intellectual moments of this totality into separate branches of knowledge.[45]

Similarly, in defending Marx and Engels against the assertion that they had a dualistic notion of the relationship between mind and matter, he insisted that "the *coincidence of consciousness and reality* characterizes every dialectic, including Marx's dialectical materialism."[46] In other words, there are homologous relationships among the various levels of the totality, at least during revolutionary periods. Much of Korsch's later theoretical difficulties, which led him at times to question the validity of Marxism itself, stemmed from his inability to construe those relationships in non-revolutionary times when process and praxis were non-identical.

Here Lukács proved the more subtle dialectician. As Mihály Vajda pointed out,[47] he was truer to Hegel than was Korsch because of his retention of the critical distinction between essence and appearance. Filtered through Weber's category of "objective possibility," this opposition was transformed into the difference between empirical and "ascribed" or "imputed" class consciousness. By recognizing the gap between the two, however much he may have felt it was being narrowed in the early 1920s,[48] Lukács was able to avoid the embarrassment of reducing theory to the vagaries of proletarian practice at any one historical moment. He was thus able to think far more concretely than Korsch about questions of mediation and organization. He was also more alert to the persistent grip of ideology than was Korsch with his naive belief in the "coincidence" of consciousness and reality. And he was able as well to speculate more imaginatively about the normative goal of socialism as the end of reification and alienation, concepts that Korsch in fact rarely employed.[49]

45. Korsch, *Marxism and Philosophy*, p. 57.

46. Ibid., p. 88.

47. Vajda, "Karl Korsch's Marxism," p. 138. More recently, Vajda has revised his evaluation of Lukács and Korsch, arguing that Korsch's greater awareness of sociological realities prevented him from resolving problems philosophically as did Lukács. See his *The State and Socialism: Political Essays* (London, 1981), p. 20.

48. There were, in fact, times when Lukács also described Marxist theory as the expression of working class practice. In *History and Class Consciousness*, trans. Rodney Livingstone (Cambridge, Mass., 1971) for example, he wrote that Marxist theory "is essentially the intellectual expression of the revolutionary process itself" (p. 3). And in *Lenin*, trans. Nicholas Jacobs (Cambridge, Mass., 1971) he argued that the essence of historical materialism is "an intellectual synthesis of the social existence which produces and fundamentally determines the proletariat" (p. 9). But these Korschian sentiments proved to be only temporary for Lukács.

49. Korsch's negative attitude towards the concept of reification appeared in a letter he wrote on December 16–17, 1935, to his friend Paul Partos:

You still always use the Lukácsian concept of 'reification.' Now to be sure Marx in fact occasionally speaks of a 'thinglike disguise' and a 'thingification' (*Versachlichung*) of the social character of production. But the expression 'fetishism' is infinitely better for materialist and sociological conception and

Lukács' greater dialectical agility brought with it, to be sure, certain dangers. As we have seen, imputing class consciousness to a class which may not subjectively achieve it could easily lead to substituting the party for the class. One of Korsch's most telling criticisms of the Soviet Union was directed precisely against this temptation. In his 1930 "Anti-Critique" of *Marxism and Philosophy*, he charged both Lenin and Kautsky (and, as is generally overlooked, Rosa Luxemburg as well) with making "a virtue out of temporary necessity"[50] in denying that the working class could achieve on its own anything but trade union consciousness. Korsch's greater sensitivity to the authoritarian potential in this assumption led him to recognize as well the Jacobin residues in Marx's theory, residues to which Lukács seems to have been oblivious.[51] By insisting on the primacy of practice over theory and by collapsing the revolutionary process into proletarian praxis, Korsch avoided that ambiguous "reconciliation" with reality endorsed by Lukács in the mid-1920s.[52]

And yet, it would be mistaken to assume that Korsch was completely

---

description of this form of thought. With Lukács, who extends the use of this concept without measure, it is at bottom a matter of a protest of a 'philosophy of life' against the cold, rigid, fixed factual and material world. (Kellner, p. 110)

Alienation seems to have been even less central to his thought. Significantly, he made little of the importance of the *Paris Manuscripts* and contended that fetishism was the "scientific" rendering of alienation (*Karl Marx*, p. 133).

It would, however, be incorrect to say that Korsch lacked any vision of the normative totality at the end of the revolutionary process. In particular, he seems to have stressed the withering away of the state and the integration of the social and the individual. One commentator, Leszek Kolakowski, goes so far as to say that "this Messianic era of the perfect integration of all human powers is the essence of Marx's Utopia, and Korsch deserves credit for reviving awareness of it" (*Main Currents of Marxism* vol. 3: *The Breakdown*, trans. P. S. Falla [Oxford, 1978], p. 316). And Hedda Korsch reports that before his death he worked on a manuscript dealing with the abolition of all divisions between classes, town and country, mental and physical labor, etc. (p. 45).

50. Korsch, *Marxism and Philosophy*, p. 114. Korsch, in fact, was generally hostile to Luxemburg, even after his Leninist period. See, for example, the remarks in Kellner, pp. 176f, 185. For attempts to defend Luxemburg against some of Korsch's charges, see Marramao, "Theory of the Crisis and the Problem of Constitution," *Telos* 26 (Winter 1975–76), pp. 149–150, and Norman Geras, *The Legacy of Rosa Luxemberg* (London, 1976).

51. See, in particular, Korsch's essay on "State and Counterrevolution" (1939) in Kellner.

52. Korsch, to be sure, on occasion felt defeated by his impotent protest against the Soviet Union, as demonstrated by his 1935 unpublished paper, "Position on Russia and the Communist Party," in Kellner. In fact, as early as 1928, Korsch could write to Partos of his retreat from a completely anti-Soviet position:

I came to see that one could not carry out a struggle against the whole world and the whole age with nothing behind oneself except nothing, and thus with the prospects of nothing as nothing; not because I was in itself against carrying out hopeless struggles—for, yes, I have already consciously done that earlier—but because I thought that there is no value in doing something only in thought, that even the worst reality would be better than merely standing in thought. (Kellner, p. 148)

It is instructive to compare this position to that of the Frankfurt School, which had much less difficulty "standing in thought."

consistent in his adherence to these principles. For in his faith in the existence of a revolutionary proletariat whose practice was the sole source of
radical theory, he constructed a highly idealized and unrealistic vision of
the working class.[53] If this image prevented him from compromising with
Stalinism, it also led him into the type of sectarian purism that traditionally characterizes ultra-Left ideologues. Because he was convinced of the
revolutionary role of the proletariat, Korsch held on to that organic view
of the revolution that Lukács had come to repudiate in the second essay on
Rosa Luxemburg in *History and Class Consciousness*. Even though he
praised Lukács for precisely this repudiation when he reviewed the latter's
Lenin in 1924,[54] and despite his brief support of the Comintern's "united
front" policy when he was a minister in the coalition government of
Thuringia in 1923–1924, Korsch moved leftward shortly thereafter and
never looked back. After the coalition was shattered, he attacked the SPD
as "social fascists." Rejecting the notion that capitalism had been stabilized, he praised Trotsky's intransigent doctrine of "permanent revolution." During the 1930s, he condemned the Popular Front as a hoax, and
when the war came, he exhorted the mythical working class of his imagination to avoid choosing sides between the Allies and the Axis. Instead, he
argued, "to fight against fascism means for the workers in the hitherto
democratic countries to fight first of all against the democratic branch of
fascism in their own countries."[55] By stubbornly holding on to an expressive view of the totality, even after his brief Hegelian flirtation in the early
1920s, Korsch grew further and further removed from the realities of
twentieth-century development.

The great irony of this quixotic dogmatism was that it accompanied a
reversion to the empirical inclinations of Korsch's youth. Indeed, he defended his anti-Leninist critique of party substitutionism by rejecting the
Hegelian distinction between essence and appearance. By 1939, he was
writing to his friend Paul Mattick about Hegel in these terms:

It is really a shame that the nonsense, overcome by the bourgeoisie, of a genuinely
'German' mystic from a hundred years ago, who at best mirrored the experience of
the great *bourgeois* revolutions from 1789 to 1830 in a *distorted form*, is still
today hindering again the activity of the workers and their thoughts.[56]

53. For a discussion of Korsch's tendency to idealize the working class, see Gian Enrico
Rusconi, "Korsch's Political Development," *Telos* 27 (Spring 1976).
54. "Georg Lukács: Lenin, Studie über den Zusammenhang seiner Gedanken," *Internationale* 12 (June 15, 1924); reprinted in *Die materialistische Geschichtsauffassung und andere Schriften*, ed. Erich Gerlach (Frankfurt, 1971), p. 148.
55. "The Fascist Counterrevolution" (1940) in Kellner, p. 258.
56. Kellner, p. 111.

Whether or not Korsch became an outright positivist is in dispute—he himself rejected the term with scorn[57]—nonetheless he defended a version of Marxism that he claimed was based on strict empirical verification. As early as his 1930 "Anti-Critique," Korsch expressed his uneasiness with the distinction between method and content in Marxist theory that Lukács had defended in *History and Class Consciousness*. Interestingly, he raised the issue in criticizing those who accented materialism over dialectics, but his complaint could easily be turned in the other direction; the privileging of either one over the other, he argued,

> prevents materialist philosophy from contributing to the further development of the empirical sciences of nature and society. In the dialectic *method and content are inseparably linked*; in a famous passage Marx says that "form has no value when it is not the form of its content." It is therefore completely against the spirit of the dialectic, and especially of the materialist dialectic, to *counterpose* the dialectical materialist "method" to the substantive results achieved by applying it to philosophy and the sciences. This procedure has become very fashionable in Western Marxism.[58]

In distancing himself from this fashion in "Western Marxism" (perhaps the first time that this term was used), Korsch was clearly rejecting the idealist indifference to empirical reality that Lukács had defended immediately after his conversion to Marxism. He was, in a sense, returning to the empirical impulse within classical historicism, that "*wie es eigentlich gewesen*" in Ranke's celebrated phrase, which linked historicism to positivism rather than to rationalism. All throughout the remainder of his career, Korsch insisted on the empirical verifiability of Marxism, arguing, to take an example from his 1935 essay "Why I am a Marxist,"

> As a matter of fact the revolutionary proletariat cannot, in its practical fight, dispense with the distinction between *true* and *false* scientific propositions. . . . In this sense and within these limits the *critical* principle of materialistic, revolutionary Marxism includes strict, empirically verifiable knowledge, marked by "all the precision of the natural science," of the economic laws of the movement and development of capitalist society and the proletarian class struggle.[59]

That the principle of "*true* and *false* scientific propositions" may not have been totally compatible with Korsch's revolutionary historicist injunction to ground knowledge in the historical process seems not to have

---

57. See his defense of Marxism as critical rather than positive in "Why I am a Marxist" in *Three Essays on Marxism*, p. 65; and his attack on Karl Popper in a letter to J. A. Dawson, May 3, 1948, in Kellner, p. 293.
58. Korsch, *Marxism and Philosophy*, p. 134.
59. Korsch, "Why I am a Marxist," pp. 67–68.

troubled him. The relativistic implications of the latter, which were drawn out most clearly in the non-revolutionary historicism of Karl Mannheim, were never fully reconciled with the demand to seek the precision of the natural sciences. In fact, in *Karl Marx*, where Marx's scientific status was staunchly defended, Korsch still claimed that its truth value was grounded in its proletarian class character.[60]

What does seem to have been called into question by Korsch's anti-Hegelian turn was his earlier faith in the longitudinal nature of the totality. In his 1937 essay "Leading Principles of Marxism," Korsch contended:

The false idealistic concept of evolution, as applied by bourgeois social theorists, is *closed* on both sides, and in all past and future forms of society rediscovers only itself. The new critical and materialistic Marxist principle of development is, on the other hand, *open* on both sides. Marx does not deal with Asiatic, Antique, or Feudal society, and still less with those primitive societies which preceded all written history, merely as "preliminary stages" of contemporary society. He regards them, in their totality, as so many independent historical formations which are to be understood in terms of their own categories.[61]

What may well account for this reversal of his earlier position was Korsch's bitter realization that Marxism, beginning with its founder, had underestimated the power of counter-revolutionary tendencies in society, which rendered untenable any optimism about the coherence of the whole historical process.[62]

Although Korsch may therefore have grown wary about longitudinal totalities, he still maintained great faith in the existence of latitudinal ones. Once again, his empiricism was compatible with an anti-Hegelian historicism. In "Leading Principles of Marxism" and again in *Karl Marx*, he defended what he called Marx's "principle of historical specification."[63] By this principle Korsch meant first, that Marxism was not a general science seeking timeless and immutable laws, and second, that it "comprehends all things social in terms of a definite historical epoch."[64]

60. Korsch, *Karl Marx*, p. 86. Kolakowski, who upholds the traditional view of truth as *adaequatio intellectus atque rei*, argues that this position entails a radical epistemological relativism that expressed "the latent anti-intellectualism of Marxism and Communism" (p. 321). In the light of Zinoviev's attack on the professorial Korsch, this charge may seem ironic, but it points to a very real difficulty in Korsch's position. In the terms of Oskar Negt, a commentator far more friendly to Marxism than is Kolakowski, it is the problem of "constitution" in Korsch's theory. By "constitution," Negt means both the epistemological ground of theory and the self-creation of the proletariat as a revolutionary class, which are related for Korsch. See his "Theory, Empiricism, and Class Struggle: On the Problem of Constitution in Karl Korsch," *Telos* 26 (Winter 1975–76).
61. Korsch, "Leading Principles of Marxism" in *Three Essays on Marxism*, p. 35–36.
62. See his essays on the counterrevolution in Kellner.
63. Korsch, "Leading Principles of Marxism," p. 16; *Karl Marx*, p. 24.
64. "Leading Principles of Marxism," p. 16.

This epoch was to be understood as a unified and coherent whole. How unified Korsch made clear in his 1932 introduction to *Capital*, where he discussed Marx's dialectical use of contradiction:

In many such cases a closer inspection reveals that the alleged "contradiction" is not really a contradiction at all, but is made to seem so by a symbolically abbreviated, or otherwise misleading, mode of expression. . . . It is not always possible, however, to resolve the contradictions so simply. Where the contradiction endures, and the anti-dialectician persists in his objection to it even as a function of a strictly systematic logical–deductive treatment of concepts, then this opponent will have to be placated with Goethe's remark on metaphorical usage, which Mehring refers to in his interesting study of Marx's style:

"Do not forbid me use of metaphor;
I could not else express my thoughts at all."[65]

Korsch then concluded in a manner that showed how far he had come from the Hegelian Marxism of *Marxism and Philosophy* in one sense, but how close he remained in another: "These tensions are all pictured as 'contradictions,' and this can be thought of as a sophisticated kind of metaphorical usage, illuminating the profounder connections and interrelation between things."[66] Korsch may no longer have held to the Hegelian view that contradictions nested in reality and were not only metaphors, but he still believed in a centered totality in which a connectedness could be discerned beneath the surface of apparent disjunctions. However much he may have shared an anti-Hegelian emphasis on the scientificity of Marx's work with later Western Marxists such as Althusser, he never anticipated their notion of a decentered totality. He was far closer to the Della Volpean recovery of the Kantian dimension in Marx's epistemology, as the following very important passage from *Karl Marx* makes clear:

We know that all these apparently separated and widely different spheres form together a universe of society in which, just as in a living organism, every part is connected with every other part. This "just as," by the way, is to be read as meaning "just as much as just as *little*." The author does not want in either case to be regarded as adhering to that mystic and unscientific theory of "whole-ism" according to which this connection is previously granted and needs only to be discovered in detail by the endeavor of the investigator. He would rather, with old Kant, regard the idea of whole-ism as a working principle which guides our strictly empirical research and may or may not hold in a given instance.[67]

If contradictions were metaphors and totality merely a Kantian regulative idea, Korsch was indeed thrown back on an empirical methodology

65. "Introduction to *Capital*," p. 58.
66. Ibid.
67. Korsch, *Karl Marx*, p. 214.

that could not guarantee the practical results he wanted. Not surprisingly, his last years were marked by growing uncertainty and equivocation. In fact, even while he was preparing *Karl Marx*, in which his solidarity with Marxist theory was insistently proclaimed, Korsch was already evincing serious doubts about its validity.[68] His critique of Hegel's philosophy was carried over into an attack on the political legacy of Hegelianism in Marx's adherence to bourgeois statist forms. He began to move closer to the anarchist tradition and planned for a while a study of Bakunin's theory of the state. Finally, in 1950, his disillusionment with Marxism reached its high point in his "Ten Theses on Marxism Today,"[69] where he ruefully concluded that "all attempts to restore the Marxist doctrine as a whole and in its original function as a theory of the working-class social revolution are reactionary utopias."[70]

Although his letters show that Korsch never completely abandoned his hope for a proletarian revolution or his belief that a reconstituted Marxism would help in this endeavor,[71] he remained theoretically uncertain and practically impotent until his death in 1961, five years after the onset of a debilitating attack of sclerosis. It is difficult to avoid agreeing with the somber conclusion of Eric Hobsbawm, however one may feel about the Leninist *Schadenfreude* underlying it, that Korsch "was left isolated, theoretically and practically sterile and not a little tragic, an ideological St. Simeon on his pillar."[72] The first flush of new enthusiasm for his ideas during the New Left era now past, it is possible to understand this outcome. For all his stress on practice, defense of empiricism, and criticism of the dogmatism of the orthodox Left, Korsch was himself dogmatic in his insistence on the priority of practice over theory, his idealization of the working class, and his refusal to probe the tensions between his revolutionary historicist and scientific readings of Marxism. One of the casualties of this rigidity was his concept of totality, which, as we have seen, remained expressive and harmonistic even though its genetic center became ambiguous and its epistemological ground unsatisfactorily defined.

These judgments are perhaps harsher than they should be, for in at least one respect Korsch's thinking about totality can be judged an advance over

68. See the articles in the section "The Crisis of Marxism," in Kellner.
69. "Ten Theses on Marxism Today," in Kellner. The article was written in 1950, but published nine years later in the French journal *Arguments*. In her *New Left Review* interview, Hedda Korsch insisted it was not a complete rejection of Marxism (p. 45).
70. Ibid., p. 281.
71. See, in particular, his letter of December 16, 1956, to Erich Gerlach, in Kellner, p. 295.
72. E. J. Hobsbawm, "Karl Korsch" in *Revolutionaries: Contemporary Essays* (New York, 1973), p. 160.

Lukács'. The issue is the role of nature in Marxist holism. Lukács, it will be recalled, based his resolution of the antinomies of bourgeois culture on the end of reification, which he conflated with the process of objectification. The social totality was thus understood as the creation of an immanent version of the transcendental subject, the proletariat as the universal class. Once it understood itself as both the subject and object of the historical process, reification and alienation would be overcome.

To make this analysis plausible, Lukács had to bracket the independent role of nature, which he claimed could only be a "societal category" for man. Dialectics was an affair of subjects and objects, or—more precisely—of subjects and their objectifications. Engels, therefore, had been wrong to argue for a dialectics of nature. As the neo-Kantians had argued, the methods of the cultural and the natural sciences were very different. The implications of all of this were blatantly idealist, as Lukács himself came to recognize, but these were the assumptions underlying his insistence in *History and Class Consciousness* on totality as the central category of Marxist thought.

Korsch, who was never convinced by the methodological arguments of the neo-Kantians, remained wedded to the Enlightenment belief that the natural sciences were on a continuum with the social sciences. In his 1932 introduction to *Capital*, he endorsed the controversial comparison made by Engels at Marx's grave between Marx and Darwin, contending that "unlike some of the modern obscurantists and demi-theologians of the so-called 'humanities,' [Marx] did not draw the conclusion that the description of man's social life permits a lesser degree of intellectual and empirical rigour and a higher ratio of subjectivity than the natural sciences themselves."[73] Even at his most Hegelian, in *Marxism and Philosophy*, Korsch refused to pit Marx against Engels and quoted the *Anti-Dühring* as an expression of their joint position:

Engels took all socio-historical phenomena (including socio-historic forms of consciousness) which were determined "in the last instance" by the economy, and added to them yet another, even more final "determination by nature." This last twist of Engels develops and sustains historical materialism; but . . . it in no way alters the dialectical conception of the relationship between consciousness and reality.[74]

When Korsch wrote his "Anti-Critique" in 1930, he specifically defended himself against the charge that he, like Lukács, had committed an "idealist deviation" by denying Engels' dialectics of nature. *Marxism and*

73. "Introduction to *Capital*," p. 42.
74. Korsch, *Marxism and Philosophy*, p. 92.

Philosophy, he boasted, "refrained in general and also with respect to this particular question ... from the one-sided fashion in which Lukács and Revai treated the views of Marx and Engels, as if they were completely at variance,"[75] although it did not assume their perfect identity. Later, in a 1935 letter to Paul Mattick, Korsch expressed his continued hostility to the denigration of nature in the more idealist variants of Western Marxism: "To me it appears that *nothing is primary here*; that *man–nature* and *man–man* are to be coordinated, that both are equiprimordial and fundamental, historically, logically, and practically."[76]

Korsch's resistance to the exclusion of nature from dialectics had its indirect costs, perhaps most notably his relative indifference to the concept of reification. But it allowed him to avoid the clearly idealist implications of Lukács' attempt to "out-Hegel Hegel" in *History and Class Consciousness*. It also meant that despite his intentions, the expressive unity of the latitudinal totalities of history was called into question by the role of nature within them. This implication was later drawn out in the work of the Frankfurt School, whose relations with Korsch were in most respects uneasy.[77] It also appeared in the earlier work of the two other figures in the Western Marxist tradition whose contribution must now be examined, Antonio Gramsci and Ernst Bloch. For, like Korsch, they offered models of totality alternative to Lukács, at the very time when the apparently coherent paradigm of Western Marxism was launched.

75. Ibid., p. 122.
76. Quoted in Kellner, p. 97.
77. This is not the place to examine Korsch's complicated relations with the Frankfurt School, but some points can be made. Although Korsch was influential in the founding of the Institute of Social Research in 1923, at least as a theoretical stimulus to its financial sponsor, Felix Weil, his role in Institute affairs during the 1920s was marginal. His activist political involvement contrasted with the detachment of most of the Institute's major figures. When both Korsch and the Institute were together in exile in the United States, he was invited to contribute some reviews, and plans were made for a possible collaboration on a book on dialectics that never materialized. Korsch's bitter reaction to the Institute is documented in his letter of November 20, 1938, to Paul Mattick, reprinted in Kellner, pp. 283–285. For some examples of the Frankfurt School's attitude towards Korsch, see the letters of Benjamin and Adorno quoted in Susan Buck-Morss, *The Origin of Negative Dialectics: Theodor W. Adorno, Walter Benjamin and the Frankfurt Institute* (New York and London, 1977), p. 207. In *Negative Dialektik* (Frankfurt, 1966), Adorno singled out Korsch as an example of identity theory because of his collapse of theory into practice (p. 144).

CHAPTER FOUR

The Two Holisms of Antonio Gramsci

The legacy of Antonio Gramsci, no less than that of Karl Korsch, has been vigorously contested by competing claimants.[1] But in Gramsci's case, the stakes have been immeasurably higher. For Gramsci, unlike Korsch, became the patron saint of a mass political movement, the powerful Communist Party which emerged from the anti-Fascist resistance in postwar Italy to become the vanguard of Eurocommunism. The official spokesmen of that movement soon transformed Gramsci into an indispensable source of theoretical legitimacy. But to do so, they had to tailor the implications of his work to the changed political demands of the postwar era. Led by Gramsci's university friend and later Party comrade, Palmiro Togliatti, the PCI (*Partito Comunista Italiano*) interpreted Gramsci as a forerunner of its own gradualist, coalition-building, national political line. His links to the earlier Neapolitan Hegelian tradition of Spaventa and Croce were underplayed in order to emphasize his adherence to a watered-down version of Leninism. Gramsci's central concept of "hegemony" was understood to imply the slow, progressive education of the population to socialism through an essentially democratic process of enlightenment.

The PCI's tendentious rendering of Gramsci's legacy was abetted by its monopoly of his work, most notably of the thirty-three notebooks containing some 2,848 pages that Gramsci's sister-in-law had smuggled out of his hospital room and sent to Moscow after his death in 1937. Selective publication of parts of his writings, especially his earlier works, helped color his

---

1. For a thorough discussion of the battles over Gramsci's legacy, see A. B. Davidson, "The Varying Seasons of Gramscian Studies," *Political Studies* 20, 4 (December 1972). For a more recent summary, see the articles and reviews in the special Gramsci issue of *Telos* 31 (Spring 1977).

reception until well into the 1960s. It was not, in fact, until 1975 that a complete critical edition of the *Quaderni del Carcere* (*The Prison Notebooks*) was finally published in four volumes by Valentino Gerratana.[2] The difficulties in assessing Gramsci's significance were not, however, produced solely by his publishing history. The conditions of intellectual production under which he labored also contributed greatly to the ambiguity of his inheritance. His earlier works were short and often hurried articles, over a thousand in number, for socialist newspapers such as *Il Grido del Popolo, Avanti!* and *L'Ordine Nuovo*.[3] Rarely more than a few pages in length, these essays and editorials were also too journalistic to allow him to develop any ideas reflectively. His mature writings, although intended "*für ewig*,"[4] were limited to fragmentary and elliptical entries in the notebooks allowed him by Mussolini's warders. Moreover, because of the constant threat of censorship, he often masked his arguments in euphemisms and vague generalizations. What has been called the "desituated"[5] mode of his discourse resulted from the need to allow a multiplicity of possible meanings to his remarks. Thus, while ranging over a wide variety of subjects, but never definitively or exhaustively exploring any, Gramsci bequeathed an enormously rich yet inconclusive body of thought to Italian and Western Marxism.

This very inconclusiveness has been accounted by some a source of strength. Just as Gramsci's incarceration meant he was spared the agonizing political choice between Stalinism and Left-oppositionism forced on Korsch and Lukács,[6] so too the unsystematic nature of his writings neces-

2. Gramsci, *Quaderni del Carcere. Edizione Critica a cura di Valentino Gerratana,* 4 vols. (Turin, 1975). For a discussion of this edition, see the review by Alastair Davidson in *Telos* 32 (Summer 1977).

3. Selections in English translation of these articles have appeared as *History, Philosophy and Culture in the Young Gramsci,* ed. Pedro Cavalcanti and Paul Piccone (St. Louis, 1975); *Antonio Gramsci: Selections from Political Writings 1910–1920,* with additional texts by Bordiga and Tasca, ed. Quintin Hoare, trans. John Mathews (New York, 1977); and *Antonio Gramsci: Selections from Political Writings (1921–1926),* with additional texts by other Italian Communist leaders, ed. and trans. Quintin Hoare (New York, 1978).

4. Letter to his sister-in-law, Tatiana Schucht, March 19, 1927, in *Antonio Gramsci, Letters From Prison,* ed., trans., intro. Lynne Lawner (New York, 1973), p. 79. The German term means "for eternity."

5. Perry Anderson, "The Antinomies of Antonio Gramsci," *New Left Review* 100 (November 1976–January 1977), p. 20. One can, of course, overemphasize Gramsci's ambiguity. At times, his intended meaning could be distorted by those interpreters who preferred to ignore it for their own purposes.

6. In prison, Gramsci did balk at the Comintern's shift in line in 1929 and the shake-up of the PCI that followed, but his qualms were not made public until after his death. See the discussion in Giuseppe Fiori, *Antonio Gramsci: Life of a Revolutionary,* trans. Tom Nairn (New York, 1971), chapter 26, and Paolo Spriano, *Antonio Gramsci and the Party: The Prison Years,* trans. John Fraser (London, 1979). Spriano is less convinced by the testimony of Gramsci's brother Gennaro than Fiori, who implies it shows Gramsci would have probably broken with or been expelled by the Party.

sitated by that same imprisonment allowed him to avoid certain theoretical choices as well. Put schematically, the major decision he never decisively made was between Croce and Lenin, neo-Hegelian humanism and
Bolshevism. Gramsci, to be sure, seems to have thought a creative synthesis of these two impulses could be forged. And indeed, many of his later
admirers found in his work this very integration, just as they claimed that
he had overcome such traditional tensions within Marxism itself as voluntarism versus spontaneism and economism versus Jacobinism. But for
others, Croce and Lenin seemed too unnatural a pair to be married for
very long in a true synthesis. For them, the real Gramsci was either a
Crocean humanist, whose intentions were ultimately irreconcilable with
Bolshevik theory and practice, or a flexible Leninist, who had overcome
the idealist impulses of his youth. Within these broad camps, there were
further and more subtle distinctions. Some Croceans uncoupled the Togliattian linkage of humanism with political reformism, stressing instead
Gramsci's Left-oppositionist, revolutionary dimension; whereas certain
Leninists, arguing that Gramsci had not gone far enough in the direction
of a real vanguard party, sought to "correct" him by reference to his main
PCI competitor, Amadeo Bordiga.[7] Moreover, when Gramsci was filtered
through later Western Marxist polemics over Althusserianism in France
or Critical Theory in Germany,[8] his legacy became even more vulnerable
to partisan and tendentious readings.

It would not, of course, be possible or even desirable now to rehearse the
still vigorous polemics surrounding Gramsci or to produce a fully articulated resolution of all the issues involved. What can be attempted instead
are the more modest tasks of isolating his contribution to the Western
Marxist tradition of holism and spelling out his similarities to and differences from the other figures we have already encountered. In so doing,
some of the ambiguities of his legacy may be resolved, while others may be
recognized as the irreconcilable antinomies that they in fact were.[9]

7. For examples of the former position, see Paul Piccone, "Gramsci's Hegelian Marxism," *Political Theory* 2, 1 (February 1974) and "Gramsci's Marxism: Beyond Lenin and
Togliatti," *Theory and Society* 3, 4 (Winter 1976); for an example of the latter, see Gwyn A.
Williams, *Proletarian Order: Antonio Gramsci, Factory Councils and the Origins of Communism in Italy, 1911–1921* (London, 1975). For a critique of Williams from a position
close to Piccone's, see the extended review by Carl Boggs in *Telos* 31 (Spring 1977).

8. The most important Althusserian reading of Gramsci is Christine Buci-Glucksmann,
Gramsci and the State, trans. David Fernbach (New York, 1980). See also the study by the
former Althusserian, Maria Antonietta Macciocchi, *Per Gramsci* (Bologna, 1974). On the
reception of Gramsci in France, see Chantal Mouffe and Anne S. Sassoon, "Gramsci in
France and Italy," *Economy and Society* 6 (February 1968); on the debate in Germany, see
Raymond Morrow, "Gramsci in Germany," *Telos* 22 (Winter 1974–75), which deals mainly
with Christian Riechers, *Antonio Gramsci: Marxismus in Italien* (Frankfurt, 1970).

9. The article by Perry Anderson cited in note 5 points to certain of these antinomies on a
political level; we will be interested primarily in their theoretical counterparts.

No commentator can deny that Gramsci was indeed an adherent of Marxist holism. There were few words in his vocabulary as frequently and positively used as "organic," whether in reference to the course of history, the value of democratic as opposed to bureaucratic centralism, the relation of certain intellectuals to their class, the unity of theory and practice, or the integrated nature of societies. In both his early and late writings, the same enthusiasm for organicism can be found. In 1918, for example, he contended:

Like man, society is always and only an ideal and historical unity which develops by negating and always overcoming itself. Politics and economics, environment and social organisms are always one, and one of the greatest merits of Marxism is to have affirmed this dialectical unity.[10]

More than a decade later, in "The Study of Philosophy" section of his notebooks, he argued in the same vein:

The individual does not enter into relations with other men by juxtaposition, but organically, in as much, that is, as he belongs to organic entities which range from the simplest to the most complex.[11]

Gramsci was in fact so unambiguously holistic that he frequently employed the term "totalitarian" to define his own position, even in the 1930s when it had begun to acquire sinister connotations.[12]

Gramsci's holism informed his image of Marxism both as a theory and as an historical force. As the materialist inheritor of what he called the "immanentist" tradition in bourgeois philosophy, Marxism for Gramsci fought any attempt at positing a realm of transcendence outside of history and, by extension, outside of its own theoretical ken. When he came to define "orthodoxy," which Lukács had equated with using the dialectical method, Gramsci contended that it lay in

the fundamental concept that the philosophy of praxis is "sufficient unto itself," that it contains in itself all the fundamental elements needed to construct a total and integral conception of the world, a total philosophy and theory of natural science, and not only that but everything that is needed to give life to an integral practical organization of society, that is, to become a total integral civilization.[13]

10. Gramsci, "Economic Organization and Socialism," *Il Grido del Popolo* (February 9, 1918); reprinted in Cavalcanti and Piccone, *Young Gramsci,* p. 88.

11. Gramsci, *Selections from the Prison Notebooks,* ed. and trans. Quintin Hoare and Geoffrey Nowell Smith (New York, 1971), p. 352.

12. See the references in *Selections from the Prison Notebooks,* pp. 147, 265 and 335. For a short history of the term's origins in Italy in the mid-1920s, see Bertram D. Wolfe, "Some Reflections on the Origins and Nature of Totalitarianism," *Lugano Review* (March 1973). For a defense of Gramsci's use, see Augusto del Noce, *Il Suicidro della Rivoluzione* (Milan, 1978), pp. 272–285.

13. Ibid., p. 462.

"Socialism," he claimed as early as 1917, "is an integral vision of life. It has a philosophy, a mysticism, and a morality."[14] This Sorelian emphasis on the global quality of Marxism as a kind of secular religion with irrational as well as rational appeal never left Gramsci, even as he distanced himself from the Council Communist inclinations of his earlier years. Like Lukács, Gramsci had come to the socialist movement after an immersion in the anti-positivist bourgeois culture of prewar Europe.[15] Born in Sardinia in 1891, the son of a lower-middle-class bureaucrat, he was educated in literature and linguistics at the University of Turin at a time when Croce's historicist idealism was at the height of its influence.[16] Croce had himself passed through a Marxist phase in the 1890s, during which he criticized positivist Marxists like Achille Loria with a number of the same arguments Gramsci would later marshal against similar targets.[17] Many years later, in 1947, Croce would in fact recognize in Gramsci "one of our own."[18]

Bergson's subjectivist voluntarism, filtered through Sorel, also seems to have impressed the young Gramsci,[19] who had little interest in the fatalistic economism and ontological materialism of the orthodox Marxism of the Second International. The only figure of that era to whom he was drawn was Antonio Labriola, whose practical emphasis he applauded. The phrase Gramsci borrowed from Labriola as a euphemism for Marxism in his

14. Gramsci, "Toward a Cultural Association," *Avanti!*, Turin ed. (December 18, 1917); reprinted in Cavalcanti and Piccone, p. 98.

15. Walter L. Adamson makes the interesting suggestion that Gramsci's dislike of positivism grew out of his interest in the Southern Question in Italian politics. "For Gramsci," he writes, "a pro-Southern stance also implied antipositivism because of the tendency of some positivists to explain the backwardness of the *Mezzogiorno* in terms of the biological inferiority of the inhabitants." "Toward the Prison Notebooks: The Evolution of Gramsci's Thinking on Political Organization, 1918–1926," *Polity* 12, 1 (Fall, 1979), p. 43.

16. The best general biography of Gramsci is by Fiori; see also Alastair Davidson, *Antonio Gramsci: Towards an Intellectual Biography* (London, 1977); Carl Boggs, *Gramsci's Marxism* (London, 1976); James Joll, *Antonio Gramsci* (London, 1977); Walter L. Adamson, *Hegemony and Revolution: A Study of Antonio Gramsci's Political and Cultural Theory* (Berkeley, 1980); as well as the older but still very useful book by John Cammett, *Antonio Gramsci and the Origins of Italian Communism* (Stanford, 1971). For a more specific treatment of Gramsci's indebtedness to Croce, see Maurice A. Finocchiaro, "Gramsci's Crocean Marxism," *Telos* 41 (Fall 1979). Other helpful treatments of Gramsci can be found in Chantal Mouffe, ed., *Gramsci and Marxist Theory* (London, 1979).

17. Gramsci, *Selections from the Prison Notebooks*, p. 458.

18. Croce, "Gramsci era uno die nostri," *Quaderni della Critica* (July, 1947).

19. In a meeting of the Socialist party on November 18, 1917, Gramsci was attacked by Mario Trozzi for the Bergsonian undercurrents in his extreme voluntarism. Gramsci seems to have taken the criticism to heart and reexamined the Bergsonian dimension of Sorel's work. See the discussion by the editors of *Selections from the Prison Notebooks*, p. 343. It should also be noted that Gramsci was attracted to similar ideas in other figures, such as the American syndicalist Daniel De Leon, whose theories on factory councils he admired. He was also impressed by the English shop steward movement after the war.

prison notebooks, "the philosophy of praxis," captured the activist impulse in his thought, which meant a keen awareness of the relative autonomy of politics from the economy. This impulse was so strong that in 1914, Gramsci briefly (and to his subsequent embarrassment) endorsed Mussolini's renegade socialist attack on Italy's "absolute neutrality" in the name of an "active and operative neutrality."[20] History, Gramsci always insisted, was the arena of conscious activity, practical will, subjective intervention, and political initiative, even if, *contra* Croce, the idea "finds its justification, the vehicle of affirmation in economic reality."[21]

In the years from 1913 to 1919 in particular, when the young Gramsci grew active in the Italian Socialist Party and became involved in the concrete struggles of the Turin proletariat, the idealist roots of his Marxism were most apparent. During this period, which invites comparison with Lukács' "revolutionary culturist"[22] phase, Gramsci insisted on the centrality of culture for socialism. Dismissing the reduction of the superstructure to a reflection of the socio-economic base, he invoked the notion of a cultural totality:

Persuaded that all human historical activity is one, that thought is one, I see in the resolution of any cultural problem the potential resolution of all others, and I believe that it is useful to accustom the intellect to grasping this unity in the manifold aspects of life, to accustom it to the organic search for truth and understanding, and to apply the fundamental principles of a doctrine to all contingencies.[23]

When the Russian Revolution took place, Gramsci eagerly welcomed it as a vindication of his activist and totalistic reading of Marxism. In his most celebrated early essay, "The Revolution Against *Capital*,"[24] he interpreted Lenin's achievement as the resurrection of political will against the economic determinism of those who reduced Marxism to the historical laws of Marx's best-known work. The Bolsheviks, he claimed, "live the Marxist thought that never dies, which is the continuation of Italian and Ger-

20. Gramsci, "Active and Operative Neutrality," *Il Grido del Popolo* (October 31, 1914); reprinted in Cavalcanti and Piccone, p. 166f. See the discussion of its implications in Adamson, p. 17f.

21. Gramsci, "Our Marx," *Il Grido del Popolo* (May 4, 1918); reprinted in Cavalcanti and Piccone, p. 10.

22. Alastair Davidson calls it Gramsci's period of "cultural messianism" in "Gramsci and Lenin, 1917–1922," *The Socialist Register*, ed. Ralph Miliband and John Saville (London, 1974), p. 127.

23. Gramsci, "Universal Language and Esperanto," *Il Grido del Popolo* (February 16, 1918); reprinted in Cavalcanti and Piccone, p. 29.

24. *Avanti!*, Milan ed. (November 24, 1917) and *Il Grido del Popolo* (January 5, 1918); reprinted in Cavalcanti and Piccone, p. 122f. (For a discussion of Gramsci's idealization of Lenin based on fragmentary knowledge of the Revolution, see Davidson, "Gramsci and Lenin, 1917–1922.")

man idealist thought, which in Marx was contaminated with positivist and naturalistic encrustations."[25] Although in later years Gramsci would grow uncertain about the fidelity of the Soviet leadership to these principles, he himself never completely abandoned them. In his prison notebooks, like Lukács and Korsch before him he singled out Bukharin's sociologistic and anti-dialectical version of Marxism for attack. "There is no doubt," he wrote, "that Hegelianism is (relatively speaking) the most important of the philosophical motivations of our author [Marx], particularly because it attempted to go beyond the traditional conceptions of idealism and materialism in a new synthesis."[26] He then added, in criticism of Bukharin's regression to ontological materialism:

It has been forgotten that in the case of a very common expression [historical materialism] one should put the accent on the first term—"historical"—and not on the second, which is of metaphysical origin. The philosophy of praxis is absolute "historicism," the absolute secularization and earthliness of thought, an absolute humanism of history.[27]

The Crocean phrase "absolute historicism" has come to be used as a convenient label for Gramsci's theory as a whole, and in fact it does capture a major ingredient in his thought. If its content is examined closely, however, it also betrays a critical ambiguity in his position, and one, moreover, that cannot be reduced to the opposition between his Crocean and Leninist inclinations. Instead, it reveals a perhaps even more fundamental conflict between the idealist and what might be called the communicative or linguistic underpinnings of his epistemology. The former is apparent in his generally receptive attitude towards the notion of history as a longitudinal totality, a coherent whole with an implicit telos. In an early essay arguing for the mastery of the culture of the past, he wrote:

If it is true that universal history is a chain of efforts by man to free himself from privileges, prejudices, and idolatries, then it is not clear why the proletariat, which wants to add another link to this chain, should not know how, why, and by whom it has been preceded, and what benefit it may derive from this knowledge.[28]

In a similar vein, he contended in 1918 that "there is in history a logic superior to contingent facts, to the will of single individuals, to the activity of particular groups, and to the industrious contributions of single na-

25. Ibid.
26. Gramsci, *Selections from the Prison Notebooks*, p. 465.
27. Ibid.
28. Gramsci, "Socialism and Culture," *Il Grido del Popolo* (January 29, 1916); reprinted in Cavalcanti and Piccone, p. 23.

tions."[29] Later still, in the prison notebooks, he defended the idea of progress against pessimists like Leopardi,[30] arguing that

The process of historical development is a unity in time through which the present contains the whole of the past and in the present is realized that part of the past which is "essential"—with no residue of any "unknowable" representing the true "essence." The part which is lost, i.e., not transmitted dialectically in the historical process, was in itself of no import, casual and contingent "dross," chronicle and not history, a superficial and negligible episode in the last analysis.[31]

History, in other words, is not merely a unified whole, but also one in which survival implies normative validation. This very idealist assumption, most cogently expressed in Schiller's remark that "world history is the world court," was soon called into question by other Western Marxists such as Benjamin and Adorno. But for Gramsci, it remained an article of faith, which sustained him during the long years in Mussolini's prison. It was combined, however, with a certain caution about the outcome of the historical process that set him apart from the more dogmatic Marxists who implicitly retained Hegel's defense of historical necessity. In arguing against those who believed in the preordained course of history, he wrote:

They do not understand history as free development of freely born and integrated energies, as something unlike natural evolution. . . . They have not learned that freedom is the force immanent in history which blows up all pre-established schemes.[32]

This formulation is, to be sure, highly ambiguous—what, after all, does it mean to call freedom a "force immanent in history" beyond the obvious point that some things are not predetermined?—but it does capture Gramsci's uneasiness over certain residues of the idealist position. Most notably, it expresses his reservations about the equation of rationality with the entire historical process and the premise that history is made by the objectification of a meta-subject. Gramsci never seems to have

29. Gramsci, "Wilson and the Russian Maximalists," *Il Grido del Popolo* (March 2, 1918); reprinted in Cavalcanti and Piccone, p. 129.
30. Gramsci, *Selections from the Prison Notebooks*, p. 357f.
31. Ibid., p. 409. Gramsci's stress on the present containing the whole of the past is related to his approval of Croce's famous dictum that "all history is contemporary history," which he expressed in "The Beard and the Band," *Avanti!*, Turin ed. (February 5, 1918); reprinted in Cavalcanti and Piccone, p. 86. If one were to ask where the center of gravity of Gramsci's notion of longitudinal totality can be found, the answer would be, in the present. He shared none of that nostalgia for a totalized past found in the early Lukács, nor did he bank as heavily on a future totalization as did Ernst Bloch.
32. Gramsci, "The Russian Utopia," *Avanti!*, Milan ed. (July 25, 1918) and *Il Grido del Popolo* (July 27, 1918); reprinted in Cavalcanti and Piccone, p. 153.

adopted the Lukácsian assumption that the proletariat is the surrogate for Hegel's Absolute Spirit, the genetic origin of the objective world. Despite the claims of Althusser and some of his followers,[33] a fully expressive notion of the totality was absent from Gramsci's theory.

Gramsci's neo-idealist historicism was in fact crossed with another set of intellectual assumptions, which were derived from the rival tradition of rhetoric in Italian history. It was these assumptions that led to what might be called a second, non-Crocean holism in his thought. To understand their implications for his "absolute historicism," a short detour through his philosophy of nature and the natural sciences is necessary. Korsch, it will be recalled, had taken Lukács to task for restricting dialectics too exclusively to society in *History and Class Consciousness.* Gramsci, although having no use for the naturalization of history,[34] shared Korsch's qualms over Lukács' utter rejection of Engels' dialectics of nature. Although he seems to have had only limited knowledge of Lukács' work and probably never met him, he did spend several months in Vienna in 1924 when *History and Class Consciousness* was being widely discussed. In the *Prison Notebooks,* he tentatively criticized Lukács:

> It would appear that Lukács maintains that one can speak of the dialectic only for the history of men and not for nature. He might be right and he might be wrong. If his assertion presupposes a dualism between nature and man he is wrong because he is falling into a conception of nature proper to religion and to Graeco-Christian philosophy and also to idealism which does not in reality succeed in unifying and relating man and nature to each other except verbally. But if human history should be conceived also as the history of nature (also by means of the history of science) how can the dialectic be separated from nature? Perhaps Lukács, in reaction to the baroque theories of [Bukharin's] *Popular Manual,* has fallen into the opposite error, into a form of idealism.[35]

In thus questioning Lukács' absolute separation of history and nature, Gramsci was in general accord with Korsch, but there was one crucial difference. Korsch had increasingly abandoned the Hegelianism of *Marxism and Philosophy* for a version of Marxism based on scientific verification. Thus, while continuing to insist on the class status of knowledge, he defended a Marxism that was methodologically continuous with the natural sciences. The dichotomy between the *Geisteswissenschaften* and the *Naturwissenschaften,* which was fundamental for Lukács, was rejected

---

33. For Althusser's critique of Gramsci's "historicism," see *Reading Capital* (with Etienne Balibar), trans. Ben Brewster (New York, 1970), p. 126f.

34. See, for example, his critique of this error in the *Action Française* in "Mysteries of Poetry and Culture," *Il Grido del Popolo* (October 19, 1918); reprinted in Cavalcanti and Piccone, p. 16f.

35. Gramsci, *Selections from the Prison Notebooks,* p. 448.

by Korsch. Gramsci, on the other hand, overcame the dualism implicit in Lukács' theory by assimilating the methods of the natural sciences to those of the cultural sciences. Scientific objectivity, he claimed, was not the correspondence of an external reality to man's conception of it. "Objective," he asserted,

always means "humanly objective" which can be held to correspond exactly to "historically subjective:" in other words, objective would mean "universal subjective." Man knows objectivity in so far as knowledge is real for the whole human race *historically* unified in a single unitary cultural system. But this process of historical unification takes place through the disappearance of the internal contradictions which tear apart human society. . . . There exists therefore a struggle for objectivity (to free oneself from partial and fallacious ideologies) and this struggle is the same as the struggle for the cultural unification of the human race.[36]

The very ideal of scientific objectivity, he insisted, was a residue of a religious faith in the existence of a truth outside of man created by God.[37]

Gramsci's alternative was what Kolakowski has called "species subjectivism and historical relativism."[38] Gramsci abandoned the traditional notion of truth as congruence between thought and its object in favor of a stress on rationality as demonstrated by historical efficacy and ultimate consensus. "Mass adherence or non-adherence to an ideology," he wrote, "is the real critical test of the rationality and historicity of modes of thinking. . . . Constructions which respond to the demands of a complex organic period of history always impose themselves and prevail in the end."[39]

Although the final remarks in this passage suggest a residual Hegelian faith in the rational outcome of history, its general tenor implies something very different. Rationality and objectivity for Gramsci are to be constructed in a process of cultural unification, a kind of collective *Bildung*. Instead of a meta-subject at the beginning of the process, who creates the totality expressively, there is an intersubjective totalization which is to be completed in the future, if at all. The ground of that totalization is no less cultural than it is economic. In fact, it entails the achievement of a linguistically unified community with shared meanings. "Great importance," he

36. Ibid., p. 445.

37. Gramsci, "Science and 'Scientific' Ideologies," *Telos* 41 (Fall 1979), p. 154.

38. Leszek Kolakowski, *Main Currents of Marxism*, vol. 3: *The Breakdown*, trans. P. S. Falla (Oxford, 1978), p. 249. For a more favorable account, see Adamson, who calls this aspect of Gramsci's work his "pragmatological dialectic" and contrasts it with Gramsci's idealist teleology, especially evident in his faith in the proletariat.

39. Gramsci, *Selections from the Prison Notebooks*, p. 341. In so arguing, Gramsci showed how naive he was about the irrational appeal of ideologies. Indeed, as Adamson points out (pp. 33 and 143), Gramsci, like Croce and Lukács, lacked any appreciation of psychology in general.

argued, "is assumed by the general question of language, that is, the question of collectively attaining a single cultural 'climate.'"[40]

As Ernesto Grassi has argued,[41] Gramsci shared with Vico and the rhetoricians of the Renaissance, such as Lorenzo Valla and Mario Nizolio, a view of language that was more hermeneutic and pragmatic than idealist or empiricist. Although certain modern idealists have tried to assimilate Vico to their own position, he actually diverged from idealism in several crucial respects. Unlike Hegel, he had no belief in the superiority of rational over poetic discourse. Nor did he assume that history was the objectification of a meta-subject. For Vico the intersubjective construction of shared meanings, the creation of a "sensus communis," was more important than the a priori postulation of truth. Theory and practice were thus intimately joined in a linguistic community, a totality without a constitutive totalizer.

Besides Croce, the other major interpreter of Vico in the period of Gramsci's intellectual development was Sorel. His notion of collective social myths was truer to Vico's intentions than Croce's idealist rationalization of the *New Science*. It is tempting to speculate that Gramsci, who was hostile to Sorel's anti-Jacobinism,[42] may have nonetheless absorbed his pragmatic view of language. There is, however, no evidence to support this assumption. What we do know is that Gramsci studied linguistics at the University of Turin at a time when the theories of pragmatists like Giovanni Vailati (1863–1909) were highly influential. Although Gramsci never fully identified with their position,[43] he seems to have built his own theory of language partly on pragmatic foundations. Even more important, as Franco lo Piparo has recently shown,[44] was the influence of Matteo Bartoli, who taught Gramsci "glottologia" at the University of Turin. A fervent enemy of the neo-grammarians with their search for formal linguistic regularities, Bartoli emphasized the specific historical and social contexts in which language developed. Although Gramsci disappointed his teacher by ultimately rejecting a career in linguistics, he remained indebted to Bartoli's anti-formalist theories. Arguing against the illusion of a pure language that would transparently reveal the objective world in its true light, Gramsci followed his mentor in asserting that language was inevitably historical and metaphorical:

40. Ibid., p. 349.
41. Ernesto Grassi, *Humanismus und Marxismus: Zur Kritik der Verselbtständigung von Wissenschaft* (Reinbek bei Hamburg, 1973), p. 65f.
42. Gramsci, *Selections from the Prison Notebooks*, p. 130.
43. See his criticisms in *Selections from the Prison Notebooks*, pp. 348–49.
44. lo Piparo, *Lingua Intellettuali Egemonia in Gramsci* (Bari, 1979).

The whole of language is a continuous process of metaphor, and the history of semantics is an aspect of the history of culture; language is at the same time a living thing and a museum of fossils of life and civilizations.[45]

It was thus folly to attempt to construct an artificial universal language like Esperanto, which was no more than "the delusion of a cosmopolitan, humanitarian and democratic mentality that has not yet been rendered fertile and not yet disenchanted by historical criticism."[46] It was also perhaps futile to expect that popular language could attain the precision of philosophy, at least in the near future. Thus, the word "materialism," although inappropriate in any strictly philosophical sense as a definition of Marxism, was permissible as an expression of the common man's rejection of transcendentalism.[47]

In so arguing, Gramsci anticipated the view associated with the later Wittgenstein and the hermeneutics tradition in Germany culminating in Hans-Georg Gadamer that language was its use, a social process of continuing development, a source of commonly accepted cultural conventions. But because of his optimistic belief that a broadly based cultural consensus could be created he came even closer to the position more recently advocated by Jürgen Habermas. Habermas, like Gramsci, derived some of his ideas from the pragmatic tradition—in his case, that of C. S. Pierce, who argued for the grounding of truth in a community of scientists. He also shared Gramsci's discursive view of language as an intersubjective practice, as well as his insistence on a future consensus as the ground of rationality and truth. Like Gramsci, he jettisoned the idealist belief, still held by Lukács, that the proletariat was the meta-subject of history.

Habermas differed from Gramsci, however, in his relative neglect of the metaphoricality of language in favor of its rationalist potential. In fact, Habermas' notion of a perfect speech situation as the telos of communication, to which we will return later, implied the overcoming of linguistic ambiguity, even if only as a regulative ideal. Although this is not the place to enter into a discussion of the complex meaning of metaphoricality, it can be said that one of its functions is to resist the idea that language is univocal. The implications of this resistance have been drawn less by Habermas than by the French post-structuralists such as Jacques Derrida and Jacques Lacan, who have built on Nietzsche's idea of infinite metaphoricality to emphasize what might be called language's decen-

45. Gramsci, *Selections from the Prison Notebooks*, p. 450.
46. Gramsci, "Universal Language and Esperanto," p. 32.
47. Gramsci, *Selections from the Prison Notebooks*, p. 454.

tering and detotalizing effects. Although it would be very misleading to equate Gramsci's position with theirs, there is perhaps a hint of their rejection of closure in his statement made in 1917:

> We distinguish ourselves from other men because we conceive of life as *always* revolutionary, and consequently tomorrow we shall not declare as definite a world realized by us, but we shall always leave the door open for betterment and for superior harmonies. We shall never be conservative, not even in a socialist regime, but we want the watchmaker of revolutions not to be a mechanical fact such as the uneasiness [sic], but the audacity of thought which creates always higher and more brilliant social myths.[48]

If not a foreshadow of post-structuralism, this statement is at least an anticipation of the preference for open-ended totalizations over fixed totalities in the later Sartre—although Gramsci was less pessimistic about the inevitability of detotalizations.

In fact, Gramsci never thematically developed the detotalizing implications of the metaphoricality of language. Instead, the importance of building a new speech community remained the dominant impulse of his work. Only by understanding its prominence can we make sense of two crucial contributions Gramsci made to the Western Marxist tradition of holism: his emphasis on national differences, and his stress on the role of intellectuals in building a new cultural hegemony.

Although Gramsci did not entirely isolate national class struggles from their international context,[49] he was far more sensitive to their uniqueness than a host of Marxist theorists, from Luxemburg to Bordiga. As such, he was a legitimate progenitor of Togliatti's policy of "polycentrism," which lay the groundwork for the Eurocommunism of the 1970s. In his studies of Italian history, he always pointed to the cosmopolitan role of the Church and the particularist resistance of local dynasties as impediments to the creation of a unified state.[50] While fulminating against artificial universal languages like Esperanto, he nonetheless advocated the overcoming of regional dialects as a critical step towards the cultural unification of Italy. And most important of all, he argued for the specific nature of revolutionary situations in different countries. For all his apparent acquiescence in the Bolshevization of the PCI and his admiration for Lenin's achievement, he insisted that Western European Communist movements

48. Gramsci, "The Watchmaker," *Il Grido del Popolo* (August 18, 1917); reprinted in Cavalcanti and Piccone, p. 37.
49. See, for example, his remarks in "The Return to Freedom . . . ," *Avanti!*, Piedmont ed. (June 26, 1919); reprinted in *Selections from Political Writings (1910–1920),* p. 69. For a critique of the limitations of Gramsci's national focus, see Alberto Asor Rosa, "Gramsci on Italian Cultural History," *Praxis* 4 (1978).
50. Gramsci, *Selections from the Prison Notebooks,* p. 117f.

should adopt tactics suited to their own situations. In so arguing, Gramsci may be called the first self-conscious "Western Marxist." In the now celebrated military metaphors of the *Prison Notebooks*,[51] he contrasted the Russian "war of maneouvre" with the Western European "war of position." The latter, he claimed, was necessitated by the much stronger role played by bourgeois civil society outside of Russia in perpetuating capitalist rule. Although the precise relationship between state and civil society in the West was never consistently worked out by Gramsci,[52] the notion that national differences mattered remained a central tenet of his thought.

A striking example of this commitment can be seen in his contrast of Trotsky with Lenin. The former, he argued, "apparently 'Western,' was in fact a cosmopolitan—i.e., superficially national and superficially Western or European. Ilitch [Lenin] on the other hand was profoundly national and European."[53] This attack on Trotsky, which was also directed at Bordiga, was aimed at his doctrine of "permanent revolution," which implied an unceasing application of offensive revolutionary pressure no matter what individual circumstances prevailed. Korsch, it will be recalled, found "permanent revolution" congenial, in part because of his tendency to homogenize the international proletariat. Although Gramsci's critique of it was a veiled defense of Stalin's notion of "revolution in one country," its real importance can only be appreciated in the context of Italian politics.

"Permanent revolution," Gramsci maintained, was inappropriate as a policy in a country like Italy, where a gradual building of coalitions among oppressed groups was absolutely essential.[54] Strongly influenced in his youth by Gaetano Salvemini's writings on the "southern question," Gramsci always insisted on the importance of the peasants of the *Mezzogiorno* as allies of the proletariat. Unlike Bordiga, he did not adopt that "organic" view of the revolution as a purely proletarian act that was characteristic of Marxist holism at its most expressive. If anything, he supported what might be called a more decentered notion of the totality, which inclined him to the position held by Lukács when he wrote the "Blum Theses." Not surprisingly, later commentators even discerned anticipations of Althusser's views in this stance, despite Althusser's initial disdain for Gramsci's historicism.[55]

51. Ibid., p. 229f.
52. For a discussion of the inconsistencies, see Anderson, "The Antinomies of Antonio Gramsci."
53. Gramsci, *Selections from the Prison Notebooks*, p. 237.
54. Nor was he in favor of Trotsky's program of forced industrialization in Russia at the cost of the peasants, a policy later, of course, adopted by Stalin. See Fiori, *Antonio Gramsci*, p. 213f.
55. John Merrington, "Theory and Practice in Gramsci's Marxism" in *Western Marx-*

Whether or not this comparison is completely valid, it is clear that Gramsci had little use for the "workerist" purism of the Left opposition to Communism. Arguing for what he called an "historic bloc,"[56] Gramsci generally supported tactical alliances such as the "united front from below," which he promoted after Mussolini's victory showed him the bankruptcy of proletarian sectarianism. He deliberately borrowed the name *L'Unita* from Salvemini's earlier review of the same name for the paper he edited from 1924 to 1926 in the hope of mending relations with Giacinto Menotti Serrati's Socialist Party. Accordingly, he had little use for putchist tactics like those followed in the abortive "March Action" in Germany in 1923 or for Bordiga's purist abstentionism from parliamentary politics. And unlike the more opportunist Togliatti, he opposed the Comintern's left turn in 1928, when the socialists were damned as "social fascists." Although, as Colletti has pointed out,[57] Gramsci's defense of unity was not the same as the Popular Front strategy of the 1930s, which was more concerned with preserving bourgeois institutions and defending the Soviet Union than in sparking a revolution, he nonetheless felt that revolution could come only through a national coalition of oppressed groups— led, to be sure, by the working class.

Gramsci's stress on the national issue was in part due to the example of nineteenth-century Italian idealism. As Paul Piccone has observed,[58] Italian neo-Hegelians were split over the question of nationalism, Bertrando Spaventa defending Italian unification against Augusto Vera's abstract universalism. Very much in the spirit of Spaventa, Gramsci interpreted Hegel's call for a "concrete universal" in national terms. Yearning for the creation of an "ethical state," a term Gramsci would use approvingly,[59] the neo-Hegelians had emphasized the crucial need to build a national culture. Gramsci's celebrated concept of hegemony was an outgrowth of this

---

ism: A Critical Reader, ed. *New Left Review* (London, 1978), pp. 144. Althusser himself came to appreciate Gramsci in his later work. See, for example, his remarks in *Lenin and Philosophy and Other Essays,* trans. Ben Brewster (New York, 1971), p. 12.

56. As was the case with many of Gramsci's other terms, "historic bloc" had several meanings. In addition to a coalition of oppressed groups, it was used to denote unities of nature and spirit, superstructure and substructure, and subjective and objective moments of the historical process. As Adamson argues (pp. 178–79), it was used to circumvent the privileging of one dimension of the totality over any other.

57. Lucio Colletti, "Gramsci and the Revolution," *New Left Review* 65 (January–February 1971).

58. Paul Piccone, "From Spaventa to Gramsci," *Telos* 31 (Spring, 1977), p. 44f.

59. Gramsci, *Selections from the Prison Notebooks,* pp. 258–59. Gramsci, to be sure, recognized that insofar as the ethical state was posited as a present reality above class conflict, it was an ideology. See his remarks in "Three Principles, Three Orders," *Avanti!* (June 6, 1918); reprinted in Cavalcanti and Piccone, p. 72. For more on Gramsci and the "ethical state" tradition, see Adamson, *Hegemony and Revolution,* p. 167f.

concern. "It is in the concept of hegemony," he claimed, "that those exigencies which are national in character are knotted together."[60] Although Gramsci himself accorded Lenin the honor of having conceived the notion of hegemony, and indeed it was current in Russian Marxist circles before the Revolution,[61] it received in Gramsci's hands a new emphasis on cultural consensus that was generally muted in the Bolshevik usage. Here Gramsci's interest in building a linguistic community as the basis for socialism must be taken into account. The Western "war of position" was to be fought largely, although not entirely, on the field of culture.

Gramsci contrasted hegemony or "direction," which he tended to associate with the power of cultural institutions in civil society, to "domination," which meant the directly coercive force of the state. Both operated to support the bourgeois state's continuing control of society. In the early 1920s, he tried to transcend the sterile alternative between the culturalist tactics of Tasca and the power-political strategy of Bordiga,[62] because he felt the Italian "war of position" might soon develop into a more dynamic "war of maneouvre," as had happened in Russia. But in the period of proletarian retreat after 1922, a revolutionary situation no longer prevailed, a fact gradually, if reluctantly, acknowledged by most socialist militants. As a result, although Gramsci continued to call for a "dual perspective"[63] in politics, the emphasis in his prison writings was more on the need to prepare the ground for a new totality through the creation of proletarian hegemony than on the violent overthrow of the state. More precisely put, what was required was a prefigurative counter-hegemony, which would undermine the power of bourgeois ideology over the masses through a process of political education.

Even after the revolution, Gramsci intimated, the need to instill a new hegemonic consciousness in the masses would still exist for some time. But then hegemony would not be an affair of civil society alone. In terms reminiscent of Fichte's call for a tutelary state, he argued,

60. Gramsci, *Selections from the Prison Notebooks*, p. 241. Gramsci's concept of hegemony has been among the most widely discussed aspects of his thought. See, for example, Joseph Femia, "Hegemony and Consciousness in the Thought of Antonio Gramsci," *Political Studies* 23:1 (March 1975); and Thomas Bates, "Gramsci and the Theory of Hegemony," *Journal of the History of Ideas* 36, 2 (April–June 1975).

61. Anderson, "The Antinomies of Antonio Gramsci." p. 15f.

62. Some of the arguments of Tasca and Bordiga are contained in Gramsci, *Selections from Political Writings (1910–1920)*.

63. Gramsci, *Selections from the Prison Notebooks*, p. 169. As the editors explain in a footnote, the term meant the "dialectical unity of the moments of force and consent in political action." First used by Zinoviev at the Fifth World Congress of the Comintern in 1923, "dual perspective" became Gramsci's watchword against the "rightist" stress on consent alone in the 1926–28 period and the "leftist" emphasis on force in the so-called "third period" of the Comintern that followed.

The State must be conceived of as an "educator," in as much as it tends precisely to create a new type or level of civilization. Because one is acting essentially on economic forces, reorganizing and developing the apparatus of economic production, creating a new structure, the conclusion must not be drawn that superstructural factors should be left to themselves, to develop spontaneously, to a haphazard and sporadic germination. The State, in this field, too, is an instrument of "rationalization," of acceleration and of Taylorization.[64]

With the disastrous experience of Communist cultural "Taylorization" behind us, it is hard not to detect in this statement a license for repression. But Gramsci meant by the post-revolutionary state something very different from the rule of Party bureaucrats. Instead, the "educators" of the new hegemonic totality were to be the intellectuals, the vanguard of the coming linguistic and cultural community.

No other Western Marxist was as keenly interested in the role of the intellectuals in the social whole as was Gramsci, and none acknowledged their links with the concept of totality as candidly as he did. For all his indebtedness to Sorel's global notion of socialism as an integral worldview, he did not share the Frenchman's hostility to intellectuals, a hostility that animated Bordiga and many of his socialist contemporaries.[65] Nor did Gramsci have much use for the "workerist" celebration of the proletariat's intrinsic wisdom, which so often infused Korsch's analysis. A better Hegelian than Korsch, he recognized the importance of mediation in history and frankly acknowledged the role of intellectuals as mediators of the new socialist totalization, bridging the gap between the old society and the new.

In the literature on Gramsci, there has been considerable debate over whether this mediation should be understood as "external" or "internal" to the working class.[66] If the former, then Gramsci would be open to Korsch's charge against Lenin, Kautsky, and Luxemburg, that he wanted to bring class consciousness to the proletariat from without. If "internal," he risked regressing to the naive belief that proletarian *praxis* autonomously generated its own theory. Gramsci's solution to this di-

64. Ibid., p. 247. "It is possible to imagine the coercive element of the State withering away by degrees," he wrote, "as ever-more conspicuous elements of regulated society (or ethical state or civil society) make their appearance" (p. 263).

65. Davidson, *Antonio Gramsci: Towards an Intellectual Biography,* p. 84. As Davidson points out, Bordiga's animus towards intellectuals was also shared by Mussolini. For an excellent treatment of Gramsci's views on this question, see Jerome Karabel, "Revolutionary Contradictions: Antonio Gramsci and the Problem of Intellectuals," *Politics and Society* 6, 2 (1976).

66. Piccone, for example, contends that Gramsci meant an "internal mediator" ("Gramsci's Hegelian Marxism," p. 35). But Boggs argues the opposite (*Gramsci's Marxism,* p. 99).

lemma was a subtle and complicated one. Very much aware of the elite theories of Pareto and Mosca then current in Italy, he sought to avoid their cynical naturalization of hierarchy without, however, endorsing the spontaneism of certain pre-Leninist theoreticians. "All men are intellectuals," he contended, "but not all men have in society the function of intellectuals."[67] The absolute distinction between intellectuals and non-intellectuals was thus an historical construct that would disappear with the achievement of socialism. Even before that event, intellectuals were not to assume total control over the revolutionary struggle. For "the popular element 'feels' but does not always know or understand; the intellectual element 'knows' but does not always understand and in particular does not always feel."[68] Intellectuals must, therefore, integrate their knowledge with the passions of the masses in order to avoid becoming a caste or priesthood. They must form an "intellectual/moral bloc"[69] with the populace.

Gramsci further nuanced this analysis by distinguishing between organic and traditional intellectuals. The former had emerged directly out of the class whose consciousness they helped articulate; the latter had once been organic, but later assumed a certain autonomy in relation to the class of their origin. The medieval clerics of the Catholic Church and the modern figure of Croce, who fancied themselves above all class ties, were typical traditional intellectuals. It was Gramsci's fervent hope that the proletariat would generate its own organic intelligentsia, which would be the internal mediator of its revolutionary struggle, the herald of a new hegemony. But he recognized that in the period of transition certain traditional intellectuals, exemplified by Marx and Engels themselves, would make common cause with the working class.

The transition has, to put it mildly, lingered far longer than Gramsci would have hoped, and his optimism about the emergence of organic intellectuals from within the working class has not been justified, at least not yet. With the odd exception, such as Raymond Williams in Britain, the leading intellectuals of twentieth-century Marxism have been renegades from the middle class. And as critics of the New Left never tire of repeating, most of its members came from relatively privileged strata of society. Although some attempts were made in the 1960s to talk of a "new working class"[70] of technocrats, engineers, and middle-level managers, it is not

67. Gramsci, *Selections from the Prison Notebooks*, p. 9.
68. Ibid., p. 418.
69. Ibid., pp. 332–33. See also his statement on p. 350, which anticipates Habermas' stress on the mutuality of education between leaders and workers.
70. The major theorists of the "new working class" were André Gorz and Serge Mallet. For an account of their thought, see Dick Howard, "New Situation, New Strategy: Serge

at all clear that Gramsci would have considered them the organic intellectuals of the proletariat. Within Communist societies, moreover, recent
commentators have noted a tendency for intellectuals to represent their
own interests rather than those of the totality.[71]

Gramsci's reflections on the role of the intellectuals were also based on
the naive assumption that converted traditional and organic intellectuals
would come together in a less exclusively vanguardist party. "That all
members of a political party should be regarded as intellectuals," he
wrote, "is an affirmation that can easily lend itself to mockery and caricature. But if one thinks about it nothing could be more exact. . . . What
matters is the function, which is directive and organizational, i.e., educative, i.e., intellectual."[72] In the long section of the *Prison Notebooks* entitled "The Modern Prince," Gramsci attempted to trace the lineage of the
Communist Party back through Jacobinism to Machiavelli's *Prince*. With
virtually no reference to the councils that he had championed in 1919 and
1920, when he was explicitly anti-Jacobin,[73] he defended the Party as the
"proclaimer and organizer of an intellectual and moral reform, which also
means creating the terrain for a subsequent development of the national–
popular collective will towards the realization of a superior, total form of
modern civilization."[74] In short, the Party, as he told his fellow prisoner,
Athos Lisa, in 1933, was the collective expression of the organic intellectuals of the working class.[75]

Because Gramsci so closely identified the Communist Party with the
organic intellectuals—even though it had been such a party which had
denounced Korsch and Lukács in 1924 precisely for their intellectualism—there was no place in his theory for the unattached, yet critical,
intellectuals, the Sartres, Adornos, and Goldmanns, who would later
emerge as the leading voices of Western Marxism. Believing that the Party
was the central mediator of the proletariat's drive for totalization, he
failed to see how external to the consciousness of the working class it
could become, especially when Communism came to power, and concomitantly, how vital a role might still be played by critical traditional intellectuals who did not pretend to be organic. Nor did he appreciate the tension

Mallet and André Gorz" in *The Unknown Dimension: European Marxism Since Lenin*, ed.
Dick Howard and Karl Klare (New York, 1972).
    71. See George Konrád and Ivan Szelényi, *The Intellectuals on the Road to Class Power:
A Sociological Study of the Role of the Intelligentsia in Socialism* (New York, 1979).
    72. Gramsci, *Selections from the Prison Notebooks*, p. 16.
    73. See, for example, his remarks in "Notes on the Russian Revolution," *Il Grido del
Popolo* (April 29, 1917); reprinted in Cavalcanti and Piccone, p. 127.
    74. Gramsci, *Selections from the Prison Notebooks*, p. 133.
    75. Ibid., p. xci.

between the Party's instrumental attitude towards the masses and its educative role, a tension his own work embodied in its uneasy juxtaposition of military and pedagogical metaphors. Thus, despite his intentions, Gramsci's concept of the Party could be accused of harboring totalitarian implications.[76]

Yet another difficulty in Gramsci's theory of the intellectuals concerned the type of education they were supposed to foster.[77] In 1917, when he was still very deeply immersed in Croce's thought, he argued that proletarian training should be in the liberal arts:

In essence, we need a humanistic school, as was understood by the ancients and more recently by the men of the Renaissance. . . . Even the sons of proletarians must have before them all the possibilities, all the areas open, in order to best realize their own individuality and thus develop in the most profitable way for themselves and for the collectivity.[78]

But in the *Prison Notebooks*, he claimed instead that "in the modern world, technical education, closely bound to industrial labor even at the most primitive and unqualified level, must form the basis of the new type of intellectual."[79] In accord with his definition of the intellectual's function as practical organizer and director of the production process, he argued in characteristic totalizing fashion for the continuity of humanistic and technical knowledge: "From technique-as-work one proceeds to technique-as-science and to the humanistic conception of history, without which one remains 'specialized' and does not become 'directive' (specialized and political)."[80]

---

76. The most extensive critique of the totalitarian potential in Gramsci is A. Garosci, "Totalitarismo e storicismo nel pensiero di Antonio Gramsci" in *Pensiero politico e storiografia moderna* (Nistri-Lischi, 1954). The same position is defended by Neil McInnes, *The Western Marxists* (London, 1972), George Lichtheim, *Marxism: An Historical and Critical Study* (New York, 1961), and H. Stuart Hughes, *Consciousness and Society* (New York, 1958). For attempted refutations, see the articles by Femia and Merrington cited above, and Adamson, *Hegemony and Revolution*, pp. 240–41.

77. For an extended discussion of Gramsci's theories of education, see Harold Entwistle, *Antonio Gramsci: Conservative Schooling for Radical Politics* (Boston and London, 1979). See also the critical review by Henry A. Giroux in *Telos* 45 (Fall 1980).

78. Gramsci, "Men or Machines?," *Avanti!*, Turin ed. (December 24, 1917); reprinted in Cavalcanti and Piccone, p. 35. Fiori, however, quotes the memoir of Annibale Pastore, one of Gramsci's philosophy professors at Turin, which suggests the young Gramsci's impatience with a purely Crocean humanism:

Another very important thing which drew him towards me was my emphasis on experimental logic, on technical innovation, on the transition from *homo sapiens* to *homo faber*, that is, from the logician to the engineer, to the technician, the mechanic, the worker who controls a machine: from mental labor to manual labor. In short, like the outstanding pragmatist that he was, Gramsci was concerned above all else at this time to understand *how ideas become practical forces*. (p. 93)

79. Gramsci, *Selections from the Prison Notebooks*, p. 9.
80. Ibid. p. 10.

Gramsci's optimism about unifying technical and humanistic education was reflected as well in his controversial attitude towards the techniques of improving worker efficiency associated with the American Frederick Winslow Taylor. How avidly Gramsci embraced Taylorization has
been disputed,[81] but it does seem clear that he was intrigued by its potential as a means to discipline the working class, especially the Italian working class, to achieve higher levels of productivity. As a result, he seems to
have underestimated the dehumanizing implications of Taylorization,
which Lukács, with his sharper eye for manifestations of reification, more
clearly perceived.[82] Nor did he rigorously conceptualize, as Habermas
was to do, the possible tensions between technological and hermeneutic
cognition. For all his insight into the rhetorical dimensions of language,
he never fully worked out the potential conflict between an instrumental
and an intersubjective cultural practice. Thus, he naively relied on an idealized version of the Communist Party to act as both the organizer of
production and the creator of a new hegemony. As the sorry history of the
Soviet Union demonstrated, it was far better suited to the former than the
latter task.

Another way of understanding this problem can be found by returning
to Gramsci's attitude towards nature. His "absolute historicism," as we
have seen, meant a totally anthropocentric epistemology, which virtually
reduced the natural sciences to a variant of the cultural sciences. In the
name of a rigorously anti-transcendental humanism, Gramsci tended to
reduce nature to an object for human exploitation. In fact, he frequently
asserted that socialism meant the rational domination of nature.[83] The
result of this assumption was what might be called "species imperialism,"[84] an attitude whose dangers were not fully understood by Western

81. Piccone, for example, distinguishes between Lenin's approval of Taylorism and
Gramsci's on the grounds that the latter situated it in a more complicated social matrix and
recognized its dehumanizing potential ("Gramsci's Marxism: Beyond Lenin and Togliatti,"
p. 499). In contrast, Martin Clark argues that Gramsci saw Taylorism as fully compatible
with his advocacy of Factory Councils and indeed endorsed it as a way to discipline the
Italian working class (*Antonio Gramsci and the Revolution that Failed* [New Haven 1977],
p. 70). See also the discussions in Enzo Rutigliano, "The Ideology of Labor and Capitalist
Rationality in Gramsci," *Telos* 31 (Spring 1977), and Adamson, pp. 54–55. The relevant
texts are translated in the "Americanism and Fordism" section of the *Selections from the
Prison Notebooks*. It is difficult not to read them as essentially a defense of the socialist
potential in Taylorism.
82. Lukács, *History and Class Consciousness,* trans. Rodney Livingstone (Cambridge,
Mass., 1971), p. 88.
83. Gramsci, *Selections from the Prison Notebooks,* pp. 358 and 360.
84. This term is a variation of Alvin W. Gouldner's "humanistic imperialism" in his
critique of *History and Class Consciousness*. See *For Sociology: Renewal and Critique in
Sociology Today* (New York, 1973), p. 420. Interestingly, it was also used by Julien Benda in
his controversial *The Treason of the Intellectuals,* trans. Richard Aldington (New York,

Marxists until the Frankfurt School's critique of the "dialectic of enlightenment"[85] in the 1940s. Among the founding fathers, only Ernst Bloch seems to have been sensitive to its potential difficulties. For Bloch, the utopian nature of a natural subject was needed to counter the arrogance of an unchecked humanism.

Before turning to Bloch's idiosyncratic contribution to the tradition of Marxist holism, one final point must be made about Gramsci concerning his image of a normative totality. As we have seen, Gramsci was less consistently idealist than the Lukács of *History and Class Consciousness*. Lacking a firm belief in the existence of a meta-subject which objectified itself in the social world, he paid far less attention to the question of reified objectification than did his Hungarian counterpart. As a result, he never posited a totally dereified identity of subject and object as the normative whole promised by socialism. That Fichtean impulse in the early Lukács, which led to his mythologizing the active meta-subject of history, was absent in Gramsci, who challenged a similar idealization of action in the Italian philosopher Giovanni Gentile. Marxism, he contended with reference to Gentile, is "philosophy of the act (praxis, development), but not of the 'pure' act, but rather of the real 'impure' act, in the most profane and worldly sense of the word."[86] As we noted before, Gramsci insisted on the progress of mankind towards newer and better harmonies, but never felt that a final harmony would be achieved. The linguistic consensus that he hoped would accompany a new socialist hegemony was always tempered by the inevitable metaphoricality of language, which implied an open-ended process of hermeneutic discourse.

Only once in his career did Gramsci explicitly define the institutional framework which would embody a normative totality. Before his turn to the Leninist party as the "modern Prince," the collective intellectual, Gramsci had gone through a brief but intense period of support for the workers' council as the proper organizational form for the proletariat. In the 1919–1920 period of mass strikes and occupied factories, the so-called *bienno rosso*, Gramsci and his collaborators Angelo Tasca, Umberto Terracini, and Palmiro Togliatti turned their newly founded journal *L'Ordine Nuovo* into the major organ of the council movement centered

---

1969), p. 202. Benda with his idealist defense of transcendental spirit attacked "imperialism of the species" as a mere universalization of nationalist aggressiveness.

85. Max Horkheimer and Theodor W. Adorno, *Dialectic of Enlightenment*, trans. John Cumming (New York, 1972). There were, to be sure, scattered references to this issue in the earlier work of Walter Benjamin.

86. Gramsci, *Selections from the Prison Notebooks*, p. 372.

in Turin.[87] In opposition to the trade unions, which the syndicalists supported, and the party, which the parliamentary revisionists defended, only
the councils truly prefigured a social order beyond capitalism:

The Factory Council is the model of the proletarian State. All the problems inherent in the organization of the proletarian State are inherent in the organization of
the Council. In the one as in the other, the concept of citizen gives way to the
concept of comrade. Collaboration in effective and useful production develops
solidarity and multiplies bonds of affection and fraternity. Everyone is indispensable, everyone is at his post, and everyone has a function and a post. . . . Whereas in
the union, workers' solidarity was developed in struggle against capitalism in suffering and sacrifice, in the Council this solidarity is a positive, permanent entity
that is embodied in even the most trivial moments of industrial production. It is a
joyous awareness of being an organic whole, a homogeneous and compact system
which, through useful work and the disinterested production of social wealth,
asserts its sovereignty and realizes its power and its freedom to create history.[88]

Unfortunately, as Sergio Bologna has pointed out,[89] the social and economic basis for the councils as organizations of industrial craftsmen was
being undermined at the very moment Gramsci was celebrating their prefigurative role. Unlike the Council Communists in Germany and Holland,[90] he seems to have reconciled himself to this change, especially because they had failed politically in 1921. When the councils were
undermined by a combination of nationwide socialist ambivalence and the
successful maneuverings of the Turin capitalists led by Gino Olivetti,
Gramsci turned his attention to the building of a vanguard political party
on the Russian model. Despite his qualms about splitting the socialist
movement, he became a member of the PCI when it was founded in January, 1921, at the historic congress in Leghorn. Because, like Korsch and so
many others, he idealized the Russian example, he apparently came to accept what might be called the Bolshevization of non-Russian parties, including his own.[91] In 1924, after returning from eighteen months in the
Soviet Union, he was rewarded for his efforts with the leadership of the PCI,
which the Comintern had withdrawn from the unpliable Bordiga. Al-

    87. The fullest account of Gramsci's *Ordine Nuovo* period is by Clark. See also Franklin
Adler, "Factory Councils, Gramsci and the Industrialists," *Telos* 31 (Spring 1977).
    88. Gramsci, *Selections from Political Writings (1910–1920),* p. 100.
    89. Sergio Bologna, "Class Composition and the Theory of the Party at the Origin of the
Workers-Councils Movement," *Telos* 13 (Fall 1972).
    90. For a comparison of Gramsci and the Council Communists, see Richard Gombin,
The Radical Tradition; A Study in Modern Revolutionary Thought, trans. Rupert Dwyer
(New York, 1979), chapter III.
    91. Thomas R. Bates, "Antonio Gramsci and the Bolshevization of the PCI," *Journal of
Contemporary History* 2, 2–3 (July 1976). Adamson, however, argues that Bates general-
izes too much from the 1923–25 period and thus underplays Gramsci's later turn against
Stalin's version of Bolshevization. See his remarks in "Towards the Prison Notebooks," p. 55.

though he had qualms about the policies of the Soviet leadership while in prison, he never publicly repudiated the international Communist movement. With the more sober attitude of his mature years went a dampening of enthusiasm for the councils, which were virtually ignored in the *Prison Notebooks*. As a consequence, Gramsci's image of a normative totality was never again expressed with the certainty of his *Ordine Nuovo* period.

Speculating on the content of the realm of freedom from within the realm of necessity has, of course, long been suspect in Marxist circles. In fact, the very distinction between utopian and scientific socialism was often based on precisely this reticence. But one of the ways in which Western Marxism tended to diverge from its orthodox predecessor was through the willingness of some of its adherents to break the taboo. The integration of utopian with scientific socialism was nowhere as insistently advocated as in the work of Ernst Bloch, to whose contribution to the discussion of totality we can now turn.

CHAPTER FIVE

Ernst Bloch and the Extension of Marxist Holism to Nature

If, as the young Gramsci insisted, socialism is an "integral vision of life" with "a philosophy, a mysticism and morality,"[1] none of the Western Marxists expanded the boundaries of that vision with as much persistent and imaginative audacity as Ernst Bloch. Nor did any drive the totalizing impulse in Marxism to the imprudent extremes found in his extraordinary body of work. Whereas all other twentieth-century Marxists postulated totalities with boundaries, boundaries defined by the distinctions between history and nature or reason and the irrational, Bloch's concept of totality was all-encompassing. Although on one level anthropocentric, it was ultimately rooted in a cosmic vision of wholeness that clearly transcended anything to be found in Marx or any of his other followers.

As a result, Bloch became and generally remained a scandal and embarrassment to most of his contemporaries in both orthodox and heterodox Marxist circles. Throughout his long life, which extended from 1885 to 1977, he was an anomaly, a permanent outsider, the quintessential prophet wandering, as the title of one of his own books put it, "through the desert."[2] Exiled no fewer than three times,[3] Bloch enjoyed sustained

1. Antonio Gramsci, "Toward a Cultural Association" in *History, Philosophy and Culture in the Young Gramsci*, ed. Pedro Cavalcanti and Paul Piccone (St. Louis, 1975), p. 98.
2. Bloch, *Durch die Wüste* (Frankfurt, 1964); original publication, 1923.
3. During the First World War, Bloch left Germany for Switzerland because of his pacifist beliefs. In 1933 he left again, settling successively in Vienna; Paris; Prague; New York; Marlborough, New Hampshire; and Cambridge, Massachusetts before returning to Germany in 1949. He then exiled himself from East Germany in 1961, to live out the remainder of his life in Tübingen. For biographical details of Bloch's life, see Erhard Bahr, *Ernst Bloch* (Berlin, 1974), Wayne Hudson, *The Marxist Philosophy of Ernst Bloch* (London, 1982), and David Gross, "Ernst Bloch: The Dialectics of Hope" in *The Unknown Dimension: European Marxism Since Lenin*, ed. Dick Howard and Karl Klare (New York, 1972).

institutional support and public recognition only at the end of his life,[4] and then in a society whose foundations he still vigorously contested. And, paradoxically, he came to be honored more by theologians than by Marxists who remained resistant to the indigestible religious elements in his thought.

Bloch's marginal status was earned in part by what must be frankly acknowledged as his penchant for highly fanciful ruminations on such esoteric topics as metempsychosis and reincarnation, which were clearly outside the traditional Marxist pale. Although paying lip service to the scientific side of Marxism—its "cold current," as he called it—Bloch drew far greater sustenance from the "warm current" whose source was in pre-scientific, even pre-philosophical thought. Proudly wearing the label of utopian, Bloch endeavored to claim the heritage of mythic, religious, irrationalist, and mystical speculations for a Marxism that thought itself clearly beyond them. And in so doing, on the basis of an astounding mastery of disparate traditions, Bloch revealed the extent to which Marxism, including its concept of totality, was ultimately rooted in a cultural tradition, or a variety of traditions, that extended back well before the Enlightenment. He was thus a scandal not merely because of his fascination with alternatives to mainstream Marxism, but also because he exposed the often unacknowledged indebtedness of that mainstream to those very alternatives. Although it would be wrong to accept Bloch's claims that everything he attributed to Marxism legitimately belonged to it, he nonetheless did illuminate the continuities between Marxism and a host of other modes of thought. In particular, he showed that the distinction between a specifically Marxist concept of totality and its non-Marxist competitors was not as water-tight as some of his peers supposed.

Bloch was also an anomalous figure because of his peculiar resistance to historical change. Although he often wrote about contemporary issues, he did so from a perspective that remained doggedly constant. To use with some license the phrase he himself applied to modern German society, he

4. During his first years in the D.D.R., Bloch was given official support and recognition. But it was not until his final emigration to Tübingen that he was discovered by a wider international audience composed largely of New Leftists and theologians. The vast majority of commentaries on his work date from that period; see the excellent bibliography compiled by Burghart Schmidt for the collection dedicated to his ninetieth birthday, *Ernst Blochs Wirkung: Ein Arbeitsbuch zum 90. Geburtstag* (Frankfurt, 1975). The Suhrkamp Verlag began republishing his collected works in 1959 and issuing composite selections at about the same time. A West German *Festschrift, Ernst Bloch zu Ehren: Beiträge zu seinem Werk*, ed. Siegfried Unseld (Frankfurt, 1965), soon followed, as did a collection of essays, *Über Ernst Bloch* (Frankfurt, 1968). For a discussion of his role in the interchange between Marxists and theologians, see James Bentley, *Between Marx and Christ: The Dialogue in German-Speaking Europe, 1870–1970* (London, 1982).

was "non-synchronous"[5] (*Ungleichzeitig*), outside of the historical mainstream, like his friend Siegfried Kracauer,[6] living a chronologically extraterritorial existence. More precisely, Bloch's intellectual and political
character seems to have matured at a specific moment in time and remained relatively unchanged for the remainder of his life. That moment
was 1917, the year of the Russian Revolution, which Bloch observed with
keen excitement from afar. In Oskar Negt's phrase, Bloch was "the German philosopher of the October Revolution."[7] And both terms of this
characterization remained accurate for virtually the rest of his life.

Politically, Bloch was a fervent supporter of Lenin and the Russian
Revolution and remained so well after most other Western Marxists had
turned at least in part against them. In 1937, at a time when even Lukács
was prudently silent, he staunchly defended the Moscow trials against
"renegades"[8] among the leftist émigrés in America. And after the Second
World War, he chose to return to the Soviet zone of Germany rather than
the Western in the belief that socialism could still be built according to the
Russian model. Although never a slavish follower of every twist and turn
in the Party line, he played the role of loyal opposition in a system he felt
was basically valid. Not until the growing pressure to conform within
Ulbricht's dictatorship led him to accept refuge in the Federal Republic,
which he was fortuitously visiting when the Berlin Wall went up in 1961,
did his faith in the October Revolution finally sour. Only in his eighth
decade did Bloch come to the reluctant conclusion that his philosophy of
hope needed another concrete embodiment.

Bloch's status as a "German philosopher" of the 1917 era did not,
however, suffer a comparable alteration. His idiosyncratic world-view
had been profoundly shaped by the creative turmoil of pre-war European,
especially German, culture. Like Lukács, with whom he was both personally and intellectually close during the 1910s, he was attracted to the full
spectrum of anti-positivist cultural phenomena that vied for prominence
in this period of spiritual crisis. Borrowing freely from *Lebensphilosophie*

5. The concept of non-synchronicity was developed in *Erbschaft dieser Zeit* (Zurich,
1935). A representative chapter has been translated as "Nonsynchronism and the Obligation to its Dialectics" in *New German Critique* 11 (Spring 1977), with an excellent introduction by Anson Rabinbach.
   6. For a discussion of Kracauer, which treats in passing his relations with Bloch, see
Martin Jay, "The Extraterritorial Life of Siegfried Kracauer," *Salmagundi* 31–32 (Fall
1975–Winter 1976).
   7. Oskar Negt, "Ernst Bloch: The German Philosopher of the October Revolution,"
New German Critique 4 (Winter 1975). Bahr notes that "theologian of the revolution"
might be even more accurate (p. 32).
   8. Bloch, "A Jubilee for Renegades," *New German Critique* 4 (Winter 1975); the article
first appeared in *Die neue Weltbühne* in December, 1937.

and neo-Kantianism, Russian mysticism and Jewish cabalism, neo-Platonic gnosticism and theosophy,[9] Bloch created a highly unusual speculative synthesis that exceeded even that of the early Lukács in its apocalyptic extremism. And like his Hungarian friend, he came to see the Russian Revolution and Marxism as providing the ultimate answer to the deeply troubling questions raised by the crisis of bourgeois culture.

Lukács, however, quickly set about distancing himself from the pre-Marxist origins of his thought. Not only in terms of content, but also in the style of expression, there is a significant gap between the essays collected in *Soul and Form* and those in *History and Class Consciousness*, a gap which for the most part continued to widen as Lukács grew more "realistic" in his attitudes and expectations. Bloch, on the other hand, remained true to the original, improbable synthesis of the 1910s. When Gershom Scholem first met Bloch in 1919, he noted in his diary that conversation with him was like talking to "a real iron wall."[10] In later years, Bloch would admit that he was inordinately obstinate in his opinions, identifying himself with Schiller's Don Carlos who "honored the dreams of his youth."[11]

Stylistically, Bloch's loyalty was to a richly metaphorical mode of non-linear prose, which was deeply indebted to the Expressionism of the 1910s and early 1920s.[12] As Jürgen Habermas later observed,

It is the style of the first decades of our century, which in its middle now has become antiquarian, though with signs of maturation and relaxation. There are erratic blocks of hyphenated terminology, luxuriant growths of pleonastic turns, the heaving of dithyrambic breath, a choice of metaphors that is reminiscent of Arnold Böcklin rather than of Walter Benjamin. All this still shows forcefulness and greatness, but it has become obsolete.[13]

Whether the results were obsolete or not, he continued to play what Adorno called "great Bloch music"[14] until the end of his life. To sceptics

9. For a full account of Bloch's early intellectual passions, see Hudson and Bahr. For the general context, see Ivo Frenzel, "Utopia and Apocalypse in German Literature," *Social Research* 39, 2 (Summer 1977).

10. Gershom Scholem, *Walter Benjamin—die Geschichte einer Freundschaft* (Frankfurt, 1975), p. 103.

11. Bloch interview in *Le Monde*, October 30, 1970; reprinted in *Ernst Blochs Wirkung*, p. 230.

12. For discussions of Bloch's style, see Jörg Drews, "Expressionismus in der Philosophie" and Renate Kübler, "Die Metapher als Argument: Semiotische Bestimmung der Blochschen Sprache" in *Ernst Blochs Wirking*; and George Steiner, "The Pythagorean Genre" in *Language and Silence: Essays on Language, Literature and the Inhuman* (New York, 1967).

13. Jürgen Habermas, "Ernst Bloch—A Marxist Romantic" in Robert Boyers, ed., *The Legacy of the German Refugee Intellectuals* (New York, 1972), p. 297.

14. Theodor W. Adorno, "Grosse Blochmusik," *Neue deutsche Hefte* 69 (April 1960). *Blochmusik* is a pun on the German word *Blechmusik*, which means brass band music.

like Leszek Kolakowski, it produced the dizzying sensation of being
"amid the fumes of an alchemist's laboratory,"[15] while in those it
charmed, like Eric Hobsbawm, it inspired rapturous descriptions of a "remarkable style, where concise and gnomic foothills blank sinewy mountain ranges of prose, broken by cascades of noble rhetoric, and on which
the glaciers of wit sparkle and glow."[16] Whether one judges it gaseous,
monumental, or both, Bloch's unique prose bore witness to the remarkable persistence of his early vision.

No less stable was the content of Bloch's thought, which never lost its
apocalyptic and utopian impulse. Although he did occasionally tamper
with his earlier political views when republishing his older essays, Bloch
was able to bring out works composed decades apart that could appear
side by side without inconsistencies. In the 1970s, he was still espousing
ideas that originated a half century earlier during the initial explosion of
Western Marxist thought. With only minor variations, such as the extent
to which Marx either needed to be supplemented or contained all the
right ideas himself, Bloch's first work, *Spirit of Utopia*, written in 1918,
was of a piece with his last, *Experimentum Mundi* of 1975.[17] Themes
were developed, terms clarified, examples given in endless profusion, but
the basic contours of Bloch's system remained firmly in place.

Within those contours, Bloch developed variations on the concept of
totality that are of special importance in the history of Western Marxism.
To understand them, it is perhaps best to begin by comparing his thought
with that of Lukács in the years of their closest friendship.[18] Both men
were born in 1885, the sons of assimilated Jewish parents. But whereas
Lukács grew up in a wealthy section of Budapest, Bloch spent his youth in

15. Leszek Kolakowski, *Main Currents of Marxism*, vol. 3: *The Breakdown*, trans. P. S.
Falla (Oxford, 1978), p. 422.
16. E. J. Hobsbawm, *Revolutionaries* (New York, 1973), p. 140.
17. Bloch's major works were *Geist der Utopie* (1918; rev. 2nd ed., 1923); *Thomas
Münzer als Theologe der Revolution* (1921); *Durch die Wüste* (1923); *Spuren* (1930); *Erbschaft dieser Zeit* (1935); *Subjekt-Objekt. Erläuterungen zu Hegel* (1951); *Das Prinzip Hoffnung* (1954–1959); *Naturrecht und menschliche Würde* (1961); *Verfremdungen I* and *II*
(1962 and 1964); *Tübinger Einleitung in die Philosophie* (1963 and 1964); *Atheismus im
Christentum* (1968); *Vom Hasard zur Katastrophe* (1972); *Das Materialismusproblem,
seine Geschichte und Substanz* (1972); *Experimentum Mundi* (1975). English translations
of Bloch's work include *Atheism in Christianity*, trans. J. T. Swann (New York, 1972); *A
Philosophy of the Future* (the first volume of *Tübinger Einleitung in die Philosophie*), trans.
John Cumming (New York, 1972); *Man On His Own* (the essay collection *Religion im
Erbe*), trans. E. B. Ashton (New York, 1970); and *On Karl Marx* (the essay collection *Über
Karl Marx*), trans. John Maxwell (New York, 1971).
18. For discussions of the Bloch–Lukács friendship, see Sandor Radnoti, "Bloch and
Lukács: Two Radical Critics in a 'God-Forsaken World'," *Telos* 25 (Fall 1975); Paul Breines,
"Bloch Magic," *Continuum* 7, 4 (Winter 1970). See also the interview conducted by Michael
Löwy with Bloch in 1974 in *New German Critique* 9 (Fall 1976).

the Rhenish industrial town of Ludwigshafen, where, as he liked to boast,[19] he came into frequent contact with Social Democratic workers. Nonetheless, like Lukács, he had little use for the scientific orthodoxies of the Second International, preferring instead the same bourgeois critics of bourgeois culture that Lukács found so fascinating. In 1908 Bloch, having completed his studies with Theodor Lipps in Munich and Oswald Külpe in Würzburg,[20] came to Berlin to work under Georg Simmel. It was through Simmel two years later that he met Lukács, whom he soon visited in Budapest. "We quickly discovered," he later reminisced, "that we had *the same opinion on everything,* an identify of viewpoints to complete that we founded a 'wildlife preserve' (*Naturschutzpark*) for our differences of opinion, so that we wouldn't always say the same things."[21] In what Bloch called their "mutual apprenticeship," Lukács persuaded Bloch to read more deeply in Kierkegaard and the German mystics, and in return was encouraged to join Bloch in Heidelberg, where they presented a common front in the discussions of the circle surrounding Max Weber.[22]

This virtual identity of positions seems to have lasted until near the end of the war, which Bloch spent in self-imposed exile in Switzerland. Lukács' unexpected decision to return to Budapest when he was drafted (although his physical condition prevented him from actually serving) dismayed the more resolutely pacifist Bloch. Their first significant theoretical difference surfaced over the figure of Schopenhauer, whose radical resistance to the world Bloch found more attractive than Lukács. As Lukács progressively distanced himself from the common heroes of their youth, such as Kierkegaard and Dostoevsky, he also estranged himself from Bloch. Although both men welcomed the Russian Revolution, which seemed to confirm their expectation of mystical greatness from the East, Bloch chose not to follow Lukács into the Communist Party. In fact, later he would blame that decision for the narrowing of Lukács' horizons and the deadening of his utopian inclinations. Looking back on the period of their closest collaboration, Bloch would come to detect a neoclassical "passion for order"[23] in Lukács, a resemblance to the Weberian "inner-worldly ascetic" character type, that he had previously overlooked. For his part, Lukács came to scorn what he called the unholy

19. Löwy interview with Bloch, p. 40.
20. For a discussion of his early training with Lipps and Külpe, see Hudson, pp. 5–6. Bloch wrote his doctoral dissertation under Külpe on Rickert (*Kritische Erörterungen über Rickert und das Problem der modernen Erkenntnistheorie* [Ludwigshafen, 1909]).
21. Löwy interview with Bloch, p. 36.
22. Paul Honigsheim, "Memories of Max Weber," in his *On Max Weber,* trans. Joan Rytina (New York, 1968).
23. Löwy interview with Bloch, p. 39.

fusion of "left" ethics and "right" epistemology[24] in both Bloch and his own early work.

If Lukács approximated Weber's inner-worldly ascetic, Bloch hovered between what Weber had called an "outer-worldly" and inner-worldly mystic."[25] The ambiguity in his position followed from his desire to preserve the world-denying power of mystical intuition without, however, merely collapsing into mysticism *per se*, crossed by his equally intense insistence that the content of that intuition was immanent in the world on the level of potentiality or possibility. Bloch spent the rest of his life working out the implications of this ambiguity, in what he came to call his ontology of "non-yet-being" or philosophy of hope. Its tension with Lukács' more sober variant of Marxism was apparent as early as Bloch's first book, *Spirit of Utopia* of 1918, whose composition actually antedated Lukács' commitment to the Party. In criticizing certain aspects of Lukács' pre-Marxist work, Bloch gave intimations of the qualms he would have about his later thought as well. Against Lukács, he defended the role of religion as a repository of utopian hope, questioned Lukács' socially immanent view of tragedy, and extolled music, to which Lukács was essentially indifferent, as a vehicle of immanent transcendence. In addition, Bloch chastised Marx for reducing the totality to only one of its elements, production, thus reproducing the very impoverishment of reality Marx had been at pains to counter:

And so the man who expelled any element of fetishism from the process of production; who would analyze and exorcise all irrationalities of history as merely unclarified, uncomprehended (and thus, in effect, fateful) obscurities of the class situation and productive process; who banished all dreams, effective utopias, and religiously garbed teleologies from history: the same man now treated the "productive forces" in the same over-constitutive, pantheistic, and mythicizing way; and accorded to the design of a "productive process" ultimately the same power of using and guiding which Hegel had granted the "idea," and even Schopenhauer his a-logical "will."[26]

Although it was manifest in economics and politics, Bloch claimed that there was a more primal reality: "The soul, the Messiah, the Apocalypse which represents the act of awakening in totality—these impart the final impulses to action and cognition, and make up the *a priori* of all politics and of all culture."[27]

    24. Lukács, *The Theory of the Novel*, trans. Anna Bostock (Cambridge, Mass., 1971), p. 21.
    25. Weber, "Religious Rejections of the World and Their Directions" in *From Max Weber: Essays in Sociology*, eds. Hans Gerth and C. Wright Mills (New York, 1958).
    26. Bloch, *Man on His Own*, p. 35; originally in *Geist der Utopie*.
    27. Ibid., p. 72.

Lukács, when he did convert to Marxism, saw that a dangerous challenge had been hurled to the integrity of Marx's thought. In *History and Class Consciousness*, he directly took up Bloch's assertion that Marxism needed to be supplemented by religion, which had been developed further in Bloch's 1921 study of Thomas Münzer's chiliastic "theology of revolution:"[28]

When Ernst Bloch claims that this union of religion with socio-economic revolution points the way to a deepening of the "merely economic" outlook of historical materialism, he fails to notice that his deepening simply by-passes the real depth of historical materialism. When he then conceives of economics as a concern with objective things to which soul and inwardness are to be opposed, he overlooks the fact that the real social revolution can only mean the restructuring of the real and concrete life of man. He does not see that what is known as economics is nothing but the system of forms objectively defining this real life.[29]

Bloch seems to have taken to heart the reproach that Marx needed no supplement, and for a while he contended that the ideas he had wanted to add to Marxism were already latent in it. But, as he ultimately acknowledged, he continued to graft on to Marxism ideas from other traditions which were only imperfectly compatible with it.

Bloch's continuing estrangement from Lukács' version of Marxism can be seen in the lengthy and essentially positive review of *History and Class Conciousness* he wrote under the title "Actuality and Utopia" in 1924.[30] It was here that his specific disagreements with Lukács' concept of totality were first spelled out. In general, the review was highly laudatory, as Bloch identified himself with Lukács' theory of reification and warned that it would be anathema to doctrinaire Soviet theoreticians. But on the issue of totality, Bloch had certain critical reservations. Lukács, he claimed, was too anxious to conceive of reality as a fully immanent and concrete whole, which left no place for mystery or the hidden. He tended to reduce the totality to its socio-economic dimension alone—the sin for which Marx had been chastised in *Spirit of Utopia*—thereby missing the polyrhythmic fluidity of history:

Not only the social achievement of the still hidden social men, but also the artistic, religious, metaphysical achievement of the hidden transcendental men is a

28. See note 17.
29. Lukács, *History and Class Consciousness*, trans. Rodney Livingstone (Cambridge, Mass., 1971), p. 193.
30. Bloch, "Aktualität und Utopie. Zu Lukács' *Geschichte und Klassenbewusstsein*," reprinted in *Philosophische Aufsätze zur Objektiven Phantasie, Gesamtausgabe* 10 (Frankfurt, 1969). For a good discussion of the review, see Dick Howard, *The Marxian Legacy* (New York, 1977), p. 69f.

thought of Being, a *new* deep relationship of Being. . . . But with the limitation or homogenization to purely *social* material (which rules Lukács, despite all will to totality), neither life nor nature nor the almost completely eccentric content of the dianetically related process of understanding can be adequately grasped.[31]

Instead of trying to find the totality's genetic center in the meta-subjective creator of the objective world, Lukács should have conceptualized the whole as a mediation of distinct spheres irreducible to a common genesis. These spheres, such as religion, nature and art, were not mere alienations produced by capitalism and thus immediately sublatable after its demise. They were instead a "consequence of the laboriousness of the founding of the Kingdom (*Mühseligkeit der Reichsgründung*), which expresses itself in the temporal process, as well as spatially in the creation of spheres."[32] History should thus be understood not as the objectification of a meta-subject, which returns to itself after a journey through estrangement, but as an experimental process driven by the goal of a possible future totalization. Because Lukács fails to grasp the utopian dimension of reality, he underplays the still unfinished quality of the whole. Although he correctly understands that the progressive humanization of reality is a crucial step on the road to this final totality, he underestimates the extent to which that state is still "not-yet," still only on the level of possibility. Lukács is thus blind to the interpenetration of actuality and utopia, and thus overly concerned with the "totality of the empirical,"[33] to use the phrase Lukács approvingly borrows from Lassalle's description of Hegel.

In this remarkable review of *History and Class Consciousness*, Bloch expressed many of the key themes of his career. For the question of totality, the following issues are paramount. In a general sense, Bloch joined Lukács in conceiving all of human history as a longitudinal totality, a coherent whole. "*The metaphysical total theme of history*," he wrote, "is revealed in Lukács' book with other means, but substantially in full conformity with *The Spirit of Utopia*."[34] Bloch also shared Lukács' vision of a normative totality, at the end of that process, as a fully achieved community in which all alienation and reification would end. The ultimate identity of subject and object was at the root of his normative utopia no less than Lukács'. Indeed, if anything, Bloch's concept of that identity was even more cosmically encompassing than Lukács' because it extended, as we will see momentarily, beyond history to nature as well.

31. Bloch, "Aktualität und Utopie," p. 618.
32. Ibid., p. 619.
33. Lukács, *History and Class Consciousness*, p. 154.
34. Bloch, "Aktualität und Utopie," p. 620.

Despite these general agreements, however, Bloch challenged Lukács' concept of totality at several fundamental levels. For Lukács, as we have seen, the genetic origin of the whole was critically important; "dereification" was a process of recollecting the human roots of the seemingly natural social system. The proletariat had to be aware of its role as the meta-subjective maker of history in order to overcome the antinomies of bourgeois thought and the alienations of bourgeois life. In other words, for Lukács, at least in the earlier essays of *History and Class Consciousness*, totality was an expressive concept with a genetic center.

Although Bloch endorsed Lukács' view of the proletariat as the "we-subject" of history and agreed that the humanization of the historical process was progressive, he stressed the teleological power of its end rather than the genetic creativity of its beginning. As he later put it in *The Principle of Hope*, "*The true genesis is not at the begining, but at the end.*"[35] The Archimedean point of the longitudinal totality was thus in the future, not in the present, which lacked plenitude and substance, and certainly not in an imagined fulfilled past (as in Lukács' *Theory of the Novel*). Totality today had to be understood as what Althusser would later call "decentered," although in the future it would not. Rather than basing his ontology and epistemology on a variant of Plato's doctrine of anamnesis, or recollection, Bloch chose the religious concept of eschatology instead. The God—or better put, the intentional content of the "God" concept— he hoped to reconcile with Marxism was less God as Creator than the God of Exodus and promised homecoming.

Lukács, Bloch contended, lacked a sense of the still unfinished quality of the totality. Thus, when referring to the actual whole—what we have called the latitudinal totality—Lukács concentrated too much on its present status. Although he used Hegel's distinction between appearance and essence, Lukács failed to understand the "not-yet" quality of the latter, which was still to be achieved. "The real of the essence," Bloch later insisted, "is that *which does not yet exist, which is in quest of itself in the core of things, and which is awaiting its genesis in the trend latency (Tendenz-Latenz) of the process.*"[36] In a reproach that could have been even more appropriately leveled at Korsch's "revolutionary historicism" and Gramsci's "absolute historicism," Bloch criticized Lukács for his presentist bias and capitulation to the empirical realities of the current whole. Fichte's defiant "so much the worse for the facts," which the young Lukács

35. Bloch, *On Karl Marx*, p. 44; originally *Das Prinzip Hoffnung*.
36. Ibid., p. 41.

had embraced but then abandoned, Bloch doggedly defended to the end of his life.[37] However much he may have tried to adjust to life under Soviet-style Communism, he remained persistently critical of stable "facts" in the name of fluid processes.

Bloch, to be sure, frequently tried to distinguish the abstract utopianism of the Fouriers and Saint-Simons attacked by Marx from his own "concrete utopia"[38] based on real tendencies in history. But the level on which those real tendencies was supposed to exist was other than, or at least not equivalent to, the socio-economic, where Marx (and Lukács) had argued they should be sought. As a result, Bloch could argue that even an analysis that distinguished between apparent and essential levels of the socio-economic whole was still too empirical because it failed to grasp the deeper level of possibility, of "objective hope," beneath. "S," he always protested, "is not yet P."[39]

In later years, Bloch's divergence from Lukács on this issue would manifest itself in many ways, a salient example being their very different interpretations of Hegel.[40] In *The Young Hegel* of 1948, Lukács sought to counter the charge that Hegel was a proto-fascist idealist by de-emphasizing the religious dimension of his thought, stressing his continuity with the Enlightenment rather than the Romantics, and demonstrating his astute and realistic grasp of political economy. Rather than the reactionary defender of the Prussian state pilloried by contemporary Stalinist thought, Lukács' Hegel was a progressive critic of nascent bourgeois society who anticipated the young Marx in many crucial respects. Bloch's *Subject–Object* of 1951 also defended the continuity between Marx and Hegel, but on entirely different grounds. Rather than suppressing the religious, even mystical, roots of Hegel's thought, Bloch sought to rescue them for a Marxism that would also benefit from an acknowledgement of its irrationalist, or at least a-rationalist, dimension. Less interested than Lukács in demonstrating Hegel's revolutionary credentials, or his realistic appraisal of contemporary society, Bloch was anxious to situate dialectical thought in traditions that were on the surface less overtly political. Among these was the nature philosophy of figures like Jacob Boehme, whose vision of natural subjectivity Bloch frequently praised.

Bloch's attitude towards nature was, in fact, a source of disagreement

37. See, for example, *A Philosophy of the Future*, p. 109; and Löwy interview with Bloch, p. 38, where Bloch wrongly attributes the phrase to Hegel.
38. See, for example, the discussion in *A Philosophy of the Future*, p. 89–90.
39. Bloch, "Dialectic and Hope," *New German Critique* 9 (Fall 1976), p. 8.
40. For a discussion of their differences over Hegel, see Iring Fetscher, *Marx and Marxism* (New York, 1971), p. 104f.

with Lukács from the first. In the 1924 review of *History and Class Consciousness*, as we have seen, he included nature as one of the spheres Lukács had ignored in his over-emphasis of the socio-economic realm. Lukács, it will be recalled, restricted the interaction of subject and object to history, leaving nature and natural scientific methods as residual categories outside of dialectics. Korsch responded to this radical separation of history from nature by reappropriating the methods of the natural sciences for historical study, while at the same time somewhat inconsistently holding on to the view that all knowledge was class bound. Gramsci followed the opposite tack of extending the methods of the cultural sciences to nature, arguing that nature was an historical category and that scientific objectivity was an intersubjective construct.

Bloch's solution was far bolder and more radical than any of the other Western Marxists.[41] Rather than dismissing Engels' dialectics of nature out of hand because nature lacked subjectivity, as had Lukács, or ignoring the subjective component of dialectics in favor of scientific objectivity, as had the later Korsch, or reducing nature and natural science to a *humanly* subjective construct, as had Gramsci, Bloch insisted on the existence "not-yet" of a subject in nature. Drawing on the underground tradition of nature philosophy stretching back through Schelling to Boehme, Paracelsus and the Renaissance, he speculated on the possible resurrection of that natural subject. The ultimate totalization at the end of the historical process would thus reconcile not merely men with themselves and their objectifications, but also men with nature, which would itself be a subject. Engels was thus right in extending dialectics to nature,[42] although he was not utopian enough to recognize that the ultimate ground for this extension was the potential for a subject in nature.

Bloch's inclusion of natural subjectivity into the dialectical process of totalization set him apart from the other members of Western Marxism's first generation, although it anticipated some of the concerns of slightly younger figures like Walter Benjamin and Herbert Marcuse. While it would not be entirely correct to follow Fredric Jameson in seeing Bloch's

41. For a discussion and critique of Bloch's philosophy of nature, see Alfred Schmidt, *The Concept of Nature in Marx* (London, 1971).
42. In the East German attack on Bloch, *Ernst Blochs Revision des Marxismus* (Berlin, 1957), Engels is contrasted with Bloch. For a critique of this view, see Schmidt, p. 210, where it is argued that "Bloch's further development of Engels' conception of matter in the direction of a romantic nature-speculation only reveals what is, at bottom, already true of the latter." For a more positive view of Engels' interpretation of nature, which stresses its awareness of the costs of dominating nature, see Alvin W. Gouldner, *The Two Marxisms: Contradictions and Anomalies in the Development of Theory* (New York, 1980), p. 264.

Marxism as indebted more to Goethe that to Hegel,[43] it is arguable that his interest in natural subjectivity prevented him from merely Hegelianizing Marx. Here, as in so many other instances, Western Marxism was more than just Hegelian Marxism.

Whether or not Bloch's syncretic system was entirely true to Marx himself is another question. Bloch liked to quote the famous passage from the *1844 Manuscripts* in which Marx described Communism as the "humanization of nature and the naturalization of man" as evidence of the compatibility of their views. But there seems to be very little evidence in Marx's work to show that he shared Bloch's vision of an ultimate reconciliation of man and nature based on a non-exploitative, non-Euclidean technology. Nor is there much cause for believing that Marx shared the idiosyncratic variant of ontological materialism that Bloch insisted was at the root of his hope for the possible emergence of a natural subject. Following the so-called "left Aristotelians" Avicenna, Averroës and Giordano Bruno,[44] Bloch argued that matter itself was creative, containing an entelechy or telos which ultimately reconciled it with consciousness. The hunger that Bloch saw as the primary human drive, his replacement for Freud's notion of libido, was, he claimed, an instance of a more general lack in nature. "Nature," he argued, "is the veiled image of itself, a symbol from within and not only for us, an allegory of her hidden future."[45] In addition to and intertwined with the mechanical, quantitative natural temporality of Newtonian science, is a substantial, qualitative time, which yearns for fulfillment. [46] This can be achieved once history and nature are reconciled, for it is through historical time that the substantive temporality of nature is realized.

It is easy to scoff at Bloch's highly speculative philosophy of nature and his ontology of creative matter as an illegitimate extrapolation of the human onto the natural, a revival of the questionable practice of analogizing from microcosm to macrocosm. But there can be no doubt that he was

43. Fredric Jameson, *Marxism and Form: Twentieth-Century Dialectical Theories of Literature* (Princeton, 1971), p. 140. Bloch, however, warns against too quick an acceptance of Goethe's naturalism in "A Jubilee for Renegades," where he writes:

Nature, employed by Schiller in a new way as a shibboleth for repudiation, is no longer the "unviolated" nature of Rousseau, which breaks off the social contract the moment it goes bad. Here nature has become the patriarchal nature of the Restoration; it is ancestral tradition, "ancient law." It is the same "slowly forming," completely non-"volcanic" nature which sustained Schiller's mentor, Goethe, for an entire lifetime, and which led him to have more tolerance for injustice than for disorder. In this regard, Goethe very clearly led Schiller astray. (p. 22)

44. Bloch, *Avicenna und die Aristotelische Linke* (East Berlin, 1952); for a discussion of Bloch's materialism, see Burghart Schmidt, "Vom teleologischen Prinzip in der Materie," in *Ernst Blochs Wirking.*

45. Michael Landmann interview with Bloch, 1968, in *Telos* 25 (Fall 1975), p. 175.

46. Bloch, *A Philosophy of the Future*, p. 133f.

sensitive to a serious weakness in the type of holism supported by Lukács in *History and Class Consciousness*. The threat of species imperialism, which we have also seen latent in Gramsci's historicist call for the domination of nature, lurked in Lukács' restriction of totality to the purely social and his exclusion of nature from dialectics. Well before the theme of the domination of nature was introduced into the work of the Frankfurt School, Bloch was detailing the domination's costs. Likewise, his call for a new type of technology anticipated their critique of technological rationality, as well as the unfortunate vagueness of their alternative.

If Bloch's insistence on the open-endedness of the totality, his suspicion of the myth of collective genesis, and his reintroduction of nature into dialectics can all be accounted advances over Lukács' position, so too can his sensitivity to what he called the "spheres" of reality outside the social. For Bloch, the present totality, the latitudinal whole, was irreducible to a homologous set of relationships and functions with one center of gravity, such as the mode of production. However homogeneous it may appear on the surface, or even on the level of socio-economic essentiality, it also contained explosive intimations of the future, figural traces (*Spuren*,[47] as he entitled one of his books) of the "not-yet," which undermine the dominant trends of the present. In what many consider his *magnum opus*, the massive three-volume work, *The Principle of Hope*,[48] Bloch demonstrated his genius for finding these *figurae* in a multitude of cultural phenomena ranging from myths to fairy tales, occult fantasies to the adventure stories of Karl May, musical compositions to the costumes of the Ku Klux Klan. All these and more he took as expressing the daydreams of mankind which, unlike their night-time counterparts investigated by psychoanalysis, were anticipations of the future, not recollections of the past.

Because of his desire to reveal these traces of the "not-yet" through a kind of hermeneutics of prefiguration, Bloch was far less inclined than Lukács to look for the typical in literature or other cultural phenomena. In his spirited defense of Expressionism in the 1930s,[49] Bloch insisted that great art need not be found only in periods when a class was on the ascendent. It could also emerge in periods of cultural crisis and class dissolution. Thus, modernist art, which Lukács rejected for its "decadent" inability to grasp the totality of social reflections, could express yearn-

47. See note 17.
48. See note 17.
49. The relevant essays are collected in Hans-Jürgen Schmitt, *Die Expressionismusdebatte* (Frankfurt, 1973); several of the contributions are translated in *Aesthetics and Politics*, ed. Ronald Taylor, with an afterword by Fredric Jameson (London, 1977).

ings for a better future even while apparently complicitous with the unfulfilled present. Although some critics have found conservative elements in Bloch's aesthetics, in particular because of his preference for the symbolic over the allegorical,[50] it is clear that his more decentered view of the totality gave him an openness to modern art that Lukács woefully lacked. Like his friends Benjamin, Adorno and Kracauer, at least in their less pessimistic moods, he was willing to sift through the ruins of detotalizing cultures in search of the forgotten dreams, the "cultural surplus," that might anticipate the future. With them, he shared an appreciation of micrological cultural analysis that valued the atypical as much as the typical.

Bloch's sensitivity to the decentered nature of the latitudinal totality extended as well to its temporal dimension. As he had put it in his 1924 review of *History and Class Consciousness*, "the laboriousness of the foundation of the Kingdom" effected the flow of time as well as space. In the 1930s, Bloch's interest in temporal discontinuity allowed him to approach the phenomenon of Fascism with an originality that was absent among orthodox Marxist defenders of the stale formula that equated Fascism with the last stage of monopoly capitalism. In the essays collected in 1935 as *Inheritance of Our Times*,[51] Bloch introduced the notion of nonsynchronicity (*Ungleichzeitigkeit*) to explain the powerful lure of Fascism for large numbers of the German population. In addition to the synchronous contradiction between capitalists and workers which reflected the contemporary stage of social development, there were also potent nonsynchronous contradictions between vestiges of pre-capitalist modes of life and modern ones. "The *objectively* non-synchronous," he wrote, "is that which is far from and alien to the present; it includes both *declining remnants* and, above all, uncompleted *past*, which has not yet been 'sublated' by capitalism."[52] Although addressing these non-synchronous contradictions cannot in itself resolve the dilemmas of the present, the kernel of legitimate protest contained in them must be used to that end. For the yearnings of the uncompleted past express "sentimentally or romantically, that wholeness and liveliness from which communism draws genuine material against alienation."[53] In short, even Fascism contains a utopian element, however distorted, that cannot be ignored.

50. Habermas, "Ernst Bloch" in Boyers, ed., *Legacy*, p. 302; Jeffrey L. Sammons, *Literary Sociology and Practical Criticism* (Bloomington, 1977), p. 107.
51. See note 5. For an excellent analysis of it, see Tony Phelan, "Ernst Bloch's 'Golden Twenties': *Erbschaft dieser Zeit* and the Problem of Cultural History" in Keith Bullivant, ed., *Culture and Society in the Weimar Republic* (Manchester, 1977).
52. Bloch, "Nonsynchronism and the Obligation to its Dialectics," p. 31.
53. Ibid., p. 35.

Optimistically, Bloch insisted that this element could be won for Marxism through a "triple alliance"[54] of the workers, peasants and discontented petit-bourgeoisie. It was foolish, he warned, to cede to Fascism by default the perverted expressions of protest and hope in non-synchronous contradictions; Marxism must claim the heritage of even allegedly irrationalist figures like Nietzsche and Dostoevsky, who were too quickly dismissed as proto-fascist by unthinking dogmatists. Even typically rightwing terms like *"Heimat"* (home) and *"Reich"* (empire or kingdom) should be "refunctioned," to use Brecht's celebrated expression, in a leftist direction. A true utopianism understands that the future is latent in uncompleted remnants of the past as well as in the cutting edge of the present.

In more general terms, Bloch's appreciation of the persistence of the past in the present means that he rejected the simplistic longitudinal view of totality as a succession of discrete wholes, each with its central, overriding contradiction. On one level, this meant an intensive view of totality, in which past, present, and future all somehow existed at once, a view of simultaneous temporality that he shared with Nicholas of Cusa and, in some moods, Hegel. But in less mystical terms in which chronological development was assumed to be meaningful, it meant an openness to the complexity of historical change. In his later work, most notably the *Tübingen Introduction to Philosophy* of 1963,[55] Bloch extended his discussion of time to a critique of the dominant view of progress, which, like Walter Benjamin, he associated with social democracy.[56] Extrapolating from the nineteenth-century mathematician G. F. B. Riemann's concept of non-Euclidean space, Bloch argued for a neo-Riemannian notion of time as a heterogeneous multitude of different chronologies that were not reducible to a unilinear temporal flow. Only as the goal of the process was time a totalizable unity:

Progress itself does not advance as a homogeneous succession of events in time; it moves forward on different levels of time that are below and above one another. It proceeds in a *humanum*-unity of passing and gain that is still only processing itself out in diverse ways. The really common uniform time of the process of history and, indeed of the world process, springs and is springing forth universally

54. Ibid., p. 36.
55. Bloch, *A Philosophy of the Future*, p. 112f.
56. See Walter Benjamin, "Eduard Fuchs—Collector and Historian," *New German Critique* 5 (Spring 1975), originally in the *Zeitschrift für Sozialforschung* 6, 2 (1937); and "Theses on the Philosophy of History" in *Illuminations*, trans. Harry Zohn with intro. by Hannah Arendt (New York, 1968).

only as a temporal form of emergent identity: that is, of non-estrangement between men, and of non-alienation between men and Nature.[57]

Because of his concept of time as more than an organic, homogeneous
flow, Bloch rejected the evolutionary view of certain orthodox Marxists
who relied on the inexorable transition from one historical stage to another, higher one as the guarantee of socialism. Instead, he emphasized
the possibility of the sudden appearance of the *Novum*, or the radically
new, in the historical process, very much like the religious experience of
the *Eschaton* intersecting the course of profane time. Bloch, to be sure,
contended that the *Novum* was often prefigured by the traces of the future
in the past, but he contended that it also transcended its figural anticipation. Thus, in accord with his critique of Platonic *anamnesis*, he revived
the alternative notion of *anagnorisis*, or recognition, which meant that
the *Novum* produced a shock of familiarity, but was more than merely an
experience of *déjà vu*.[58]

In certain important respects, Bloch's speculations about time paralleled those of his friends Benjamin and Kracauer.[59] Perhaps of even greater
interest, they were similar in unexpected ways to those defended by Louis
Althusser in the 1960s.[60] Skeptical about the utopian consummation posited by Bloch, Althusser nonetheless stressed the heterogeneity of different times that were irreducible to one over-riding chronology; like Bloch
he questioned the expressivist notion of totality in which one creator–
subject exfoliated itself in time and space. Here as in so many other instances, the simple dichotomy of Hegelian or Critical and non-Hegelian or
Scientific Western Marxists proves a distorting simplification.

Bloch cut across that division in other ways as well, as we've seen in his
unfashionably favorable attitude towards Engels' dialectics of nature. Although there can be no doubt that he enthusiastically endorsed the humanism of the young Marx and welcomed the emergence of a collective
"we-subject" of history in the proletariat, there was a strong counter-current in his thought that suggested a reliance on extra-human forces in
history. One critic has even detected in his writing a "highly typical stylis-

57. Bloch, *A Philosophy of the Future*, pp. 132–133.
58. Landmann interview with Bloch, p. 178.
59. Siegfried Kracauer, *History, the Last Things Before the Last* (New York, 1969).
When Bloch sent Kracauer a copy of *Tübinger Einleitung*, Kracauer replied, "You are to my
knowledge the only one who presents the problem of time. And what you say about it
strongly touches my own ideas on the antinomy at the center of the chronological concept of
time" (Letter of June 17, 1963, in the Kracauer Archive, Schiller Nationalmuseum, Marbach
am Neckar).
60. Louis Althusser, *Reading Capital*, with Etienne Balibar, trans. Ben Brewster (New
York, 1970), p. 94f.

tic strategy of making an inanimate force the subject of an action for which the human being is a vehicle."[61] As Wayne Hudson has shown,[62] the young Bloch was deeply indebted to process philosophers such as Eduard von Hartmann, Henri Bergson, and the more obscure Jakob Frohschammer, from whom he absorbed a faith in a cosmic movement larger than man. As Bloch admitted in an interview in 1968:

> Anthropology is not a key word for me. It is a false key that locks more doors than it opens. It sets a part for the whole. What is special about man does not exist in him exclusively. A mountain can have a greater future than a man. "Man" is therefore too narrow a category.[63]

The larger category was the cosmic process of fulfillment, the teleological drive embodied in creative matter, of which man was only a part. While often stressing that man was to become the ultimate master of that process, indeed to fill the place vacated by the death of God, Bloch intimated that before concrete utopia was achieved, the process itself was self-propelling. This assumption allowed him to embrace both Marxist Humanism and Dialectical Materialism at a time when most Western Marxists (and orthodox Marxist-Leninists)[64] thought them incompatible.

Bloch's non-humanist interpretation of the underlying process of reality did not, however, mean that he always privileged the socio-economic sphere in the manner of most conventional Marxists, although he sometimes tended to do so in his mature writings. As we saw in his critique of *History and Class Consciousness*, he objected to Lukács' sociologism in the name of a more multifarious ontology of spheres, including nature, religion, art, and the dianoetic (the realm of reason and the intellect). In fact, as Habermas has pointed out (albeit with some exaggeration), he paid virtually no attention at all to social, economic, and political relations, confining himself instead "entirely to the sphere which Hegel reserves for Absolute Spirit."[65] By refusing to bathe in the cold current of Marxism, he avoided having to ponder its socio-economic analysis, which

---

61. Sammons, *Literary Sociology*, p. 45. Wayne Hudson argues in response that "Bloch does not make the human being the vehicle for the action of an inanimate force. He means that *human beings* could act to release as yet unrealized possibilities in nature" (Letter to the author, November 15, 1980).

62. Hudson, *Marxist Philosophy*, chapter 3.

63. Landmann interview with Bloch, p. 182.

64. The leading orthodox critic of Bloch was his former student in Leipzig, Rugard Otto Gropp. See the discussions in Jürgen Rühle, *Literature and Revolution: A Critical Study of the Writer and Communism in the Twentieth Century*, trans. Jean Steinberg (New York, 1969), p. 291; and Fetscher, *Marx and Marxism*, p. 117f.

65. Jürgen Habermas, *Theory and Practice*, trans. John Viertel (London, 1974), p. 240. See also his remarks in "Ernst Bloch—A Marxist Romantic," p. 299.

he seems to have taken as a given. Accepting the orthodox Communist line on class struggle and the introduction of capitalism, he spared himself the effort, with the major exception of his essays on Nazism, of testing them against historical reality. For all his stress on ontological materialism, there was thus a strongly idealist impulse in Bloch's assumption that ideological, theoretical, or artistic expressions of hope, desire, and hunger have objective correlatives on the ontological level of the "not-yet" expressed in, but more basic than, socio-economic relations. As a result, the differences between his vision of a concrete utopia, ostensibly rooted in real historical trends, and the abstract utopias of Fourier *et al.* were far less critical than Bloch believed.

To put this difficulty in another way, there was more than a hint in Bloch of the traditional ontological proof of God, which argues from the thought of God to His existence. Relying uncritically on an implicit argument by analogy rather than deduction or induction, Bloch moved too quickly from subjective intention to objective tendency, the realm of "not-yet becoming." Questioning, like that other great anti-dualist of his generation, Martin Heidegger, the very opposition between subject and object, Bloch assumed that "subjective" desires and intentions were part of the "objective" world. As a result, if Korsch can be faulted for reducing Marxism too rigidly to the class consciousness of the proletariat, Bloch can be said to have committed the opposite error of severing it too drastically from any concrete ground. The streak of gnosticism, which many observers have detected in his thought, ultimately prevented him from answering satisfactorily the epistemological problem of constitution that we have seen haunting Western Marxism.[66]

It also can be seen as influencing Bloch's troubled political history. As Kolakowski has pointed out,[67] there is an interesting parallel between Bloch and Heidegger on the issue of the link between politics and philosophy. At times in each of their careers, both men endorsed totalitarian political practices in ways that proved an ultimate embarrassment to them and their supporters. As in Heidegger's case, there has been a tendency to defend Bloch by uncoupling his political mistakes, which are excused as the product of naivete, from his philosophy.[68]

66. Howard, in *The Marxian Legacy*, p. 70, claims that in his review of *History and Class Consciousness*, "what Bloch is presenting is a theory of constitution; the Now is mediated, constituted, by the we-subject which can only seize itself precisely in its act of constitution and as its act of constitution." But this anthropological emphasis in Bloch is constantly in tension with his process philosophy, which lacks a satisfactory epistemological constitution.
67. Kolakowski, *The Breakdown*, p. 444.
68. See, for example, Kolakowski, p. 444; Negt, "Ernst Bloch," p. 9; and Douglas

Something can be said for this defense, but it should be noted that whereas Heidegger embraced Nazism for no longer than two years, Bloch supported the Soviet Union from 1917 to at least 1956, if not 1961, and was an outspoken defender of Stalinism for most of that period. During the worst period of Stalin's crimes, he mocked other refugees such as the members of the Frankfurt School for their failure to see that the only choice was between Hitler and Stalin.[69] And as late as *The Principle of Hope*, he could still write:

Without choosing a party in love, without a very concrete pole of hatred, there can be no true love; without the *party standpoint* in the revolutionary class struggle, there is only an idealism turned backwards instead of praxis aiming forward.[70]

Although one may attribute this and other like statements in *The Principle of Hope* to his bitter belief that capitalism entailed Fascism and therefore had to be fought at all costs, or more cynically, to the pressures of publishing in the DDR, there can be little doubt that Bloch was politically deluded for much of his career.

And yet, for all his distrust of non-commitment, Bloch never actually took the fateful step of joining the Communist Party, which, as we saw, he blamed for the narrowing of Lukács' horizons. Nor did he have much success reconciling his philosophy of hope with the realities of East German life after he answered the call to Leipzig in 1949. In fact, by the critical year of 1956, the *Deutsche Zeitschrift für Philosophie*, which he had helped found three years earlier, was taken from his control, his students Wolfgang Harich, Günther Zehm, and Manfred Hertweg were imprisoned, and Bloch himself was discharged from his teaching post and threatened with arrest.[71] Despite a grudging rehabilitation two years later, Bloch remained a vulnerable hostage to the whims of Ulbricht's regime. Clearly, a philosophy that insisted on so utopian a future was hard pressed to celebrate the bleak present of Soviet bloc existence.

There were, however, two ways in which Bloch's philosophy did lend itself to a favorable reading of that situation, and which may in part account for his lengthy acceptance of Stalinism. First, because of his desire to rescue the legitimate dimension of protest and hope in the non-syn-

---

Kellner and Harry O'Hara, "Utopia and Marxism in Ernst Bloch," *New German Critique* 9 (Fall 1976), p. 14.
    69. Negt, "Ernst Bloch," p. 5. As late as 1976, he could refer to the Frankfurt School as the "Institute of Social Falsification" because of its non-revolutionary pessimism. Quoted in Zoltan Tar, *The Frankfurt School: The Critical Theories of Max Horkheimer and Theodor W. Adorno* (New York, 1977), p. 206.
    70. Quoted in Howard, p. 83.
    71. Rühle, *Literature and Revolution*, pp. 292–293.

chronous contradictions feeding Fascism, which dimension was paradoxically denied by orthodox Marxists, he possessed no real standard by
which to judge the elements that were analogous to Fascism in Stalin's
perversion of Marxism. As he admitted in 1968, "In 1940 we (the leftist
emigrants) in the USA all thought that Fascism was the inevitable last
stage of capitalism and that Russia would never become fascist. This prognosis turned out to be false. The *citoyen* of the French Revolution became
the *bourgeois* of capitalism. Who know what the Soviet *comrade* will
become?"[72] Anxious to claim the explosive potential in the irrationalist
heritage of the past, he disregarded the extent to which Stalinism was
itself dependent on authoritarian irrational appeals, not to mention outright terror. The apocalyptic tradition Bloch so fervently embraced had a
sinister as well as benign dimension, which he seems to have ignored. The
Dostoevskyan salvation coming from the East to which he so long sub-
scribed proved far less utopian than he originally believed.

The second, and more important, source of his political delusions arose
from his indebtedness to process philosophy, which allowed him to argue
that Dialectical Materialism and Marxist Humanism were compatible. Because he conceived of history as a cosmic process of "not-yet-becoming"
and the proletariat as its "we-subject," he failed to recognize the critical
importance of intersubjectivity,[73] which Gramsci and later Habermas investigated largely in linguistic terms. Although Bloch's method of reading
the traces of the future in the present and past was often hermeneutic, he
neglected the rhetorical tradition of intersubjective discourse underlying
modern hermeneutic theory. While often writing about language,[74] he
never really confronted the implications of the linguistic turn in philosophy,
yet another example of the extent to which he remained beholden to the
thought of the early decades of this century. By neglecting the importance of
building an intersubjectively grounded consensus, Bloch was able to delude
himself into thinking that the Party was the most likely concrete embodiment of hope, an institutional prefiguration of the Communist "kingdom"
still to come. And when he tried to find a standard by which to criticize the
Party, he fell back on the questionable tradition of natural law, which he
tried to give a Marxist turn in *Naturrecht und menschliche Würde*. Like
Heidegger and so many other German intellectuals of this era, he had no

72. Landmann interview with Bloch, p. 166.
73. Helmut Fleischer, *Marxism and History*, trans. Eric Mosbacher (New York, 1973),
p. 101.
74. See, for example, his essay "Zerstörte Sprache—zerstörte Kultur" in *Verbannung:
Aufzeichnungen deutscher Schriftsteller im Exil*, ed. Egon Schwarz and Matthias Wegner
(Hamburg, 1964). This essay, written in 1939, deals with the effects of emigration on German writers.

real theory of politics per se to temper his judgments about the realization of philosophy in concrete historical terms.

Bloch's awakening came only near the end of his long life. For most of his ninety-two years, he seems to have remained relatively indifferent to historical change, doggedly playing the role of "the German philosopher of the October Revolution." Although as we have seen, his concept of totality differed from Lukács in its openness to the future, non-expressivity, inclusion of nature, and sensitivity to the spheres of religion, modern art, and myth, he nonetheless shared with his Hungarian counterpart a fervent hope in normative totality as the end of all alienation and reification and a belief in the coherence of the process of history leading to that end. And he remained far truer to those ideals than did Lukács in the years after their friendship dissolved. In this sense, he preserved in non-synchronous fashion the moment of Western Marxism's messianic and utopian birth.[75]

If Bloch can be seen as a kind of fossilized remnant of Western Marxism's earliest years, resisting historical change with obstinate determination, the figures we will examine in the following chapters demonstrate how quickly the assumptions and hopes of that era could be called into question by Bloch's successors. Instead of ignoring historical transformation, the members of what later became known as the Frankfurt School reacted, perhaps even over-reacted, to the rapid and cataclysmic events of modern life, especially during the fascist era. And in so doing, they progressively dismantled the concepts of totality bequeathed to Western Marxism by its founding fathers, Lukács, Korsch, Gramsci and Bloch.

75. In fact, one might say that Bloch also preserved the moment *before* the birth of Western Marxism as a distinct tradition. Not only did he remain a convinced Leninist for most of his life, but he also tried to combine Second International Dialectical Materialism with the Hegelian and other non-materialist currents that would nurture most later Western Marxists. In this sense, Bloch was never fully a Western Marxist.

CHAPTER SIX

Max Horkheimer and the Retreat from Hegelian Marxism

In May, 1922, a small gathering of leftist intellectuals was convened in the Thuringian town of Ilmenau by Karl and Hedda Korsch and their young friend Felix J. Weil. Intended as the first in a series of Marxist "work weeks" devoted to the theoretical evaluation of recent revolutionary events, the meeting brought together leading thinkers from the German and Hungarian Communist parties, as well as others closely affiliated with them. Although no second such gathering ensued, the "summer academy," as it became known, was an important milestone in the early history of Western Marxism. For not only did it bring face-to-face for the first time Korsch and Lukács, whose fortunes were to be so closely entwined during the next few years, but it also provided an important stimulus to the creation of the Institute of Social Research, the institutional matrix of what later became known as the Frankfurt School.[1] In addition to Weil, whose wealthy father sponsored the Institute, Friedrich Pollock and Karl August Wittfogel were among the meeting's participants. With Max Horkheimer, they provided the initial nucleus of the Institute, which

---

1. For accounts of the emergence of the Frankfurt School out of the Institute of Social Research, see Martin Jay, *The Dialectical Imagination: A History of the Frankfurt School and the Institute of Social Research, 1923–1950* (Boston, 1973); Phil Slater, *Origin and Significance of the Frankfurt School: A Marxist Perspective* (London, 1977); Susan Buck-Morss, *The Origin of Negative Dialectics: Theodor W. Adorno, Walter Benjamin, and the Frankfurt Institute* (New York, 1977); Zoltan Tar, *The Frankfurt School: The Critical Theories of Max Horkheimer and Theodor W. Adorno* (New York, 1977); Andrew Arato and Eike Gebhardt, eds., *The Essential Frankfurt School Reader,* intro. Paul Piccone (New York, 1978); Paul Connerton, *The Tragedy of Enlightenment: An Essay on the Frankfurt School* (Cambridge, 1980); David Held, *Introduction to Critical Theory: Horkheimer to Habermas* (Berkeley, 1980); George Friedman, *The Political Philosophy of the Frankfurt School* (Ithaca, 1981).

was officially opened in June, 1924, as an autonomous affiliate of the University of Frankfurt.

The links between the Ilmenau meeting and the founding of the Institute, which have been detailed elsewhere,[2] bear repeating now because they focus our attention on the early connections between the Frankfurt School and Lukács and Korsch. The Institute emerged out of the same milieu that produced *Marxism and Philosophy* and *History and Class Consciousness*; its members shared with the authors of those works an initial excitement over the Russian Revolution as well as their hopes for its imminent spread westward. Although the Institute's first director, the Austro-Marxist Carl Grünberg, was not an advocate of Hegelian Marxism, its ranks soon included several younger thinkers who looked to Lukács and Korsch for theoretical solutions to the errors of Second (and Third) International Dialectical Materialism. Foremost among the younger members was the philosopher Max Horkheimer,[3] who succeeded Grünberg as Institute director in 1930 and became the major architect of the Frankfurt School's idiosyncratic "Critical Theory." He was supported by the sociologist of literature Leo Lowenthal, who joined in 1926; the philosopher, sociologist, and musicologist Theodor W. Adorno, who was involved in Institute affairs for a decade before becoming an official member in 1938; and the philosopher Herbert Marcuse, who entered the ranks of the Institute on the eve of its forced departure from Germany in 1933. Along with Pollock, who was an economist and the Institute's main administrator, and the psychologist Erich Fromm, who was associated from 1930 to 1939, they formed the Institute's inner core, the first generation of what later became known as the Frankfurt School.

Although the Institute's inner circle did not remain faithful to the arguments of Lukács and Korsch for very long, its initial sympathies were with the type of alternative to orthodox Marxism presented in their work. Never as directly involved in political practice as Western Marxism's founding fathers, Horkheimer and his colleagues nonetheless shared many of the same attitudes that we have encountered in earlier chapters.

2. Andrew Arato and Paul Breines, *The Young Lukács and the Origins of Western Marxism* (New York, 1979), pp. 175–76; G. L. Ulmen, *The Science of Society: Toward an Understanding of the Life and Work of Karl August Wittfogel* (The Hague, 1978), p. 47. Based on Wittfogel's memory, Ulmen records the date of the meeting as Whitsuntide, 1923. The earlier date was confirmed by both Hedda Korsch and Felix Weil.

3. For discussions of Horkheimer's work and career, see Helmut Gumnior and Rolf Ringguth, *Max Horkheimer in Selbstzeugnissen und Bilddokumenten* (Reinbek bei Hamburg, 1974); Anselm Skuhra, *Max Horkheimer: Eine Einführung in sein Denken* (Stuttgart, Berlin, Cologne and Mainz, 1974); and Franz Lienert, *Theorie und Tradition: Zum Menschenbild im Werke Horkheimers* (Bern, 1977).

No better evidence of this initial fidelity, as well as of their subsequent apostasy, can be adduced than the history of their use of the concept of totality. For like the other progenitors of Western Marxism, they insisted that totality was an absolutely essential tool of Marxist as opposed to bourgeois analysis. But unlike those older thinkers, they came increasingly to doubt the efficacy of the concept in its Hegelian Marxist guise. Thus, by tracing the history of the Frankfurt School's critique of Western Marxist holism, we can understand better the tensions and ambiguities in the new Marxist paradigm presented by Lukács, Korsch, Gramsci, and Bloch. Although the Frankfurt School's alternative was not without problems of its own, its demolition of the legacy of Western Marxism's first generation was potent enough to force more recent inheritors of the tradition, most notably Jürgen Habermas, to try to reconstitute Marxist holism on entirely new grounds. Combined with the very different critiques made by more anti-Hegelian Western Marxists in France and Italy after World War II, the Frankfurt School's dismantling of the theoretical premises of Western Marxism made it impossible for contemporary Marxist thought to revert to its original formulations.

The best way to understand the Frankfurt School's initial indebtedness to Lukács and Korsch as well as its progressive disenchantment is to focus on the work of three figures in particular: Horkheimer, Marcuse, and Adorno. Although there was a considerable amount of overlapping in their thought, each brought a special emphasis to Critical Theory. All considered the question of totality central, but each dealt with it in a different way. Even though it does violence to strict chronology, it is most revealing to trace the Frankfurt School's attitude toward Marxist holism by first examining the work of Horkheimer and Marcuse and then turning to Adorno, for it was the last of these figures who most explosively demonstrated its inadequacies.

During the Institute's initial decade in Frankfurt, there were few signs of the coming theoretical crisis. Under Grünberg's leadership, the Institute focused on the history of the workers' movement and provided a meeting place for Western Marxists and such Eastern Marxists as David Ryazanov, the director of the Marx–Engels Institute in Moscow. In his September, 1922, memorandum to the curator of the University of Frankfurt proposing the creation of the Institute, Felix Weil had characterized its goal as "knowledge and understanding of social life in its totality."[4] But there was as yet

4. Quoted in Paul Kluke, *Die Stiftungsuniversität Frankfurt am Main 1914–1932* (Frankfurt, 1972), p. 489.

little attempt to go beyond the conventional Marxist stress on the socioeconomic substructure and the political struggles of the proletariat. Still, the Lukácsian-Korschian insistence on knowing the social whole, which Weil had defended in his memorandum, was already implicit in the very structure of the Institute as it was constituted. In its charter, the director was expressly given "dictatorial"[5] powers to coordinate the work of its various members. Although under Grünberg centralized control was exercised only sparingly, his successor assumed a much more active role in organizing, one might say totalizing, the Institute's efforts.

At his inauguration as director on January 24, 1931, Horkheimer spoke on "The Contemporary Situation of Social Philosophy and the Tasks of an Institute of Social Research."[6] Social philosophy, he contended, should be understood today as "a part of the philosophical and religious attempts to reinsert hopeless individual existence once again into the womb or—to speak with Sombart—in the 'golden ground' of meaningful totalities."[7] Social philosophy was thus more than a single specialized discipline, such as sociology. It inherited the traditional philosophical impulse to know the whole. It ought not, however, to be confused with philosophy pure and simple, which normally remains hostile to "mere" empirical research. Instead, Horkheimer claimed,

the problems of empirical research and theoretical synthesis can only be solved by a philosophy which, concerned with the general, the "essential," provides the respective research areas with stimulating impulses, while itself remaining open enough to be impressed and modified by the progress of concrete studies.[8]

In other words, the abstract antithesis between totalistic philosophy and analytic empirical research had to be transcended.

As Helmut Dubiel has shown,[9] the way in which this transcendence was carried out by the Institute followed in broad outlines the dialectic of "*Forschung*" and "*Darstellung*" pioneered by Marx. The former meant concrete research conducted by relatively traditional sociological techniques, such as the surveys employed by the Institute in the project on the

5. Carl Grünberg, "Festrede gehalten zur Einweihung des Instituts für Sozialforschung an der Universität Frankfurt a.M. am 22 Juni 1924," *Frankfurter Universitätsreden* 20 (Frankfurt, 1924), p. 7.

6. Max Horkheimer, "Die Gegenwärtige Lage der Sozialphilosophie und die Aufgaben eines Instituts für Sozialforschung," *Frankfurter Universitätsreden* 37 (January, 1931).

7. Ibid., p. 8.

8. Ibid., p. 11.

9. Helmut Dubiel, *Wissenschaftsorganisation und politische Erfahrung: Studien zur frühen Kritischen Theorie* (Frankfurt, 1978). For a discussion of another model of interdisciplinary research later influencing the Institute's work, see Martin Jay, "Positive and Negative Totalities: Implicit Tensions in Critical Theory's Vision of Interdisciplinary Research," *Thesis Eleven* 3 (1982).

consciousness of white-collar employees and workers begun in the years before the Institute left Frankfurt.[10] The latter signified the totalizing "representation" of that work in a new theoretical synthesis, most often in the ambitious essays of Horkheimer himself. In the process of representation, the conceptual framework within which future empirical work would be defined was itself changed and strengthened. Conversely, while the empirical findings were never to be taken as verification or falsification of the theory in a traditionally positivist sense, they helped modify and enrich the Institute's Critical Theory.

The initial issue of the Institute's new journal, the *Zeitschrift für Sozialforschung*, which began publication in 1932, concretely demonstrated the totalizing impulse behind the Institute's work. Its opening article was a general survey by Horkheimer of the relations between science (in the broad German sense of *Wissenschaft*) and the contemporary social crisis.[11] Chastising science for failing to address the fundamental questions confronting contemporary society, Horkheimer insisted that the contradictions within science were a function of the larger ones in society as a whole. "At the present time," he asserted from a still faithful Marxist perspective, "scientific effort mirrors an economy filled with contradictions."[12] His article was followed by a series of others designed to back up this claim programmatically in various areas of the social whole: Lowenthal wrote on literature, Adorno on music, Fromm on psychology and Pollock on the contemporary situation of the capitalist economy itself. In later years, their analyses would be supplemented by others on cultural issues by Walter Benjamin and on legal and political ones by Franz Neumann and Otto Kirchheimer. In addition, the Institute would collectively mount ambitious research projects on a variety of topics, which culminated in the five-part series of *Studies on Prejudice* conducted with various American collaborators in the 1940s.[13]

The integration of these investigations of various dimensions of the totality was not, of course, without its difficulties, as the dialectic of *Forschung* and *Darstellung* proved less smoothly reciprocal in practice than

10. For an account of this project, which was never fully completed, see Jay, *The Dialectical Imagination*, p. 116f. Its title was, "The Authoritarian Character Structure of German Workers and Employees Before Hitler." It has recently been edited by Wolfgang Bonss and issued under Fromm's name as *Arbeiter und Angestellte am Vorabend das Dritten Reichs: Ein Sozialpsychologische Untersuchung* (Stuttgart, 1980).

11. Horkheimer, "Notes on Science and the Crisis," in *Critical Theory: Selected Essays*, trans. Matthew J. O'Connell and others; intro. Stanley Aronowitz (New York, 1972).

12. Ibid., p. 8.

13. For discussions of the Institute's empirical work, see the literature cited in note 1, as well as Alfons Söllner, *Geschichte und Herrschaft: Studien zur Materialistischen Sozialwissenschaft, 1929–1942* (Frankfurt, 1979).

in theory.[14] But the Institute's stubborn maintenance of its institutional integrity, despite the vicissitudes of emigration and isolation, bore witness to its strong commitment to a totalizing methodology. The postwar concept of a Frankfurt School with Horkheimer as its "master," for all its unwarranted homogenizing of figures who in many respects went their separate ways, correctly captures this integrating impulse. Although by no means without its internal disputes, both serious and petty, the Institute struggled to create a kind of normative totality of its own, a community of scholars prefiguring the cooperative world of the socialist future.

In more specifically theoretical terms, the early formulations of Horkheimer's position, which became known as "Critical Theory" after a seminal article in 1937,[15] also expressed considerable indebtedness to the holism of Lukács and Korsch. Although reluctant to repudiate statements about the primacy of the economy, such as that quoted above, Horkheimer nonetheless invoked the category of totality as an antidote to economic reductionism:

Economism, to which Critical Theory is often reduced, does not consist in giving too much importance to the economy, but in giving it too narrow a scope. The theory is concerned with society as a whole, but this broad scope is forgotten in economism where limited phenomena are made the final court of appeal.[16]

Similarly, he derided the fetishism of isolated, unmediated facts in positivism for lacking a totalistic perspective:

Dialectics, too, notes empirical material with the greatest care. The accumulation of solitary facts can be most incisive if dialectic thought manipulates them. Within dialectical theory such individual facts always appear in a definite connection which enters into every concept and which seeks to reflect reality in its totality.[17]

Accordingly, he cited Hegel's celebrated aphorism that the true is the whole, against the analytic agnosticism of positivist critics of metaphysics, such as the logical empiricists.[18] And although impatient with metaphysical justifications of the world as an already achieved normative totality, he nonetheless insisted that "harmony and significant existence, which metaphysics wrongly designates as true reality as against the con-

14. For a discussion of some of the problems, see Martin Jay, "The Frankfurt School in Exile," *Perspectives in American History* 6 (Cambridge, 1972). Söllner claims that the original interdisciplinary program of the Institute was already in trouble by the time of Horkheimer's "Traditional and Critical Theory" essay of 1937. See his discussion on p. 188f.

15. Horkheimer, "Traditional and Critical Theory" in *Critical Theory: Selected Essays.*

16. Horkheimer, "Postscript" to "Traditional and Critical Theory" in *Critical Theory: Selected Essays*, p. 249.

17. Horkheimer, "The Latest Attack on Metaphysics" in *Critical Theory: Selected Essays*, p. 161.

18. Ibid., p. 177.

tradictions of the phenomenal world, are not meaningless."[19] But they were, to be sure, only a future possibility because, so Horkheimer contended in true Lukácsian fashion, men

experience the fact that society is comparable to nonhuman natural processes, to pure mechanisms, because cultural forms which are supported by war and oppression are not the creations of a unified, self-conscious will. That world is not their own but the world of capital.[20]

In short, in these and other instances too numerous to mention, Horkheimer invoked the same arguments forwarded by the first generation of Western Marxists to defend the necessity of a totalistic perspective.

In fact, in several ways his work can be said to have extended the scope of Marxist holism beyond that envisaged by the founders of that tradition. For the more messianic of the first Western Marxists, and here Bloch is the exemplary figure, totality was basically an anti-empirical category. To try to grasp the whole as an empirical aggregate was to seek what Hegel would have damned as a "bad infinity." If the facts contradicted the deeper knowledge of an essential reality—and here the classic case was the Revisionists' observation about empirical class consciousness—then, in Fichte's phrase, "so much the worse for the facts." In the more apocalyptic moments of the immediate post-revolutionary era, such a defiance of mere facts seemed justified to Marxist intellectuals believing themselves in touch with the deeper process of social (or in Bloch's case, even ontological) transformation. But a decade later, when Horkheimer began to articulate Critical Theory, such confidence was no longer easily maintained. Thus for him, Marxist holism would have to take into account the stubborn facts that ran counter to the revolutionary expectations of the earlier period.

Like the later Korsch, but without his scientific inclinations, Horkheimer insisted on taking unpleasant facts into account. He fully endorsed the importance of mediating such facts through a dialectical theory that grasped reality on the level of essence as well as appearance. He did not yet feel, as would Adorno in his more bitter moods, that a micrological analysis of the fragments of the social whole could be all that a critical theorist might achieve in the present era. Although as we will see, the seeds of such an outlook were present in the 1930s, he still reserved judgment about the ultimate validity of the Hegelian Marxist premises he had inherited from Lukács and Korsch. A totalizing social research, he continued to believe, could take into account empirical data without losing its holistic perspective.

19. Ibid., p. 178.
20. Horkheimer, "Traditional and Critical Theory," pp. 207–08.

Because of this persistent belief, another modification of the original Hegelian Marxist position must be accounted an enrichment of Marxist holism rather than, as it was considered later, an obstacle to it. The modification in question was Horkheimer's introduction of a psychological component into the Institute's analysis of the social totality. Lukács, it will be recalled, was fiercely hostile to psychology, Korsch only marginally less antagonistic, and Gramsci relatively indifferent. Bloch, although of all the early Western Marxists the one best acquainted with Freud and Jung, substituted hunger for sexual libido as the basic human motivation and prefigural daydreams for their nocturnal counterparts as the object of his hermeneutics of hope. In general, the first generation of Western Marxists accepted that equation of psychology with a natural scientific reduction of the subject made by most defenders of historicism and the *Geisteswissenschaften*. Dilthey's abortive attempt to ground his critique of historical reason in psychology was considered an exemplary failure. Like Husserl, the Western Marxists argued that psychologism in any form was an intrusion into philosophy properly speaking, and by extension into a philosophically informed Marxism as well. Indeed, with the notable exception of Wilhelm Reich, who was relatively indifferent to philosophical questions, Western Marxists in the 1920s were generally hostile to the psychological dimension of class consciousness, which accounts in large measure for their often schematic treatment of it as a theoretical category imposed on reality.

Horkheimer and his colleagues at the Institute were thus breaking new ground in arguing for the possibility of integrating psychology and Marxism. The primary stimulus to their interest, reinforcing the more purely intellectual effects of Horkheimer's work with the Gestaltist Adhemar Gelb[21] and Adorno's years in Vienna in the mid-twenties, was the waning of revolutionary hopes during the course of the Weimar Republic. The philosophically engendered models of class consciousness informing the work of the first generation of Western Marxists were inadequate to explain the persistence of working-class passivity; the psychological dimension of reification had to be explored in ways that Lukács and Korsch had neglected. In an essay entitled "History and Psychology," in the first volume of the *Zeitschrift*,[22] Horkheimer contended that the traditional

21. Horkheimer was also drawn to Gestalt psychology through his work with Hans Cornelius, who had become interested in it as early as the 1890s, well before the movement officially began. See the discussion in David F. Lindenfeld, *The Transformation of Positivism: Alexius Meinong and European Thought, 1880–1920* (Berkeley, 1980), pp. 118–119.
22. Horkheimer, "Geschichte und Psychologie," *Zeitschrift für Sozialforschung* 1, 1–2 (1932).

Marxist equation of false consciousness with ideologies must be supplemented by a psychological analysis of the motivations behind their acceptance. Old social forms, which should be left behind, persist because of the psychic needs which they fulfill. Liberal utilitarian psychology, with its naive assumption of a rationally egoistic individual driven solely by self-interest, was bankrupt, but orthodox Marxism provided no real guidance in replacing it. Although economics was still the primary motor of human behavior, the psychological mediations between the substructure and the actions and beliefs of real men must also be investigated.

The proper psychological method for doing so, Horkheimer contended, did not posit a mass soul or collective consciousness. Instead, it must respect the integrity of the individual psyche, however much it was shaped and penetrated by social forces. Although Horkheimer had been schooled in Gestalt psychology and in fact invoked the theories of Koffka and Wertheimer in discussing epistemological questions,[23] the approach he favored was that of Freudian psychoanalysis, to which Adorno had also been drawn in the 1920s.[24] Its systematic integration into Critical Theory was originally assigned to Erich Fromm, who spelled out the grounds of that integration in a series of contributions to the *Zeitschrift*.[25] In later years, when Critical Theory came to question the holistic premises of its earlier formulations, Fromm's interpretation of the Freud-Marx relationship would be subjected to blistering criticism,[26] but during the 1930s it remained an expression of the Institute's collective thinking on this subject.

In his contribution to the first issue of the *Zeitschrift*, "The Method and Function of an Analytic Social Psychology," Fromm argued for a smooth transition from Marxism to psychoanalysis. Claiming that psychoanalysis provided the concept of human nature that was absent from historical materialism, Fromm optimistically concluded:

23. Horkheimer, "Materialism and Metaphysics" in *Critical Theory: Selected Essays*, p. 43.
24. Adorno wrote a study of Kant and Freud entitled "Der Begriff des Unbewussten in der transzendentalen Seelenlehre" in 1927 for Cornelius, who did not accept it for Adorno's *Habilitation*. It was published posthumously in the first volume of Adorno's *Gesammelte Schriften*, ed. Rolf Tiedemann (Frankfurt, 1973). See the discussion in Buck-Morss, *The Origin of Negative Dialectics*, p. 17f.
25. For a discussion of Fromm's Institute period, see Jay, *The Dialectical Imagination*, chapter 3. For a general discussion of his life's work, see Rainer Funk, *Erich Fromm: The Courage to Be Human*, trans. Michael Shaw (New York, 1982).
26. The most public attack came in the epilogue of Marcuse's *Eros and Civilization* (Boston, 1955), but it was anticipated in an unpublished paper written by Adorno in 1946 entitled "Social Science and Sociological Tendencies in Psychoanalysis." For a not very convincing defense of Fromm, see Ken O'Brien, "Death and Revolution; A Reappraisal of Identity Theory" in *On Critical Theory*, ed. John O'Neill (New York, 1976).

(1) The realm of human drives is a natural force which, like other natural forces (soil fertility, natural irrigation, etc.), is an immediate part of the substructure of the social process. Knowledge of this force, then, is necessary for a complete understanding of the social process. (2) The way ideologies are produced and function can only be understood correctly if we know how the system of drives operates. (3) When economically conditioned factors hit upon the realm of drives, some modifications occur; by virtue of the influence of drives, the social process operates at a faster or slower tempo than one would expect if no theoretical consideration to the psychic factors is given.[27]

The key institution that mediated between the socioeconomic realm and the individual was the family, which Fromm claimed was historically mutable. Although traditional psychoanalysis had absolutized it in its patriarchal form, Fromm, like Reich,[28] contended that the family would be transformed under socialism. In the present, it served as an avenue of socialization into the prevailing order, although it also functioned at least to some extent as a haven of comfort and human warmth in an increasingly regimented world. This last argument, which Horkheimer was later to find particularly compelling,[29] contributed to the nostalgic dimension of Critical Theory. But in Fromm's work in the 1930s, it was never very powerful. Instead, he emphasized the liberating potential of harnessing psychoanalysis (stripped to be sure of some of its more pessimistic features, such as the death instinct[30]) to a humanist Marxism. The Institute's early integration of Freud and Marx was thus consonant with its still-Lukácsian optimism about a holistic dialectical method.

That fundamental optimism was demonstrated in another crucial aspect of Critical Theory, its attitude toward the link between the concept of totality and praxis. Although the Frankfurt School's position on the traditional Marxist unity of theory and practice was always highly complicated, and became even more so in later years, during the 1930s Horkheimer consistently called for a Marxism that was practical rather than contemplative.

27. Fromm, "The Method and Function of an Analytic Social Psychology," in *The Essential Frankfurt School Reader*, p. 492.

28. For a selection of Reich's early works synthesizing Marx and Freud, see *Sex-Pol: Essays, 1929–1934*, ed. Lee Baxandall; intro. Bertell Ollman, trans., Anna Bostock, Tom DuBose and Lee Baxandall (New York, 1972). For a defense of Reich against Fromm's criticisms, see Slater, *Origin and Significance of the Frankfurt School*, p. 104f.

29. See, for example, his general essay for the Institute's collective project *Studien über Autorität und Familie* (Paris, 1936), trans. as "Authority and the Family" in *Critical Theory: Selected Essays*, p. 114.

30. Erich Fromm, "The Method and Function of an Analytic Social Psychology," pp. 522–523. Horkheimer was equally hostile to the death instinct. See his disparaging remarks in his essay, "Egoismus und Freiheitsbewegung; Zur Anthropologie des bürgerlichen Zeitalters," *Zeitschrift für Sozialforschung* 5, 2 (1936), pp. 225–26.

While inviting the charge of hypocrisy because of his refusal to align with any specific party or sect, Horkheimer insisted that "activity is not to be regarded as an appendix, as merely what comes after thought, but enters into theory at every point and is inseparable from it."[31] Carefully distinguishing his theory of truth from that of the pragmatists, whose criterion of validity was tied too closely to success in the present society, he nonetheless linked the verification of a theory to its ultimate efficacy.

Accordingly, Horkheimer contrasted his concept of totality with that of conventional intellectuals who were concerned more with knowledge than with practice. The most prominent target of this reproach was Karl Mannheim, whose sociology of knowledge became the object of a series of Frankfurt School critiques.[32] Mannheim, who had been a close friend and at times even disciple of Lukács in Budapest during the 1910s,[33] did not follow his fellow Hungarian into the Communist Party in 1918. But he did adopt Lukács belief in the supreme importance of the concept of totality, which he agreed was essential to any knowledge of humanity. He also concurred with Lukács' assessment of the links between cognitive and social totalization, writing in 1924:

The present trend toward synthesis, toward the investigation of totalities, may be regarded as the emergence, at the level of reflection, of a force which is pushing social reality into more collectivist channels.[34]

Even in *Ideology and Utopia*, composed when he had moved closer to Weber than to Lukács on many questions, Mannheim continued to argue for a holistic method of analysis:

The study of intellectual history can and must be pursued in a manner which will see in the sequence and co-existence of phenomena more than mere accidental

31. Horkheimer, "On the Problem of Truth" in *The Essential Frankfurt School Reader*, p. 420.

32. For discussions of the Frankfurt School's critiques of Mannheim, see Martin Jay, "The Frankfurt School's Critique of Karl Mannheim and the Sociology of Knowledge," *Telos* 20 (Summer 1974); James Schmidt, "Critical Theory and the Sociology of Knowledge: A Response to Martin Jay," *Telos* 21 (Fall 1974); Martin Jay, "Crutches vs. Stilts: A Reply to James Schmidt on the Frankfurt School," *Telos* 22 (Winter 1975); James Schmidt, "Reification and Recollection: Emancipatory Intentions and the Sociology of Knowledge," *Canadian Journal of Political and Social Theory* 2, 1 (Winter 1978); and Helmut Dubiel, "Ideologiekritik versus Wissenssoziologie: Die Kritik der Mannheimschen Wissenssoziologie in der Kritischen Theorie," *Archiv für Rechts-und Sozialphilosophie* 61, 2 (1975).

33. For Mannheim's relations with Lukács, see David Kettler, "Culture and Revolution: Lukács in the Hungarian Revolution of 1918," *Telos* 10 (Winter 1971); see also A. P. Simonds, *Karl Mannheim's Sociology of Knowledge* (Oxford, 1978), pp. 2–5, and Jay, "The Frankfurt School's Critique of Karl Mannheim and the Sociology of Knowledge." Several of Mannheim's worshipful letters to Lukács of the 1910–1916 period have been translated in *The New Hungarian Quarterly* 16, 57 (Spring 1975).

34. Karl Mannheim, "Historicism" in *Essays on the Sociology of Knowledge*, ed. Paul Kecskemeti (New York, 1952), p. 96.

relationships, and will seek to discover in the totality of the historical complex the role, significance, and meaning of each component element. It is with this type of sociological approach to history that we identify ourselves.[35]

But where Mannheim clearly diverged from Lukács was over the social ground of totalistic knowledge. Instead of seeing the proletariat as the universal class, both subject and object of history, and thus Marxism as a comprehensive theory of the social whole, he demoted the working class to only one class among others and Marxism, concomitantly, to a partial viewpoint. In fact, he claimed, no theory could arrogate to itself a total perspective, because all were the expressions of specific class positions. Ideology was therefore a total concept applicable to every theory, not merely an attribute of the false consciousness of a minority class.

Mannheim did not, however, draw the conclusion that all cognition was therefore irreparably relativist. Instead, he believed that partial knowledge, although not absolutely true, contained aspects of the truth that could be combined in a dynamic synthesis with other partial viewpoints. This synthesis, which he called "relationism," could be achieved by the harmonious integration of all the perspectives represented by the more reflective spokesmen of each social group: the intellectuals. In what one observer has seen as a latter-day resurrection of the nineteenth-century German mandarins' claim to represent society as a whole,[36] Mannheim argued that the "free-floating intelligentsia" could transcend its members' social origins and integrate their perspectives into a holistic knowledge of the current totality. Like many other critics of both liberalism and Marxism in the Weimar era—one thinks here of Kurt Hiller's call for an aristocracy of *Geist*, a "Logokratia," or Leonard Nelson's elitist defense of a *Bund* of spiritual leaders—Mannheim turned the intellectuals into the functional equivalent of a universal class whose disinterested concern for the whole would end social conflict.[37]

In a 1930 review of *Ideology and Utopia*,[38] Horkheimer rejected virtually all of Mannheim's contentions. Like Lukács, he defended the traditional Marxist notion of true and false consciousness, denouncing Mannheim's concept of total ideology as a suppression of the validity of class struggle. Mannheim's sociology of knowledge, Horkheimer charged,

35. Karl Mannheim, *Ideology and Utopia,* trans. Louis Wirth and Edward Shils (New York, 1936), p. 93.
36. Fritz Ringer, *The Decline of the German Mandarins* (Cambridge, 1969), p. 425f.
37. See Walter Struve, *Elites Against Democracy: Leadership Ideals in Bourgeois Political Thought in Germany, 1890–1933* (Princeton, 1973). Struve discusses the specific debt of the conservative thinker Hans Zehrer, of the *Tat* circle, to Mannheim, p. 358f.
38. Horkheimer, "Ein neuer Ideologiebegriff?" *Archiv für die Geschichte des Sozialismus und die Arbeiterbewegung* 15 (1930).

lacked any sense of the link between theory and practice. Unlike Marx, who wanted to change the world, Mannheim was content with only knowing it in its present state. In the terms of Horkheimer's later distinction, Mannheim's sociology of knowledge was thus a "traditional" rather than "critical" theory. It was, moreover, premised on the already achieved meaningfulness, or truthfulness, of the world as it was—a world in fact rent by contradictions and irrationality. Like Hegel with his notion of a *Volksgeist* or the Gestalt psychologists with their harmonizing holism, Mannheim assumed that these contradictions could be reconciled on the level of knowledge. But as long as men did not collectively plan history in a rational way, social reality would remain contradictory and cognition necessarily untotalizable. As Adorno later put it, "Mannheim's use of the concept of the social totality serves not so much to emphasize the intricate dependence of men within the totality as to glorify the social process itself as an evening-out of the contradictions of the whole."[39] A more critical concept of truth would recognize that the present totality could not be its ultimate ground, for in a very important sense it was itself "untrue." Truth, therefore, was a critical, negative concept, rather than an affirmative one. Its verification was a practical, not merely cognitive task. Or, as Marcuse contended many years later, "No method can claim a monopoly of cognition, but no method seems authentic which does not recognize that these two propositions are meaningful descriptions of our situation: 'The whole is the truth,' and the whole is false."[40]

Whether or not Horkheimer's criticisms of Mannheim's position were always fair to the latter's intentions,[41] they clearly expressed the Frankfurt School's caution about grounding truth in the current social whole. Although stressing the link between theory and practice, Horkheimer and his colleagues had no illusions about that impending normative totalization of the world by the proletariat celebrated in *History and Class Consciousness*. In fact, in Horkheimer's review of *Ideology and Utopia* and in his subsequent essays in the *Zeitschrift*, the epistemological ground of totalistic knowledge in the working class, or indeed in any existing social agent, was absent. In so arguing, Horkheimer was closer to Lukács with his Leninist disdain for the empirical consciousness of the proletariat than, say, Korsch with his "revolutionary historicist" reliance on actual

39. Theodor W. Adorno, "The Sociology of Knowledge and its Consciousness" in *Prisms*, trans. Samuel and Shierry Weber (London, 1967), p. 38. This was the final version of an essay that Adorno first drafted in 1937.
40. Herbert Marcuse, 1960 preface to second ed. of *Reason and Revolution: Hegel and the Rise of Social Theory* (Boston, 1960), p. xiv.
41. For a defense of Mannheim that makes him into a forerunner of Gadamerian hermeneutics, see Simonds, *Karl Mannheim's Sociology of Knowledge*, pp. 180f.

class consciousness. And so, not surprisingly, a later commentator has claimed to find a residual Leninism in Horkheimer's position, despite his clear distaste for Bolshevik politics.[42] But unlike Lukács, Horkheimer unequivocally rejected the fiction of an essential class consciousness reflecting the "objective possibility" of the working class. And he had no use at all for a vanguard party that arrogated to itself the right to express that deeper level of class consciousness.

This rejection, however, presented Horkheimer with a dilemma. If the social ground of truth was absent in the present, who was to be the guardian of a future truth? Horkheimer's answer, at least in 1937, was that "under the conditions of later capitalism and the impotence of the workers before the authoritarian state's apparatus of oppression, truth has sought refuge among small groups of admirable men."[43] Were these isolated figures, selected as Adorno would later admit by a "stroke of undeserved luck,"[44] like Mannheim's "free-floating intelligentsia," beyond their class origins? That far Horkheimer would not go: "Critical Theory is neither 'deeply rooted' like totalitarian propaganda nor 'detached' like the liberalist intelligentsia."[45] But precisely how it was related to contemporary social forces or agents, Horkheimer did not say. Without Gramsci's hope in the eventual emergence of "organic" intellectuals from within the ranks of the working class, all Horkheimer could do was contend that there was some vaguely defined relationship between certain intellectuals' judgments and the movement of history and historical practice:

Conceptual development is, if not parallel, at least in verifiable relation to the historical development. But the essential relatedness of theory to time does not reside in the correspondence between individual parts of the conceptual construction and successive periods of history; that is a view on which Hegel's *Phenomenology of Mind* and *Logic* and Marx's *Capital*, examples of the same method, are in agreement. It consists rather in the continuous alteration of the theoretician's

42. Arato, introduction to Part 1 of *The Essential Frankfurt School Reader*, pp. 7–8. The Frankfurt School was, in fact, often contemptuous of what it saw as the manipulated economistic consciousness of the contemporary working class. See, for example, Marcuse's remark in "On Hedonism" in *Negations: Essays in Critical Theory*, trans. Jeremy J. Shapiro (Boston, 1968), p. 191: "It appears that individuals raised to be integrated into the antagonistic labor process cannot be judges of their own happiness. They have thus been prevented from knowing their true interest."
43. Horkheimer, "Traditional and Critical Theory," pp. 237–38.
44. Theodor W. Adorno, *Negative Dialectics,* trans. E. B. Ashton (New York, 1973), p. 41.
45. Horkheimer, "Traditional and Critical Theory," pp. 223–24; compare this statement with Adorno's remark in "The Sociology of Knowledge and its Consciousness" that

The answer to Mannheim's reverence for the intelligentsia as "free-floating" is to be found not in the reactionary postulate of its "rootedness in Being" but rather in the reminder that the very intelligentsia that pretends to float freely is fundamentally rooted in the very being that must be changed and which it merely pretends to criticize. (p. 48)

existential judgment on society, for this judgment is conditioned by the conscious relation to the historical practice of society.[46]

The notion of an "existential judgment" is not a fully self-evident one, as evidenced by the fact that one misguided critic of the Frankfurt School took it to mean that Critical Theory was, despite all its protestations to the contrary, a variant of existentialism.[47] In a footnote to the essay in which it first appeared, "Traditional and Critical Theory," Horkheimer explained:

The classificatory judgment is typical of prebourgeois society: this is the way it is, and man can do nothing about it. The hypothetical and disjunctive forms belong especially to the bourgeois world: under certain circumstances this effect can take place; it is either thus or so. Critical Theory maintains: it need not be so; man can change reality and the necessary conditions for such change already exist.[48]

Why this faith in the possibility of change is called an "existential judgment" is not fully clear—its implications are really Hegelian—but what is certain is that it involved a still-Marxist belief in the inevitability of capitalism's collapse:

The basic form of the historically given commodity economy on which modern history rests contains in itself the internal and external tensions of the modern era; it generates these tensions over and over again in an increasingly heightened form. . . . After an enormous extension of human control over nature, it finally hinders further development and drives humanity into a new barbarism.[49]

Believing in this course of history was what Horkheimer called the "unfolding of a single existential judgment" that was the basis of Critical Theory. In other words, he still maintained a Luxemburgist confidence in the breakdown of capitalism and the subsequent alternative of barbarism or socialism, an outcome to be decided on the basis of collective human will.

In the 1930s, Horkheimer continued to believe that this "existential judgment" was still "conditioned by the conscious relation to the historical practice of society," although he could not spell out precisely what this relation in fact was. By the end of the decade, however, the "existential judgment" of Critical Theory had radically shifted in a more pessimistic direction, which was most dramatically expressed in the dark pages of *Dialectic of Enlightenment*, written jointly with Adorno from 1942 to 1944. The transformation of the Frankfurt School's concept of totality was no less striking, as we will see when turning to Adorno's work in a later chapter. But even in Horkheimer's *Zeitschrift* essays of the 1930s,

46. Horkheimer, "Traditional and Critical Theory," pp. 233–234.
47. Tar, *The Frankfurt School*, p. 205.
48. Horkheimer, "Traditional and Critical Theory," p. 227.
49. Ibid.

certain anticipations of his later disillusionment can be discerned. Although, as we have seen, he relied heavily on a Lukácsian notion of totality and indeed began his tenure as Institute director with the intention of translating it into a research program, there were significant ways in which even the early Horkheimer distanced himself from Hegelian Marxist holism.

One indication of this distance, paradoxically, was Horkheimer's attempt to introduce psychology into Critical Theory. Although its inclusion can, as we have seen, be accounted in one sense as an attempt to flesh out the Lukácsian concept of totality and fill in one of its gaps, in another sense it served to undermine it. In stressing the superiority of an individual psychology over a mass one, Horkheimer expressed his loyalty to one of the most fundamental premises of his thought: the irreducibility of the individual to the collective. While acknowledging the inevitable end of the liberal era, he nonetheless retained its individualist concept of man. Although in the future a harmonious equilibrium between individual and collective might be achieved, in the present era of growing authoritarianism, the balance was shifting in the direction of oppressive collectivities.

Horkheimer's concern for individual emancipation, which developed during his early rebellion against his parents' authority, initially had an expressionist coloration.[50] Unlike Bloch, he quickly passed beyond this stage of his intellectual maturation, but he remained committed to the value of the individual even as he grew attached to Hegelian Marxism. An important influence in this regard was his major professor in Frankfurt, the heterodox neo-Kantian Hans Cornelius,[51] who taught Pollock and Adorno as well. For Cornelius, the epistemological subject was more individual than transcendental, philosophy was an open system with no absolute point of origin, and concrete experience was the ultimate ground of knowledge. Even when Horkheimer began studying Hegel, "the philosopher to whom we are most indebted in many respects,"[52] he retained Cornelius' distrust of absolute idealism in any form. One of his first publications was a contribution to Grünberg's *Festschrift* entitled "Hegel and Metaphysics,"[53] which attacked the idealist premise of the perfect unity of

50. See his juvenilia collected in *Aus der Pubertät: Novellen und Tagebüchblatter,* ed. with afterword by Alfred Schmidt (Munich, 1974); and the discussion in Helmut Gumnior and Rolf Ringguth.
51. The best discussion of Cornelius is in Buck-Morss, *The Origin of Negative Dialectics,* p. 7f.
52. Horkheimer, "The Social Function of Philosophy" in *Critical Theory: Selected Essays,* p. 270.
53. Horkheimer, "Hegel und die Metaphysik" in *Festschrift für Carl Grünberg zum 70. Geburtstag* (Leipzig, 1932).

subject and object and defended individuals against the hypostatization of an absolute subject. In later essays, such as "Materialism and Morality,"[54] he criticized Kant for numerous failings, but continued to invoke his notion of the individual against organic sociologies of community that were indifferent to its importance.

Reinforcing Horkheimer's suspicion of epistemological anti-individualism was an equally vehement rejection of the ascetic moment in idealist philosophies. Like Nietzsche, he distrusted the Kantian opposition between duty and interest as a cruel suppression of the value of human happiness. Perhaps because of an early fascination with Schopenhauer, he was particularly sensitive to the denial of individual suffering implicit in idealist theodicies.[55] Despite his distaste for narrow utilitarian philosophies of self-interest, he granted a certain legitimacy to the bourgeois concept of egoism with its demand for personal gratification.[56] As a result, he condemned the identification of labor with man's quintessential ontological activity as an ascetic ideology inherited by Marxism from the bourgeois apotheosis of the work ethic.[57] The hedonist tradition in philosophy, which Marcuse discussed at some length in the *Zeitschrift*,[58] should be understood as a corrective to the idealist indifference to corporeal happiness. Indeed, the very essence of materialism, rightly understood, was a protest against the denial of personal gratification. Nothing condemned contemporary organic holism more than its specious justification of heroic self-sacrifice on behalf of the whole.[59]

Many of these strictures were aimed at right-wing, *völkisch* ideologies, but insofar as Lukács' anti-individualist celebration of the proletariat as the meta-subject of history partook of the same ascetic impulses, Horkheimer questioned it as well. The Lukács who could say to Paul Honigsheim that "all this individualism is just humbug"[60] and call for strict party discipline in *History and Class Consciousness*[61]—the Lukács,

54. Horkheimer, "Materialismus und Moral," *Zeitschrift für Sozialforschung* 2, 2 (1933), p. 176.

55. See, for example, his critique of such theodicies in *Anfänge der bürgerlichen Geschichtsphilosophie* (Stuttgart, 1930), p.92.

56. Horkheimer, "Egoismus und Freiheitsbewegung," pp. 229–31.

57. Horkheimer, *Dämmerung* (Zurich, 1934), under pseud. Heinrich Regius, p. 181. Connerton, in his otherwise often very insightful study, misses the importance of this passage when he claims that "the concept of work becomes for Horkheimer an ontological category; it designates the primary process" (p. 65).

58. Marcuse, "On Hedonism," *Negations*, originally *Zeitschrift für Sozialforschung* 7, 1 (1938).

59. Horkheimer, *Dämmerung*, p. 67.

60. Paul Honigsheim, *On Max Weber*, trans. Joan Rytina (Toronto, 1968), p. 25.

61. Georg Lukács, *History and Class Consciousness: Studies in Marxist Dialectics*, trans. Rodney Livingstone (Cambridge, Mass., 1971), p. 315f.

in short, who could be the model for Thomas Mann's Naphta—was anathema to Horkheimer and his colleagues.[62] In fact, their refusal to compromise their own individuality, which was translated into an abstinence from all direct political involvement, often invited the reproach that they wanted to preserve what Hegel would have called their "beautiful souls," or Sartre their "clean hands," as indeed was argued by a host of critics from Brecht to Hans-Jürgen Krahl.[63] But whatever its cost, their concern for individual autonomy spared them the terrible compromises with authoritarianism marking Lukács' tortured political history.

It also permitted them to escape several of the inadequacies of Lukács' concept of totality. Rather than transferring the categories of idealism directly to Marxism, as Lukács tended to do in his "attempt to out-Hegel Hegel" in *History and Class Consciousness*, Horkheimer recognized that materialism meant something different. Instead of privileging concept over reality, claiming that the former encompassed the latter, materialism should acknowledge the non-identity of the two. Against idealism, it "maintains the irreducible tension between concept and object and thus has a critical weapon of defense against belief in the infinity of the mind."[64] However much Horkheimer may have admired Vico,[65] he never completely accepted the *verum-factum* principle as the basis of a Marxist epistemology, as Lukács had in *History and Class Consciousness*. He argued instead that such a principle underlay metaphysics, whose secret

generally may be seen in the immanent motif which dominates German idealism and is expressed as early as the Preface to the *Critique of Pure Reason*, namely that "nothing in *a priori* knowledge can be ascribed to objects save what the thinking

62. Horkheimer, "Egoismus und Freiheitsbewegung," p. 220, where Robespierre and the Terror of the French Revolution are discussed in terms of petit-bourgeois asceticism. It should be noted, however, that in *Dämmerung*, Horkheimer admitted the necessity of some suffering in a revolution: "When the cynical member of the ruling class reproaches the ascetic revolutionary for causing nameless suffering, he is not even incorrect. That is the world" (p. 258).

63. Brecht's comments came in the notes he wrote for his so-called "Tuinovel," in which the Institute was held up as a model of pseudo-revolutionary impotence. See Brecht, *Arbeitsjournal 1938–1942/1942–1955* (Berlin, 1973), p. 103f. Krahl was a leading member of the German New Left in the 1960s; for his critique of the Frankfurt School's politics, see his "The Political Contradictions in Adorno's Critical Theory," *Telos* 21 (Fall 1974). Phil Slater's book on the Frankfurt School continues this kind of attack based on a crude, ritualistic insistence on the unity of theory and practice. Slater reviews all the political options open to Germans of their generation, grudgingly concludes that they were without much success, and then still complains that the Frankfurt School should have been politically engaged nonetheless. For a defense of their political abstinence, see Russell Jacoby, review of Slater, *Telos* 31 (Spring 1977).

64. Horkheimer, "Materialism and Metaphysics," p. 28.

65. Horkheimer's most extensive discussion of Vico came in *Anfänge der bürgerlichen Geschichtsphilosophie*. For discussions of his attitude towards Vico, see Joseph Maier,

subject derives from itself," in other words, that reason can attain absolute knowledge only of itself.[66]

There was therefore even in Horkheimer's most Lukácsian work of the 1930s a dissonant impulse that called into question the messianic humanism of the first generation of Western Marxists. Brooding on the implications of religion and coming to very different conclusions than had the utopian Bloch, he warned:

In a really free mind the concept of infinity is preserved in an awareness of the finality of human life and of the inalterable aloneness of men, and it keeps society from indulging in a thoughtless optimism, an inflation of its own knowledge into a new religion.[67]

Because Horkheimer distrusted absolute meta-subjects, whether idealist or Marxist, he was also implicitly critical of the expressive concept of totality employed by Lukács to overcome the antinomies of bourgeois thought. The notion of a unified genetic creator of history was, he claimed, an idealist fiction:

In materialism, individuals and social groups, working and struggling, of course, with such capabilities as previous historical development affords them, have an effect, in turn, on current economic relationships. In idealism, on the contrary, an intellectual force whose essential traits are antecedently fixed is the originator of events; history, consequently, is not a process of interaction between nature and society, already existent and emerging cultures, freedom and necessity, but is the unfolding or manifestation of a unitary principle.[68]

In contrast, materialism, for Horkheimer, always acknowledged the existence of a natural object irreducible to the objectification of a creator subject and resistant to all attempts to master it conceptually.

As a result, even though his early writings often endorsed the domination of nature as a task of socialism,[69] Horkheimer never completely adopted the justification for species imperialism latent in Lukács and Gramsci. By the 1940s, Horkheimer came to recognize more explicitly the dangers in the domination of nature itself, which only Bloch of the first

---

"Vico and Critical Theory," and Fred R. Dallmayr, " 'Natural History' and Social Evolution: Reflections on Vico's *Corsi e Riscorsi,* " both in *Social Research* 43, 4 (Winter 1976), and Martin Jay, "Vico and Western Marxism" in *Vico: Past and Present,* ed. Giorgio Tagliacozzo (New York, 1981).
    66. Horkheimer, "Materialism and Metaphysics," p. 27.
    67. Horkheimer, "Thoughts on Religion," in *Critical Theory: Selected Essays,* p. 131. For a discussion of Horkheimer's attitude toward religion, see Rudolf Siebert, "Horkheimer's Sociology of Religion," *Telos* 30 (Winter 1976–77).
    68. Horkheimer, "Authority and the Family," p. 51.
    69. See, for example, his defense in "Traditional and Critical Theory," of "that function of knowledge which will continue to be necessary even in a future society, namely the mastering of nature" (p. 240).

generation of Western Marxists had understood. Now, instead of accepting the continuity of nature and history underlying Fromm's attempt to
integrate Freud and Marx, he stressed the tensions between them, tensions which had been suppressed by Marxist Humanist anthropocen-
trism. Although he did not rule out entirely an ultimate reconciliation
between man and nature—indeed, he called for at least a dialectical rapprochement in which each respected the integrity of the other—
Horkheimer warned, nevertheless, against a forced unification rooted in
the dominating power of subjective human rationality. In such works as
Dialectic of Enlightenment, written jointly with Adorno, and *Eclipse
of Reason*,[70] he spelled out his doubts about the optimistic assumptions of
the Marxist holism that, at least in part, he had himself accepted during
the 1930s. By the time of his return to Frankfurt after the Second World
War, when the Institute was reconstituted in a building near its former
home, Horkheimer had virtually abandoned all of the attitudes he had
inherited from Lukács and Korsch. Not surprisingly, they responded by
growing increasingly scornful of his political and theoretical development, which they saw leading, in Lukács' memorable phrase, to "the
Grand Hotel Abyss."[71]

In part, the shift in Horkheimer's position reflected the growing influence of Adorno on his thinking, which intensified when both left the
Institute's New York office for southern California in 1941. "It would be
difficult to say which of the ideas originated in his mind and which in my
own," Horkheimer wrote in 1946. "Our philosophy is one."[72] Even accounting for some hyperbole in this statement, it is true that many of the
new ideas espoused by Horkheimer in the 1940s had been defended by
Adorno more than a decade earlier. But beyond the purely personal impact of his friend's thought, the transformation of Horkheimer's Critical
Theory must be understood as a response to the changed historical circumstances of this highly turbulent era.

If Bloch can be said to have remained permanently fixated on the revolutionary events of the post-1917 period, Horkheimer and his colleagues
were similarly affected by the catastrophes of the 1930s and 1940s. The
historical experiences they returned to again and again as justification for
their melancholy view of reality were the failure of the working-class
movement to prevent Fascism, the horrors of the concentration camps,

70. Horkheimer and Adorno, *Dialectic of Enlightenment*, trans. John Cumming (New
York, 1972) and Horkheimer, *Eclipse of Reason* (New York, 1947).
71. Georg Lukács, *The Theory of the Novel*, trans. Anna Bostock (Cambridge, Mass.,
1971), p. 22.
72. Horkheimer, *Eclipse of Reason*, p. vii.

and the devastation of Hiroshima. Traumatized by these events which they interpreted as emblematic of capitalism's dogged power to survive, the Frankfurt School lost virtually all hope for the realization of normative totality either in the immediate or in the distant future. However much they may have still used holistic arguments in their methodological polemics against positivism, they no longer relied on similar ones in their oblique references to what Horkheimer called "the entirely other." Instead, totality became a concept used almost exclusively to denote the oppressive integration of contemporary society, an "administered world" of one-dimensional homogeneity, rather than a true community of fulfilled subjects in a socialist society.

The hope for this latter outcome was not, however, completely lost to Critical Theory. Sober realism, they contended, did not mean resignation or total despair.[73] In fact, at times Horkheimer and his colleagues would juxtapose expressions of apparently total pessimism with outbursts of utopian hope in ways that could only appear paradoxical. The *locus classicus* of this paradox was the essay Horkheimer wrote in 1940 for a privately reproduced collection of memorial tributes to Walter Benjamin, whose recent suicide had deepened his friends' gloom. "The Authoritarian State"[74] is also of particular interest because in it, Horkheimer conclusively rejected the implicit assumption of history as a longitudinal totality which we have seen was the basis of Critical Theory's "existential judgment" in the 1930s.

The foundation of Horkheimer's argument was the model of state capitalism that Pollock had developed in several essays in the *Zeitschrift*.[75] The dialectic of inevitable economic collapse posited by orthodox Marxism, Pollock had argued, was no longer operative. Through political intervention and technological innovation, advanced capitalism had been able to forestall the worsening of the contradictions, including the falling rate of profit, that Marx had assumed would necessarily destroy bourgeois society. The Soviet Union, Pollock suggested, provided no real alterna-

73. Theodor W. Adorno, "Resignation," *Telos* 35 (Spring 1978).

74. Horkheimer, "The Authoritarian State" in *The Essential Frankfurt Reader*.

75. Pollock, "State Capitalism: Its Possibilities and Limitations," *Studies in Philosophy and Social Sciences* (the English continuation of the *Zeitschrift*) 9, 2 (1941), reprinted in *The Essential Frankfurt School Reader*; idem, "Is National Socialism a New Order?," *Studies in Philosophy and Social Sciences* 9, 3 (1941). For discussions of Pollock's contribution to Critical Theory and the Institute's economic work in general, see Jay, *The Dialectical Imagination*, chapter 5; Giacomo Marramao, "Political Economy and Critical Theory," *Telos* 24 (Summer 1974); Barbara Brick and Moishe Postone, "Friedrich Pollock and the Primacy of the Political: A Critical Reexamination," *International Journal of Politics* 6, 3 (Fall 1976); Helmut Dubiel, intro. to Friedrich Pollock, *Stadien des Kapitalismus* (Munich, 1975); and Andrew Arato, intro. to Part 1 of *The Essential Frankfurt School Reader*.

tives; instead of being a truly socialist experiment, it had degenerated into a repressive form of authoritarianism little different from Fascism. Although Pollock was careful to call state capitalism only a Weberian "ideal type" and cautiously listed a number of limitations to its indefinite expansion, the burden of his argument was that socialists could no longer look to the objective laws of capitalist disintegration to bring about the crisis from which they would benefit.

In "The Authoritarian State," Horkheimer extended this argument to challenge the basic assumption of historical coherence underlying Marxism in both its scientific and Hegelian guises:

According to Hegel, the stages of the *Weltgeist* follow one another with logical necessity and none can be omitted. In this respect Marx remained true to him. History is represented as an indivisible development. The new cannot begin before its time. However, the fatalism of both philosophers refers to the past only. Their metaphysical error, namely, that history obeys a defined law, is cancelled by their historical error, namely, that such a law was fulfilled at its appointed time. The present and past are not subject to the same law.[76]

In fact, Horkheimer argued, the very belief in inevitable progress was a dangerous delusion which perpetuated unhealthy trends in the present and ignored the radical break with the past which revolution required:

Dialectic is not identical with development. Two contradictory moments, the transition to state control and liberation from it, are seized as one in the concept of social revolution. Revolution brings about what would happen without spontaneity in any case: the socialization of the means of production, planned management of production, and unlimited control of nature. And it also brings about what will not happen without resistance and constantly renewed efforts to strengthen freedom: *the end of exploitation.* Such an outcome is not a further acceleration of progress, but a qualitative leap out of the dimension of progress.[77]

Appropriately introduced in a volume dedicated to the memory of Benjamin, who also vigorously denounced linear notions of progress,[78] Horkheimer's distinction between dialectic and development indicated his complete abandonment of the optimistic longitudinal concept of totality so essential to the first generation of Western Marxists.

It did not, however, yet mean an embrace of a new pessimistic longitudinal view in which global progress was understood to mean global regression, a position which could be attributed with some justification to

76. Horkheimer, "The Authoritarian State," p. 105.
77. Ibid., p. 107.
78. Walter Benjamin, "Eduard Fuchs: Collector and Historian" in *The Essential Frankfurt School Reader*; idem, "Theses on the Philosophy of History," in *Illuminations: Essays and Reflections,* ed. with intro. Hannah Arendt, trans. Harry Zohn (New York, 1968).

the Frankfurt School's later work like *Dialectic of Enlightenment*.[79] For Horkheimer endorsed with truculent bravado Pollock's caution about the limited permanence of state capitalism; however difficult it might be to overcome, it was only "an antagonistic, transient phenomenon."[80] He even argued that "the law of its collapse is readily visible: it is based on the limitation of productivity due to the existence of the bureaucracies."[81]

But it was not really to any laws of collapse that Horkheimer looked for salvation. Pointing to the tradition of workers' councils in previous revolutions as a model for a future transformation, Horkheimer insisted with a vehemence that would have done credit to Lenin in his battle with the Mensheviks that "present talk of inadequate conditions is a cover for the tolerance of oppression. For the revolutionary, conditions have always been ripe."[82] The material conditions for a break in the course of progress have been achieved; all that is needed is the exercise of human will.

This rather melodramatic appeal to the power of human will, buried, significantly, in an essay Horkheimer chose not to publish, was in effect the last expression of his revolutionary fervor. In fact, in the essay itself there are clear indications that he knew he was addressing a nonexistent audience. Instead of specifying a social agent to bring about the "qualitative leap out of the dimension of progress," he resorted once again to a defense of the "isolated individual" who "is a power because everyone is isolated" and whose "only weapon is the word."[83] And rather than positing a link between critical thought and specific social contradictions or the concrete praxis of a social class, he grounded Critical Theory in the method of immanent critique: "The difference between concept and reality—not the concept itself—is the foundation for the possibility of revolutionary praxis."[84]

Soon after writing "The Authoritarian State," Horkheimer came to recognize that immanent critique was not really a sufficient ground for the possibility of meaningful praxis. By *The Eclipse of Reason* in 1947, he was warning against any instrumentalization of Critical Theory in the present. "Is activism, then, especially political activism," he asked, "the sole means of fulfillment, as just defined? I hesitate to say so. This age needs no added stimulus to action. Philosophy must not be turned into propaganda, even for the best possible purpose."[85] Repressing the minor

79. Connerton, p. 114.
80. Horkheimer, "The Authoritarian State," p. 109.
81. Ibid.
82. Ibid., p. 106.
83. Ibid., pp. 112–13.
84. Ibid., p. 109.
85. Horkheimer, *Eclipse of Reason*, p. 184.

theme of Pollock's analysis of state capitalism, the limitations on its indefinite expansion,[86] Horkheimer froze the conditions of the present into an endless repetitive pattern with no apparent way out. In this view, totality became little more than a synonym for totalitarianism, and religion rather than social action was seen as the major repository of hopes in what Horkheimer called "the entirely other."[87]

Still, the tensions present in "The Authoritarian State" and in Horkheimer's essays of the 1930s, the explosive mixture of bleak despair and utopian optimism, were by no means absent from the Frankfurt School's work as a whole. In both Marcuse and Adorno, if in different ways and to varying degrees, the combination of yearning for a normative totality in the future and pessimism about its denial in the "false totality" of the present remained potent. So too did the vacillation we have seen in Horkheimer between a Lukácsian emphasis on the virtue of totalistic knowledge and a more modest admission that in the present it was impossible to see things whole. The tensions generated by these contradictory impulses ultimately led to the collapse of Critical Theory in its classical form and the subsequent attempt by Jürgen Habermas to ground it anew. But in the process, they also conclusively demolished the paradigm introduced by the first generation of Western Marxists, and with it, its concept of totality.

86. In his introduction to Part 1 of *The Essential Frankfurt School Reader* (p. 23), Arato makes the interesting point that Pollock's doubts about the limitless stability of state capitalism, which were shared by Kirchheimer and Neumann, were only later recovered by Habermas in his analysis of the "rationality crisis" of contemporary capitalism.
87. Horkheimer, *Die Sehnsucht nach dem ganz Anderen* (Hamburg, 1970).

CHAPTER SEVEN

Anamnestic Totalization: Memory in the Thought of Herbert Marcuse

For none of the major architects of Critical Theory was the lure of totality as intense and seductive as it appears to have been for Herbert Marcuse.[1] More deeply and consistently committed to Marxist Humanism and the activist politics it generated than either Horkheimer or Adorno, Marcuse remained loyal to the holistic vision that had first attracted him to radicalism in the years after World War I when Western Marxism was launched. More resolutely Hegelian than his colleagues, even while expanding Hegel's concept of reason to include sexual and aesthetic dimensions, he stubbornly resisted the detotalizing implications of their work. More doggedly faithful to the utopian potential in Marxism—indeed, like Bloch, sometimes berating it for not being utopian enough—he refused to accept as final the dystopian analysis of the modern world offered by the other Frankfurt School members. In short, however much Marcuse may have emphasized the importance of negative thinking, he never lost his original hope for a dialectic that might have a positive resolution.

That Marcuse did, to be sure, absorb a great deal of his colleagues' pessimistic analysis cannot be denied. In his bleaker moods, as when, for example, he composed his controversial portrayal of *One-Dimensional Man* in 1964,[2] Marcuse developed the argument of *Dialectic of Enlightenment* to claim that the advance of technological rationality and the integration of the proletariat had rendered the opportunities for revolutionary

---

1. For a complete bibliography of works by and about Marcuse up until 1980, see Morton Schoolman, *The Imaginary Witness: The Critical Theory of Herbert Marcuse* (New York, 1980). For a full-scale treatment of his career, see Barry Kātz, *Herbert Marcuse and the Art of Liberation: An Intellectual Biography* (London, 1982).
2. Marcuse, *One-Dimensional Man: Studies in the Ideology of Advanced Industrial Society* (Boston, 1964).

change virtually nugatory. Rather than talking about totality as a normative goal, he joined with Horkheimer and Adorno in bemoaning the oppressive totalization that was contemporary society:

By virtue of the way it has organized its technological base, contemporary industrial society tends to be totalitarian. For "totalitarian" is not only a terroristic
political coordination of society, but also a non-terroristic, economic-technical
coordination which operates through the manipulation of needs by vested interests. It thus precludes the emergence of an effective opposition against the whole.[3]

But unlike Horkheimer and Adorno, he restlessly searched for ways
out of this apparent impasse. Quick to identify with the New Left, which
drew sustenance from even his most pessimistic works, Marcuse refused
to rest content with a politics that dismissed all activism as misplaced
instrumental rationalism or self-indulgent psychodrama. Although he
soon recognized the inadequacies of the New Left and the accompanying
counter-culture of the 1960s, he continued to look for cracks in the facade
of one-dimensional "totalitarianism" until the end of his life in 1980 at
the age of 81. And in so doing, he insisted on the necessity of a totalistic
analysis which would conceptualize society as a whole and demand its
complete replacement. For, as he put it in a review of Karl Popper's *The
Poverty of Historicism* in 1959,

Contemporary society is increasingly functioning as a rational whole which over-
rides the life of its parts, progresses through planned waste and destruction, and
advances with the irresistible force of nature—*as if* governed by inexorable laws.
Insistence on these irrational aspects is not betrayal of the liberalistic tradition, but
the attempt to recapture it. The "holism" which has become reality must be met
by a "holist" critique of this reality.[4]

In many respects, what Marcuse meant by a "holist" critique remained
close to the Hegelian Marxism of Lukács, Korsch, Gramsci and the early
Horkheimer. In the first book he wrote in English, *Reason and Revolution*, which appeared in 1941, he took pains to dissociate Hegel from the
right-wing appropriation of him, insisting instead that he was more properly understood as the philosophical inspiration for Marx and Marxism.
Stressing Marx's indebtedness to Hegel's idea of determinate negation—
the dialectical tension between apparent, positive reality and its essential,
negative opposite—Marcuse contended: "For Marx, as for Hegel, 'the
truth' lies only in the whole, the 'negative totality.'"[5] There was only one

3. Ibid., p. 3.
4. Marcuse, *Studies in Critical Philosophy*, trans. Joris de Bres (Boston, 1973), p. 208.
5. Marcuse, *Reason and Revolution: Hegel and the Rise of Social Theory*, 2nd ed. (Boston, 1960), p. 313.

basic difference between the ways in which the two thinkers conceived this whole:

For Hegel, the totality was the totality of reason, a closed ontological system, finally identical with the rational system of history. Hegel's dialectical process was thus a universal ontological one in which history was patterned on the metaphysical process of being. Marx, on the other hand, detached dialectic from this ontological base. In his work, the negativity of reality becomes an *historical* condition which cannot be hypostatized as a metaphysical state of affairs.[6]

In other words, for Marcuse the primary, perhaps the sole, distinction between the Hegelian and Marxist views of totality was that the latter historicized the metaphysical viewpoint of the former, substituting class struggle for the clash of ideas. Otherwise, the dialectical method, including its crucial concept of totality, was shared by both men. History for Marx thus operated in Marcuse's eyes very much like Hegel's "notion," which "evolves only by virtue of its contradictory forces."[7] History, like the "notion," was "an objective totality in which every particular moment appears as the 'self-differentiation' of the universal (the principle that governs the totality) and was therefore itself universal. That is to say, every particular moment contained, as its very content, the whole, and must be interpreted as the whole."[8] For Marcuse, at least in *Reason and Revolution*, the Hegelian and Marxist concepts of totality, aside from the issue of metaphysics versus history, were virtually identical.

Thus, Marcuse retained the longitudinal concept of totality that we have noted earlier in Hegelian Marxism, without any of its fatalistic or theodicy-promoting residues.[9] He was no less certain that the present latitudinal totality should also be understood in holistic terms. As he put it in *Reason and Revolution,*

Marxian theory is of its very nature an integral and integrating theory of society. The economic process of capitalism exercises a totalitarian influence over all theory and all practice, and an economic analysis that shatters the capitalist camouflage and breaks through its 'reification' will get down to the subsoil common to all theory and practice in this society.[10]

And as his reference to a reification that hides an essential reality "common to all theory and practice in this society" demonstrates, he was also deeply indebted, at least initially, to Lukács' expressive concept of totality, in which a subject-object unity embodied the ultimate goal of socialism.[11]

---

6. Ibid., p. 314.   7. Ibid., p. 159.   8. Ibid.
9. Ibid., p. 318–19.   10. Ibid., p. 320.
11. In his later years, to be sure, he qualified his allegiance to subject-object unity in its pure form. See, for example, his critique of Norman O. Brown in *Negations: Essays in Critical Theory*, trans. Jeremy J. Shapiro (Boston, 1968).

Although he came to insist on the "material," that is, erotic and aesthetic dimensions of that unity in ways that married Schiller's ideal of the aesthetic state with Fourier's insistence on the gratification of desire, he nonetheless always relied on a definition of rationality that drew at its deepest level on Hegel's identity theory. However much he may have defended the rights of the concrete individual against the demands of a hypostatized collective, the utopian telos of his thought was reconciliation, harmony, the *Aufhebung* of contradictions. In ways that would frustrate later Frankfurt School figures like Jürgen Habermas,[12] Marcuse continued to think like a Hegelian even when he seemed to be moving as far away as he could from idealism into some ill-defined instinct theory.

Because Marcuse remained so close in these ways to the initial Western Marxism paradigm, it would be redundant to detail all aspects of his variant of Marxist holism. Moreover, the general contours of his intellectual career are more likely to be known to an English-speaking audience than perhaps those of any other figure in this account. For, in a sense, Marcuse was "our" Western Marxist. Although his ideas certainly derived from non-native traditions, they were expressed for the most part initially in the language of his adopted country and thus had a more immediate impact on America and England than did the work of those who needed to be translated before they could be read. In addition, as a teacher at Brandeis University and the University of California, San Diego, during the 1950s, 1960s and 1970s, Marcuse was a direct participant in the growth of the New Left, and indeed was labeled its "guru" by the popular media.[13]

Rather than follow his well-known intellectual career, we will concentrate on one somewhat idiosyncratic element in the development of Marcuse's concept of totality, which was nonetheless of considerable importance for his own work and indeed for the Western Marxist discourse on totality as a whole. That element is his theory of remembrance, or what

12. In a conversation recorded in 1978, Habermas chastised Marcuse for his residual Hegelianism:

I object to the fact that, on the one hand, you base your definition of reason and what is rational on Hegel. You develop that in all your books, even in *Eros and Civilization* in a peripheral chapter on the *Phenomenology of the Mind*. On the other hand, knowing full well that Hegelian logic is no longer so readily acceptable, you push Hegel aside. The concept of reason becomes anonymous, so to speak, denies its idealist origins, and is transplanted into the context of Freudian instinct theory.

("Theory and Politics: A Discussion with Herbert Marcuse, Jürgen Habermas, Heinz Lubasz and Tilman Spengler," *Telos* 38 [Winter 1978–1979], p. 137.) In response, Marcuse claimed, "No, that's too slick. The concept of reason is inherent in the instinctual drives to the extent that Eros is identical to the efforts to contain destructive energy" (ibid.).

13. The best discussion of Marcuse and the New Left remains Paul Breines' two articles, "Marcuse and the New Left in America" in *Antworten auf Herbert Marcuse*, ed. Jürgen Habermas (Frankfurt, 1968) and "From Guru to Spectre: Marcuse and the Implosion of the Movement" in *Critical Interruptions: New Left Perspectives on Herbert Marcuse*, ed. Paul Breines (New York, 1970).

might be called anamnestic totalization. Many of his earlier commentators have noted its importance.[14] One of the more astute, Fredric Jameson, has gone so far as to claim that the theoretical foundation of Marcuse's philosophy

takes the form of a profound and almost platonic valorization of memory, anamnesis, in human existence. Indeed, it is not too much to say that Mnemosyne occupies something of the same emblematic and mythopoetic position in Marcuse's thinking that the deities of Eros and Thanatos hold in Freud's late metapsychology.[15]

From his earliest writings, beginning with *Hegels Ontologie* in 1932, until his very last, *The Aesthetic Dimension* in 1978,[16] Marcuse returned again and again to what he saw as the liberating power of remembrance. In almost all of his major works, most notably *Eros and Civilization, One-Dimensional Man*, and *Counterrevolution and Revolt*, he introduced a virtually identical defense of that power and expressed alarm at its current weakened status. Matched among twentieth-century Marxists perhaps only by Walter Benjamin,[17] Marcuse attempted to harness the energies of recollection for revolutionary purposes.

The sources of his persistent fascination with memory can be traced for analytical purposes to four separate stimuli: his early philosophical training, his adherence to Critical Marxism, his special concern for aesthetics

14. See, for example, Fredric Jameson, *Marxism and Form: Twentieth-Century Dialectical Theories of Literature* (Princeton, 1971), p. 112f; Trent Shroyer, *The Critique of Domination: The Origins and Development of Critical Theory* (New York, 1973), p. 208f; John O'Neill, "Critique and Remembrance" in *On Critical Theory*, ed. John O'Neill (New York, 1976); and Alison Pogrebin Brown, "Marcuse: the Path of his Thought" (Ph.D. Diss., Cornell U., 1978). For a very suggestive discussion of the role of memory in the Frankfurt School as a whole, which curiously ignores Marcuse's contribution in favor of Horkheimer's and Benjamin's, see Christian Lenhardt, "Anamnestic Solidarity: the Proletariat and its *Manes*," *Telos* 25 (Fall 1975). See also Russell Jacoby, *Social Amnesia: A Critique of Conformist Psychology from Adler to Laing* (Boston, 1975) for an attempt to apply the Frankfurt School's theory of remembrance to the history of psychology in this century.

15. Jameson, p. 112.

16. Marcuse, *Hegels Ontologie und die Grundlegung einer Theorie der Geschichtlichkeit* (Frankfurt, 1932) and *The Aesthetic Dimension: Toward a Critique of Marxist Aesthetics* (Boston, 1978).

17. Benjamin's theory of memory has been widely discussed in the context of his philosophy of history. See, for example, Peter Bulthaup, ed., *Materialien zu Benjamins Thesen "Über den Begriff der Geschichte"* (Frankfurt, 1975); Jeanne M. Gagnebin, *Zur Geschichtsphilosophie Walter Benjamins. Die Unabgeschlossenheit des Sinnes* (Erlangen, 1978). There are also suggestive treatments of Benjamin's theory of memory in Jameson, op. cit.; Jürgen Habermas, "Consciousness-Raising or Redemptive Criticism: The Contemporaneity of Walter Benjamin," *New German Critique* 17 (Spring 1979); and Irving Wohlfarth, "Walter Benjamin's Image of Interpretation," *New German Critique* 17 (Spring 1979).

Another figure whose meditations on memory warrant mention is Siegfried Kracauer, a close friend of Adorno's and Benjamin's. See my discussion in "The Extraterritorial Life of Siegfried Kracauer," *Salmagundi* 31–32 (Fall 1975–Winter 1976).

and his radical appropriation of psychology. Although often conflated in his discussions of anamnesia, these different sources contributed distinctive elements to his argument, elements which can be isolated and critically analyzed. In so doing, we can more accurately assess the strengths and weaknesses of Marcuse's theory of remembrance.

From its beginning, Western philosophy has been drawn to the issues raised by present knowledge of past events.[18] From Plato's *Meno* and *Theaetetus* through Aristotle's *De Memoria et Reminiscentia*, Augustine's *Confessions*, Hume's *Treatise on Human Nature*, Bergson's *Matter and Memory* and on up to Russell's *The Analysis of Mind* and Ryle's *The Concept of Mind*, the greatest philosophers of the Western tradition have wrestled with the epistemological puzzles presented by memory. Contemporary philosophers such as E. J. Furlong, W. von Leyden, Brian Smith and Norman Malcolm continue to devote long and learned studies to the same, still unresolved issues.[19] Marcuse, however, seems to have paid little attention to this body of what might be called mainstream speculation about memory. Aside from an occasional vague reference to the "ancient theory of knowledge as recollection,"[20] he ignored the arguments of these thinkers. Instead, as might be expected, he relied far more on the less technical treatments of the problem in the German idealist and phenomenological traditions.

Although no firm evidence appears in his writings, it is likely that the latter first impressed upon him the importance of remembrance. In particular, his philosophical apprenticeship under Martin Heidegger in the late 1920s should probably be considered decisive in this regard. For in Heidegger's *Being and Time* of 1927, a work whose influence on his early development Marcuse has freely acknowledged, memory played a central role. To characterize the wayward course of Western philosophy since the pre-Socratics, Heidegger introduced the notion of *Seinsvergessenheit*, the forgetting of Being.[21] This forgetting, he contended, was so pervasive that language itself had lost the capacity to treat Being as a meaningful reality.

18. For a brief survey of Western philosophy up to Bergson that deals with this issue, see Michael Wyschograd, "Memory in the History of Philosophy" in *Phenomenology of Memory*, ed. Erwin W. Straus and Richard M. Griffith (Pittsburgh, 1970). For a brilliant discussion of artificial inducements to memory or mnemotechnics, from the classical period to Leibniz, see Frances A. Yates, *The Art of Memory* (Chicago, 1966). On twentieth-century analytic philosophy and memory, see W. von Leyden, *Remembering: A Philosophical Problem* (New York, 1961), which deals with Russell and Ryle.

19. E.J. Furlong, *A Study in Memory* (London, 1951); von Leyden, op. cit.; Brian Smith, *Memory* (London, 1966); and Norman Malcolm, *Memory and Mind* (Ithaca, 1977).

20. Marcuse, *Counterrevolution and Revolt* (Boston, 1972), p. 69.

21. Martin Heidegger, *Being and Time*, trans. John Macquarrie and Edward Robinson (New York, 1962).

His own philosophy, Heidegger claimed, was an effort to reverse this collective amnesia and restore consciousness of Being to its proper place. Although Marcuse soon came to recognize the vacuous nature of Heidegger's notion of Being, he nonetheless retained his teacher's insistence that something extraordinarily important had been forgotten in the modern world. Because remembrance was a window on this fundamental reality, it had ontological as well as epistemological implications.

What these implications were became clearer to Marcuse in his first prolonged study of Hegel, directed by Heidegger, which appeared as *Hegels Ontologie* in 1932. In examining Hegel's *Logic* with its central category of negativity, Marcuse argued:

This "not," this negativity which Being is, is itself never present in the sphere of immediacy, is itself not and is never *present*. This "not" is always precisely the *other* of immediacy and the other of presence, that which is never as *present* precisely *never* is and what, however, constitutes its *Being*. This "not," this negativity, is the immediate present always already past at every moment. The Being of present being resides therefore always already in a past, but in a, to a certain degree, "intemporal" past (*Logic*, II, 3), in a past which still always is present and *out* of which precisely Being *is*. A being is at each moment what it is in its immediate present through memory. . . . With the phenomenon of memory, Hegel opens the new dimension of Being which constitutes Being as authentic having-beenness (*Gewesenheit*): the dimension of essence.[22]

Memory, *Erinnerung*, in other words, permits access to an essential, "negative" level of reality, that "intemporal past" preserved on a second ontological plane more basic than that of "positive" and immediate appearance. The German language itself, so Hegel had noted, captured this relationship: "In the verb *Sein* (to be) language has conserved essence (*Wesen*) in the past participle of the verb, '*gewesen*.'"[23]

As Alison Pogrebin Brown has perceptively noted,[24] Marcuse's later stress on two-dimensionality was foreshadowed here in his discussion of the temporal aspect of Hegel's doctrine of essence. But whereas in *Hegels Ontologie* Marcuse identified essence entirely with the "intemporal past," in his later work it was ambiguously related to the future as well. In his 1936 essay, "The Concept of Essence," written after his break with Heidegger and his entrance into the Institute of Social Research, Marcuse linked essence with the Aristotelian notion of potentiality. "All historical struggles," he argued,

22. Marcuse, *Hegels Ontologie und die Grundlegung einer Theorie der Geschichtlichkeit*, p. 76.
23. Ibid., p. 78.
24. Brown, *Marcuse*, p. 153.

for a better organization of the impoverished conditions of existence, as well as all of suffering mankind's religious and ethical ideal conceptions of a more just order of things, are preserved in the dialectical concept of the essence of man, where they have become elements of the dialectical practice linked to dialectical theory. There can also be experiences of potentialities that have never been realized. . . . In idealist philosophy the timeless past dominates the concept of essence. But when a theory associates itself with the progressive forces of history, the recollection of what can authentically be becomes a power that shapes the future.[25]

The identification of essence with the past as well as the future remained a powerful premise of Marcuse's. Returning to Hegel in *Eros and Civilization*, he enthusiastically endorsed his cyclical view of time, remarking:

The fact that remembrance here appears as the decisive existential category for the highest form of Being indicates the inner trend of Hegel's philosophy. Hegel replaces the idea of progress by that of a cyclical development which moves, self-sufficient, in the reproduction and consummation of what *is*. This development presupposes the entire history of man (his subjective and objective world) and the comprehension of his history—the remembrance of his past. The past remains present; it is the very life of the spirit; what has been decides on what is. Freedom implies reconciliation—redemption of the past.[26]

And in *Counterrevolution and Revolt*, he contended, now with special reference to Goethe's view of science, "The Marxian vision recaptures the ancient theory of knowledge as *recollection*: 'science' as the *re*discovery of the true *Forms* of things, distorted and denied in the established reality, the perpetual *materialistic core of idealism*."[27]

Of course, what made it imperative for Marcuse to link essence with both the past and the future was his adherence to Marxism. At first glance, Marxism seems like an unlikely stimulant to the notion that re-capturing the past, whether or not understood as the repository of es-sence, would be a revolutionary project. For all his stress on grasping real-ity historically, Marx himself appears to have had little use for memory as a radical tool. In the *Eighteenth Brumaire of Louis Bonaparte*, he pointed out that earlier revolutions, such as the English and French, had sought legitimacy by cloaking themselves in the mantles of their historical pre-decessors. However, "The social revolution of the nineteenth century," he argued,

cannot draw its poetry from the past, but only from the future. It cannot begin with itself before it has stripped off all superstition in regard to the past. Earlier

25. Marcuse, "The Concept of Essence" in *Negations*, pp. 75–76.
26. Marcuse, *Eros and Civilization: A Philosophical Inquiry into Freud* (Boston, 1955), p. 106.
27. Marcuse, *Counterrevolution and Revolt*, p. 69.

revolutions required recollections of past world history in order to drug themselves concerning their own content. In order to arrive at its own content, the
revolution of the nineteenth century must let the dead bury the dead.[28]

Although one might, as Christian Lenhardt has suggested,[29] read Marx's
labor theory of value as a reminder to see the capital of the present as the
coagulated labor power of previous generations, Marx himself never
seems to have explicitly drawn the conclusion that remembering of the
past was a key to revolutionary consciousness. Instead, he contended,
"The tradition of all the dead generations weighs like a nightmare on the
brain of the living."[30]

It was not really until Georg Lukács introduced the idea of reification in
History and Class Consciousness that the emancipatory potential of memory was tapped by a Marxist thinker of note. Lukács had, in fact, still earlier
pointed to the power of remembrance in his pre-Marxist *The Theory of the
Novel* while discussing time in Flaubert's *Sentimental Education*:

Only in the novel and in certain epic forms resembling the novel does memory
occur as a creative force affecting the object and transforming it. The genuinely
epic quality of such memory is the affirmative experience of the life process. The
duality of interiority and the outside world can be abolished for the subject if he
(the subject) glimpses the organic unity of his whole life through the process by
which his living present has grown from the stream of his past life dammed up
within his memory.[31]

After Lukács' conversion to Marxism in 1918, he no longer stressed the
retrospective nature of totalization, as he had in *The Theory of the Novel*. A
true totality would be achieved only when the proletariat, the universal
class, dereified the objective structures of the social world and recognized
them as its own creations. Totalization was thus a practical activity of the
future, not a contemplative one directed towards the past. And yet, the
concept of dereification implied a certain type of remembering, for what
had to be recaptured were the human origins of a social world that had been
mystified under capitalism as a kind of "second nature."

28. *Karl Marx: Selected Writings*, ed. David McLellan (Oxford, 1977), p. 302.
29. Lenhardt, "Anamnestic Solidarity," p. 149.
30. *Karl Marx: Selected Writings*, p. 300.
31. Georg Lukács, *The Theory of the Novel*, trans. Anna Bostock (Cambridge, Mass.,
1971), p. 127. It should be noted here that Lukács' epic theory of memory with its assumption that the past could be recovered as a meaningful narrative leading up to the present was
implicitly attacked by Benjamin in his "Eduard Fuchs: Collector and Historian," *New German Critique* 5 (Spring 1975), where he writes: "The historical materialist must abandon
the epic element in history. For him history becomes the object of a construct (*Konstruktion*)
which is not located in empty time but is constituted in a specific epoch, in a specific life, in a
specific work. The historical materialist explodes the epoch out of its reified 'historical continuity,' and thereby lifts life out of this epoch and the work out of the life work" (p. 29).
Marcuse's attitude towards memory seems to have vacillated between these two alternatives.

Marcuse recognized the link between memory and dereification, at least implicitly, in his 1932 essay "The Foundations of Historical Materialism," where he reviewed Marx's newly published Paris manuscripts. "Because it is dependent on the conditions pre-established by history," he argued,

the praxis of transcendence must, in order to be genuine transcendence, reveal these conditions and appropriate them. Insight into objectification as insight into the historical and social situation of man reveals the historical conditions of this situation and so achieves the *practical force and concrete form* through which it can become the level of revolution. We can now also understand how far questions concerning the *origin* of estrangement and insight into the *origin* of private property must be an integrating element in a positive theory of revolution.[32]

The explicit linkage of dereification with remembrance came somewhat later in the work of Marcuse's colleagues at the Institute of Social Research. In an important letter of February 29, 1940, to Walter Benjamin, Adorno responded with considerable enthusiasm to the theory of forgetting propounded in Benjamin's essay "On Some Motifs in Baudelaire."[33] In that essay, Benjamin had introduced his now celebrated contrast between the integrated, meaningful experience he called "*Erfahrung*" and the atomizing, incoherent alternative he called "*Erlebnis.*" Benjamin tied the former to Proust's idea of "involuntary memory," which he claimed was possible only when men were immersed in an ongoing, communal tradition. In the modern world, such a tradition was lacking; the only experience thus possible was the impoverished disorientation of *Erlebnis*.
    In his letter to Benjamin, Adorno asked,

Wouldn't it be the task to connect the entire opposition between *Erlebnis* and *Erfahrung* to a dialectical theory of forgetting? One could also say: to a theory of reification. For every reification is a forgetting: objects become thinglike at the moment when they are seized without all their elements being contemporaneous, where something of them is forgotten.[34]

Although Marcuse did not know of this letter, one of the aphorisms included in Horkheimer and Adorno's *Dialectic of Enlightenment*, entitled "Le Prix du Progrès," repeated the key phrase "all reification is a forgetting."[35] Significantly, it was linked to the issue of the domination of

32. Marcuse, "The Foundations of Historical Materialism" in *Studies in Critical Philosophy*, trans. Joris de Bres (Boston, 1972), p. 35.
33. Benjamin's essay is translated in *Illuminations*, ed. Hannah Arendt, trans. Harry Zohn (New York, 1968); Adorno's letter is reprinted in Theodor W. Adorno, *Über Walter Benjamin* (Frankfurt, 1970).
34. Ibid., p. 159.
35. Horkheimer and Adorno, *Dialektik der Aufklärung* (Amsterdam, 1947), p. 274; the English translation by John Cumming (New York, 1972) unfortunately renders "*Verdingli-*

nature, one of the Frankfurt School's central concerns. The lines preceding it read: "Perennial domination over nature, medical and non-medical techniques, are made possible only by the process of oblivion. The loss of memory is a transcendental condition for science."[36]

In Marcuse's later work, the same linkages between forgetting, reification and the domination of nature appear. The passage quoted above from *Counterrevolution and Revolt,* with its veiled reference to Goethe's theory of science as the recovery of primary forms, follows directly a discussion of the redemption of nature as a "subject–object" with intrinsic value in its own right. The implication is that forgetting the suffering of men is akin to forgetting the pain caused nature by its human domination; remembrance somehow permits us to see the connections and honor the subjective side of both nature and man.

"All reification is a forgetting" also served another function in Marcuse's theory of remembrance: as a reminder of the negative potential in art. The final paragraph of *The Aesthetic Dimension* begins by quoting the phrase from *Dialectic of Enlightenment* and continues: "Art fights reification by making the petrified world speak, sing, perhaps dance. Forgetting past suffering and past joy alleviates life under a repressive reality principle. In contrast, remembrance spurs the drive for the conquest of suffering and the permanence of joy."[37]

The third source of Marcuse's celebration of memory was, in fact, the role it played in his vision of aesthetics. For much Western art, as for Western philosophy, memory has proven an object of singular fascination. To the Greeks, Mnemosyne was the mother by Zeus of the nine Muses. Proust, to whom Marcuse himself referred approvingly,[38] also comes immediately to mind in this regard, but he was by no means alone in associating art with remembrance. The Romantics, towards whom Marcuse was always drawn, were intensely interested in the links between memory, personal identity and imagination.[39] In Germany, Schlegel was particu-

---

chung" as objectification, which destroys the meaning of the aphorism. It should be emphasized that the Frankfurt School did not believe that reification was *only* a forgetting, which could be undone by memory alone. Clearly, dereification, to the extent that it was possible, was a practical task.

36. Ibid.

37. Marcuse, *The Aesthetic Dimension: Toward a Critique of Marxist Aesthetics* (Boston, 1978), p. 73.

38. Marcuse, *Eros and Civilization,* p. 213.

39. For discussions of these links, see M. H. Abrams, *Natural Supernaturalism* (New York, 1973), pp. 80–83; Robert Langbaum, *The Mysteries of Identity: A Theme in Modern Literature* (New York, 1977), Chapter 1; Marshall Brown, *The Shape of German Romanticism* (Ithaca, 1979), pp. 186–87; Carl Dawson, *Victorian Noon: English Literature in 1850* (Baltimore, 1979), p. 123f; and Georges Poulet, "Timelessness and Romanticism" in *Ideas in*

larly fascinated with memory as a vehicle for overcoming fragmentation, while in England, Wordsworth sought ways to recapture and render intelligible his personal past in such works as *The Prelude*. His friend Coleridge defined "the primary imagination" as "a repetition in the finite mind of the eternal act of creation,"[40] and later Victorian writers, such as Ruskin in *The Seven Lamps of Architecture*, advocated lighting what he called "the lamp of memory" to escape the dreary present and renew contact with a more beautiful past.

Although after his 1922 dissertation on the *Künstlerroman* (novels about artists),[41] Marcuse never directly acknowledged the influence of the Romantic tradition on his thought, he was clearly in its debt, as the following passage from *Counterrevolution and Revolt* demonstrates:

On a primary level, art is recollection: it appeals to a preconceptual experience and understanding which re-emerge in and against the context of the social functioning of experience and understanding—against instrumentalist reasoning and sensibility.[42]

No less Romantic was his privileging of music among all the arts as the most essential repository of recollected truth:

These extreme qualities, the supreme points of art, seem to be the prerogative of music . . . and within music, of melody. Here the melody—dominant, *cantabile*, is the basic unit of recollection: recurring through all variations, remaining when it is cut off and no longer carries the composition, it sustains the supreme point: in and against the richness and complexity of the work. It is the voice, beauty, calm of another world here on earth.[43]

In *The Aesthetic Dimension*, Marcuse introduced memory into the very heart of artistic form itself:

The medium of sensibility also constitutes the paradoxical relation of art to time—paradoxical because what is experienced through the medium of sensibility is present, while art cannot show the present without showing it as past. What has become form in the work of art has happened: it is recalled, re-presented. The mimesis translates reality into memory.[44]

In short, for Marcuse the promise of future happiness embodied in art was dialectically related to its retention of past instances of joy and fulfillment.

Cultural Perspective, ed. Philip P. Wiener and Aaron Holland (New Brunswick, N.J., 1962). For a treatment of Marcuse's general indebtedness to Romanticism, see Michael Löwy, "Marcuse and Benjamin: The Romantic Dimension," *Telos* 44 (Summer 1980).

40. Coleridge, *Biographia Literaria*, ed. J. Shawcross (Oxford, 1965), p. 202.
41. Marcuse, *Der deutsche Künstlerroman* in *Schriften*, vol. 1 (Frankfurt, 1978).
42. Marcuse, *Counterrevolution and Revolt*, p. 99.
43. Ibid., p. 100.
44. Marcuse, *The Aesthetic Dimension*, p. 67.

In combatting the "affirmative character of culture"[45] as a realm of transcendent values, Marcuse insisted on the sensuous, material, even erotic nature of artistic pleasure. His linkage of art and Eros was abetted by his radical appropriation of psychology into his version of Critical Theory, an appropriation that also strengthened his interest in the liberating power of remembrance. Psychology thus joined philosophy, Critical Marxism and aesthetics as an especially potent source of his theory of memory. In *Hegels Ontologie*, he had warned against reducing memory to a psychological category,[46] but after his entrance into the Institute of Social Research, where psychology was a subject of considerable interest, he grew increasingly open to the psychological dimension of anamnesia. The psychology of memory to which Marcuse was drawn was not, to be sure, that of the experimentalists, such as Hermann Ebbinghaus,[47] whose scientific data on the functioning of memory he chose to ignore. It was instead the psychoanalysis of Freud that provided him with a psychological theory of memory to complement those he had derived from philosophy, Marxism and aesthetics.

Beginning with his 1898 paper, "On the Psychic Mechanism of Forgetfulness"[48] and elaborating in later works such as *The Psychopathology of Everyday Life*, Freud advanced the now familiar argument that the loss of memory was due to the repression of traumatic experiences or unpleasant thoughts that had engendered pain or anxiety in the past, most of which were sexual or aggressive in nature. One of the fundamental objectives of psychotherapy was thus the anamnestic recovery of forgotten and repressed experiences, thoughts, desires or impulses. Once remembered, they could be dealt with in a conscious and responsible fashion, rather than being allowed to fester as the source of unconsciously generated neurotic symptoms.

Marcuse adopted Freud's linkage of forgetting and repression, but drew on an essay on childhood amnesia by his former Institute colleague, Ernst Schachtel,[49] to give it a subtle twist. Instead of emphasizing the

45. Marcuse, "The Affirmative Character of Culture" in *Negations*. The phrase was Horkheimer's invention.

46. Marcuse, *Hegels Ontologie*, p. 77.

47. Ebbinghaus, *Über das Gedächtnis* (Leipzig, 1885). Ebbinghaus was the pioneer of the experimental psychology of memory.

48. *The Standard Edition of the Complete Psychological Works of Sigmund Freud*, trans. James Strachey and Anna Freud, vol. 3 (London, 1962).

49. Schachtel, "Memory and Childhood Amnesia" in *A Study of Interpersonal Relations*, ed. Patrick Mullahy (New York, 1950) and in Schachtel, *Metamorphosis: On the Development of Affect, Perception, Attention and Memory* (New York, 1959). Marcuse singled out for special praise Schachtel's discussion of the "conventionalization" of memory by society. He might also have mentioned Schachtel's linkage of memory with artistic creation and his depiction of childhood as dominated by the pleasure principle and "polymor-

forgetting of painful or traumatic episodes in the past, he stressed the repression of pleasurable activities that society could not willingly tolerate. The source of forgetting was thus not so much the intrapsychic needs of repression as the external demands of a repressive society. Citing Nietzsche's link in *The Genealogy of Morals*[50] between the training of memory and the origins of morality, Marcuse condemned

the one-sidedness of memory-training in civilization: the faculty was chiefly directed toward remembering duties rather than pleasures; memory was linked with bad conscience, guilt and sin. Unhappiness and the threat of punishment, not happiness and the promise of freedom, linger in memory.[51]

What should be remembered by man instead, Marcuse contended, are those promises and potentialities "which had once been fulfilled in his dim past."[52] There was a time, he claimed, in the "archaic" prehistory of the species before socially induced surplus repression, a time controlled largely by the pleasure principle, which remembrance should labor to rescue. As he put it in his later essay, "Freedom and Freud's Theory of Instincts,"

Originally,* the organism in its totality and in all its activities and relationships is a potential field for sexuality, dominated by the pleasure principle.

*The notion of "origin" as Freud uses it has simultaneously structural-functional—and temporal, ontogenetic, and phylogenetic significance. The "original" structure of the instincts was the one which dominated in the prehistory of the species. It is transformed during the course of history but continues to be effective as a substratum, preconscious and unconscious, in the history of the individual and the species—most obviously in early childhood. The idea that mankind, in general and in its individuals, is still dominated by "archaic" powers is one of Freud's most profound insights.[53]

Although in this essay[54] Marcuse acknowledged that freedom from certain of these archaic powers, most notably those associated with the death

---

phous perversity." Marcuse went beyond Schachtel in linking childhood amnesia with the repression of the species "childhood," which Freud had discussed in his speculations about the "archaic heritage." Marcuse felt both were forgotten for social reasons, and argued, as Schachtel did not, that a different social order would allow the repressed to return in a healthy way.

50. Friedrich Nietzsche, *The Genealogy of Morals*, trans. Walter Kaufmann (New York, 1967) Part 2, pp. 1–3; Marcuse did not, however, acknowledge Nietzsche's defense of a certain kind of forgetfulness in *The Genealogy* as a mark of the noble man "beyond good and evil." For discussion of the positive role of forgetting in Nietzsche, see Alphonso Lingis, "The Will to Power;" Eric Blondel, "Nietzsche: Life as Metaphor;" and Pierrre Klossowski, "Nietzsche's Experiences of the Eternal Return," all in *The New Nietzsche: Contemporary Styles of Interpretation*, ed. with intro. David B. Allison (New York, 1977).

51. Marcuse, *Eros and Civilization*, p. 212.

52. Ibid., p. 18.

53. Marcuse, *Five Lectures: Psychoanalysis, Politics, and Utopia*, trans. Jeremy J. Shapiro and Shierry M. Weber (Boston, 1970), p. 8.

54. Ibid., p. 29.

instinct, would be itself a liberation, the burden of his argument was that remembering still others was a precondition for a utopian future.

With the psychological component introduced in *Eros and Civilization*, Marcuse's theory of remembrance was essentially complete. It provided him with a potent weapon in his attempt to find an Archimedean point for a Critical Theory no longer able to rely on the praxis of a revolutionary proletariat as its ground. For insofar as recollecting a different past prevents men from eternalizing the status quo, memory subverts one-dimensional consciousness and opens up the possibility of an alternative future. Moreover, it does so in a way that avoids the traditional bourgeois and social democratic ideology of history as evolutionary progress. As Benjamin often pointed out,[55] the belief in a smooth, unilinear flow of time helps preserve the tendencies for domination existent in the present. In *Eros and Civilization*, Marcuse approvingly quoted Benjamin's observation that clocks were shot at during the July Revolution as evidence of the link between stopping ongoing temporality and achieving revolutionary change.[56] And in *One-Dimensional Man*, he cited Adorno's similar insight that "the spectre of man without memory . . . is more than an aspect of decline—it is necessarily linked with the principle of progress in bourgeois society."[57] By depreciating the past to mere preparation for the future and seeing that future as an extrapolation of tendencies in the present, the ideology of progress justified the suffering of past generations. It also made it impossible to recapture past moments of happiness and fulfillment which memory preserved as beacons for the future. In fact, so Marcuse argued, the very notion of progress with its never-ending dissatisfaction with the present and impatient yearning for an improved tomorrow was one of the earmarks of a repressive society. In a true utopia, "time would not seem linear, as a perpetual line or rising curve, but cyclical, as the return in Nietzsche's idea of the 'perpetuity of pleasure.'"[58] Memory, by restoring the forgotten past, was thus a model of the utopian temporality of the future. In other words, it was not merely the content of what is remembered that constitutes the liberating power of memory, but also the very fact of memory's ability to reverse the flow of time that makes it a utopian faculty. If there is to be a true human totality in the future, anamnesis in the present is one of its prefigurations.

55. Benjamin, "Eduard Fuchs: Collector and Historian," and "Theses on the Philosophy of History," in *Illuminations*.
56. Marcuse, *Eros and Civilization*, p. 213.
57. Marcuse, *One-Dimensional Man*, p. 99.
58. Marcuse, "Progress and Freud's Theory of Instincts" in *Five Lectures*, p. 41.

The claims Marcuse made for the liberating power of remembrance were obviously very large ones. What can be said about their validity? Any answer to this question must begin with a consideration of precisely what Marcuse thought should be remembered. For it is clear that emancipatory remembrance was far more than that indiscriminate preservation of everything in the past condemned by Nietzsche in his "Use and Abuse of History" and by Benjamin in his "Eduard Fuchs: Collector and Historian." If memory has been trained by civilization to preserve duties and guilt, it must be retrained to recover something else.

Marcuse's notion of that alternative contained, however, a certain ambiguity. At times, the Marxist in him protested the ontologization of the content of memory; the dialectical concept of essence, we have seen him argue in his 1937 essay, contains only the historical struggles of past generations. In *Counterrevolution and Revolt*, he protested in a similar vein that recollection "is not remembrance of a Golden Past (which never existed), of childhood innocence, primitive man, et cetera."[59] In contrast, what must be remembered are the real historical experiences and desires of our actual ancestors, not some imagined prehistorical era of perfect bliss. Indeed, as Benjamin once noted,[60] revolutionary motivation may well stem more from outrage over the indignities suffered by our fathers than hope for the comfort of our children.

But despite the historical intentions of these passages, at other times in his work Marcuse fell back on what must be called an ontological theory of anamnesis. Although he abandoned Heidegger's notion of a Being that had to be recollected and criticized Hegel's idea of essence as an "intemporal past," in his appropriation of psychoanalysis he retained their ontological biases. Freud's archaic heritage meant that an individual's promises and potentialities "had once been fulfilled in his dim past,"[61] or as he put it elsewhere, the sensuous form of beauty preserved "the memory of happiness that once was."[62] Jameson captures this aspect of Marcuse's theory of remembrance when he writes:

It is because we have known, at the beginning of life, a plenitude of psychic gratification, because we have known a time before all repression, a time in which, as in Schiller's nature, the elaborate specializations of later, more sophisticated consciousness had not yet taken place, a time that precedes the very separation of subject from its object, that memory, even the obscured and unconscious memory

59. Marcuse, *Counterrevolution and Revolt*, p. 70.
60. Benjamin, "Theses on the Philosophy of History," p. 262.
61. Marcuse, *Eros and Civilization*, p. 18.
62. Marcuse, *The Aesthetic Dimension*, p. 68.

of that prehistoric paradise in the individual psyche, can fulfill its profound therapeutic, epistemological, and even political role. . . . The primary energy of revolutionary activity derives from this memory of prehistoric happiness which the individual can regain only through its externalization, through its re-establishment
for society as a whole.[63]

Although on the surface, this type of remembrance seems to be historical
in the sense that it recaptures a reality that allegedly existed in the past, a
closer look at Marcuse's use of the archaic heritage shows it to be something else. For when confronted with the anthropological evidence that
Freud's theories cannot be corroborated, he retreated into the explanation that "We use Freud's anthropological speculation only in this sense:
for its *symbolic* value. The archaic events that the hypothesis stipulates
may forever be beyond the realm of anthropological verification: the alleged consequences of these events are historical facts."[64] What this admission implies, as he put it in *An Essay on Liberation*, is "not regression
to a previous stage of civilization, but return to an imaginary *temps perdu*
in the real life of mankind."[65]

But if the plenitude "remembered" is only symbolic and the *temps
perdu* merely "imaginary," can one really talk of memory in the same way
one does when recalling the actual defeats and struggles of our historical
predecessors? How, in fact, can we distinguish a true memory from what
Brian Smith calls a "mnemic hallucination,"[66] if the reality remembered
never actually occurred? What Marcuse was obviously doing here was
introducing a myth of original wholeness, of perfect presence, of the "remembering"[67] of what had been dismembered, whose roots, if in memory
at all, were in remembered desire rather than remembered fulfillment.
Very much in the spirit of his problematic call for a "biological foundation for socialism,"[68] Marcuse's exhortation to remember an "imaginary
temps perdu" allowed him to smuggle an a priori philosophical anthropology into Critical Theory.

His symbolic adoption of Freud's archaic heritage also allowed him to
sidestep another troubling aspect of his theory of remembrance: its undefended identification of individual and collective memory. "Individual
psychology," he wrote in *Eros and Civilization*, "is thus *in itself* group

63. Jameson, *Marxism and Form*, p. 113.
64. Marcuse, *Eros and Civilization*, pp. 54–55.
65. Marcuse, *An Essay on Liberation* (Boston, 1969), p. 90.
66. Brian Smith, p. 19.
67. In a translator's footnote in *Negations* (p. 177), Jeremy J. Shapiro points out: "'Sich
erinnern,' the word for 'to remember' or 'to recollect,' literally means 'to go into oneself.'
That is, in remembering, one is re-membered or re-collected by returning to oneself from a
state of externality, dispersion, or alienation."
68. Marcuse, *An Essay on Liberation*, chap. 1.

psychology insofar as the individual itself still is in archaic identity with the species. This archaic heritage bridges the 'gap between individual and mass psychology.'"[69] But precisely how far the individual was in fact in archaic identity with the species Marcuse did not say. For all of Marcuse's contempt for Jung, a certain affinity can perhaps be discerned here. Assuming too quickly that individual and collective memory were virtually the same, he never conducted those experiments in personal recollection so painstakingly attempted by Benjamin. Marcuse's own *Berliner Kindheit um neunzehnten Jahrhundert* remained unwritten. Nor did he rigorously investigate the differences between personal memory of an actual event or thought in a person's life and the collective historical memory of events antedating all living persons. Because the latter is preserved in the archival records of past men and the often opaque processes of collective behavior and belief, rather than in the living memories of present ones, the hermeneutic process of recovery is different in each case. The dialectic of restitution between the present and past is more than mere remembrance of things past. As Benjamin understood,[70] there is both a destructive and a constructive move necessary to explode a previous epoch out of the continuum of history and make it active in the present. At times— when, for example, he linked memory to imagination as a synthetic epistemological faculty "reassembling the bits and fragments which can be found in the distorted humanity and distorted nature"[71]—Marcuse seemed to sense this. But he never adequately developed the dynamics of mnemonic praxis.

One final difficulty in Marcuse's appropriation of anamnesis for revolutionary purposes was the problem of accounting for the new in history. Although Marcuse was firm in insisting that remembrance did not simply mean retrogression—a mistake for which Jung was chastened in *Eros and Civilization*[72]—he did not entirely escape the reproach that recollection is too close to repetition. The inadequacies of anamnestic totalization were perhaps nowhere as clearly perceived as in the work of Ernst Bloch, who preferred another Greek term, *anagnorisis*, or recognition. In an interview given at the 1968 Korcula summer school, which Marcuse also attended, Bloch spelled out his reasons:

The doctrine of *anamnesis* claims that we have knowledge only because we formerly knew. But then there could be no fundamentally new knowledge, no future knowledge. The soul merely meets in reality now what it always already knew as

69. Marcuse, *Eros and Civilization*, p. 51.
70. Benjamin, "Eduard Fuchs: Collector and Historian;" see note 31.
71. Marcuse, *Counterrevolution and Revolt*, p. 70.
72. Marcuse, *Eros and Civilization*, pp. 134–35.

idea. That is a circle within a circle and just as inaccurate as the other theory *(anagnorisis)* is revealing: that the new is never completely new for us because we bring something with us to measure by it. .... *Anamnesis* provides the reassuring evidence of complete similarity; *anagnorisis,* however, is linked with reality by only a thin thread; it is therefore alarming. *Anamnesis* has an element of attenuation about it; it makes everything a gigantic *déjà vu,* as if everything had already been, *nil novi subanamnesi.* But *anagnorisis* is a shock.[73]

Based on Bloch's idiosyncratic ontology of the "not-yet," *anagnorisis* meant that one could recognize figural traces of the future in the past, but the past itself contained no archaic heritage of plenitude.

Whether or not Bloch's alternative seems superior to Marcuse's depends on one's confidence in his highly speculative philosophy of hope, whose difficulties we have already encountered. His criticism of anamnesis makes an important point, however, which is clarified still further if we turn to Paul Ricoeur's well-known dichotomy, applied to hermeneutics as a whole,[74] between mnemonics as a recollection of meaning and mnemonics as an exercise of suspicion. Ricoeur placed Freud, Nietzsche and Marx as the great exemplars of the interpretative art of suspicious demystification. The recollectors of meaning were mainly men of religion, for the opposite of suspicion was faith, faith in a primal word that could be recovered. In Bloch's terms, *anamnesis* is a doctrine that derives from the belief in an original meaning that can be recollected, whereas *anagnorisis,* while holding out hope for a plenitude in the future, is suspicious of claims that it existed in the past.

If one were to survey the Frankfurt School as a whole, one would conclude that its attitude towards these alternatives was mixed. In Benjamin's search for an *Ursprache,* a perfect language in which words and things are one, there is an elegiac impulse for recollected meaning. But in his stress on the constructive and destructive aspects of memory properly applied there was an awareness that simple recollection does not suffice. Similarly, in Adorno's warning against a philosophy of origins, in his stubborn insistence on a negative dialectic of non-identity, and in his acceptance of the inevitability of some reification, the mnemonics of suspicion were paramount. When Horkheimer speculated on religion and concluded that no matter how utopian the future might be, the pain of past generations could never be redeemed through remembrance,[75] he too questioned the

73. Michael Landmann, "Talking with Ernst Bloch: Korcula, 1968," *Telos* 25 (Fall 1975), p. 178.
74. Paul Ricoeur, *Freud and Philosophy: An Essay on Interpretation,* trans. Danis Savage (New Haven, 1970), p. 28f.
75. Max Horkheimer, "Thoughts on Religion" in *Critical Theory: Selected Essays,* trans. Matthew J. O'Connell and others (New York, 1972), p. 130.

possibility of recovering a primal wholeness. Especially in his more Schopenhauerian moods, he despaired of mankind ever fully awakening from
the "nightmare" weighing on the brain of the living which Marx had seen
as the legacy of the past.

Marcuse seems to have been attracted to both types of mnemonics.
The philosophical legacy he inherited from Heidegger and Hegel led him
to argue that something essential had been forgotten, whose content he
thought he saw in Freud's archaic heritage. But his tenure at the Institute
of Social Research, where the critique of ideology was a far more frequent
practice than the postulating of utopian alternatives, seems to have tempered his search for recollected meaning with a suspicion that it might
never be found. At the very end of the main argument of *Eros and Civilization*, his most utopian book, he borrowed Horkheimer's argument
against memory as redemption:

> But even the ultimate advent of freedom cannot redeem those who died in pain. It
> is the remembrance of them, and the accumulated guilt of mankind against its
> victims, that darken the prospect of a civilization without repression.[76]

Remembrance must, in other words, always retain its demystifying critical impulse, bearing sober witness to the sufferings of the past, even as it
offers up images of utopian fulfillment as models for the future.

For Marcuse, then, anamnestic totalization was never quite as complete
a source of normative wholeness as his philosophical forebears had intimated. And, *a fortiori*, harnessed to a political practice in the present it
could never lead to a perfectly harmonious totality in the future. For as he
admitted in one of his last works when considering the possibility of transforming life into an organic work of art, "no matter in what form, art can
never eliminate the tension between art and reality. Elimination of this tension would be the impossible final unity of subject and object: the materialist version of absolute idealism."[77] Indeed, as he warned his more utopian
friend Norman O. Brown a few years earlier, "Tension can be made nonantagonistic, nondestructive, but it can never be eliminated, because (Freud
knew it well) its elimination would be death—not in any symbolic but in a
very real sense."[78]

But if Marcuse did admit, however grudgingly, the necessity of some
tension even under Communism, he nonetheless held out real hope for the
reduction of its unnecessary—or what he would call its "surplus"—manifestations. For his Frankfurt School colleague Theodor Adorno, however,

76. Marcuse, *Eros and Civilization*, p. 216.
77. Marcuse, *Counterrevolution and Revolt*, p. 108.
78. Marcuse, *Negations*, pp. 236–37.

a certain kind of tension was less a regrettable necessity than a positive virtue. In so arguing, Adorno called into question the fundamental premises of the Western Marxist tradition, which still nurtured Marcuse's thought, and, most notably, its essentially Hegelian concept of totality. Indeed, as we shall see in the next chapter, Adorno's critique of Lukács' original paradigm was sufficiently powerful to render it no longer truly viable. In surprising concord with the scientific Marxist contentions of Althusser and the Della Volpeans, which we will examine later, Adorno's arguments against the holistic assumptions we have traced in earlier chapters marked a critical watershed in the development of Western Marxism.

CHAPTER EIGHT

Theodor W. Adorno and the Collapse of the Lukácsian Concept of Totality

The dawning sense of freedom feeds upon the memory of the archaic impulse not yet steered by any solid I. . . . Without an anamnesis of the untamed impulse that precedes the ego—an impulse later banished to the zone of unfree bondage to nature—it would be impossible to derive the idea of freedom, although that idea in turn ends up reinforcing the ego.[1]

This argument, so reminiscent of those we have just been examining, did not flow from the pen of Herbert Marcuse. Instead, it was expressed by his former colleague at the Institute of Social Research, Theodor W. Adorno, in the work that is often seen as the bleakest expression of his "melancholy science,"[2] *Negative Dialectics*, written three years before his death in 1969. "As a sense of nonidentity through identity," he wrote elsewhere in that work,

dialectics is not only an advancing process but a retrograde one at the same time. To this extent, the picture of the circle describes it correctly. The concept's unfold-

1. Theodor W. Adorno, *Negative Dialectics*, trans. E. B. Ashton (New York, 1973), pp. 221–22.

2. "Melancholy science" is the phrase used by Adorno in *Minima Moralia*, trans. E. F. N. Jephcott (London, 1974), p. 15, to contrast his own position with Nietzsche's "joyful science." Gillian Rose has chosen it for the title of her study of Adorno, *The Melancholy Science: An Introduction to the Thought of Theodor W. Adorno* (New York, 1978). For other extended treatments of his work, see Kurt Oppens et al., *Über Theodor W. Adorno* (Frankfurt, 1968); Friedemann Grenz, *Adornos Philosophie in Grundbegriffen: Auflösung einiger Deutungsprobleme* (Frankfurt, 1974); Susan Buck-Morss, *The Origin of Negative Dialectics: Theodor W. Adorno, Walter Benjamin, and the Frankfurt Institute* (New York, 1977); and Burkhardt Lindner and W. Martin Lüdke, eds., *Materialien zur ästhetischen Theorie Theodor W. Adornos: Konstruktion der Moderne* (Frankfurt, 1979). The last of these contains an annotated bibliography of other works on Adorno. The most important work since its compilation is Eugene Lunn, *Marxism and Modernism: An Historical Study of Lukács, Brecht, Benjamin, and Adorno* (Berkeley, 1982).

ment is also a reaching back, and synthesis is the definition of the difference that perished, "vanished," in the concept—almost like Hölderlin's anamnesis of the doomed naturalness.[3]

For Adorno, then, just as for Marcuse and Benjamin, some form of anamnesis was an important dialectical force. Even amidst the seemingly most pessimistic passages of his writings, there often appeared residues of a utopian insistence on the possibility of radical change. The paradoxical Frankfurt School dialectic of despair and hope that we have seen in its most acute form in Horkheimer's "The Authoritarian State" was evident throughout his friend's work as well. But whereas in Marcuse's case the balance between the two impulses was relatively even, with admitted fluctuations from work to work, in Adorno's utopian hope was by far the weaker and more muted of the two. Often little more than a ritualized gesture of affirmation added on to an argument whose clear import was the reverse, Adorno's expressions of belief in the possibility of normative totality were the most tenuous of all the Western Marxists. If anything, his concept of totality was far more negative than positive in a variety of ways that will become clear shortly. Indeed, his stress on negation dictated not only the content of his thought, but the form in which it was expressed, a form that refused to hide the irreconcilability of its generating energies. Thus, despite his protestations to the contrary, Adorno's work consistently invited the charge that he had abandoned the confidence in the possibility of human emancipation which underlay the Marxist tradition in all its forms.

The most explicit expression of that alleged abandonment came in Adorno's writings of the 1940s and after, most notably in his collaborative effort with Horkheimer, *Dialectic of Enlightenment*, and what he called its "extended appendix," *Philosophy of Modern Music*; his reflections on a "damaged life," *Minima Moralia*; the essay collections *Prisms* and *Notes on Literature I, II, III and IV; Negative Dialectics; The Jargon of Authenticity*; and finally his uncompleted and posthumously published *Aesthetic Theory*.[4] In several of these works, Adorno contemplated the

3. Adorno, *Negative Dialectics*, 157. For a somewhat more cautious view of memory, see *Minima Moralia*, p. 166. Adorno's appropriation of the anamnesia motif has led one critic, Gunter Rohrmoser, to compare him with the late Heidegger. See his *Das Elend der Kritischen Theorie* (Freiburg, 1970), p. 37. For a refutation of this comparison, which points to the weakness of Adorno's faith in anamnestic totalization, see W. Martin Lüdke, *Anmerkungen zu einer "Logik des Zerfalls": Adorno-Beckett* (Frankfurt, 1981), pp. 66, 70.
4. Max Horkheimer and Theodor W. Adorno, *Dialectic of Enlightenment*, trans. John Cumming (New York, 1960); *Philosophy of Modern Music*, trans. Anne G. Mitchell and Wesley V. Blomster (New York, 1973); *Prisms*, trans. Samuel and Shierry Weber (London, 1967); *Noten zur Literatur I* (Berlin, 1958), *II* (Frankfurt, 1961), *III* (Frankfurt, 1965), *IV*

bitter implications of the Holocaust, and concluded in a widely discussed phrase, "To write poetry after Auschwitz is barbaric."[5] To certain commentators,[6] it has seemed as if Adorno's personal trauma as a Jewish (or, more precisely, half-Jewish) survivor of the Final Solution permanently blackened his perception of the world, obliterating the Marxist optimism of his earlier period. Adorno himself encouraged this interpretation by raising the question "whether after Auschwitz you can go on living— especially whether one who escaped by accident, one who by rights should have been killed, may go on living," and answering it: "His mere survival calls for the coldness, the basic principle of bourgeois subjectivity, without which there could have been no Auschwitz; this is the drastic guilt of him who was spared."[7]

There was, in fact, another kind of coldness in Adorno's later work, a deliberate withholding of positive feeling almost ascetic in intensity. As his frequent criticisms of humanism, whether bourgeois or Marxist, demonstrated,[8] he scorned the forgiving celebration of mankind that would lessen the impact of the Holocaust's horrible meaning. Unlike Marcuse, he refused to transform Freud's tragic vision into an almost fully redemptive one. Nor did he have any illusions about the realization of a more truly humane society through political means of any kind. As he put it in the frequently cited first sentences of *Negative Dialectics*, "Philosophy, which once seemed obsolete, lives on because the moment to realize it was missed. The summary judgment that it had merely interpreted the world, that resignation in the face of reality had crippled it in itself, becomes a defeatism of reason after the attempt to change the world miscarried."[9]

Adorno's perception of that miscarriage was surely intensified by the horrors of the 1930s and 1940s, but it would nonetheless be mistaken to derive it solely from the guilt of a Jewish survivor "after Auschwitz." For

---

(Frankfurt, 1974); *The Jargon of Authenticity*, trans. Knut Tarnowski and Frederic Will (London, 1973); *Aesthetische Theorie*, ed. Gretel Adorno and Rolf Tiedemann (Frankfurt, 1970). Adorno's *Gesammelte Schriften* are being brought out by Suhrkamp Verlag in twenty-three volumes edited by Rolf Tiedemann.

5. Adorno, *Prisms*, p. 34. Later he would amend this view somewhat and concede that "literature must resist this verdict, in other words, be such that its mere existence after Auschwitz is not a surrender to cynicism." "Commitment," *New Left Review* 87–88 (September–December 1974), p. 84.

6. See, for example, Arnold Künzli, *Aufklärung und Dialektik: Politische Philosophie von Hobbes bis Adorno* (Freiburg, 1971), p. 146.

7. Adorno, *Negative Dialectics*, pp. 362–63.

8. For a discussion of Adorno's critique of humanism, see Martin Jay, "The Frankfurt School's Critique of Marxist Humanism," *Social Research* 39, 2 (Summer 1972).

9. Adorno, *Negative Dialectics*, p. 3.

virtually all of the same arguments can be discerned, at least embryonically, in Adorno's work from its very beginnings during the Weimar Republic. In fact, as Susan Buck-Morss has perceptively noted,[10] many of
the themes developed in *Negative Dialectics* were already present in "The
Actuality of Philosophy" the inaugural lecture the twenty-eight-year-old
Adorno gave to the philosophy faculty of the University of Frankfurt in
1931.[11] Published only after Adorno's death, the lecture demonstrates
that many of the ideas that would emerge later in the work of the Frankfurt School, which Adorno officially joined only in 1938, were already
articulated outside of the Institute of Social Research.

The lecture, to which we will return shortly, also shows the effects of
what, broadly speaking, might be called a counter-current in leftist
thought during the Weimar Republic. Although, as we have had ample
opportunity to note, there was a "hunger for wholeness" on the Left as
well as the Right during that turbulent era, a hunger that fed the holistic
impulse in Western Marxism, there was a less vocal, but nonetheless important, reaction against it. Despite the Hegel Renaissance of the 1920s
and the apparent demise of neo-Kantianism as the major strain in German philosophy, there were still vital residues of Kant's influence that
might have an impact on heterodox Marxist thought. The legacy of
figures like Simmel, who died in 1919, was potent enough to convince
some that the "tragedy of culture" was an unalterable condition. The faith
in history, which was characteristic of both Rankean and Hegelian historicist thought, was challenged by former adherents, such as the Jewish
thinker Franz Rosenzweig. Turning to a faith in faith instead, Rosenzweig, and others drawn to what later would become known as existentialism, bitterly rejected the concept of totality.[12] However strong the
desire for a "concrete" philosophy, a philosophy that would break through
the formal abstractness of neo-Kantianism to a more "authentic" existence beneath it, some thinkers remained skeptical about the possibility of
achieving such immediacy. For all the fascination with the new phenomenological and existentialist claims to recover Being, most influentially expressed in Heidegger's *Being and Time* of 1927, there were some who

10. Buck-Morss, *The Origin of Negative Dialectics*, p. 24f.
11. Adorno, "The Actuality of Philosophy," *Telos* 31 (Spring 1977) with a useful introduction by "Benjamin Snow," a pseudonym for Buck-Morss.
12. For Rosenzweig's critique of the Hegelian concept of totality, see *The Star of Redemption*, trans. William W. Hallo (New York, 1970); Buck-Morss discusses its possible
impact on Adorno in *The Origin of Negative Dialectics*, p. 5. For a discussion of the distance
between Adorno and Rosenzweig on other issues, see Martin Jay, "Politics of Translation:
Siegfried Kracauer and Walter Benjamin on the Buber–Rosenzweig Bible," *The Leo Baeck
Yearbook* 20 (1976).

warily refused the lure. The young Marcuse may have thought for a while that Heidegger provided the ontological supplement necessary to complete Marxism, but others soon perceived their incompatability.

Among those who resisted both the neo-Hegelian and phenomenological trends of the 1920s was Hans Cornelius, who taught Adorno as well as Horkheimer and Pollock in Frankfurt. He directed Adorno's first study of psychoanalysis, which tried to find a place for Freud's unconscious in Kant's transcendental mind, as well as his first study of Husserl, the forerunner of a more extensive critique of phenomenology not published until the 1950s.[13] Cornelius' unorthodox brand of anti-ontological, even quasi-empiricist idealism prevented Adorno, as well as Horkheimer and Pollock, from completely embracing the arguments of Lukács' Hegelian Marxism, which in so many ways they found attractive.

The fact that Adorno was even more wary of them than Horkheimer was can perhaps be attributed to the impact of his "education" outside of normal academic circles. From two older friends in particular, Siegfried Kracauer and Walter Benjamin, he learned to distrust the totalistic claims of Hegelian Marxism. Adorno had become friends with Kracauer in 1918, when he was only fifteen years of age and Kracauer twenty-nine.[14] For a year, they informally studied Kant together every Saturday afternoon. Kracauer helped Adorno appreciate the hidden social content in Kant's texts, as well as their claims to truth. He also aroused in Adorno an interest in the possibility of examining less exalted cultural phenomena for the same revelations. Influenced by Simmel's micrological analyses of a wide variety of social and cultural phenomena, Kracauer nurtured Adorno's ability to read and interpret the seemingly insignificant details of modern life, which more global perspectives, such as Lukács', often passed over in silence. Although he was more visually adept than Adorno and concentrated on such phenomena as film and architectural space, Kracauer's half-philosophical and half-sociological style of analysis provided a model for Adorno's later forays into a variety of cultural areas, most notably music.

13. Adorno's early study of Freud and Kant was entitled "Der Begriff des Unbewussten in der Transzendentalen Seelenlehre"; written in 1924, it was published only in the first volume of his *Gesammelte Schriften* (Frankfurt, 1973). His critique of Husserl, entitled "Die Transzendenz des Dinglichen und Noematischen in Husserls Phänomenologie," written in 1927, was likewise unpublished until that same volume. His later study of Husserl, itself written primarily in the 1930s, was published in 1956 as *Zur Metakritik der Erkenntnistheorie: Studien über Husserl und die phänomenologischen Antinomien* (Stuttgart, 1956), in English as *Against Epistemology: A Metacritique*, trans. Willis Domingo (Cambridge, Mass., 1983).

14. For a discussion of their relationship, see Martin Jay, "Adorno and Kracauer: Notes on a Troubled Friendship," *Salmagundi* 40 (Winter 1978).

So too did his general distrust of metaphysical systems, collectivist denigrations of the individual, and faddish solution to what Lukács had called the "transcendental homelessness"[15] of modern existence. Although a man of the Left, profoundly discontented with the quality of bourgeois life, Kracauer resisted joining any political party or faction. Instead, he remained, to use his self-description, an "extra-territorial"[16] outsider, a quintessentially homeless intellectual of the type so often pilloried by partisans of both the Left and Right. Here too, Kracauer seems to have served as a role model for his younger friend.

Perhaps an even more potent example for Adorno's theoretical development was presented by Walter Benjamin,[17] to whom he was introduced by Kracauer in 1923. Eleven years older than Adorno, Benjamin had already made his mark as a leader of the radical Jewish student movement during the 1910s, where he developed a distaste for the communitarian *Lebensphilosophie* of Martin Buber. He was drawn instead to unorthodox theological themes in Judaism, in particular those associated with the cabalistic tradition whose rediscovery by his close friend, Gershom Scholem, was then only beginning.[18] Combined with an interest in linguistic philosophy and a fascination with symbolist poetics, Benjamin's religious concerns were to remain a potent force in his thinking even after he embraced Marxism in the later 1920s. Philosophically, Benjamin, a student of the neo-Kantian Heinrich Rickert, had never been sympathetic to Hegelianism. Thus, even though he valued Lukács' pre-Marxist works highly and found aspects of *History and Class Consciousness* to admire,[19]

15. This phrase from Lukács' *The Theory of the Novel* was echoed in the chapter of Kracauer's *Die Angestellten: Aus dem neuesten Deutschland* (Frankfurt, 1930), entitled "Asylum for the Homeless," which treated the metaphysical disorientation of the *Mittelstand*.

16. The term appears frequently in Kracauer's work; for a discussion of its importance, see Martin Jay, "The Extraterritorial Life of Siegfried Kracauer," *Salmagundi* 31–32 (Fall 1975–Winter 1976).

17. For the best discussions of the Adorno–Benjamin relationship, see Buck-Morss, *The Origin of Negative Dialectics*; Richard Wolin, *Walter Benjamin: An Aesthetic of Redemption* (New York, 1982); and Lunn, *Marxism and Modernism*. Adorno's writings on Benjamin have been collected as *Über Walter Benjamin* (Frankfurt, 1970). The literature on Benjamin himself is now immense; the best recent bibliography was compiled by Gary Smith for the special Benjamin issue of *New German Critique* 17 (Spring 1979).

The reader may wonder why a separate chapter has not been devoted to Benjamin's concept of totality. The main reason, aside from the difficulty of doing justice to the complexity of his thought in so short a compass, is the fact that Adorno brought most of Benjamin's ideas on the subject into the mainstream of Western Marxism.

18. For Scholem's version of his friendship with Benjamin, see his *Walter Benjamin—Die Geschichte einer Freundschaft* (Frankfurt, 1975); see also their exchange of letters, *Walter Benjamin—Gershom Scholem: Briefwechsel 1933–1940*, ed. Scholem (Frankfurt, 1980).

19. Scholem, *Walter Benjamin—Die Geschichte einer Freundschaft*, p. 155.

he was never a Hegelian Marxist of any kind. Precisely what kind of Marxist he actually became has been the source of considerable controversy. But what is of more importance in understanding his impact on Adorno's development is his earliest, least Marxist work, most notably his extraordinary study of *The Origin of German Tragic Drama*.[20]

Originally intended as a *Habilitationsschrift* in 1925, it was rejected by, among others, the uncomprehending Cornelius, thus marking the end of Benjamin's academic hopes. Published nonetheless in 1928, it struck Adorno with uncommon force as methodologically suggestive for the type of heterodox Marxist analysis he was himself trying to develop. Whether or not *The Origin* had a Marxist dimension has been heatedly contested.[21] Although it is true that Benjamin discerned certain similarities between his own epistemology and Lukács',[22] precisely what these were he did not say. In any case, Adorno clearly felt that Benjamin's method was compatible with a materialism of the kind he was beginning to develop in what must be seen as an essentially anti-Lukácsian direction. Almost immediately after the publication of *The Origin*, its impact was apparent in Adorno's musical writings, his study of Kierkegaard and his inaugural lecture.[23]

Many of the features of Benjamin's work that impressed Adorno bore directly on the issue of holism. The highly cryptic "Epistemo-Critical Prologue" opening the book begins with a quotation from Goethe:

Neither in knowledge nor in reflection can anything whole be put together, since in the former the internal is missing and in the latter the external; and so we must necessarily think of science as art if we expect to derive any kind of wholeness from it. Nor should we look for this in the general, the excessive, but, since art is always wholly represented in every individual work of art, so science ought to reveal itself completely in every individual object treated.[24]

20. Walter Benjamin, *The Origin of German Tragic Drama*, trans. John Osborne, intro. George Steiner (London, 1977). The best discussion of Benjamin's early works appears in Bernd Witte, *Walter Benjamin—Der Intellektuelle als Kritiker: Untersuchungen zu seinem Frühwerk* (Stuttgart, 1974); see also Wolin, chapters 1 and 2.
21. See Steiner's introduction to *The Origin of German Tragic Drama*, p. 14.
22. See his September, 1924, letter to Scholem, quoted and discussed in Wolin, *Walter Benjamin*, pp. 112–15.
23. For a discussion of that impact, see Buck-Morss, *The Origin of Negative Dialectics*, p. 23.
24. Benjamin, *The Origin of German Tragic Drama*, p. 27. For a suggestive interpretation of this quotation, which contends that it shows Benjamin had not abandoned his desire for totality, see Sandor Radnoti, "The Early Aesthetics of Walter Benjamin," *International Journal of Sociology* 7, 1 (Spring 1977). Radnoti argues that "Benjamin can be compared only to Lukács to the extent that he sought and placed at the center of his analysis an objective category of totality" (p. 91). Wolin makes the same claim (p. 114). However true this may be for Benjamin, it certainly does not express what Adorno absorbed from him.

Benjamin developed the implications of these remarks in several telling ways. The method of philosophy, he claimed, must eschew the totalizing pretensions of most nineteenth-century thought:

Inasmuch as it is determined by this concept of system, philosophy is in danger of accommodating itself to a syncretism which weaves a spider's web between separate kinds of knowledge in an attempt to ensnare the truth as if it were something which came flying in from outside. But the universalism acquired by such philosophy falls far short of the didactic authority of doctrine. If philosophy is to remain true to the law of its own form, as the representation of truth and not as a guide to the acquisition of knowledge, then the exercise of this form—rather than its anticipation in the system—must be accorded due importance.[25]

Defending the loose form of the treatise with its use of authoritative quotations, digressive, non-deductive mode of reasoning, and lack of a coherent, purposeful organization, Benjamin contended that philosophy's "representation of truth" best proceeds by immersion in "the most minute details of subject-matter."[26] Such an immersion was not, however, that of the empiricists' "acquisition of knowledge" through inductive generalization. The traits of the proper philosophical style were rather "the art of interruption in contrast to the chain of deduction; the tenacity of the essay in contrast to the single gesture of the fragment; the repetition of themes in contrast to shallow universalism; the fullness of concentrated positivity in contrast to the negation of polemic."[27]

Dialectical mediation with its goal of *Aufhebung* (sublation) too quickly forced a unity where none in fact existed. Classical German Idealism with its emphasis on the subjective synthesis of reality was less effective than its Platonic predecessor in grasping the objective dimension of truth. Such truth appeared, Benjamin claimed, in what he called "ideas." Rather than subsuming particular examplars under a general rubric, ideas preserved the integrity of concrete objects, which they organized into patterned configurations. To explain this process, Benjamin chose the analogy of constellations and stars:

Ideas are timeless constellations, and by virtue of the elements' being seen as points in such constellations, phenomena are subdivided and at the same time redeemed; so that those elements which it is the function of the concept to elicit from phenomena are most clearly evident at the extremes. The idea is best explained as the representation of the context within which the unique and extreme stands alongside its counterpart.[28]

Although accepting the role of the interpreter in discovering the proper constellations, Benjamin was adamantly opposed to the notion that truth

25. Benjamin, *The Origin of German Tragic Drama*, p. 28.
26. Ibid., p. 29.   27. Ibid., p. 32.   28. Ibid., p. 35.

was a function of subjectivity. Against the nineteenth-century hermeneutics of Schleiermacher and the early Dilthey, with its stress on recapturing the intentionality of an initial author, Benjamin insisted that "truth is an intentionless state of being, made up of ideas. The proper approach to it is not therefore one of intention and knowledge, but rather a total immersion and absorption in it. Truth is the death of intention."[29] Because of his hostility to constitutive subjectivity, there was a trace of positivism in Benjamin's method, which was the reverse side of his Platonizing inclinations. Questioning the idealist challenge, "so much the worse for the facts," which we have seen Bloch and the early Lukács defend, he introduced an idiosyncratic notion of non-genetic origin:

This genuinely idealist attitude pays for its confidence by abandoning the central feature of the idea of origin. For every proof of origin must be prepared to face up to the question of its authenticity. If it cannot establish this, then it does not merit the name.[30]

The investigator, to be sure, must not take every "fact" at face value, but rather search for the authentic structure of the idea of which it is an element. This search is a process of discovery and recognition, rather than construction or abstraction. Its goal is what Benjamin calls "redemption" through revelation of the "origin," which he defined as something other than simple genesis. "Philosophical history," he wrote, "the science of the origin, is the form which, in the remotest extremes and the apparent excesses of the process of development, reveals the configuration of the idea—the sum total of all possible meaningful juxtapositions of such opposites."[31] Once this search ends, the idea will be revealed as a monad; "The pre-stabilized representation of phenomena resides within it, as in their objective interpretation."[32]

In the body of his treatise, Benjamin attempted to apply his anti-idealist, anti-subjectivist, anti-historicist method to one idea in particular, that of the long-neglected tragic drama (*Trauerspiel*) of the German Baroque era. Among the sources of his fascination with this esoteric form was the similarity he saw between the period of its popularity and Benjamin's own era, both of which were ages of "so-called decadence"[33] without that sense of communal existence Lukács had described in *The Theory of the Novel* as the ground of the epic. Although the artistic will to wholeness still existed in these periods, the means to achieve it were lacking. Accordingly, the dominant stylistic mode of these eras was allegorical rather than symbolic.

Contemporary criticism, Benjamin contended, had been prevented

29. Ibid., p. 36.   30. Ibid., p. 46   31. Ibid., p. 47.
32. Ibid., p. 47.   33. Ibid., p. 55.

from reaching this understanding by its dogged insistence on the priority of the symbol, which was a legacy of both romantic and classical aesthetics and ultimately traceable to the degeneration of a religious tradition:

> The unity of the material and the transcendental object, which constitutes the paradox of the theological symbol, is distorted into a relationship between appearance and essence. The introduction of this distorted conception of the symbol into aesthetics was a romantic and destructive extravagance which preceded the desolation of modern art criticism. As a symbolic construct, the beautiful is supposed to merge with the divine into an unbroken whole.[34]

In opposition to the symbolic notion of the perfect individual incarnation of the whole, which would reappear in Lukács' aesthetics with its stress on typicality, Benjamin defended the allegorical alternative presented by baroque art:

> In contrast the baroque apotheosis is a dialectical one. It is accomplished in the movement between extremes. In this eccentric and dialectic process the harmonious inwardness of classicism plays no role.[35]

The non-harmonizing of the two extremes of the allegorical relationship meant that the *Trauerspiel* was an untotalized, open art form:

> In the field of allegorical intuition the image is a fragment, a rune. Its beauty as a symbol evaporates when the light of divine learning falls upon it. The false appearance of totality is extinguished.[36]

Because of the inevitably splintered nature of the allegory, works based on it, such as the *Trauerspiel*, were composed of the ruins of past totalizations. Not surprisingly, they expressed a melancholic nostalgia for lost wholeness—the sadness (*Trauer*) of the *Trauerspiel*—which could not be recaptured by aesthetic fiat. Indeed, Benjamin contended, the decay to which they bore witness was part of a larger process of degeneration, which he claimed was natural. In terms reminiscent of Schelling,[37] he talked of the "collapse of physical, beautiful nature"[38] which precludes historical totalization. In accounting for this natural decay, he could only revert to theological explanations, in particular the Christian concept of the Fall:

> Allegory itself was sown by Christianity. For it was absolutely decisive for the development of this mode of thought that not only transitoriness, but also guilt

34. Ibid., p. 160.
35. Ibid., p. 160.
36. Ibid., p. 176.
37. For a discussion of the similarity between the motif of natural decay in Benjamin (and later in Adorno) and Schelling, see Perry Anderson, *Considerations on Western Marxism* (London, 1976), p. 81.
38. Op. cit., p. 176.

should seem evidently to have its home in the province of idols and of the flesh. The allegorically significant is prevented by guilt from finding fulfillment of its meaning in itself. Guilt is not confined to the allegorical observer, who betrays the world for the sake of knowledge, but it also attaches to the object of his contemplation. This view, rooted in the doctrine of the fall of the creature, which brought down nature with it, is responsible for the ferment which distinguishes the profundity of western allegory from the oriental rhetoric of this form of expression. Because it is mute, fallen nature mourns. But the converse of this statement leads even deeper into the essence of nature: its mournfulness makes it become mute.[39]

Beauty, therefore, is not communicable as a formed whole, but rather as the debris, the torso, of a past unity whose loss could only be mourned. Redemption meant a recognition of the loss, a calling of the unspoken decay by its right name, and not the reversal of its direction. Unlike what Bloch would call *Spuren* (traces), the detritus to be redeemed were not prefigurations of a future plenitude. Redemption is thus a category of a more "negative" than positive theology.

The only totalization, Benjamin seemed to be saying, was that of the unmediated constellation, the objective representation of ideas which monadically mirrored the "discontinuous finitude"[40] of the world. Truth thus appeared more in concrete, material images related to each other spatially than in abstract philosophical concepts. Rather than collapsing the distance between subject and object in the manner of an expressive totality, the constellation redeemed its disparate elements by maintaining their irreducible heterogeneity. Although Benjamin sometimes contended that his was a "dialectical" method, it was a far cry from the positive dialectics of subject-object unity introduced into Western Marxism by Lukács and the other Hegelianizers examined above. Instead, it contained the seeds of what Adorno would later call his own "negative dialectics."

There were, to be sure, elements in Benjamin's approach that Adorno found questionable. For example, he warned that its extreme anti-subjectivism turned Benjamin's philosophy into "no less a source of terror than a promise of happiness."[41] And he found much to criticize in Benjamin's quasi-positivist rejection of mediation and his Platonizing, ahistorical search for "eternal constellations." Thus, aside from their widely discussed differences over politics and technology,[42] there were certain fun-

39. Ibid., p. 224.
40. Ibid., p. 37.
41. Adorno, *Prisms*, p. 235. Elsewhere Adorno would chastise Benjamin for the opposite sin of missing the objective moment in subjectivity. See his letter of August 2, 1935, in *Aesthetics and Politics: Debates Between Bloch, Lukács, Brecht, Benjamin, and Adorno* (London, 1977), p. 110f. Here his animus is directed against Benjamin's sympathy for Jung's notion of a collective consciousness.
42. For summations of the debate, see Buck-Morss, *The Origin of Negative Dialectics*: Wolin, *Walter Benjamin*; and Lunn, *Marxism and Modernism*.

damental theoretical tensions between the two friends. But even if, consequently, it is problematic to speak of a full-fledged "conversion"[43] after
Adorno read *The Origin*, it is nonetheless clear that his early work cannot
be grasped without reference to Benjamin's example.

Nor can it be fully understood without one final stimulus, which was
less directly philosophical. The Goethe quotation cited by Benjamin to
open *The Origin* stressed the links between artistic and philosophical
cognition. In choosing it to begin his study, Benjamin was at one with
Bloch, Kracauer, Horkheimer and Adorno, all of whom emphasized the
cognitive power of art and introduced aesthetic elements into their philosophical method. Although Adorno warned against a philosophy that im-
itated art too closely,[44] he nonetheless acknowledged a strongly aesthetic
dimension in his own thought.

The specific artistic field he mastered both as a participant and critic
was, of course, music. Aside from Bloch, he was, in fact, the only Western
Marxist who commented extensively on music as part of his cultural criticism. And perhaps more important, he was the only one who drew from
the principles of musical composition inspiration for this theorizing. The
musical milieu which nurtured him was that of the Schoenberg school in
Vienna, where he was a student from 1925 to 1927. More accurately, he
was influenced by Schoenberg's "new music" before it spawned an orthodox following, which developed after the adoption of the twelve-tone row
as the basis of composition. Adorno's relationship to Schoenberg was always a complicated one—he was personally much closer to Alban
Berg[45]—and he did not shy away from criticizing Schoenberg's later development, even as he was favorably contrasting his general achievement
to Stravinsky's.[46]

What attracted Adorno to Schoenberg in the mid-twenties was the
"free atonality" of his so-called expressionist phase, which began with
the *Georgelieder (Das Buch der hängenden Gärten)* in 1910 and lasted
until approximately 1925, when his serial compositions began replacing
it. Schoenberg's expressionism did not, however, mean the self-indulgent
articulation of his subjective emotions, in the manner of much nineteenth-century romantic music. Instead, it signified a necessary, if painful,
withdrawal into the objective logic of musical development, a withdrawal
which, Adorno insisted, was linked through a complicated mimetic pro-

43. Buck-Morss, p. 23. For a good discussion of the early differences between Adorno
and Benjamin underplayed by Buck-Morss, see Lunn, p. 200f.

44. Adorno, *Negative Dialectics*, p. 15.

45. Berg was his teacher of composition in Vienna in the mid-1920s. Adorno wrote of
his relationship in *Alban Berg: Der Meister des kleinsten Übergangs* (Vienna, 1968).

46. See, for example, his linking of Schoenberg's twelve-tone row with the domination
of nature in *Philosophy of Modern Music*, p. 64.

cess with general social trends outside of music itself. Schoenberg believed that music was a vehicle for the representation of truth, not merely for the expression of affect. Like Benjamin with his denigration of the communicative function of language, Schoenberg insisted that musical language did more than convey feeling or excite an emotional response in the listener. He was thus willing to forego immediate audience "understanding" of his work and withhold the pleasurable experience music traditionally supplied. As Adorno himself later approvingly put it,

The purity and sovereignty with which Schoenberg always entrusts himself to the demands of his subject-matter has restricted his influence; it is precisely because of its seriousness, richness and integrity that his music arouses resentment. The more it gives its listeners, the less it offers them. It requires the listener spontaneously to compose its inner movement and demands of him not mere contemplation but praxis.[47]

There was, therefore, in Schoenberg a strongly ascetic moment, a distrust of play and ornament, that Adorno justified by reference to developments outside of music itself. The objective truth revealed by Schoenberg's musical innovations, which accounts for its identification with the anguished suffering of expressionism, was the collapse of the basis for traditional artistic totalization, the active bourgeois subject.

In musical terms, this breakdown was expressed in the overthrow of tonality, the logical culmination of the process of disintegration already set into motion by Wagner's chromaticism. Schoenberg's refusal to force a new type of coherence on music in his atonal phase, a refusal that was similar to the allegorical liquidation of the false appearance of totality celebrated by Benjamin, meant that his compositions were true to the unreconciled dissonances of modern life. As Adorno later put it, in praising Schoenberg's inability to complete an ambitious Oratorio:

The whole, as a positive entity, cannot be antithetically extracted from an estranged and splintered reality by means of the will and power of the individual; if it is not to degenerate into deception and ideology, it must assume the form of negation. The *chef d'oeuvre* remained unfinished and Schoenberg's admission of failure, his recognition that it was "a fragment, like everything else," says perhaps more for him than any success.[48]

On those occasions when Schoenberg remained faithful to the classical ideal of a fully rounded work, Adorno did not hesitate to criticize him.[49]

47. Adorno, *Prisms*, pp. 149–50.
48. Ibid., p. 164.
49. In his first *Zeitschrift* essay in 1932, Adorno questioned "whether the ideal of the hermetic work of art, resting within itself, which Schönberg inherited from classicism and to

But in comparison with other contemporary composers, most notably
Stravinsky, whose music Adorno tendentiously damned as the equivalent
of *völkisch* mythologizing, Schoenberg staunchly resisted the lure of organic totality. Nor did he embrace the superficial optimism of the *Neue
Sachlichkeit*, which pervaded the work of Hindemith and other defenders
of *Gebrauchsmusik* (utility music). However much his music moved towards objectivism, especially in its dodecaphonic form, it always registered the anguish of the suppressed subject.

Schoenberg was therefore more genuinely progressive than any other
composer in more than merely musical terms. For instead of being complicitous with the growing facade of universalism, the false totality that
Adorno and his colleagues saw as dominating contemporary consciousness, truly progressive music, indeed art in general, had to preserve the
determinate negations of this illusory, yet pervasive whole.

The concept of determinate negation is, of course, Hegelian, and
Adorno did not hesitate to apply Hegelian categories to Schoenberg, "the
dialectical composer,"[50] as he once called him. There was, in fact, an un-
deniably Hegelian element in his aesthetic theory, indeed in his entire philosophy, which drew him at times closer to Lukács than to Benjamin or
Kracauer.[51] In musical terms, this meant a belief that whereas music in the
present could not achieve a genuinely organic totality, at times in the past
it had been able to and would possibly in the future as well. As he put it in
a 1938 essay in the *Zeitschrift*, the greatness of music

is shown as a force for synthesis. Not only does the musical synthesis preserve the
unity of appearance and protect it from falling apart into diffuse culinary moments, but in such unity, in the relation of particular moments to an evolving
whole, there is also preserved the image of a social condition in which above those
particular moments of happiness would be more than mere appearance.[52]

The wholeness of art, including music, was thus a prefiguration of the

which he remains true, can be reconciled with the means which he has defined, and further,
whether such a concept of art, as totality and cosmos, can still be upheld at all." "On the
Social Situation of Music," *Telos* 35 (Spring 1975), p. 136.

50. Adorno, "Der dialektische Komponist" in *Arnold Schönberg zum 60. Geburtstag,
13 September 1934* (Vienna, 1934); reprinted in *Impromptus: Zweite Folge neu gedruckter
musikalischer Aufsätze* (Frankfurt, 1969).

51. For an argument stressing his similarities to Lukács, see Ferenc Feher, "Negative
Philosophy of Music—Positive Results," *New German Critique* 4 (Winter 1975).

52. Adorno, "On the Fetish Character of Music and the Regression of Hearing," reprinted in *The Essential Frankfurt School Reader*, ed. with intros. Andrew Arato and Eike
Gebhardt (New York, 1978), p. 273.

normative totality of the future society, or as Marcuse following Stendhal would have put, "*une promesse de bonheur.*"[53]

The classical example of musical totalization for Adorno was always Beethoven, in particular his middle period. Like Hegel and Goethe, Beethoven represented the fragile and ephemeral synthetic moment of bourgeois ascendency that had existed for perhaps a generation in the early nineteenth century before the proletariat emerged to challenge its hegemony. In his person, Beethoven expressed the highest achievement of the recently emancipated autonomous subject of bourgeois society. However, by the time of his *Missa Solemnis*, composed in 1818–19, the synthesis had already begun to unravel:

The musical experience of the late Beethoven must have become mistrustful of the unity of subjectivity and objectivity, the roundness of symphonic successes, the totality emerging from the movement of all the parts; in short, of everything that gave authenticity up to now to the works of his middle period. He exposed the classical as classicizing. He rejected the affirmative, that which uncritically endorsed Being in the idea of the classically symphonic.[54]

Beethoven thus began the process of negating totality in music that would culminate in Schoenberg's atonal revolution.

In philosophy as in music, atonality was more "truthful" than an "extorted reconciliation."[55] For all of Adorno's interest in Lukács and Hegelian Marxism, for all his fascination with the concepts of reification, mediation and second nature, for all his attraction to the totalizing methodology of Horkheimer's Institute, he stubbornly maintained that under present circumstances, the anti-holistic lessons he learned from Kracauer, Benjamin and Schoenberg were of equal, if not greater, value. The most explicit and extended formulation of that position came in *Negative Dialectics*, a book which he acknowledged would allow his enemies to "proclaim that they knew it all the time and now he was confessing."[56] But, as we have noted above, many of the same themes appeared in his earlier work in the waning years of the Weimar Republic.

The document that most clearly demonstrates this point is his inaugural lecture of 1931, "The Actuality of Philosophy," which would have been

53. Herbert Marcuse, "The Affirmative Character of Culture" in *Negations: Essays in Critical Theory*, trans. Jeremy J. Shapiro (Boston, 1968), p. 115.
54. Adorno, "Alienated Masterpiece: The *Missa Solemnis*," Telos 28 (Summer 1976), p. 122.
55. "Erpresste Versöhnung" was the title of Adorno's critique of Lukács' anti-modernist aesthetics in *Noten zur Literatur II*.
56. Adorno, *Negative Dialectics*, p. xxi.

dedicated to Benjamin had it been published in Adorno's lifetime.[57] It opens with a bold denial:

Whoever chooses philosophy as a profession today must first reject the illusion that earlier philosophical enterprises began with: that the power of thought is sufficient to grasp the totality of the real. No justifying reason could rediscover itself in a reality whose order and form suppresses every claim to reason; only polemically does reason present itself to the knower as total reality, while only in traces and ruins is it prepared to hope that it will ever come across correct and just reality.[58]

Tracing the recent history of holistic thinking in philosophy, Adorno located its breakdown in the terminal crisis of idealism. He then discussed efforts to reconstitute totality in existentialist and phenomenological circles, which culminated in the work of Scheler and Heidegger, efforts that were all in vain.

Turning to the argument that science would somehow replace philosophy as the method of totalization, an assumption often held by vulgar Marxists, he contended that the two were fundamentally incompatible modes of cognition:

The separate sciences accept their findings, at least their final and deepest findings, as indestructible and static, whereas philosophy perceives the first finding which it lights upon as a sign that needs unriddling. Plainly put: the idea of science (*Wissenschaft*) is research; that of philosophy is interpretation.[59]

In so arguing, Adorno was implicitly criticizing the contention made by Horkheimer in his own inaugural address a few months before that social philosophy and scientific research could combine to give knowledge of the social whole.

The alternative he was presenting, philosophy as interpretation, did not, however, mean embracing traditional hermeneutics of the Schleiermacherian or Diltheyan kind. Instead, following Benjamin and suppressing his own neo-Hegelian inclinations, Adorno denied that interpretation meant the recovery or recollection of an intended meaning. There was no "real world" behind the veil of appearance, no fixed meaning to be exposed. Anamnesis was not an *Erinnerung* of an original subject-object

57. The intended dedication is mentioned in the editor's first note to the English translation of the text in *Telos*. Why Adorno chose not to publish the lecture during his life is not clear, although he may have felt uncertain of the response it would evoke. In letters to Kracauer of May 29, 1931, and June 8, 1931, he complained of the misunderstandings aroused by his talk, the stupidest of which was Karl Mannheim's assumption that he had gone over to the Vienna Circle. (Letters in the Kracauer *Nachlass*, Schiller Nationalmuseum, Marbach am Neckar.)
58. Adorno, "The Actuality of Philosophy," p. 120.
59. Ibid., p. 126.

unity. Truth could only be discovered through permitting constellations of existing elements to become illuminations, sudden and momentary revelations of a non-totalized reality. Through such constructions, philosophy would become materialist:

Here one can discover what appears as such an astounding and strange affinity existing between interpretive philosophy and that type of thinking which most strongly rejects the concept of the intentional, the meaningful: the thinking of materialism. Interpretation of the unintentional through a juxtaposition of the analytically isolated elements and illumination of the real by the power of such interpretation is the program of every authentically materialist knowledge, a program to which the materialist procedure does all the more justice, the more it distances itself from every "meaning" of its objects and the less it relates itself to an implicit, quasi-religious meaning.[60]

Materialist interpretation also meant rejecting the symbolizing mode of thought characteristic of idealism, which Benjamin had demonstrated was less appropriate than allegory to times of fragmentation:

If philosophy must learn to renounce the question of totality, then it implies that it must learn to do without the symbolic function, in which for a long time, at least in idealism, the particular appeared to represent the general.[61]

By calling for such a renunciation, Adorno was implicitly criticizing the premises of Hegelian Marxism, in particular those articulated in *History and Class Consciousness*. This challenge was made explicit in a thought experiment he proposed which was aimed at Lukács' solution of the antinomies of bourgeois thought:

Suppose it were possible to group the elements of a social analysis in such a manner that the way they came together made a figure which certainly does not lie before us organically, but which must first be posited: the commodity structure. This would hardly solve the thing-in-itself problem, not even in the sense that somehow the social conditions might be revealed under which the thing-in-itself problem came into existence, as Lukács even thought the solution to be; for the truth content of a problem is in principle different from the historical and psychological conditions out of which it grows.[62]

In other words, the reliance on Vico's *verum—factum* principle to collapse truth into class origin, which we have seen in Gramsci as well as Lukács,

60. Ibid., p. 127.
61. Ibid., p. 127. Here, we might note in passing, Adorno was at odds with Marcuse's aesthetics, which remained indebted to classical ideals of symbolism rather than to allegory. For a contrast of Marcuse and Benjamin on this issue, which also suggests a contrast between Marcuse and Adorno, see Jürgen Habermas, "Consciousness-Raising or Redemptive Criticism: The Contemporaneity of Walter Benjamin," *New German Critique* 17 (Spring 1979), p. 35f.
62. Adorno, "The Actuality of Philosophy," p. 128.

was ultimately untenable, as genesis and truth value are unrelated. Similarly, Mannheim's attempt to salvage truth by grounding it entirely in the social being of the contemporary totality misfired, for truth is a function more of the content of thought than of the social status of its thinkers.

In severing truth from its social origins, Adorno did not, however, turn the search for it entirely into a contemplative enterprise. With an optimism that would be absent from his later work, he called for a certain unity of theory and practice:

The interpretation of given reality and its abolition are connected to each other, not, of course, in the sense that reality is negated in the concept, but that out of the construction of a configuration of reality the demand for its [reality's] real change always follows promptly. The change-causing gesture of the riddle process—not its mere resolution as such—provides the image of resolutions to which materialist praxis alone has access. Materialism has named this relationship with a name that is philosophically certified: dialectic. Only dialectically, it seems to me, is philosophic interpretation possible.[63]

The precise nature of the link between his anti-intentionalist hermeneutics and concrete praxis Adorno did not, however, specify. Instead, he intimated that philosophic interpretation, presiding as it did over the liquidation of traditional philosophy, would be a form of praxis itself. To achieve this goal, interpretation would have to derive certain of its insights from sociology, without capitulating to what Adorno called its nominalist inclinations. Here he came close to endorsing Horkheimer's program for the Institute, which his earlier insistence on the tension between philosophy and scientific research had implicitly questioned. Interpretation would have to manipulate the findings of sociology into constellations whose truth value would be "legitimated in the last analysis alone by the fact that reality crystallizes about them in striking conclusiveness."[64] This rather empty and tautological principle of verification—who was to say what constituted "striking conclusiveness"?—showed that for all his insistence that the demand for "real change always follows promptly" the construction of an idea, he had little confidence in the practical validation of that idea. The complicated dialectic of verification and practice, defended by Horkheimer in the 1930s against both contemplative scientism and pragmatism, was absent from Adorno's epistemology.

In general, "The Actuality of Philosophy" revealed a cautious and prudent mind. Whereas, for example, Marcuse would celebrate the power of rationality as a legacy from idealism that Marxism had to preserve, Adorno emphasized its limits, which were not merely historical:

63. Ibid., p. 129.   64. Ibid., p. 131.

Philosophy which no longer makes the assumption of autonomy, which no longer believes reality to be grounded in the *ratio*, but instead assumes always and forever that the law-giving of autonomous reason pierces through a being which is not adequate to it and cannot be laid out rationally as a totality—such a philosophy will not go the entire path to the rational presuppositions, but instead will stop there where irreducible reality breaks in upon it.[65]

The "always and forever" of this statement betrays Adorno's deepest qualms about the possible achievement of normative totality, despite his occasional protestations of belief in it. The philosophy that was true to these qualms would have to be less systematic than essayistic, a traditional term of opprobrium that Adorno happily accepted to describe his own work. Like Benjamin and Kracauer, he was convinced that the uncompleted and broken form of the essay was far more appropriate than the massive volume of conventional philosophy, "for the mind (*Geist*) is indeed not capable of producing or grasping the totality of the real, but it may be possible to penetrate the detail, to explode in miniature the mass of merely existing reality."[66] Schoenberg's praiseworthy inability to complete a finished masterpiece of the type mandated by traditional musical practice could serve as well as a model for philosophy, which should admit its experimental and tentative nature.

With this final expression of doubt about the totalizing power of philosophy, Adorno closed what must be seen as the most explicitly Benjaminian of his works.[67] Its implications were clearly opposed to the type of holism promoted by Lukács and the first generation of Western Marxists. The expressive concept of totality, in particular, was ruled out by Adorno's reluctance to link epistemological validity and social genesis; the symmetry of making and knowing posited by the *verum—factum* principle was a fallacy. Marxist theory, contrary to the tenets of Korsch's "revolutionary historicism," could never be reduced to the consciousness of a progressive class.[68] In fact, the very notion of a meta-subject capable of totalizing reality was an illegitimate hypostatization taken over from idealism's notion of a transcendental subject.

In his later writings, Adorno contended that such a hypostatization was not merely dubious philosophy, but pernicious as well. Its ultimate

65. Ibid., p. 132.
66. Ibid., p. 133.
67. Another essay written during the same period and also unpublished until after Adorno's death, "Die Idee der Naturgeschichte," is perhaps equally Benjaminian. It first appeared in print in volume 1 of Adorno's *Gesammelte Schriften* (Frankfurt, 1973).
68. In the German version of *Negative Dialectics* (but inexplicably absent from the English), there is a direct attack on Korsch for this failing. See *Negative Dialektik* (Frankfurt, 1966), p. 144.

ground, he argued, could be found in the domination of exchange value in
social relations, a domination that reduced individuals to interchangeable exemplars of an abstract subjectivity. As he put it in one of his
last essays,

What shows up faithfully in the doctrine of the transcendental subject is the priority of the relations—abstractly rational ones, detached from the human individuals and their relationships—that have their model in exchange. If the exchange
form is the standard social structure, its rationality constitutes people; what they
are for themselves, what they seem to be to themselves, is secondary.[69]

Because exchange value was in fact so pervasive in capitalism, indeed
throughout Western civilization, meta-subjects did reflect reality, but reality of the most oppressive kind.

The solution, however, was not the emergence of another, more genuine kind of collective subject favored by most Marxists—the "we-subject"
that Sartre was to posit as an antidote to serialization—but rather the
dialectical non-identity of subjects, which were at once individual and
collective, empirical and transcendental. Because the integrity of the individual subject was now in such danger of liquidation, not through some
dialectical sublation but rather through the triumph of what Marcuse
would call "one-dimensional" consciousness, it was necessary to criticize
all varieties of meta-subjectivism. As Adorno put it in the preface to *Negative Dialectics*, "To use the strength of the subject to break through the
fallacy of constitutive subjectivity—this is what the author felt to be his
task ever since he came to trust his own mental impulses."[70] For Adorno,
therefore, saving "the subject" did not mean reducing objectivity to the
intentional objectification of a collective subject.

But in defending the legitimacy of empirical and individual subjectivity, Adorno demonstrated his distance from one of Benjamin's more troubling biases. Whereas Benjamin had seemed to move from a completely
objectivist denigration of the subject, whether individual or collective, in
The Origin of German Tragic Drama to a crudely Marxist defense of
collective subjectivity alone in such later works as "The Author as Producer,"[71] Adorno always defended a complicated balance among collective subjectivity, individual subjectivity and objectivity. Determined to resist the collapse of any one of these elements into any of the others, he
argued for a "force-field" of non-identity that would preserve the integrity

69. Adorno, "Subject and Object" in *The Essential Frankfurt School Reader*, p. 501.
70. Adorno, *Negative Dialectics*, p. xx.
71. Benjamin, "The Author as Producer" in *The Essential Frankfurt School Reader*. It
would be wrong, however, to see this work as completely representative of Benjamin's more
materialist period. See the discussion in Wolin, *Walter Benjamin*, p. 154f.

of the parts against even the most apparently liberating totalization. True to Benjamin's metaphor of a constellation, but including individual subjectivity among the component stars, he called for a dialectics that would resist the positive negation of the negation, the perfect identity of subject and object, celebrated by Hegelianism and Hegelian Marxism.

Adorno's concern for the dangers of collective meta-subjectivity grew out of more than a protective attitude towards the individual; it stemmed as well from his keen awareness of the costs of subjugating objective nature. Unlike Horkheimer in the 1930s, he seems to have been sensitive to the risks involved in dominating nature, whether by capitalist or socialist means. In a talk he presented to the Frankfurt Kant Society in 1932, entitled "The Idea of Natural History,"[72] he called into question the privileging of either nature over history or history over nature as an ontological first principle. Although he considered Hegel's concept of "second nature," which Lukács developed in *The Theory of the Novel*, a useful way to conceive the pseudo-naturalism of human relations under capitalism, he nonetheless rejected the belief that subjective human praxis could completely denaturalize the social world. The assumption of an "absolute historicism," to use Gramsci's phrase that Adorno could not have yet known, was as mythicizing as the naturalization of human relations favored in certain right-wing circles. In the spirit of Benjamin's early work, Adorno insisted that history and nature were too intertwined to be completely separated. The passing away of nature, its own "historical" decay, was thus a part of human history. Mourning for its loss could not be overcome in the theodicy of an idealist or Hegelian Marxist faith in history. As Horkheimer also pointed out in numerous places, the suffering of past generations, the pain inflicted on nature itself, could not be redeemed by any future totalizations.

In the joint work written by Horkheimer and Adorno during the war, *Dialectic of Enlightenment*, the theme of the unredeemable suffering of nature achieved a new urgency. Although integrated in imprecise fashion with a still Marxist critique of bourgeois society, it became the dominant explanatory device by which they attempted to analyze the ills of contemporary society, indeed of all of Western history. In this analysis, the concept of totality lost virtually all of its positive connotations and became almost a synonym for totalitarianism. Idealism alone was no longer singled out as the primary example of subjective human arrogance. Now, reason itself, in particular its instrumental and formal variants, was seen as responsible for the domination of nature. Initially arising as an antidote

72. See note 67.

to myth, reason had itself become a new form of myth. The enlightenment, broadly understood as Western civilization's rationalizing imperative, had treated nature as if it were an objective "other" to be exploited
for the benefit of the subject. The result was the concomitant objectification of men themselves, who were treated as if they were natural objects to
be mastered. Fascism, the final result of this dialectic, combined a distorted revolt of oppressed nature with a cynical use of the very means
instrumental rationalization had perfected.

In this process, Horkheimer and Adorno contended, the Jews played a
tragically complex role. At once the supreme rationalizers and the victims
of that rationalization, they suffered from a special fate that was determined by the totalistic pretensions of rationalism, both as an ideology and
a social imperative. As stubborn examples of non-identity, the irreducible
"other" that totalitarian reason sought to bring under its control, they
were the targets of special hatred. "From the outset," they wrote, "there
has always been an intimate link between anti-Semitism and totality."[73]
Although after the defeat of Fascism anti-Semitism per se no longer was a
political threat, the rage against non-identity that spawned it was still a
powerful reality. Totality was no less oppressive a tendency in allegedly
democratic societies than in avowed authoritarian ones.

The animus towards totality expressed in *Dialectic of Enlightenment*
was especially directed against its longitudinal form, the belief in universal history as a coherent whole. Benjamin, as we noted earlier, had been
deeply critical of the concept of progress, in both its bourgeois and its
socialist guises. Believing that history was more a process of decay than of
development, he hoped for relief only though messianic intervention, the
sudden incursion of what he called *Jetztzeit* or *nunc stans* (mystically
fulfilled time) into the empty movement of chronology. This essentially
religious hope for ruptures in historical continuity was married to his later
Marxism with questionable results. As Habermas pointed out,

An anti-evolutionary conception of history cannot be tacked onto historical materialism as if it were a monk's cowl—tacked onto a historical materialism, which
takes account of progress not only in the dimension of the forces of production,
but in that of domination too. . . . Benjamin did not realize his intention to bring
together enlightenment and mysticism, because the theologian in him could not
accept the idea of making his messianic theory of experience serviceable to historical materialism.[74]

73. Horkheimer and Adorno, *Dialectic of Enlightenment*, p. 172. For a discussion of
links between the Jewish question and the Frankfurt School's attitudes toward totality, see
Martin Jay, "The Jews and the Frankfurt School: Critical Theory's Analysis of Anti-Semitism," *New German Critique* 19 (Winter 1980).
74. Habermas, "Consciousness-Raising or Redemptive Criticism," p. 51.

The more religious dimensions of his thought were also considered questionable by Horkheimer and Adorno, who therefore could not share his desperate optimism about sudden messianic interruptions in the historical totality. As we have seen, Horkheimer adopted Benjamin's critique of progress in "The Authoritarian State," but stressed collective human will rather than messianic intervention as the way to disrupt historical continuity. In that work, he still held out hope for the exercise of revolutionary will. But by *Dialectic of Enlightenment,* virtually all such hope was abandoned. Whether because of Adorno's growing influence or the pressure of events, that work not merely questioned the Enlightenment's faith in progress, but actually turned it on its head. Now instead of seeing history as the arena for the realization of normative totality, they viewed it as the site of an ever-worsening disaster. The counter-evolutionary image of decay underlying Benjamin's mournful vision, that "single catastrophe which keeps piling wreckage upon wreckage"[75] seen by the angel in Klee's painting "Angelus Novus," was now shared by Horkheimer and Adorno. As Adorno would later put it in *Negative Dialectics,*

After the catastrophes that have happened, and in view of the catastrophes to come, it would be cynical to say that a plan for a better world is manifested in history and unites it. Not to be denied for that reason, however, is the unity that cements the discontinuous, chaotically splintered moments and phases of history—the unity of the control of nature, progressing to rule over men, and finally to that over men's inner nature. No universal history leads from savagery to humanitarianism, but there is one leading from the slingshot to the megaton bomb.[76]

Clearly, Adorno eschewed any optimistic image of longitudinal totality, but did he nonetheless retain it as a pejorative concept? A number of commentators have thought so, arguing that in so doing, Adorno revealed his hidden indebtedness to the immanentist teleology of orthodox Marxism.[77] In Paul Connerton's words,

What was criticized in Marx as an apotheosis of history is transformed by Adorno into a "diabolisation" of history. What was condemned in Hegel is once more turned on its head: radical evil—Evil as such—is promoted to the status of the World-Spirit. The history of salvation is replaced by the history of damnation.[78]

---

75. Benjamin, "Theses on the Philosophy of History" in *Illuminations,* trans. Harry Zohn (New York, 1968), p. 259.
76. Adorno, *Negative Dialectics,* p. 320.
77. See, for example, Peter Bürger, *Theorie der Avantgarde* (Frankfurt, 1974); Paul Piccone, "The Changing Function of Critical Theory," *New German Critique* 12 (Fall 1977), p. 30; and Russell Berman, "Adorno, Marxism and Art," *Telos* 34 (Winter 1977–78), p. 158f.
78. Paul Connerton, *The Tragedy of Enlightenment: An Essay on the Frankfurt School* (Cambridge, 1980), p. 114.

There is some truth in this charge, but it must be qualified in two respects. First, although the burden of Adorno's argument is that history is a
"Satanic" process of worsening oppression, he did occasionally evince a
guarded hope for the sudden reversal of this trend. The utopian moment
in Critical Theory, which remained particularly potent in Marcuse's
thought, was never entirely extinguished in that of his friend. Even *Dialectic of Enlightenment* was written in order to pave the way for a more defensible notion of enlightenment. Like Benjamin with his hope for messianic
intervention, albeit without the theological basis for that hope, Adorno
protested against seeing history as completely predetermined. Thus, to
take an example from his 1951 article on "Freudian Theory and the Pattern of Fascist Propaganda," he concluded that the increase in collective
control of the masses through psychological manipulation

may well terminate in sudden awareness of the untruth of the spell, and eventually
in its collapse. Socialized hypnosis breeds within itself the forces which will do
away with the spook of regression through remote control, and in the end awaken
those who keep their eyes shut though they are no longer asleep.[79]

And in an essay entitled "Resignation," written in 1969, the year of his
death, he insisted,

As long as thinking is not interrupted, it has a firm grasp on possibility. Its insatia-
ble quality, the resistance against petty satiety, rejects the foolish wisdom of resignation. The utopian impulse in thinking is all the stronger, the less it objectifies
itself as utopia—a further form of regression—whereby it sabotages its own realization. Open thinking points beyond itself.[80]

Such statements of course might be called external to Adorno's real argument, introduced like a utopian *deus ex machina*, as Kracauer sus-
pected,[81] to save him from the inevitable reproach of political quietism. And
it is certainly true that a vague hope for the sudden collapse of the system as
a whole provides little real impetus to political action of any kind either
now or in the future, especially as Adorno never endorsed the "great refusal" Marcuse would derive from a similar analysis. Adorno, therefore,
seemed to be open to the charge of inconsistency because he combined an
increasingly gloomy analysis of the totality on the macrological level with a

    79. Adorno, "Freudian Theory and the Pattern of Fascist Propaganda," in *The Essential
Frankfurt School Reader*, p. 137.
    80. Adorno, "Resignation," *Telos* 35 (Spring 1975), p. 168. For other examples of this
refusal to rule out change, see "Culture Industry Reconsidered," *New German Critique* 6
(Fall 1975) and "Transparencies on Film," *New German Critique* 24–25 (Fall-Winter
1981–82).
    81. See the memoranda of August 12, 1960 and July 27–28, 1964 in the Kracau-
er *Nachlass*, which are discussed in Jay, "Adorno and Kracauer: Notes on a Troubled
Friendship."

call for theoretical and artistic resistance to it on the micrological. Either the totality was completely watertight in its reifying power and resistance could only be co-opted, or the totality still contained negations and Adorno's descriptions of its Satanic "falseness" were exaggerations.

Clearly, Adorno did not accept the former alternative, for in the very art of writing he affirmed the possibility of some escape from co-optation. Indeed, and this is also the second reason why it is not completely accurate to say that Adorno retained an inverted Hegelian concept of longitudinal totality, Adorno himself would agree that such descriptions were hyperbolic. As he put it in *Minima Moralia,*

While thought relates to facts and moves by criticising them, its movement depends no less on the maintenance of distance. It expresses exactly what is, precisely because what is is never quite as thought expresses it. Essential to it is an element of exaggeration, of overshooting the object, of self-detachment from the weight of the factual, so that instead of merely reproducing being it can, at once rigorous and free, determine it.[82]

In other words, as Gillian Rose has perceptively noted,[83] Adorno's use of totality must be taken as an example of his general anti-realist use of concepts. The inevitable gap between concept and object, which he claimed materialism preserved and idealism denied, meant that Adorno's own concepts were themselves not to be taken as perfectly true to reality. Thus, when Adorno spoke, for example, of "our totally organized bourgeois society, which has forcibly been made over into a totality,"[84] he should be understood as positing a conceptual object that was not fully equivalent to its real counterpart. In fact, before remarking on the universal history leading from the slingshot to the megaton bomb, he argued that "universal history must be construed and denied,"[85] and elsewhere in *Negative Dialectics* he asserted, "Totality is to be opposed by convicting it of nonidentity with itself—of the nonidentity it denies, according to its own concept."[86] In short, even in those statements where Adorno described the

82. Adorno, *Minima Moralia,* pp. 126–27; see also his defense of exaggeration in his introduction to *The Positivist Dispute in German Sociology,* trans. Glyn Adey and David Frisby (London, 1976), pp. 35–36.
83. Rose, *The Melancholy Science,* p. 79. Rose, however, is not fully convincing when she claims that the concept of totality "adds little or nothing ... to the theory of value (reification) and to the theory of identity and non-identity thinking. It is simply another way of stating the basic characteristics of non-identity thinking." What Rose neglects is the extent to which the frequent use of totality in Adorno's work brings with it a freight of associations that derive from the tradition we have been examining in this book. Although Adorno certainly rejected many aspects of that tradition, as we have noted, he nonetheless never fully escaped from it.
84. Adorno, *Philosophy of Modern Music,* p. 25.
85. Adorno, *Negative Dialectics,* p. 320.
86. Ibid., p. 147.

latitudinal totality of the present or the longitudinal totality of Western history in the bleakest of terms, there is always the saving grace that concept and object are necessarily non-identical.

There were, to be sure, frequent expressions of alarm in Adorno's writings concerning the narrowing of the gap between non-identical entities, including concepts and objects. At times, he even seems to have thought that the immanent method dependent on exploiting such gaps was in danger of losing its critical power.[87] But elsewhere in his work, he would retreat from his more extreme expressions of pessimism about the totalitarian omnipotence of the present whole.[88] Adorno's negative dialectics must itself be understood as an untotalized "forcefield" of apparently contradictory statements, which both reflects and resists the reality it tries critically to analyze. The disdain for traditional logic manifested in the Hegelian tradition allowed Adorno to hold opposing, even incompatible, positions simultaneously without worrying about their coherence. Indeed, at times he seemed to suggest that the fetish of logical consistency was a manifestation of the very identitarian thinking to which he was so adamantly opposed. To his more orthodox philosophical critics, negative dialectics thus offered little more than what Leszek Kolakowski called "a blank check"[89] on which any judgment freed from logical validation or empirical verification could be written. How valid this charge may be depends on one's criteria for verification, always a point of dispute between Critical Theory and its opponents.

What is clear is that Adorno's attitude towards normative totality manifested a certain lability that resulted from his distaste for perfect consistency. Although, as we have noted, he sometimes saw the organic wholeness of great works of art as promises of future happiness, he generally tended to deny that it would appear in the form of a fully integrated community without alienation. As he put it in his debate with Karl Popper and his followers, "Totality is not an affirmative but rather a critical category. Dialectical critique seeks to salvage or help to establish what does not obey totality, what opposes it or what first forms itself as the potential

87. This concern was perhaps most clearly voiced in the collective Institute publication, *Aspects of Sociology*, trans. John Viertel (Boston, 1972), especially in the section entitled "Ideology," which was written by Adorno.

88. A prime example of this partial retreat was his essay "Freizeit" in *Stichworte: Kritische Modelle 2* (Frankfurt, 1969), where he conceded that the integration of consciousness was not as complete as he had previously believed.

89. Kolakowski, *Main Currents of Marxism*, vol. III: *The Breakdown*, trans. P. S. Falla (Oxford, 1978), p. 364. This remark is one of the milder charges hurled at Adorno, whose *Negative Dialectics* he calls a "model of professorial bombast concealing poverty of thought" (p. 368). Kracauer had similar qualms. See the memoranda cited in note 81.

of a not yet existent individualization. . . . A liberated mankind would by no means be a totality."[90]

Adorno therefore seems not to have hoped for the complete overcoming of reification, that special bugbear of Hegelian Marxism. Yet in much of his writing, he used reification as a term of opprobrium, contending, for example, that "dialectics means intransigence towards all reification."[91] In his vocabulary, reification was linked with other pejorative terms such as fetishism, myth and second nature (far more, one might add, than with the more specifically Marxist Humanist term alienation, which Adorno tended to avoid).[92] It was, in fact, so central a term in his version of Critical Theory that one commentator has gone so far as to say that "Adorno's thought depends fundamentally on the category of reification."[93]

All the more surprising then are the following passages from *Negative Dialectics:*

The thinker may easily comfort himself by imagining that in the dissolution of reification, of the merchandise character, he possesses the philosopher's stone. But reification itself is the reflexive form of false objectivity; centering theory around reification, a form of consciousness, makes the critical theory idealistically acceptable to the reigning consciousness and to the collective unconscious. This is what raised Marx's early writings—in contradistinction to *Das Kapital*—to their present popularity, notably among theologians.

There is a good deal of irony in the fact that the brutal and primitive functionaries who more than forty years back damned Lukács as a heretic, because of the reification chapter in his important *History and Class Consciousness*, did sense the idealistic nature of his conception. We can no more reduce dialectics to reification than we can reduce it to any other isolated category, however polemical.[94]

Later in his book, Adorno returned to the same theme:

90. Adorno, introduction to *The Positivist Dispute in German Sociology*, p. 12. In so arguing, Adorno may not have been as distant from Marx as might appear at first glance. As Moishe Postone has argued, Marx himself may have conceived totality as an expression of social alienation under capitalism. In other words, capital acts like Hegel's Subject to dominate individual, contingent subjects. Hegelian Marxism thus merely inverts this domination by searching for a new totalizing subject in the proletariat. See Postone, "The Present as Necessity: Towards a Reinterpretation of the Marxian Critique of Labor and Time" (Ph.D. diss., University of Frankfurt, 1983), p. 82.

91. Adorno, *Prisms*, p. 31.

92. Adorno, in fact, preferred the mature Marx to his earlier version, contrary to the sympathies of most Western Marxists. See, for example, his discussion in *Negative Dialectics*, p. 192. He thus never made as much of the concept of alienation as did many of his peers. In his *Introduction to the Sociology of Music*, trans. E. B. Ashton (New York, 1976), he called it "a term that is gradually becoming hard to bear" (p. 220).

93. Rose, *The Melancholy Science*, p. ix.

94. Adorno, *Negative Dialectics*, p. 190.

The category of reification, which was inspired by the wishful image of unbroken subjective immediacy, no longer merits the key position accorded to it, over-zealously, by an apologetic thinking happy to absorb materialist thinking. . . . The total liquefaction of everything thinglike regressed to the subjectivism of the pure act. It hypostatized the indirect as direct. Pure immediacy and fetishism are equally untrue.[95]

How to reconcile these statements with Adorno's previous reliance on reification is a source of some controversy. Buck-Morss contends that in *Negative Dialectics* Adorno "was criticizing his own earlier position,"[96] whereas Rose argues that after 1932, reification was "the centrifuge of all of his major works,"[97] including *Negative Dialectics*. Indeed, passing over in silence the remarks quoted above, Rose develops a theory of reification that she claims derives from that very work. Her interpretation is ingenious, but it succeeds only at the cost of forcing a consistency on Adorno's writings that was not there.

In certain of Adorno's more casual references to reification before *Negative Dialectics*, its Lukácsian resonances are still active. Thus, for example, when he writes in *The Positivism Dispute* that "despite all the experience of reification . . . critical theory is oriented towards the idea of society as subject,"[98] the clear implication is that a subject has forgotten his objectification and allowed it to become an external other. Here the component of reification that is related to consciousness, indeed a transindividual consciousness, is unmistakable. In *Negative Dialectics*, however, Adorno criticizes reification as an idealistic category precisely because it is a function of collective consciousness. If, then, he persists in employing the category of reification, as Rose contends, it must be in a very non-Lukácsian way.

To make her case for such an alternative, Rose argues that Adorno equated reification with identity theory, the non-dialectical claim that concepts are perfectly adequate to their objects. Although drawing on Nietzsche's critique of conceptual realism, Adorno derived his animus against identity theory and reification largely from Marx, she claims, in particular the Marx of *Das Kapital*. For the model of identitarian reification is the exchange principle that Marx saw at the root of capitalism, the reduction of concrete acts of human labor into abstract units of labor time and the transformation of use values into interchangeable commodities in

95. Ibid., p. 374.
96. Buck-Morss, *The Origin of Negative Dialectics*, p. 213.
97. Rose, *The Melancholy Science*, p. 43.
98. Adorno, introduction to *The Positivist Dispute in German Sociology*, p. 34.

the market place. Reification is thus more than a property of false con-sciousness; it is a social category. Or, as Rose puts it,

To say that something is reified is not to emphasize that a relation between men appears as a relation between things. It is to emphasize that a relation between men appears in the form of a property of a thing. To be non-reified, then, is really to be a property of a thing, or, by analogy, to be a use-value.[99]

To call a use-value "the property of a thing" and not a relation between people and things may well be a simplification, as usefulness is always in reference to a user, but Rose is correct to point to the importance of objec-tivity in Adorno's anti-Lukácsian concept of reification.

She does, however, neglect to bring out the major difference between Marx and Adorno over the universality of the exchange principle. Whereas the former restricted it solely to capitalism, the latter extended it to a property of the entire Enlightenment, broadly understood. The re-duction of nature into interchangeable units was a fundamental premise of its domination, which began in ancient times. In *Dialectic of Enlight-enment*, Horkheimer and Adorno contended that the exchange principle was at work in Odysseus' proto-bourgeois behavior, in particular his de-ceptive assumption of the anonymous "Nobody" as his name in the battle with the Cyclops.[100] The implication of this extension of the exchange principle before capitalism is, of course, that it would be much harder to abolish. So it is not surprising to find Adorno admitting that

Humanity includes reification as well as its opposite, not merely as the condition from which liberation is possible, but also positively, as the form in which, how-ever brittle and inadequate it may be, subjective impulses are realized, but only by being objectified.[101]

The cautious realism of such passages, which led to the denunciations of the category of reification as an alleged "philosopher's stone" in *Negative Dia-lectics*, must be read as a rejection of the specifically Lukácsian notion of reification, which the younger Adorno at times found appealing. As we have noted earlier, Adorno was highly suspicious of the idealist assumption of a collective meta-subject who could totalize the social world and thereby shatter the illusion of society as second nature. The nonidentical constella-tions that he claimed were the representation of truth contained irreducible moments of objectivity that resisted subsumption under the subject. Op-posing the species imperialism of the Marxist Humanists, he wrote:

99. Rose, *The Melancholy Science*, p. 47.
100. Horkheimer and Adorno, *Dialectic of Enlightenment*, p. 60f.
101. Adorno, *Prisms*, p. 106.

The dichotomy of subject and object is not to be voided by a reduction to the human person, not even to the absolutely isolated person. The question of man, a question whose present popularity extends all the way to Marxism of the Lukács persuasion, is ideological because its pure form dictates the invariant of the possible answer, even if that invariant is historicity itself.[102]

Although never as categorically anti-subjectivist as the early Benjamin or the later structuralist Marxists in France, Adorno nonetheless warned against the primacy of philosophical anthropology:

The more concrete the form in which anthropology appears, the more deceptive will it come to be, and the more indifferent to whatever in man is not all due to him, as the subject, but to the de-subjectifying process that has paralleled the historic subject formation since time immemorial.[103]

Because Adorno agreed with Benjamin's contention that truth was not a function of intentionality, he rejected Lukács' Hegelian answer to the relativism of bourgeois thought, an answer which was intimately tied to the possibility of an expressive totality. Instead of seeing meaning as a result of making and recognition, he argued that

the concept of sense involves an objectivity beyond all "making": a sense that is "made" is already fictitious. It duplicates the subject, however collective, and defrauds it of what it seemingly granted.[104]

Indeed, if Rose is right in linking Adorno's theory of reification with Marx's distinction between exchange and use-value, it might be said that his major difference with Lukács followed from the grounding of the latter's theory of reification in Marx's third concept of "value" per se, which is produced by the labor of a subject. Thus, for Lukács dereification is a function of a collective unalienated practice based on the value-creating power of labor (which, in his more idealistic moments, he seems to have understood solely in terms of the objectification of subjectivity). For Adorno, on the other hand, the labor theory of value was never as central. Like Horkheimer, he saw it as an ascetic reflection of the bourgeois work

102. Adorno, *Negative Dialectics*, p. 51. It is statements like this that show how wrong more scientistic Western Marxists were to assimilate Adorno and Critical Theory to Lukácsian Hegelian Marxism. See, for example, the misguided reading of the Swedish Althusserian Göran Therborn, "The Frankfurt School," in *Western Marxism: A Critical Reader*, ed. *New Left Review* (London, 1977). Therborn argues that Critical Theory is a variant of historicism for which "society is always reducible to its creator-subject, and history is the continuous unfolding of this subject. At every given point in time, society is a unique manifestation of Man" (p. 97). However much this characterization may approach the work of Marcuse and even Horkheimer, it was never remotely valid for Adorno's.
103. Adorno, *Negative Dialectics*, p. 124.
104. Ibid., p. 376.

ethic. In *Negative Dialectics*, he quoted the later Marx against the ontologization of labor apparent in his early manuscripts:

When Marx, in his critique of the Gotha Program, told the Lassalleans that in
contrast to the customary litany of popular socialists labor was not the sole source
of social wealth, he was philosophically—at a time when the official philosophical thematics lay already behind him—saying no less than that labor could not be
hypostatized in any form, neither in the form of diligent hands nor in that of mental production. Such hypostasis merely extends the illusion of the predominance
of the productive principle.[105]

Because Adorno so fundamentally opposed the apotheosis of labor and
so persistently questioned a hypostatized collective subjectivity, his notorious inability to find a real link between theory and practice must be understood as more than merely a reflection of historical failures; it was, rather,
built into his negative dialectics at its most fundamental level. His abhorrence of identity theory and the domination of the exchange principle
meant that he could scarcely conceive of collective totalization in anything
but the most critical terms. Indeed, in *The Jargon of Authenticity*, his critique of Heidegger, he went so far as to link totality with death itself:

Throughout history, identity thinking has been something deathly, something that
devours everything. Identity thinking is always virtually out for totality. . . . In
Heidegger, as in idealism, that which tolerates nothing beyond itself is understood
to be the whole. The least trace which went beyond such identity would be as
unbearable as anyone who insists on his own individuality is to the fascist. . . .
Totality is also the moving principle of Heidegger's observations about death.[106]

Adorno, to be sure, continued to intersperse utopian passages throughout his work, such as his claim in *Negative Dialectics* that "dialectical
reason's own essence has come to be and will pass, like antagonistic society."[107] But it is clear from the general import of his work that such a
passing would never produce a normative totality of the type envisaged by
the first generation of Western Marxists. Moreover, by ruling out in advance the possibility of a liberating collective subject, he made it extremely difficult to see how any utopia at all might be achieved short of the
messianic intervention on which Benjamin seems to have placed his
hopes. The very stress on the virtue of non-identity meant that Adorno
could only rely on the most individualistic of actors to resist the pressure
of the whole. Despite his stress on mediation, he made little real attempt

105. Ibid., pp. 177–78. (Translation corrected.)
106. Adorno, *The Jargon of Authenticity*, pp. 139–40.
107. Adorno, *Negative Dialectics*, p. 141.

to investigate the concrete social forces and forms between such an individual and the totality. Micrological stress on the smallest detail went hand in hand with macrological emphasis on the largest whole.

What Adorno lacked was any analysis of a possible intermediate level between the collective subject of the idealists and Hegelian Marxists, on the one hand, and the isolated, defensive individual of the bourgeois empiricists on the other. Although in places in his work he continued to repeat the Marxist formula that "society remains class society, today just as in the period when that concept originated,"[108] his theory undercut in advance the transformation of classes-in-themselves into classes-for-themselves. As a number of critics have noted,[109] the possibility of a non-hypostatized intersubjectivity, a public realm in which non-coercive, rational discourse might take place among equals, was absent from his thinking, as it was in Critical Theory as a whole until Habermas. That hostility to the dialogic, communicative function of language he inherited from Benjamin and Schoenberg meant he gave short shrift to the generalizable intersubjective potential that even the "administered world" of the present had not entirely destroyed.

Instead of probing the possibility that such a potential might still exist, Adorno damned "the liberal fiction of the universal communicability of each and every thought"[110] and withdrew increasingly into a defense of autonomous art as what he liked to call the *"Statthalter"* (representative) of non-identity. The art he particularly valued in this regard was that most hostile to easy communication, best exemplified in the plays of Samuel Beckett. It was to Beckett that he intended to dedicate his last major effort, posthumously published as *Aesthetic Theory* in 1970.[111] In that work, he developed a complicated dialectical analysis of art as the mimesis of natural beauty that harked back more to Kant than to Hegel. As in

108. Adorno, "Society," *Salmagundi* 10–11 (Fall 1969–Winter 1970), p. 149. Translation corrected. The original is *Klassengesellschaft*, not *Klassenkampf*. See "Gesellschaft," *Gesammelte Schriften 8* (Frankfurt, 1972), p. 15.

109. See, for example, Connerton, *The Tragedy of Enlightenment*, p. 75, and Axel Honneth, "Communication and Reconciliation: Habermas' Critique of Adorno," *Telos* 39 (Spring 1979), p. 49. Interestingly, Habermas himself claims that there are hints in Adorno's work, for example his remarks on Eichendorff's "distant nearness" in *Minima Moralia*, to show that he in fact "returns to categories of intersubjectivity from which he philosophically abstains." "The Dialectics of Rationalization, An Interview with Jürgen Habermas," *Telos* 49 (Fall 1981), p. 9.

110. Adorno, *Minima Moralia*, p. 80.

111. See note 4. See also his 1961 essay "Trying to Understand *Endgame*," *New German Critique* 26 (Spring–Summer 1982). The best extensive treatment of *Aesthetic Theory* in English is Lambert Zuidervaart, *Refractions: Truth in Adorno's Aesthetic Theory* (Toronto, 1981). See also Richard Wolin, "The De-Aestheticization of Art: On Adorno's *Aesthetische Theorie*," *Telos* 41 (Fall 1979), and Peter Uwe Hohendahl, "Autonomy of Art: Looking Back at Adorno's *Aesthetische Theorie*," *The German Quarterly* 54, 2 (March 1981).

his early talk on "The Idea of Natural History," he warned against giving priority either to human history over nature or vice versa. And as in *Negative Dialectics*, he cautioned against giving too much precedence to constitutive subjectivity over objectivity, to the intentions of the artist over the work itself. Finally, as in *Dialectic of Enlightenment* he valued those works of art, like Beckett's *Endgame*, that registered the sorry history of mankind's *Zerfallsgeschichte* (history of decay) without flinching.

The result was an aesthetic theory that reversed the direction of German thought since Kant's *Critique of Judgment*, where art was understood as the mediating organon of reconciliation between man's contradictory status as both noumenal and phenomenal being. As W. Martin Lüdke has put it,

If for German idealism art was the final expression of a positivity, where alienation was overcome, art therefore having the place and function of an indication of absolute affirmation, for Adorno this relationship was reversed: the place of art as well as its function consisted precisely in its expression of absolute negativity. In art, the alienation of positivity is not overcome, the antagonisms of reality are not healed, art is no longer primarily (Bloch's) *Vor-schein* [appearance and anticipation] of a possible reality, anticipation of reconciliation.[112]

If art thus has an anamnestic dimension, it is not, *contra* Marcuse, the memory of an original plenitude that it reveals, but rather the remembrance of a non-identical origin in natural beauty, a beauty that was not entirely "for others."[113] If part of what is remembered by art is also the unredeemable suffering of mankind in its negative progress from the slingshot to the atomic bomb, art can do little more than bear witness to the horror of this history, even if its combination of sensuousness and conceptual truth foreshadows a better social order based on non-identity. The utopian impulse in art may be contained in its capacity to transcend the status quo, which it more than merely reflects, but the limits of that utopian transcendence are no less surely contained in its inevitable mimesis of non-identical natural beauty, a beauty not created by men. Although such a mimesis may be seen as portending a new, non-exploitative relationship between man and nature,[114] one in which conceptual domination of otherness is suppressed, and by extension a non-exploitative social order, it also suggests a sober recognition of humanity's diminished role in shaping its destiny. Moreover, if genuine works of art, like Beckett's

112. Lüdke, *Anmerkungen zu einer "Logik des Zerfalls,"* p. 86. For a more positive view of the redemptive moment in Adorno's aesthetics, see Wolin, "The De-Aestheticization of Art."

113. Adorno, *Aesthetische Theorie*, p. 116.

114. Wolin, "The De-Aestheticization of Art," p. 118.

Endgame, can be understood as "messages in bottles on the flood of barbarism,"[115] to use the vivid phrase Adorno applied to his own negative
dialectics, it is hard to know who the shapers of that destiny will be, if
indeed they will exist at all.

In a certain sense, then, Adorno's work inevitably led into a kind of
cul-de-sac, at least from a political point of view. As Susan Buck-Morss
put it,

Adorno ensured perhaps too successfully that reason did not become "instrumental." For instrumental reason preserved a moment of "use-value" which negative
dialectics had to abandon. The result was that as opposites, they too converged:
instrumental reason lost sight of rational goals, ceased to be a means and became
an end in itself; but negative dialectics abrogated political utility, and thus became
an end in itself as well.[116]

One cause of this dilemma must be traced to his overwhelmingly critical
use of the concept of totality, which turned into a fear of anything collective, communitarian or intersubjective. It also was due to his insistence on
the utter "falseness" of the present totality, which, even allowing for the
gap between concept and object, left little sense of the persistence of unresolved tensions and contradictions beyond the isolated negations of art
and critical philosophy. As we have already pointed out, it was left to
Habermas to pick up the analysis of unreconciled and displaced contradictions in Pollock's theory of State Capitalism, which both Horkheimer
and Adorno ignored. It was also left to him to re-establish a more affirmative concept of totality.

Habermas could only do so, however, on the basis of a completely new
set of assumptions. For Critical Theory, and Adorno's work in particular,
had irrevocably demolished the foundations of Western Marxism's initial
concepts of totality. Or if a more historically materialist explanation is
preferred, negative dialectics correlated theoretically with fundamental
changes in social reality, and these made the weaknesses of the Lukácsian
paradigm too obvious to ignore. No longer could a Western Marxist defend an expressive view of the whole in which a meta-subject was both the
subject and object of history. No longer could history itself be seen as a
coherent whole with a positive conclusion as its telos. No longer could
totality ignore the non-identity of the historical and the natural and subordinate the latter to human domination. And no longer could the totalizing epistemology of the Hegelian tradition be invoked with confidence
against the antinomies of bourgeois thought.

115. Adorno, *Minima Moralia*, p. 134.
116. Buck-Morss, *The Origin of Negative Dialectics*, p. 189.

Significantly, at the same time as Critical Theory was undermining the assumptions of the first generation of Western Marxists, including early Critical Theorists themselves, a similar process of disenchantment was underway in France and Italy, where the concept of totality was also the focus of a lively debate. Despite the very different intellectual traditions feeding those discussions, not to mention the dissimilar fates of their working class movements, the trajectory we have traced from Lukács to Adorno had rough parallels in those nations as well. However great the insularity of Western Marxists from each other, a common pattern can be discerned in the ways in which totality was treated in all three of these contexts. The Hegelian Marxist origins of Western Marxism were progressively dismantled as the paradigm inaugurated by Lukács, Gramsci, Korsch and Bloch played itself out against the tragic backdrop of twentieth-century European history.

CHAPTER NINE

Henri Lefebvre, the Surrealists and the Reception of Hegelian Marxism in France

The relative poverty of Marxist theory in France before World War II has often been remarked.[1] Lacking access to most of Marx's early texts,[2] even less conversant with Hegel's writings, French Marxists tended to repeat the tired formulae of Second International Orthodoxy as they were appropriated by Lenin and his followers. For most non-Marxist intellectuals, in and out of the university system, Marxism was more an object of ridicule than a stimulus to serious thought. As Sartre remembers his days at the Ecole Normale.

In 1925, when I was twenty years old, there was no chair of Marxism at the University, and Communist students were very careful not to appeal to Marxism or even to mention it in their examinations; had they done so they would have failed. The horror of dialectic was such that Hegel himself was unknown to us. . . . Without the Hegelian tradition, without Marxist teachers, without any planned program of study, without the instruments of thought, our generation, like the preceding ones and like that which followed, was wholly ignorant of historical materialism.[3]

1. See, for example, the discussions in Mark Poster, *Existential Marxism in Postwar France: From Sartre to Althusser* (Princeton, 1975); George Lichtheim, *Marxism in Modern France* (New York, 1966); and David Caute, *Communism and the French Intellectuals, 1914–1960* (London, 1964).
2. Norbert Guterman did, in fact, translate the *1844 Manuscripts* into French in 1927, but they were not widely read. August Cornu, who wrote a dissertation on the young Marx in 1934 entitled *Karl Marx: l'homme et l'oeuvre*, does not even mention them. See the discussion in Albert Rabil, Jr., *Merleau-Ponty: Existentialist of the Social World* (New York, 1967), p. 275.
3. Jean-Paul Sartre, *Search for a Method*, trans. Hazel B. Barnes (New York, 1973), p. 17. See also Louis Althusser's similar lament in *For Marx*, trans. Ben Brewster (New York, 1970), p. 23.

The first notable circle of French Marxist philosophers coalesced only slowly in the twenties around a series of journals, the first of which, *Philosophies* (1924–1925), gave it its name.[4] Led by Pierre Morhange, Georges Politzer, Paul Nizan, Henri Lefebvre, Norbert Guterman, and Georges Friedmann, the *Philosophies* group was initially very eclectic in its interests; Morhange for instance advocated a kind of mysticism while others defended Gidean *actes gratuits* and toyed with violence. In their confused philosophy and arrogant demand for an intellectual aristocracy, they bore certain resemblances to Kurt Hiller's Activists in Weimar Germany.

It was not really until 1929 and another of their journals, *La Revue Marxiste*, which lasted only from February to September, that they began to espouse Marxism with any rigor—in fact with too much rigor. For despite their earlier infatuation with spiritualist and proto-existentialist concerns, as Marxists they proved exceedingly doctrinaire and unimaginative. Rather than questioning the scientific and crudely materialist reading of Marxism sponsored by orthodox Marxists, they merely adopted it as a weapon against the subjectivism of Bergson and the neo-Kantianism of Léon Brunschvicq, both of which they damned for having religious implications. Nor did they systematically explore the differences between Marxism and Communism, in particular the brand defended by the Bolshevized Parti Communiste Français (PCF).[5] Fighting what might be seen as a rearguard action against the residues of Jaurèsian eclecticism in the French party, they tended to overemphasize the ontologically materialist and methodologically scientific aspects of Marxism. Because of their subsequent personal histories—Politzer was killed by the Nazis, Nizan left the Party after the Hitler–Stalin pact, Morhange returned to more literary interests, Friedmann became a liberal sociologist and Guterman lived in relative obscurity in American exile—the *Philosophies* group, with the major exception of Lefebvre (to whom we will return shortly), played only a marginal role in the development of a truly innovative French Marxism.

4. For treatments of the *Philosophies* groups, see W. F. Redfern, *Paul Nizan: Committed Literature in a Conspiratorial World* (Princeton, 1972), pp. 12–20; Roger Garaudy, *Perspectives de l'homme* (Paris, 1969); and Henri Lefebvre, *La Somme et le reste*, 2 vols. (Paris, 1959). There was an earlier group of French Marxist intellectuals, mostly Trotskyists, around the journal *Clarté*, but they cannot be called genuine theorists.

5. For histories of the PCF in this period, see Robert Wohl, *French Communism in the Making 1914–1924* (Stanford, 1966) and Ronald Tiersky, *French Communism 1920–1972* (New York, 1974). For an account of the general process of Bolshevization, see Helmut Gruber, *Soviet Russia Masters the Comintern: International Communism in the Era of Stalin's Ascendancy* (Garden City, New York, 1974).

It was in fact not until the 1950s, when the Resistance's infusion of new intellectual blood into the Party and its ambiance had a theoretical effect, that French Marxism reached the conceptual level of its Central European counterpart. Only then were the distinctions between Marxism and Communism systematically developed by figures who were in varying degrees distanced from the PCF. Only then did non-partisan Marxologists like Maximilian Rubel provide the materials for a considered assessment of the distinctions between Marx and Marxism.[6] Following the disclosures of Stalin's crimes and the events in Eastern Europe they helped precipitate, it was now possible to speak of a distinctly "Western" Marxism not beholden to the tenets of Marxism–Leninism. Indeed, the term itself, as we have noted before, gained widespread currency only in 1955 with the publication of Merleau-Ponty's *Adventures of the Dialectic*. Thus, not surprisingly, the concept of totality, which was so central to the development of Central European Western Marxism, was relatively peripheral in French Marxist theory until those years. With isolated exceptions such as Henri Lefebvre and Lucien Goldmann, who was generally an outsider in Marxist circles, the French Left did not consider totality a theoretical concept of critical significance.

It was not, however, entirely absent from French intellectual life more broadly conceived. As we briefly indicated in Chapter One, there were two traditions in which totality was vigorously defended: the Comtean positivism that culminated in Durkheim's allegedly scientific sociology, and the Pascalian intuitionism that fed the anti-scientific irrationalism of Bergson, Sorel, Péguy and the Surrealists. During the interwar years, French Marxists were hostile to both—Paul Nizan's celebrated critique of establishment philosophy, *The Watchdogs*,[7] pilloried Bergson and Durkheim alike—but in subtle ways, their concepts of totality had an impact

6. For an account of Rubel's contribution, see Bruno Bongiovanni, "Maximilian Rubel," *Telos* 47 (Spring 1981) and the introduction to *Rubel on Marx: Five Essays*, ed. J.J. O'Malley and K. Algozin (Cambridge, 1981). Rubel, it should be noted, stressed the ethical aspect of Marx's work and had little use for the Hegelian concept of totality in its Lukácsian form. See his remarks in *Marx Critique du Marxisme* (Paris, 1974), pp. 399, 421.

7. Paul Nizan, *The Watchdogs: Philosophers and the Established Order*, trans. Paul Fittingoff (New York, 1971). Poster claims that the book "could be viewed equally as a Marxist or vaguely surrealist-existentialist critique of the established philosophical order" (p. 138). Although it is true that Nizan, like the Surrealists, mocks bourgeois philosophy's pretensions to rationality, he has little use for what he calls "cathartic philosophies preaching Nothingness" (p. 124) or "philosophies relating exclusively to the Inner Life, philosophies that will probe the innermost convolutions of the human psyche" (p. 125). If there is a Surrealist-existentialist moment in his work, it is clearly subordinate to the Marxist. Redfern, in fact, points out Nizan's aloofness from the attempted rapprochement between the Surrealists and the *Philosophies* group in 1925 (p. 14).

on its later recovery by a new generation of leftists. The filiation can be seen most clearly in the specific cases of Durkheim and the Surrealists.

Emile Durkheim was himself a socialist of sorts, although of a type closer to the moralist Jean Jaurès than to the materialist Jules Guesde.[8] Around the turn of the century, he flirted with the so-called "solidarism" propounded by Léon Bourgeois and his followers, which was one of the ideological mainstays of the Third Republic.[9] Allegedly scientific, solidarism drew parallels between biological models of organic wholeness and social community. Rejecting class conflict, it called for a moral resolution of social differences in a way that would ultimately leave the class structure of society intact. Durkheim, whose first major work, *The Division of Labor*, began by trying to prove that modern "organic solidarity" provided just such a community and ended by admitting that it did not,[10] shared solidarism's fear of the corrosive effects of unchecked individualism. In practical terms, Durkheim's solution, the fostering of occupational corporations between the individual and the state, was sterile. Theoretically, however, his concern for community proved far more fertile.

This is not the place for a full-scale appreciation of Durkheim's pioneering contribution to sociology, but several points can be made in connection with the theme of totality. Durkheim, as we noted earlier, examined the concept itself in *The Elementary Forms of the Religious Life*, where he concluded that "the concept of totality is only the abstract form of the concept of society: it is the whole which includes all things, the supreme class which embraces all other classes."[11] Whether called society or totality, this notion had to be understood as expressing a reality that was irreducible to its component parts. As he insisted in the preface to the second edition of his *Rules of Sociological Method*, "Whenever certain elements combine and thereby produce, by the fact of their combination,

8. For discussions of Durkheim's socialism, see Steven Lukes, *Emile Durkheim: His Life and Work: A Historical and Critical Study* (London, 1973), chapter 17; Alvin W. Gouldner, "Emile Durkheim and the Critique of Socialism," in *For Sociology: Renewal and Critique in Sociology Today* (New York, 1973); and Jean-Claude Filloux, "Durkheim and Socialism," *The Review* 10 (1963).

9. Lukes, p. 350f. For a good general introduction to Solidarism, see Theodore Zeldin, *France 1848–1945: Politics and Anger* (Oxford, 1979), chapter 8.

10. Durkheim, *The Division of Labor in Society*, trans. George Simpson (New York, 1933); the reversal came less in the body of the work than in the preface to the second edition in 1902, where Durkheim introduced occupational groups as a possible remedy.

11. Durkheim, *The Elementary Forms of the Religious Life*, trans. Joseph Ward Swain (New York, 1915), p. 490.

new phenomena, it is plain that these new phenomena reside not in the original elements but in the totality formed by their union."[12] Sociology, as Comte had originally stressed, was thus concerned with a reality *sui generis*, reducible neither to individual psychology nor to biology.

Durkheim's struggle to devise a method to analyze this generic reality is now generally conceded to have produced a brilliant failure; his defense of an epistemology at once positivist and idealist, empiricist and a priori has not stood the test of time. But however inadequate their methodological ground must ultimately be judged, Durkheim's reflections on totality did anticipate the later arguments of one strand of French Western Marxism in particular: that derived from the work of Louis Althusser, whose praise for Comte and Durkheim we have already noted. In the appreciative words of the English Althusserian Paul Hirst,

Durkheim's position is a sociological *anti-humanism*; it insists that the human subject is neither the author of society nor a purely social being. This anti-humanist position is central to his critique of the anthropocentric fallacy and the teleological forms of explanation which follow from it.[13]

Despite what the Althusserians would call his naively realist epistemology and his evident antipathy to class struggle, Durkheim thus clearly laid the groundwork for Althusser's critique of the subjective origins of the social whole. As he put it in *The Rules of Sociological Method*,

It displeases man to renounce the unlimited power over the social order he has so long attributed to himself; and on the other hand, it seems to him that, if collective forces really exist, he is necessarily obliged to submit to them without being able to modify them. This makes him inclined to deny their existence. In vain have repeated experiences taught him that this omnipotence, the illusion of which he complacently entertains, has always been a cause of weakness in him; that his power over things really began only when he recognized that they have a nature of their own, and resigned himself to learning this nature from them.[14]

From the point of view of more dialectically minded Marxists like Adorno, Durkheim's stress on social facts as objective "things" legitimized reification,[15] but from Althusser's anti-Hegelian perspective, it meant a sober recognition of the priority of structure over praxis. Moreover,

12. Durkheim, *The Rules of Sociological Method*, trans. Sarah A. Solovay and John H. Mueller (New York, 1938), p. xlvii. Interestingly, Durkheim suggests a temporal priority here to the elements in a combination, but he always opposed the genetic fallacy that would try to understand results in terms of origins.

13. P. Q. Hirst, *Durkheim, Bernard and Epistemology* (London and Boston, 1975), pp. 137–38.

14. Durkheim, *The Rules of Sociological Method*, p. lviii.

15. For a discussion of Adorno's views on Durkheim, see Gillian Rose, *The Melancholy Science: An Introduction to the Thought of Theodor W. Adorno* (New York, 1958), p. 82f.

Durkheim, unlike Comte with his Religion of Humanity, had little use for the longitudinal concept of totality that we have seen was so central to Central European Marxist Humanism. Although his early discussion of the transition from "mechanical" to "organic" solidarity had an evolutionary dimension, Durkheim came increasingly to deny any progressive universal history. Instead, anticipating Althusser, he spurned the notion of an overarching, unified temporality in favor of the specific chronologies of different societies.

The two differed, however, in their conceptions of the internal articulation of the social whole. Durkheim's emphasis on the generic irreducibility of the social whole was directed not only against psychologism, but against economism as well. When he said social facts, he generally meant norms, beliefs, and values—in short, "collective representations"—rather than economic structures. The chief antithesis in his work is between the individual and the moral community.[16] For him, economics generally meant the atomizing individualism of the utilitarian tradition, rather than the more relational structuralism of Marxism, with its stress on modes of production. As a result, he tended to homogenize society in ways that Marxists, even anti-historicist ones like Althusser, would find lacking in historical specificity. The differentiation among substructures of society, ultimately determined by a "structure in dominance," which we will examine when we turn to Althusser, was thus absent from his work. Ironically, at the same time as he worried about the lack of intermediate organizations between the individual and the social whole, he failed to examine those economically determined mediations that did exist in the society of his day.

In this sense, Durkheim was clearly aligned with solidarism, which, as we have seen, was very much an ideology of the Third Republic. As a number of commentators have noted,[17] Durkheim's intellectual influence was closely tied to the Third Republic's fortunes. When they waned, so did his prestige. After Durkheim's death in 1917, the talented group of his

16. Because of Durkheim's stress on the moral community, the Swedish Althusserian Göran Therborn contends that "Durkheim and Marx part company precisely at the point where Marx left the young Hegelians to develop historical materialism. It was Karl Marx the Young Hegelian with whom Emile Durkheim the sociologist had most in common" (*Science, Class and Society: On the Formation of Sociology and Historical Materialism* [London, 1976], p. 251). Therborn's stress on Durkheim's moralism is absent from Hirst's account, which demonstrates that the Althusserian view of Durkheim is by no means uniform.

17. See, for example, H. Stuart Hughes, *The Obstructed Path: French Social Thought in the Years of Desperation, 1930–1960* (New York, 1969), p. 14; and Therborn, *Science, Class and Society*, p. 262f. See also the discussion in Terry Nichols Clark, *Prophets and Patrons: The French University System and the Emergence of the Social Sciences* (Cambridge, Mass., 1973), p. 229f.

disciples around the *Année sociologique* who had survived the war managed to maintain the momentum of his thought for a decade or so. But in the late 1920s and 1930s French intellectuals began to look for inspiration elsewhere, often abroad or from emigrés like Kojève who came from abroad. Durkheim's concept of totality, which equated it with society as a whole, was thus called into question when the moral authority of the society he had defended, the Third Republic, grew weaker.

It was not, however, entirely abandoned, for in the work of his nephew and collaborator, Marcel Mauss, totality remained a central concern. In his highly influential *Essay on the Gift* of 1924, Mauss introduced the concept of the "total social fact" to account for the reciprocal relations underlying the exchange of gifts in primitive societies:

In these "early" societies, social phenomena are not discrete; each phenomenon contains all the threads of which the social fabric is composed. In these *total* social phenomena, as we propose to call them, all kinds of institutions find simultaneous expression: religious, legal, moral, and economic.[18]

Unlike his uncle, Mauss focussed on the variety of structural levels within the all-encompassing social reality. As Merleau-Ponty would later put it,

This social fact, which is no longer a massive reality but an efficacious system of symbols or a network of symbolic values, is going to be inserted into the depths of the individual. But the regulation which circumvents the individual does not eliminate him. It is no longer necessary to choose between the individual and collective. . . . There are no longer just absolutes or mere summations, but everywhere totalities or articulated wholes of varying richness.[19]

In Mauss's hands, the "total social fact" was an aid to research, not yet the foundation of a full-fledged theory. Only with the synthesis of Saussurean linguistics, Gestalt psychology and Maussian ethnology that became known as structuralism was such a theory proposed. Its primary founder, Claude Lévi-Strauss, acknowledged Mauss's significance for his own development:

In the theory of the total fact, the notion of totality is less important than the very special way in which Mauss conceived it; foliated as it were and made up of a multitude of distinct yet connected planes. Instead of appearing as a postulate, the

18. Marcel Mauss, *The Gift: Forms and Functions of Exchange in Archaic Societies*, trans. Ian Cunnison, intro. E. E. Evans-Pritchard (New York, 1967), p. 1. For an account of his concept of totality, see Chito Guala, "Uso e Significato del Concetto di Totalita' nel Pensiero e nell' Opera di Marcel Mauss," *Sociologia: Rivista di Studi Sociali* 7, 1 (January 1973).

19. Maurice Merleau-Ponty, "From Mauss to Claude Lévi-Strauss" in *Signs*, trans. with intro. Richard C. McCleary (Evanston, Ill., 1964), p. 115.

totality of society is manifested in experience. . . . The totality consists finally of the network of functional interrelations among all these planes.[20]

Although Althusser was to question the functionalist implications of Mauss's theory, it is clear that a line can be drawn from the *Essay on the Gift* through Lévi-Strauss to his own structuralist reading of Marx, which we will examine in a later chapter.

The second non-Marxist source of French Marxist concepts of totality, the Pascalian tradition that led to Surrealism, was in certain ways related to the one we have just examined. The primary link grew out of the subject matter of interwar ethnology. Whereas Durkheim had been relatively indifferent to the distinction between sociology and anthropology, applying his method equally to both, his successors gravitated increasingly to the study of primitive societies. Perhaps as a result of their inability to find a normative totality in the Third Republic, they sought it elsewhere in less apparently conflicted cultures. As Jacques Derrida once remarked, if with some exaggeration:

One can assume that ethnology could have been born as a science only at the moment when a decentering had come about: at the moment when European culture—and, in consequence, the history of metaphysics and of its concepts— had been *dislocated*, driven from its locus, and forced to stop considering itself as the culture of reference.[21]

In more specifically political terms, as Perry Anderson argued in reference to British anthropology in the same period,[22] it was far less threatening to investigate a totality in exotic and distant lands than to confront the reasons for its absence at home.

In France, to be sure, the process of displacement was not as severe as in Britain because there was a larger and more militant working-class movement, which at least for some intellectuals could serve as the repository of their holistic desires. The flight from the Third Republic could

20. Claude Lévi-Strauss, *The Scope of Anthropology* (London, 1967), p. 12. For discussions of Mauss's importance for Lévi-Strauss, see Miriam Glucksmann, *Structuralist Analysis in Contemporary Social Thought: A Comparison of the Theories of Claude Lévi-Strauss and Louis Althusser* (London, 1974), p. 28f.; and Simon Clarke, "The Origins of Lévi-Strauss's Structuralism," *Sociology* 12, 3 (September 1978), p. 417.

21. Jacques Derrida, *Writing and Difference*, trans. with intro. Alan Bass (Chicago, 1978), p. 282. For a critique of this argument, see Dell Hymes, "De-centering Linguistics: A Comment on Lemert," *Theory and Society* 7, 3 (May, 1979), p. 317.

22. Perry Anderson, "Components of the National Culture," *New Left Review* 50 (July–August 1968), p. 47.

therefore lead either abroad or into the myth of proletarian redemption. In fact, for some figures, like André Malraux,[23] the two often succeeded each other in ways that recalled Sorel's volatile search for collective moral regeneration. An even more striking example of this dizzy search for totality in a wide variety of places was the tumultuous aesthetic modernist movement known as Surrealism.[24]

As many observers have noted, the disparate aesthetic phenomena grouped wholesale under the rubric of modernism contained both nihilistic and constructivist impulses in varying measure. Contemptuous of traditional culture and the bourgeois sensibility which it supported, modernism often mockingly repudiated all that had hitherto been exalted as art and seen as somehow superior to prosaic reality. In certain instances, the most extreme being that of Dadaism, this destructive moment overwhelmed its regenerative antithesis, resulting at times in a celebration of cultural, and even personal, suicide.[25] In others, the nihilistic impulse in modernism was transcended in favor of a positive, indeed often immoderately ambitious, drive for cultural renovation. Before the war, perhaps the most explicit expression of this latter alternative came in what John Berger has called "the moment of cubism," when artists tried for the first time "to paint totalities rather than agglomerations."[26] After the war, however, purely aesthetic solutions seemed less satisfactory; a variety of modernist movements, most notably Expressionism and Futurism, sought political as well as cultural change. In the early days of the Soviet Union, a brief and unstable alliance between the Bolsheviks and artists like Mayakovsky, Eisenstein, and El Lissetsky testified to the possibility of integrating the aesthetic and political avant-gardes.

In postwar France, the movement that most insistently asserted this possibility, as well as demonstrating its ultimate disappointment, was Surrealism, which emerged out of the embers of Dadaism in 1924. André

23. For a discussion of Malraux's Sorelian quest for moral regeneration, see David Wilkinson, *Malraux, An Essay in Political Criticism* (Cambridge, Mass, 1967), p. 117f.

24. The literature on Surrealism is enormous. For representative accounts, see Maurice Nadeau, *The History of Surrealism*, trans. Richard Howard, intro. Roger Shattuck (New York, 1965); Anna Balakian, *Surrealism* (New York, 1959); Herbert S. Gershman, *The Surrealist Revolution in France* (Ann Arbor, 1969); and Patrick Waldberg, *Surrealism* (New York, 1971). Gershman also compiled a *Bibliography of the Surrealist Revolution in France* (Ann Arbor, 1969).

25. For a discussion of the suicidal impulse in Dada, see A. Alvarez, *The Savage God: A Study of Suicide* (London, 1971), p. 215f. On its residual impact in Surrealism, see Wallace Fowlie, *Age of Surrealism* (Bloomington, 1966), p. 21f.

26. John Berger, *The Moment of Cubism and Other Essays* (New York, 1969), p. 26. For another recent treatment of modernist yearnings for totality, see Steven A. Mansbach, *Visions of Totality: Laszlo Moholy-Nagy, Theo van Doesberg, and El Lissitzky* (Ann Arbor, 1980).

Breton, Louis Aragon, Philippe Soupault, Robert Desnos, Paul Eluard and the shifting cast of characters around them actively sought an aesthetic practice of reconstruction that would transform life as well as art. Initially, to be sure, the techniques they advocated, most notably automatic writing, were less collective than individual in nature. Drawing more on Freud, understood tendentiously, than on Marx, they claimed that wholeness would come from access to a dream world hitherto suppressed by mundane ratiocination. Privileging states of madness over conventional sanity, celebrating primitive and exotic cultures over that of a moribund Europe, praising the sanctifying power of love and the innocent wisdom of the child, they retraced many of the steps followed by the more prophetic participants in the Romantic Movement a century before.[27]

And like many of their Romantic predecessors, they soon came to the realization that individual liberation would only be attainable in the context of communal transformation. To Rimbaud's injunction "to change life" they added Marx's "to transform the world."[28] In 1930, they founded a journal entitled *Surrealism in the Service of the Revolution*, which superseded their earlier organ, *The Surrealist Revolution*. Calling for a total revolt against bourgeois society, they loudly proclaimed their belief in the justifiable use of violence, the most notorious example being Breton's defense of firing a pistol blindly into a crowd. The tragicomic story of how, from 1925 to the later 1930s, the Surrealists sought an alliance with Marxism, first with the PCF and then in certain cases with Trotsky, has been told too often to bear repeating here.[29] As a test case of the coalition of artists and intellectuals with the working class, it makes depressing reading. What is important for us to note is that in making the attempt, the Surrealists elaborated a concept of totality that would have subtle reverberations within French Marxism in the decades that followed.

On the most general level, the Surrealists were among the first in France to recover the importance of Hegel for revolutionary thought.[30]

27. In the Second Surrealist Manifesto of 1929, Breton himself identifies Surrealism with the "tail" of the Romantic movement. See André Breton, *Manifestoes of Surrealism*, trans. Richard Seaver and Helen R. Lane (Ann Arbor, 1972), p. 153. They also had links with late nineteenth-century Decadence. See Jean Pierrot, *The Decadent Imagination, 1880–1900*, trans. Derek Coltman (Chicago, 1981), pp. 256–64.

28. In 1935, Breton wrote, "Marx said, 'Transform the world'; Rimbaud said, 'Change life'; these two mottoes are for us one and the same." *Position politique du surréalisme* (Paris, 1935), p. 97.

29. See, for example, the accounts in Nadeau and Gershman, as well as Roger S. Short, "The Politics of Surrealism, 1920–1936" in *Left-wing Intellectuals Between the Wars*, ed., Walter Laqueur and George L. Mosse (New York, 1966).

30. For discussions of the French reception of Hegel, see Roberto Salvadori, *Hegel in Francia* (Bari, 1974); John Heckman, "Hyppolite and the Hegel Revival in France," *Telos* 16

Victor Cousin's eclectic appropriation of German Idealism in the mid-nineteenth century had long since lost its power; attempts by Renan and Taine to marry Comte and Hegel were no more successful, especially after the Franco-Prussian War. Although an interest in Hegel can be discerned in later figures on the Left, such as Sorel, Jaurès, Charles Andler, and Lucien Herr, French thought remained stubbornly wedded to its Cartesian heritage. Significantly, Hegel's *Phenomenology* was not translated until Jean Hyppolite's version in 1939–1941 (the first English translation by Baillie having appeared in 1910 and the first Italian by Novelli in 1863).

In their zeal to overthrow the bourgeois reason dominating French thought, the Surrealists naturally sought an alternative to Cartesianism. Not surprisingly, they found it, at least in part, in Hegel. For Breton in particular, Hegel seemed to provide a philosophy of immanent synthesis that would reveal the underlying wholeness of reality. How seriously he and his friends really understood Hegel is, of course, not certain.[31] But by invoking his name in connection with their own radical philosophy, such as it was, they helped prepare the ground for the far more sophisticated recovery of Hegel accomplished by Alexandre Kojève and Jean Hyppolite a decade later.

In two important respects, however, the Surrealists developed a concept of totality that was at variance with Hegel's. First, they rejected the rationalist logocentrism at the heart of his thought. The synthesis they hoped to achieve would include both the rational and the irrational, sanity and madness, waking consciousness and the dream. In the view of a latter, somewhat unsympathetic observer, Albert Camus, it was precisely this all-inclusiveness that doomed the alliance of Surrealism and Marxism:

The definitive rupture is explained if one considers that Marxism insisted on the submission of the irrational, while the surrealists rose to defend irrationality to the death, Marxism tended toward the conquest of totality, and surrealism, like all spiritual experiences, tended toward unity. Totality can demand the submission of the irrational, if rationalism suffices to conquer the world. But the desire for unity is more demanding. It does not suffice that everything should be rational. It wants, above all, the rational and irrational to be reconciled on the same level. . . . For

---

(Summer 1973); and Poster, *Existential Marxism in Postwar France*, chapter 1. A recent corrective to the view that Hegel was virtually unknown in France before 1930 can be found in Michael Kelly, "Hegel in France to 1940: A Bibliographical Essay," *Journal of European Studies* 11, 1 (March, 1981).

31. For an insider's critique of the seriousness of Breton's understanding of Hegel, see Ferdinand Alquié, *The Philosophy of Surrealism*, trans. Bernard Waldrop (Ann Arbor, 1965), p. 34f.

André Breton, totality could be only a stage, a necessary stage perhaps, but certainly inadequate, on the way that leads to unity.[32]

Ultimately, the Surrealists had to choose between the two, Aragon and Eluard opting for Marxist rationalism and Breton, among others, returning to Rimbaudian irrationalism. It is difficult to avoid feeling, however, that much of the later French Marxist ambivalence about the omnipotence of totalizing rationality, which we will encounter in particular in Sartre and Merleau-Ponty, had its anticipation in the Surrealist struggle with Hegel. "To win the energies of intoxication for the revolution,"[33] as Walter Benjamin once characterized the Surrealist project, remained a potent desire in heterodox French Marxism, as the events of May, 1968, clearly demonstrated.

If the Surrealists' concept of totality (or unity, as Camus would have it) differed from Hegel's and that of the more rationalist Hegelian Marxists, so too did their understanding of the process of totalization. Instead of a dialectical interplay of mediations culminating in a final synthesis (*Aufhebung*) of contradictions, the Surrealists argued for an unmediated juxtaposition of seemingly discordant elements. Through such an unexpected convergence of the dissimilar, they argued, a new whole, what Breton called the "marvelous," would be revealed. In the manner of Lautréamont's celebrated "chance meeting of a sewing machine and an umbrella on a dissecting table,"[34] an image they frequently evoked with admiration, the Surrealists wanted to disrupt the conventional expectations of bourgeois consciousness. In more traditional Marxist terms, the results could be seen as a challenge to reification. As Fredric Jameson put it,

The Surrealist image is thus a convulsive effort to split open the commodity forms of the objective universe by striking them against each other with immense force.[35]

Whether or not this procedure was legitimately revolutionary generated

32. Albert Camus, *The Rebel: An Essay on Man in Revolt*, trans. Anthony Bower (New York, 1956), pp. 96–97.
33. Walter Benjamin, "Surrealism," in *Reflections: Essays, Aphorisms, Autobiographical Writings* ed., with intro. Peter Demetz, trans. Edmund Jephcott (New York, 1978), p. 189. For an excellent discussion of this essay, see Richard Wolin, *Walter Benjamin: An Aesthetic of Redemption* (New York, 1982), p. 126f.
34. The phrase comes from Canto VI of *Les Chants de Maldoror*. For a discussion of Lautréamont's significance for the Surrealists, see Fowlie, Chapter 2. For a treatment of his anticipation of more recent deconstructionist tendencies in French literature and criticism, see Leo Bersani, *A Future for Astyanax: Character and Desire in Literature* (Boston, 1976), p. 189f.
35. Fredric Jameson, *Marxism and Form: Twentieth-Century Dialectical Theories of Literature* (Princeton, 1971), p. 96.

an intense controversy, among Western Marxists in France and elsewhere, which deserves a brief excursion.

The so-called "Expressionism Debate" of the mid-1930s, despite its general focus on German modernism, contained frequent references to Surrealism.[36] The defenders of realism, socialist or critical, were hostile to the Surrealists' destruction of narrative coherence and the integrity of the ego; Lukács in particular was outraged by the convergence of naturalism and Surrealism he detected in writers like James Joyce. Bloch, defending Surrealism as the heir of Expressionism, praised its ability to render the chaos of life as experienced by modern man. Like the similar polemic over the implications of montage in the cinema sparked by the great Russian filmmakers of the 1920s, the argument centered on the allegedly un-dialectical consequences of an anti-narrative aesthetic of virtual simultaneity. To those like Lukács, who were upholders of an essentially linear view of time (the historical temporality of the longitudinal totality), Surrealism seemed like a regression to the mythic time of endless repetition. To the critics of uniform temporality, on the other hand, Surrealism seemed sensitive to the ways in which utopian time might intersect with that of quotidian existence.

Outside of the "Expressionism Debate" properly speaking, a similar polemic was carried on over Surrealism between Walter Benjamin and Theodor W. Adorno.[37] For Benjamin, who had vigorously rejected all historicist residues in Marxism, Hegelian or otherwise, Surrealism came as a revelation; as early as 1926 and his reading of Aragon's *Le Paysan de Paris*, he was enchanted by its liberating potential as a means to overcome the gap between esoteric art and life. Surrealism, he wrote in 1929, provided brilliant examples of "profane illuminations,"[38] which were incursions of messianically charged "now time" into the mundane course of history. What Benjamin was to call "dialectical images" in his own work,

36. H.-J. Schmitt, *Die Expressionismusdebatte* (Frankfurt, 1973), pp. 193–209 *passim*. One way to conceptualize the incompatibility of Surrealism and Lukács' brand of realism, or indeed any for that matter, is to introduce the distinction between metaphor and metonymy developed by Roman Jakobson. Roland Barthes does precisely this in *Elements of Semiology* (London, 1964), p. 66.

37. For a discussion of Benjamin's interest in Surrealism and his quarrel with Adorno over it, see Susan Buck-Morss, *The Origin of Negative Dialectics: Theodor W. Adorno, Walter Benjamin, and the Frankfurt Institute* (New York, 1977), p. 124f; Gershom Scholem, *Walter Benjamin—Die Geschichte einer Freundschaft* (Frankfurt, 1975), p. 169f; and Eugene Lunn, *Marxism and Modernism: An Historical Study of Lukács, Brecht, Benjamin, and Adorno* (Berkeley, 1982), p. 269f.

38. Benjamin, "Surrealism," p. 179.

most notably employed in his unfinished "*Passagenwerk*" on nineteenth-century Paris, were deeply indebted to the Surrealist model. Moreover, like Breton he agreed with Fourier that corporeal gratification must be included in any legitimately revolutionary theory.

Benjamin's enthusiasm was not, however, shared by Adorno, who otherwise concurred with his (and Bloch's) defense of modernism against realism. Although Adorno's stress on non-identity bore many marks of his friend's influence, he never accepted the wholesale rejection of subjectivity which underlay Benjamin's attraction to Surrealism. For Adorno, Surrealism fetishized unmediated images from the archaic world of the psyche. Instead of bridging the gap between subject and object,

the dialectical pictures of surrealism are those of a dialectic of subjective freedom in a situation of objective unfreedom. . . . Its montages are the true still lifes. In as much as they arrange the archaic they create *nature morte*. These pictures are not so much those of an inner essence; rather they are object-fetishes on which the subjective, the Libido, was once fixated.[39]

Static and frozen, the images of the Surrealists, and to the extent that he followed them, the dialectical images of Benjamin as well, smelled of death and reification.[40] Instead of providing a model for uniting art and life, the Surrealists' gleeful destruction of art's aura, which Benjamin applauded, was less in the service of ultimate liberation than was such resolutely esoteric art as Schoenberg's music. The latter resisted the commer-

39. Theodor Adorno, "Looking Back on Surrealism" in *The Idea of the Modern in Literature and the Arts*, ed., Irving Howe (New York, 1967), p. 223. In his essay on Benjamin in *Prisms*, trans. Samuel and Shierry Weber (London, 1967), Adorno used the phrase "*nature morte*" to describe Benjamin's own work (p. 233), and added, "his aim was not merely for philosophy to catch up to surrealism but for it to become surrealistic."

40. Another way to express this same reservation is to connect Surrealism with what Ortega y Gassett made famous as the modernist "dehumanization of art." The Marxist cultural historian Arnold Hauser does precisely this when he writes of the movement:

Art is seized by a real mania for totality. It seems possible to bring everything into relationship with everything else, everything seems to include within itself the law of the whole. The disparagement of man, the so-called "de-humanization" of art, is connected above all with this feeling. In a world in which everything is significant or of equal significance, man loses his pre-eminence and psychology its authority.

(*The Social History of Art*, Vol. 4, trans. Stanley Goodman [New York, 1958], p. 237.) Adorno was in general supportive of modern art's refusal to "humanize" its subject matter, but in the case of Surrealism, he clearly felt it had gone too far in affirming the dehumanization of modern society. As he put it in contrasting Surrealism with Expressionism:

Surrealism is anti-organic and rooted in lifelessness. It destroys the boundary between the body and the world of objects, in order to convert society to a hypostatization of the body. Its form is that of montage. This is totally alien to Schoenberg. With regard to Surrealism, however, the more subjectivity renounces its right over the world of objects, aggressively acknowledging the supremacy of that world, the more willing it is to accept at the same time the traditionally established forms of the world of objects.

(*Philosophy of Modern Music*, trans. Anne G. Mitchell and Wesley Blomster [New York, 1973], p. 51.)

cialization of art in ways that Surrealism, with its premature collapse of the tension between art and life, did not.

What particularly galled Adorno was an aspect of Surrealism that paradoxically brought it close to the Durkheimian tradition to which it seemed so uncompromisingly opposed. The Surrealists yearned for subjective freedom but tried to achieve it through the suppression of the conscious self. Automatic writing was designed to allow the atemporal unconscious to overwhelm the ego and express itself directly. Following Rimbaud's famous dictum that "je est un autre,"[41] the Surrealists wanted to become the vessels of a higher reality. The artist, they contended, should be understood as a seer through whom that reality spoke. How precisely this passive image of the self with its elitist overtones could be reconciled with the Marxist stress on mass praxis was not easy to say, as the debacle of the Surrealist-Marxist relationship demonstrates. But it could more easily fit with the structuralist and post-structuralist denigration of the self in the name of a more impersonal linguistic system.

Indeed, one of the most controversial aspects of the Surrealist project was its attitude towards language. In Jean Paulhan's celebrated terms, they were "language terrorists" rather than "rhetoricians."[42]

Their aim is to avoid the danger of using the image to communicate some point. The image must not be useful; it must be innocent. Surrealist art must be stripped of rhetoric: it must never seek to prove anything. The great common error which the surrealists never ceased attacking was the belief that language was created in order to help men in their relationships with one another. This was an aberration, for André Breton. The highest goal of language, for which it was created, was the attainment to a disinterested purity.[43]

For many Marxist humanists, this denigration of the linguistic function of communication signaled Surrealism's complicity in the breakdown of meaningful discourse in the culture of late capitalism. But others saw in it a covert sign of protest. Herbert Marcuse, for example, argued that Surrealism's refusal to pretend that such communication was possible had a critical function. Also admiring the Surrealists' radical reading of Freud,[44] he praised their linguistic intransigence:

Prior to their incorporation into the material development, these possibilities [of

41. This assertion is from Rimbaud's celebrated "Lettre du Voyant" of May 15, 1871 to Paul Demeny.
42. Jean Paulhan, *Les Fleurs de Tarbes* (Paris, 1941).
43. Fowlie, pp. 142–43.
44. Herbert Marcuse, *Eros and Civilization: A Philosophical Inquiry into Freud* (Boston, 1955), p. 135.

libertarian revolution] are "sur-realistic": they belong to the poetic imagination, formed and expressed in the poetic language. It is not, it cannot be, an instrumentalist language, not an instrument of revolution.[45]

For many Western Marxists, such as Benjamin and Marcuse, who were generally pessimistic about the possibility of building a linguistic consensus in the present or near future, Surrealism's groping for a new non-instrumental language of images rather than concepts therefore had its attractions. For others who were less saturnine, like Habermas, Surrealism did not.[46]

Within France itself, Surrealism was also at the center of a heated controversy on the Left. Aside from the more conventional denunciations of it by orthodox Marxists both in and out of the party, such as the Trotskyist Pierre Naville's *The Revolution and the Intellectuals* of 1926, one critique stands out as having particular importance. From his earliest phenomenological writings on the imagination in 1936 through his defiant call for artistic engagement in *What Is Literature?* in 1947, Jean-Paul Sartre relentlessly condemned Surrealism.[47] Perhaps out of a desire to exorcise similar pseudo-rebellious impulses in his own youth, perhaps because of the need to define himself against the cultural radicalism of the previous generation, or perhaps even as a result of a general hostility to the political claims of poetry, Sartre excoriated Breton and his friends for a wide variety of sins. Hostile to the very idea of an unconscious, Freudian or otherwise, Sartre rejected automatic writing as a negation of the active consciousness that was necessary for both art and politics. Mocking the Surrealists' pretensions to have transcended literature, he contended that "Literature as Negation became Anti-Literature; never had it been more *literary*: the circle was completed."[48] Nor did he find the Surrealist "destruction" of bourgeois life any more convincing. Their flamboyant invocation of violence became, so Sartre charged, an end in itself, which bore a disturbing resemblance to the proto-fascist politics of the Action Française.

45. Herbert Marcuse, *An Essay on Liberation* (Boston, 1969), p. 33; see also the remarks on Surrealism in his *One-Dimensional Man: Studies in the Ideology of Advanced Industrial Society* (Boston, 1964), p. 68.

46. For Habermas' thoughts on Surrealism, see *Legitimation Crisis*, trans. Thomas McCarthy (Boston, 1973), p. 83, and "Modernity versus Post-modernity," *New German Critique* 22 (Winter 1981), pp. 10–11. Habermas was also wary about the Surrealist attempt to integrate de-auraticized art and everyday life. Here, paradoxically, it was Adorno's more cautious attitude towards the prospects of emancipation that he adopted against Benjamin and Marcuse.

47. For a discussion of Sartre's critique of Surrealism, see Michel Beaujour, "Sartre and Surrealism," *Yale French Studies* 30 (1964).

48. Jean-Paul Sartre, *What Is Literature?*, trans. Bernard Frechtman, intro. Wallace Fowlie (New York, 1949), p. 127.

Most interesting for our purposes, Sartre singled out the Surrealists' concept of totality for special attack. Referring to the argument of two defenders of the movement, that Surrealism wanted to assert "the rights of the human totality without omitting anything," Sartre replied,

I am in complete agreement with them. That is what surrealism *wanted*; that is certainly the greatness of its enterprise. It should again be noted that the "totalitarian" idea is typical of the age; it animates the Nazi, the Marxist and, today, the "existentialist" attempt. It must certainly go back to Hegel as the common source of all these efforts. But I discern a serious contradiction at the origin of surrealism: to use Hegelian language, this movement had the *concept* of totality . . . and *realized* something quite different in its concrete manifestations. The totality of man is, indeed, necessarily a synthesis, that is, the organic and schematic unity of all his secondary structures. A liberation which proposes to be *total* must start with a total knowledge of man by himself.[49]

Surrealism, however, lacked such a knowledge, for without the synthesis of subjective mediation, the totality it promoted was little more than a collection of dead images. In words that Adorno could have written, Sartre contended that:

Surrealism is haunted by the ready-made, the solid; it abhors genesis and births; it never regards creation as an emanation, a passing from the potential to the act, a gestation; it is the surging up *ex nihilo*, the abrupt appearance of a completely formed object which enriches the collection.[50]

And also like Adorno, Sartre concluded that Surrealism was thus still caught in the very objective dialectic of unfreedom that it had attempted to overcome: "What it liberates is neither desire nor the human totality, but pure imagination."[51]

How Sartre himself conceived of a more genuinely emancipatory concept of totality will occupy us later. Whether or not his diatribe against Surrealism was fully justified,[52] it helped to discredit the movement among leftists for almost a generation until the Situationists and other revolutionaries of the imagination rediscovered its liberating power in the late 1960s. What must not be lost sight of, however, is that much earlier, Surrealism had played a decisive role in directing French Marxist thought towards the issue of totality. A clear example of this influence can be seen

49. Ibid., p. 187.
50. Ibid., p. 190.
51. Ibid., p. 191.
52. For defenses of Surrealism against Sartre, see Gershman, *The Surrealist Revolution in France*, p. 118f., and Dominick LaCapra, *A Preface to Sartre: A Critical Introduction to Sartre's Literary and Philosophical Writings* (Ithaca, 1978), p. 85. It should also be noted that Sartre softened his views of Surrealism considerably when discussing its effect on African poetry, most notably that of Aimé Césaire, in "Orphée noir," *Situations III* (Paris, 1949).

in the career of the most important member of the *Philosophies* group, Henri Lefebvre, who never fully accepted the scientistic materialism of his fellow members.[53]

One of the first articles Lefebvre, then in his early twenties, published for *Philosophies* in 1924 was an appreciation of Dada, which earned him the friendship of Tristan Tzara and entrance into the circle that was about to coalesce around Breton.[54] He was particularly attracted to their interest in psychoanalysis, then virtually ignored in France, and their understanding of the linguistic crisis in the modern world. As a result of this initial contact, the *Philosophies* group was present at the discussions that led to the formation of the Bureau of Surrealist Inquiries in 1924. Lefebvre recounts an important meeting with Breton during that same year:

> He showed me a book on his table, Vera's translation of Hegel's *Logic*, a very bad translation, and said something disdainfully of the sort: "You haven't even read this?" A few days later, I began to read Hegel, who led me to Marx.[55]

It was this initial reading, Lefebvre recalls, that directed him in particular to the key concept of alienation, which he was later to make the centerpiece of his widely influential reading of Marx.

Lefebvre joined the PCF in 1928, at about the same time as several Surrealists. His conversion to Marxism proved, however, far closer in seriousness to that of Aragon and Eluard than to that of Breton, and like the former, he soon began to distance himself from Surrealism. The estrangement seems to have been mutual. In Breton's Second Surrealist Manifesto of 1929, Lefebvre, along with Morhange and Politzer, was sharply criticized for committing acts of bad faith.[56]

In the next decades, when he became one of the Party's leading philosophical spokesmen, writing on a wide variety of subjects, Lefebvre's early links with Surrealism were discreetly forgotten.[57] Only after his

53. For discussions of Lefebvre, see his autobiographical studies *La Somme et le reste* and *Le temps des méprises* (Paris, 1975); Alfred Schmidt, "Henri Lefebvre and Contemporary Interpretations of Marx" in *The Unknown Dimension: European Marxism Since Lenin*, ed. Dick Howard and Karl E. Klare (New York, 1972); Poster, *Existential Marxism in Postwar France, passim*; Edith Kurzweil, *The Age of Structuralism: Lévi-Strauss to Foucault* (New York, 1980), chap. 3; and Arthur Hirsh, *The French New Left: An Intellectual History from Sartre to Gorz* (Boston, 1981), chapter 4.

54. Lefebvre, review of *7 Manifestes Dada* by Tristan Tzara, ed. Jean Budry, in *Philosophies* 4 (November 15, 1924).

55. Lefebvre, *Le temps des méprises*, p. 49.

56. Breton, *Manifestoes of Surrealism*, p. 145.

57. During the height of the Cold War, for example, he published a short work entitled *Contribution à l'esthétique* (Paris, 1953) in which there is no reference at all to Surrealism.

long-delayed break with the Party in 1958 did overtly Surrealist motifs return to center stage in his work, in particular in his celebrated discussions of everyday life, urbanization, modernity, and the festival.[58] Well before his departure from the PCF, however, Lefebvre had fought to open its mind to a more philosophically and less scientistically inclined version of Marxism. And well before the impact on other Marxists of the Hegel Renaissance led by Kojève and Hyppolite, he had taken to heart the lesson he had first learned from Breton, that Hegel was crucial for the understanding of Marx. In fact, whereas the more academic discoverers of Hegel at the Ecole Pratique des Hautes Etudes were to read him largely in phenomenological and existentialist terms, Lefebvre immediately focussed on his importance for Marxism per se. As one of the first in France to read and appreciate the importance of the *1844 Paris Manuscripts*, he was able to see the links between the young Marx and Hegel, in particular the Hegel of the *Phenomenology* rather than the *Logic*. He thus far outdistanced the Surrealists in his grasp of dialectical thought, and left behind their concept of a totality of juxtapositions.

The major expression of Lefebvre's Hegelian reading of Marx came in *Dialectical Materialism*, written in 1934–35 and published four years later.[59] Stressing the unity of Marx's thought and the continued vitality of his humanist origins, upholding the philosophical as opposed to strictly scientific status of Marx's work, arguing for the primacy of subjective praxis over objective determinism, Lefebvre implicitly came into conflict with the Stalinist version of Dialectical Materialism then dominant in the PCF. However, at a time when the Party was willing to tolerate certain deviations from its official line, if the deviants were prestigious enough intellectuals,[60] the work caused Lefebvre little official trouble. During the

---

The tenor of the work is contained in its opening epigraphs, a short one by Marx and a longer one by Zhadnov, the Soviet guardian of socialist realism. "Liberty," Lefebvre writes in orthodox Marxist (and anti-Surrealist) fashion, "is not defined outside of necessity, but by knowledge and mastery of objective laws" (p. 147).

58. Many of these themes are developed in his multi-volume *Critique de la vie quotidienne* (Paris, 1947–1962); they are most accessible in English in *Everyday Life in the Modern World*, trans. S. Rabinovitch (New York, 1971). One aspect of Surrealism, which it shared with ethnology, Lefebvre steadfastly rejected: its fascination with the exotic and primitive. In stressing the importance of everyday life in the modern world as the correct object for critical social inquiry, he attacked the escapism he detected in the Surrealist-ethnological search for the "entirely other."

59. Lefebvre, *Dialectical Materialism*, trans. John Sturrock (London, 1968).

60. Caute argues (*Communism and the French Intellectuals*, p. 267) that the Party's response to the book was an incarnation of what he calls one of five principles of utility employed by the PCF in its attempt to use intellectuals: "professional excellence, if possible within the framework of a Marxist-communist philosophy, with the primary object of influencing politically other intellectuals and the educated community in general" (p. 35).

years of the Resistance, it proved to be one of the most important intellectual stimuli to membership in the Party for younger figures like Edgar Morin, Roger Garaudy, and Jean Duvignaud.[61]

The general argument of *Dialectical Materialism*, which has since become common coin among Marxist Humanists, does not bear repeating in detail, but a few comments are in order. Without mentioning Lukács, Korsch, or Gramsci, Lefebvre repeated their evocation of the concept of concrete totality as an antidote to economism:

The analysis of the given reality, from the point of view of political economy, leads to "general abstract relations": division of labor, value, money, etc. If we confine ourselves to the analysis we "volatilize" the concrete representation into abstract determinations, and lose the concrete presupposed by the economic categories, which are simply "abstract, one-sided relations of an already given concrete and living whole." This whole must be recovered by moving from the abstract to the concrete. The concrete totality is thus the conceptual elaboration of the content grasped in perception and representation; it is not, as Hegel thought, the product of the concept begetting itself above perception and representation.[62]

Lefebvre, anxious to distance himself from any hint of idealism, stressed that this "conceptual elaboration" was anything but a human construct imposed on the world; "The dialectic," he insisted, "far from being an inner movement of the mind, is real, it precedes the mind, in Being. It imposes itself on the mind."[63] He thus resisted the temptation to view the totality expressively, as the product of a meta-subjective creator, a view which we have seen implicit in certain arguments of the first generation of Western Marxists. "The totality of the world, the infinite–finite of Nature," he contended,

has a determinable structure, and its movement can become intelligible for us without our having to attribute it to an organizing intelligence. Its order and structure emerge from reciprocal action, from the complex of conflicts and solutions, destructions and creations, transcendings and eliminations, chances and necessities, revolutions and involutions.[64]

If anything, and here Lefebvre sounded more like Bloch than like Lukács, totality was open to the future. "All reality," he wrote, "is a totality, both one and many, scattered or coherent and open to its future, that is to its end."[65]

At that end, Lefebvre contended, was the possibility of achieving what

61. Caute, p. 267; Hirsh, *The French New Left*, p. 106.
62. Lefebvre, *Dialectical Materialism*, p. 87.
63. Ibid., p. 109.
64. Ibid., p. 108.
65. Ibid.

he called "total man," which he contrasted to the alienated "economic man" of capitalism. In terms reminiscent of Lukács' vision of normative totality, he described "total man," the telos of Communism, as

both the subject and the object of the Becoming. He is the living subject who is opposed to the object and surmounts this opposition. He is the subject who is broken up into partial activities and scattered determinations and who surmounts this dispersion. He is the subject of action, as well as its final object, its product even if it does seem to produce external objects. The total man is the living subject–object, who is first of all torn asunder, dissociated and chained to necessity and abstraction. Through this tearing apart, he moves towards freedom; he becomes Nature, but free. He becomes a totality, like Nature, but by bringing it under control. The total man is "de-alienated" man.[66]

That this vision was originally indebted to idealism, however much Marxism had transcended it, Lefebvre freely admitted: "The total man is the Idea, that idea which idealism reduced one-sidedly to the theoretical activity, and which it thought of as outside life, ready-made in the absolute."[67] That it was vague and imprecise enough to be used by fascists as well as Marxists—an exemplary case being Marcel Déat in 1944[68]—Lefebvre did not pause to consider. But in many of his later writings which stressed the fragmentary nature of modern life, Lefebvre would return to these themes. In 1955, for example, he published a piece specifically devoted to "The Notion of Totality in the Social Sciences,"[69] which once again stressed its vital importance for understanding reality. Perhaps the article's most interesting emphasis was on the distinction between closed and open totalities. Lukács, he complained, had failed to understand the difference in *History and Class Consciousness*, where he applied the term in a closed manner to the proletariat's class consciousness.[70] The proper concept of totality, Lefebvre contended, recognized its dynamic, open-ended, undetermined quality.

66. Ibid., pp. 161–62.
67. Ibid., p. 165.
68. Marcel Déat, *Pensée allemande et pensée française* (Paris, 1944), p. 110.
69. Lefebvre, "La notion de totalité dans les sciences sociales," *Cahiers internationaux de Sociologie* 18 (January–June 1955).
70. Ibid., p. 68. Interestingly, Lefebvre absolved Gramsci of the same charge, but later changed his mind in *The Sociology of Marx*, trans. Norbert Guterman (New York, 1968), where he wrote, "Both Marxist theoreticians have conceived the *end* of philosophy without its *realization*—a very widespread error" (p. 37). It should also be noted that Lefebvre's distinction between open and closed totalities did not actually begin in 1955; in *Dialectical Materialism*, he wrote, "the exposition of dialectical materialism does not pretend to put an end to the forward march of knowledge or to offer a closed totality, of which all previous systems had been no more than the inadequate expression. . . . No expression of dialectical materialism can be definitive, but, instead of being incompatible and conflicting with each other, it may perhaps be possible for these expressions to be integrated into an open totality, perpetually in the process of being transcended" (p. 111).

Whether or not this charge was fully fair to Lukács, it expressed one of the essential themes of postwar French Marxism: its abhorrence of premature closure. In the writings of the so-called *Arguments* group,[71] as well as in Sartre's *Critique of Dialectical Reason*, totality was expressly understood as an experimental and open concept. Perhaps because of the polemical identification of totality with totalitarianism by anti-Marxists such as Camus and the phenomenologist Emmanuel Levinas,[72] the indeterminacy of the totality was defensively stressed by those Marxists, like Lefebvre, who were anxious to establish the credentials of Marxist Humanism as an alternative to Stalinism.

Although signaling a healthy flexibility, this opening up of the concept of totality was often accompanied by a certain loss of theoretical clarity and rigor. The tendency, always latent in Marxist holism, for totality to become a vague and all-embracing notion that permitted its user to avoid making hard choices seems to have come to the fore. In his 1955 essay, for example, Lefebvre dealt with the issue of history and nature, which we have seen was so troublesome for other Western Marxists, by swallowing both in the concept of totality:

The "totality" envelops nature and its becoming, man and his history, his consciousness (*conscience*) and his knowledge, his ideas and ideologies. It determines itself as "sphere of spheres," infinite totality of moving, partial totalities, reciprocally and deeply implicated in and by conflicts themselves. At the limit, the totality of knowledge coincides with the universe itself.[73]

From one point of view, Lefebvre continued, phenomena could be understood as objects; from another, they were the products of subjective human praxis. A truly holistic perspective, he ecumenically concluded,

71. Lefebvre was one of the directors of *Arguments* when it first appeared in 1956, along with other former Communists Pierre Fougeyrollas, Jean Duvignaud, and Edgar Morin. It ceased publication in 1962, although its major figures, who also included Kostas Axelos and François Chatelet, continued to write for some time on similar themes. Significantly, their books often dealt with the concept of totality, e.g., Fougeyrollas, *Contradiction et totalité* (Paris, 1964). For a good treatment of their work, see Poster, *Existential Marxism in Postwar France*, chap. 5.

72. Emmanuel Levinas, *Totality and Infinity: An Essay on Exteriority*, trans. Alphonos Lingi (Pittsburgh, 1969). The French original appeared in 1961. Levinas, a Jewish philosopher very much influenced by Franz Rosenzweig's critique of totality in *The Star of Redemption*, criticized the totalitarian implications of Hegelian and Heideggerian holism. He defended the concept of infinity as more in touch with the ongoing desire that characterizes man's thrust into the future. Not surprisingly, Levinas was an inspiration for Derrida. See the appreciative essay in the latter's *Writing and Difference*.

73. Lefebvre, "La notion de totalité dans les sciences sociales," p. 73. This passage calls into question Alfred Schmidt's assertion, which he applies to Lefebvre, that "The necessity, expressed for the first time by the early Lukács, of limiting the validity of the dialectic to the historical and social world has since then become the unspoken presupposition of every serious interpretation of Marx" (p. 331).

would embrace both perspectives. Although he stressed that within a dialectical concept of totality, contradictions were an essential reality, he did
not question their ultimate harmonization. To be sure, he admitted in *The
Sociology of Marx* that "the totality of human knowledge can no longer
be encompassed as it could in Marx's epoch, at once from the inside and
from the outside (both as a reality and as a possibility), critically and descriptively."[74] But he refused to agree that our "broken-up totality, fragments of which confront one another and sometimes separate when they
do not enter into conflict,"[75] could not be overcome. Thus, "the indispensable presuppositions in the social sciences remain the unity of knowledge
and the total character of reality."[76]

And at the end of the process, for all its openness, there still loomed the
normative prospect of "total man," which Lefebvre admitted played the
same role in dialectical social theory as the idea of the absolute did in
epistemology. It was not, however, "an abstraction, a dream, an ideal
empty of meaning, but on the contrary, a full and rich notion, implicated
in that of social development."[77] Although by no means an already
achieved reality—Lefebvre was careful to distinguish his position from
Feuerbach's philosophical anthropology—normative totality was still the
telos of history. Like the Surrealists who first sparked his interest in totality, Lefebvre remained doggedly optimistic in his belief that alienation
could be overcome. In the 1940s, he attacked the existentialists for their
pessimism on this issue; in the 1960s, he was no less hostile to the structuralists, whose "new Eleatism" threatened the Heraclitean awareness of
historical flux underlying the Marxist tradition.[78] Even in his more recent
work, in which he incorporated the insights of semiology and structural
linguistics, and acknowledged the failure of the proletariat to fulfill its
historical mission, he never fully abandoned the hope that men might recapture the direct intersubjective communication in their daily lives that
the achievement of "total man" suggested. Nor did he give up his insistence on the liberating power of the idea of totality.[79]

Although it might be argued that the events of 1968 somehow validated Lefebvre's optimism,[80] there can be little doubt that the essentially

74. Lefebvre, *The Sociology of Marx*, p. 23.
75. Ibid.
76. Ibid., pp. 23–24.
77. Lefebvre, "La notion de totalité dans les sciences sociales," p. 76.
78. Lefebvre, "Claude Lévi-Strauss et le nouvel éléatisme" in *Au-delà du structuralisme*
(Paris, 1971). The volume also contains a lengthy critique of "Les paradoxes d'Althusser."
79. See the concluding sentences of Lefebvre, *The Survival of Capitalism: Reproduction
of the Relations of Production* (London, 1976), p. 127.
80. So Poster argues, p. 255. Lefebvre's ideas were, in fact, very influential on certain
French New Leftists, for example, the Situationists. Guy Debord's *Society of the Spectacle*

Hegelian view of totality he advocated, that Lukácsian image of the total man as "both the subject and object of Becoming," was increasingly called into question by other Western Marxists in France. The process of disillusionment, which we have traced in Central Europe, can be discerned as well in postwar France. Its progress can best be understood if we ignore strict chronology and look first at Lucien Goldmann, who was born in 1913, and then at Jean-Paul Sartre, eight years his elder. Our justification is that Sartre came to both Marxism and the concept of totality somewhat later than did Goldmann. After examining Sartre's fellow existentialist Marxist, Maurice Merleau-Ponty, we will pass on to Louis Althusser, who played a role in the French debate over totality surprisingly analogous to that of Adorno in the German, at least in certain respects. For paradoxically, by returning to the Durkheimian concept of totality, filtered through a linguistically inspired structuralism that bore a certain resemblance to the Surrealists' concept of non-communicative language,[81] Althusser exposed many of the same difficulties in the Hegelian Marxist concept of totality which Adorno had found so troubling.

(Detroit, 1970), originally written in 1967, attacked the current "spectacular" totality as false and in need of total revolution. His goal of a completely different totality drew on Lefebvre's concept of the festival and on earlier Surrealist concepts of liberation, in which separation would be overcome and community realized.

81. One possible link between Surrealism and structuralist Marxism, whose impact on Althusser we will examine later, was the philosopher of science, Gaston Bachelard. The similarities between his "poetics of revery" and that of the Surrealists has been explored in Mary Ann Caws, *Surrealism and the Literary Imagination* (The Hague, 1966). There were, in fact, also many important links between the Surrealists and the ethnologists of the interwar era. See the discussion in James Clifford, "On Ethnographic Surrealism," *Comparative Studies in Society and History* 23, 4 (October 1981). Yet another connection can be discerned in the influence of Surrealism on Jacques Lacan, whose reading of Freud, as we will see, was adopted by Althusser.

CHAPTER TEN

Totality and Marxist Aesthetics: The Case of Lucien Goldmann

As we have had many opportunities to remark, the concept of totality has often been evoked in considerations of aesthetics. Ever since Plato's *Phaedrus* and Aristotle's *Poetics*, aestheticians have employed the metaphor of organic unity to characterize a "true" work of art. The greater the work, they have argued, the more adequate a sense of fullness and completeness it conveys and the more economical the means to achieve that end. For Aristotle, each of the parts of an aesthetic whole should play a functional role in the constitution of its essential unity, thus helping to reveal what he called, following the organic metaphor, its "soul." Details were thus artistically valid when they expressed a work's essential nature, its coherent form.

With certain variations of emphasis, the Platonic and Aristotelian concept of art as an organic unity can be detected in most Western notions of aesthetic validity. When systematic aesthetic theory emerged during the Enlightenment, reaching its crowning achievement in Kant's *Critique of Judgment*, Aristotle's insistence on the immanently purposive nature of the artistic whole was given even wider currency. The Romantics, most notably August Wilhelm Schlegel in Germany and Coleridge in England, freely extrapolated from biological notions of organic wholeness to aesthetic ones. And as noted in Chapter One, the model of aesthetic unity became in Schiller the norm for social totality as well. With the birth of the idea of the Aesthetic State, the interpenetration of artistic and social models of totality became securely established. Although Hegel subordinated art to rational philosophy, his *Aesthetics* nonetheless emphasized the totalistic character of art as the sensuous representation of the Idea, whose classical embodiment was to be found in Greek art.

The impact of classical aesthetics on Karl Marx has been widely acknowledged.[1] Although like the Romantics, he preferred Shakespeare to Schiller, it was largely out of a preference for sensuous over moralizing art, rather than out of any rejection of Schiller's view of artistic wholeness. In his famous discussion of the continuing power of Greek art in the *Grundrisse*[2] he contrasted the childlike ability of the ancients to give us a sense of perfect structural totality with the one-sided distortions of modern life and art. Stressing the importance of *Mass* (measure or proportion), Marx contended that genuine works of art were prefigurations of the normative society of the future. Indeed, at times he seemed to envisage the de-alienation of man in terms of the liberation of man's aesthetic potential.[3]

Marx's aesthetic writings were, to be sure, fragmentary and incomplete, and so subject to a number of different, even conflicting, interpretations. For example, did Marx feel that the unity of a work of art mimetically reflects or reproduces the actual totality of its creator's epoch? Or did that unity anticipate a social coherence still to be achieved? Were the criteria for unity the same for all periods of art and for all artistic genres and modes? Or was it possible to create coherence in different ways at different historical moments? How important were the conscious intentions and prejudices of the artist in determining his ability to express or capture the whole in artistic form? Did the criteria for judging this importance change when a holistic social theory and a totalizing social movement actually appeared in history?

These and similar questions were posed with particular urgency in the period after 1917. In Eastern Marxism, they had special weight because of the growing prescriptive power of the state to determine what was legitimate art and what was not. In Western Marxism, they were of great importance because of the general shift in its focus from political and economic to cultural and philosophical concerns. In fact, as we have seen, it was in a work on aesthetic issues, *The Theory of the Novel*, that Lukács first introduced the concept of totality as a key to understanding the relations between culture and the world. Although he came to repudiate many of the

1. See, for example, S. S. Prawer, *Karl Marx and World Literature* (Oxford, 1978). For a good selection of Marx's writings on aesthetics, see *Marx and Engels on Literature and Art*, ed. Lee Baxandall and Stefan Morawski, intro. Stefan Morawski (St. Louis, 1973). For general considerations of the organic metaphor, see the essays in G. S. Rousseau, ed., *Organic Form: The Life of an Idea* (London, 1972).

2. Karl Marx, *Grundrisse: Introduction to the Critique of Political Economy*, trans. with foreword Martin Nicolaus (New York, 1973), p. 110.

3. For a discussion of this point, see Robert C. Tucker, *Philosophy and Myth in Karl Marx* (London, 1961) and the critique of his position in Morawski's intro. to *Marx and Engels on Literature and Art*, p. 6.

concerns of his early period as excessively idealist, Lukács nonetheless retained the concept of totality as the basis of his theory of realism. Although it might be argued that, robbed as it was of its expressivist dimension as the product of a meta-subjective universal class, totality became, in Ferenc Feher's words, an "increasingly meaningless category,"[4] it nonetheless served Lukács well in the polemical wars of the 1930s and 1940s.[5] Stressing Marx's links with classical German aesthetics,[6] Lukács attempted to build bridges between Marxism and bourgeois humanism on cultural issues, thus paralleling the popular front strategy he had defended as early as the Blum Theses in 1928. Insisting on realism as the only proper form for a progressive aesthetics, Lukács assimilated the concept of organic unity to that of mimesis in ways that nonetheless excluded certain bourgeois artistic currents from the Humanist coalition. Most vigorously expelled were naturalism and modernism,[7] both of which, Lukács claimed, failed to reflect the meaningful social totality that true realism, with its sensitivity to the hierarchy of essence and appearance, was able to capture. Drawing on Engels' celebrated letter to Mrs. Harkness,[8] he contended that the ability of realist authors to reveal the workings of the whole was not dependent on their avowed political sympathies. Following Engels' distinction between Balzac and Zola, he contended that the narrative power of the former was inherently more progressive than the flatly descriptive ability of the latter, which betrayed a positivist inability to reveal the dialectical relations beneath the surface of society.

Although Lukács' defense of realism was not in perfect harmony with the official socialist realism then being propagated in Moscow,[9] it nonetheless served to circumscribe the options of Marxist aesthetics, both as a practice and a critical method, during the 1930s and after. In a series of

4. Ferenc Feher, "Lukács in Weimar," *Telos* 39 (Spring 1979), p. 123.

5. For treatments of these battles, see Helga Gallas, *Marxistische Literaturtheorie: Kontroversen im Bund proletarisch-revolutionärer Schriftsteller* (Neuwied, 1971); Henri Arvon, *Marxist Esthetics*, trans. Helen Lane, intro. Fredric Jameson (Ithaca, 1973); *Aesthetics and Politics: Debates Between Bloch, Lukács, Brecht, Benjamin, Adorno*, ed. *New Left Review* (London, 1977); Rob Burns, "Theory and Organisation of Revolutionary Working-Class Literature in the Weimar Republic" in Keith Bullivant, ed., *Culture and Society in the Weimar Republic* (Manchester, 1977); and Eugene Lunn, *Marxism and Modernism: An Historical Study of Lukács, Brecht, Benjamin, and Adorno* (Berkeley, 1982).

6. See in particular his essays "The Ideal of the Harmonious Man in Bourgeois Aesthetics" in *Writer and Critic and Other Essays*, trans. Arthur D. Kahn (New York, 1970) and "Karl Marx und Friedrich Theodor Fischer" in *Beiträge zur Geschichte der Aesthetik* (Berlin, 1954).

7. Lukács' linkage of modernism with naturalism is developed *inter alia* in *The Meaning of Contemporary Realism*, trans. J. and N. Mander (London, 1963).

8. Engels to Margaret Harkness, April, 1888, in Baxandall and Morawski, p. 114f.

9. For a discussion of the differences, see George Bisztray, *Marxist Models of Literary Realism* (New York, 1978).

highly charged battles with a variety of figures, including Ottwalt, Bredel, Seghers, Brecht, and Bloch, Lukács helped forge the dominant position on Marxist aesthetics for a generation. At its center was the essentially Aristotelian concept of the art work as an organic totality.[10] Indeed, aside from certain relatively minor changes, such as his rethinking of the contrast between intensive and extensive totalities,[11] Lukács remained constant in his emphasis on totality, from *The Theory of the Novel* to the treatise on aesthetics he left unfinished at his death in 1971.

By then, however, alternative versions of Marxist aesthetics, some of which included new concepts of totality, had proliferated, so that Lukács' defense of realism was subjected to increasing critical scrutiny. The general process of disillusionment with Lukács' philosophical position that we have traced in this book can be discerned as well in the reception of his aesthetics. Figures as varied as Adorno, Althusser, Della Volpe and Sartre came to question his formulations. His earlier debates with opponents like Bloch and Brecht were revived and the verdict, which had initially gone his way, was generally reversed. His political compromises were reexamined for the effect they had on his aesthetic judgments. The cognitive bias of his aesthetics was called into question by a younger generation of Marxists anxious to harness the practical possibilities of art for immediate political purposes. The charge of formalism that he had hurled at modernism was turned back on him because of his insistence that only one form, that of the nineteenth-century realistic novel, was truly progressive for contemporary literature as well. All in all, Lukacs' variant of Hegelian (or Aristotelian) Marxist aesthetics went the way of his philosophical attempt to revive Marxism on essentially Hegelian lines in *History and Class Consciousness*. Much to his chagrin, the massive theoretical effort he made before his death to summarize his life-long thoughts on aesthetics was greeted with relative indifference by younger Western Marxists.[12]

10. Lukács emphasized the importance of Aristotle, in particular in his *Über die Besonderheit als Kategorie der Ästhetik* (Neuwied, 1967).
11. In *The Theory of the Novel,* it will be recalled, Lukács wrote of the epic as depicting the "extensive" totality of life, whereas the drama portrayed only the "intensive" totality, by which he meant a split between the "is" and the "ought." But in his 1954 essay "Art and Objective Truth," translated in *Writer and Critic,* he wrote:

The extensive totality of reality necessarily is beyond the possible scope of any artistic creation; the totality of reality can only be reproduced intellectually in ever-increasing approximations through the infinite process of science. The totality of the work of art is rather intensive: the circumscribed and self-contained ordering of those factors which objectively are of decisive significance for the portion of life depicted, which determine its existence and motion, its specific quality and its place in the total life process. In this sense the briefest song is as much an intensive totality as the mightiest epic. (p. 38)

12. Although his students in Budapest were active in promoting the importance of his later aesthetics, their efforts were largely in vain. As Agnes Heller reported, "Goldmann, Bloch and Adorno admitted to me that they never read the Aesthetics, and their unanimous

This is not to say, of course, that Lukács' theories fell on entirely barren ground.[13] In addition to the gifted circle of students around him during his last years in Budapest—Agnes Heller, Ferenc Feher, György Márkus, Mihály Vajda, and Andras Hegedüs, most of whom ultimately migrated from Hungary[14]—Lukács had one major foreign disciple of note,[15] who developed his aesthetic theory in imaginative ways: the sociologist of literature, Lucien Goldmann.[16] Born in Rumania in 1913, the son of a lawyer, Goldmann had his greatest impact in France after the Second World War. Indeed, insofar as Mark Poster is correct in claiming that "the link between Lukács and the French was in great measure forged by Lucien Goldmann,"[17] pausing with his work now will give us an important insight into the ways in which Western Marxism developed in France. In

------

objection was that it was too long" ("Marxist Ethics and the Future of Eastern Europe: An Interview with Agnes Heller," *Telos* 38 [Winter 1978–79], p. 166). For an extensive discussion of Lukács' later aesthetics, see Béla Királyfalvi, *The Aesthetics of György Lukács* (Princeton, 1975). In Eastern Europe, Lukács' star also waned after his participation in the abortive Hungarian revolution of 1956. See Peter Uwe Hohendahl, "Georg Lukács in the GDR: On Recent Developments in Literary Theory," *New Germany Critique* 12 (Fall 1977).

13. For a general discussion of his impact, see Andrew Arato and Paul Breines, *The Young Lukács and the Origins of Western Marxism* (New York, 1979), Conclusion.

14. For a discussion of the Budapest School, see Serge Frankel and Daniel Martin, "The Budapest School," *Telos* 17 (Fall, 1973) and Joseph Gabel, "Hungarian Marxism," *Telos* 25 (Fall 1975). Another prominent Lukács student, who left Hungary before the school coalesced (the term itself dates only from a letter Lukács wrote in 1971, which appeared in the *Times Literary Supplement* [London] on February 2, 1972), is István Mészáros.

15. There have been, to be sure, others of some importance, for example the Polish-born Leo Kofler who, although he never actually met Lukács, acknowledges his importance for his work. See his *Zur Theorie der modernen Literatur* (Neuwied, 1962), p. 8. Also the Yugoslavian writers associated with the journal *Praxis* were indebted to Lukács, although as Gershon S. Sher points out, "It would be an oversimplification to characterize *Praxis* Marxism as a whole as a mere imitation or a direct development of the idea of Lukács, Bloch or indeed of any single school of thought." *Praxis: Marxist Criticism and Dissent in Socialist Yugoslavia* (Bloomington, 1977), p. 65.

16. There is now a wealth of secondary literature on Goldmann. See especially, Pierre V. Zima, *Goldmann: Dialectique de l'immanence* (Paris, 1973); Sami Naïr and Michael Löwy, *Goldmann ou la dialectique de la totalité* (Paris, 1973); Hermann Baum, *Lucien Goldmann: Marxismus contra vision tragique?* (Stuttgart, 1974); and Mary Evans, *Lucien Goldmann* (Brighton, 1981). For an excellent bibliography of Goldmann's works and of works on him, see Lucien Goldmann, *Cultural Creation in Modern Society,* trans. Bart Grahl, intro. William Mayrl, bibliography compiled by Ileana Rodriguez and Marc Zimmerman (St. Louis, 1976). See also the important introductory essay to Lucien Goldmann, *Essays on Method in the Sociology of Literature,* trans. and ed. William Q. Boelhower (St. Louis, 1980). I am also indebted to Mme. Annie Goldmann, herself a distinguished film critic, for an interview on her late husband in Paris on December 30, 1974.

17. Mark Poster, *Existential Marxism in Postwar France: From Sartre to Althusser* (Princeton, 1975), p. 47. One should also acknowledge the efforts of the *Arguments* group, who translated *History and Class Consciousness* into French in 1960, and of Joseph Gabel, whose *La fausse conscience* (Paris, 1962) attempted to render Lukács' category of reification into psychological terms. And one cannot, of course, forget the seminal chapter on Western Marxism in Merleau-Ponty's *Adventures of the Dialectic* of 1955, which presented Lukács as the originator of that tradition.

fact, apart from Henri Lefebvre, Goldmann was the first Hegelian Marxist to prosper in the essentially hostile environment of France, if only for a short period of time.

If Goldmann brought Lukács to France, he nonetheless subtly transformed certain of the implications of Lukács' position which directly concerned the issue of totality. Thus, although Goldmann was a staunch advocate of the Hegelian Marxist alternative to orthodox Dialectical Materialism, signs of the ultimate disintegration of that problematic and its aesthetic correlate can be discerned in his texts. In this chapter we will explore the ways in which Goldmann, in the very act of translating Lukács into French, undercut the power of his argument, or more precisely put, unintentionally exposed many of its weaknesses.

Goldmann's first acquaintance with Lukács' work came when he was twenty, in 1933. Already involved in leftist politics in Bucharest,[18] where he had just earned a degree in law, Goldmann came to Vienna to study with the leading Austro-Marxist theoretician Max Adler. Although the Austro-Marxists were far more interested in Kant and Mach than Hegel, Lukács' early work was certainly known to them. Goldmann read *Soul and Form, The Theory of the Novel* and *History and Class Consciousness* and, disregarding their repudiation by Lukács himself, he was overwhelmed by their power. For the rest of his life, he remained faithful, at least on the surface, to the "young Lukács," rarely if ever turning to his later writings for inspiration.[19] As late as 1970, Goldmann would call Lukács "simply the most important philosopher of the first half of the twentieth century."[20] Even though he came to see the pre-Marxist Lukács as the harbinger of existentialism,[21] a philosophy he generally rejected, Goldmann continued to draw sustenance from those texts until the end of his life in 1970, one year before Lukács' own death.

18. Naïr and Lowy claim that Goldmann was involved in a clandestine para-Communist group in Rumania and may have spent some time in prison for his activities (p. 11). He never had any other direct political affiliations.

19. Lukács, in fact, was very dismayed by Goldmann's indifference to his mature work. In October, 1959, he wrote to Goldmann,

If I had died around 1924 and my unchanged soul had observed your literary activity from some beyond, it would be filled with a veritable gratitude at seeing you occupied so intensely with the works of my youth. But as I am not dead and for 34 years have been creating what must be called my life's work and for you this work does not exist at all, it is hard for me as a living being whose interests are, of course, directed toward its own present activity, to take a stand on your reflection.

Apparently, this letter marked the end of their cordial relations. It is quoted in Nicolas Tertulian, "On the Later Lukács," *Telos* 40 (Summer 1979), p. 139.

20. See his article on Lukács in the *Encyclopaedia Universalis*, vol. 10 (Paris, 1971), p. 138.

21. Goldmann, "The Early Writings of Georg Lukács," *Tri Quarterly* 9 (Spring 1967), p. 168.

In 1934, Goldmann moved to Paris to study political economy at the faculty of law, and then German literature and philosophy at the Sorbonne. Six years later, when the Nazis invaded France, Goldmann, who was both a Jew and an outspoken, if unaffiliated, leftist, fled Paris for Toulouse in the unoccupied zone, where he was interned for a brief period. When the Nazis overran the Vichy-controlled region in November, 1942, he clandestinely moved to Switzerland, where once again he was placed in a refugee camp, this time for almost a year. His release from Swiss internment in September, 1943, seems to have been due in part to the efforts of the figure who, after Lukács, most influenced his subsequent work, the psychologist Jean Piaget.[22] Through Piaget, he was also given a scholarship to the University of Zurich, where he wrote his doctoral dissertation in philosophy on *Mensch, Gemeinschaft and Welt in der Philosophie Immanuel Kants.*[23] While working on this project, he also served as Piaget's assistant in Geneva, at the time of the psychologist's seminal experiments on the genetic development of perception and intelligence in children.[24]

After the liberation of France, Goldmann moved once again to Paris where he hoped to make a scholarly career. "Isolated, crossing borders, acquiring new tongues, addressing invisible audiences," as Andrew Arato and Paul Breines have put it, "Lucien Goldmann symbolized the situation of critical Marxism at mid-century.[25] Goldmann's isolation, like that of Critical Marxism, was not to be permanent. Supported by the Centre National de Recherche Scientifique, he began research under the direction of the great scholar of Descartes, Henri Gouhier, on what was to become his most celebrated study, *The Hidden God.*[26] Accepted at the Sorbonne for his second doctorate, it was published in book form in 1956, four years after he brought out a shorter treatise on method entitled *The Human Sciences and Philosophy.*[27] In 1959, Goldmann collected a number of his essays, most of them also methodological, as *Recherches dialectiques,*[28] and became a director of studies at the sixth section of the Ecole Pratique des Hautes Etudes, where he taught the sociology of literature and

22. For Piaget's version of their friendship, see his brief memorial tribute appended to *Cultural Creation in Modern Society.*
23. (Zurich, 1945); English translation as *Immanuel Kant,* trans. Robert Black (London, 1971).
24. For Piaget's account of these years, see his autobiographical sketch in Richard I. Evans, *Piaget: The Man and His Ideas,* trans. Eleanor Duckworth (New York, 1973), p. 134f.
25. Arato and Breines, *The Young Lukács,* p. 219.
26. Goldmann, *The Hidden God: A Study of Tragic Vision in the Pensées of Pascal and the Tragedies of Racine,* trans. Philip Thody (New York, 1964).
27. Goldmann, *The Human Sciences and Philosophy,* trans. Hayden V. White and Robert Anchor (London, 1969).
28. Goldmann, *Recherches dialectiques* (Paris, 1959).

philosophy. While retaining that post until his death, Goldmann also organized a center for the study of the sociology of literature in Brussels in 1961. There he turned his attention to contemporary themes and prepared his next major work, *Towards a Sociology of Literature*,[29] which appeared in 1964. Before his sudden death in 1970 he brought out several more collections of essays, which added to the reputation he earned through the books mentioned above and several shorter studies such as his 1956 treatment of *Racine*.[30]

Although Goldmann had great sympathy for the student movement of the 1960s, supported the "new working class" theories of Mallet, Gorz, Foa and Trentin, and praised the self-management experiments in Yugoslavia, he was far more a scholar than a political activist. As such, he exemplified the widening gap within Western Marxism between theory and practice that we have already noted, most clearly in the case of the Frankfurt School. Like them and in clear contrast to Lukács, Goldmann had no illusions about the revolutionary role of the proletariat in late capitalist society and thus felt no compunction for not supporting the parties that claimed to speak in its name.

Goldmann, however, did remain loyal to Lukács in many other ways, in particular through the emphasis he placed on the concept of totality. Perhaps the most uncritically Lukácsian of his studies was his Zurich doctoral dissertation on Kant. The admiring Goldmann went so far as to include Lukács, in a judgment he would soon qualify,[31] with Hegel and Marx in the pantheon of genuinely dialectical thinkers. What was perhaps even more striking was the central argument of the book: that Kant also belonged in that company. Here, without really admitting it,[32] Goldmann was dissenting from Lukács' own judgment in *History and Class Consciousness*. But ironically, he based his case on the argument that Kant was "the first modern thinker to recognize anew the importance of

29. Goldmann, *Towards a Sociology of the Novel*, trans. Alan Sheridan (London, 1975).
30. Goldmann, *Racine*, trans. Alastair Hamilton, intro. Raymond Williams (London, 1969) and *Structures mentales et création culturelle* (Paris, 1970), part of which is in English as *The Philosophy of the Enlightenment: The Burgess and the Enlightenment*, trans. Harry Maas (London, 1973). After his death, a collection of unfinished lectures was edited by Youssef Ishaghpour and published as *Lukács et Heidegger* (Paris, 1973), English translation *Lukács and Heidegger: Towards a New Philosophy*, trans. William Q. Boelhower (London, 1977), without Ishaghpour's valuable introduction.
31. In the preface to the first French edition of the book in 1948 (in the English translation, p. 17).
32. There is only one place in the book where Lukács comes in for mild criticism. In speaking of Lukács' charge that Kant failed to transcend reification, Goldmann writes, "One might just as well take him to task for having written in 1790 and not in 1940, or for having lived in Königsberg and not in Paris. To me this seems quite pointless and secondary" (p. 128). For a discussion of Goldmann's disagreement with Lukács over Kant, see Sami Naïr, "Goldmann's Legacy," *Telos* 48 (Summer 1981), p. 142f.

totality as a fundamental category of existence, or at least to recognize its problematic character."[33]

In opposition to the still influential neo-Kantian interpretation of Kant as a dualist hostile to the totalizing claims of speculative reason (*Vernunft*), Goldmann insisted that even in the *Critique of Pure Reason* totality played a central role. The very dichotomy of pure and practical reason, assumed by most commentators to be central to Kant, was not required by the logic of his system, which led towards their reconciliation. Rejecting the sterile alternative of empiricism or rationalism, Kant had pointed the way to their dialectical synthesis. Not even Emil Lask, whom Goldmann praised for his distinction between emanatist and formal logic, had appreciated the impulses in Kant leading from the latter to the former.

Totality, Goldmann contended, appeared in Kant in the dual form of the concepts of the universe and the human community. The latter was of particular importance because it anticipated the Marxist goal of a normative whole. The links between Kant and Marx had been seen by the earlier thinkers, including the Austro-Marxists with whom Goldmann had studied in Vienna,[34] but he was perhaps the first to argue that they existed as well in Kant's seemingly most ahistorical studies, including his critical epistemology:

In synthetic *a priori* judgments the community is postulated from the outset. The categories are, in spite of their reification, the theoretical expression of the human spirit and the human community.[35]

Kant, to be sure, was aware of the present inadequacy of the human community, and posited it as a regulative ideal to be achieved in the future. But in so doing, Goldmann contended, he was the first theorist to make it a practical task. Indeed, except for his indifference to the importance of classes, his short works on history strongly anticipated historical materialism.

Moreover, unlike a wide variety of irrationalist defenders of holism from Böhme to Heidegger,[36] Kant was careful not to subordinate the individual to the collective. Instead, he defended a totality

---

33. Ibid., p. 36.

34. I owe this observation to Agnes Heller, with whom I spoke in San Francisco in November, 1980.

35. Goldmann, *Immanuel Kant*, p. 154.

36. Ibid., p. 52. In the literature on Goldmann, it is sometimes argued that Heidegger was important for his thought, e.g., in Poster, *Existential Marxism in Postwar France*, p. 49 and Arato and Breines, *The Young Lukács*, p. 219. If this is so, Goldmann kept it well hidden in his dissertation. In addition to his criticism of Heidegger's mystical intuitionism, he also attacked him for seeing the whole as already given, whereas Kant understood it as still to be made (p.57). The only positive idea he seems to have taken from Heidegger is the distinction

where the *autonomy* of the parts and the *reality* of the whole are not only reconciled but constitute reciprocal conditions, where in place of the partial and one-sided solutions of the individual *or* the collective there appears the only total solution: that of the *person and the human community*.[37]

Kant was prevented from achieving a fully developed dialectical theory of totality, Goldmann admitted, by two obstacles, the first intellectual and the second social. As a Christian, Kant was deeply committed to a transcendent God; to have replaced him with an immanent one, as was necessary for a genuine dialectics, would have invited the unwelcome charge of Spinozan pantheism. And as a citizen of a "backward" and "sick" European nation still decades away from a democratic or industrial revolution, Kant could only register the yawning gap between totalistic desires and the lamentably fragmented state of affairs then prevalent in Germany. The distance between his essentially "tragic" view of the limits of totalizing reason and the more optimistic alternative in Hegel and Marx was thus largely a function of their different social situations.

Goldmann's unorthodox interpretation, for all its tendentious homogenizing of Kant's intellectual career and trivializing of his differences with his dialectical successors, was a provocative departure from previous attempts to link Kant and Marx on either universalistic moral grounds (Bernstein) or scientific epistemological ones (Max Adler). Unlike the first generation of Western Marxists, he was able to distinguish clearly between Kant and the neo-Kantians and to recognize in the former a legitimate source of Marx's thought. Goldmann's emphasis on the embryonic notion of totality in Kant did cast light on the practical-historical themes shared by the two thinkers. And his emphasis on the preservation of the individual component in both of their views of totality was a valuable corrective to those Marxists who identified the whole with the domination of the collective. Perhaps because of this insistence, Goldmann neglected to examine Kant's indebtedness to Rousseau, which was being explored at about the same time by Ernst Cassirer.[38] Rousseau's concept of the general will in *The Social Contract* may have seemed too inimical to

---

between authentic and inauthentic existence, which he saw as a synonym for Lukács' true and false consciousness. Although it is true that in *Immanuel Kant* Goldmann first advanced the controversial thesis that *Being and Time* was the bourgeois answer to *History and Class Consciousness*, this does not seem to me to indicate that Goldmann was influenced in a meaningful way by it.

37. Ibid., p. 53.

38. Ernst Cassirer, *Rousseau, Kant, Goethe* (Princeton, 1947); for a more recent treatment of the Rousseau-Kant relationship, see George Armstrong Kelly, *Idealism, Politics and History: Sources of Hegelian Thought* (Cambridge, 1969).

individualism for Goldmann to have considered it proto-Kantian. In any event, if he had probed the impact of Rousseau on Kant, it would have only made his case stronger.

More tellingly absent, as Goldmann himself later recognized,[39] was a consideration of the critical issue of subject-object identity, which as we have seen was central to Hegelian expressive views of totality. In his 1967 preface to the second French edition of his study of Kant, Goldmann claimed that his "Copernican Revolution" in epistemology "constituted a not insignificant step"[40] in the elaboration of that identity. Goldmann's omission in the original edition, however, may have had sounder reasons than he was willing to admit. For even if Kant's constitutive transcendental subjectivity may have partly overcome Cartesian dualism, he nonetheless firmly rejected the possibility of achieving full knowledge of things-in-themselves. The complete identity of subject and object on a human level was thus ruled out for Kant, who insisted on the separation of epistemology and ontology. Goldmann's "neglect" of this issue may have been just as well for his general argument. Moreover, as we will see shortly, Goldmann himself was soon to question the Hegelian identity theory of *History and Class Consciousness* and press for only a "partial identity"[41] of subject and object, which brought him in certain ways closer to Kant than to Hegel or Lukács.

Kant's own recognition of the non-identity of subject and object, for all his positing of totality as a regulative ideal, meant that he held to what Goldmann called a "tragic vision" of the world. This term, like totality, Goldmann admitted deriving from the young Lukács, indeed from the "younger," pre-Marxist author of the essay on "The Metaphysics of Tragedy" in *Soul and Form*. It was, as we have noted, appropriate to Kant's social situation, but, according to Goldmann, not to his alone:

The tragic vision of the world which sees the grandeur of man in his aspirations and his pettiness in the impossibility of realizing them, and which in German formed the ideology of the most advanced strata of the bourgeoisie, could develop in France only in one very specific part of the bourgeoisie, that of the *noblesse de robe*. The institution which most clearly expressed that ideology was Port-Royal, and it is no accident that the two great French tragic writers, Pascal and Racine, both came from there.[42]

39. In the preface to the second French edition of 1967.
40. Goldmann, *Immanuel Kant*, p. 14.
41. Goldmann, "Reflections on *History and Class Consciousness*," in *Aspects of History and Class Consciousness*, ed. István Mészáros (London, 1971), p. 73.
42. Goldmann, *Immanuel Kant*, p. 48.

After completing his dissertation on the German instance of the tragic vision, Goldmann turned his attention to the French and began the project that would culminate in his most important work, *The Hidden God*. Before its publication in 1956, more than a decade later, he composed the methodological studies that culminated in *The Human Sciences and Philosophy*.[43] In these statements, he spelled out the basic principles of all his later work, which remained remarkably consistent even with the shift, which we will discuss shortly, to a more Piagetian vocabulary.

In his 1948 essay "Dialectical Materialism and the History of Philosophy," Goldmann immediately made clear his adherence to the Lukácsian category of totality, approvingly citing the passage from *History and Class Consciousness* in which it is called the "bearer of the principle for revolution in science."[44] Accordingly, he claimed it was the first task of the researcher to ascertain the immanent coherence in the work of the thinker examined. Such coherence, he claimed, was most likely to be found in the work of truly great thinkers, who articulated the "world view"[45] of the social group from which they emerged far more clearly than did lesser thinkers. Lukács' notion of form in his earliest work, Goldmann contended, was, once divorced from its idealist origins, the key to grasping cultural phenomena. For there was a formal parallel between great works of philosophy and the world-views of social groups. World-views, he added, were finite in number, including for example rationalism, empiricism, dialectics, mystical intuitionism, pantheism and the tragic vision. Depending on the social circumstances of a specific group, one or another of these was most likely to suffuse its mentality. To demonstrate the links between the group and its world-view required, Goldmann admitted, a certain amount of schematization, but through a constant oscillation between whole and parts, the researcher could approach valid knowledge of the totality he chose to examine.

In so arguing, Goldmann was essentially faithful to Lukács, but in one important respect he was not. Lukács, it will be recalled, had justified his own ability to see things whole as an expression of the imputed class consciousness of the proletariat. Gramsci and Korsch, in different ways, had

43. See note 27.

44. Goldmann, "Materialisme dialectique et histoire de la philosophie," *Revue philosophique de la France et de l'étranger*, 138, 4–6 (April–June 1948), p. 162.

45. Ibid., p. 168. The term "*Weltanschauung*" was, of course, Dilthey's and may well have come to Goldmann through the work of Bernard Groethuysen, who was a prominent exile in France during the early 1940s. Goldmann always insisted it was more rigorously developed by Lukács than by Dilthey. See his discussion in *The Hidden God*, p. 14.

each assumed a similar relationship between his own views and that of the universal totalizer. Goldmann, however, never really reflected on the links between his totalistic claims and that of any collective social agent. Although he constantly emphasized the immanent character of dialectics, his own position was unmistakably transcendent to the social reality of his day. "In the great Marxist works," he would later write, ". . . the history of theories is bound to the development of totality where those theories are born as functional realities for collective subjects who are in the world,"[46] but it was never clear precisely for whom his totalizing perspective was functional. Thus, in Goldmann's hands, historical materialism became a mere research tool rather than the embodiment of the unity of theory and practice.

In *The Human Sciences and Philosophy*, he spoke approvingly of the importance of Lukács' concept of potential consciousness, which he felt was vital for an analysis of the relations between a work of philosophy and the essential, but not necessarily apparent, world-view of the group it expressed. But he added:

> In 1918 Georg Lukács referred to a reality-horizon (*réalité limite*) which seemed at that time to be near realization or even already present. This was contained in the *potential consciousness (conscience possible)* of the revolutionary proletariat. . . . Today we know (even Lukács knows it) that this reality-horizon, far from being present, was almost an apocalyptical vision. In any case, for us it has value primarily as an ideal concept, not as a practical reality.[47]

The implications of this development seem not to have fully appeared to Goldmann until sometime later and his confrontation with Adorno, who drew the radical consequence that truth and social genesis were unrelated. According to Goldmann in a lecture he gave in the late 1960s:

> If one does not accept Adorno's "critical consciousness," which judges and scans reality from on high, or the individual relation to global history as Lukács currently conceives it, if one wishes to maintain, no longer the idea of the revolutionary proletariat, but the requirements of Marx's dialectical thought (which always demands that one knows who is speaking and from where), of the subject-object totality, then the basic question arises of knowing who is, now, the subject of speech and action.[48]

46. Goldmann, *Lukács and Heidegger*, p. 76.
47. Goldmann, *The Human Sciences and Philosophy*, p. 51.
48. Goldmann, "The Topicality of the Question of the Subject" in *Lukács and Heidegger*, p. 96. Agnes Heller points out that the implication of this argument is that the intellectuals are the totalizing group, although the success of their cultural objectifications depends on their reception among non-intellectuals. See Heller, "Group Interest, Collective Consciousness, and the Role of the Intellectual in Lukács and Goldmann," *Social Praxis* 6, 3–4 (1979), p. 186.

This was indeed the question his method required, but his response was woefully inadequate:

There are situations in which one cannot give an answer because the group, from which speech and action come, is not yet manifest. In these situations, on the basis of a modified tradition, individuals speak by formulating perspectives and positions for which the group, the true subject, if it is not yet there, is in gestation or waiting to be elaborated.[49]

Goldmann's defense, with its almost Blochian reliance on a consciousness that anticipates a "true subject ... in gestation," did little to solve the problem of epistemological constitution that we have seen haunting the Western Marxist tradition from its inception.

Be that as it may, in the 1940s and 1950s Goldmann seems to have been little troubled by the implications of the separation of his own use of totality from the activity of a collective totalizer. Instead, bracketing the social roots of his own holistic vision, he concentrated on its power as a tool of research. Perhaps one reason that he neglected to reflect on the implications of his isolation was the subtle shift in his understanding of the relationship between totality and world-view away from that of Lukács'. For the latter, only the proletariat, both the subject and object of history, could have a truly total vision of reality; all other class perspectives were partial and thus ideological. For Goldmann, on the other hand, all true world-views, whether they be dialectical or not, were totalistic in their truth claims. In *The Human Sciences and Philosophy*, he suggested that

Perhaps the distinction between *ideologies* and *world-views* might be based pre-cisely on the *partial*—and for that reason distorting—character of the former, and the *total* character of the latter. At least for medieval and modern society that would allow us to link *world-views* to *social classes* so long as they still possess an ideal bearing on the totality of human community; and to link *ideologies* to all other social groups, and to classes in *decline*.[50]

There is an important uncoupling here of the concept of totality from that of the proletariat that shows Goldmann's distance from his mentor. Still, like Lukács, he wanted to argue that world-views were generated only by

49. Ibid., p. 97.
50. Goldmann, *The Human Sciences and Philosophy*, p. 103. As Alan Swingewood has observed, "It would seem impossible, given this definition, for world views to exist today unless they are Marxist, and since the vision creates the values which determine the aesthetic unity of the literary text, it would follow that modern literature is wholly ideological and partial" (Diana Laurenson and Alan Swingewood, *The Sociology of Literature* [London, 1972], p. 83). Goldmann, however, was never willing to draw this very Lukácsian conclusion.

collective subjects, which were pre-eminently but not exclusively social classes. The sociology of culture would therefore have to concern itself with the "trans-individual subjects" underlying the apparently individual artistic creator. The great creators, for reasons that Goldmann never really developed,[51] were able to express the *"maximum of potential consciousness"*[52] of their groups or classes. In their works was to be found that integral coherence, understood, to be sure, functionally rather than logically, which was the characteristic of true art. The researcher, Goldmann insisted, should not feel defensive about dwelling on the cultural products of an elite rather than on those of the masses, because only the former expressed the deepest level of a group's potential consciousness.

These precepts, first developed in the 1940s, were, with certain relatively superficial modifications, occasioned by his increasing use of Piaget, the basis of all his later work. With a doggedness that seemed to many observers excessive—as David Caute once remarked with gentle sarcasm, "Goldmann believed that a sound doctrine was worth repeating"[53]—he defended his methodology again and again. The centerpiece of his case was the only truly magisterial study of his career, *The Hidden God*. Published in the same year as the dramatic events unleashed by Khrushchev's de-Stalinization speech at the twentieth party congress of the CPSU, it coincided with the emerging French turn to a more critical and less orthodox Marxism. In this context, it created quite a stir and for a short while captured the fickle imaginations of Parisian intellectuals. Although soon surpassed by other infatuations, *The Hidden God*, among its other effects, brought the concept of totality squarely to the center of French Marxist concerns for the first time.

In his preface, Goldmann spelled out the "central idea" of his book:

that facts concerning man always form themselves into significant global structures, which are at one and the same time practical, theoretical and emotive, and that these structures can be studied in a scientific manner, that is to say they can be both explained and understood, only within a practical perspective based upon the acceptance of a certain set of values.[54]

The particular global structure he chose, as we have seen, was that of the "tragic vision," whose configuration was derived from Lukács' essay in *Soul and Form*, Hegel's discussion of tragedy in his *Aesthetics* and the

51. Goldmann theoretically reserved a place for psychological literary criticism, but never developed it in his own work. As a result, he saw genius solely in terms of representability; the greater the writer, the more he expressed the potential consciousness of his class.

52. Goldmann, *The Human Sciences and Philosophy*, p. 129.

53. David Caute, *Collisions: Essays and Reviews* (London, 1974), p. 220.

54. Goldmann, *The Hidden God*, p. ix.

chapter on ethical order in the *Phenomenology*. In essence, the tragic vision was that of a world from which God had fled (the *Deus absconditus* of his title) and was thus a world without its bearings. Although incapable of conceiving an historical transformation of this situation, holders of this world-view were nonetheless adamant in their refusal to accept it with equanimity. Instead they demanded the unattainable, a life of absolute meaningfulness, what we have called normative totality. This demand was seen as coming from their "hidden God," who in Goldmann's words:

forbids the slightest degree of compromise, and constantly reminds man—who lives in a universe where life is made possible only by approximations—that a true calling is one devoted to the quest for wholeness and authenticity.[55]

Put schematically, Goldmann attempted to show that this world view was the meaningful structure underlying both Pascal's *Pensées* and Racine's tragedies, that it more generally expressed the religious philosophy of the Jansenists at Port-Royal, and that ultimately it reflected the consciousness of the *noblesse de robe*, at that time engaged in a losing struggle to resist the growing absolutist power of the French monarchy. How successful Goldmann was in defending this argument we will leave to students of the seventeenth century. Nor will we trouble ourselves with deciding its originality.[56] What will interest us instead are certain methodological aspects of the book that bear most closely on the question of totality.

In many ways, *The Hidden God* was a continuation of the argument of *Immanuel Kant*, but his change of focus from Kant to Pascal had an important result. By moving back the starting point of the dialectical tradition—the tragic vision being for Goldmann more genuinely proto-dialectical than any other world-view—he subtly introduced a new emphasis in his explanation of Marxist holism. The concept of totality, he now claimed, was already present in the work of Pascal, to whom he also gave the honor of being called "the first modern man."[57] It was, of course, expressed in the *Pensées* more as a desideratum than an accomplished fact, but as the following passage shows it was central to Pascal's world-view:

55. Ibid., p. 38. The existentialist term "authenticity" has sometimes been taken as evidence of Heidegger's impact on Goldmann; see, for example, Ferenc Feher, "Is the Novel Problematic? A Contribution to the Theory of the Novel," *Telos* 15 (Spring 1973), p. 60.

56. George Lichtheim contended that virtually all of the same arguments could be found in Franz Borkenau's *Der Übergang vom feudalen zum bürgerlichen Weltbild* (Paris, 1934). See his review of *The Hidden God* in *The Concept of Ideology and Other Essays* (New York, 1967), p. 279. According to Mme. Goldmann in my interview with her, Goldmann had not known Borkenau's book when he wrote *The Hidden God*. Henri Lefebvre had also already developed the connection between Pascal and Jansenism in his *Pascal* (Paris, 1949).

57. Goldmann, *The Hidden God*, p. 171.

If man were to begin by studying himself, he would see how incapable he is of going beyond himself (*passer outre*). How could it be possible for a part to know the whole? But he may perhaps aspire to a knowledge of at least those parts which are on the same scale as he himself. But the different parts of the world are all so closely linked and related together that I hold it to be impossible to know one without knowing the other and without knowing the whole.[58]

Because Pascal recognized the necessity of holistic knowledge, he was more progressive than Descartes and the Enlightenment tradition that he spawned.

In the seemingly liberating act of denying God, the rationalists had also destroyed the concept of totality, in particular "the two closely connected ideas of the community and the universe, and had replaced them by the totally different concepts of the isolated individual and of infinite space."[59] Although a rationalist attempt to grasp the totality had been made by Spinoza, the mainstream of rationalist thought had led to its suppression. Rationalism and totalistic thinking, Goldmann concluded, were thus deeply at odds. Goldmann, to be sure, carefully distinguished between Cartesian *raison*, which he identified with the German *Verstand*, and the synthesizing, dialectical reason (*Vernunft*), to which Pascal's "heart" led. But the implication of his argument was that the Enlightenment and dialectical thinking were ultimately opposed.

With this Pascalian view of the limits of *raison*, Goldmann was not surprisingly able to admit the irrationalist underpinnings of dialectical holism. This admission appeared most clearly in his discussion of Pascal's celebrated wager on divine existence. Like Bloch, whose work he did not know (or at least did not acknowledge), Goldmann was willing to emphasize the similarities between Marxism and religion. Just as Pascal had bet on God, so the Marxist, Goldmann contended, bet on history and the future. Marxism could therefore arguably be understood as a kind of faith, although one without transcendental values:

Marxist faith is faith in the future which men make for themselves in and through history. Or more accurately, in the future that we make for ourselves by what we do, so that this faith becomes a "wager" which we make that our actions will, in fact, be successful. The transcendental element present in this faith is not supernatural and does not take us outside or beyond history; it merely takes us beyond the individual. This is sufficient to enable us to claim that Marxist thought leaps over six centuries of Thomist and Cartesian rationalism and renews the Augustinian tradition.[60]

58. Quoted in ibid., p. 5.
59. Ibid., p. 27.
60. Ibid., p. 90.

Marxism, therefore, is "certainly a religion, but a religion with no God, a religion of man and of humanity."[61]

Such an irrationalist view of the ultimate ground of Marxism, which can perhaps be detected as well in Goldmann's insistence elsewhere on the similarities between Lukács' notion of totality and Heidegger's concept of Being,[62] may be a franker explanation of its appeal to certain adherents than is generally found in Marxist writings. Lukács, for example, had damned Pascal only two years earlier in *The Destruction of Reason* as a forerunner of fascist irrationalism.[63] But by admitting the elements of irrationalism at the root of Marxism, Goldmann opened himself up to the charge of decisionism, which, as we will see when examining Habermas, was a troublesome issue for other Western Marxists.

More broadly understood, Goldmann's admission of the wager underlying Dialectical Materialism can be seen as part of his general retreat from that confidence in the power of holistic thought we observed at the outset of the Western Marxist paradigm. Thus, for example, rather than embracing the longitudinal view of history as a coherent and meaningful totality, Goldmann conceded that

It is impossible for man to know history as a whole, both because his interpretation of the past always depends upon future events, and because he himself is inside history and therefore cannot achieve the "objective" knowledge available to the physical scientist.[64]

Accordingly, the researcher had to be satisfied with only relative totalities and eschew the meta-totality linking them all together, for "we can never actually reach a totality which is no longer an element or part of a greater whole."[65]

61. Ibid., p. 172.

62. In *Lukács and Heidegger,* he wrote, "In order to express approximate, at times nearly identical, ideas, Lukács will speak about 'totality' where Heidegger will use the word 'Being'; about 'man' where Heidegger will create the term 'Being-there'; about 'praxis' where Heidegger will use the term '*Zuhandenheit*' (approximately: 'manipulability')" (p. 10). In so arguing, Goldmann tended to minimize the differences between Heidegger and Marxism that were emphasized by other Western Marxists, such as Lukács and Adorno.

63. George Lukács, *The Destruction of Reason,* trans. Peter Palmer (London, 1980), pp. 114–16. Lukács' own connection to Marxism had, as we have seen, something of the irrational quality of a Pascalian wager, and in some of his earlier work he argued for making a decision to embrace Marxism. For a comparison of his more specific wager on the proletariat with Goldmann's more general bet on the future of mankind, see Heller, "Group Interest, Collective Consciousness, and the Role of the Intellectual in Lukács and Goldmann," pp. 190–91.

64. Goldmann, *The Hidden God,* p. 95. There are, to be sure, other passages in Goldmann's work where he does seem to adopt the notion of longitudinal totality. See, for example, *Lukács and Heidegger,* p. 76, where he talks of current theories taking their place "as a stage in the history of a totality which is evolving."

65. Goldmann, *The Hidden God,* p. 12.

Implied in this concession was a criticism of Lukács' attempt in *History and Class Consciousness* to restrict the totality to human history and exclude the natural world. Although it is clear that Goldman did not want to restore the dialectics of nature of Engels or Stalin,[66] he recognized the inadequacy of Lukács' overly historicist alternative. In *The Human Sciences and Philosophy*, he had remarked that human behavior "concerns a *relative* totality which is only one element of the totality men-nature."[67] In *The Hidden God*, he added that

It is, in my view, interesting to note that this problem of the relationship between dialectical thought and the possibility of arriving at an understanding of the physical universe is still far from being solved today. Most dialectical thinkers, Marx, Lenin and Lukács, have not even dealt with it, preferring to limit their enquiries to a purely historical domain.[68]

But precisely how one should treat the man-nature relationship, which we have seen troubling so many other Western Marxists, Goldmann did not say. Perhaps because of his almost complete indifference to the materialist dimension of Dialectical Materialism, he never really probed the implications of this disturbing issue for Marxist holism.

It was, however, in the very act of raising the question that he showed a certain wavering in his allegiance to Lukács' argument. In fact, *The Hidden God* contains several hints of his uneasiness with the Hegelian-Marxist recipe for overcoming the tragic vision. Commenting on the popularity of existentialism in France during the period of the book's inception, he wrote,

Once again, the most honest thinkers have been compelled to recognize the existence of the dichotomy which had already struck Pascal between justice and force, between man's hopes and the human predicament.

It is also our present historical situation which has not only made us more aware of the ambiguity of the world and of the inauthentic nature of daily life, but which has also revived our interest in the tragic writers and thinkers of the past.[69]

Later in the book, he added,

From the medieval masters of the spiritual life to Marx, Engels, Lenin and Lukács, all such thinkers tend to overestimate the chances of success and to underestimate

66. Ibid., p. 195.
67. Goldmann, *The Human Sciences and Philosophy*, p. 143.
68. Goldmann, *The Hidden God*, p. 244.
69. Ibid., p. 61. He then added in a footnote, "This was written in 1952. Since then, the historical situation has changed, and both Sartre and Merleau-Ponty have modified their respective ideological attitudes—in opposite directions, it may be added."

the opposition of reality. They all continue to think that victory is just around the corner at the very moment that reality comes and destroys their illusions.[70]

It is perhaps because of the doubts that passages like these betray that Goldmann after *The Hidden God* turned more explicitly to Piaget in defining his methodology.[71] For although he never abandoned his contention of a wager at the heart of Marxism, Goldmann was able to use Piaget's genetic epistemology as a more scientifically secure anthropological ground for his work, which was then coming under attack for its lack of scientificity by the emerging structuralist movement. As William Boelhower has put it,

Goldmann collected certain macro-analytical categories (totality, world view, form, the transindividual subject and possible consciousness-objective consciousness) from Lukács and grounded them in a series of positive and anthropological categories taken from Piaget (significant structure, function, the structuration-destructuration process, the epistemological circle of the subject and object, equilibrium). His intention was to convert the categories Lukács used in a philosophical and merely descriptive way into methodological prototypes that would prove to be highly functional, rather than ideological instruments.[72]

The change seems to have come, or at least was publicly announced, in the collection of essays, *Recherches dialectiques*, Goldmann published in 1959 and dedicated to Piaget. In addition to two earlier essays containing references to Piaget's ideas, the volume included a new piece entitled "The Concept of Significant Structure in the History of Culture,"[73] in which a more distinctly structuralist vocabulary appeared.

Goldmann, however, always insisted that there was no radical break between his early and later periods. Like Piaget himself,[74] he denied the antithesis between dialectical and structuralist thought. Both challenged the assumption that the only variety of structuralism was the synchronic

70. Ibid., p. 187.
71. There were, it should be acknowledged, places in Goldmann's earlier work where Piaget's importance was mentioned, for example, in *The Hidden God*, pp. 15, 94, 100, 132, 187, and 258. But he remained overshadowed by Lukács until later in Goldmann's development.
72. Boelhower, intro. to *Essays on Method in the Sociology of Literature*, p. 8.
73. In English in *Essays on Method in the Sociology of Literature*.
74. According to Piaget, "In the domain of the sciences themselves structuralism has always been linked with a constructivism from which the epithet 'dialectical' can hardly be withheld—the emphasis upon historical development, opposition between contraries, and "*Aufhebungen*" ("*dépassements*") is surely just as characteristic of constructivism as of dialectic, and that the idea of wholeness figures centrally in structuralist as in dialectical modes of thought is obvious." Jean Piaget, *Structuralism*, trans. and ed. Chaninah Maschler (New York, 1970), p. 121.

kind associated with Claude Lévi-Strauss. Instead, they argued for a diachronic, genetic alternative. It was this image of structuralism that allowed Goldmann to claim that Lukács was actually a genetic structuralist *avant la lettre*,[75] an honor that one doubts the Hungarian would have found to his liking.

What drew Goldmann to Piaget was less his psychology per se than its epistemological implications, in particular his demonstration that structures, which he saw as irreducible wholes rather than aggregates of component elements, were constituted through active intervention in the world. Rather than being derived from a transcendental, ahistorical rationality, as they were for Lévi-Strauss, structures for Piaget were generated through a dialectical process of assimilation and accommodation. As early as *The Hidden God*,[76] Goldmann had noted the parallels between Piaget's argument and that of Marx in *Capital* concerning the labor process as a reciprocal interaction of man and nature. For Goldmann, Piaget provided a deeper understanding of this interaction than even Marx had been able to provide.

Goldmann was also impressed with Piaget's contention that human action had as its telos the achievement of a new homeostatic equilibrium.[77] Here, it seemed, was anthropological evidence for that aspiration for totality so much a part of the Western Marxist tradition. In Goldmann's words:

One of the essential tenets of both psychoanalysis at the level of the individual subject and of dialectical thought at the social and historical level is precisely the assumption that all human acts—resulting from the behavior of an individual or transindividual subject whose action is directed to transforming the world surrounding it in such a way as to create an equilibrium more in keeping with its aspirations—possess as such the quality of functional structures or significant structures.[78]

Or to put it differently, there was no structuralism without an accompanying functionalism, an entailment that purely synchronic structuralism obscured. Only a Marxist genetic structuralism, combining the insights of Lukács and Piaget, was thus adequate to the complexity of social reality.

In adopting Piaget's vocabulary to reformulate Lukács' holism, Goldmann, as we have noted, insisted on the continuity of his thought. There was, however, a subtle weakening of his fidelity to Hegelian Marxism,

---

75. Goldmann, "Lukács" in *Encyclopaedia Universalis,* p. 138.
76. Goldmann, *The Hidden God,* pp. 15–16.
77. Piaget recognized a tight fit between his own views on this issue and cybernetics, which Goldmann seems not to have acknowledged. See Piaget's remarks in Evans, *Piaget: the Man and his Ideas,* p. 48.
78. Goldmann, "Reflections on *History and Class Consciousness,*" p. 75.

which went beyond that we have already observed in *The Hidden God*. In moving away from emphasizing the philosophical dimension of Marxism in favor of its social scientific side, Goldmann subtly transformed the concept of the collective subject that we have seen was so crucial to Hegelian Marxism in general and the early Lukács in particular. Distancing himself from the idealist roots of *History and Class Consciousness*, he now spoke only of a partial identity of subject and object as the very best the human sciences might attain.[79] Even more tellingly, he attempted to exorcise all remnants of transcendentalism from his definition of the transindividual subject, which he now discussed in strictly behavioral terms. When challenged at a 1966 conference on structuralism at the Johns Hopkins Humanities Center to defend the ontological status of his transindividual subject, Goldmann replied,

I would like to specify that I did not use the term transindividual consciousness. There is no consciousness except in the individual. But I say that to understand the consciousness of the individual, his youth, his transformations, I must link them to behavior, not to his behavior, but to behavior in which he does not have the status of the subject.[80]

Such behavior, Goldmann contended, was intrasubjective rather than intersubjective. That is, "Individual subjects—or individual consciousnesses—by acting within behavior patterns which in turn go through the division of labor—become transindividual."[81]

If, however, this transindividual subject was constituted behaviorally rather than through a shared consciousness, what was its status when it was not actually engaged in a collective task? Did it immediately dissolve into its constituent individual subjects and thus detotalize or destructure itself? For Goldmann, in fact, as for Piaget, the process of structuration had its reverse side, as destructuration was always a possibility. Thus like Sartre, whose concepts of totalization and detotalization we will examine in the next chapter, Goldmann's faith in the permanence of totalization was far shakier than had been that of Lukács, whose definition of collective subjectivity was far more philosophical, that is, essentialist, than behavioral or empirical. Although Lukács' version was prone to idealist hypostatizations of meta-subjects that never really existed, Goldmann's courted nominalist disintegration.

In addition and perhaps more seriously, by insisting on a purely behavioral definition of intrasubjectivity Goldmann risked rendering his sociol-

79. Ibid., p. 73.
80. Goldmann, discussion following his paper in *The Structuralist Controversy*, ed. Richard Macksey and Eugenio Donato (Baltimore and London, 1972), p. 114.
81. Goldmann, "Structure: Human Reality and Methodological Concept" in *The Structuralist Controversy*, p. 102.

ogy of literature, with its dependence on collective world-views, incoherent. For what were the behavioral criteria by which the researcher might identify such common visions? Surely, they could only be inferred from the cultural traces left behind by acts of objectifying consciousness. Insofar as Goldmann always demanded that these acts be understood as communal rather than purely individual, he depended on a notion of collective consciousness that his behavioral definition of intra-subjectivity appeared to deny.

This difficulty was only one of many that plagued his sociology of literature, as it was developed in the years after *The Hidden God*. Its most important statement was his 1964 study *Towards a Sociology of the Novel*, which drew heavily on Lukács' typology in *The Theory of the Novel*, supplemented by the work of René Girard.[82] Once again, he argued for a close relationship between the form of the novel and the structure of society. His working hypothesis was that

The novel form seems to be *the transformation on the literary plane of everyday life in individualistic society born of production for the market*. There is a *rigorous homology* between the literary form of the novel as we have just defined it following Lukács and Girard, and the everyday relationship of men with goods in general—and, by extension, of men with other men—in a society producing for the market.[83]

Goldmann's main analysis was directed at twentieth-century texts, most notably those of Malraux and Robbe-Grillet. Without Lukács' rancorous hostility to modernism, he probed the ways in which these works were homologously related to the social tendencies of the modern world.

Without going into Goldmann's specific treatments of these writers, or his later discussions of other modernists such as Genet, Gombrowicz or Saint-John Perse,[84] one central problem which troubled many of his critics[85] must be mentioned. In stressing the "rigorous homology" between literature and society, Goldmann was vulnerable to the reproach of reverting to that crudely reductionist derivation of the superstructure from the base, that the Western Marxist stress on totality had been introduced to overcome. Some commentators, in fact, even detected a trace of Hippolyte

82. In particular, Girard's *Deceit, Desire and the Novel; Self and Other in Literary Structure*, trans. Yvonne Freccero (Baltimore, 1965).
83. Goldmann, *Towards a Sociology of the Novel*, p. 7.
84. For a list of Goldmann's treatments of these authors, see the bibliography in *Cultural Creation in Modern Society*.
85. For example, Terry Eagleton, *Marxism and Literary Criticism* (Berkeley, 1976); Raymond Williams, "From Leavis to Goldmann: In Memory of Lucien Goldmann," *New Left Review* 67 (May–June 1971); Robert Weimann, "French Structuralism and Literary History: Some Critiques and Reconsiderations," *New Literary History* 4, 3 (Spring 1973); and Miriam Glucksmann, "Lucien Goldmann, Humanist or Marxist?," *New Left Review* 56 (July–August 1969).

Taine's positivist reduction of literature to its social milieu.[86] The charge was given further credence by Goldmann's willingness to discern homologies not only between literature and society, but between literature and philosophy as well. The specificity of the literary and the speculative disappeared as he turned them respectively into imaginative and cognitive versions of the same structure, which was then seen as rigorously homologous to a social structure.

These, of course, had been the working assumptions of *The Hidden God*, but now applied to more recent cultural phenomena, their forced and arbitrary quality became blatant. Goldmann divided the history of Western capitalism into three separate periods, each with its own characteristic philosophy and literature. The first, which began with the origins of bourgeois society and lasted until around 1910, was the individualist period of "liberal capitalism" in which the concept of totality was missing from consciousness. In philosophy, this period was marked by empiricism and rationalism, and in literature by the classical novel of the problematic hero who sought community but was thwarted in his efforts. The second era was that of "capitalism in crisis," or imperialism, which extended from the 1910s until World War II. Its representative philosophy was existentialism and its literature the modernism of Kafka, Musil, Sartre and Camus. The third stage, that of the Gaullist present, Goldmann characterized as "organized or technocratic capitalism," in which economic crises were contained through the self-regulating integration of society. In philosophy its correlate was non-genetic structuralism, and in literature, the *nouveau roman* of Robbe-Grillet, Sarraute, etc., which registered the total reification of consciousness. Unlike the earlier periods, "in organizational capitalism the awareness of totality appears to be the fundamental phenomenon, at least on the level of the will and behavior of managers and directors."[87]

Goldmann's periodization was tempered by occasional qualifications, but even regarded generously, it does not bear close scrutiny. Aside from the fact that historians now tend to see the beginnings of "organized capitalism" in the reactions to the Great Depression of 1873–96 or at least in the mobilization of economies during the First World War,[88] the notion

86. Serge Doubrovsky, *The New Criticism in France*, trans. Derek Coltman, intro. Edward Wasiolek (Chicago and London, 1973), p. 180; and Elizabeth and Tom Burns, introduction to *Sociology of Literature and Drama* (London, 1973), p. 20. Taine, it should be noted, spoke not only of milieu, but also of race and historical moment.

87. Goldmann, "The Revolt of Arts and Letters in Advanced Civilizations," in *Cultural Creation in Modern Society*, p. 55.

88. See, for example, the essays in *Organisierter Kapitalismus*, ed. Heinrich August Winkler (Göttingen, 1974). The term was first used by Rudolf Hilferding in 1915. Goldmann seems to have had a narrowly French perspective in identifying it with the onset of Gaullism in 1958.

that the concept of totality disappeared during the period of liberal capitalism is false, as we had ample opportunity to observe in Chapter One. Moreover, as Goldmann himself admitted, the novel of the problematic hero "is not homologous to empiricism, to rationalism, or to Enlightenment philosophy,"[89] but can rather be seen as a critical genre in which yearning for totality was a potent impulse. As for the era of "capitalism in crisis," it can be argued that Western Marxism was just as representative of the culture of the period as was existentialism. If we stress the Heideggerian rather than Sartrean version of the latter, the concept of totality, as Goldmann himself argued, was already present in distorted form in the idea of Being. Moreover, since neither existentialism nor Western Marxism made much headway in two of the most advanced capitalist countries, Britain and America, the whole notion of a homology between philosophy and social structure on a global level seems highly problematic. In literary terms, as Goldmann admitted in discussing Malraux (and in mentioning Martin du Gard, Galsworthy and Mann), modernist novels of despair were by no means the only "representative" works of this period.

Finally, Goldmann's characterization of the contemporary period, in addition to its being completely dominated by a provincial French perspective, fails to account for the events of May, 1968, and the New Leftist counterculture in general. Although he tried to salvage his argument by using Genet as an example of a critical avant-garde in opposition to Robbe-Grillet (whose alleged complicity with reification is by no means so certain[90]), the effort was fraught with difficulties. The basis of these was his insistence that totalities were organized homologously. As one critic more favorable to non-genetic structuralism put it, "Goldmann appears to be ignorant of Lévi-Strauss's analysis of myth, which conceives of many possible relations between the structure of this cultural product and other structures: homologous, inverse, mirror image or transposed in some other way."[91] There was, in other words, little appreciation in Goldmann of the temporal pluralities and discontinuities that we have seen discussed in Bloch and will encounter again in Althusser.

Goldmann, to be sure, vigorously resisted the accusations made against him of simplistic reductionism, contending:

The reproach of being a partisan of reflection theory and of neglecting mediation by the collective consciousness is entirely without foundation. I have in the totality of my works criticized and permanently refuted reflection theory and insisted on taking into account in a genuinely dialectical manner *all* the multiple and complex

89. Goldmann, "The Revolt of Arts and Letters in Advanced Civilizations," p. 53.
90. See the defense of Robbe-Grillet in Glucksmann, p. 59.
91. Ibid.

aspects of mediation through the collective consciousness as well as its active and dynamic character.[92]

But, in addition to the problems we have noted in his concept of the collective consciousness, Goldmann's bias towards homologies, his Piagetian faith in the telos of equilibration, meant that he underplayed the real complexity of the whole. It was as if he transposed that bias for aesthetic order, which is central to Platonic and Aristotelian notions of art, to culture as a totality and then sought to do the same for the relationship between culture and society.

Although Goldmann may have begun to assimilate some of the criticisms directed towards this problem in his later work,[93] in general he remained a staunch supporter of Lukács' concept of totality as filtered through Piaget. In an essay on "The Dialectic Today," delivered at the *Praxis* summer school on the island of Korcula in August, 1970, only a month before his death, he energetically defended it once again:

The first, principal idea of dialectical thought is the category of totality. This is no accident: a dialectician cannot do the history of ideas outside the history of society: as Hegel, I think, or Lukács said, the history of the problem is the problem of history; or, the history of ideas forms part of the history of facts. Totality is the idea that a phenomenon can be comprehended only by first inserting it in the broader structure of which it is part and in which it has a function, the latter being its objective meaning independently of whether or not the men acting and creating it are conscious of it. It is the category of meaningful structure, which can be comprehended only by inserting it in a broader meaningful structure and in the whole of history.[94]

In his last years, Goldmann perceived two major threats to this idea from within Western Marxism itself: the Frankfurt School's non-identity theory and Althusser's anti-humanism.[95]

In many ways, Goldmann identified himself with Critical Theory, defending for example its appreciation of modernism against Lukács' rigid repudiation and agreeing with its analysis of the manipulation of working-class consciousness. But he balked at what he saw as its one-dimensionally negative, pessimistic side. Still committed to his own wager on the future, he could never bring himself to accept the Frankfurt School's

92. Goldmann, "Reponse à MM. Elsberg et Jones" in *Structures mentales et création culturelle*, pp. 392–93.

93. This is the argument of Marc Zimmerman, "Exchange and Production: Structuralist and Marxist Approaches to Literature," *Praxis* 2, 4 (1978), p. 163.

94. Goldmann, "The Dialectic Today" in *Cultural Creation in Modern Society*, p. 112.

95. See Zima for a good discussion of Goldmann's two-front war with these opponents. For a comparison of Goldmann with the Frankfurt School's major sociologist of knowledge, see Robert Sayre, "Lowenthal, Goldmann and the Sociology of Literature," *Telos* 45 (Fall 1980).

bitter realization that all bets were off. "I would say," he remarked at the Royaumont conference on the sociology of literature in 1968,

that perhaps the greatest difference between Theodor Adorno and me is that I have always insisted on the necessity of accounting for two parallel elements, dogmatism and criticism, and on the danger of neglecting either of them. I have explained that even on the level of scientific thought, it is impossible to bypass the creation of objects. Correlating certain sensations involved in creating an object, and from that, creating world views and systems—this is the order of dogmatism, introduced by the spirit in order to orient itself.[96]

One aspect of this "dogmatism" was Goldmann's insistence that dialectics was both monistic and immanent; there were no Archimedean points, he claimed, outside of the totality. Because Adorno failed to understand this impossibility, because he misunderstood the importance of a positive dialectics, he regressed to "Neo-Kantian thought and to the dualism of subject and object which Lukács and Heidegger had transcended, thus taking up the position of Bruno Bauer's and Max Stirner's *Critical Consciousness*."[97] Likewise, so Goldmann contended, Adorno's defense of art as fragmentary and devoid of immediate meaning failed to see that every fragment could be put into a larger meaningful framework. Adorno's claim that such meaning had to be brought from without by the critic himself was incorrect; for the "truth value" of works of art could be discovered by recognizing the larger context in which they belonged.[98] Nor was Adorno right in calling for a partially mediated juxtaposition of sociological and psychological methods in approaching that larger context. If any psychology were necessary, it would be better to employ Piaget's genetic structuralism, which could be smoothly integrated into a sociological analysis, than a Freudian psychoanalysis that could not.[99]

Goldmann's criticism of the Frankfurt School's failure to grasp a positive dialectics led him to claim it damaged not only Adorno's aesthetics, but even such works as Marcuse's *Reason and Revolution*, that most apparently Hegelian of all Critical Theory texts. Rereading it in the late 1960s, he concluded:

One can see that it is not truly "dialectical": it uses Hegel and an Hegelian language to return to a Kantian and Fichtean position, brought up to date and radicalized, and in some respects close to Sartre. For, though *Reason and Revolution*

    96. "Goldmann and Adorno: To Describe, Understand and Explain" in *Cultural Creation in Modern Society*, pp. 137–38.
    97. Goldmann, *Lukács and Heidegger*, p. 92.
    98. Goldmann, *Cultural Creation in Modern Society*, p. 147.
    99. See, for example, his critique of Freud in "Genetic-Structuralist Method in History of Literature" in *Marxism and Art: Writings in Aesthetics and Criticism*, ed. Berel Lang and Forrest Williams (New York, 1972), p. 251.

may be radical and critical, nowhere does it contain the idea of the identity of subject and object, of reason and reality, fundamental to the belief that the only valid and realizable goals are those discoverable within the real tendencies of the social process.[100]

Although, as we have seen, Goldmann was hard pressed himself to identify the genuinely revolutionary agent in the contemporary world,[101] settling instead for only a partial subject-object identity, he nonetheless rejected what he called the complete abandonment of the Hegelian belief in those "real social tendencies of the social process" leading to radical change. Resisting the Frankfurt School's withdrawal from politics, he conflated their analysis with that of the liberal "end-of-ideology" theorists of the 1950s and early 1960s:

Must we acknowledge as correct what Raymond Aron, Daniel Bell, Herbert Marcuse, Claude Lévi-Strauss, or Roland Barthes have said? I do not think so. Social reality is much more complex than it appears to these theoreticians who are confusing a relatively short period of transition with an historical period or with a fundamental and "a-historical" state of humanity.[102]

Goldmann's own practical response to this quietism, which drew largely on "new working class" theorists, was what he called "revolutionary reformism." Spurning Leninist forms of party organization, while trying to avoid falling back into parliamentary reformism, he contended that radicalized technocrats and white-collar workers would begin to demand the rights of self-management characteristic of workers' soviets. Radical political change would then follow the economic transformation produced by the meeting of this demand. There was a great deal of wishful thinking in all of this, as even some of Goldmann's supporters have acknowledged,[103] and it is clear that his ultimate reputation will not rest on his concrete economic or political arguments. As an antidote to the Frankfurt School's "strategy of hibernation," they proved sadly ineffective.

100. Goldmann, "Understanding Marcuse," *Partisan Review* 38, 3 (1971), p. 252.
101. Richard Wolin thus seems to me to be mistaken in his otherwise excellent essay "The De-aestheticization of Art: On Adorno's *Aesthetische Theorie*," *Telos* 41 (Fall 1979), in arguing that Goldmann differed from Adorno in believing "in the proletariat as the legitimate agent of social transformation" (p. 125). Goldmann needed a functional equivalent for the proletariat in his theory, but he had difficulty finding one.
102. Goldmann, *Power and Humanism,* trans. Brian Trench (London, 1974), p. 26. In so arguing Goldmann was implicitly criticizing his own position during the Gaullist era. See Naïr, "Goldmann's Legacy," p. 147.
103. See, for example, William W. Mayrl's intro. to *Cultural Creation in Modern Society*, p. 25. Goldmann himself shortly before his death called his analysis "not false but schematic and unilateral" ("The Dialectic Today," p. 115). It should be noted that the concept of "revolutionary reformism" was not new in French socialist theory. It had been used by certain syndicalists in the nineteenth century. See Theodor Zeldin, *France, 1848–1945: Ambition and Love* (Oxford, 1979), p. 233.

328 Totality and Marxist Aesthetics: Goldmann

On Goldmann's other flank was a different adversary from the Frankfurt School, far more influential on the French scene: the structuralist Marxism of Althusser and his followers.[104] Like Lefebvre, Garaudy, Sartre and other defenders of a humanist or existentialist Marxism, he excoriated the ahistorical, anti-subjectivist, anti-praxis implications of what he saw as a new attempt to restore the nondialectical, rationalist holism of Spinoza.[105] As part of his general defense of a genetic as opposed to linguistic structuralism, Goldmann interpreted the latter's privileging of *langue* over *parole* as a symptom of the dehumanizing ideology of the era of organized capitalism. Although he did acknowledge that Althusser's critique of the ubiquitous use of the concept of alienation had its force,[106] he steadfastly held to the Lukácsian notion of reification as a key explanatory tool. And, needless to say, he remained deeply committed to an essentially Lukácsian notion of totality, however much he may have watered it down.

Goldmann's efforts against these opponents enjoyed only a limited success, especially in France. The orthodox Marxist critics around such journals as *La Nouvelle Critique* were never won over to his methods.[107] Students of seventeenth-century literature in the 1960s were more likely to turn to the studies of Racine by Roland Barthes or Charles Mauron than to *The Hidden God*.[108] Sartreans like Serge Doubrovsky challenged Goldmann's assumption of a trans-individual subject.[109] Pierre Macherey's *A Theory of Literary Production* converted still others to a more Althusserian method of cultural criticism, while the *Tel Quel* group around Julia Kristeva and Philippe Sollers demonstrated the power of combining Marxism with semiotics,[110] and in the process undermined the Aristotelian premises of Goldmann's conception of art. Increasingly interested in the "materiality" of texts, they protested against Goldmann's reduction of literary products to mere microcosms of world-views. Even

104. For a discussion of Goldmann and Althusser, see Hermann Baum, "Humanismus und Ideologie bei Lucien Goldmann und Louis Althusser," *Philosophisches Jahrbuch* 1 (Halbband, 1972).
105. Goldmann, "The Social Structure and the Collective Consciousness of Structures" in *Essays on Method in the Sociology of Literature*, p. 87.
106. Goldmann, *Lukács and Heidegger*, p. 90.
107. The November 1956 issue of the journal was devoted to a critique of *The Hidden God*. For Goldmann's response, see "*Le Dieu Caché, 'la Nouvelle critique' et le Marxisme*" in *Structures mentales et création culturelle.*
108. Roland Barthes, *Sur Racine* (Paris, 1963); Charles Mauron, *Inconscient dans l'oeuvre et la vie de Racine* (Paris, 1957).
109. Doubrovsky, *The New Criticism in France*, p. 212f.
110. Pierre Machery, *A Theory of Literary Production*, trans. Geoffrey Wall (London, 1978); for a discussion of the *Tel Quel* circle, see Jonathan Culler, *Structuralist Poetics: Structuralism, Linguistics and the Study of Literature* (London, 1975), chapter 10.

Henri Lefebvre, who might be seen as Goldmann's Hegelian Marxist bed-fellow, wrote disparagingly of genetic structuralism for dealing only with mental structures. "It abuses the concept of totality taken in itself," he complained. "It risks becoming neither genetic nor structural."[111]

Politically, despite the enthusiasm of Serge Mallet,[112] Goldmann's "revolutionary reformism" proved a non-starter. Although Goldmann did have appreciative students both in Paris and Brussels who attempted to carry forward his methods, it is significant that several of the best, such as Pierre Zima and Michael Lowy,[113] were like him not native Frenchmen. In France, as David Caute observed, "At congresses and seminars, young radical audiences were usually baffled by the clinical jargon he employed, and nowhere glimpsed within his doctrines that gleam of revolutionary hope provided by Marcuse."[114] In short, it is hard to contest George Lichtheim's verdict that Goldmann's efforts to acclimatize Lukács in France proved ultimately "fruitless,"[115] although he did earn the respect of foreign Marxists such as Raymond Williams and Agnes Heller.[116]

In conclusion it should be remembered that Goldmann himself had already called into question a great deal of Lukács' theory. Aside from the fact that he was indifferent to everything Lukács wrote after 1923, never embraced his Leninist politics, and rejected his critical realist dismissal of modernism, Goldmann subtly challenged the argument of the "young Lukács" as well. His Piagetian reading of Lukács shifted the ground of Marxist holism away from philosophy to social science. His admission of the religious element in Marxism and his emphasis on the wager at its heart undermined the rationalist premises of Lukács' work. His interpretation of the trans-individual subject in terms of behavior rather than consciousness undercut Lukács' semi-idealist reading of the meta-totalizer of history, as did his uncertainty about the coherence of history as a longitudinal whole. And finally, by severing knowledge of the totality from the self-knowledge, imputed or otherwise, of a collective creator-subject, Goldmann restored the dichotomy of theory and practice that Lukács had been at such pains to overcome.

111. Lefebvre, *Au-delà du structuralisme* (Paris, 1971), p. 218.
112. For a discussion of Goldmann's influence on Mallet, see Dick Howard, "In Memory of Serge Mallet," *Telos* 20 (Summer 1974), p. 123.
113. Zima was from Czechoslovakia and Löwy from Brazil. Many of Goldmann's students, so Mme. Goldmann told me, were non-French.
114. Caute, *Collisions*, p. 221.
115. Lichtheim, *From Hegel to Marx* (New York, 1971), p. 46. For a more positive assessment of Goldmann's impact, see Joseph Gabel, "Hungarian Marxism," p. 189.
116. See Williams' article cited in note 84 and Agnes Heller, "Marxist Ethics and the Future of Eastern Europe," p. 159. For a far less friendly discussion, see Terry Eagleton, *Criticism and Ideology: A Study in Marxist Literary Theory* (London, 1976).

Although Goldmann always insisted that Piaget's genetic structuralism was merely a way to improve Lukács' holism, in certain ways it rendered it more vacuous. For whereas Lukács, in the classical Marxist fashion, had identified the proletariat as the only possible universal totalizer because of its unique role in the production process, Goldmann, following Piaget, began to claim that all groups sought homeostatic equilibrium as an anthropological constant. In some ways, this made his Marxism more open and less doctrinaire, but it also caused it to be less historically specific. As was the case with Goldmann's assumption about "rigorous homologies" in literature, philosophy, world-views and social structures, it tended to introduce an a priori element into what he insisted were inductive enterprises.

As a result, although genetic structuralism was designed to hold together the synthesis proposed by the first generation of Western Marxists, it ultimately registered its approaching breakdown. At the risk of adopting some of Goldmann's schematism, it might be said that the subjective impulse in that synthesis came to the fore in existentialist Marxism, most notably in the later work of Sartre, whereas the objective impulse emerged most strongly in Althusser's structuralist antithesis. And if a new mediation of the two can be detected in certain so-called post-structuralist thinkers in France, it certainly looks very different from that proposed by the early Lukács and his uneasy epigone, Lucien Goldmann. As was the case in the German discussion which led to Adorno, French Western Marxists also progressively dismantled the paradigm inaugurated in the early 1920s. Precisely how this occurred with reference to the central concept of totality will be the focus of the following chapters—the first two on existentialist Marxism, the third on Althusser.

CHAPTER ELEVEN

From Totality to Totalization: The Existentialist Marxism of Jean-Paul Sartre

In his 1945 doctoral dissertation on Kant, Lucien Goldmann put forward the provocative thesis that Martin Heidegger's *Being and Time* "cannot be understood without the realization that it constitutes largely, although perhaps implicitly, a debate with Lask, and above all with Lukács' work, *History and Class Consciousness*. In the latter, however, philosophy, sociology and politics are almost inextricably intertwined, whereas Heidegger has transported the whole debate into the realm of 'metaphysics'."[1] Throughout the remainder of his career, culminating in the lectures he gave in the late 1960s that were published posthumously as *Lukács and Heidegger: Towards a New Philosophy*,[2] Goldmann insisted on the importance of Heidegger's "debate" with Lukács, whose victor, as we have seen, he clearly felt was the latter.

In making his case that such an implicit confrontation had taken place, Goldmann introduced an argument that is of special significance for our own study. Heidegger's celebrated notion of *Sein* (Being) and Lukács' concept of totality, he claimed, were employed "to express approximate, at times nearly identical, ideas."[3] Both were introduced as antidotes to dualistic ontologies of whatever kind, serving as synonyms for that ultimate wholeness and community which would overcome what Lukács called reification and Heidegger called "inauthenticity." Both, moreover, recognized that such wholeness had to encompass historical change, rather than negate it as had traditional metaphysics. And finally, both questioned

1. Lucien Goldmann, *Immanuel Kant*, trans. Robert Black (London, 1971), p. 25.
2. Lucien Goldmann, *Lukács and Heidegger: Towards a New Philosophy*, trans. William Q. Boelhower (London, 1977).
3. Ibid., p. 10.

the ontological priority of subject over object or vice versa, arguing instead for a synthetic unity of the two.

Goldmann, to be sure, also acknowledged the obvious differences between Being and totality, in particular the contrast between Heidegger's sense of a wholeness that already existed, but had been forgotten, and Lukács' faith in a wholeness yet to be achieved. Lukács, Goldmann also recognized, understood the ground of totality to be a concrete, collective historical subject which would be reunited with its objectifications through revolutionary praxis, whereas Heidegger posited *Being* as prior to the differentiation of subject and object, collective or otherwise. And finally, Goldmann emphasized the still-potent individualism in what Heidegger called *Dasein* (Being-there), the human dimension of *Sein* (Being); in fact, by contrasting *Sein* and *Dasein*, Goldmann contended, Heidegger had reintroduced the two-dimensional historical structure Lukács' more Hegelian viewpoint had sought to transcend.

Goldmann's reading of the relationship between Heidegger and Lukács has not won universal acceptance,[4] but his insight into the similarities between the concepts of Being and totality is highly suggestive. Lukács' later fulminations against Heidegger in *The Destruction of Reason* and elsewhere, as an irrationalist forerunner of Fascism, should not mask the commonality of their positions (including, one might add, their equally ambiguous relations to totalitarian politics). Nor should Heidegger's generally hostile attitude to Marxism be allowed to obscure his relations to the milieu of early Western Marxism. As George Steiner recently remarked, "Even where Heidegger is most dismissive of Marxism and where he advocates a 'far more radical conception of overthrow' (namely, the overthrow of Western metaphysics and the return to a remembrance of Being), he is closely in tune with the revisionist, partly messianic Marxism of the 1920s."[5]

It is thus not surprising that in the subsequent history of Western Marxism, Heidegger has shadowed Lukács as a potent, if sometimes unacknowledged, stimulus to holistic thought. As we noted when examining Marcuse, Heidegger's argument for the remembrance of Being was a formative influence on his student's faith in anamnestic totalization, even after Marcuse's repudiation of other aspects of his philosophy. Echoes of Heidegger's position can also be found in the phenomenological Marxism of Enzo Paci, Pier Aldo Rovatti and the *Aut-Aut* circle in Italy, although

4. Heideggerians, in particular, have not been convinced by it. But see the defense of Goldmann in Rainer Rochlitz, "Lukács et Heidegger," *L'Homme et la société* 43–44 (January–July, 1977).
5. George Steiner, *Martin Heidegger* (London, 1980), p. 148.

they often preferred Husserl's earlier formulation of phenomenology.[6] Less ambiguous in their support for a synthesis of Marx and Heidegger were the *Arguments* group around Kostas Axelos in France, who endorsed not only Heidegger's holism but also his critique of technology.[7] And finally, Heidegger deeply influenced the work of two East European philosophers, the Czech, Karel Kosík, and the Yugoslav, Gajo Petrović.[8] Moreover, as Adorno's excoriation of the links between death, totality and Being in *The Jargon of Authenticity* vividly demonstrates,[9] when a Western Marxist turned against Lukács' notion of totality, he was just as likely to repudiate Heidegger's Being. Further examples of this pattern, as we will see, can be found in the anti-Hegelian Marxisms of Althusser, Della Volpe and Colletti.

The full measure of Heidegger's impact on Western Marxism cannot, however, be reduced to the question of Being and totality. In interwar France, well before Goldmann posited the similarities between these two concepts, Heidegger became known largely for his ancillary idea of *Dasein*, which was understood to have very different implications.[10] If any-

6. Paci's major work is *The Function of the Sciences and the Meaning of Man*, trans. Paul Piccone and James E. Hansen (Evanston, 1972); for an example of Rovatti's position, see his "A Phenomenological Analysis of Marxism: The Return to the Subject and to the Dialectic of the Totality," *Telos* 5 (Spring 1970). Paul Piccone, the founder and editor of *Telos*, has been the major American supporter of their argument. See, for example, his "Phenomenological Marxism" in *Towards a New Marxism*, ed. Bart Grahl and Paul Piccone (St. Louis, 1973). Another figure who attempted to combine Husserl and Marx was the Vietnamese philosopher Tran Duc Thao, who lived in Paris in the 1930s. His major work is *Phénoménologie et Matérialisme Dialectique* (Paris, 1951); for a discussion of his position, see Silvia Federici, "Viet Cong Philosophy: Tran Duc Thao," *Telos* 6 (Fall 1970). For a critical appraisal of the movement, see Efraim Shmueli, "Can Phenomenology Acccommodate Marxism?," *Telos* 17 (Fall 1973).
7. Kostas Axelos, *Einfuhrung in ein künftiges Denken: Über Marx und Heidegger* (Tübingen, 1966). See the discussion of the *Arguments* group in Mark Poster, *Existential Marxism in Postwar France: From Sartre to Althusser* (Princeton, 1975), p. 220f.
8. Karel Kosík, *Dialectics of the Concrete: A Study on Problems of Man and World*, trans. Karel Kovanda and James Schmidt (Dordrecht, 1976). Kosík's view of Heidegger, it should be understood, was by no means uncritical. For an interesting discussion of his position, see James Schmidt, "Praxis and Temporality: Karel Kosík's Political Theory," *Telos* 33 (Fall 1977). Gajo Petrovic, *Marx in Mid-Twentieth Century: A Yugoslav Philosopher Considers Karl Marx's Writings* (Garden City, N.Y., 1967); for a general discussion of the importance of Heidegger for the *Praxis* circle, see Gerson S. Sher, *Praxis: Marxist Criticism and Dissent in Socialist Yugoslavia* (Bloomington, 1977), p. 66.
9. Theodor W. Adorno, *The Jargon of Authenticity*, trans. Knut Tarnowski and Frederic Will (London, 1973), p. 140f. Sartre, it should be noted, shared Adorno's distaste for Heidegger's treatment of death. See his discussion in *Being and Nothingness: An Essay on Phenomenological Ontology*, trans. Hazel E. Barnes (New York, 1966), pp. 650–77.
10. For a general treatment of the initial reception of phenomenology in France, see Herbert Spiegelberg, *The Phenomenological Movement: An Historical Introduction*, vol. 2; John Heckman, "Hyppolite and the Hegel Revival in France," *Telos* 16 (Summer 1973); and Ian W. Alexander, "The Phenomenological Philosophy in France: An Analysis of its Themes, Significance and Implications," and George L. Kline, "The Existentialist Rediscovery of Hegel and Marx," both in *Sartre: A Collection of Critical Essays*, ed. Mary Warnock (Garden City, 1971).

thing, the earlier (and as we will argue in the case of Sartre, the most lasting) impact of Heideggerian thought was in an anti-totalistic direction. To understand how the advocate of a Being that was prior to the differentiation of subject and object became a key stimulus to the radical subjectivism that was French existentialism, we must dwell for a while on the curious history of his reception in France.

The initial French interest in Heidegger was sparked by a meeting between German and French philosophers in Davos, Switzerland, in March and April, 1929. The ground had already been prepared by Georges Gurvitch's lectures on Husserl at the Sorbonne in 1928 and Husserl's short visit to Paris in February of the following year, which helped acquaint the French with phenomenology in general. Max Scheler's variant of it had been known since 1924, when he made the first of several visits to Paris. At Davos, Germany was represented by Ernst Cassirer, whose reputation as a major neo-Kantian was already established, and by Heidegger, who was still only a name to the French. From Paris came Léon Brunschvicg, the dean of French neo-Kantians, and Albert Spaier who, with Alexandre Koyré and Henri-Charles Puech, was to found the influential *Recherches philosophiques* in 1931. The conference is perhaps best remembered for the celebrated "disputation"[11] between Cassirer and Heidegger over Kant, but for French philosophy, it had another meaning. For among the French party were a number of young students from the Ecole Normale Supérieure, who brought back with them the news of a non-positivist but nonetheless "concrete" alternative to the neo-idealism then dominant in French academic circles. That alternative was phenomenology, which meant both the philosophy of Husserl and that of his recent successor in the chair of philosophy at Freiburg, Heidegger. Several young French philosophers, including Emmanuel Levinas, Raymond Aron, and Maurice de Gandillac, soon went to Germany to study at the source. In 1930, Levinas published *La Théorie de l'intuition dans la phénoménologie de Husserl* and Gurvitch collected the lectures he had been giving on Husserl, Lask and Heidegger as *Les tendances actuelles de la philosophie allemande.*[12]

11. Ernst Cassirer and Martin Heidegger, *Débat sur le Kantisme et la Philosophie* (Davos, March 1929), ed. with intro. by Pierre Aubenque (Paris, 1972). For a summary of the debate in English, see "A Cassirer-Heidegger Seminar," *Philosophy and Phenomenological Research* 25 (1964). For an account by one of the young French philosophers in the audience, see Maurice de Gandillac, "Entretiens avec Martin Heidegger," *Les Temps Modernes* (January 1946).

12. Emmanuel Levinas, *La Théorie de l'intuition dans le phénoménologie de Husserl* (Paris, 1930) and Georges Gurvitch, *Les tendances actuelles de la philosophie allemande* (Paris, 1930). There was also a resumé of Husserl's Paris lectures published in the *Revue de métaphysique et de morale* in 1928. See the general discussion of this period in Theodore F. Geraets, *Vers une nouvelle philosophie transcendentale: La genèse de la philosophie de*

From this beginning, phenomenology began to permeate French philosophical life to mingle in ways too complicated to spell out here with the
religious existentialism of Gabriel Marcel, the Personalism of Emmanuel
Mounier, and the rediscovery of Hegel by Jean Wahl, Alexandre Kojève and
Jean Hyppolite. Whereas in Germany, phenomenology, existentialism and
Hegelianism were separate and often opposing positions, in France they
tended to blur together in creative, if often questionable, fashion. What is
important for our purposes is that Heidegger was understood by the French
primarily as a phenomenologist of human existence who was specially sensitive to such concrete questions as personal authenticity, anguish, care and
dread. In the hands of commentators like Wahl, he was turned into a version of Kierkegaard, the individualist and irrationalist critic of Hegelian
holism.[13] Ironically, in this guise Heidegger could have merited comparison
with the pre-Marxist Lukács of *Soul and Form*, if that work had been
known in France,[14] rather than with the author of *History and Class Consciousness*. In any event, the French almost universally understood Heidegger as a diagnostician of the irrationality of the human condition. In fact, as
late as 1942 and *The Myth of Sisyphus*, Albert Camus could include him
with Kierkegaard, Jaspers and Chestov as a philosopher of the absurd for
whom "existence is humiliated."[15]

Much to Heidegger's ultimate chagrin, the category of *Dasein*, which
the French translator, Henri Corbin, rendered as *réalité humaine*,[16] was
given primacy over *Sein* in their reading of his work, with the result that he
was understood as far more of a humanist than in fact he was. Because he
seemed to be stressing the concrete realities of human existence, rather
than searching for timeless essences, as had Husserl, Heidegger was assimilated, despite his larger ontological concerns, to what soon became
known as existentialism. It was not, in fact, until an essay by Jean Beaufret
and the partial translation of Heidegger's "Letter on Humanism" in 1947,
that the French realized their error.[17]

Maurice Merleau-Ponty jusqu'à la Phénoménologie de la Perception (The Hague, 1971),
Chapter 1.
    13. Jean Wahl, *Etudes Kierkegaardiennes* (Paris, 1938). Sartre cites this work in *Being
and Nothingness*, p. 35, as proof that Heidegger was influenced by Kierkegaard.
    14. The early Lukács was only introduced in France by Goldmann in 1962 in his "Intro-
duction aux premiers écrits de George Lukács," *Les Temps Modernes* 195 (August 1962;
later appended to the French translation of *The Theory of the Novel* in 1963).
    15. Albert Camus, *The Myth of Sisyphus and Other Essays*, trans. Justin O'Brien (New
York, 1960), p. 18.
    16. For a discussion of the mistranslation of *Dasein* as *réalité humaine*, see Denis Hol-
lier, ed., *Le collège de sociologie (1937–1939)* (Paris, 1979), p. 55.
    17. The fragment appeared with Beaufret's "M. Heidegger et le problème de la vérité,"
Fontaine 63 (November 1947).

Perhaps no body of work contributed to this misinterpretation more than that of Jean-Paul Sartre who, in a legendary meeting in 1933 with his fellow *normalien*, Raymond Aron, had discovered phenomenology and, according to Simone de Beauvoir, "turned pale with emotion."[18] After then reading Levinas' account of Husserl, Sartre applied for and was awarded a research fellowship to travel to Germany. In Berlin and then Freiburg during 1933 and 1934, he studied Husserl's *Ideas* very closely and attended a few of Heidegger's lectures. Even though this was the year Heidegger served as Nazi-appointed rector of the University of Freiburg and delivered his notorious address on "The Self-assertion of the German University," Sartre, then vaguely leftist, seems to have ignored his politics and focussed only on his philosophy. When he returned to Paris, his first major work, *The Transcendence of the Ego*, deeply indebted to Husserl, was already near completion.[19] It was now Sartre's turn to impress the importance of phenomenology on other Frenchmen, most notably his younger colleague from the Ecole Normale, Maurice Merleau-Ponty, whose appetite had been already whetted by Husserl's visit to Paris in 1929 and Gurvitch's lectures.[20] Merleau-Ponty became another convert, leaving his earlier Catholic preoccupations behind to merge phenomenology with the Marxist-oriented Hegelianism he was then absorbing from Kojève's lectures.

It is, of course, largely through the subsequent efforts of Sartre and Merleau-Ponty that a specifically existentialist variant of Western Marxism was fashioned. Although in important respects congruent with the more systematically Hegelian Marxist paradigm constructed by Lukács, Korsch and Gramsci, it contained energies, derived primarily from the French reception of phenomenology, that helped explode that paradigm.

18. Simone de Beauvoir, *The Prime of Life*, trans. Peter Green (Cleveland, 1962), p. 112. The literature on Sartre is too lengthy to list here. See Robert Wilcocks, *Jean-Paul Sartre: A Bibliography of International Criticism* (Alberta, 1975); and François Lapointe, *Jean-Paul Sartre and His Critics: An International Bibliography (1938–1980)* (Bowling Green, Ohio, 1981). Especially helpful are Raymond Aron, *History and the Dialectic of Violence: An Analysis of Sartre's "Critique de la Raison Dialectique,"* trans. Barry Cooper (New York, 1976); Pietro Chiodi, *Sartre and Marxism*, trans. Kate Soper (New York, 1976); Dominick LaCapra, *A Preface to Sartre: A Critical Introduction to Sartre's Literary and Philosophical Writings* (Ithaca, 1978); Joseph P. Fell, *Heidegger and Sartre: An Essay on Being and Place* (New York, 1979); Mark Poster, *Sartre's Marxism* (London, 1979); István Mészáros, *The Work of Sartre*, vol. 1: *Search for Freedom* (Atlantic Highlands, N.J., 1979); Ronald Aronson, *Jean-Paul Sartre: Philosophy in the World* (London, 1980); Hugh J. Silverman and Frederick A. Elliston, eds., *Jean-Paul Sartre: Contemporary Approaches to His Philosophy* (Pittsburgh, 1980).

19. Jean-Paul Sartre, *The Transcendence of the Ego: An Existentialist Theory of Consciousness*, trans. Forrest Williams and Robert Kirkpatrick (New York, 1957); first published in French in 1936. *L'imagination* also appeared in that same year.

20. See the account in *Geraets*, Chapter 1.

Central to this development was the existentialist critique of the Hegelian concept of totality. If, as we have argued, the early Lefebvre and Goldmann can be understood as attempting to graft that concept onto the tree of French Marxist thought, Sartre and Merleau-Ponty bear witness to its ambiguous success.

The complex and tension-filled relationship between Sartre and Heidegger has been widely discussed in the voluminous literature on existentialism, most recently and with greatest acuity in the work of Joseph Fell.[21] Despite having attended Heidegger's lectures during his German visit, Sartre seems to have read *Being and Time* with real rigor only when he was interned in a prisoner-of-war camp in 1940. Although he had already published several works of philosophy as well as the philosophical novel, *Nausea*, which earned him popular recognition, it was only after immersing himself in Heidegger that Sartre could express his existentialist position in ontological terms. The result was *Being and Nothingness: An Essay on Phenomenological Ontology*, published in 1943[22] and immediately recognized as a work of major importance comparable to *Being and Time*. The comparison was particularly apt, for Sartre was clearly in agreement with Heidegger on a number of fundamental issues. Both relied on the non-deductive, descriptive method of Husserl's phenomenology—shorn, to be sure, of its "eidetic" reductions. Both sought to use that method to overcome traditional philosophical alternatives, such as that between idealism and realism, and both agreed that transcendental notions of subjectivity were metaphysical fictions. And in substantive terms, both viewed the present world as deeply alienated in a myriad of ways.

But it would be certainly wrong to consider *Being and Nothingness*, as some early commentators were wont to do, as little more than a French translation of *Being and Time*. On the most basic level, Sartre shifted the emphasis away from *Sein* to *Dasein*, and then criticized Heidegger for resolving the alienations that existed on the level of the latter by claiming that they did not exist on the level of the former. For Heidegger, estrangement was merely a surface phenomenon masking a more basic, if forgotten, unity; for Sartre, it was a frightening and unredeemable dimension of existence. Although Heidegger included negation in his phenomenological description of reality, he nonetheless overlooked its central importance. "The characteristic of Heidegger's philosophy," Sartre charged, "is

21. See note 18.
22. See note 9.

to describe *Dasein* by using positive terms which hide the implicit negations."[23] For Sartre, it was incorrect to oppose negation as merely an absence or privation of Being; instead, as he put it in a vivid and memorable
metaphor, "Nothingness lies coiled in the heart of being—like a worm."[24]

Being and Nothingness was devoted in large measure to exploring the
ways in which that "worm," which Sartre identified with consciousness,[25]
gnawed at the heart of Being. For Sartre, Being was divisible into what
following Hegel he called objective "Being-in-itself" (*être-en-soi*) and
subjective "Being-for-itself" (*être-pour-soi*). In his earlier philosophical
works he had explored the nature of this opposition epistemologically in
the realms of perception and the imagination; in *Being and Nothingness*,
he posited it as more fundamentally ontological. The ontology he presented was resolutely dualistic, even Cartesian to many observers.[26]
Sartre, in fact, explicitly rejected any dialectical overcoming of Descartes'
opposition between consciousness and the world; "Hegel's failure," he
insisted, "has shown us that the only point of departure possible is the
Cartesian *cogito*."[27] But unlike Descartes, he understood the subjective
pole of the dualism as negative rather than positive, as an absence that felt
itself to be a lack. Whereas the "in-itself" was fully self-sufficient, a completed positivity that was identical with itself, the "for-itself" was totally
dependent on what it was not and yet desired to be. Rather than identity,
it implied non-identical difference. Its appearance in the world, Sartre
claimed (but never really proved), emerged only with "the upsurge of human reality."[28] Indeed, the very nature of that reality was a lack, as demonstrated by the existence of the human desire to transcend mere negativity and become positive. Thus, "human reality is its own surpassing
toward what it lacks; it surpasses itself toward the particular being which
it would be if it were what it is. Human reality is not something which
exists first in order afterwards to lack this or that; it exists first as lack and
in immediate, synthetic connection with what it lacks."[29]

23. Ibid., p. 22.
24. Ibid., p. 26.
25. *The Worm of Consciousness and Other Essays*, ed. Miriam Chiaramonte (New
York, 1976), it might be noted in passing, was a collection of essays by Nicola Chiaramonte,
an exile from fascist Italy who became a friend of Camus in the 1940s and later migrated to
New York.
26. See, for example, the arguments in Wilfred Desan, *The Tragic Finale: An Essay on
the Philosophy of Jean-Paul Sartre* (New York, 1960), *passim*, and Desan, *The Marxism of
Jean-Paul Sartre* (Garden City, 1966), p. 260f. In *Adventures of the Dialectic*, trans. Joseph
Bien (Evanston, 1973), Merleau-Ponty makes a similar charge (pp. 193–96), which is repeated in many other places in the literature on Sartre.
27. Sartre, *Being and Nothingness*, p. 308.
28. Ibid., p. 105.
29. Ibid., p. 109.

At once the ground of human freedom and the source of human frustration, this incessant lacking and desiring could never be overcome, for there was no meta-Being, no overarching totality, prior to the split between "for-itself" and "in-itself," as Heidegger posited. Nor was there a way to create a totality in the future through a Hegelian or Marxist resolution of contradictions. As Sartre put it, in denying the Hegelian *Aufhebung* of opposites:

While the For-itself *lacks* the In-itself, the In-itself does not *lack* the For-itself. There is then no reciprocity in the opposition. In a word, the For-itself remains non-essential and contingent in relation to the In-itself. . . . In addition, the synthesis or value would indeed be a return to the thesis, then a return upon itself; but as this is an unrealizable totality, the For-itself is not a moment which can be surpassed. As such its nature approaches much nearer to the "ambiguous" realities of Kierkegaard.[30]

Very much in the spirit of Kierkegaard, Sartre contended that the ultimate stage of human development was what Hegel in *The Phenomenology* had seen as merely transitional, that of the "unhappy consciousness":

The being of human reality is suffering because it rises in being as perpetually haunted by a totality which it is without being able to be it, precisely because it could not attain the in-itself without losing itself as for-itself. Human reality therefore is by nature an unhappy consciousness with no possibility of surpassing its unhappy state.[31]

Because Sartre so emphatically denied any reconciliation, he rejected Heidegger's portrayal of the human world as a community, a world of "*Mit-sein*," or "Being-with." Characterizing human interaction in terms of objectifying gazes, which he called "the look," Sartre claimed that struggle and confrontation rather than cooperation were the essence of human relations. "Conflict," he insisted, "is the original meaning of being-for-others."[32] Individual consciousness inevitably saw other people as an "undifferentiated totality"[33] like the inert "in-itself" that the "for-itself" tried to attain, but could never become. Although Sartre admitted that experiences of belonging to a community do exist for the individual, he insisted that "the 'we' is not an inter-subjective consciousness nor a

30. Ibid., p. 115.
31. Ibid., p. 110.
32. Ibid., p. 445. It should be noted that Heidegger's own notion of "*Mit-sein*" was equivocal, as his celebrated emphasis on the importance of death as an inalienable individual experience demonstrated. More dialogically inclined existentialists were critical of him precisely for this ambiguity. See, for example, Martin Buber, *Between Man and Man*, trans. Ronald Gregor Smith (New York, 1965), p. 169.
33. Sartre, *Being and Nothingness*, p. 359.

new being which surpasses and encircles its parts as a synthetic whole in the manner of the collective consciousness of the sociologists."[34] The temporary sense of community among individuals was produced only by the objectifying gaze of an external observer, who created an "us-object." Because there was no meta-observer outside of the human race as a whole, a possibility that was denied for Sartre by the non-existence of God, humanity must remain forever fragmented and in conflict. There was no totalizing dialectic of reciprocity that might create meaningful wholes beyond the isolated self; "Here as everywhere else," Sartre wrote, "we ought to oppose to Hegel Kierkegaard, who represents the claims of the individual as such."[35]

Thus, the Heideggerian faith in the recovery through memory of a wholeness prior to the alienation of the present, which Marcuse had found a stimulus to recovering it in the future, was a false consolation. In *Nausea*, Sartre had his hero Roquentin reject the Proustian assumption that at the end of the story a retrospective totalization could occur; it is impossible, Roquentin says, to "catch time by the tail."[36] And in *Being and Nothingness*, he insisted that "between past and present, there is an absolute heterogeneity; and if I cannot enter the past, it is because the past *is*. The only way by which I could be it is for me myself to become in-itself in order to lose myself in it in the form of identification; this by definition is denied me."[37] Thus Hegel's celebrated assertion that "essence is what has been," which Marcuse had found an inspiration to anamnestic totalization, suggested the opposite for Sartre: "'*Wesen ist was gewesen ist.*' My essence is in the past; the past is the law of its being."[38] But because man's existence was future-oriented, a project whose outcome was undetermined, the very attempt to reconcile essence and existence was a betrayal of human freedom.

Perhaps even more fundamental in thwarting the possibility of achieving totality in Sartre's work was his analysis of nature. Although he accepted the argument advanced by both Lukács and Kojève that nature was undialectical and therefore not to be confused with history, he did not draw the conclusion that history could be completely segregated from nature and understood as the realm of a potential subject-object unity. If anything, as his celebrated discussion of the body showed, Sartre thought that non-dialectical nature permeated the human sphere in irremediable

34. Ibid., p. 506.
35. Ibid., p. 294.
36. Jean-Paul Sartre, *Nausea*, trans. Lloyd Alexander (New York, 1949), p. 59.
37. Sartre, *Being and Nothingness*, p. 144.
38. Ibid., p. 145.

ways. Here he was at his least Cartesian, emphasizing that consciousness was inevitably situated in the body and thus inseparable from its vulnerable contingency. "I exist my body,"[39] he insisted, which means that corporeality precedes self-consciousness. Although the for-itself incessantly tried to surpass the facticity of its contingent status in the body, it could not succeed in this endeavor. The result was that "a dull and inescapable nausea perpetually reveals my body to my consciousness."[40] Moreover, the body served as an impediment to any possible intersubjective totalization because what Sartre calls "the body-for-others" was inevitably frozen into an object by the look of other subjectivities. This objectified perception was then internalized by the original consciousness as the reified reality of its body, which then became alienated from the for-itself rather than its preconceptual ground.

In short, the radical heterogeneity between history and nature that was posited by Hegelian Marxists like Lukács and Kojève in order to save dialectical totalization for human practice was interiorized within the realm of human history itself by Sartre. As a result, Vico's *verum-factum* principle, which was so central to the early Western Marxist paradigm, was ruled out by Sartre as a solution to the antinomies of existence, bourgeois or otherwise. Instead of being able to recognize himself in the world around him, man was constantly confronted by an alien world not of his own making. Indeed, in his very self-understanding man was prevented from achieving complete lucidity by his interiorization of the objectified view of his body in the eyes of other people. Even in the seeming identity of the self, there lurked an irreducible difference.

Sartre, however, was not fully consistent in drawing this bleak conclusion, for elsewhere in *Being and Nothingness* he insisted that it was possible to gain a coherent and totalized sense of the self. Totality does, in fact, appear in the work in a positive guise in Sartre's discussion of existential psychoanalysis,[41] which grew largely out of Heidegger's distinction between authentic and inauthentic existence. Existential psychoanalysis was sharply contrasted with its Freudian competitor because of the latter's positing of the unconscious, which is used to explain behavior in terms that reduce individual responsibility for it. Freud, Sartre argued, was also wrong in dividing the psyche into separate compartments, most notably

39. Ibid., p. 430.
40. Ibid., p. 415.
41. Ibid., p. 682f. For a discussion of the general attempt to create an existentialist psychoanalysis, which began before Sartre in the work of the Swiss psychiatrist Ludwig Binswanger, see Gerald N. Izenberg, *The Existentialist Critique of Freud: The Crisis of Autonomy* (Princeton, 1976).

the id and ego, which "introduces into my subjectivity the deepest inter-subjective structures of the *Mit-sein*."[42] Existential psychoanalysis, in contrast, insists on the unified integrity of the self and the complete responsibility of each man for his acts:

> The *principle* of this psychoanalysis is that man is a totality and not a collection. Consequently he expresses himself as a whole in even his most insignificant and his most superficial behavior.[43]

What is revealed, Sartre claimed, are the ultimate choices that man, condemned as he is to his inescapable freedom, has made. If these choices are hidden it is not because man is controlled by his unconscious, but rather because he deceives himself and lives inauthentically, a victim of "bad faith." Past choices are not, however, inescapably binding in the sense of creating some sort of essence from which man cannot depart; the for-itself can always choose anew.

Choosing a project, deciding on a course of action, taking responsibility for the consequences that ensue did not, however, mean for Sartre that success would follow. For what existential psychoanalysis will reveal to man is "the real goal of his pursuit, which is being as a synthetic fusion of the in-itself with the for-itself; existential psychoanalysis is going to acquaint man with his passion."[44] But since no unity of this kind was possible short of that assumed to exist in an imaginary God, man, in the frequently quoted words of Sartre's penultimate chapter, was a "useless passion."[45]

Why the early Sartre came to hold such a chilling view of reality has been the subject of considerable conjecture, much of it fueled by Sartre's own ruminations on his past in his autobiography, *The Words*, and elsewhere.[46] Inevitably, much attention has been paid to the peculiar circumstances of Sartre's youth: his isolation and escape into the imaginary world of literature, his personal sense of superfluity and complementary yearning for adventure, his dislike of nature and his own flesh, his disgust with the vacuous humanism of his grandfather, Charles Schweitzer, all of

42. Sartre, *Being and Nothingness*, p. 62.
43. Ibid., p. 696.
44. Ibid., p. 767.
45. Ibid., p. 754.
46. Jean-Paul Sartre, *The Words*, trans. Bernard Frechtman (New York, 1964); *Sartre by Himself*, text of a film made by Alexander Astruc and Michel Contat, trans. Richard Seaver (New York, 1978); see also the interviews in Sartre, *Between Existentialism and Marxism*, trans. John Mathews (New York, 1974) and Sartre, *Life/Situations: Essays Written and Spoken*, trans. Paul Auster and Lydia Davis (New York, 1977); for a very helpful aid to piecing together Sartre's intellectual life, see Michel Contat and Michel Rybalka, *The Writings of Jean-Paul Sartre*, 2 vols. (Evanston, 1974). See also the useful essay by István Mészáros, "From 'The Legend of Truth' to a 'True Legend': Phases of Sartre's Development," *Telos 25* (Fall 1975).

which combined to produce what Sartre himself called his "writer's neu-
rosis," the ideological belief that salvation, such as it was, could only come
through the pen. In the terms of *Being and Nothingness*, the result was
living in "bad faith," in which the misunderstood conditions of Sartre's
own existence were projected onto mankind. As he put it in *The Words*,

> At the age of thirty, I executed the masterstroke of writing in *Nausea*—quite sin-
> cerely, believe me—about the bitter unjustified existence of my fellowmen and of
> exonerating my own. I *was* Roquentin; I used him to show, without complacency,
> the texture of my life. At the same time, I was *I*, the elect, the chronicler of Hell, a
> glass and steel photomicroscope peering at my own protoplasmic juices . . . . Fake
> to the marrow of my bones and hoodwinked, I joyfully wrote about our unhappy
> state. Dogmatic though I was, I doubted everything except that I was the elect of
> doubt. I built with one hand what I destroyed with the other, and I regarded anxi-
> ety as the guarantee of my security; I was happy.[47]

There is, of course, a great deal of validity in this personal explanation
for Sartre's idiosyncratically bleak attitude towards reality. But what
should not be forgotten is that his version of existentialism struck a very
respondent chord in the France of his day. Sartre, as we have seen, was not
alone in turning Heidegger's account of *Dasein*, in which living with others played a central role, into a *réalité humaine* ruled by conflict and absurdity. As has often been remarked, even those French thinkers who discovered Hegel in the 1930s concentrated on the violent struggle which
they saw at the heart of his system.[48] Indeed, the theme of terror, which
was later to play such a role in the Marxist work of both Sartre and Merleau-Ponty, can be seen already in Kojève's account of the master-slave
relationship. Although the French were discovering history and the concrete during the interwar era, they were far less sanguine than, say, Lukács,
Korsch or Marcuse about the prospects of reconciling history and reason.
For every Lefebvre writing of a "total man" who could overcome alienation, there were a dozen writers proclaiming the absurdity of that quest.

The frightening attraction of Fascism or related reactionary doctrines
for so many French intellectuals of genuine talent—Céline, Drieu la Rochelle, Brasillach, Bernanos—testifies to the general malaise of French
cultural life during the last decades of the Third Republic. The "strange
defeat" of 1940, as Marc Bloch called it, was not a surprise to those who

47. Sartre, *The Words*, pp. 157–58.
48. For a discussion of the irrational and violent implications of Kojève's interpretation
of Hegel, see Vincent Descombes, *Modern French Philosophy*, trans. L. Scott-Fox and J. M.
Harding (Cambridge, 1980), p. 13f. Significantly, one of the books on Sartre's *Critique*, that
by R. D. Laing and D. G. Cooper, is called *Reason and Violence: A Decade of Sartre's Philosophy 1950–1960* (New York, 1971).

had been proclaiming the decadence of France for so many years.[49] Although it would certainly be unfair to make Sartre the bed-fellow of right-wing fanatics and ignore his friendship with Marxists like Nizan, it is nonetheless true that the context out of which his ideas emerged was radically ambiguous; the ethic of authenticity, as many critics have pointed out, could justify many different political stances. There is nothing intrinsically leftist about the argument of *Being and Nothingness*.[50]

That Sartre himself soon came to this conclusion is obvious from the remainder of his intellectual career. In fact, the major quest of Sartre's work after *Being and Nothingness* can be seen as an attempt to square his increasingly radical political sympathies with his philosophy. How successful he was in this endeavor, how completely he overcame the antinomian terms of his early position instead of merely reformulating them, has been the source of spirited debate.[51] To follow all of its ramifications is impossible, but insofar as Sartre sought to overcome his earlier hostility to holistic thinking by embracing heterodox Marxism, we must pursue his general development. For, as one commentator has remarked:

To the extent to which, in his post-war works, existence became increasingly freed of its wholly fantastic isolation in the exceptional and the incommunicable, the principal problem of Sartre's philosophy became not that of the individual but of the *whole*, in the sense of being the problem of a totality in which the individual finds himself placed within the perspective of the *totalized*, while yet preserving his own particularity as *totalizing* existent.[52]

The experience that seems to have moved Sartre out of the cul-de-sac of *Being and Nothingness* was the solidarity he felt as a member of the Resistance, when it was possible for the first time to be politically commit-

49. Bloch, *Strange Defeat*, trans. Gerard Hopkins (London, 1949). For discussions of the malaise of French life in the interwar era, see H. Stuart Hughes, *The Obstructed Path: French Social Thought in the Years of Desperation* (New York, 1966) and the special issue of *MLN* 95, 4 (May 1980) devoted to the 1930s. For a more general treatment of the theme of decline in French thought, see Koenraad W. Swart, *The Sense of Decadence in Nineteenth-Century France* (The Hague, 1964).

50. As Herbert Marcuse pointed out in his review of *Being and Nothingness*, "French Existentialism revives many of the intellectual tendencies which were prevalent in the Germany of the twenties and which came to naught in the Nazi system." "Sartre's Existentialism" in *Studies in Critical Philosophy* (Boston, 1973), p. 162. Marcuse, it should be noted, also recognized in this review the contradictory impulses in Sartre's position that tied him to the Left.

51. For arguments stressing continuity, see Aronson, *Jean-Paul Sartre*; LaCapra, *A Preface to Sartre* (who talks of displaced repetitions and continuities within discontinuities rather than straightforward recapitulation); and Raymond Aron, *Marxism and the Existentialists*, trans. Robert Addis and John Weightman (New York, 1969); for the counter-argument, see Poster, *Sartre's Marxism*, and the chapter on Sartre in Fredric Jameson, *Marxism and Form: Twentieth-Century Dialectical Theories of Literature* (Princeton, 1971).

52. Chiodi, *Sartre and Marxism*, pp. 112–13.

ted. It was in fact during the Occupation that he began his curious relationship with the French Communist Party, whose journal *Action* asked
him to defend existentialism in its pages.[53] Although the hand it extended
to him was soon withdrawn in the first of many rebuffs, Sartre was now
irreversibly embarked on his own pursuit of a politically viable alternative
to *Being and Nothingness*. The first major theoretical statement expressing his tentative rejection of that work came in his 1945 lecture "Existentialism is a Humanism."[54] Although still loyal to the conceptual structure
of his earlier argument, Sartre introduced a note of truculent optimism
that suggested a new departure. Whereas his previous work had mocked
the humanist pretensions of bourgeois "men of good will" such as his
grandfather or the Auto-didact in *Nausea*, he now sought to demonstrate
that his own position was compatible with a certain kind of humanism,
indeed one with politically active implications.

Sartre's argument was premised on the existentialist insistence that
men were free to make their lives themselves; they were therefore defined
through their action, rather than through any externally determining constraints. Men were compelled to choose their destinies, however limited
the range of their possibilities might seem. The anguish of which existentialists spoke was a function of the profound implications of such choices,
for rather than merely deciding for himself, man was "at the same time a
legislator deciding for the whole of mankind."[55] Instead of being a radically individualist subjectivism, existentialism, therefore, had universal
implications. Moreover, rather than advocating capricious choices in the
manner of Gide's notorious *actes gratuits*, existentialism recognized the
contextual implications of specific decisions: "Man finds himself in an
organized situation in which he is himself involved: his choice involves
mankind in its entirety, and he cannot avoid choosing. . . . Doubtless he
chooses without reference to any pre-established values, but it is unjust to
tax him with caprice. Rather let us say that the moral choice is comparable to the construction of a work of art."[56]

In so arguing, Sartre was obviously introducing a note of Kantian universalism to supplement the radical individualism of his earlier ethic of

53. On Sartre's relationship with the Communist Party, see Michel-Antoine Burnier,
Choice of Action, trans. Bernard Murchland (New York, 1968); David Caute, *Communism
and the French Intellectuals 1914–1960* (London, 1964); and Poster, *Existential Marxism
in Postwar France*.
54. This was originally a lecture given on October 28, 1945 and published the following
year. The English translation can be found in Walter Kaufmann, ed., *Existentialism from
Dostoevsky to Sartre* (Cleveland, 1963).
55. Ibid., p. 292.
56. Ibid., p. 305.

authenticity.[57] But precisely how the two fit together was by no means certain, nor did his comparison between moral decisions and artistic creativity illuminate the ground of choice very brightly. Indeed, the vacuity that plagued his earlier, more individualist position remained in this revised version, in which the stakes involved were higher but the criteria by which to choose remained obscure. Nonetheless, if one takes seriously the argument that Goldmann was advancing at precisely this time about the underlying holistic and communitarian assumptions in Kant's philosophy, then Sartre's attempt to universalize the ethics of authenticity can be considered a halting step in the direction of a more genuinely holistic position.

Sartre, however, was still a long distance from Marxism, as evidenced by his rigorous rejection of "all kinds of materialism," which "led one to treat every man including oneself as an object."[58] In an article entitled "Materialism and Revolution"[59] in the new journal he helped found, *Les Temps Modernes*, he made his hostility to ontological materialism even clearer, arguing that revolution was conceivable only as a subjective transcendence of the material world. But insofar as materialism meant something other than the ontological priority of matter to spirit—as indeed Marx, if not many later Marxists, assumed it did—then Sartre was moving towards a kind of materialism, the materialism that recognized the external constraints on human freedom. As Sartre himself later acknowledged, he had learned after *Being and Nothingness* that freedom must be situated in the world; "Life," he explained, "had taught me *la force des choses*—the power of circumstances."[60]

He also soon learned that the hesitant reformulation of his earlier position in "Existentialism is a Humanism" had not gone far enough in opening up his work to this new realization. Ironically, one of the stimuli to this understanding came from Martin Heidegger, who finally spoke out against the French misappropriation of his position in 1947.[61] What makes Heidegger's role in Sartre's transformation particularly surprising is that it appeared in the context of an attack on Sartre's inappropriately humanist reading of *Being and Time*. In his "Letter on Humanism," Heidegger made clear his objection to being included in the existentialist

57. For a discussion of the Kantian dimension in his ethics, see Frederick A. Olafson, "Authenticity and Obligation" in Warnock, ed., *Sartre: A Collection of Critical Essays*.
58. Sartre, "Existentialism is a Humanism " in Kaufmann, ed., *Existentialism*, p. 303.
59. Sartre, "Materialism and Revolution" in *Literary and Philosophical Essays*, trans. Annette Michelson (London, 1955).
60. Sartre, "The Itinerary of a Thought" in *Between Existentialism and Marxism*, p. 33. The phrase "la force des choses" was adopted by Simone de Beauvoir as the title of one volume of her memoirs.
61. See note 17. The essay "Letter on Humanism" appears in English in Martin Heidegger, *Basic Writings*, ed. David Krell (New York, 1977).

camp because of his firm belief in the priority of Being to man. To make his point, he called on an unexpected ally:

Because Marx by experiencing estrangement attains an essential dimension of history, the Marxist view of history is superior to that of other historical accounts. But since neither Husserl nor—so far as I have seen till now—Sartre recognizes the essential importance of the historical in Being, neither phenomenology nor existentialism enters that dimension within which a productive dialogue with Marxism first becomes possible.[62]

To begin that dialogue, Heidegger contended, a more sophisticated notion of materialism than that held by Sartre would be imperative, one that would understand the relation of materialism to labor and production. "The modern metaphysical essence of labor is anticipated in Hegel's *Phenomenology of Spirit*," Heidegger argued, "as the self-establishing process of unconditioned production, which is the objectification of the actual through man experienced as subjectivity. The essence of materialism is concealed in the essence of technology."[63]

Although Sartre was never to focus on the issue of technology to the extent Heidegger suggested, he did slowly abandon his simplistic notion of materialism and began to include labor in his concept of action. The hesitancy he evinced in moving towards a full-fledged Marxism in the 1940s must in part be attributed to the vituperative attacks aimed at his philosophy by official spokesmen of the doctrine. The dialogue Heidegger had called for between Marxism and existentialism had begun after the war, but it was initially very sterile.[64] The alternative presented by Communist Party figures like Jean Kanapa, Roger Garaudy, Henri Mougin and the then-still-militant Henri Lefebvre to what Lefebvre indelicately called Sartre's "magic and metaphysics of shit"[65] was the orthodox Dialectical Materialism of Stalinism. Nothing very different was offered by foreign critics of *Being and Nothingness* like Lukács,[66] who was at the nadir of his intellectual development.

Nonetheless, Sartre did struggle to find a philosophical position commensurate with his "radical conversion."[67] The late 1940s and early

62. Ibid., pp. 219–20.
63. Ibid., p. 220.
64. For discussions of the debate, see Chiodi, *Sartre and Marxism*; Caute, *Communism and the French Intellectuals, 1914–1960*; and Poster, *Existential Marxism in Postwar France*.
65. Quoted in Poster, p. 117.
66. Lukács, *Existentialisme ou Marxisme?*, trans. E. Keleman (Paris, 1948); see also the 1947 article "Existentialism" in Lukács, *Marxism and Human Liberation*, ed. E. San Juan, Jr. (New York, 1973). One exception to this generalization was the review by Marcuse cited in note 50.
67. *Being and Nothingness*, p. 504.

1950s were the years of his most intense commitment to Left politics, first as a member of David Rousset's short-lived Rassemblement Démocratique Révolutionnaire in 1947, and then after abandoning his hope for a "third way" between capitalism and Communism, as a fellow-traveller of the French Communist Party from 1951 to 1956. These were also the years of his most politically engaged theater, most notably *Les Mains Sales* of 1948 and *Le Diable et le bon Dieu* of 1951,[68] as well as his highly publicized political quarrels with his former friends Aron, Camus and Merleau-Ponty. Although stridently supportive of the Soviet Union, at least until its invasion of Hungary, and willing to discount bourgeois "moralizing" about its failings, he was nonetheless unwilling to take the final step and submit himself to Party discipline.

The same caution can be discerned in his embrace of Marxism as a completely adequate alternative to existentialism. Here, too, Sartre remained a kind of fellow-traveller. Clear evidence of his hesitation can be seen in his attitude towards the concept of totality. As we saw in his critique of Surrealism in *What is Literature?*, Sartre was deeply suspicious of the links between a certain kind of holism, one based on the juxtaposition of reified entities whose human creation was forgotten, and totalitarianism. Even as he moved closer to heterodox Marxism in the 1950s, he retained this distaste for finished wholes of any kind. In fact, in the works that can be seen as his most significant contributions to Western Marxist theory, his *Search for a Method* of 1957 and the *Critique of Dialectical Reason* published three years later,[69] Sartre still resisted that meta-totality whose possibility had been so emphatically denied in *Being and Nothingness*.

Nonetheless, these works were intended as theoretical refutations of the antinomian pessimism of Sartre's existentialist period and, as such, should be examined for their solutions to the dilemmas of that earlier stage in his development. It would be tempting to interpret these answers either in terms of a covert restitution of Heidegger's notion of Being or as an uneasy acceptance of what Goldmann saw as its Lukácsian alternative, the Hegelian Marxist concept of totality. The former argument has, in fact, been advanced by the Italian critic, Pietro Chiodi, who claims that "in many important ways the *Critique* is a straightforward return to the Heideggerian position after the attack on it in *Being and Nothingness*."[70]

68. For discussion of Sartre's theater, see Pierre Verstraeten, *Violence et éthique: Esquisse d'une critique de la morale dialectique à partir du théâtre politique de Sartre* (Paris, 1972); and Aronson, *Jean-Paul Sartre*, p. 180f.

69. Sartre, *Search for a Method,* trans. Hazel E. Barnes (New York, 1963); *Critique of Dialectical Reason*, vol. 1: *Theory of Practical Ensembles*, trans. Alan Sheridan-Smith, ed. Jonathan Ree (London, 1976).

70. Chiodi, p. 8.

But, as Chiodi is forced to admit,[71] Sartre was never able to abandon the subject-object dialectic in favor of a prior, if forgotten, unified Being. In the *Critique*, Sartre addressed this issue with specific reference to the passage in Heidegger's "Letter on Humanism" dealing with Marx:

But how can we ground *praxis*, if we treat it as nothing more than the inessential moment of a radically non-human process? How can it be presented as a real material totalization if the whole of Being is totalized through it? Surely man would become what Walter Beimel, in his commentary on Heidegger, calls "the bearer of the Opening of Being." This is not a far fetched comparison. The reason why Heidegger paid tribute to Marxism is that he saw Marxist philosophy as a way of showing, as Waelhens says (speaking of Heideggerian existentialism), "that Being is Other in me . . . (and that) man . . . is himself only through Being, which is not him." But any philosophy which subordinates the human to what is Other than man, whether it be an existentialist or Marxist idealism, has hatred of man as both its basis and its consequence. History has proved this in both cases.[72]

Nor was Sartre willing to accept that Hegelian identification of subject and object that had underlain the argument of *History and Class Consciousness*. In fact, *Search for a Method* has a specific critique of Lukács' use of totality as an instrument of terror:

The totalizing investigation has given way to a Scholasticism of the totality. The heuristic principle—"to search for the whole in its parts"— has become the terrorist practice of "liquidating the particularity." It is not by chance that Lukács— Lukács who so often violates history—has found in 1956 the best definition of this frozen Marxism. Twenty years of practice give him all the authority necessary to call this pseudo-philosophy *a voluntarist idealism*.[73]

Sartre's animus here was obviously directed at Lukács' Stalinist works of the 1930s and 1940s, which he failed to distinguish from the earlier argument of *History and Class Consciousness*, a work which in certain respects, such as its rejection of a dialectics of nature, was closer to his own position. Was this failure merely a function of ignorance and would Sartre have found the Western Marxist Lukács more to his liking than his "scholastic" replacement? Although there is no direct evidence showing that Sartre had read *History and Class Consciousness* in 1957, he certainly must have known of its importance from Merleau-Ponty's *Adventures of the Dialectic*, published two years earlier. In the "Western Marxism" chapter of that book, Merleau-Ponty had specifically argued that the Lukács of the 1920s had propounded a non-dogmatic Marxism in which open-ended totalizations predominated over closed totalities:

71. Ibid., p. 24–25.
72. Sartre, *Critique of Dialectical Reason*, p. 181.
73. Sartre, *Search for a Method*, p. 28.

The totality of which Lukács speaks is, in his own terms, "the totality of observed facts," not of all possible and actual beings but of our coherent arrangement of all the known facts. When the subject recognizes himself in history and history in himself, he does not dominate the whole, as the Hegelian philosopher does, but at least he is engaged in a work of totalization.[74]

Sartre, however, inexplicably passed over this defense in silence and chose to ignore whatever sustenance his position might have received from Merleau-Ponty's reading of the early Lukács. In fact, there is virtually no trace of any other Western Marxist in Sartre's texts, with the one exception of Lefebvre, whose "progressive–regressive" method of historical analysis he endorsed in the *Search for a Method*.[75] The struggles with Lukács' problematic that we have traced in Korsch, Gramsci, Bloch and the Frankfurt School were either unknown to or ignored by Sartre. And yet by virtue of his still potent animus against Hegelianism of any kind, he recapitualated many of the earlier arguments directed against the original Hegelian-Marxist syntheses.

Sartre's appropriation of Marxism was, in fact, limited by his understanding of it in essentially orthodox terms. Rather than drawing on the heterodox tradition to which he was generally oblivious, he claimed Marxism had to be saved from without, by the remnants of his earlier existentialism. As he put it in the *Search*, "Marxism, while rejecting organicism, lacks weapons against it."[76] It is thus the task of existentialism, Sartre argued, to provide such weapons, even though in the process it is dissolved as an independent theoretical position. Most importantly, existentialism offers a sense of the primary and irreducible concreteness of the individual who resists collective hypostatization. "Kierkegaard," Sartre claimed still very much in the spirit of *Being and Nothingness*, "has as much right on his side as Hegel has on his own."[77] Lived existence stubbornly defies absorption into an abstract system.

Because of his continued hostility to the Hegelian answer to Kierkegaardian individualism, Sartre remained as critical of the concept of totality as he had been in *Being and Nothingness*. Whether in the hands of Gestaltists like Kurt Lewin, cultural anthropologists like Abraham Kardiner or "scholastic" Marxists like Lukács, totality, he insisted, is a category of undialectical hypostatization. As he put it in the *Critique*,

74. Merleau-Ponty, *Adventures of the Dialectic*, p. 31.
75. Sartre, *Search for a Method*, p. 51; Lefebvre rejected the honor of having invented the method and gave the credit to Marx. See his remarks in *Le temps des méprises* (Paris, 1975), p. 144.
76. Sartre, *Search for a Method*, p. 77.
77. Ibid., p. 12.

A totality is defined as a being which, while radically distinct from the sum of its parts, is present in its entirety, in one form or another, in each of these parts, and which relates to itself either through its relation to the relations between all or some of them. If this reality is *created* (a painting or a symphony are examples, if one takes integration to an extreme), it can exist only in the imaginary (*l'imaginaire*), that is to say, as the correlative of an act of imagination. The ontological status to which it lays claim by its very definition is that of the in-itself, the inert. The synthetic unity which produced its appearance of totality is not an activity, but only the vestige of a past action.[78]

Totality for Sartre is equivalent to the dead exteriority produced by human action. In the new terms of the *Critique*, it belongs to the realm of the "practico-inert," the worked-over matter that presents an obstacle to human spontaneity. Like Marx's concept of capital as dead labor or Sartre's own earlier notion of the in-itself, the practico-inert confronts man as an irreducible other, despite his role in its creation.

The term that Sartre counterposes to the practico-inert, a term which carries with it many of the same connotations as the for-itself in *Being and Nothingness*, is praxis, the subjective process of self-definition through action in the world. Whether or not all praxis for Sartre inevitably leads to the practico-inert, which would mean he collapses the Marxist distinction between alienation and objectification into a more Hegelian unity of the two, has engendered considerable debate.[79] Without going into its intricacies, it seems fair to say that Sartre extends alienation beyond the realm of labor to all aspects of human objectification which produce the practico-inert; hence the overcoming of alienation requires far more than the end of alienated labor under capitalism. Furthermore, lacking any normative notion of an essential man comparable to the early Marx's concept of "species–being," Sartre has no real model of what a completely de-alienated man would be like. It is thus difficult to attribute to him a clearcut theory of de-alienated objectification.

If totality and the practico-inert are related in Sartre's conceptual scheme, praxis has as its counterpart the notion of totalization. Like totality, totalization considers "each part an expression of the whole," but it differs from it in being a "*developing* activity which cannot cease without the multiplicity reverting to its original statute."[80] Whereas totality is inert and thing-like, totalization is dynamic, alive, and most significantly, inherently unstable. Totalization, to be sure, was not Sartre's invention.

78. Sartre, *Critique of Dialectical Reason*, p. 45.
79. See Chiodi, p. 23f; Poster, *Sartre's Marxism*, p. 61f; and Richard Schacht, *Alienation* (New York, 1971), p. 226f.
80. Sartre, *Critique of Dialectical Reason*, p. 47.

Lefebvre had already distinguished it from totality in his 1955 essay on the subject and, according to Georges Gurvitch,[81] the word was used as early as Proudhon's *De la création de l'ordre dans l'humanité* of 1843. It was left, however, to Sartre to elaborate in extraordinarily rich detail the processes of totalization and detotalization that constituted what he called "the intelligibility of dialectical Reason."[82]

Volume I of the *Critique*, the only one actually completed, was designed to spell out in abstract terms this alleged intelligibility, to lay the foundations, as Sartre put it with self-conscious reference to Kant, for a "prolegomena to any future anthropology."[83] The second volume, which remained unfinished like so many of Sartre's ambitious projects, was to show how in concrete, historical terms "there is *one* human history, with *one* truth and *one* intelligibility."[84]

If in *Being and Nothingness* Sartre played Descartes off against Heidegger and vice versa, the combatants of the *Critique* were Descartes and Marx, with the latter gaining only apparent ascendency. In the *Search*, Sartre identified "the most important theoretical contribution of Marxism" as the "wish to transcend the opposition of externality and internality, of multiplicity and unity, of analysis and synthesis, of nature and anti-nature."[85] Sartre clearly shared this wish, but the Cartesian (or on another level, the Kierkegaardian) in him prevented him from ever really believing that the wish could be fulfilled. The tensions generated by this internal struggle are perhaps in large measure accountable for the prolix, repetitive, tedious way in which the *Critique* was written and ultimately left unconcluded.

There have been many attempts to summarize and analyze what was finished, and this is not the place to try yet another. But its implications for the question of totality can be spelled out in the following terms. Because Sartre remained insistent on the priority of the individual over the collectivity, claiming that "individual practices are the sole ground of totalizing temporality,"[86] there was no possibility for him to adopt a truly expressive view of the whole in the manner of the early Lukács. For there could be no original meta-subject who created history, forgot its original creative act through the mystifying effects of reification, and then would regain it in the revolutionary act of becoming both subject and object of the whole. The historical process, Sartre contended, should be under-

81. Georges Gurvitch, *Dialectique et Sociologie* (Paris, 1962), p. 173.
82. Sartre, *Critique of Dialectical Reason*, p. 46.
83. Ibid., p. 66.
84. Ibid., p. 69.
85. Sartre, *Search for a Method*, p. 87.
86. Sartre, *Critique of Dialectical Reason*, p. 64.

stood instead as a "human work without an author,"[87] a "totalization without a totalizer."[88] The argument that he had made in *Being and Nothingness* about the absence of an external observer in the form of a transcendent God, who could totalize humanity as a whole through His gaze, was echoed in the *Critique*. Returning to that position he had had only partly modified in "Existentialism is a Humanism," he excoriated humanism as a bourgeois form of inert solidarity, which he called the aggregate collectivity of the series rather than the fused group.[89] What kept it together, he claimed, was the tacit exclusion of the worker. Whether or not a socialist humanism could replace it, Sartre did not explicitly say, but the burden of his argument, contrary to the reading of his later structuralist critics, was that it could not. Humanity as a collective "we-subject" was still an unattainable goal.[90]

If there was no meta-subject at the root of an expressive totality and no truly universal human subjectivity was indeed possible, how was it then meaningful to talk of history as a unified and intelligible whole, or what we have called a "longitudinal totality"? Sartre's response, although he seems to have been unaware of the similarity, harkened back more to Ernst Bloch than to Lukács. He wrote in the *Search*,

The plurality of the meanings of History can be discovered and posited for itself only upon the ground of a future totalization—in terms of the future totalization and in contradiction with it. It is our theoretical and practical duty to bring this totalization closer every day. . . . Our historical task, at the heart of this polyvalent world, is to bring closer the moment when History will have *only one meaning*.[91]

Here we see how far Sartre had come from Heidegger's nostalgia for a lost Being and how close he was not only to Bloch, but also to Goldmann with his irrational wager on the future.[92]

87. Sartre, *Search for a Method,* p. 100.
88. Sartre, *Critique of Dialectical Reason,* p. 805.
89. Ibid., p. 752f.
90. In the last interview before his death, Sartre returned to the question of humanism, which clearly continued to vex him. "If one views beings as finished and closed totalities," he argued, "humanism is not possible in our time. On the contrary, if one considers that these pre-men have within them certain principles that are human, I mean, certain germs which lead to man and which anticipate the being that constitutes the pre-man, then to think the relations from individuals to individuals by the principles that are imperative today, we will be able to call that a humanism. There is essentially the morality of the relation with the other. That is a moral theme that will remain when man will be. A theme of that kind can give rise to a humanist affirmation" ("Today's Hope: Conversations with Sartre" by Benny Lévy, *Telos* 44 [Summer 1980], pp. 161–62). In this rather muddled way, Sartre showed a certain nostalgia for the Kantian universalism he tied to existentialism in his 1945 essay.
91. Sartre, *Search for a Method,* p. 90.
92. Sartre had, in fact, read *The Hidden God* and cited it approvingly in *Search,* pp. 112–13. Goldmann, for his part, was relatively cool to existentialist Marxism. See his critical comments throughout *Essays on Method in the Sociology of Literature,* trans. and ed.

He was, however, careful to couch his faith in the future in conditional terms:

If History really is to be the totalization of all practical multiplicities and of all their struggles, the complex products of conflicts and collaborations of these very diverse multiplicities must themselves be intelligible in their synthetic reality, that is to say, they must be comprehensible as the synthetic products of a totalitarian *praxis*. This means that History is intelligible if the different practices which can be found and located at a given moment of the historical temporalization finally appear as partially totalizing and as connected and merged in their very oppositions and diversities by an intelligible totalization from which there is no appeal.[93]

That Sartre may have felt ambivalent about the complete desirability of this potential state of affairs can be intuited from his choice of words in this passage. Whereas Gramsci in the 1920s could employ "totalitarian" in an innocent way, Sartre in 1960 was certainly aware of its sinister connotations, yet chose to use it. There is, in fact, obviously something chilling in his talk of a totalization "from which there is no appeal." And yet, he did seem to feel that an intelligible total history was a real possibility. Volume II of the *Critique*, in fact, was designed to move from the conditional to the declarative. As he put it as late as 1969, when the project was not yet abandoned, "My aim will be to prove that there is a dialectical intelligibility of the singular. For ours is a singular history."[94]

But the second volume of the *Critique* remained unfinished. Devoted primarily to Soviet history during its Stalinist phase, the manuscript ran to six hundred or so pages before Sartre gave up on it, never to return. The reason for his failure, as one reader of the unpublished text has remarked, is that "he never begins his account of how a *multiplicity* of hostile or unrelated *praxes* cohere."[95] The only explanation he finally offered was the personal despotism of Stalin, who totalized Russian history through his coercive power. Making sense of the internal history of the Soviet Union was problematic enough for Sartre; how much more so must it have been to fit it into an intelligible total history of mankind?

It was, moreover, not only the intractability of actual history that defeated Sartre's ambitions, for in the abstract analysis of Volume I, there were equally severe obstacles to success. Despite his wager on the future,

William Q. Boelhower (St. Louis, 1980), and his essay "The Theater of Sartre," *The Drama Review* 15 (Fall 1970).
    93. Sartre, *Critique of Dialectical Reason*, p. 817.
    94. Sartre, "The Itinerary of a Thought," p. 54.
    95. Aronson, *Jean-Paul Sartre*, p. 285. A similar conclusion is reached in the editorial introduction to a portion of the manuscript, *New Left Review* 100 (November 1976 – January 1977), p. 139.

Sartre never really felt comfortable with the traditional Marxist reliance on History as the court of last judgment. Thus, for example, he resisted the tendency of Marxism to achieve "the totalization of human activities within a homogeneous and infinitely divisible continuum which is nothing other than the 'time' of Cartesian rationalism."[96] Radically subjectivizing the concept of temporality, he argued that

Neither men nor their activities are *in time*, but . . . time, as a concrete quality of history, is made by men on the basis of their original temporalization. Marxism caught a glimpse of true temporality when it criticized and destroyed the bourgeois notion of "progress"—which necessarily implies a homogeneous milieu and coordinates which would allow us to situate the point of departure and the point of arrival. But—without ever having said so—Marxism has renounced these studies and preferred to make use of "progress" again for its own benefit.[97]

In thus criticizing the homogeneous notion of univocal temporality, Sartre was in good company among Western Marxists. We have encountered similar arguments in Bloch, Benjamin, Horkheimer, and Adorno, and will see yet another in Althusser. But what set Sartre apart (or perhaps linked him only with Adorno) was his sober assessment of the repetitive and nonprogressive dimension of human temporality. Marcuse, to be sure, had also pondered the returns in history, but he did so essentially in the spirit of Heidegger's celebration of memory. Sartre, however, saw the implications of repetition very differently:

For us the reality of the collective object rests on *recurrence*. It demonstrates that the totalization is never achieved and that the totality exists at best only in the form of a *detotalized totality*.[98]

In the micrological analysis of group creation and destruction that occupied Sartre throughout the *Critique*, the ephemerality of totalization was in fact a constant theme. Commenting, for example, on the conflict of competing individual sovereignties, Sartre concluded:

The group itself, insofar as it is totalized by the practice of a given common individual, is an objective quasi-totality and, as a negated multiplicity of quasi-sovereignties, it is in a state of perpetual *detotalization*.[99]

Thus, Sartre's macrological wager on a future common totalization in which history would gain a single intelligibility was insidiously undermined by his more pessimistic appraisal, not terribly different from that in *Being and Nothingness*, of the dynamics of small group formation.

96. Sartre, *Search for a Method*, p. 91.
97. Ibid., p. 92.
98. Ibid., p. 98.
99. Sartre, *Critique of Dialectical Reason*, p. 579.

Sartre, to be sure, did attempt to include an "anti-dialectic" of passivity, in which groups constituted by collective subjective praxis were transformed back into the serial relations of the practico-inert, in his definition of his-torical intelligibility. But even if history might be seen as meaningful in these terms, the results were a far cry from the normative model of fulfilled totality that had inspired earlier Western Marxists. For Sartre, as most commentators have remarked, there seemed to be no really basic difference, as there had been for Hegelian Marxists, between objectifica-tion and alienation. All praxis, he implied, leads to the practico-inert; subjective *élan* always turns into reified institutions.

That Sartre felt the need to fight against these implications is evident, for example in his occasional evocation, very much against the grain of *Being and Nothingness*, of Vico's *verum—factum* principle. In his 1964 essay on "Kierkegaard: the Singular Universal," he chastised his former idol (and perhaps his own earlier acceptance of that idol's arguments) in the following terms:

Pitting himself against Hegel, he occupied himself over-exclusively with transmit-ting his instituted contingency to the human adventure and, because of this, he neglected *praxis*, which is rationality. At a stroke, he denatured *knowledge*, for-getting that the world we know is the world we make.[100]

But for all his bravado in pitting Vico against Kierkegaard, Sartre himself never really thought of the historical world as the knowable product of a collective human praxis, as had Lukács in *History and Class Conscious-ness*. When asked in 1969 by the editors of *Il Manifesto* if he believed that the proletariat could "transcend the level of seriality to become effectively and totally the subject of collective action," he bluntly replied, "This is an impossible condition; the working class can never express itself com-pletely as an active political subject; there will always be zones or regions or sectors which, because of historical reasons of development, will re-main serialized, massified, alien to the achievement of consciousness."[101]

In fact, the *Critique's* general analysis of human interaction demon-strated Sartre's awareness of how frequently group solidarity was a product of coercion, fear, even terror.[102] Although it may be an exaggeration to speak of a covert Hobbesianism in his analysis,[103] Sartre clearly felt that

    100. Sartre, "Kierkegaard: The Singular Universal" in *Between Existentialism and Marxism*, p. 168.
    101. Sartre, "France: Masses, Spontaneity, Party" in *Between Existentialism and Marx-ism*, p. 123.
    102. For Sartre's discussion of terror, see in particular, *Critique of Dialectical Reason*, p. 430f.
    103. The analogy with Hobbes is made by Aron, *Marxism and the Existentialists*, p.

instances in human history of true reciprocity and intersubjective consensus were rare indeed. The reason, he claimed, lay in material reality itself, or more specifically in scarcity, as a constraint on human cooperation and a source of violence. Whether or not Sartre considered scarcity an ontological fact, which would persist even after the attainment of socialism, or merely a human project that could thus be changed, has been heatedly contested.[104] From the evidence of the writings, he seems to have been uncertain in his own mind. "Man is violent," he wrote, "*throughout* History right up to the present day (until the elimination of scarcity, should this ever occur, and occur in *particular circumstances*)."[105] Once again a conditional phrasing expressed a deep ambivalence about the utopian dimension of his position. But it is a rare reader who could come away from the *Critique* thinking that Sartre had much faith in the possibility of achieving those "particular circumstances" in which scarcity would really end.

One final manifestation of the persistent desolation of Sartre's thought even during his most Marxist period can be discerned in what is a relatively minor aspect of his philosophy: the question of language. Here Sartre's distance from Heidegger, especially after the latter's "turn,"[106] was particularly acute. For the later Heidegger, language was the privileged locus of access to Being; prior to the split between subject and object, language "speaks" man rather than the reverse. For Sartre, in contrast, language (like time) was a human totalization, albeit one that quickly escapes human control. In an important sense, he claimed, language should be understood as part of the material world of the practico-inert:

Language might well be studied on the same lines as money: as a circulating, inert materiality, which unifies dispersal; in fact this is partly what philology does. Words live off the death of men, they come together through men; whenever I form a sentence its meaning escapes from me, is stolen from me; meanings are changed *for everyone* by each speaker and each day; the meanings of the very words in my mouth are changed by the others.[107]

Sartre, to be sure, acknowledged that language should also be understood as a "constantly developing organic totalization" so that "incommunica-

169, and by George Lichtheim, "Sartre, Marxism and History" in *Collected Essays* (New York, 1973), p. 387. It is criticized by Poster, *Sartre's Marxism*, p. 55; at least in part by Chiodi, p. 58f; and by Perry Anderson, *Considerations on Western Marxism* (London, 1976), p. 86.

104. Most of the literature, especially from the Left, attacks Sartre for ontologizing scarcity. Poster, *Sartre's Marxism*, and Jameson, *Marxism and Form*, are exceptions.

105. Sartre, *Critique of Dialectical Reason*, p. 736.

106. For a discussion of Heidegger's philosophy of language, see Joseph J. Kockelmans, ed., *On Heidegger and Language* (Evanston, 1972).

107. Sartre, *Critique of Dialectical Reason*, p. 98.

bility—insofar as it exists—can have meaning only in terms of a more fundamental communication, that is to say, when based on mutual recognition and on a permanent project to communicate."[108] But in general, he never thematically developed the implications of this "permanent project to communicate," a task left to Merleau-Ponty and then Habermas. His philosophy resolutely resisted the linguistic turn of much twentieth-century thought and remained wedded instead to the more traditional categories of subject and object, even as he was defining them in unorthodox ways. In fact, as one commentator put it, for Sartre, "The radical distinction between language and things is a condition of truth."[109] Because of his reluctance to abandon this distinction, Sartre remained within the problematic bequeathed to Western Marxism by Lukács, however much he may have modified it. Where he differed from Lukács, as we have seen, was in his refusal to follow the path from *Soul and Form* through *The Theory of the Novel* to *History and Class Consciousness*. Instead, he remained torn between his existentialist instincts and his Marxist aspirations, unable, despite his best intentions, to transcend the former in the name of the latter.

In fact, it is arguable that after the failure of the second volume of the *Critique*, Sartre covertly and remorsefully returned to the individualist concerns of his earlier period. "For a long time," he had reproached himself in *Search for a Method*, "we confused the *total* and the *individual*. Pluralism, which had served us so well against M. Brunschvicg's idealism prevented us from understanding the dialectical totalization."[110] But now after his inconclusive efforts to achieve that understanding, Sartre once again pursued the problem of individual totalization, or what he frequently called the "singular universal." Although still militant politically, indeed even a defender of Maoist activism, he withdrew in his purely theoretical work into the role of traditional intellectual. The massive but unfinished study of Flaubert, to which he devoted the remainder of his active life, rested on the method of existential psychoanalysis he had outlined in *Being and Nothingness* and honed in earlier studies of Baudelaire and Genet.[111] Although he now grasped the mediations of Flaubert's historical situation with greater concreteness than would have been possible before he wrote the *Critique*, his decision to focus on an individual artist,

108. Ibid.,
109. Fell, *Heidegger and Sartre*, p. 275.
110. Sartre, *Search for a Method*, p. 20.
111. Sartre, *The Family Idiot*, trans. Carol Cosman (Chicago, 1981); his earlier biographies were *Baudelaire*, trans. Martin Turnell (New York, 1950) and *Saint Genet, Actor and Martyr*, trans. Bernard Frechtman (New York, 1963). For a study of his work in this area, see Douglas Collins, *Sartre as Biographer* (Cambridge, 1980).

especially one whose anti-social contempt for group solidarity was no-
toriously vehement, strongly suggests the defeat of that book's hopes.
Lefebvre would speak for many in calling *The Idiot of the Family* "fundamentally an expression of despair, an admission of defeat, a bearer of
nihilism."[112] Like the later Frankfurt School, Adorno in particular, Sartre
registered the exhaustion of the Lukácsian paradigm in Western Marxism, or to put it in the terms of the *Critique*, the detotalization of the
concept of totality itself. It cannot come as much of a surprise to learn
that near the end of his life, he ceased calling himself a Marxist.[113]

It might be possible to read the *Critique* as the theoretical correlate of a
new type of political praxis closer to that of the New Left than to Lukács'
totalistic Leninism. In 1971, Fredric Jameson, for example, argued that:

Sartre's *Critique*, at the beginning of the 1960s written during the Algerian revolution and appearing simultaneously with the Cuban revolution, the radicalization
of the civil rights movement in the United States, the intensification of the war in
Vietnam, and the worldwide development of the student movement, therefore corresponds to a new period of revolutionary ferment.[114]

This ferment, Jameson and later observers like Mark Poster contended,[115]
achieved its quintessential expression in the May, 1968, events in France,
which in Jameson's words, was a "corroboration of Sartre's theory."[116]

But with the passage of more than a decade since the events, it is possible to see that what was "corroborated" was as much the darker elements
of that theory as the more hopeful. For no less startling and unexpected
than the outbreak of the student/worker rebellion was the manner of its
end. De Gaulle, having covertly assured the loyalty of the French army,
went on television to announce new elections, and, as if by magic, the
revolutionary fever broke. Although it was not fully clear until ten years
later with the bitter failure of the electoral alliance between the Socialists
and Communists, 1968 was less the portent of the future than the high
point of an historical era of unfulfilled hopes. The *Critique*'s emphasis on
the fragility of totalization and the likelihood, indeed the inevitability, of a

112. Lefebvre, *Le temps des méprises*, p. 149.
113. Reported by Michel Rybalka in a review of Poster, *Existential Marxism in Postwar
France*, in *Telos* 30 (Winter 1976–77), p. 226.
114. Jameson, *Marxism and Form*, p. 299.
115. Poster, *Existential Marxism in Postwar France*, p. 361f. In *A Preface to Sartre* La-
Capra, in contrast, argues that Derrida may be a better guide to the events:

One of the more promising features of the anticapitalistic and antibureaucratic protest during the May-
June 1968 events in France was the attempt to assert the need for more "supplementarity" and even
"carnivalesque" forms of relationship in modern institutional life. To this extent, these events may have
been more "advanced" than the analysis in Sartre's *Critique* that is often seen as their theoretical analogue. (p. 223)

116. Jameson, p. 272.

detotalizing regression of communal groups back into practico-inert series was no less confirmed by the outcome of events than was Sartre's analysis of revolutionary totalization.

Although future 1968s may occur, there is little reason to assume that
results will be different. Indeed, if the argument of Sartre's *Critique* is to be
taken seriously, it is hard to imagine they will be otherwise. In the last years
before his death in 1980, Sartre seems to have felt the weight of this conclusion. The last interview he gave ended with the following admission:

> With this third world war, which is going to break out one day, with this miserable
> ensemble that our planet is, despair returns to tempt me again: the idea that we
> will not ever finish it, that there is not any goal, that there are only individual goals
> for which people struggle. People start small revolutions, but there is not a goal for
> humanity, there is nothing that interests mankind, there are only disruptions.[117]

But like Adorno, who also refused to turn a pessimistic appraisal of contemporary possibilities into complete resignation, Sartre still struggled
against his desolation:

> The world seems ugly, bad, and without hope. That is the tranquil despair of an old
> man who will die within it. But that is precisely what I resist, and I know that I will
> die in hope; but it is necessary to create a foundation for this hope.[118]

But such a foundation, he seemed to be admitting, had not been achieved
through that forced marriage between existentialism and Marxism to
which he had devoted his remarkable energies since the Resistance.

Sartre, to be sure, was not the only French student of Husserl and
Heidegger who had turned to Marxism. In the work of his friend and
critic, Maurice Merleau-Ponty, another variant of existential Marxism
had been crafted, one which some commentators saw as avoiding the aporias of Sartre's position. How new difficulties developed, difficulties which
ultimately also led Merleau-Ponty away from Marxism, must be discussed in the next chapter.

117. Sartre, "Today's Hope," p . 180.
118. Ibid., 181.

Phenomenological Marxism:
The Ambiguities of
Maurice Merleau-Ponty's Holism

Insofar as Sartre overcame his initial antinomian dualism and drew closer to a more holistic social philosophy, credit must be given to his friendship with Maurice Merleau-Ponty. Reflecting on the meaning of that bond shortly after Merleau-Ponty's unexpected death in 1961, Sartre claimed:

> In a word, it was Merleau who converted me. At heart, I was a throwback to anarchy, digging an abyss between the vague phantasmagoria of collectivities and the precise ethic of my private life. He enlightened me.[1]

Even though Sartre's conversion may not have been complete—Merleau-Ponty, as we will see, thought not—his transformation from the existentialist of *Being and Nothingness* to the existentialist Marxist of *The Critique of Dialectical Reason* cannot be understood without acknowledging the impact of Merleau-Ponty's more insistently social philosophy.

Sartre, to be sure, never did fully commit himself to holism, Marxist or otherwise. In contrast, Merleau-Ponty's philosophy, indeed his entire outlook on the world, was deeply holistic from the beginning,[2] so much so

---

1. Jean-Paul Sartre, *Situations*, trans. Benita Eisler (New York, 1965), p. 255.
2. The literature on Merleau-Ponty, while not as extensive as on Sartre, is nonetheless very substantial. I have found the following works particularly useful: Thomas Langan, *Merleau-Ponty's Critique of Reason* (New Haven, 1966); Albert Rabil, Jr., *Merleau-Ponty: Existentialist of the Social World* (New York, 1967); John F. Bannan, *The Philosophy of Merleau-Ponty* (New York, 1967); Xavier Tilliette, *Merleau-Ponty ou la mesure de l'homme* (Paris, 1970); Theodore F. Geraets, *Vers une nouvelle philosophie transcendentale: La genèse de la philosophie de Maurice Merleau-Ponty jusqu'à la Phénoménologie de la perception* (The Hague, 1971); Garth Gillan, ed., *The Horizons of the Flesh: Critical Perspectives on the Thought of Merleau-Ponty* (Carbondale, Ill., 1973); Laurie Spurling, *Phenomenology and the Social World: The Philosophy of Merleau-Ponty and its Relation to the Social Sciences* (London, 1977); Barry Cooper, *Merleau-Ponty and Marxism: From Terror to Reform* (Toronto, 1979); Samuel B. Mallin, *Merleau-Ponty's Philosophy* (New Haven, 1979);

that when he finally abandoned Marxism, he did so in the name of a competing holism. Can it then be said that his variant of existentialist Marxism successfully avoided the problems that we have seen shipwreck Sartre's? Did he find a way to salvage the Lukácsian concept of totality from that process of disintegration we have been tracing in this book?

There can be no question that Merleau-Ponty was far more suited than Sartre for the task of rescuing Marxist holism. Whether or not we accept Sartre's contention that their differences can ultimately be traced to Merleau-Ponty's far happier childhood,[3] it is clear that he was never drawn, as was Sartre, to the bleak, anti-social individualism of those proto-existentialists Kierkegaard and Nietzsche. Even more than Heidegger, he stressed the sociality of mankind, the "*Mit-sein*" that the early Sartre had dismissed as only a mask for the deadly conflict of opposing subjectivities. Whereas Sartre rejected Descartes' rationalism but remained uneasily beholden to his dualism of subject and object, Merleau-Ponty relentlessly attacked both in the name of an enlarged concept of reason grounded in an ontology of monistic ambiguity.[4] Taking Kojève's Marxist reading of Hegel more seriously than Sartre did,[5] he realized far sooner that existence was an histori-

---

James Miller, *History and Human Existence: From Marx to Merleau-Ponty* (Berkeley, 1979); Sonia Kruks, *The Political Philosophy of Merleau-Ponty* (Atlantic Highlands, N.J., 1981). The relevant chapters in the following books are also worth consulting: Herbert Spiegelberg, *The Phenomenological Movement: An Historical Introduction*, vol. 2 (The Hague, 1960); Edward N. Lee and Maurice Mandelbaum, eds., *Phenomenology and Existentialism* (Baltimore, 1967); Joseph J. Kockelmans, ed., *Phenomenology: The Philosophy of Edmund Husserl and its Interpretations* (Garden City, N.Y., 1967); H. Stuart Hughes, *The Obstructed Path: French Social Thought in the Years of Desperation 1930–1960* (New York, 1969); Mark Poster, *Existential Marxism in Postwar France: From Sartre to Althusser* (Princeton, 1975); Dick Howard, *The Marxian Legacy* (New York, 1977); Fred R. Dallmayr, *Twilight of Subjectivity: Contributions to a Post-Individualist Theory of Politics* (Amherst, Mass., 1981).

3. Sartre, *Situations*, p. 296. As Merleau-Ponty's father was killed in action in 1914, when the son was six years old, it is difficult to talk of a really idyllic childhood.

4. The nature of this ambiguous monism can be captured from the following remarks in Merleau-Ponty's unpublished prospectus of his work written in the early 1950s, which appeared posthumously in *The Primacy of Perception*, ed. James M. Edie (Evanston, 1964):

The study of perception could only teach us a "bad ambiguity," a mixture of finitude and universality, of interiority and exteriority. But there is a "good ambiguity" in the phenomenon of expression, a spontaneity which accomplishes what appeared to be impossible when we observed only the separate elements, a spontaneity which gathers together the plurality of monads, the past and the present, nature and culture into a single whole. To establish this wonder would be metaphysics itself and would at the same time give us the principle of an ethics. (p. 11)

The importance of ambiguity in Merleau-Ponty's work has been a constant theme of his commentators ever since Ferdinand Alquié's "Une philosophie de l'ambiguité: l'existentialisme de M. Merleau-Ponty," *Revue Fontaine* 59 (April 1947).

5. Contrary to earlier accounts of Kojève's audience, Sartre was not among his regular listeners, whereas Merleau-Ponty was. For a good account of Kojève's importance, see Vincent Descombes, *Modern French Philosophy*, trans. L. Scott-Fox and J. M. Harding (Cambridge, 1980), Chapter 1. Spiegelberg largely blames Kojève for the confusion of Husserl

cal phenomenon in which concrete situations always enveloped individual subjectivities. Rather than insisting that men were condemned to a frustrating freedom with only absurd implications, he optimistically argued that "we are *condemned to meaning*."[6]

For Merleau-Ponty, subjective consciousness was embedded in two primordial and meaning-laden contexts: the sensual reality of the body and the intersubjective reality of the social world. From Gabriel Marcel, he took the insight that man "existed" his body as a pre-reflective condition of all consciousness, and he combined it with Bergson's stress on sensual perception as the means by which knowledge was initially generated. From the Gestaltists, who had been introduced in France by his friend Aron Gurwitsch,[7] he took the idea that perception was always prestructured in a meaningful and coherent way and integrated it with the phenomenological stress on objects in the world that were likewise significantly structured. From the later Husserl, whose *Crisis in the European Sciences* he had been the first in France to read in its entirety,[8] he absorbed the notion of a fundamental *Lebenswelt* (life-world) of meaningful symbols and actions prior to transcendental egos and objectifications. All of these influences he combined with Hegel's concept of a relational totality in which parts were mediated by larger wholes. The result was a philosophy of inclusion rather than exclusion that emphasized the dialectical interpenetration of mind and body, man and the world, individual and community, present action and historical context.

Merleau-Ponty never passed through a radically existentialist phase, dominated by a belief in the absurdity of isolated individual existence, before becoming a Marxist.[9] In fact, his interest in Marxism emerged in the 1930s, the same time he turned away from his youthful fascination

---

and Hegel in the minds of many French thinkers in the 1930s (*The Phenomenological Movement*, p. 413f).

6. Merleau-Ponty, *Phenomenology of Perception*, trans. Colin Smith (London, 1962), p. xix.

7. For a discussion of the introduction of Gestalt psychology to France, see Spiegelberg, p. 529. One of the Gestaltists most often quoted by Merleau-Ponty was the same Adhemar Gelb who had been Horkheimer's teacher in Frankfurt.

8. The first part of the *Crisis* was published in 1936. Shortly thereafter, Merleau-Ponty consulted the unpublished materials in the Husserl archive in Louvain, Belgium, which he cited in *Phenomenology of Perception*. See the discussion in H. L. van Breda, "Merleau-Ponty et les Archives-Husserl à Louvain," *Revue de Métaphysique et de Morale* 67 (October–December, 1962).

9. It is erroneous to argue, as do Raymond Aron and others, that all versions of existentialism are inherently incompatible with Marxism because of their individualist premises. For a critique of this alleged incompatibility, see Spurling, *Phenomenology and the Social World*, p. 93f.

with Catholicism towards phenomenology.[10] The publication in 1934 by Lefebvre and Guterman of selections from Marx's early writings gave him access to another Marx besides that promulgated by official spokesmen of the Communist Party. Thus, whereas Sartre could still identify Marxism with Dialectical Materialism in its crudest form as late as "Materialism and Revolution" in 1946, Merleau-Ponty came much earlier to appreciate its potential compatability with a non-individualist existentialist phenomenology. Indeed, Sartre was later to claim that his friend was never as close to Marxism as in the years before the Second World War.[11]

Although his first major writing, *The Structure of Behavior* of 1942, gave no evidence of this concern, his next work, *Phenomenology of Perception*, published in 1945, did demonstrate a growing identification with historical materialism.[12] The experience that seems to have convinced Merleau-Ponty to make manifest his political inclinations and allow them to permeate his philosophy was the Resistance, that brutal but inspirational political school for a generation of French intellectuals.[13] Unlike Sartre, whose Resistance involvement initially taught the absolute freedom of men whatever their objective circumstances, Merleau-Ponty learned that men were immersed in the ambiguities of history, whether they wanted to be or not. There was no pure freedom above the fray. Indeed, freedom and power, truth and violence were intimately related, or to use a phrase Sartre would later make his own, "no one's hands are clean."[14]

Merleau-Ponty was not, however, repelled by the impurity of man's immersion in history, but rather emboldened by it. For the Resistance, which he interpreted as a movement of genuine intersubjective solidarity, had also shown him that effective intervention in history was possible. "It is a question not of giving up our values of 1939," he exulted at the war's end, "but of realizing them."[15] For the next five years, Merleau-Ponty dedicated himself to his endeavor. In the roles of editor and major political

10. For a discussion of Merleau-Ponty's religious interests, which were stirred again near the end of his life, see Rabil, chapter 9.

11. Sartre, *Situations*, p. 242.

12. Merleau-Ponty, *The Structure of Behavior*, trans. Alden L. Fisher, foreword by John Wild (Boston, 1963) does contain isolated references to Hegel, but Marx is never mentioned. *Phenomenology of Perception*, in contrast, has important discussions of class consciousness and historical materialism, where Marx is specifically cited.

13. For Merleau-Ponty's reflections on the Resistance, see his essay "The War Has Taken Place" in *Sense and Non-Sense*, trans. Hubert L. Dreyfus and Patricia A. Dreyfus (Evanston, 1964). For a general account of intellectuals and the Resistance, with a discussion of Merleau-Ponty's role, see James D. Wilkinson, *The Intellectual Resistance in Europe* (Cambridge, 1981).

14. Merleau-Ponty, *Sense and Non-Sense*, p. 147. The same phrase appears in *Humanism and Terror: An Essay on the Communist Problem*, trans. John O'Neill (Boston, 1969), p. 60. Sartre was, of course, to adopt it in his play, *Dirty Hands*, in 1948.

15. Merleau-Ponty, *Sense and Non-Sense*, p. 152.

columnist for *Les Temps Modernes,* participant with Sartre in David Rousset's short-lived Rassemblement Democratique Revolutionnaire, and cautious fellow-traveller of the French Communist Party, he threw himself into the turbulent politics of postwar France. In 1947, he published *Humanism and Terror,* perhaps his most controversial book, which criticized Arthur Koestler's anti-Communist novel *Darkness at Noon* and offered a convoluted and essentially defensive analysis of the Moscow purge trials of the 1930s.[16] *Sense and Nonsense,* a series of essays on aesthetic, intellectual and political themes written from 1945 to 1947, appeared in the following year.[17]

But almost simultaneously with his entrance into public life began a subtle process of disillusionment. In 1945, he advocated a cautious identification with the Soviet Union and its allied Communist Parties in the hope that a proletarian revolution would follow the Second World War as it had the First. But in a footnote to an essay of that year reprinted in *Sense and Nonsense,* he soberly concluded:

Since then, while the West was shaping up a war machine, the U.S.S.R.—having returned to pessimism, pure authority, and ultimatums—made it necessary for the non-Communist left to state clearly, under pain of mystification, why it was not Communist, and would not in any case put up a liberal front for the system.[18]

By 1950, in fact, Merleau-Ponty's period of guarded political optimism was at an end. The Korean War, which many on the French Left, including Sartre, blamed on the United States, he saw instead as evidence of Russian bellicosity. As one of his main arguments for supporting the Soviet Union had been its peaceful intentions, the war's origin as he understood it left him deeply embittered. Following his resignation from the editorial board of *Les Temps Modernes* over a minor squabble,[19] he lapsed into a period of unwonted silence, which seems to have been prolonged by the death of his mother in 1952.

At approximately the same time, Sartre was moving politically in the opposite direction, aligning himself more closely than ever with the Soviet Union and the French Communist Party, whose policies he defended unflinchingly in *The Communists and the Peace,* a series of articles published in *Les Temps Modernes* between 1952 and 1954.[20] In the following year, Merleau-Ponty broke his silence with a major work of political philoso-

16. See note 14. For an extensive discussion of *Humanism and Terror* and its reception, see Cooper.
17. See note 13.
18. Merleau-Ponty, *Sense and Non-Sense,* p. 171.
19. For an account of the dispute, see Sartre, *Situations,* p. 297f.
20. Sartre, *The Communists and the Peace: With a Reply by Claude Lefort,* trans. Martha H. Fletcher, John Klemschmidt and Philip R. Berk (New York, 1968).

phy, *Adventures of the Dialectic*, which was aimed in large measure at what he termed Sartre's "Ultrabolshevism."[21] Rejecting the "expectant Marxism" of the postwar period, he now defended a "new liberalism" which drew on Max Weber as much as on Marx. Although he resisted the role of Cold War anti-Communist, preferring to label his position "a-communism," he had clearly lost his willingness to wager on Marxism as the handmaiden of progressive historical change.

Although he did return to political commentary, now as a supporter of Pierre Mendès-France in the pages of the left-liberal mass circulation journal *L'Express,* most of his energies went into more purely philosophical work. Elevated in 1953 to the chair once held by Bergson at the Collège de France, he lectured on a wide variety of philosophical topics, while reestablishing his links with non-Marxist philosophical schools, most notably Husserlian phenomenology.[22] His last works also showed an openness to the penetration of linguistics into social thought and philosophy that marked the nascent structuralist movement, about which he wrote sympathetically in *Signs,* which appeared in 1960.[23] After his sudden death at the age of 53 in May, 1961, selections from his uncompleted final projects were published as *The Visible and the Invisible, The Primacy of Perception* and *The Prose of the World,* while several volumes of his lectures were compiled by former students.[24]

Although Merleau-Ponty influenced a number of young political theorists on the Left, most notably Claude Lefort and Cornelius Castoriadis,[25] and had several philosophical disciples such as Alphonse de Waelhens and Mikel Dufrenne,[26] his star waned in the mid-1960s when new ones arose to dazzle the French intellectual scene.[27] The events of 1968 can certainly be

21. Merleau-Ponty, *Adventures of the Dialectic,* trans. Joseph Bien (Evanston, 1973), chap. 5.

22. For evidence of Merleau-Ponty's renewed interest in traditional philosophical schools, see his inaugural lecture at the Collège de France, *In Praise of Philosophy,* trans. John Wild and James E. Edie (Evanston, 1963).

23. Merleau-Ponty, *Signs,* trans. Richard C. McCleary (Evanston, 1964). The essay in which he wrote about structuralism was entitled "From Mauss to Claude Lévi-Strauss."

24. Merleau-Ponty, *The Visible and the Invisible: Followed by Working Notes,* ed. Claude Lefort, trans. Alphonso Lingis (Evanston, 1968); *The Prose of the World,* ed. Claude Lefort, trans. John O'Neill (Evanston, 1973); *Themes from the Lectures at the Collège de France 1952–1960,* trans. John O'Neill (Evanston, 1970); "Philosophy and Non-Philosophy Since Hegel," *Telos* 29 (Fall 1976). See also the essays collected by James Edie in *The Primacy of Perception,* which appeared as a book only in English.

25. For a discussion of Lefort and Castoriadis and their relations with Merleau-Ponty, see Dick Howard, *The Marxian Legacy.* See also his introduction to an interview with Castoriadis in *Telos* 23 (Spring 1975) and his introduction to an essay by Lefort in *Telos* 22 (Winter 1974–75).

26. For discussions of their indebtedness to Merleau-Ponty, see Spiegelberg, *The Phenomenological Movement.*

27. For a good account of the shift, see Descombes, *Modern French Philosophy.* The

understood as owing something to the open and experimental Marxism he had propounded after World War II, but the vexing ambiguities of his later work did little to nurture the activism of the French New Left. In fact, he was adopted by the so-called "New Philosophers" of the 1970s as a fellow anti-totalitarian "moraliste" in the tradition of Kant and Camus.[28]

If, then, Merleau-Ponty can be said to have made a significant contribution to the Western Marxist discourse on totality and perhaps to have found solutions to the dilemmas of Sartre and others in the tradition, it could only have happened during the relatively short period of his Marxist militancy from 1945 until the Korean War. It was then that the concept of totality was at the center of his concerns. Merleau-Ponty was one of the first French thinkers to appreciate the significance of *History and Class Consciousness*, from which he approvingly quoted as early as his 1946 essay on "Marxism and Philosophy."[29] Even earlier, in a long footnote on historical materialism in *The Phenomenology of Perception*, he implicitly invoked the concept of totality as an antidote to vulgar Marxist economism. Marxism, he argued,

does not bring the history of ideas down to economic history, but replaces these ideas in the one history which they both express, and which is that of social existence. . . . In this sense there is never any pure economic causality, because economics is not a closed system but is a part of the total and concrete existence of society.[30]

---

extent of the change can be measured by comparing his portrayal of modern French philosophy, written in the late 1970s, with that of Colin Smith, *Contemporary French Philosophy* (London, 1964). Smith's sub-title is *A Study in Norms and Values* and his main figures are existentialists and phenomenologists. He also treats philosophers like Lalande, Polin, Jankélévitch, Le Senne and Parain, who are completely absent from Descombes' account. Saussure, in contrast, is never even mentioned by Smith.

28. Bernard-Henri Lévy, *Barbarism with a Human Face*, George Holoch (New York, 1979), pp. 196–97. For a critique of the tendencies in the late Merleau-Ponty that allowed him to be used in this way, see Kruks, chapters 6 and 7.

29. Merleau-Ponty, *Sense and Non-Sense*, p. 126. Merleau-Ponty seems to have discovered *History and Class Consciousness* independently of Goldmann, whose work is not mentioned by him until *Adventures of the Dialectic*, p. 66. where *The Human Sciences and Philosophy* is cited. Interestingly, Merleau-Ponty was also aware of the importance of Piaget's psychology in the early 1940s, as several references to him in *Phenomenology of Perception* demonstrate. But he seems to have been more critical of the evolutionary implications of Piaget's work, which Goldmann, and later Habermas, would find attractive. See his remarks on p. 355, where he writes: "It must be the case that the child's outlook is in some way vindicated against the adult's and against Piaget, and that the unsophisticated thinking of our earliest years remains as an indispensable acquisition underlying that of maturity, if there is to be for the adult one single intersubjective world." See also his critique of Piaget for not being Gestaltist enough in *Sense and Non-Sense*, p. 85. The less evolutionary implications of Lévi-Strauss's version of structuralism attracted him more than they did Goldmann. See their contributions to "Sur les rapports entre la mythologie et le rituel," *Bulletin de la société française de la philosophie* 3 (October–December 1956).

30. Merleau-Ponty, *Phenomenology of Perception*, pp. 171–72.

And in an essay written in 1945, he asserted that "the greatness of Marxism lies not in its having treated economics as the principal or unique cause of history but in its treating cultural history and economic history as two abstract aspects of a single process."[31] A year later, he put it even more directly in criticizing the Trotskyist Pierre Naville: "The notion of structure or totality, for which P. Naville has nothing but mistrust, is one of the basic categories of Marxism."[32]

Like the first generation of Western Marxists, Merleau-Ponty contended that Hegel was vitally important for Marxism; but his Hegel was also that of Kojève, Wahl, and especially Hyppolite, that is, basically compatible with existentialism as well.[33] In "Hegel's Existentialism," published in *Les Temps Modernes* in 1946, he defended the Hegel of *The Phenomenology of Mind* period against the strictures of Kierkegaard. Rather than trying to fit history into a preconceived logical pattern, the young Hegel was "concerned with recapturing a total sense of history, describing the inner workings of the body social, not with explaining the adventures of mankind by debates among philosophers."[34] Moreover—and here Merleau-Ponty repeated the arguments of the Surrealists without acknowledgement—Hegel's rationalism, which some existentialists had scorned as incompatible with lived experience, provided an enlarged concept of reason transcending the earlier intellectualist notion of an abstract, ahistorical *Logos*. This enlarged concept was fully compatible with the phenomenological concept of reason, which Merleau-Ponty outlined in *The Phenomenology of Perception*:

Probably the chief gain from phenomenology is to have united extreme subjectivism and extreme objectivism in its notion of the world or of rationality. Rationality is precisely measured by the experiences in which it is disclosed. To say that there exists rationality is to say that perspectives blend, perceptions confirm each other, a meaning emerges. But it should not be set in a realm apart, transposed into absolute Spirit, or into a world in the realist sense. . . . Rationality is not a *problem*. There is behind it no unknown quantity which has to be determined by deduction, or beginning with it, demonstrated inductively. We witness every minute the miracle of related experiences, and yet nobody knows better than we how this miracle is worked, for we are ourselves this network of relationships. The world and reason are not problematical.[35]

31. Merleau-Ponty, *Sense and Non-Sense*, p. 107.
32. Ibid., p. 126.
33. For a discussion of the subtleties of his Hegel interpretation, see Sonia Kruks, "Merleau-Ponty, Hegel and the Dialectic," *Journal of the British Society for Phenomenology* 7, 2 (May 1976).
34. Merleau-Ponty, *Sense and Non-Sense*, p. 64.
35. Merleau-Ponty, *Phenomenology of Perception*, pp. xix–xx.

To the extent that the early Hegel had not yet equated reason with the Absolute Spirit, he was true to this phenomenological sense of reason immanent in human relations. It was therefore wrong to see him as an opponent of existentialism, for

A more complete definition of what is called existentialism than we get from talking of anxiety and the contradictions of the human condition might be found in the idea of a universality which men affirm or imply by the mere fact of their being and at the very moment of their opposition to each other, in the idea of a reason immanent in unreason, of a freedom which comes into being in the act of accepting limits and to which the least perception, the slightest movement of the body, bear incontestable witness.[36]

In short, reason was revealed in history, as even, so Merleau-Ponty contended, the late Husserl had recognized.[37] The full realization of that reason, he hastened to add, was dependent on human praxis, for

It is consciousness which *definitively* puts reason into history by linking the constellation of facts in a particular way. Every historical undertaking is something of an adventure, since it is never guaranteed by any *absolutely* rational structure of things.[38]

Marxism, therefore, had a "completely empirical and experimental character."[39] Or to employ the influential distinction Bergson had made in 1932 in *The Two Sources of Morality and Religion*, it was an "open" rather than "closed" system.[40] "The contingency of history," Merleau-Ponty insisted with characteristic caution, "means that even if the diverse orders or events form a single intelligible text, they are nonetheless not rigorously bound together, that there is a certain amount of free play in the system."[41]

Merleau-Ponty's unwillingness to make reason a guarantor of the coherence of history as a longitudinal totality extended as well to his normative notion of totality. Whether or not the perfect unity of subject and object posited by Hegel and Hegelian Marxists like Lukács could ever be fully achieved, Merleau-Ponty refused to say. Against the dogmatic insistence of Lefebvre that Communism would realize the "total man," he cautioned

Whether it bears the name of Hegel or Marx, a philosophy which renounces the absolute Spirit as history's motive force, which makes history walk on its own feet

36. Merleau-Ponty, *Sense and Non-Sense*, p. 70.
37. Ibid., p. 135.
38. Ibid., p. 166.
39. Ibid., p. 120.
40. For a discussion of the general impact of Bergson's distinction on French thought, see Colin Smith, p. 143f.
41. Merleau-Ponty, *Sense and Non-Sense*, p. 121.

and which admits no other reason in things than that revealed by their meeting and interaction, could not affirm *a priori* man's possibility for wholeness, postulate a final synthesis resolving all contradictions or affirm its inevitable realization. . . . Although synthesis exists *de jure* in Hegel, it can never be more than *de facto* in Marxism. . . . It cannot assign history a particular end in advance; it cannot even affirm the dogma of "total man" before he actually comes into being.[42]

If from the very beginning, then, there was a strong note of caution in Merleau-Ponty's Marxism, he nonetheless was willing in the years after the war to place that Pascalian bet which Goldmann later claimed was at the root of every intellectual conversion to historical materialism. In *Humanism and Terror*, he boldly proclaimed,

To be a Marxist is to believe that economic problems and cultural or human problems are a single problem and that the proletariat, as history has shaped it, holds the solution to that problem. In modern language, it is to believe that history has a *Gestalt*, in the sense German writers give to the word, a holistic system moving towards equilibrium.[43]

Indeed, because history has such a potential resolution, it is possible to apply a standard to judge violence and terror in the present. That standard, Merleau-Ponty contended, was not an ahistorical condemnation of all violence as incompatible with humanist goals, the mistaken position of those "beautiful souls" whose hands remained unsullied by historical compromise. Instead, it was the somber recognition that some acts of violence serve the cause of historical progress, while others do not. Terror—and here Merleau-Ponty was very much the student of Kojève[44]—was an irreducible dimension of politics, at least in the present. What had to be judged was the use to which it was put, or else one fell into "Quaker hypocrisy."[45]

During the period of his Marxist militancy, Merleau-Ponty resolutely contended that the only possible agent of human progress was the working class. Indeed, in *Humanism and Terror*, he answered the liberal reproach that Marxist holism was virtually indistinguishable from its fascist counterpart by pointing to its reliance on the proletariat:

It is the theory of the proletariat which radically distinguishes Marxism from every so-called "totalitarian" ideology. Of course, the idea of totality plays an

42. Ibid., pp. 81–82.
43. Merleau-Ponty, *Humanism and Terror*, p. 130.
44. According to Descombes, "Kojève bequeathed to his listeners a *terrorist conception of history*" (p. 14). It is significant that Georges Bataille and Pierre Klossowski were also in his audience in the 1930s. Their fascination with Nietzschean notions of power, violence and madness were later influential on the post-structuralists. The Kojèvean theme of terror thus provides another link between Merleau-Ponty and the current masters of French thought in addition to those to be mentioned shortly.
45. Merleau-Ponty, *Humanism and Terror*, p. 107.

essential role in Marxist thought. It is the concept of totality which underlies the whole Marxist critique of the "formal," "analytic," and pseudo-objective nature of bourgeois thought. . . . The opponents of Marxism never fail to compare this "totalitarian" method with the Fascist ideology which also pretends to go from the formal to the actual, from the conceptual to the organic. But the comparison is in bad faith. . . . For if the proletariat is the force on which revolutionary society is based and if the proletariat is that "universal class" we have described from Marx, then the interests of this class bring human values into history and the proletariat's power is the power of humanity. Fascist violence, by contrast, is not the violence of a universal class, it is the violence of a "race" or late-starting nation; it does not follow the course of things, but pushes against them.[46]

In so arguing, as many commentators have noted, Merleau-Ponty was betraying his own best instincts. The harsh critic of all anti-empirical, essentialist systems, the bitter opponent of all idealist "high-altitude thinking,"[47] the advocate of irreducible historical ambiguities had allowed himself to turn the proletariat of his imagination into the transcendental ground of his historical optimism. Like Gramsci and Korsch, he tacitly made history into an absolute itself and assigned it an inherent direction. Although hedging his bets by couching his description of the proletariat as a universal class in conditional terms, he nonetheless made an irrational decision to justify certain acts of violence on the grounds that the "ifs" of history would come true. As he put it in *Sense and Nonsense*, "Faith—in the sense of an unreserved commitment which is never completely justified—enters the picture as soon as we leave the realm of pure geometrical ideas and have to deal with the existing world."[48]

But faith can easily be shaken, especially when it rests on an assumption so deeply at odds with the rest of a thinker's world-view. By 1947, Merleau-Ponty had abandoned the slim hopes he entertained after the war in the rising of the American working class.[49] The Soviet Union's refusal to jeopardize its own security in the cause of a European proletarian uprising soon soured him on its claim to represent true working-class interests. And the French Communist Party's authoritarian inflexibility, expressed among other ways in its unremittingly hostility to his own work,[50] made

46. Ibid., pp. 123–24.
47. Cited in Sartre, *Situations*, p. 229.
48. Merleau-Ponty, *Sense and Non-Sense*, p. 179.
49. In the preface to *Sense and Non-Sense*, he wrote, "Just after the war one again had reason to hope that the spirit of Marxism would reappear, that the movement of the American masses would take up the banner" (p. 4). It is difficult to know on what grounds Merleau-Ponty might have held such an unlikely hope.
50. For a discussion of the Communist reaction to Merleau-Ponty, see Cooper, *Merleau-Ponty and Marxism*, chapter 4. One of his most vocal critics was Lukács, who attacked him at length as a covert Trotskyist in *Existentialisme ou Marxisme?* (Paris, 1948). In that work, Lukács also defended once again the category of totality against both its fascist abusers, like

fellow-travelling increasingly problematic. By the late 1940s, Merleau-Ponty could no longer apologize for every distasteful aspect of Soviet practice, such as the forced labor camps,[51] on the basis of his tentative historical theodicy. Stalinism, he came to see, was a variant of Bonapartism, rather than the embodiment of proletarian activism. The final straw, as we have noted, was the invasion of South Korea, which taught him that "proletarian" violence could not always be justified as inherently progressive. By 1950, he realized that the emergence of reason from unreason, sense from nonsense, was far less likely than he had thought a few years before.

Without a faith in the proletariat as the universal class of history, Merleau-Ponty was also forced to acknowledge that Husserl and Hegel were less compatible than he had previously contended. Even an existentialist version of Hegel had assumed too rational a course of history. The phenomenology of the twentieth century, that of Husserl and Heidegger, was closer to the truth, Merleau-Ponty reluctantly concluded, than that of the nineteenth. The impact of this conclusion on his concept of totality was readily apparent in his next work, *Adventures of the Dialectic*, which dramatically broke his self-imposed silence. "Politics," he ruefully admitted at the beginning of the book, "is never able to see the whole directly."[52] In fact, "Marxism does not have a total view of universal history at its disposal; and its entire philosophy of history is nothing more than the development of partial views that a man situated in history, who tries to understand himself, has of his past and of his present."[53] According to Merleau-Ponty, the early Lukács had understood the contingent nature of Marxism's claim to total knowledge, a claim that could be redeemed only in the practical activity of the proletariat. For Lukács, the working class was a totality only in "intention."[54] But, as Josef Revai had argued in his 1924 review of *History and Class Consciousness*, there was a certain "conceptual mythology" in Lukács' assumption that the proletariat represented the subject and object of history even tendentially. "This hold on the future," Merleau-Ponty concluded with Revai, "—and moreover, on the past, which remains to be unveiled in its true light—was, for Lukács, guaranteed to the proletariat because the proletariat is the work of nega-

---

Othmar Spann, and its existentialist critics, like Karl Jaspers (p. 273f). Merleau-Ponty obliquely responded to Lukács in a short piece written in December 1949 entitled "Marxism and Superstition," in *Signs*, which concluded "thus communism goes from historical responsibility to naked discipline, from autocriticism to repudiation, from Marxism to superstition" (p. 262).

51. Merleau-Ponty, "The U.S.S.R. and the Camps" in *Signs*.
52. Merleau-Ponty, *Adventures of the Dialectic*, p. 4.
53. Ibid., p. 51.   54. Ibid., p. 45.

tivity. If the proletariat is nothing but a carrier of myths, the whole meaning of the revolutionary enterprise is in danger."[55]

Because Merleau-Ponty no longer could believe in Lukács' myth of the proletariat as the subject and object of history, he concluded that however superior *History and Class Consciousness* may have been to what followed, "there was something justified in the opposition it encountered."[56] More precisely, what Lukács, "Western Marxism," and indeed the young Marx himself had failed to understand were the limits of subjective humanism:

The Marxism of the young Marx as well as the "Western" Marxism of 1923 lacked a means of expressing the inertia of the infra-structures, the resistance of economic and even natural conditions, and the swallowing up of "personal relationships" in "things." History as they described it lacked density and allowed its meanings to appear too soon. They had to learn the slowness of mediations.[57]

In short, they lacked an appreciation of that intractible historical reality known as the "institution," the web of constraining, if ultimately meaningful, historical residues that were reducible neither to spirit nor to matter. Nor would such inertial institutions, Merleau-Ponty contended, be overcome by the proletarian revolution:

Marx was able to have and to transmit the illusion of a negation realized in history and in its "matter" only by making the non-capitalistic future an absolute Other. But we who have witnessed a Marxist revolution well know that revolutionary society has its weight, its positivity, and that it is therefore not the absolute Other.[58]

It was precisely because he had failed to learn this lesson and appreciate the density of institutional mediations that Sartre was the special target of Merleau-Ponty's ire in *Adventures of the Dialectic*. Still beholden to his early dualistic ontology, Sartre, according to his erstwhile friend, had transformed the Leninist Party into the incarnation of a totally unconstrained transcendental subject outside of history, which could then manipulate the masses like so much passive matter. The result was an advocacy of pure action, a radical voluntarism that was all the more absurd because of Sartre's studied refusal to join the Party himself. His "ultrabolshevism" was thus the result of an inability to appreciate the "interworld" of symbols, institutions and incarnated meanings that enveloped the opposition of active subjects and passive objects. Even as an apologist for Communist policies, Sartre remained an unregenerate existentialist trapped in the antinomies of *Being and Nothingness*.

55. Ibid., p. 55.   56. Ibid., p. 57.
57. Ibid., p. 64.   58. Ibid., p. 90.

In her heated rebuttal of Merleau-Ponty's charges,[59] Simone de Beauvoir claimed that he had created a straw man in his portrayal of Sartre, whose movement away from the stark antinomies of his earlier work had been profound. There may have been some truth to this defense, but Sartre still had a long way to go before completely overcoming his Cartesian past. Even in the later *Critique of Dialectical Reason*, strong residues remained. We cannot say whether or not Merleau-Ponty, who began a halting rapprochement with Sartre before his death, would have seen in that work a resolution of Sartre's earlier problems. In fact, Sartre's *Critique* might have alienated Merleau-Ponty by holding on to certain Western Marxist notions, such as the possibility of longitudinal totality. As Paul Ricoeur noted in his memorial tribute, "It is doubtful . . . that the idea of totalization—even detotalization—would have found favor in his eyes, to the extent that it saved what Merleau-Ponty wanted to lose in order to see more clearly: the idea of universal history."[60]

In fact, the vehemence of Merleau-Ponty's attack on Sartre in *Adventures of the Dialectic* may well have reflected a covert desire to exorcise the demons of his own Marxist past. In disparaging the "ultrabolshevik" idea of the Party as the surrogate of transcendental consciousness, he was also belittling the role the proletariat had played in his own thought as the covertly transcendental ground of historical meaning. In his epilogue, he posed the key question, "Is it then the conclusion of these adventures that the dialectic was a myth?"[61] His answer was very revealing:

The illusion was only to precipitate into an historical fact—the proletariat's birth and growth—history's total meaning, to believe that history itself organized its own recovery, that the proletariat's own power would be its own suppression, the negation of the negation. . . . What then is obsolete is not the dialectic but the pretention of terminating it in an end of history, in a permanent revolution, or in a regime which, being the contestation of itself, would no longer need to be contested from the outside and, in fact, would no longer have anything outside it.[62]

Like Adorno, Merleau-Ponty proposed an essentially negative dialectic without the likelihood of any positive resolution. The expressive view of totality, which had been uneasily combined with his phenomenological

59. Simone de Beauvoir, "Merleau-Ponty et le pseudo-Sartrisme," *Les Temps Modernes* 10, 114–115 (June–July 1955). See also Mikel Dufrenne, "Sartre and Merleau-Ponty" in *Jean-Paul Sartre: Contemporary Approaches to His Philosophy*, eds. Hugh J. Silverman and Frederick A. Elliston (Pittsburgh, 1980). He argues that even *Being and Nothingness* was more of a philosophy of ambiguity than Merleau-Ponty understood.
60. Paul Ricoeur, "Hommage à Merleau-Ponty," *Esprit* 29, 296 (June–July 1961), p. 1119.
61. Merleau-Ponty, *Adventures of the Dialectic*, p. 205.
62. Ibid., pp. 205–6.

critique of any meta-subjective constitution of the world, was now completely abandoned. As Ricoeur noted, with it went the hope, always a
shaky one, of understanding history as a unified system with an underlying temporal homogeneity. As Merleau-Ponty put it in the preface to *Signs*
in 1960, "There is no universal clock."[63] Although during the 1950s he
struggled to find a formula that would capture a contingently determined
pattern of history,[64] it is clear that the quasi-Hegelian optimism of the
previous decade was behind him. Although he occasionally permitted
himself a nostalgic glance backwards at the proletariat,[65] his new allegiance was to a non-Communist leftism that approached what he called
Max Weber's "heroic liberalism."[66]

Now, instead of saying that if the unity of subject and object were not
guaranteed by history, at least it was a possible and desirable goal, he
criticized even the possibility. To rethink Marxism, he wrote in *Signs*,

is not a matter of classifying men and societies according to their approximation
to the canon of the classless society or the man without conflicts; these negative
entities cannot be used to think about existing men or societies. . . . The "healthy"
man is not so much the one who has eliminated his contradictions as the one who
makes use of them and drags them into his vital labors. . . . Human history is not
from this moment on so constructed as to one day point, on all its dials at once, to
the high noon of identity.[67]

There was, in other words, no normative totality which could be used as
the critical vantage point from which the present might be judged and, as
he had argued in *Humanism and Terror*, in whose name proletarian violence might be justified. In fact, and here he sounded very much like
Adorno, the concept of a harmonistic end of history was "an idealization
of death,"[68] rather than the realization of life.

In so arguing, Merleau-Ponty moved subtly away from the humanist
bias of his militant Marxist period, which he now began to see had led him
to neglect a crucial dimension of reality as a complete whole. Previously, he
had attacked only bourgeois humanism with its questionable belief in a

63. Merleau-Ponty, *Signs*, p. 35.
64. See, for example, his "Materials for a Theory of History," in *Themes from the
Lectures*.
65. In the Preface to *Signs*, he wrote: "Perhaps one day, after incredible detours, the
proletariat will rediscover its role as the universal class, and will once more take over that
universal Marxist criticism which for the moment has no historical impact or bearing"
(p. 8).
66. Merleau-Ponty, *Adventures of the Dialectic*, p. 226.
67. Merleau-Ponty, *Signs*, pp. 130–31.
68. Merleau-Ponty, *Adventures of the Dialectic*, p. 206. Where he differed with Adorno
was in not attributing this fetish of death to Heidegger.

human nature outside of history. Like Sartre, he had wanted to defend another kind of non-essentialist humanism. In 1951 he had written,

Even those among us today who are taking up the word "humanism" again no longer maintain the *shameless humanism* of our elders. What is perhaps proper to our time is to disassociate humanism from the idea of a humanity fully guaranteed by natural law, and not only reconcile consciousness of human values and consciousness of the infrastructures which keep them in existence, but insist upon their inseparability.[69]

But soon after, he began to question even a socialist humanism in which man's alleged species-being would be realized in a Communist future. In his inaugural address at the Collège de France in 1953, he argued that philosophy "eludes both Promethean humanism and the rival affirmations of theology. The philosopher does not say that a final transcendence of human contradictions may be possible, and that the complete man awaits us in the future. Like everyone else, he knows nothing of this."[70] To make man the key explanatory principle of philosophy was mistaken, he continued, because

One explains nothing by man, since he is not a force but a weakness at the heart of being. . . . His existence extends to too many things, in fact to all, for him to become the object of his own delight, or for the authorization of what we can now reasonably call a "human chauvinism."[71]

Not surprisingly, as Merleau-Ponty began to question "human chauvinism," he also came to stress the importance of nature, which he claimed (without any apparent knowledge of Bloch or the Frankfurt School) had been ignored by previous Marxist philosophers.[72] Implicitly rejecting Kojève's view of nature as an inert other to be dominated by man, a view which Sartre still seemed to hold, he began to recognize the damage done to nature by unchecked humanism. To the uncomprehending Sartre, he quoted Whitehead's remark "Nature is in tatters,"[73] and proceeded to search for manifestations of its potential rehabilitation. Returning to his early stress on the incarnated body-subject, he emphasized the existence of a primary natural truth that was prior to the split between subject and object. "At the root and in the depths of Cartesian nature," he told his students at the Collège de France, "there is another nature, the domain of an 'originary presence' (*Urpräsenz*) which, from the fact that it

69. Merleau-Ponty, *Signs*, p. 226.
70. Merleau-Ponty, *In Praise of Philosophy*, p. 43.
71. Ibid., p. 44.
72. Merleau-Ponty, *Themes from the Lectures*, p. 63.
73. Quoted in Sartre, *Situations*, p. 309.

calls for the total response of a single embodied subject, is in principle present to every other embodied subject."[74]

Merleau-Ponty's new—or, better put, renewed—interest in nature meant a subtle de-emphasis of history, which was no longer the privileged locus of all meaning. The "flesh of history" had to be understood as continuous with the "flesh of nature." As he put it in his lectures,

The ontology of life, as well as that of "physical nature," can only escape its troubles by resorting, apart from all artificialism, to brute being as revealed to us in our perceptual contact with the world. It is only within the perceived world that we can understand that all corporeality is already symbolism.[75]

His disillusionment with history as the realm of a progressive realization of reason and sense was expressed in the last essay published before his death, "The Eye and the Mind": "The whole of human history is, in a certain sense, stationary."[76]

Moving away from his Hegelian Marxist faith in history meant, as we have noted, a reaffirmation of his roots in Husserlian phenomenology. Even more interesting for our purposes, he increasingly acknowledged his closeness to Heidegger, whose notion of Being he seems to have found especially attractive.[77] Recognizing the mistake made by Heidegger's early French interpreters, he noted:

Commentators have missed what, from the Preface to *Sein und Zeit*, was the declared aim of his thought: not to describe existence, *Dasein* (which has been incorrectly translated in French as "human reality"), as a fundamental and autonomous sphere—but, through *Dasein*, to get at Being, the analysis of certain human attitudes being undertaken only because man *is* the interrogation of Being.[78]

Merleau-Ponty also now called his own philosophy interrogative and argued that man possessed "a natural light or opening to being."[79] Although Sartre, betraying his own bias, insisted that for all his changes, Merleau-Ponty's "principal concern remained man,"[80] in his later work man was

74. Merleau-Ponty, *Themes from the Lectures*, p. 83.
75. Ibid., p. 98.
76. Merleau-Ponty, *The Primacy of Perception*, p. 190.
77. For a thorough discussion of Merleau-Ponty's closeness to Heidegger as well as their differences, see Mallin, *Merleau-Ponty's Philosophy*. Whereas the early Merleau-Ponty tended to link Heidegger and Hegel, as for example in his remark in *Sense and Non-Sense* that "Heidegger—like Hegel—makes Spirit or Unity a future and a problem" (p. 134), the later Merleau-Ponty came to recognize their differences.
78. Merleau-Ponty, *Themes from the Lectures*, pp. 109–10.
79. Merleau-Ponty, *Signs*, p. 239.
80. Sartre, *Situations*, p. 314. Rabil makes a similar argument, p. 190. It is hard to reconcile with Merleau-Ponty's rejection in *The Visible and the Invisible* (p. 274) of "any compromise with *humanism*."

decentered in relation to the whole. However much he may have continued to insist on the primacy of perception in a way that Heidegger never did, his philosophy moved further and further away from that subjective bias of early French existentialism. In short, from the Hegelian Marxist concept of totality, he moved ever closer to the Heideggerian concept of Being, thus reversing the choice Goldmann had made.

Merleau-Ponty's abandonment of Hegelian Marxism manifested itself in more than just an increased respect for Heideggerian ontology. From his earliest work, he had been attracted to the Gestaltist concept of structure as an antidote to atomistic and sensationalist theories of perception. His first major book, it will be recalled, was entitled *The Structure of Behavior.* In the 1950s, while he was accusing Western Marxism of failing to acknowledge the inertia of social institutions, a heightened interest in the already structured nature of those institutions began to emerge in French intellectual life. Although Merleau-Ponty always preferred the vocabulary of intersubjectivity and situations and never gave up his search for meaning, he was strongly receptive to the new structuralist movement that grew out of the appropriation of Saussure's linguistics by ethnologists and other social scientists. In fact, he was one of the first French philosophers to appreciate Saussure's importance, commenting on him as early as 1947 in his essay on "The Metaphysical in Man."[81] In his 1953 inaugural lecture, he suggested that "Saussure, the modern linguist, could have sketched a new philosophy of history" and added:

> Just as language is a system of signs which have meaning only in relation to one another, and each of which has its own usage throughout the whole language, so each institution is a symbolic system that the subject takes over and incorporates as a style of functioning, as a global configuration, without having any need to conceive it at all. . . . It is in this way, as is also true of logics of behavior, that the forms and processes of history, the classes, the epochs, exist.[82]

Not only did Merleau-Ponty recognize the importance of structuralist linguistics, he also respected the ways in which its implications for the social sciences were drawn by other theorists. According to Sartre, "He must have agreed with Lacan's formula: 'The unconscious is structured like a language.'"[83] And in an essay written in 1959 and published in *Signs,*[84] he

81. Merleau-Ponty, *Sense and Non-Sense,* where he admires Saussure's understanding of language as a totality rather than a causal system (p. 87).

82. Merleau-Ponty, *In Praise of Philosophy,* pp. 55–56.

83. Sartre, p. 306. In *The Visible and the Invisible,* Merleau-Ponty approvingly cites Lacan's dictum (p. 126).

84. Merleau-Ponty, "From Mauss to Claude Lévi-Strauss" in *Signs.*

praised the introduction of Saussurean motifs into anthropology by Lévi-Strauss.

In the light of later developments in French culture, when structuralism served for many as the grave-digger of phenomenology,[85] Merleau-Ponty's approbation may seem misplaced. In fact, at times it did reflect an imperfect understanding of the implications of what he was embracing.[86] But Merleau-Ponty's enthusiasm makes sense in the light of his growing disenchantment with Hegelian Marxism. And insofar as post-structuralist philosophers in the 1970s were able to cross-fertilize themes from Heidegger with those from Saussure, Merleau-Ponty's groping attempt to do the same ought not to be seen as a barren enterprise. As several recent commentators have noted,[87] he should be recognized as an important bridge between the generation of French intellectuals dominated by Hegel, Husserl and Heidegger to the one enthralled by Saussure and Nietzsche.

That later generation, to be sure, was resolutely anti-holistic, whereas Merleau-Ponty's absorption of structuralist and Heideggerian ideas did not lead him away from holism per se, only from its Hegelian Marxist variant. His continued allegiance is demonstrated in "From Mauss to Claude Lévi-Strauss," which begins by praising Mauss for going beyond Durkheim's collective conscience as a hypostatization external to the individual subject. Mauss's "social fact" was superior because it transcended the sterile opposition of individual and collectivity: as a network of symbols it both penetrated the individual and encompassed him. For Mauss, Merleau-Ponty wrote approvingly, "There are no longer just absolutes or mere summations, but everywhere totalities or articulated wholes."[88] Even more attractive, Merleau-Ponty suggested, was Lévi-Strauss's enrichment of Mauss's insight through the introduction of structural linguistics:

85. See, for example, Eugenio Donato, "The Two Languages of Criticism" in Richard Macksay and Eugenio Donato, eds., *The Structuralist Controversy: The Languages of Criticism and the Sciences of Man* (Baltimore, 1972), which begins, "The works of Lévi-Strauss and Lacan have taken the place of the works of Sartre and Merleau-Ponty" (p. 89). The belief that structuralism is the antithesis of Merleau-Ponty's position remains in more recent work as well, e.g. Kruks *The Political Philosophy of Merleau-Ponty*, p. 135.

86. For a discussion of the misunderstandings, see Spurling, *Phenomenology and the Social World*, pp. 59, 187. Although Lévi-Strauss dedicated *The Savage Mind* to Merleau-Ponty, he claimed that their relationship was not reciprocal "in that Merleau-Ponty, from his writings and what he said to me personally, had a much stronger impression that what I was doing derived from his philosophical work than I had of the possibility of joining him." "A Confrontation," *New Left Review* 62 (July–August 1970), p. 72. See also Lévi-Strauss, "On Merleau-Ponty," *Graduate Faculty Philosophy Journal* 7, 2 (Winter 1978).

87. Hugh J. Silverman, "Re-Reading Merleau-Ponty," *Telos* 29 (Fall 1976); and Dallmayr, *Twilight of Subjectivity*.

88. Merleau-Ponty, *Signs*, p. 115.

This notion of structure, whose present good fortune in all domains responds to an intellectual need, establishes a whole system of thought. For the philosopher, the presence of structure outside us in natural and social systems and within us as symbolic function points to a way beyond the subject—object correlation which has dominated philosophy from Descartes to Hegel. By showing us that man is eccentric to himself and that the social finds its center only in man, structure particularly enables us to understand how we are in a sort of circuit with the socio-historical world.[89]

Merleau-Ponty, however, remained still fundamentally in the phenom-enological camp, never accepting, for example, the scientific pretensions of Lévi-Strauss and his followers or their privileging of language's deep structure (Saussure's *langue*) over its surface level (*parole*). Nor did he agree that signifiers could be completely liberated from what they sig-nified and studied as a formal diacritical system without reference to their intended meanings. The institution that was language never completely overwhelmed its embodied speakers to become the sole object of his in-quiry. If no longer a truly humanist philosophy, it would be wrong to call his later work strongly anti-humanist either. As in so many other respects, Merleau-Ponty's ambiguity prevented him from unreservedly embracing either term in an opposition. Man may be "eccentric to himself," but "the social finds its center only in man."

In any event, by shifting from an uneasy amalgam of phenomenology and Hegelian Marxism to a no less problematical combination of phe-nomenology and structuralism, Merleau-Ponty significantly altered his notion of totality. From an essentially critical concept capable of provid-ing a vantage point from which the present might be judged and found wanting, it became an essentially descriptive one used to make sense of what was. As Merleau-Ponty put it in his praise of Lévi-Strauss,

What interests the philosopher in anthropology is just that it takes man as he is, in his actual situation of life and understanding. The philosopher it interests is not the one who wants to explain or construct the world, but the one who seeks to deepen our insertion in being.[90]

Or as he argued in his critique of Sartre,

The dialectic does not, as Sartre claims, provide finality, that is to say, the presence of the whole in that which, by its nature, exists in separate parts; rather it provides the global and primordial cohesion of a field of experience wherein each element opens onto the others. . . . The adventures of the dialectic . . . are errors through which it must pass, since it is in principle a thought with several centers and several points of entry, and because it needs time to explore them all.[91]

89. Ibid., p. 123.   90. Ibid.
91. Merleau-Ponty, *Adventures of the Dialectic*, p. 204.

Such an exploration, he contended, was an infinite task, whose result would be the revelation of ontological differences, the visible and the invisible, chiasmically[92] intertwined but not identical.

The implications of Merleau-Ponty's shift are admirably summarized by Albert Rabil, Jr.:

> The idea that the task of philosophy is to describe how men who have intentions (i.e. who are free) are related to the world (i.e. "totality") which is always already there before them is a fundamental constant in Merleau-Ponty's philosophy. The presupposition underlying such a task is that, despite the multiplicity of perspectives which men have on the world ... there is a discernible human unity. Such a presupposition allied to a descriptive metaphysics can lead in either one of two directions. On the one hand, descriptive metaphysics might attempt to evaluate the concrete meanings that men find in the world with a view to judging between them on the basis of the degree to which a particular meaning of an individual or group is at the same time an expression of a genuinely universal meaning. An evaluatively descriptive metaphysics of this kind is likely to be politically oriented and to assume that the attainment of a universal meaning is an immanent human possibility. ... On the other hand, a descriptive metaphysics might attempt to comprehend the various meanings men discover in the world, not in order to evaluate their relative merits, but rather in order to uncover the *basis* on which all these meanings inhere together in the same world. ... The first alternative ultimately sacrifices multiplicity to unity; the second seeks to found unity on multiplicity.[93]

As we have seen, Merleau-Ponty's rapid disillusionment with the Soviet Union after World War II led him to embrace the second alternative. Linking the validity of Marxism too closely with the actions of the U.S.S.R. and its allied parties, unable to conceptualize social alternatives to the debunked proletariat which he had mythologized into the savior of mankind, moving away from anthropocentric historicism to a nuanced defense of the continuity between history and nature, the later Merleau-

---

92. Chiasm, from the Greek letter chi (χ), suggests a crossing of two terms without their being fully reconciled in a dialectical sense. The grammatical figure chiasmus entails a reversal of the order of words from one clause to the next, e.g., "history is nature, nature is history." This example is taken from the work of Adorno, who, as Gillian Rose points out in *The Melancholy Science* (New York, 1978), p. 13, often used chiasmus to represent the related, but non-identical linkages between seemingly opposite terms. Marx also was fond of this figure, especially in his least Hegelian works such as *The Eighteenth Brumaire*. See the analysis in John Paul Riquelme, "*The Eighteenth Brumaire* of Karl Marx as Symbolic Action," *History and Theory* 19, 1 (1980), where it is argued that chiasmus suggests a non-linear causality in which effects and causes reciprocally influence one another. Merleau-Ponty's most extensive discussion of it comes in chapter 4 of *The Visible and the Invisible*, which is entitled "The Intertwining—The Chiasm." The last words of that book are "Worked-over-matter—man = chiasm" (p. 275). Like Adorno, Merleau-Ponty wanted to avoid the extremes of separating subject and object too drastically or reconciling them too completely. Instead, he called for a reversability of the terms without their collapse into each other.

93. Rabil, *Merleau-Ponty*, pp. 85–86.

Ponty subtly withdrew from the Western Marxist camp. His withdrawal, however, was not of the kind associated with so many apostates of the "God that failed" variety. In the preface to *Signs* he wrote that it was foolish to argue that a theory with the historical power of Marxism could be "refuted" or "verified" by a few new occurrences. But what these occurrences did suggest was that "Marxism has definitely entered a new phase of its history, in which it can inspire and orient analyses and retain a real heuristic value, but is certainly no longer true *in the sense it was believed to be true*."[94] Marxism, therefore, had attained the status of what Merleau-Ponty called a "classic," no longer to be taken literally, but still able to illuminate new facts.

But in order to make sense of such facts, it was clear that Marxism in either its orthodox or its Hegelian guise no longer sufficed. The alternative he chose, that uneasy mix of phenomenology and structuralism described above, may have provided him with a more subtle vision of lived reality than offered by Hegelian Marxism, but it lacked much of the latter's critical power. In fact, by stressing the descriptive, exploratory intentions of the two movements he tried to combine, while at the same time arguing that the process of description was endless, Merleau-Ponty came perilously close to accepting what Hegel had called a "bad infinity," in which the play of perpetual ambiguity and difference was enthroned as the only historical possibility. By expanding the concept of reason to include what earlier, non-dialectical rationalists had damned as irrational, and then losing his faith in the historically immanent emergence of reason from unreason, he inadvertently ended without a criterion by which to judge the present. There was more than a grain of truth in Lefebvre's charge in his critique of *Adventures of the Dialectic*, "The philosophy of ambiguity justifies the situation instead of denouncing it."[95]

As early as *Phenomenology of Perception*, Merleau-Ponty had described Husserl's method as a "phenomenological positivism which bases the possible on the real."[96] Although it would certainly be misleading to categorize Merleau-Ponty's philosophy as positivist in any conventional sense, there was in his late work a characteristically positivist acceptance of the givenness of reality.[97] Philosophy, as an infinite interrogation of the

94. Merleau-Ponty, *Signs*, p. 9.

95. Lefebvre, in *Mésaventures de l'anti-Marxisme, les Malheurs de M. Merleau-Ponty* (Paris, 1956), p. 102.

96. Merleau-Ponty, *Phenomenology of Perception*, p. xvii. He repeated the phrase in one of his last essays, "Phenomenology and the Sciences of Man" in *The Primacy of Perception*, p. 50.

97. For discussion of the positivist moment in Merleau-Ponty's theory of perception, see Raymond Herbenick, "Merleau-Ponty and the Primacy of Reflection" in Gillan; and James Edie's introduction to *The Primacy of Perception*, p. xvi.

"wild meaning"[98] of the world, leads from speech to silence, from sense to nonsense, from the visible to the invisible and back again. But it never seems to suggest a way to escape the dilemma of the present. It is thus plausible to see, in what Sartre once called "his desperate struggle to keep digging in the same place,"[99] an anticipation of the deconstructionist fetish of unending repetition.[100] In fact, like the deconstructionists, Merleau-Ponty abandoned any hope for purely transparent linguistic communication. "Sometimes one starts to dream about what culture, literary life, and teaching could be if all those who participate, having for once rejected idols, would give themselves up to the happiness of reflecting together," he once mused, as if anticipating Habermas' "perfect speech situation." "But," he sadly continued, "this dream is not reasonable."[101]

No more reasonable, his later work suggested, was the dream of a normative totality. In his very last lecture in 1961, he referred scornfully to totality as the Marxist "sacred cow."[102] Indeed, his political heirs Lefort and Castoriadis were soon linking the concept of totality with totalitarianism in a manner similar to Camus' in *The Rebel*.[103] They were, however, relatively marginal voices in the Marxist debate in France in the period after Merleau-Ponty's death. Sartre, still in his militant Marxist phase, polemicised against them in *Les Temps Modernes*. Their own collaboration on the journal *Socialisme ou Barbarie*, which was spawned by their disillusionment with Trotskyism in 1948, ended in acrimony a decade later. In 1968, their ideas did enjoy a period of influence, but it was

98. Merleau-Ponty, *The Visible and the Invisible*, p. 155. By "wild" Merleau-Ponty meant a meaning that transcends its human origins. As he put it, "In a sense, as Valéry said, language is everything, since it is the voice of no one, since it is the very voice of the things, the waves, and the forests" (p. 155).

99. Sartre, *Situations*, p. 322.

100. Silverman, "Re-Reading Merleau-Ponty," p. 129. Merleau-Ponty's complicated discussions of art, which cannot be treated here, may perhaps be seen as giving evidence of his concern with repetition rather than historical progress. Opposing Lukács' variant of socialist realism in *Adventures of the Dialectic*, he wrote, "For a realist there is not a plurality of viewpoints, a center and a periphery of the dialectic, an intensive totality; there is only an historical process to be verified and to be followed" (p. 70). Elsewhere in his writings on painting, especially his essay "Cezanne's Doubt" in *Sense and Non-Sense*, he attacked a mimetic or historical theory of art and argued instead for an essentially expressive view: "Although it is certain that a man's life does not *explain* his work, it is equally certain that the two are connected. The truth is that *this work to be done called for this life*" (p. 20). And in his critique of Malraux's "imaginary museum," he argued that the unity of painting over the years "exists in that single task which all painters are confronted with" (*Signs*, p. 60). It is not so much that Merleau-Ponty denied difference in artistic achievement, it is rather that he tended to ontologize the artistic project rather than see it in historical terms. Thus, it is not surprising that his contribution to a specifically Marxist aesthetics has been regarded as very limited.

101. Merleau-Ponty, *Signs*, pp. 242–43.

102. Merleau-Ponty, "Philosophy and Non-Philosophy Since Hegel," p. 85.

103. Howard, *The Marxian Legacy*, p. 283.

short-lived.[104] For at the same time, they were faced with the rise of a new variant of French Marxism, which had little use for the phenomenological residues in their theory or the bitter rejection of Communist bureaucraticism in their politics. This new movement was structuralist Marxism, most powerfully defended by the philosopher and Communist Party stalwart, Louis Althusser.

If Sartre most clearly articulated the essentially subjective moment in the Hegelian Marxist synthesis, and Merleau-Ponty attempted to go beyond the subject-object dichotomy through ultimately non-Marxist means, then Althusser can be understood as trying to restore Marxism's objectivist intentions. Rather than finding common ground between phenomenology and structuralism, Althusser rejected the former entirely in the name of a Marxist version of the latter. And in so doing, he recast the Western Marxist discourse of totality in a radically new form. How successful he was in this endeavor will be considered in the following chapter.

104. For a discussion of their impact on Daniel Cohn-Bendit and the student movement at Nanterre, see Arthur Hirsh, *The French New Left: An Intellectual History from Sartre to Gorz* (Boston, 1981), pp. 146–47.

CHAPTER THIRTEEN

Louis Althusser and the
Structuralist Reading of Marx

In 1946, Merleau-Ponty chastised Pierre Naville for failing to acknowledge that "the notion of structure or totality . . . is one of the basic categories of Marxism."[1] But a generation later it had become clear that structure and totality were by no means as synonymous as Merleau-Ponty had assumed. And Marxism, it became no less obvious, would have to choose between them. Merleau-Ponty, as we have seen, welcomed the nascent structuralist movement in the 1950s and sought to find common ground between it and phenomenology. By the mid-1960s, the futility of this endeavor was apparent to everyone, as the structuralists, taking their cue from Claude Lévi-Strauss's attack on Sartre's *Critique* in *The Savage Mind* in 1962,[2] defined themselves in strict—one might say diacritical—opposition to phenomenology and existentialism. Underlying continuities between these movements and structuralism—such as that between Sartre's description of desire as a lack and the analysis of desire in the work of Jacques Lacan, or that between Jean Hyppolite's existentialist reading of Hegel and Michel Foucault's critique of closed totalities[3]—

1. Maurice Merleau-Ponty, *Sense and Non-Sense*, trans. Hubert L. Dreyfus and Patricia A. Dreyfus (Evanston, 1964), p. 126.
2. Claude Lévi-Strauss, *The Savage Mind* (Chicago, 1966), Chap. 9.
3. For a discussion of Lacan and Sartre, see Anthony Wilden's commentary on Jacques Lacan, *The Language of the Self: The Function of Language in Psychoanalysis*, trans. Anthony Wilden (New York, 1968), p. 192f. For an acknowledgement of Foucault's debt to Hyppolite, see his lecture "The Discourse on Language" in *The Archaeology of Knowledge*, trans. A. M. Sheridan Smith (New York, 1972), p. 236, where he notes that philosophy for Hyppolite was "the thought of the inaccessible totality." Foucault's early interest in existentialist psychoanalysis should also be mentioned. See the introduction he wrote to his translation of Ludwig Binswanger, *Le Rêve et l'existence* (Paris, 1954). For an account of Foucault that suggests his covert debt to Heidegger, see Hubert L. Dreyfus and Paul Rabinow, *Michel Foucault: Beyond Structuralism and Hermeneutics* (Chicago, 1982).

were now ignored as structuralism was claimed to represent a radically new departure in French intellectual life.[4]

Although unremittingly hostile to phenomenology and existentialism, the structuralists were by no means equally dismissive of the Marxism that Sartre and Merleau-Ponty had tried to combine with those philosophies. Lévi-Strauss, in fact, called Marxism his "point of departure,"[5] while other structuralists like Roland Barthes were deeply indebted to the Marxist critique of bourgeois culture. Even Foucault, who was soon to reduce Marxism to a minor variation of Ricardian economics,[6] went through a Marxist phase and briefly joined the Communist Party. Although in many ways an oversimplification, Edmund Leach's observation therefore contains a grain of truth: "Existentialism and Structuralism have common Marxist roots and the distinction between the two is by no means as sharp as some tidy-minded critics would like us to believe."[7]

But as a rule, the structuralists and "post-structuralists," as Foucault, Lacan and others soon became known, were only fleetingly and superficially concerned with Marxism. In contrast, there was among them a small group of thinkers whose allegiance to Marxism and, in many cases, the PCF was far more serious. Frequently denying that they belonged to the structuralist movement per se, they nonetheless drew on many structuralist precepts in an attempt to rescue Marxism from what they saw as the cul-de-sac into which it had been forced by both orthodox dialectical materialists and their existentialist-phenomenological critics. Sensitive not only to the inadequacies of the Sartrean or Merleau-Pontyan version of Western Marxism, they were also among the most insistent critics of the Hegelian-Marxist tradition as a whole. In fact, the exhaustion of this paradigm, which we have followed in earlier chapters, was first deliberately argued in their work. Although the alternative they proposed was

4. The secondary literature on structuralism is now endless. For some recent efforts, see Miriam Glucksmann, *Structuralist Analysis in Contemporary Thought* (London, 1974); Jonathan Culler, *Structuralist Poetics* (London, 1975); Terence Hawkes, *Structuralism and Semiotics* (London, 1977); John Sturrock, ed. *Structuralism and Since* (Oxford, 1979); and Edith Kurzweil, *The Age of Structuralism: Lévi-Strauss to Foucault* (New York, 1980).

5. Lévi-Strauss, p. 246.

6. Michel Foucault, *The Order of Things: An Archaeology of the Human Sciences* (New York, 1970), p. 261. Elsewhere, Foucault, who was Althusser's student, has a more positive reading of Marx. See, for example, his remarks in *The Archaeology of Knowledge*, pp. 12–13, and his admission in *Power/Knowledge: Selected Interviews and Other Writings, 1972–1977*, ed. Colin Gordon, trans. Colin Gordon et al. (New York, 1980), p. 53, that "it is impossible at the present time to write history without using a whole range of concepts directly linked to Marx's thought and situating oneself within a horizon of thought which has been defined and described by Marx." For an Althusserian critique of Foucault, see Dominique Lecourt, *Marxism and Epistemology: Bachelard, Canguilhem, Foucault*, trans. Ben Brewster (London, 1975).

7. Edmund Leach, *Claude Lévi-Strauss* (New York, 1970), p. 7.

even more deeply flawed, the French structuralist Marxists were insightful critics of many of the failings of their Western Marxist predecessors.

Led by Louis Althusser,[8] who was both a Communist Party stalwart
and professor of philosophy at the prestigious Ecole Normale Supérieure,
they included anthropologists like Maurice Godelier and Emmanuel
Terry, philosophers like Etienne Balibar and (the quickly disillusioned)
André Glucksmann, literary critics like Pierre Macherey and political theorists like Nicos Poulantzas. By the mid-1960s, older French Marxists
were forced to recognize, sometimes with considerable dismay, that a new
and aggressive structuralist or Althusserian school had developed at the
Rue d'Ulm, where Althusser and several of the others taught.[9] Soon, a
similar phenomenon occurred elsewhere, especially in England where Althusserianism captured (at least for a while) many of the editors of the
New Left Review and helped inspire new journals like *Theoretical Practice* and *Screen.*

Because the Althusserians were adamantly opposed to virtually everything that had previously passed as Western Marxism, there has been
some controversy over whether or not to include them in the category at
all. If, as we have argued, the family resemblances linking Western Marxists should be loosely construed, then Althusser and his followers can legitimately be seen as cousins, if unfriendly ones, of the Marxist Humanists. Indebted to Western bourgeois modes of thought, preoccupied with
methodological and philosophical questions, interested as much in superstructural as in substructural issues, and marked by that characteristic
pessimism we have seen emerge among Marxist intellectuals when the
post-World War I euphoria ended, they manifested certain obvious affinities with the Hegelian Marxists. Both camps, moreover, were composed
of unabashed intellectuals without roots in the working class and with
little ability to speak its language. More significant for this study, the Althusserians were convinced of the importance of the question of totality
for Marxism. In fact, in criticizing the specifically Lukácsian version of
totality they were in surprising harmony with its critics in the supposedly
opposing tradition. To banish the Althusserians from the Western Marx-

8. For a bibliography of works by and about Althusser, see Grahame Lock's list at the
end of his translation of Althusser, *Essays in Self-Criticism* (London, 1976). Important addi-
tions would include Alex Callinicos, *Althusser's Marxism* (London, 1976); E. P. Thompson,
The Poverty of Theory and Other Essays (New York, 1978); Perry Anderson, *Arguments
Within English Marxism* (London, 1980); Simon Clarke et al., *One-Dimensional Marxism:
Althusser and the Politics of Culture* (London, 1980); Arthur Hirsh, *The French New Left:
An Intellectual History from Sartre to Gorz* (Boston, 1981); and Alfred Schmidt, *History
and Structure,* trans. Jeffrey Herf (Cambridge, 1981).

9. For a brief discussion of the school, see Brian Singer's review of Jacques Rancière, *La
Leçon d'Althusser* in *Telos* 25 (Fall 1975).

ist camp as nothing more than crypto-orthodox Marxist-Leninists is to ignore the meaningful ties they had with it.

Still, if Althusser and his followers can be considered a variant of Western Marxists, they were certainly Western Marxists in a different key. Most decisively, they rejected those links between Marxism and the tradition of idealist "critical philosophy" that had been so enthusiastically defended by their predecessors as a bulwark against vulgar Marxism. Instead, they insisted on Marxism's claim to scientificity with a fervor that often evoked the reproach that they had reverted back to the "positivist" Dialectical Materialism of the Second International. No longer satisfied with Gramsci's equation of Marxism with the "philosophy of praxis," or content with his reading of October 1917 as a "revolution against *Capital*," they disdainfully rejected the humanist, subjectivist concept of Marxism that informed his and other early Western Marxist views. Theirs was instead a truculently objectivist Marxism that insisted on the constraining power of structures over consciousness and voluntary action.

Accordingly, they and especially their leader espoused a politics that was very different from that generally endorsed by earlier Western Marxists. Whereas Lukács and Gramsci (and Della Volpe) were content to remain within the Communist movement, despite their qualms about its policies, all other Western Marxists, beginning with Korsch in the mid-1920s, either never joined the Party or left it in disgust. Althusser not only remained a PCF member, if at times a critical one, but also defended its Leninist principles with relentless vigor. Although he struggled to dissociate himself from the Party's Stalinist past, his efforts to do so were rarely successful because of the arguably Stalinist implications of his philosophy itself.[10] When he came to revise that philosophy, it was largely at the Party's bidding and in a way that emphasized his subservience to it. Like Lukács, he was forced to make the compromises with his own theoretical integrity demanded by his acceptance of Party discipline. Not all of his followers were prepared to toe the line as strictly as he, which accounted in part for the ultimate disintegration of the school.

In short, there were substantial differences separating Althusser in particular and structuralist Marxists in general from their Hegelian or existen-

10. The extent of Althusser's Stalinism is discussed, *inter alia*, in Thompson, Anderson and Hirsh. It is also the subject of a penetrating article by Valentino Gerratana, "Althusser and Stalinism," *New Left Review* 101–102 (February–April 1977). Perhaps the most judicious, if indecisive, way of handling this problem is to conclude with Fredric Jameson that the antithetical evaluations of Althusser's Stalinism "mark out a space in which that operation is objectively and functionally ambiguous" (*The Political Unconscious: Narrative as a Socially Symbolic Act* [Ithaca, 1981], p. 39). Part of the problem, of course, is finding a shared definition of Stalinism.

tialist competitors, as the furious polemics they generated demonstrate. Nonetheless, if we focus on the Althusserian revision of the earlier Western Marxist concept of totality, significant similarities can be discerned as well, similarities that the polemicists often failed to acknowledge.

Most obviously, Althusserian Marxism like Hegelian Marxism insisted on the importance of a holistic perspective. Structuralism in general, at least in its classic phase, was anxious to establish the priority of the whole (understood as a relational system of diacritical oppositions) over the parts. Lévi-Strauss had chastised Sartre in *The Savage Mind* for failing to recognize that modern man was not the only totalizer in history. "The characteristic feature of the savage mind," he wrote, "is its timelessness; its object is to grasp the world as both a synchronic and diachronic totality."[11] Here the widely remarked influence of Saussurean linguistics, with its emphasis on a deep linguistic structure, or *langue*, underlying surface speech acts, or *parole*, was obvious. For Lévi-Strauss, linguistics "presents us with a dialectical and totalizing entity but one outside (or beneath) consciousness and will. Language, an unreflecting totalization, is human reason which has its reasons and of which man knows nothing."[12] Combining this implication of linguistics with Marcel Mauss's concept of total facts and a Gestaltist view of the psyche,[13] Lévi-Strauss sought to read all of culture and society as an "unreflecting totalization" without a totalizer.

For Althusser and other Marxists, Lévi-Strauss's highly rationalist and essentialist model, which Paul Ricoeur once characterized as "Kantianism without a transcendental subject,"[14] smacked of idealism. But in certain respects they shared its premises (and, as we will see, invited the same rebuke). Both Althusser and Lévi-Strauss were indebted, as we noted in an earlier chapter, to that anti-individualist and anti-humanist holism generated by Durkheim's sociology, although both rejected his notion of society as a moral community. Both resisted the reduction of the social or cultural whole to its component parts, stressing instead the irreducibility of its relational structure. And both rejected the privileging of historical process over static structures that had characterized Western thought since the end of the Enlightenment. Although Althusser as an historical materialist did emphasize the importance of process, what was constant and repeated in that process seemed more important than what actually

11. Lévi-Strauss, *The Savage Mind*, p. 263.
12. Ibid., p. 252.
13. For an argument that Gestalt psychology was actually more important than linguistics in Lévi-Strauss's development, see Simon Clarke, "The Origins of Lévi-Strauss's Structuralism," *Sociology* 12, 3 (September 1978).
14. Lévi-Strauss quotes and accepts this description in "A Confrontation," *New Left Review* 62 (July–August 1970), p. 61.

changed. He too, in Lefebvre's phrase, was an "Eleatic"[15] thinker more sensitive to the eternal than to the ephemeral in human affairs.

Because of this characteristically structuralist insistence on the priority of the whole over the parts, Althusser echoed the traditional Western Marxist critique of empiricism with its fetish of isolated facts. Although his Marxism aspired to scientificity, it shared none of the nominalism or phenomenalism that characterized positivism in its purer forms. Althusser may have praised Auguste Comte as a worthy predecessor, but his own version of scientific method owed little, if anything, to Comte's belief in the inductive testing of hypotheses leading to an evolutionary perfection of knowledge. Nor was he inclined towards the reductivist economism of the Second International with its simple-minded derivation of all levels of the social totality from the mode of production. Like earlier Western Marxists, Althusser tacitly abandoned the reductive base-superstructure model that governed orthodox Marxist notions of culture and ideology, and with it the reflection epistemology that had been enthroned by Lenin's *Materialism and Empirio-criticism.*[16] Although, as we will see, he tried to find a formula to avoid the pluralizing implications of this abandonment, one of the central implications of his work, as that of earlier Western Marxists, was the displacement of the economy from its causally central role as the motor of history.

But if in these ways Althusser was a characteristic Western Marxist, he clearly saw himself opposed to its other exponents. Althusserianism was, in fact, a self-conscious rejoinder to the entire Hegelian Marxist tradition, which stretched in his eyes from Lukács to Sartre. Aside from a reconsidered appreciation of Gramsci in his later work and that of his followers like Christine Buci-Glucksmann, Althusser denounced Western Marxism in wholesale terms. In doing so, however, he ignored the extent to which the tradition was itself deeply split, most notably over the question of totality. Neglecting the extent to which a critique of Lukács had been made from within the Western Marxist camp, he failed to grasp that many of his complaints had already been voiced, if in a different vocabulary, by certain Critical Marxists. Sensitized as we have become by Althusser himself to the need for a "symptomatic" rather than literal reading of texts, we can only wonder at Althusser's failure to apply his own standards of read-

15. Henri Lefebvre, "Claude Lévi-Strauss et le nouvel éléatisme" in *Au-delà du structuralisme* (Paris, 1971). This epithet is especially appropriate for the early work of Althusser's colleague, Etienne Balibar, who stressed synchrony more than Althusser himself. It is far less accurate for more historically minded Althusserians like Nicos Poulantzas.

16. Althus..er, to be sure, never could bring himself to criticize anything by Lenin in public. In fact, there are several positive references to *Materialism and Empirio-criticism* in *Lenin and Philosophy and Other Essays*, trans. Ben Brewster (New York, 1971).

ing, as Göran Therborn has pointed out,[17] to any writer other than Marx himself. If he had done so, he might have perceived the subtle parallels between his critique of the Hegelian Marxist concept of totality and that made by the erstwhile followers of Lukács.

For us to appreciate these parallels ourselves, we need a more detailed understanding of Althusser's intellectual trajectory than can be ascertained by categorizing him as the Marxist Lévi-Strauss. For the origins of Althusserianism were (to use another of his favorite terms) complexly overdetermined. Although his protestations of fundamental incompatibility with bourgeois structuralism are hard to take at face value, his work was in fact indebted to an idiosyncratically diverse number of sources. Oddly, this most tenacious defender of orthodoxy among Western Marxists was also the most promiscuous in allowing non-Marxist influences to affect his ideas.

Althusser was born in 1918 in the Algerian town of Birmendreïs, the son of a bank manager.[18] Schooled in Algiers and Marseilles, he joined the Catholic youth movement, Jeunesse Etudiante Chrétienne, in 1937—an early commitment that some of his critics would claim reappeared in the religious way he approached Marxist doctrine.[19] Drafted in 1939, he was captured by the Germans in June, 1940, and placed in a German prisoner-of-war camp for the duration of the war.[20] It was apparently here that his political education began, a process that Althusser credited largely to a friendship with Jacques Martin.[21] Martin, whom Althusser later acknowledged as the source of his concept of a problematic, was a Communist militant and seems to have been instrumental in bringing Althusser into the Party in 1948, when he was 30.

The Communist Party he entered was then hardening into the disciplined Stalinist monolith, under the stern leadership of Maurice Thorez, that was to alienate so many initially sympathetic intellectuals like Mer-

17. Göran Therborn, *Science, Class and Society: On the Formation of Sociology and Historical Materialism* (London, 1976), p. 63.

18. For biographical data on Althusser, see the brief account in Saül Karsz, *Théorie et Politique: Louis Althusser* (Paris, 1974). Like Camus before him and Derrida after, Althusser was a product of French colonial culture in Northern Africa.

19. See, for example, Thompson, *The Poverty of Theory*, p. 4, and Leszek Kolakowski, "Althusser's Marx," *Socialist Register* (London, 1971), p. 113.

20. Kurzweil (*The Age of Structuralism*, p. 35) claims that he was in the Resistance, but there is no other account that does.

21. See his dedication to Martin in *For Marx*, trans. Ben Brewster (New York, 1970). According to K. S. Karol, "The Tragedy of the Althussers," *New Left Review* 124 (November–December 1980), p. 94, it was his future wife Hélène, a Jewish Resistance fighter ten years his elder, who drew him towards Communism.

leau-Ponty. The campaign against Tito was in its early stages, the issue of the Soviet forced labor camps was causing painful divisions with other leftists, the show trials of Rajk and Kostov in Hungary were about to begin, and—perhaps most important of all for a Marxist intellectual—so too was the Lysenko affair, which was followed very closely in France.[22] Although, many years later, Althusser was to speak out vigorously against the idiocy of Lysenko's "proletarian science,"[23] in 1948 it did not deter him from joining the Party, nor did the other signs of its increased Stalinization.

The date he joined has been accounted significant for his later work. Although revolution was possible elsewhere, as the events in China illustrated, the expectation of the left wing of the French Resistance that it might happen in Europe were all but abandoned by 1948. As E. P. Thompson has pointed out, "Voluntarism crashed against the wall of the Cold War. No account can convey the sickening jerk of deceleration between 1945 and 1948. . . . In the West our heads were thrown against the windscreen of capitalist society; and that screen felt like—*a structure*."[24] Whether or not Althusser's penchant for structuralist explanations can be attributed to the date of his Party membership—these after all were the same years that nurtured Sartre's supremely voluntarist "ultrabolshevism"—it is nonetheless significant that he felt comfortable in a relatively bureaucratized, non-revolutionary party that seemed to many observers a parody of the Catholic Church he had only recently left.[25] It was not in fact until the late 1970s, as we will see, that he could contemplate criticizing the Party in public. Nor would many critics be mollified by his boast in his debate with John Lewis that he had begun writing about Stalin "already"[26] in 1965, a date which many other Western Marxists, including Lukács,[27] had beaten by many years. In short, all of Althusser's contributions to Marxist theory were made from within the confines of a rigidly Leninist party, whose line in most non-theoretical matters (except when it did not seem Leninist enough) he loyally supported.

Nineteen forty-eight was also a crucial year in Althusser's professional development. He completed his studies at the Ecole Normale, which he had entered after the war, with a dissertation on "The Notion of Content

22. See the account in Dominique Lecourt, *Proletarian Science? The Case of Lysenko,* intro. Louis Althusser, trans. Ben Brewster (London, 1977).
23. Althusser's introduction to Lecourt, entitled "Unfinished History," appeared in French in 1976.
24. Thompson, p. 73.
25. George Lichtheim, *Marxism in Modern France* (New York, 1966), p. 68.
26. Althusser, *Essays in Self-Criticism,* p. 36.
27. See, for example, his 1962 essay "Reflections on the Cult of Stalin," reprinted in *Marxism and Human Liberation,* ed. with intro. E. San Juan, Jr. (New York, 1973).

in Hegel's Philosophy."[28] His director was Gaston Bachelard, then the leading figure in the great French tradition of the philosophy of science that stretched back through Koyré, Duhem and Poincaré all the way to the eighteenth century. Bachelard's anti-evolutionist, anti-realist, anti-empiricist philosophy of science, elaborated by Georges Canguilhem and others, was to have a lasting impact on Althusser's thought, as it had on that of Foucault and many other French intellectuals.[29] Althusser's interests lay less, however, in the philosophy of natural science than in that of the social sciences (a dichotomy he called into question). In 1949, he proposed to Jean Hyppolite and Vladimir Jankélévitch a study of politics and philosophy in the Enlightenment as a topic for his *grande thèse*, and Rousseau's *Second Discourse* for his *petite thèse*.[30] Although not completed in precisely these forms, this project led to the publication of his first work, *Montesquieu: Politics and History*, in 1959, as well as a later essay on Rousseau's *Social Contract*.[31]

The intervening decade was critical for Althusser's intellectual and political maturation. In 1956, Khrushchev's Twentieth Party Congress speech had unleashed the halting process of de-Stalinization whose most dramatic outcome was the Hungarian Revolution of that year. For Marxist theoreticians, de-Stalinization meant the recovery of Marx's humanist roots and the rehabilitation of those Western Marxists, like the early Lukács and Korsch, who had understood them. Even former hard-line Stalinist apologists like Roger Garaudy, who had been the PCF's "philosophical *gendarme* and heresy-hunter,"[32] began to talk about alienation and de-humanization, without, to be sure, acknowledging the Communist Party's role in prolonging them. Not all Marxists, however, were convinced of the wisdom of forgetting Stalin. The Chinese Communists in

28. Althusser, "La notion de contenu dans la philosophie de Hegel," unpublished Diplôme at the Ecole Normale, 1948.

29. For discussions of Bachelard and Althusser, see Lecourt, *Marxism and Epistemology*, and Ben Brewster, "Althusser and Bachelard," *Theoretical Practice* 3–4 (November 1971).

30. Althusser mentions this project in *Essays in Self-Criticism*, p. 165. For a discussion of the various *thèses* expected of French scholars, see Terry Nichols Clark, *Prophets and Patrons: The French University and the Emergence of the Social Sciences* (Cambridge, 1973), p. 24.

31. These have been published together in English in *Politics and History: Montesquieu, Rousseau, Hegel and Marx*, trans. Ben Brewster (London, 1972).

32. David Caute, *Communism and the French Intellectuals, 1914–1960* (London, 1964), p. 268. For more on Althusser's battles within the PCF, see Mark Poster, *Existential Marxism in Postwar France: From Sartre to Althusser* (Princeton, 1975), p. 341; Richard Johnson, *The French Communist Party versus the Students: Revolutionary Politics in May–June 1968* (New Haven, 1972), p. 57f; and Lock's intro. to *Essays in Self-Criticism*, p. 3–4. Garaudy, it might be noted in passing, was later to break with the Party.

particular were offended by Khrushchev's deviation from the recent past. By the late 1950s the long-smoldering quarrel between Mao and his Soviet ally turned into active hostility.

Althusser was deeply influenced by these events, so much so that he later suspended his doctrine that theoretical production was carried out within theory itself, to argue that his work had to be understood in the context of the political "conjuncture"[33] of these years. Starting in 1960 with a review of a collection of Feuerbach's writings, he published a series of progressively more outspoken articles that appeared together under the pugnacious title *For Marx* in 1965.[34] Directed against what he saw as the "right-wing" critique of Stalinism, which merely attacked the "cult of personality" in the name of humanism, Althusser's book provoked an enormous storm within the PCF, whose leading theoretician was still Garaudy.[35] Identifying himself at first cautiously and then more explicitly with the Maoist "leftist" critique of Stalinism,[36] he denounced any attempt to reduce Marx to his early humanist writings, which he claimed were polluted by pre-scientific ideology. Invoking the Bachelardian concept of an "epistemological break," which he made even sharper by substituting "*coupure*" for Bachelard's "*rupture*,"[37] he insisted that Marx had become a true Marxist only after radically shifting his "problematic" in 1845.[38] Only then did he open up what Althusser liked to call "a new continent"[39] hitherto closed to science, that of history. To understand Marxism in its truly scientific guise, one had to turn from the *1844 Manuscripts* to *Capital*, which must be read "symptomatically," that is, with a

33. Althusser, *For Marx*, p. 10. Why he was not also influenced by other dimensions of the conjuncture, such as de Gaulle's coming to power in 1958 or the Hungarian uprising of 1956, is not clear.

34. In *Essays in Self-Criticism*, Althusser points out that his titles were slogans in the campaign against humanism (p. 173).

35. The controversy over Althusser reached the highest levels of the Party. Waldeck Rochet, who had replaced Maurice Thorez as its leader in 1964, wrote a book attacking Althusser called *Le Marxisme et les chemins de l'avenir* (Paris, 1966). There is some irony then in Althusser's dedication to his *Elements of Self-Criticism* in 1974: "To Waldeck Rochet who admired Spinoza and spent a long day with me talking about him in June 1966."

36. The first reference to Mao in his work came in his 1962 essay "Contradiction and Overdetermination," reprinted in *For Marx*, p. 94. Mao, it should be noted, was never very critical of Stalin; in fact, one of the sources of his dispute with Khrushchev was the latter's attempt at de-Stalinization. Thus, it is exaggerated to claim, as Anderson has done, that Althusser's Maoism demonstrates his anti-Stalinism.

37. Althusser, *Essays in Self-Criticism*, p. 114.

38. The concept of "problematic" is explained in the glossaries to *For Marx* and *Reading Capital*, with Etienne Balibar, trans. Ben Brewster (New York, 1970). For discussions of its parallels with the more familiar notion of a paradigm introduced by Thomas Kuhn, see Therborn, *Science, Class and Society*, p. 58f; and Russell Keat and John Urry, *Social Theory as Science* (London, 1975), p. 132f.

39. For Althusser's explanation of this metaphor, see his discussion in the text reproduced in Karsz, *Théorie et Politique*, p. 321f.

sensitivity to its unconscious and apparently hidden meaning. Despite the Hegelian residues in certain passages in the work, such a reading would uncover its underlying anti-humanist significance.

In a series of papers delivered to his seminar at the Ecole Normale, Althusser and his colleagues, Etienne Balibar, Pierre Macherey, Jacques Rancière, and Roger Establet attempted to demonstrate what such a reading would reveal. Published in the same year as *For Marx*, *Reading Capital*[40] established the reputation of the Althusserian school, the "Cercle d'Ulm," as it became known because of the Parisian address of the Ecole Normale. Equipped with a new and often esoteric vocabulary, they set about saving Marxism from its corrupting encounter with bourgeois humanism.

But not all Althusserians were content merely to read and reread the classical texts. Many of his students became deeply involved in the radical activism that culminated in the May, 1968, events, and one, Régis Debray, ecame an international revolutionary celebrity.[41] Giving the lie to the assumption that Althusserianism could only have one political implication—Leninist orthodoxy—they grew increasingly restless with the PCF's cautious policies. In late 1966, 600 of them were formally expelled from the Party to regroup in little Maoist cells, those "groupuscules" depicted with sympathetic irony in Godard's film, *La Chinoise*.

Althusser himself was apparently unnerved by the use to which his work was put. Unlike many of his Marxist Humanist opponents, who were enthusiastic supporters of the students, he initially greeted the events with what one unsympathetic commentator has called "deafening silence."[42] Like the majority of the non-Marxist structuralists,[43] he seems to have been unprepared for the explosion of subjective praxis that shook the Gaullist regime. Whether because he was toeing the Party line on the student movement, having been temporarily chastened by Garaudy's recent victory over him in Party circles, or because he was incapacitated by one of the severe depressions that began to disrupt his mental equilibrium in 1962, Althusser waited until after order had been established to make his views known.[44] In essence, he adopted the official PCF argument against

40. The original French version of this book appeared in two volumes in 1975 with texts by Rancière, Macherey and Establet that were deleted from the English translation.

41. Debray came to prominence when he was tried and jailed in Bolivia for revolutionary activities in 1967. He was involved with Che Guevara's ill-fated attempt to spread Castroism elsewhere in Latin America. More recently, he has reemerged as an official of Mitterand's Socialist government, a less dangerous occupation.

42. George Lichtheim, *From Marx to Hegel* (London, 1971), p. 143.

43. See the discussion in Johnson, *The French Communist Party versus the Students*, p. 84.

44. Althusser, "A Propos de l'article de Michel Verret sur 'mai étudiant'," *La Pensée* 145 (June 1969). Anderson calls this piece "a generous and eloquent defence of the role of the

the "infantile disorder" of anarchistic utopianism that had infiltrated the
student movement. Nor did he have anything unorthodox to say about the
Soviet invasion of Czechoslovakia until much later.[45]
  Not surprisingly, a process of disillusionment, which actually began as
early as Glucksmann's penetrating essay of 1967 on "A Ventriloquist
Marxism,"[46] was started by former adherents, as Rancière, Debray and
others began to attack Althusser from the Left.[47] Their criticisms seem to
have had an effect, for admissions of earlier mistakes began to appear in
Althusser's writings. Although it would be incorrect to speak of the result
of an "epistemological break" in his intellectual development (as we will
see, "epistemological breakdown" would perhaps be more accurate), a
shift significant enough for commentators to talk of an early and late Althusser did occur. Turning against what he called the "theoreticist deviation"[48] of *For Marx* and *Reading Capital,* he acknowledged that despite
his best efforts "the young pup called structuralism slipped between my
legs."[49] Now instead of contending that Marx had made a clean break
with his earlier ideological problematic in 1845, he admitted that the only
unblemished "Marxist" texts were *The Critique of the Gotha Program*
(1875) and *The Marginal Notes on Wagner's Lehrbuch der politischen*

students in the events of May 1968" (p. 111), which seems to me an even more generous
reading of the article. Although Althusser clearly wanted to reconcile the students and the
PCF, it was largely on the latter's terms. He thus insisted that the real center of the May
events was not, as Verret claims, the students, but rather the workers' strike. While claiming
that the Leninist category of "infantile leftism," which he agreed applies to the students, is
less damning that its rightist counterpart, he nonetheless attacked the students' "anarchist-
libertarian ideology" (p. 10). He used the Leninist category without the qualifying explanation in his letter of March 15, 1969 to Maria Antonietta Macciocchi, reprinted in Macciocc-
chi, *Letters from Inside the Italian Communist Party to Louis Althusser,* trans. Stephen M.
Hellman (London, 1973), p. 314. Nonetheless, he did call the students' role progressive in
what he saw as "the *most significant event in Western history* since the Resistance and the
victory over Nazism" (p. 320). For a discussion of the students' reactions to Althusser, see
Johnson, p. 84.
  45. Althusser, *Essays in Self-Criticism,* p. 77, where he denies that the Czech's slogan "socialism with a human face" meant they wanted humanism. He nonetheless claims
that "the national mass movement of the Czech people, even if it is no longer to be heard of
(and the struggle is nevertheless still going on) merits the respect and support of all Communists." These sentiments were expressed only in 1974, six years after they might have done
some good.
  46. André Glucksmann, "A Ventriloquist Marxism," reprinted in *Western Marxism: A
Critical Reader,* ed. *New Left Review* (London, 1977).
  47. Jacques Rancière, *La Leçon d'Althusser* (Paris, 1974); Régis Debray, *Prison Writings* (London, 1973), p. 187.
  48. The term was first introduced in his 1967 prefaces to *For Marx.*
  49. Althusser, *Essays in Self-Criticism,* p. 125. For Poulantzas' similar acknowledgement of a limited debt to structuralism, see his interview, "Political Parties and the Crisis of
Marxism," *Socialist Review* 48 (November–December 1979), p. 66.

Ökonomie (1882).[50] The concept of alienation, he now grudgingly conceded, did have a certain provisional usefulness, if it was not confused with the still idealist concept of reification and was subordinated to the category of exploitation.[51]

The most important work of Althusser's second period was the collection of essays published in 1969 as *Lenin and Philosophy*, whose weightiest entry was a discussion of "Ideology and Ideological State Apparatuses." It was followed four years later by *Response to John Lewis*, a rebuttal of an English Communist's defense of Marxist Humanism, and then in 1974 by a semi-apologetic *Elements of Self-Criticism*, which elaborated on his new conception of philosophy as in the last instance "*class struggle in the field of theory.*"[52]

Although Althusser wrote several later essays and continued to participate in PCF political disputes,[53] no other major theoretical statement came from his pen. The psychological troubles that had plagued him for some time became increasingly severe, interrupting not only his writing but his teaching as well. Then in November, 1980, the shocking news that he had strangled his wife, Hélène,[54] and was too incoherent to account for his actions made it tragically clear that his intellectual and political career was prematurely at its end. He was only sixty-two at the time. Following by a year the suicide of one of his most creative followers, the forty-three-year-old Greek political theorist Poulantzas, Althusser's demented act of violence spelled the end of structuralist Marxism, whose obituary some observers in fact had written as early as 1969, when the implications of

50. Althusser, *Lenin and Philosophy*, p. 94. By 1974, his colleague Etienne Balibar went even further and admitted that the "humanist Marx" was equivalent to the "Marxist Marx." See Balibar, *Cinq études du matérialisme historique* (Paris, 1974). It was Althusser's habit of speaking through Marx and claiming to know better what Marx meant than Marx himself that incurred Glucksmann's epithet "ventriloquist Marxism." For another critique of the dangers in too free a "symptomatic reading," see Sebastiano Timpanaro, *On Materialism*, trans. Lawrence Garner (London, 1975), p. 194.

51. Althusser, *Essays in Self-Criticism*, p. 70.

52. Ibid., p. 37. John Lewis' critique appeared as "The Althusser Case" in *Marxism Today* (January and February, 1972). The essay "Elements of Self-Criticism" appeared as a short book in 1974 and is included with other works in the English *Essays in Self-Criticism*. For an insightful analysis of the limits of Althusser's self-criticism, see Mark Poster's review in *Praxis*, 5 (1981).

53. See, for example, "Something New," in *Essays in Self-Criticism*; "On the Twenty-Second Congress of the French Communist Party," *New Left Review* 104 (July–August 1977); and "What Must Change in the Party," *New Left Review* 109 (May–June 1978).

54. See the discussion in Karol, "The Tragedy of the Althussers." There is also a lurid account of the event in *Time*, December 1, 1980, entitled "Marx and Murder: The Philosopher Who Failed," which is placed next to an article on the Yorkshire Ripper. Clearly, there was no lack of *Schadenfreude* in many quarters aroused by the news.

his self-critique were first understood.[55] Although aspects of Althusser's work continue to be influential in certain quarters, his system as a whole no longer commands widespread respect.

This abbreviated account of Althusser's development gives some indication of the sources of his rejection of Hegelian and humanist Marxism. Attracted to a staunchly Leninist Communist Party that relied on its possession of scientific truth to justify its ultimate authority, he labored to bring the grounds of that scientificity in line with the modern philosophy of science he had learned from Bachelard and Canguilhem. Insofar as that philosophy emphasized discontinuities and ruptures rather than cumulative development, he distrusted not only epistemologies that claimed an increasing approximation to "the truth," but also all progressive or evolutionary philosophies of history. Fascinated by Enlightenment thinkers like Montesquieu, who had argued for the natural-law-like quality of social relations rather than their human origins, and deeply indebted to the Comte-Durkheim critique of social contract theory, Althusser rejected any account of society that sought its origins in individual or collective intentionality. The distinction between a *Geisteswissenschaft* and a *Naturwissenschaft* was therefore irrelevant for Althusser, who talked about different sciences, but posited on the most general level a common scientific method.[56] In this sense, his project might be regarded as the revenge of the Marburg neo-Kantians, with their stress on Kant's first *Critique* as the source of all scientific knowledge, against the South-Western or Baden School, which differentiated between nomothetic and idiographic *Wissenschaften*.[57] Lukács, it will be recalled, began the Western Marxist discourse on totality by assimilating Marxism to the *Geisteswissenschaften* and denying its status as a natural science; Althusser rejected the very opposition as ideological.

Restoring Marxism's scientific credentials, however, did not mean a simple return to nineteenth-century Dialectical Materialist orthodoxy. In fact, Althusser gave little ground to Lukács and his followers in his dismissal of Second International vulgar Marxism. His most radical departure, in some ways more radical than that of the Hegelian Marxists, con-

55. Vincent Descombes, *Modern French Philosophy*, trans. L. Scott-Fox and J. M. Harding (Cambridge, 1980), p. 134.

56. As Brewster points out (*Althusser and Bachelard*, p. 30), the same ambiguity existed in Bachelard's work.

57. For other links between Althusser and neo-Kantianism, see Descombes, p. 120, and Gillian Rose, *Hegel Contra Sociology* (London, 1981), pp. 37–39.

cerned the verification procedures that guarantee a theory's scientificity. Orthodox Marxism generally wavered between traditional scientific realism based on a correspondence theory of truth (sometimes, to be sure, understood asymptotically) and a pragmatist notion of verification as the historical realization of predictions. Western Marxism, as we have seen, tended to base its truth claims on Vico's *verum-factum* principle, in which the ultimate identity of subject and object, maker and made, was the guarantee of truth.

Althusser rejected all of these alternatives. Instead, he relied on the work of the French logician Jean Cavaillès, who died in 1944 fighting for the Resistance two years after completing his magnum opus, *Sur La Logique*.[58] Cavaillès attempted to account for the development of science through an epistemology of conceptual self-correction. That is, rather than arguing that the mind of the scientist was stimulated by an interaction with data from the world, he saw science as proceeding entirely within the dialectical logic of the concept. Man was thus the bearer or instrument of the concept, which criticized itself. Combined with Bachelard and Canguilhem's refusal to seek guarantees of scientific truth outside of the activity of science itself, this conceptualist view of logical development gave Althusser a rigorously anti-empiricist, anti-positivist, as well as anti-subjectivist epistemology.[59]

At first glance, such an epistemology seems like a caricature of Hegelian conceptual realism and therefore hopelessly idealist. But it was less Hegel than another figure from philosophy's past who lurked behind Althusser's argument and allowed him to defend it, at least in his early period, as genuinely materialist. That figure was "Marx's only direct ancestor, from the philosophical standpoint,"[60] Baruch Spinoza. The opponent

58. Cavaillès, *Sur la Logique* (Paris, 1960). Althusser acknowledges his debt in *Reading Capital*, p. 16.

59. In *For Marx*, Althusser spelled out "the process of theoretical practice" as an interplay of three "generalities," the first of which was the ideological raw material, the second the theory of science at the time, and the third the new knowledge produced by the impact of the second on the first. See in particular the discussion beginning on p. 182. All of this pretentious anti-empiricist terminology did not prevent him from advising Maria Antonietta Macciocchi in 1968 that "The most important things you can write to me are the precise, positive materials facts you learn. . . . 'Impressions' are important, but above all it is *facts* which count" (p. 21).

60. Althusser, *Reading Capital*, p. 102. Althusser, it should be noted, was not the first French Marxist to find Spinoza attractive. Paul Nizan was also enthusiastic. See the discussion in W. D. Redfern, *Paul Nizan: Committed Literature in Conspiratorial World* (Princeton, 1972), p. 103f. Their views of Spinoza, to be sure, were not identical. Althusser in some ways was closer to the other members of the post-Hegelian generation of French thinkers who were intrigued by Spinoza, such as Gilles Deleuze, who found ways to combine him with Nietzsche. See his *Spinoza et le problème de l'expression* (Paris, 1968) and *Spinoza*

of both Descartes and Vico, Spinoza claimed that *verum index sui et falsi* (truth is its own measure), an argument that Althusser came to adopt as his own. In his *Elements of Self-Criticism*, he made clear the extent of his debt, which had been only indirectly acknowledged in his earlier work:

We made a detour *via* Spinoza in order to improve our understanding of Marx's philosophy. To be precise: since Marx's materialism forced us to *think out* the meaning of the necessary detour *via* Hegel, *we made the detour via Spinoza in order to clarify our understanding of Marx's detour via Hegel.*⁶¹

This detour showed not only that the truth is the sign of itself and not verifiable by any external criterion, but also that this sign identifies itself "not as a Presence but as a Product, in the double sense of the term 'product' (*result* of the work of a process which '*discovers*' it), as it emerges in its own production."⁶² As Cavaillès had argued, truth was the result of an activity, a practice, although not a subjective or individualist one. Theory should therefore be understood as its own productive practice, irreducible, if in certain ways related, to the other practices in which theoreticians might be engaged.

The ground for arguing that this epistemology was also Marx's came from Althusser's reading of the *Introduction to the Critique of Political Economy*, where Marx wrote:

The concrete totality as a totality of thought, as a thought concretum, is in fact a product of thought and conception; but in no sense a product of the concept thinking and engendering itself outside or over intuitions or conceptions, but on the contrary, a product of the elaboration of intuitions and conceptions into concepts.⁶³

Whether or not this passage represented Marx's method has been disputed,⁶⁴ but Althusser claimed that it did, with the result that the separation of thought objects from their referents became a cornerstone of his early work.

What made this argument materialist was Althusser's insistence on a real material world which somehow ultimately provided the real objects

---

(Paris, 1970). Althusser's own attitude towards Nietzsche was apparently positive. See, for example, his remark in *Reading Capital* that we owe our most profound knowledge to "a few men: Marx, Nietzsche and Freud" (p. 16).
    61. Althusser, *Essays in Self-Criticism*, p. 134. Whether or not Althusser got Spinoza right has been disputed. See, for example, Kolakowski, "Althusser's Marx," p. 128.
    62. Ibid., p. 137.
    63. Althusser quotes this passage in *For Marx*, pp. 182–183.
    64. Nancy Hartsock and Neil Smith, "On Althusser's Misreading of Marx's 1857 'Introduction'," *Science and Society* 43, 4 (Winter 1979–1980); David-Hillel Ruben, *Marxism and Materialism: A Study in Marxist Theory of Knowledge*, 2nd ed. (Brighton, 1979), p. 152f.

that were congruent with the objects of conceptual production. But because Althusser was adamantly opposed to any verification of this correspondence coming through the senses, there was a large measure of faith and circular reasoning in the equation. The Althusserian Göran Therborn has called this a "materialist postulate,"[65] which is all it ever was. For Spinoza with his monistic belief in *Deus siva natura*, a single substance which differentiated itself into various modes, idealist and materialist, such a position may have been defensible, but for a twentieth-century exponent of science it was not, as Althusser perhaps tacitly admitted in his later work.

For his early writings, however, it was absolutely essential because it provided the grounds for Althusser's central distinction between science and ideology, which, as we noted, he applied to Marx's own intellectual development. Science, he claimed, operates on the level of conceptual production in which experimental verification plays no role; it is nonetheless materialist because it posits an ultimate congruence between thought objects and a real world. The raw material for scientific activity is provided by ideological conceptions of the world, the "facts" that positivists innocently take as the givens of experience. Following Bachelard and Cavaillès, Althusser equated ideology with naive faith in the immediacy of sense impressions. In so arguing, he was not, of course, at odds with Hegelian Marxists like Lukács, who also decried the illusions of immediacy. However, he differed in his explanation of the origins of such illusions, as well as in his estimation of the chances for overcoming them. He also subtly undermined the equation of ideology and falsehood, preferring instead to see it as a necessary, but non-scientific, kind of knowledge. Whereas Lukács and other Hegelian Marxists had attributed ideology to the reified "false consciousness" of classes in a still contradictory society and postulated a future dereification when classes and ideology would end, Althusser located it in a more intractable source. Here he relied on yet another non-Marxist theory, that of psychoanalysis in its French form.

Traditionally, French Marxists had been wary of psychoanalysis, which had been criticized as early as Georges Politzer's *Critique des fondements de la psychologie* in 1928.[66] In 1949, eight Communist psychologists were forced to engage in humiliating auto-critiques as a result of the Party's Zhdanovist cultural policies.[67] Although the Lukácsian Joseph Gabel had

65. Therborn, *Science, Class and Society*, p. 60.
66. For a discussion of Politzer's ambivalence towards psychoanalysis, see Redfern, *Paul Nizan*, p. 18f, and Sherry Turkle, *Psychoanalytic Politics: Freud's French Revolution* (Cambridge, Mass., 1981), pp. 88–89. For Althusser's critique of Politzer, see *Reading Capital*, pp. 39 and 138.
67. Caute, *Communism and the French Intellectuals*, p. 312.

offered a psychoanalytic analysis of reification as early as 1951 and the *Arguments* group were interested in Marcuse's attempt to create a Freudo-Marxism,[68] it was not really until the linguistic reading of Freud by Jacques Lacan that the possibility for his reconciliation with Marx became widely entertained in France. Here Althusser, who was an actual patient of Lacan for a while, was the main advocate. In 1963 he invited Lacan's seminar to the Ecole Normale, when it was expelled from the orthodox analytic association. Then in the following year Althusser wrote an article entitled "Freud and Lacan" for the PCF journal *La Nouvelle Critique*.[69]

Althusser's interest in psychoanalysis for a theory of ideology may have already been whetted by Bachelard, who often explained what he called "epistemological obstacles" in psychoanalytic terms.[70] But it was to Lacan's "intransigent and lucid—and for many years isolated effort"[71] that he went for a precise analysis of the links between ideology and psyche. Although he came to have second thoughts about some of the formulations in the 1964 essay and appears to have broken personally with Lacan and his circle in the late 1970s,[72] he remained loyal to Lacan's contention that the unconscious was the thought object of a new science. What in particular he admired in Lacan's linguistic interpretation of Freud was its claim to have exposed the subject, the integrated ego, as an illusion, indeed the central illusion of all ideology. "Freud," he wrote,

has discovered for us that the real subject, the individual in his unique essence, has not the form of an ego, centred on the "ego", on "consciousness" or on "existence"—whether this is the existence of the for-itself, of the body-proper or of behavior—that the human subject is de-centred, constituted by a structure which has no "centre" either, except in the imaginary misrecognitions of the "ego", i.e. in the ideological formations in which it "recognizes" itself.[73]

The central word in this description is the "imaginary," which in La-can's specialized vocabulary is contrasted with the symbolic and the real.[74] The imaginary is a stage in human psychic development between six and eighteen months, approximately equivalent to Freud's "primary

68. Poster, *Existentialist Marxism in Postwar France*, p. 260f.
69. Reprinted in *Lenin and Philosophy*, with a qualifying note.
70. See, for example, *La Psychoanalyse du Feu* (Paris, 1938). Brewster ("Althusser and Bachelard," p. 29) accuses Bachelard of an inclination towards psychologistic explanations.
71. Althusser, *Reading Capital*, p. 76.
72. Personal communication with Michel de Certeau, Los Angeles, October, 1981.
73. Althusser, *Lenin and Philosophy*, pp. 218–219.
74. For a good discussion of Lacan's abstruse legacy and its implications for Marxism, see Fredric Jameson, "Imaginary and Symbolic in Lacan: Marxism, Psychoanalytic Criticism, and the Problem of the Subject," *Yale French Studies*, 55–56 (1977). See also Rosalind Coward and John Ellis, *Language and Materialism: Developments in Semiology and the Theory of the Subject* (London, 1977).

narcissism." The pre-verbal child, seeking his specular image in a mirror, recognizes himself as (or better put, imagines himself to be) a unified and coherent individual totality, a "self" identical over time. Here, as later, the empirical evidence of the senses is untrustworthy. Once, however, the child enters the world of language, the realm of the symbolic, this false unity is threatened, for the self is exposed as a grammatical fiction in which centeredness is a function of a linguistic convention rather than an ultimate reality. The transition from the imaginary or mirror state to the symbolic, according to Lacan, coincides with the resolution of the Oedipus Complex, in which the child learns to repress his desire for the mother through identification with the name of the father. Because the identification is only with the name, it is an inevitably mediated and incomplete victory for the child, who never really possesses his mother. The symbolic stage, therefore, is one in which learning to live with the gap between word and thing is a sign of maturity. Seeking a complete fusion of the two is akin to regression to the mirror stage; life for Lacan—and here the influence of the early Sartre is obvious—is a vain search for the fulfillment of desire. The realm of the "real," which he posits as outside of the symbolic system of language, is forever beyond our grasp. So too is the fully integrated ego, which is only an illusory remnant of the mirror stage.

For Althusser, ideology is the imaginary continued through maturity, when a false sense of individual subjectivity is preserved. Indeed,

There is no ideology except by the subject and for subjects. Meaning, there is no ideology except for concrete subjects, and this destination for ideology is only made possible by the subject: meaning, by *the category of the subject* and its functioning. . . . The category of the subject (which may function under other names: e.g. as the soul in Plato, as God, etc.) is the constitutive category of all ideology, whatever its determination (regional or class) and whatever its historical date— since ideology has no history.[75]

This relationship between ideology and subjectivity is, however, a reciprocal one, for not only does subjectivity constitute ideology, but ideology also "*hails or interpellates concrete individuals as concrete subjects*."[76] This process of hailing, the "Hey, you there!" that makes individuals imagine they are subjects, is produced by more than Lacan's glimpse in the mirror, because every child is born into a "specific familial ideological configuration in which it is 'expected' once it has been conceived."[77] As a result, men are "always already subjects."[78]

75. Althusser, *Lenin and Philosophy*, pp. 170–71.
76. Ibid., p. 173.
77. Ibid., p. 176.
78. Ibid., p. 172.

The permanence of ideology, the fact that like the unconscious it has no history, is guaranteed by these inevitable facts of human development. Man, Althusser went so far as to argue, "is an ideological animal by nature."[79] Ideology is therefore never reducible to mere "false consciousness," which can be remedied by dereification. Indeed, it is a function more of the unconscious than the conscious part of the human psyche. And what makes it even more resistant to change is its inscription in actual material practices in the world, for it is the expression of a lived relation between man and his world and not merely its reflected form in conceptual terms. Ideology, in fact, is both practical and theoretical, which makes it all the more impossible to overcome.

What does penetrate it is science, which goes beyond the immediate lived relations of everyday life. Ideology fails to reflect on itself as ideological, in Althusser's vocabulary; it "denegates"[80] or hides from itself its ideological character. It is not so much false consciousness, then, as unreflected, merely lived practical activity. Science (and what Althusser calls "authentic art")[81] is able to see through ideology, although it is unable to end its power over lived experience. History, in fact, *contra* Vico, proves harder to understand than nature because of the persistent power of ideology in hindering our grasp of it. But in opening up the continent of history to science, Marx did allow the theoretical practitioner some access to non-ideological truth.

Precisely how this knowledge would then affect the lived relations of ordinary men, however, Althusser did not make clear.[82] For while he did develop a highly controversial notion of "Ideological State Apparatuses," which drew on Gramsci's concept of hegemony to describe the ways specific ideologies were instilled by specific institutions in bourgeois society,[83] he always insisted that Ideology in general was eternal. Even under

79. Ibid., p. 171.
80. In the glossaries to *For Marx* and *Reading Capital*, this term is related to Freud's *Verneinung*, which means "an unconscious denial masked by a conscious acceptance, or *vice versa.*"
81. Althusser, *Lenin and Philosophy*, p. 222.
82. For an example of his muddle, see *Essays in Self-Criticism*, where he writes:

Knowledge of reality changes something in reality, because it *adds* to it precisely the fact that *it* is known, though everything makes it appear as if this *addition* cancelled itself out in its result. Since knowledge *of* reality belongs in advance to reality, since it is knowledge *of nothing but* reality, it adds something to it only on the paradoxical condition of adding *nothing* to it, and once produced it reverts to it without need of sanction, and disappears in it. The process of knowledge adds to reality at each step its own knowledge of that reality, but at each step reality puts it in its pocket, because this knowledge is its own. *The distinction between the object of knowledge and real object presents the paradox that it is affirmed only to be annulled. But it is not a nullity*: because in order to be annulled it must be constantly affirmed. (p. 194)

83. Althusser, *Lenin and Philosophy*, p. 143. See Gramsci, *Selections from the Prison Notebooks*, ed. and trans. Quintin Hoare and Geoffrey Nowell Smith (New York, 1978), p.

Communism, ideological practices would not end, as men would continue to see themselves as centered subjects. The differences between class society and Communism were therefore not as profound as other Western Marxists had hoped. In *For Marx,* all Althusser could suggest was that

> In a class society ideology is the relay whereby, and the element in which, the relation between men and their conditions of existence is settled to the profit of the ruling class. In a classless society ideology is the relay whereby, and the element in which, the relation between men and their conditions of existence is lived to the profit of all men.[84]

What presumably would remain, therefore, after the revolution is the separation between theoretical and other practices, which meant that the Marxist intellectual, who is able to have scientific, totalistic knowledge of society, would still be privileged over the masses. With these conclusions, it is not surprising that Althusser was regarded by many other Western Marxists as an apologist for Stalinism, despite his protestations to the contrary, or at least as a defender of inevitable political and intellectual elitism. Although certain of his followers attacked the gap between intellectual and manual labor as a class distinction, the persistence of a similar split seemed inevitable under Althusser's version of Communism.

If, however, we focus more closely on his concept of totality, to which we can now finally turn, certain unexpected similarities between his position and that of Lukács' critics within the Hegelian Marxist camp can be discerned. These similarities were apparently hidden not only to his opponents, but also to Althusser himself because of his unwillingness to discriminate among variants of Western Marxism.

In *For Marx,* he contended that there were basically only two competing holisms, Hegel's and Marx's:

> The Hegelian "totality" is not such a malleable concept as has been imagined; it is a concept that is perfectly defined and individualized by its theoretical role. Similarly, the Marxist totality is also definite and rigorous. All these totalities have in common is: (1) a word; (2) a certain vague conception of the unity of things; (3) some theoretical enemies. On the other hand, in their essence they are almost unrelated.[85]

342, for an anticipation of Althusser's ISA's. They have occasioned considerable controversy. See, for example, Ralph Miliband, *Marxism and Politics* (Oxford, 1977), p. 54f; Göran Therborn, *The Ideology of Power and the Power of Ideology* (London, 1980), p. 8f; David Silverman and Brian Torode, *The Material Word: Some Theories of Language and its Limits* (London, 1980), chapter 2.

84. Althusser, *For Marx,* p. 236.
85. Ibid., p. 203.

What characterized Hegel's totality, Althusser argued, was its reduction of the whole to the alienated exfoliation of an original simple unity. All of the elements in the totality were thus merely manifestations or "moments" of the essential genetic principle underlying the whole. Because each of these moments was equally expressive of the whole, there was no way to determine which was more important than the others. The unity they expressed was thus a spiritual one in which actual material differences were ideologically transfigured rather than genuinely reconciled. "My claim," Althusser wrote,

is that the Hegelian totality: (1) is not really, but not apparently, articulated in "spheres"; (2) that its unity is not its complexity itself, that is, the structure in dominance *(structure à dominante)* which is the absolute precondition for a real complexity to be a unity and really the object of a *practice* that proposes to transform this structure: political practice. It is no accident that the Hegelian theory of the social totality has never provided the basis for a *policy*, that there is not and cannot be a Hegelian politics.[86]

Furthermore, Althusser went on, the Hegelian totality tacitly reproduced the bourgeois myth of the social contract because of its dependence on a point of origin from which the whole emerged. Thus, to assume that memory *(Erinnerung)* could have a liberating function in Marcuse's sense was misguided.[87] There was no primary plenitude whose recovery in memory could provide a foretaste of a future totalization.

Marx's totality, Althusser contended, was very different in all critical respects:

We know that the Marxist whole cannot possibly be confused with the Hegelian whole: it is a whole whose unity, far from being the expressive or "spiritual" unity of Leibniz's or Hegel's whole, is constituted by a certain type of *complexity*, the unity of a *structured whole* containing what can be called levels or instances which are distinct and "relatively autonomous", and co-exist within this complex structural unity, articulated with one another according to specific determinations, fixed in the last instance by the level or instance of the economy.[88]

Rather than being centered in one original and still effective principle which manifested itself in all its disparate moments, the Marxist totality was a decentered whole which had neither a genetic point of origin nor a teleological point of arrival. Thus, allegedly "secondary" contradictions in, say, culture and politics were not mere epiphenomena of "primary" ones, as both orthodox superstructure-base theory and Marxist human-

86. Ibid., p. 204.
87. In *Reading Capital*, he attacks Sartre rather than Marcuse for relying on Hegelian *Erinnerung* (p. 173), but the critique would apply a fortiori to the latter.
88. Althusser, *Reading Capital*, p. 97.

ist collective subject theory had argued. In fact, economism and humanism were reverse sides of the same non-Marxist coin, for both reduced the
whole to one expressive center. A genuinely Marxist view of totality conceptualized reality as an "ever-pre-given complex whole" in which each
contradiction was "complex-structurally-unevenly determined,"[89] or to
use the simpler term Althusser borrowed from Freud, "overdetermined."

"Overdetermination," Althusser hastened to add, did not mean a pluralist chaos of multiple factors. For as Mao pointed out, at every stage in
the historical process, there was one principal contradiction which dominated the others. To grasp the import of this fact, the Freudian notions of
condensation and displacement, originally applied to dream work, were
useful. A structure in dominance remained in place, Althusser contended,
when the principal contradiction could alternate with other secondary
contradictions in a process of endless displacement. When those contradictions fused together in a process of condensation, however, then a
revolutionary moment was at hand, a moment when a new structure in
dominance could come to the fore. What Mao called "nonantagonistic
contradictions" corresponded to the first case, whereas "antagonistic
contradictions" meant the second, or to put it in traditional if still ideological terms, a shift in quantity becomes a shift in quality.

To head off the charge of non-Marxist pluralism still more vigorously,
Althusser emphasized (as we saw in the excerpt above), that the economy
was always determinate "in the last instance." Here the canonical authority was Engels' famous letter to Joseph Bloch of September 21, 1890, in
which he argued that

According to the materialist conception of history, the *ultimately* determining element in history is the production and reproduction of real life. More than this
neither Marx nor I have ever asserted. Hence if somebody twists this into saying
that the economic element is the *only* determining one, he transforms that proposition into a meaningless, abstract, senseless phrase.[90]

Althusser, however, added a qualification to this argument, which his detractors always found totally unconvincing: "The lonely hour of the 'last
instance'," he contended, "never comes."[91] What this suggested was the

89. Althusser, *For Marx*, p. 209.
90. *Marx and Engels: Selected Works* (Moscow, 1968), p. 692.
91. Althusser, *For Marx*, p. 113. For a characteristically critical response to this formula, see Simon Clarke, "Althusserian Marxism," in Clarke et al., *One-Dimensional Marxism*, where he compares the role of the economy in Althusser to that of God in Spinoza:
"Since it is only an act of faith that can establish the determination, even in the last instance,
of the economic, once a secular, bourgeois conception of society is adopted, it is hardly
surprising that Althusser's dominant philosophical inspiration is that of metaphysical theology" (p. 85).

power of structural rather than factoral causation. As Balibar put it in his contribution to *Reading Capital*:

In different structures, *the economy is determinant in that it determines which of the instances of the social structure occupies the determinant place.* Not a simple relation, but rather a relation between relations; not a transitive causality, but rather a structural causality. In the capitalist mode of production it happens that this place is occupied by the economy itself; but in each mode of production, the "transformation" must be analyzed.[92]

What made this type of causal analysis structural rather than transitive was its reliance on synchronic rather than diachronic explanation. Borrowing the key distinction between metonymy and metaphor introduced into structuralist linguistics by Roman Jakobson and employed by the Lacanian philosopher Jacques-Alain Miller to differentiate causalities,[93] Althusser further elaborated:

The structure is not an essence *outside* the economic phenomena which comes and alters their aspect, forms and relations and which is effective on them as an absent cause, *absent because it is outside them. The absence of the cause in the structure's "metonymic causality" on its effects is not the fault of the exteriority of the structure with respect to the economic phenomena; on the contrary, it is the very form of the interiority of the structure, as a structure,* in its effects. ... It implies that the structure is immanent in its effects in the Spinozist sense of the term, that the *whole existence of the structure consists of its effects.*[94]

To argue instead that causality was a mechanized result of an anterior cause on a posterior effect was, Althusser insisted, non-Marxist; instead, it was a form of ideological "historicism," whose implications for science were disastrous:

The project of thinking Marxism as an (absolute) historicism automatically unleashes a logically necessary chain reaction which tends to reduce and flatten out the Marxist totality into a variation of the Hegelian totality, and which, even allowing for more or less rhetorical distinctions, ultimately tones down, reduces, or omits the real differences separating levels.[95]

Althusser's contorted effort to combine some sort of orthodox Marxist stress on economic determination "in the last instance" with the paradoxi-

92. Balibar, *Reading Capital*, p. 224.
93. Jakobson's seminal article, "Two Aspects of Language: Metaphor and Metonymy," can be found, *inter alia*, in *European Literary Theory and Practice: From Existential Phenomenology to Structuralism*, ed. with intro. Vernon W. Gras (New York, 1973). Althusser credits Miller for applying it to causality in *Reading Capital*, p. 188. Miller, who was Lacan's son-in-law, was one of his most scientific followers, eagerly following the master in his attempt to spell out psychoanalytic insights in mathematical terms. See Turkle, p. 182.
94. Althusser, *Reading Capital*, pp. 188–89.
95. Ibid., p. 132. The specific target here is, of course, Gramsci.

cal admission that in structural causality with its Spinozan "absent cause" the "last instance never comes" was rarely convincing to his more sceptical readers. As the Foucauldian Alan Sheridan observed, it "proved, for many, to be the thin end of the wedge of its abandonment, rather than its saving grace."[96] Barry Hindess, for example, who was one of Althusser's earliest British disciples, finally concluded that holding on to that mysterious last instance meant that "his concept of structuralist causality involves an essentialism that is little different in principle from that of expressive causality."[97]

However inadequate in the long run, Althusser's stress on the relative (but never absolute) autonomy of different structural levels, which he always liked to defend to referring to Stalin's not very remarkable acknowledgement that language was more than a superstructural derivative of the economic base,[98] did have some positive effect. In *Reading Capital*, for instance, it led him to posit an intricate analysis of differential temporalities. Extrapolating from Durkheim's notion of time as a reflection of specific social structures, Canguilhem's contention that each science had its own temporality, and the differentiations between "long" and "short" time by historians like Braudel, Labrousse and Febvre, Althusser argued against the longitudinal concept of totality that was so important for many earlier Western Marxists. Different structural levels have their distinct temporalities, which "can no longer be thought in the co-existence of the Hegelian *present*, of the ideological present in which temporal presence coincides with the presence of the essence with its phenomena."[99] Therefore, "the model of a *continuous and homogeneous time* which takes the place of immediate existence, which is the place of the immediate existence of this continuing presence, can no longer be regarded as the time of history."[100] Once again, however, Althusser tried to ward off the pluralist implications of this conclusion:

96. Alan Sheridan, *Michel Foucault: The Will to Truth* (London, 1980), p. 106. For a more extensive analysis of the link between the failure of Althusser's project and Foucault, see Alex Callinicos, *Is There a Future for Marxism?* (Atlantic Highlands, N.J., 1982).

97. Barry Hindess, "Humanism and Teleology in Sociological Theory," in *Sociological Theories of the Economy*, ed. Barry Hindess (London, 1977), p. 189. For another critique of the concept of structural causality that argues it is really an "amphibology" (an ambiguous formulation that fails to resolve questions of priority and thus ends where it begins), see Glucksmann, "A Ventriloquist Marxism," p. 306f. See also Jameson, *The Political Unconscious* for an attempt to salvage structural causality as in some sense compatible with expressive causality (p. 41).

98. Althusser, *For Marx*, p. 22 and *Reading Capital*, p. 133. For a more nuanced view of the implications of Stalin on language, see Galvano Della Volpe, *Critique of Taste*, trans. Michael Caesar (London, 1978), p. 181.

99. Althusser, *Reading Capital*, p. 99.

100. Ibid.

The fact that each of these times and each of these histories is *relatively autonomous* does not make them so many domains which are *independent* of the
whole: the specificity of each of these times and of each of these histories—
in other words, their relative autonomy and independence—is based on a certain
type of articulation in the whole, and therefore on a certain type of *dependence*
with respect to the whole.[101]

Once again, his detractors were unconvinced by his attempt to have it
both ways.[102] To some, in fact, Althusser seemed little different from Lévi-
Strauss, who had also attacked the fetish of unified historical time in his
critique of Sartre in *The Savage Mind*. Where Althusser differed from
Lévi-Strauss, however, was in distinguishing between his belief in a complexly decentered "combination" of structural levels and Lévi-Strauss's
"combinatory."[103] The latter, Althusser claimed, recognized only homologous synchronic relations among levels, and was therefore another version of expressive totalism. What the Marxist "combination" combined
in its own non-homologous way were, according to Balibar's contribution
to *Reading Capital*, three invariant elements: the laborer, the means of
production (itself divided into objects of labor and means of labor) and
the non-laborer (the property connection and the real or material appropriation connection).[104] This was the specific combination defining the
mode of production, which was itself one level, albeit the most important,
of the social totality as a whole.

What precisely these elements of the mode of production mean or how
the Althusserians juggled them to explain variations in historical combination need not concern us now. What is more significant to note is that
they were taken as irreducible and invariant dimensions of every mode of
production. Under no economic system, including Communism, would
they be the intelligible and deliberate objectifications of a collective subject, as the Hegelian Marxists had hoped. Marx, so Althusser contended,
had always thought men were merely the "*Träger*" or "supports" of connections entailed by the structure. There could never be a re-centering of
the meta-subject of history, or even any meaningful intersubjective determination of the whole. For, according to Althusser, "Marx's whole analysis excludes this possibility. It forces us to think, not the multiplicity of

101. Ibid., p. 100.
102. See, for example, the critiques in Pierre Vilar, "Marxist History, a History in the
Making: Dialogue with Althusser," *New Left Review* 80 (July–August 1973), p. 78; and
Jean Chesneaux, *Pasts and Futures or What is History For?*, trans. Schofield Coryell (London, 1978), pp. 103–4. The latter is particularly critical of Althusser's separation of different
times from the felt time of political practice.
103. Althusser, *Reading Capital*, p. 310.
104. Ibid., p. 215.

centers, but the radical absence of a center."[105] Such an absence, he concluded, was, like ideology, an eternal fact of human existence. Even after the revolution, men would be mere supports of a structure whose origins they were not responsible for and whose goals they could not determine.

With these conclusions, it is not difficult to see why Althusser was anathema to so many other Western Marxists. Most obviously, his abandonment of their vision of a normative totality, in which a dereified subjectivity would recognize itself in its hitherto alien objectifications, made him appear as an apologist for bureaucratic authoritarianism masking as socialism. Although, unlike more explicit defenders of the Soviet Union, he never claimed that it was actually a society in which humanist values had been or were on the road to being realized, his denial that they could ever be realized made it difficult to fault the Soviet Union for not doing so. Indeed, because of his insistence that ideology was an eternal reality and men were forever condemned to be the supports of constraining structures, it was hard to comprehend what a classless society would really achieve. The qualms of his Hegelian or existentialist opponents were not assuaged by clarifications by his colleagues, such as the following attempt by Godelier to define the "higher" mode of production introduced by socialism:

The criterion is the fact that the *structure* of socialist relations *corresponds* functionally with the conditions of rapid development of the new, gigantic, more and more socialized productive forces created by capitalism. The criterion thus expresses the possibilities, the objective properties, of an historically determined structure. This correspondence is totally *independent* of any *a priori* idea of happiness, of "true" liberty, of the essence of man, etc. Marx demonstrates the necessity and superiority of a new mode of production, thus establishing a value-judgment *without starting* with an *a priori* criterion of rationality.[106]

What such a vision implied was a fetish of production, an inability to distinguish between *techne* and *praxis*,[107] that remained within the bourgeois problematic, despite its intentions to transcend it. Not surprisingly, Althusserianism seemed to many to be a Marxist version of the systems theory or cybernetics then becoming popular in bourgeois circles.[108]

        105. Ibid., p. 253. For an analysis that claims, nonetheless, that there is a covert anthropological assumption in Althusser, see Michael H. Best and William E. Connolly, "Politics and Subjects: The Limits of Structural Marxism," *Socialist Review* 48 (November–December 1979).
        106. Maurice Godelier, "Structure and Contradiction in *Capital*" in *Ideology and Social Science*, ed. Robin Blackburn (New York, 1973), p. 354.
        107. As we will see, this distinction plays a crucial role in the work of Habermas. For a good discussion of the limits of the production paradigm in Marx himself, see Agnes Heller, "Paradigm of Production: Paradigm of Work," *Dialectical Anthropology* 6 (1981). For critiques of Althusser's productivist bias, see Clarke, "Althusserian Marxism," p. 54, and Glucksmann, "Ventriloquist Marxism," p. 285.
        108. See, for example, Thompson, *The Poverty of Theory*, p. 201.

Nor were Althusser's critics happy with the implications for a revolutionary politics that came from his work. Because of his denial of agency and will, they seemed to some quietistic, which was an impression strengthened by Althusser's silence in 1968.[109] If men were nothing more than the supports or bearers of structural contradictions that condensed or were displaced for reasons that were outside of human control, it was difficult to see how political practice affected events in a meaningful manner. Althusser, to be sure, did include such a practice in his series of semi-autonomous practices, but it was not at all clear how it related to the others. Certain of his followers, most notably Poulantzas, probed this issue with better results, but little of real value came from Althusser's own pen. As we have noted, many young supporters who were first attracted to his militant anti-revisionism became disillusioned at the time they decided to be active demolishers rather than mere supporters of the current structure in dominance.

To others, however, Althusser's politics seemed inherently less quietistic than Leninist, or even, as we have seen, Stalinist. The elitist distinction between science for the few and ideology for the many suggested an inevitable division of labor between the vanguard and the masses. The characteristic bourgeois distinction between mental and manual labor of exchange-oriented societies was thus valorized rather than undermined in his work.[110] Although it might be argued at first glance that Althusser's call for autonomous "theoretical practice" was a declaration of independence from the Party, as indeed his Party critics felt it was,[111] a closer look suggested otherwise. For his Spinozan faith in the inherent correspondence between truth and certain institutional embodiments of it, despite all empirical evidence to the contrary, led to a perpetual defense of the wisdom of the Party, no matter how inept its specific actions or policies might be. Thus, Althusser always submitted to Party discipline whenever his criticisms were rejected by its leaders. Althusser's late self-criticism, to which we will return shortly, made this political submissiveness even more evident.

Other criticisms of Althusser by his Western Marxist opponents might be detailed, but they should not be allowed to mask the unexpected similarities mentioned above. For the absolute dichotomy between his scientific

109. See, for example, Timpanaro, *On Materialism*, p. 218.
110. Clarke, "Althusserian Marxism," p. 16. The now classic analysis showing the harmful implications of this distinction is Alfred Sohn-Rethel, *Intellectual and Manual Labor: A Critique of Epistemology*, trans. Martin Sohn-Rethel (London, 1978).
111. For a discussion of the Party's response to Althusser, see Hirsh, *The French New Left*, p. 167f.

Marxism and their critical alternative was not as watertight as both supposed. First of all, Althusser was himself mistaken in assuming that all previous Western Marxists had relied on a Hegelian expressive concept of totality. Indeed, as we have seen, Lukács held to it only for a very brief period in his development. By his 1924 essay on Lenin, he had recognized its difficulties,[112] which Revai's hostile review of *History and Class Consciousness* soon made even clearer. Although Korsch was truer than Lukács to his initial expressive holism, he waffled between seeing the genetic center of the totality as proletarian praxis or as the more objective "process" of socioeconomic change.[113] Finally, he retreated to a scientific reading of Marx that reduced holism to an heuristic methodological principle rather than an ontological truth. Gramsci, in particular in those passages of the *Prison Notebooks* where he argued for intersubjective consensus-building, also cast doubt on the idealist notion of a collective meta-subject at the beginning of the historical process. And although Bloch did join the early Lukács in talking about the proletariat as the "we-subject" of history, he argued that the Archimedean point of the whole was at the end rather than the beginning of the process. Well before Althusser attacked memory as a totalizing power, Bloch had argued against anamnesis in favor of anagnorisis or recognition of traces of a future totalization. The eschatological premise of Bloch's position was, of course, anathema to Althusser, but both shared an aversion to genetic meta-subjects.

The same can be said a fortiori of the Frankfurt School, especially Adorno, whose distaste for philosophical first principles, idealistic meta-subjects, and myths of original unity was especially keen.[114] And, as we have seen, Sartre's stubbornly individualist bias prevented him too from ever embracing a collective meta-subject, except as the possible result of a painful and indeed ephemeral process of totalization. As for Merleau-Ponty, his remarks on humanist chauvinism and his quasi-Heideggerian interest in Being show how far he ultimately travelled from his relatively brief infatuation with Hegel in the 1940s. Even Lukács' most faithful fol-

112. Not surprisingly, Althusserians generally approve of this essay. See, for example, the remarks in Robin Blackburn and Gareth Stedman Jones, "Louis Althusser and the Struggle for Marxism" in *The Unknown Dimension: European Marxism Since Lenin*, ed. Dick Howard and Karl E. Klare (New York, 1972), p. 381.

113. For a nuanced defense of Korsch's concept of totality against the charge that it was entirely expressive, see Norman Geras, "Althusser's Marxism: An Assessment" in *Western Marxism: A Critical Reader*, p. 261.

114. For a comparison of Adorno and Althusser, see Martin Jay, "The Concept of Totality in Lukács and Adorno," *Telos* 32 (Summer 1977), p. 135f, and *Varieties of Marxism*, ed. Shlomo Avineri (The Hague, 1977), p. 164f. A similar argument appears in Perry Anderson, *Considerations on Western Marxism* (London, 1976), p. 72.

lower among the later Western Marxists, Goldmann, talked only of a partial identity of subject and object and implicitly abandoned the *verum–factum* principle as the basis of correct knowledge. And as we will see in subsequent chapters, the Della Volpeans in Italy and Habermas in Germany, the latter after freeing himself from an early neo-Hegelianism, also rejected any expressive notion of the whole. In short, although there were certainly traces of expressivism in many of their theories, most Western Marxists before Althusser had become extremely sceptical of a purely Hegelian concept of totality.

This scepticism was manifested among other places in their wrestling with the thorny question of the relationship between nature and history. Lukács' pseudo-solution in which nature was bracketed as a category outside of dialectical totalization, a totalization in which subject and object identity was an attainable goal, clearly satisfied no one. Even the other founding fathers of Western Marxism—Gramsci, Korsch and Bloch— were highly critical. By the time of Horkheimer and Adorno's *Dialectic of Enlightenment*, the implications of Lukács' species imperialism were understood as of a piece with the bourgeois domination of nature, which underlay Western civilization as a whole. Thus, as one recent commentator has noted, there is "a certain unwitting convergence of Frankfurt School and Althusserian interpretations in that both emphasize the autonomy of nature as against philosophy of praxis and condemn as idealistic any doctrine that attempts to understand nature through history."[115] Althusser's Spinozan reading of Marx tended, of course, to collapse history back into nature,[116] which the Critical Theorists staunchly resisted; but what they shared was a hostility to the absolute historicism of Hegelian Marxism in its purer forms. Not surprisingly, Critical Theory also recognized the dangers in an overly humanist interpretation of Marxism, which ultimately endeared them to Althusser's former student, Foucault, if not to Althusser himself.[117]

Yet another similarity between Althusser and certain earlier Western Marxists can be discerned in their attitudes towards time. Despite the provocative rhetoric of *Reading Capital*, Althusser was by no means alone in rejecting Hegel's concept of a continuous and homogeneous time in

115. Andrew Freenberg, *Lukács, Marx and the Sources of Critical Theory* (Towota, New Jersey, 1981), p. 9. It might be more accurate to say "second nature" in Althusser's case, as the autonomy he stressed was that of social structures.
116. In *Lenin and Philosophy*, he writes, "The Marxist tradition was quite correct to return to the thesis of the Dialectics of Nature, which has a polemical meaning that history is a *process without a subject*" (p. 122).
117. Conversation with Foucault, Berkeley, October, 1980.

favor of the particular temporalities of relatively autonomous historical levels. As early as Bloch's 1924 review of *History and Class Consciousness*, the importance of distinct temporal patterns had been emphasized by a Western Marxist. Bloch's subsequent discussion of *Ungleichzeitigkeit* in his writings on Fascism showed how useful such an emphasis might be in freeing Marxism from its naively progressive view of historical movement. In the work of the Frankfurt School, especially where Benjamin's notion of revolutionary *Jetztzeit* disrupting evolutionary historicist time had its impact, a complex view of temporality was also evident. Even in Sartre's writings, which Althusser often held up as a particularly vivid example of Hegelian Marxism,[118] time was not reduced to a homogeneous continuum. As we saw, in *Search for a Method* Sartre rejected the bourgeois concept of progress as more Cartesian than dialectical. Men, he insisted, are not "in time": their specific activities constitute distinct temporalities. And although he did hold out hope for some ultimate collective totalization in which history might become an intelligible unity, his recognition of the power of recurrence and detotalization led him to a generally pessimistic conclusion resembling Althusser's insistence on the eternity of ideology.

Such a pessimism also marked Althusser as a characteristic Western Marxist. But interestingly, so too did one of the central antidotes he posited to it. In words that, aside from their celebration of science, could have come from the pen of Adorno, he wrote:

Art (I mean authentic art, not works of an average or mediocre level) does not give us a *knowledge* in the *strict sense;* it therefore does not replace knowledge (in the modern sense: scientific knowledge), but what it gives us does nevertheless maintain a certain *specific relationship* with knowledge. This relationship is not one of identity but one of difference. Let me explain. I believe that the peculiarity of art is to "make us see," "make us perceive," "make us feel" something which *alludes* to reality. . . . What art makes us *see*, and therefore gives to us in the form of "*seeing,*" "*perceiving*" and "feeling" (which is not the form of *knowing*), is the ideology from which it is born, in which it bathes, from which it detaches itself as art, and to which it *alludes.*[119]

In the work of his disciple Macherey, the privileging of art as at least a partial way out of ideology was made even more explicit. In the *Theory of Literary Production,* he wrote,

118. Althusser, to be sure, did grant Sartre the honor of being like Rousseau in his refusal to compromise with power. See the comparison in *Essays in Self-Criticism*, p. 59, which is repeated in his obituary for Sartre entitled "Our Jean-Jacques Rousseau," *Telos* 44 (Summer 1980).
119. Althusser, *Lenin and Philosophy*, p. 222.

By means of the text it becomes possible to escape from the domain of spontaneous ideology, to escape from the false consciousness of self, of history, and of time.
The text constructs a determinate image of the ideological, revealing it as an object
rather than living it from within as though it were an inner conscience.[120]

As Terry Eagleton has noted,[121] there is an obvious parallel here with the
faith placed in the "aesthetic dimension" by Marcuse and other Critical
Theorists, as well as with Goldmann's notion of a "valid" text.

No less typical of Western Marxism, at least after Lukács, was Althusser's positive attitude towards the radical implications of modernist art,
particularly the "materialist theater," as he called it, of Brecht.[122] His distance from Zhdanovite science in the Lysenko Affair extended as well to the
official socialist realism of Zhdanovite art. The fetish of narrative realism in
orthodox Marxist aesthetics (and, of course, in Lukács' moderately heterodox version) was an example of Lacan's "imaginary" and thus ideological;
"authentic art" undermined rather than supported narrative coherence.[123]
Equally suspect to Althusser was a perfectly lucid narrative style in more
theoretical work, which also smacked of ideological immediacy. What Anderson has called Althusser's "sybilline rhetoric of elusion"[124] thus also put
him in the company of most other Western Marxists, whose stylistic impenetrability was the target of innumerable complaints.

Where Althusser was a true post-Lukácsian Western Marxist, therefore, was in his critique of Hegelian Marxist expressive holism in its purest
form. Where he differed from the rest was in his attempt to present a
genuinely Marxist alternative. Rather than unflinchingly face the aporias
presented by the collapse of Lukács' problematic, he argued for the complete adequacy of that Spinozan, scientific version of the true Marx we
have outlined above. Or at least he did so until the consequences of his
"theoreticist deviation" finally became clear (or were made clear to him by
Party criticism). Although Althusser represented the self-critique that fol-

120. Macherey, *A Theory of Literary Production*, trans. Geoffrey Wall (London, 1978),
p. 132.
121. Terry Eagleton, *Criticism and Ideology: A Study in Marxist Literary Theory* (London, 1976), p. 83; and *Walter Benjamin: Or Towards a Revolutionary Criticism* (London,
1981), p. 90. For more discussion of the aesthetics of the Althusserians, see the special issue
on Art and Ideology, *Praxis* 5 (1981); and the article on *Screen* by Kevin McDonnell and
Kevin Robins in Clarke et al, *One-Dimensional Marxism*.
122. Althusser, "The 'Piccolo Teatro': Bertalozzi and Brecht: Notes on a Materialist
Theater," in *For Marx*.
123. For an extension of this argument, see Fredric Jameson, *Fables of Aggression:
Wyndham Lewis, the Modernist as Fascist* (Berkeley, 1979), p. 12f. For a critique, see Terry
Lovell, "The Social Relations of Cultural Production: Absent Centre of a New Discourse," in
Clarke et al., p. 240f.
124. Anderson, *Consideration on Western Marxism*, p. 54. It is amusing to see Althusser chastise Michel Verret for the inaccessibility of his prose to the working class. See the
remarks in "A propos de l'article de Michel Verret," p. 4.

lowed as only a minor readjustment of his earlier position, in reality it undermined its premises irreparably. And with the collapse of his theoretical framework went his attempt to locate a truly "Marxist" concept of totality.

The first hint of Althusser's second thoughts came as early as his 1967 prefaces to the Italian and English editions of *For Marx*, where he chastised himself for separating theoretical from political practice too drastically, leaving the distinction between philosophy and science unclear, and generally failing to acknowledge the centrality of the "unity of theory and practice" in the Marxist–Leninist tradition. Like Foucault at around the same time, he discovered that there were fundamental links between *savoir* (knowledge) and *pouvoir* (power) that had been occluded by an exclusively theoretical (or in Foucault's case, discursive) focus. In the 1970s, the full implications of this occlusion were spelled out in his *Essays in Self-Criticism*, which referred, in still orthodox Leninist fashion, to a "deviation"[125] from what was presumably a "correct" Party line. Although now admitting that he had been tempted by structuralism, he contended that it was merely a "secondary deviation" in comparison with "theoreticism."

"Theoreticism" was a sin with several dimensions. Basically, it grew out of the assumption that theoretical practice was a hermetically closed, conceptually generated enterprise in which contact with both empirical reality and other practices was irrelevant. The fundamental lesson of the Cavaillès–Bachelard–Canguihem tradition in the philosophy of science was implicitly acknowledged as more idealistic and rationalistic than truly materialist. Now the "materialist postulate" of his earlier work came to the fore rather than lurking uncomfortably in the background: "*Marxism–Leninism has always subordinated the dialectical Theses to the materialist Theses*," he scolded John Lewis. "Take the famous Thesis of the primacy of practice over theory: it has no sense unless it is subordinated to the Thesis of the primacy of being over thought."[126]

Secondly, theoreticism meant believing that philosophy was like a science with its own object and its own history of epistemological breaks.

125. Stalinism also now became a "deviation" for Althusser, although Stalin himself did too many positive things to be "*reduced* to the deviation which we have linked to his name; even less can this be done with the Third International which he came in the thirties to dominate" (*Essays in Self-Criticism*, p. 91). By treating Stalinism as a theoretical problem (a "deviation" from some putatively true line), Althusser mocked his own pretensions to give a materialist explanation of the phenomenon. Nowhere in his work did he ever really come to grips with the social and economic origins of Stalinism, although attempts were made by certain of his followers, such as the Maoist Charles Bettelheim: see his *Luttes de classes en URSS* (Paris, 1979). For a critique of all Althusserian analyses of Stalinism, see Alex Callinicos, *Is There a Future for Marxism?* which offers an alternative based on the Trotskyist Tony Cliff's writings.
126. Althusser, *Essays in Self-Criticism*, p. 54.

Instead, Althusser now contended, Marx's philosophical revolution had preceded his scientific one and, what was even more important, this philosophical revolution was itself based on a prior political shift:

For he was only able to break with bourgeois ideology in its totality because he took inspiration from the basic ideas of proletarian ideology, and from the first class struggles of the proletariat, in which this ideology became flesh and blood. This is the "event" which, behind the rationalist facade of the contrast between "positive truth" and ideological illusion, gave this contrast its real historical dimension.[127]

Accordingly, it was to class struggle that one had to look for those guarantees that Althusser, deluded by his previous theoreticist deviancy, had not acknowledged:

It is possible to produce (as Marx does in *Capital*) proven theoretical results, that is, results which can be verified by scientific *and* political practice, and are open to methodological practice.[128]

Never mind that he added in a footnote, "This little 'and' (scientific *and* political practice) naturally poses important problems which cannot be dealt with here,"[129] because he then alluded to certain "crucial texts" of Lenin, Gramsci and Mao that allegedly contained the solution. All that had to be remembered, and this is precisely what the theoreticist Althusser had forgotten, was that "*philosophy is, in the last instance, class struggle in the field of theory.*"[130]

For the chastened, no longer deviant Althusser, "class struggle" became a potent shibboleth, supplanting all the others in his previous work. The earlier titles of his books, he now admitted, had been slogans in "the great class struggles of contemporary history,"[131] where the main enemy, it seemed, was the humanist misreading of Marx. Stalinism, Althusser contended, was related to this misreading, even though humanism had been invoked against it. For what Stalin had forgotten was class struggle. Because of this amnesia, Stalinism could be understood as the "posthumous revenge of the Second International,"[132] whose economism, it will be

127. Ibid., p. 121.
128. Ibid., p. 110.
129. Ibid.
130. Ibid., p. 37. Althusser's work on class was, however, not very convincing. For an excellent analysis, see R. W. Connell, "A Critique of the Althusserian Approach to Class," *Theory and Society*, 8, 3 (November, 1979).
131. Althusser, *Essays in Self-Criticism*, p. 173.
132. Ibid., p. 89. For a critique of the argument that Stalinism espoused economism and was thus another form of expressive holism, see Clarke, "Althusserian Marxism," p. 83 and 93.

recalled, was the reverse side of humanism for Althusser. What must be always grasped was that the true motor of history was neither man nor the economy, but rather class struggle, which Althusser claimed, preceded classes themselves. Even the formula, the "masses make history," which Althusser invoked against John Lewis's "man makes history," was ultimately subordinate to the class struggle, for "history is an immense *natural-human* system in movement, and the motor of history is class struggle. History is a process, and a *process without a subject*."[133]

Althusser's new emphasis on class struggle as the motor of history may have preserved his anti-humanist, anti-subjectivist credentials, but it severely undermined his entire epistemological framework. For at the same time that he staunchly denied any origin or genetic center in the structural totality, he contended that everything in it, including theoretical practice, was somehow "in the last instance" a function or expression of class struggle. Thus he began surreptitiously to reproduce that very expressive concept of totality that he had been at such pains to exorcise from Marxism. Indeed, almost like Korsch with his contention that "scientific socialism is the theoretical expression of a revolutionary process,"[134] he implicitly cancelled out the relative autonomy of the separate levels of the structural whole. One indication of the resulting confusion came in his new, if still guarded, generosity towards Hegel, which surfaced as early as his 1968 essay on "Marx's Relation to Hegel"[135] and reappeared in the *Elements of Self-Criticism*. Hegel, he now conceded, had also understood that history was a process without a subject and had denied any genetic origin at the beginning of history. "Hegel's Logic," he now claimed, "is the Origin affirmed-denied: the first form of a concept that Derrida has introduced into Philosophical reflection, *erasure (rature)*."[136] In this sense, Hegel was not as far from Spinoza as he first seemed. In fact, in his better

133. Althusser, *Essays in Self-Criticism*, p. 51.
134. Karl Korsch, *Marxism and Philosophy*, trans. with intro. Fred Halliday (New York), p. 69.
135. Althusser, *Politics and History*, p. 174f. As Timpanaro argues in *On Materialism*, "The notion that in Hegel there is the idea of a 'process without a subject' is only an exaggerated and awkward way of repeating something which had already been maintained by all those Hegelian-Marxists from whom Althusser, till recently was (legitimately) eager to dissociate himself" (p. 193). This is more true of those who came after Lukács than of Lukács himself.
136. Althusser, *Politics and History*, p. 184. Althusser's new reading of Hegel did not win over all of his readers. Descombes, for example, sarcastically remarks, "Doubtless the word 'Mind,' fairly frequent in Hegel's work, had eluded Althusser's 'symptomatic reading'" (p. 77). Colletti was no less hostile; see his remarks in "A Philosophical and Political Interview" in *Western Marxism: A Critical Reader*, ed. *New Left Review* (London, 1977), p. 333.

grasp of the power of contradiction, Hegel, Althusser now admitted, had surpassed Spinoza. Hegel did differ from the latter (and from Marx as well) in positing a telos at the end of history:

There is no assignable Origin in Hegel, but that is because the whole process, which is fulfilled in the final totality, is indefinitely, in all the moments which antic- ipate its end, its own Origin. There is no Subject in Hegel, but that is because the becoming-Subject of substance, as an accomplished process of the negation of the negation, is the Subject of the process itself.[137]

For this reason, Althusser claimed, the differences between Marx and He- gel were still substantial, so much so that he now argued it was better to restrict the concept of totality to Hegel alone and to claim that of the whole for Marx. "It might be said," he admitted,

that this is a verbal quibble, but I do not think this is entirely true. If I preferred to reserve for Marx the category of the whole rather than that of the totality, it is because within the totality a double temptation is always present: that of consider- ing it as a pervasive essence which exhaustively embraces all of its manifestations, and—what comes to the same thing—that of discovering in it, as in a circle or a sphere (a metaphor which makes us think of Hegel once again), a center which would be its essence.[138]

Marx's metaphor, Althusser contended, was more that of an edifice than a circle, an edifice with a foundation and several floors. The foundation, he implied, was the site of that "last instance that never comes," but which nonetheless suggests the ultimate place where the class struggle is waged at its most consequential.

From these convoluted attempts to salvage his earlier argument and reconcile it with his new anti-theoreticist stance, it is evident that the edifice of Althusser's own system was increasingly shaky. The tensions that resulted were also apparent in his growing estrangement from PCF politics. Because of his new insistence on the subordinate role of theory to practice and science to politics, it might appear that Althusser would be even more compelled than before to recognize the Party as the historical embodiment of the class struggle. And yet, his growing impatience with many of its disastrous policies led him into ever more public criticisms of it, especially as it seemed to be slipping into a new opportunistic version of Marxist Humanism when it officially abandoned the goal of a "dicta- torship of the proletariat" in 1976. Beginning in that year with his sharply worded attack on the past actions of the Soviet Union and the PCF during the Lysenko Affair, he leveled a number of charges against the present

137. Althusser, *Essays in Self-Criticism*, pp. 180–81.
138. Ibid., p. 181.

policies of the leadership of the party in *Le Monde* (and not, significantly, in *L'Humanité*, which closed its pages to him). These culminated in "What Must Change in the Party,"[139] written after the debacle of the Union of the Left in 1978. In a direct challenge to the neo-Stalinism of Georges Marchais, he sarcastically remarked:

> Talk away! It is all very well to be heir to the October Revolution, and to preserve the memory of Stalingrad. But what of the massacre and deportation of recalcitrant peasants baptized as Kulaks? What of the crushing of the middle classes, the Gulag Archipelago, the repression that still goes on twenty-five years after Stalin's death? When the only guarantees offered are words that are *immediately contradicted* in the only possible field of verification, namely the internal practices of the Party, then it is clear that the "buffer" also lies within the Party itself.[140]

Althusser's recommended cures for the Party's hypocrisy—its covert function as a "buffer" neutralizing any real class struggle—were not, however, particularly radical. Arguing that it should leave its "fortress" of official platitudes and make more concrete analyses of political realities, he called for a critique of the Party's internal organization, without, however, abandoning the sacred Leninist principle of democratic centralism. The immediate task was a renewed effort to forge an alliance of working-class and popular forces, but one free of any reformist or sectarian bias.

Such proposals, in fact, echoed certain complaints of Party critics much further to the right, like Jean Elleinstein.[141] With the collapse of the Maoist leadership in China, Althusser seems to have lost his external model for a non-deviationist leftist politics. Because he was incapable of breaking with the Party, his frustrations seem to have mounted to the point where his mental balance, for so long precariously unstable, was finally shattered. Even if we resist allegorizing the murder of his wife, who was an even more adamant Party militant than he, into an expression of his political despair, it clearly ended his public career. In strangling Hélène Althusser, who herself seems to have grown impatient with the Party line,[142] he was thus making the break with Communism that his conscious mind told him was impossible.

The death throes of Althusserianism, as we have noted, had begun much earlier. The legacy of this controversial episode in the history of Western Marxism was not, however, an entirely negative one. For by ex-

139. Althusser, "What Must Change in the Party," *New Left Review* 109 (May–June 1978).

140. Ibid., p. 38.

141. See, for example, Elleinstein's call for a new truthfulness in Party propaganda in his "Plea to Drop 'Founding' Myths," *The Guardian* (April 30, 1978), p. 12f.

142. Karol, "The Tragedy of the Althussers," p. 94.

posing many of the questionable assumptions of Hegelian Marxism as sharply as he did, indeed in showing that in some ways it was more of a continuation than a true break with orthodox Dialectical Materialism, Althusser helped focus attention on many of its genuine weaknesses. The unexpected similarities that we have discerned between his work and that of several post-Lukácsian Western Marxists show the extent to which the original problematic of the tradition was vulnerable to attack from many different directions. The solutions Althusser proposed may not have survived careful scrutiny, but neither has the target of his wrath. Although occasional brave efforts are still made today to revive the Lukácsian concept of totality,[143] it is difficult to avoid concluding with Althusser and his unwitting allies in the Critical Marxist camp that it is no longer viable in its classical form.

The force of this negative judgment can be made even clearer if we examine one other strain in the Western Marxist tradition which, like Althusser, defended science against critique. In post-war Italy, a school emerged in and around the PCI identified with the figure of Galvano Della Volpe, which also rejected Hegelian Marxism, in particular in its Gramscian guise. In the work of Della Volpe and his most illustrious student, Lucio Colletti, the limits of the original Western Marxist model of totality were once again exposed. But no less clearly, if to be sure no more intentionally, so too were those of a scientific Marxist alternative. In turning to the work of the Della Volpeans, we can therefore observe one final way in which the Western Marxist discourse on totality was in fact unravelling at the very time when its rediscovery seemed to promise so much for the New Left of the 1960s and early 1970s.

143. See, for example, McDonnell and Robins in Clarke et al., *One-Dimensional Man*, p. 159.

CHAPTER FOURTEEN

Scientific Marxism in Postwar Italy: Galvano Della Volpe and Lucio Colletti

No national Marxist culture after World War II was as rich and vital as that which emerged from the ashes of Mussolini's Italy. Drawing on the popularity it had gained as a leading force in the partisan movement, especially in the north, the Italian Communist Party, seemingly shattered in 1926 when Gramsci and most of its other leaders were imprisoned, reconstituted itself as a powerful political force after 1944.[1] Gramsci's old Turinese comrade, Palmiro Togliatti, who had escaped jail to spend the fascist years in the Soviet Union, returned from exile to direct the Party's rapid rebirth. Although outwardly faithful to Stalin's domination—he had ruthlessly banished dissenters like Angelo Tasca and Ignazio Silone in the late 1920s for questioning the official Party line—Togliatti subtly introduced a new note into Italian Communism, which led it increasingly away from the Russian model. Anxious to avoid repeating the disasters of the pre-Mussolini era, which he attributed to the Party's maximalist rigidity under the leadership of Bordiga, he rejected an exclusively *ouvrierist* approach in favor of a more broadly based alternative. Open to coalitions with other parties and willing to play the parliamentary game, Togliatti promulgated a national strategy that would build on bourgeois democracy rather than seek to undermine it. Intent on showing his commitment to moderate means, he served as Minister of Justice in the postwar government of Alcide De Gasperi and helped write the new republican constitution after the fall of the monarchy, which the Communists in fact never vigorously sought. A specifically "Italian road to socialism,"[2] he insisted,

1. For a discussion of the PCI during the Mussolini era, see Charles F. Delzell, *Mussolini's Enemies: The Anti-Fascist Resistance* (Princeton, 1961).
   2. For an early use of this phrase, see Palmiro Togliatti, "La nostra lotta per la democra-

could be followed, which essentially meant returning to the Popular Front strategy of the 1930s in order to build a mass movement with deep roots in Italian society. Even after the Christian Democrats succeeded in shutting the PCI out of a governmental role in January 1947, Togliatti remained faithful to this long-term strategy, which his successors to this day have not abandoned.

A key element in Togliatti's approach was the construction of a broad cultural coalition to foster the counter-hegemony Gramsci had argued was a preliminary to socialist transformation. The "New Party," as Togliatti called it, was thus especially cordial to intellectuals, whose talents it hoped to use to build a new consensus.[3] In this effort, the selective manipulation of Gramsci's legacy (briefly traced in an earlier chapter) played a central role. Emphasizing his debt to the Crocean idealism that still dominated Italian culture,[4] Togliatti turned Gramsci into the patron saint of a domesticated, humanist, not-very-revolutionary Leninism that would appeal to a broad spectrum of sympathetic intellectuals. If the PCI's political center of gravity was in the industrial north, its intellectual center remained in the south, where the Neapolitan idealism of Spaventa and Croce was still particularly potent. Although Togliatti's tolerance of genuine cultural diversity would prove to have its limits, as his polemic against Elio Vittorini's *Politecnico* in 1947 demonstrated,[5] he was able to resist the worst excesses of Zhdanovite orthodoxy far more strongly than, say, the leaders of the French Communist Party. As a result, authentic intellectual life within the PCI or in its general ambience remained more alive than in any other Communist Party in Europe. It was, in fact, the only party to emerge out of the Third International, officially dissolved by Stalin in 1943, that was also significantly open to influences from the Western Marxist tradition.

After 1956, when Togliatti took advantage of Khrushchev's criticism of Stalinism to announce his own "Strategy of Reforms" at the PCI's eighth congress, the process of intellectual and cultural rejuvenation ac-

---

zia e per il socialismo" in *Critica marxista* 2 (July–October 1964). The essay was originally a talk delivered in 1947. For a good short discussion of the Togliattian line, see Stephen Hellman, "PCI Strategy and the Question of Revolution in the West" in *Varieties of Marxism*, ed. Shlomo Avineri (The Hague, 1977).

3. Maria Antonietta Macciocchi makes this point in her *Letters from Inside the Italian Communist Party to Louis Althusser*, trans. Stephen M. Hellman (London, 1973), p. 130.

4. See Cesare Vasoli, "Italian Philosophy After Croce" and Tito Perlini, "Left-Wing Culture in Italy Since the Last War," both in *Twentieth-Century Studies* 5 (September 1971).

5. For a discussion of this episode, see Jürgen Rühle, *Literature and Revolution: A Critical Study of the Writer and Communism in the Twentieth Century*, trans. Jean Steinberg (New York, 1969), p. 373f.

celerated. In Party journals like *Rinascita, Il Contemporaneo,* and *So-cietà*, theoretical and methodological issues were thrashed out with greater candor than anywhere else in the Communist movement.[6] Non-affiliated periodicals like *Aut Aut* and *Quaderni Rossi* also played a criti-cal role in opening the Italian Left to new ideas. The rediscovery of the young Marx coincided with an openness to stimuli from heterodox Marx-ists abroad that meant Italian Marxism lost its provinciality much earlier than many of its counterparts in other countries.

Some Italian Marxists like Antonio Banfi, Enzo Paci and Pier Aldo Rovatti in Milan were attracted to existentialism and phenomenology and tried, like Sartre and Merleau-Ponty, to turn them in a material direction. Others like Mario Spinella, Gian Enrico Rusconi and Giuseppe Vacca promoted and quarrelled over the significance of Karl Korsch, whose *Marxism and Philosophy* and *Karl Marx* were translated into Italian in 1966 and 1969 respectively.[7] Interest in Lukács, initially confined to his aesthetic works, soon turned to his philosophical writings, especially af-ter the translation of *History and Class Consciousness* in 1971. Mario Vacatello and others found ways to assimilate him to the humanist Marx-ism sponsored by the Party, while Alberto Asor Rosa followed Goldmann in probing Lukács' links with bourgeois culture in crisis before World War I.[8] At the same time, gifted younger scholars like Gian Enrico Rusconi, Giacomo Marramao, and Furio Cerutti began introducing the Frankfurt School's Critical Theory into Italy.[9] Cesare Luporini, Maria Antonietta Macciocchi and others were no less industrious in presenting the work of Althusser and his structuralist colleagues, even if in several cases their enthusiasm soon waned.[10]

Many of these intellectuals were at one time or another members of the PCI, but in the 1960s an increasing number of Italian Marxists found it easier to remain outside its walls. As in France in the years leading up to 1968, a wide variety of New Leftist, Trotskyist and anarchist groups set

6. See, for example, the essays collected in Franco Cassano, ed., *Marxismo e Filosofia in Italia (1958–1971)* (Bari, 1973).
7. For a good survey of the Italian reception of Korsch, see Giacomo Marramao, "Korsch in Italy," *Telos* 16 (Winter 1975–76).
8. For a treatment of Lukács in Italy, see Franco Fortini, *Verifica dei Poteri* (Milan, 1974).
9. For surveys of the Italian response to the Frankfurt School, see Enzo Rutigliano, "Qualche nota sulla recezione italiana della scuola di francoforte" in *Lo sguardo dell'angelo* (Bari, 1981), and "L'influenza della teoria critica sulla sociologia italiana," *Temi di storia della sociologia* (Trento, 1983). The reception of the Frankfurt School actually began as early as 1954 with Renato Solmi's translation of *Minima Moralia*.
10. For a survey of the early Italian literature on Althusser, see Sergio Pieri, "Althusser in Italia," *Aut Aut* 135 (May–June 1973).

themselves up in opposition to the Party. Some broke with it because of its residual Stalinism, others for its political pusillanimity, still others because of its pollution by bourgeois modes of thought. The Party itself occasionally aided the process of proliferation by insisting on the limits of internal debate. To take a particularly noteworthy example, Lucio Magri, Rosanna Rossanda and their colleagues on the journal *Il Manifesto* were expelled from the PCI in 1964 for interpreting and applying Gramsci in a more revolutionary way than was considered prudent by the Party leadership.[11] Other leftist intellectuals like Tito Perlini and Sebastiano Timpanaro, who were attracted to various forms of Trotskyism, or the distinguished political theorists Norberto Bobbio and Massimo Salvadori, who favored the more moderate socialism of the Italian Socialist Party (PSI), also remained outside the Party's orbit.

To make complete sense of the richness of postwar Italian Marxist intellectual life, one would have to understand not only the work of all of these figures, but also that of a host of other prominent leftists, such as Ludovico Geymonat, Raniero Panzieri, Franco Fortini, Lelio Basso, Nicola Badaloni, Mario Tronti, Antonio Negri and Cesare Cases, to name only a few.[12] Insofar as many of them dealt with the concept of totality, an issue of particular importance in Italy not only because of Gramsci's legacy, but also because of the recent memory of totalitarianism,[13] it might appear necessary to provide a general overview. But were such a survey attempted, many of the same arguments and problems we have already encountered would necessarily be repeated. Instead, it seems much more profitable to focus on only one strain in postwar Italian Marxism, a strain which was peculiar to it alone and which introduced a new perspective on the question of Marxist holism. That strain is the school deriving from the work of Galvano Della Volpe, whose members included Giulio Pietranera, Umberto Cerroni, Mario Rossi, Nicola Merker, and most notably, Lucio Colletti.[14] In the philosophical writings of Della Volpe and

11. For a discussion of the *Manifesto* affair, see the introduction to Lucio Magri, "Problems of the Marxist Theory of the Revolutionary Party," *New Left Review* 60 (March–April 1970).

12. For a good general account of this period, see Nicola Badaloni, *Il marxismo italiano degli anni sessanta* (Rome, 1972).

13. See, for example, the discussions of totalitarianism in Ugo Spirito, *Il communismo*, 2nd ed. (Florence, 1970), chapter 2; and Augusto del Noce, *Il suicidio della rivoluzione* (Milan, 1978), chapter 4.

14. For a short discussion of the school, see John Fraser, *An Introduction to the Thought of Galvano Della Volpe* (London, 1977), p. 14f. Fraser's is also the best general account of Della Volpe in English, despite its often tortured prose and unclear arguments. See also Giuseppe Vacca, *Scienza stato e critica di classe: Galvano Della Volpe e il marxismo* (Bari, 1970); Mario Montano, "The 'Scientific Dialectics' of Galvano Della Volpe," in *The Unknown Dimension: European Marxism Since Lenin*, eds. Dick Howard and Karl Klare

Colletti in particular, a new challenge to the Lukácsian paradigm was presented, which subtly complemented many of those developed by German and French intellectuals.

The Della Volpeans appeared as a distinct school in Italian Marxist thought during the post-Stalinist era of the late 1950s, when many intellectuals began to search for an alternative to the PCI's political strategy of reformist pseudo-Leninism and its cultural policy of ecumenical pseudo-Gramscianism. Some, such as Magri and the Manifesto group, found an answer in a fresh reading of the *Prison Notebooks*, which led them to try to rescue Gramsci from his official interpretation. But for others, Gramsci's work had been too irreparably tainted by idealist and historicist modes of thought to permit such an operation. Like the Althusserians, although with important differences we will explore later, they sought to resurrect a more genuinely scientific Marxism, which would not, however, repeat the errors of Second International Dialectical Materialism. In Galvano Della Volpe, then a little-known professor of philosophy at the obscure Sicilian University of Messina, they found an inspiration, for he had liberated himself from the coils of idealism and historicism many years before.

Born in 1895 in Imola, near Bologna, Della Volpe was the son of a financially strapped aristocrat. After serving in the war, he studied philosophy and history at the University of Bologna, where he received his doctorate in 1920. Although he came into contact with leftist ideas at the university, in particular through the influence of Rodolfo Mondolfo, a social democrat with an interest in humanist and idealist issues,[15] the young Della Volpe was soon attracted to the more powerful figure of Giovanni Gentile. His first article, written in 1924, was devoted to Gentile's philosophy of the act and his first book, *The Origins and Formation of the Hegelian Dialectic: Hegel, Romantic and Mystic (1793–1800)*, appearing in 1929, was dedicated to his teacher.[16] His ardor for Gentilean or any other form of idealism soon cooled, however, and by the mid-

---

(New York, 1972) and "On the Methodology of Determinate Abstraction: Essay on Galvano Della Volpe," *Telos* 7 (Spring 1971); and Robert A. Gorman, "Empirical Marxism," *History and Theory* 20, 4, Beiheft 20 (1981).

15. On Mondolfo, see Enzo Santarelli, *La revisione del marxismo in Italia: Studi di critica storica*, 2nd ed. (Milan, 1977).

16. Della Volpe, "L'idealismo dell'atto e il problema della categorie," *Logos* 4, 1–2 (1924) and *Le origini e la formazione della dialettica hegeliana. I: Hegel romantico e mistico (1793–1800)* (Florence, 1929).

1930s he was working on the very different philosophy of David Hume, whose hostility to a priorism of any kind left a lasting mark on him.[17] Searching for a more concrete philosophy than idealism, he was drawn to existentialism. The most permanent effect of this relatively ephemeral interest was the deepening of his awareness of the links between philosophy and political commitment, which expressed itself initially in a fascination with Rousseau's political philosophy and then, in 1944, in his decision to join the PCI. After an unsuccessful attempt to run as a Communist candidate for the senate in Reggio Calabria in 1948, he gave up active political work for the life of a professional, if still committed, philosopher.

Having taught history and philosophy in *liceos* (high schools) in Ravenna and Bologna, and then philosophy in a junior position at the University of Bologna, Della Volpe occupied the chair of Professor of the History of Philosophy at Messina after 1938, and remained there for the rest of his career (although he managed to live in Rome for most of the year). As Colletti was later to describe him, he was "an intellectual of the old style, who always worked on the assumption that there should be a division of labor between theory and politics."[18] In his own case, however, it seems as if certain compromises he had made with the fascist authorities during his early years in Messina had helped reinforce the division, as they precluded his having a major policy-making role in the Party,[19] whose political line he obediently followed.

Della Volpe's most important theoretical statement was published in 1950 under the title *Logic as a Positive Science*,[20] but it had little immediate impact in Party circles. After 1956, however, when the PCI began to rethink its philosophical and cultural policies, Della Volpe's star began to rise. Mario Alicata, who directed the PCI's cultural line, was attracted to him and admitted him to the editorial board of *Società*. According to John Fraser, "Della Volpe's acceptance of the need for intellectuals to compromise with the historical imperative of the PCI—for survival, and for hegemony—was significant. It acted as a stern appeal for Party discipline in

17. Della Volpe, *La filosofia dell'esperienza di Davide Hume*, 2 vols. (Florence, 1933 and Rome, 1935); republished in *Opere*, 2.
18. Lucio Colletti, "A Political and Philosophical Interview" in *Western Marxism: A Critical Reader*, ed. *New Left Review* (London, 1977), p. 323.
19. So Perry Anderson reports in *Considerations on Western Marxism* (London, 1976), p. 41. For a discussion of the aspects of his early philosophy compatible with Fascism, see Fraser, p. 27f.
20. *Logica come scienza positiva* (Messina, 1950); 2nd ed. 1956; republished in *Opere* 4, with all the changes from the two editions noted; a third edition was published posthumously in 1969 with the title changed to *Logica come scienza storica*, but the text intact. An English translation of the second edition by Jon Rothschild appeared in 1980 as *Logic as a Positive Science* (London, 1980); all quotations are from the translation.

accepting limitations to the political implications of debate, without sacrificing doctrinal pluralism."[21] In 1958, Della Volpe's challenge to the humanist, historicist and Gramscian orthodoxy of the Party's mainstream theorists finally surfaced through an exchange of public letters between Valentino Gerratana and Colletti over the extent and significance of Lenin's Hegelianism in his *Philosophical Notebooks*.[22] An awareness of a distinct Della Volpean school soon followed, as Colletti and Pietranera joined their mentor as editors of *Società*.

Despite Della Volpe's own conformist inclinations, his followers soon gained a reputation for rejecting the Party's line from a leftist perspective, and in 1962, *Società* was discontinued. Nonetheless, in the review *Città Futura* and in several student organizations taken over by Della Volpeans, the criticism of the Party deepened, as many of the same arguments used a few years later by the radicalized Althusserians against the PCF were directed against "rightist" versions of de-Stalinization. In 1964, Colletti, who was among the most politically vocal Della Volpeans, went so far as to leave the PCI because the break with its semi-Stalinist past was leading in what he called "a patently rightward direction."[23]

Della Volpe himself remained a loyal Party member until his death in 1968 at the age of 73. The legacy he left, in the tradition of Western Marxism as a whole, was far more theoretical than political. In addition to his *Logic*, which went through another edition in 1956 and was reissued posthumously in 1969 under the slightly revised title *Logic as an Historical Science*, his major works were *Rousseau and Marx* and *Critique of Taste*, each of which also went through several different editions.[24] Together they represented a boldly ambitious attempt to defend a viable Marxist epistemology and methodology on strictly scientific grounds, which would also have implications for political and aesthetic theory.

The full extent of Della Volpe's labyrinthine and frequently revised philosophy cannot be recapitulated here, but insofar as it bears on the question of totality, the following general observations must be made. As in the case of Althusser, it is first necessary to establish his credentials as a legitimate participant in the Western Marxist tradition, even if a heterodox one. Insofar as the Della Volpeans themselves generally employed the

21. Fraser, pp. 35–36.
22. Reprinted in Cassano, *Marxismo e Filosofia in Italia*, p. 79f.
23. Colletti, p. 319.
24. *Rousseau e Marx* went through four editions from 1957 to 1964; it was translated by John Fraser as *Rousseau and Marx and Other Writings* (London, 1978). *Critica del gusto* went through three editions from 1960 to 1964; it was translated by Michael Caesar from the third edition in 1978 as *Critique of Taste* (London, 1978).

term only in Merleau-Ponty's narrow sense as a synonym for Hegelian Marxism,[25] they clearly defined themselves in opposition to the tradition. But if we understand it in the expanded sense suggested earlier in this study, certain familiar patterns emerge. First, for all their interest in Marx's scientificity, they were no less hostile to the Dialectical Materialism of Engels and the Second International than were Lukács and the neo-Hegelians. Indeed, as we will see, Colletti was to argue that earlier Western Marxists were more deeply indebted to Diamat than they had themselves understood. Second, the Della Volpeans focused on philosophical and methodological issues to the detriment of economic and social ones in ways that harked back to Lukács' definition of orthodoxy as the use of correct method in *History and Class Consciousness*. Della Volpe in particular rarely descended from the level of lofty theoretical abstraction to deal with concrete historical or political issues. Nor did he find a way to join his theory very directly with political praxis, which he tended to leave to professional Party politicians. The tortured impenetrability of his style made it clear that he conceived of his audience in only the most elitist terms.

Third, the school insisted that the revival of a viable Marxism could only follow from a fresh reading of Marx's texts unencumbered by the intervening commentaries of his official interpreters. Significantly, the texts to be treated in this way included Marx's early writings, which Della Volpe had been among the first in Italy to translate and discuss.[26] Unlike Althusser, in fact, he defended the continuity of Marx's method throughout his life in ways that were not very different from the comparable defense by many Marxist Humanists. Fourth, Della Volpe was characteristically Western Marxist, at least of the post-Lukácsian variety, in his admiration for modernist art and interest in recent linguistic theory, in particular the glossematics of Hjelmslev.[27] However much he may have

25. See, for example, Colletti, *Marxism and Hegel*, trans. Lawrence Garner (London, 1973), p. 192.
26. Della Volpe, *La teoria marxista dell'emancipazione umana* (Messina, 1945) and *La libertà communista* (Messina, 1946). It is one of the small ironies of history that Della Volpe was first translated into English in a volume of essays edited by Erich Fromm entitled *Socialist Humanism: An International Symposium* (New York, 1965), where his unlikely bedfellows included figures like Goldmann, Marcuse, Bloch, Rubel and several editors of *Praxis*. Still, Della Volpe was never as hostile to humanism as that other major scientific Western Marxist, Althusser, and so perhaps was not entirely out of place in this collection.
27. See in particular his discussion in *Critique of Taste*. Anderson, however, notes that in comparison with other Western Marxists, Della Volpe and his followers were remarkably free of non-Marxist influences (*Considerations on Western Marxism*, p. 58). The school's indifference to Freud is a good reason for accepting this observation, although it might be argued that the Della Volpeans were covertly indebted to bourgeois modes of scientific rationalism that they then read back into Marx's work.

toed the line on political issues, he was clearly opposed to the Zhdanovite cultural policies of more orthodox Communist theoreticians. Fifth and finally, the Della Volpeans, although not their leader himself, followed a typically Western Marxist path in growing increasingly impatient with Leninism, at least as it was practiced in the Soviet Union and in its affiliated parties.

Nonetheless, despite these similarities, it is clear that Della Volpe and his school were deeply at odds with the critical wing of the Western Marxist tradition. Rejecting with almost fanatic intensity the alleged indebtedness of Marx to any Romantic, irrationalist or anti-scientific traditions of thought, they staunchly defended his scientific credentials against the charge that in so doing they were obscuring his differences with bourgeois scientism. Disregarding Lukács' and Gramsci's strictures against Bukharin, they insisted that Marxism was much closer to sociology, the science of society, than to philosophy.[28] Hostile to the putative distinction between the cultural and natural sciences, they claimed that there was only one true scientific method, which Marx shared with Galileo and other genuine scientists. Marx's "moral Galileanism,"[29] as Della Volpe liked to call it, was neither the idealist pseudo-science of Dialectical Materialism nor the positivism of bourgeois empiricists. Instead, it followed a method of "determinate abstraction," which avoided the extremes of a priorism or a posteriorism. Modeled more on Hume and Kant than on Hegel or Spinoza, Marxist science was genuinely materialist in its appreciation of the disparity between thought and its object. And concomitantly, it employed a concept of totality that in no way echoed either Hegel's or Spinoza's metaphysical holism.

To grasp what they considered the correct Marxist concept of totality requires some understanding of the substance of Della Volpe's "logic of positive science" and its application by Colletti to the relationship between Hegel and Marx. Such an understanding will also reveal certain unexpected convergences between their critique of Lukács' initial Western Marxist paradigm and those made by later Western Marxists, most notably Adorno. What makes these parallels so surprising is that the Della Volpeans were unremittingly contemptuous of all other Western Marxists, in particular the Frankfurt School, which they identified entirely with that irrationalist and Romantic repudiation of science they were at such

28. See, for example, Della Volpe, *Logic as a Positive Science*, p. 209; and *Rousseau and Marx*, p. 39.
29. Della Volpe, *Logic as a Positive Science*, p. 127. "Moral" is used in the old-fashioned sense of pertaining to the social world.

pains to refute.[30] Nonetheless, as we demonstrated in the case of Althusser, Scientific and Critical Marxism were not as diametrically opposed as their adherents normally supposed, especially when it came to undermining the holistic paradigm of the earliest Western Marxists.

A useful way to enter Della Volpe's argument is to focus on his analyses of two texts by Marx which he found especially suggestive, the *Critique of Hegel's Philosophy of Right* of 1843 and the 1857 *Introduction to a Critique of Political Economy*. Beginning in 1947 with his *Marx and the Representative State* and frequently repeating the point in his later work,[31] Della Volpe contended that Marx discovered his scientific method through his early analysis of Hegel's mystified hypostatization of the state as the embodiment of rationality. Hegel's reversal of subject and object, his idealist transformation of the state into an essential reality above civil society, had led to what Della Volpe called a "generic" rather than "determinate" abstraction. That is, the state became a pseudo-universal in which all the specific differences of society were supposedly reconciled. Hegel's political hypostatization had its economic equivalent in the work of the classical economists, whose allegedly natural economic laws were also generic rather than determinate abstractions. The commodity, which they fetishized into a mysterious and impenetrable thing, was like Hegel's hypostatized state, the result of a misleading metaphysical method. This method itself, Della Volpe hastened to add, was a reflection of the real hypostatizations that characterize capitalist society, where universality flees from civil society into a political realm hovering above it, commodities confront men as alien objects whose human origins are forgotten, and labor is bought and sold as abstract labor power.

Marx, according to Della Volpe, had understood that a scientific method capable of penetrating the generic abstractions of capitalist society would first have to dispense with their philosophical and methodological correlates, which he identified with a priori theories of whatever kind. The prime example of a dangerous theoretical hypostatization, Della Volpe contended, was the Hegelian concept of Reason (*Vernunft*), which as early as his 1929 study of the young Hegel he identified with mysticism and Romanticism.[32] In the *Logic*, he spelled out what he also saw as the concept's links with Schiller's purely aesthetic reconciliation of opposites

30. As early as 1966, Della Volpe was identifying the Frankfurt School with Huizinga, Jaspers and Ortega y Gasset as reactionary spiritualists. See "Giornale di lettura 2," *Il Contemporaneo Rinascita* 6 (1966).
    31. See, for example, "Sulla dialettica" in Cassano, *Marxismo e Filosofia in Italia*, and *Logic as a Positive Science*, p. 113f.
    32. See note 16. One of his other early works dealt with the mysticism of Meister Eckhart (*Eckart o della filosofia mistica* [Bologna, 1930], in *Opere* 1).

in a spiritual totality that overcame the immediacy of the senses in the name of a higher unity.[33] This hostility to sense experience Della Volpe further connected to the distrust of the senses that could be found as early as ancient scepticism.[34] In fact, a dogmatic notion of reason and scepticism towards the senses went hand in hand.

Because of Hegel's covert debt to sceptical, mystical and Romantic modes of thought, his concept of totality should not be identified with Marx's. Like Aristotle's demolition of Platonic idealism, Marx's denunciation of Hegel exposed the mystical kernel in the rational shell of his philosophy, despite Marx's own famous remark in the Preface to *Capital* suggesting the contrary.[35] As Colletti later put it, Marx

perceives the mysticism [of Hegel] as one of *reason*, deriving from Hegel's all-pervading logic—that is, deriving from the fact that for Hegel reason is not human thought but the Totality of things, the Absolute, and possesses (consequently) a dual and indistinct character uniting the worlds of sense and reason.[36]

The only rationality to which Marx appealed was that of the intellect (*Verstand*), which kept the two worlds apart.

In his 1857 *Introduction to a Critique of Political Economy*, according to Della Volpe,[37] Marx spelled out the implications of his alternative. Rather than arguing on the level of generic, a priori abstractions, Marx decided to focus on only one specific society, that of modern capitalism. Instead of beginning with conceptual definitions that contained their conclusions in a tautological way and thus committed the logical fallacy of *petitio principii*,[38] Marx began with the concrete and moved in a circular way through determinate abstractions back to the concrete. Hypotheses in the time-honored scientific sense thus replaced hypostatizations; experimentation and practical verification supplanted tautological and self-contained reasoning. Because it employed abstractions, Marxist science

33. Della Volpe, *Logic as a Positive Science*, p. 56f. For another attempt to link Hegel with Schiller and Romanticism, see M. H. Abrams, *Natural Supernaturalism: Tradition and Revolution in Romantic Literature* (New York, 1971).

34. Della Volpe, *Logic as a Positive Science*, p. 78.

35. Marx, *Capital*, Preface to 2nd ed. (New York, 1906), p. 25, where he writes the frequently quoted words:

The mystification which dialectic suffers in Hegel's hands by no means prevents him from being the first to present its general form of working in a comprehensive and conscious manner. With him it is standing on its head. It must be turned right side up again, if you would discover the rational kernel within the mystical shell.

As far as I can tell, Della Volpe avoided the implications of these remarks.

36. Colletti, introduction to Karl Marx, *Early Writings*, trans. Rodney Livingstone and Gregor Benton (London, 1975), p. 19.

37. Della Volpe, *Logic as a Positive Science*, p. 184f.

38. *Petitio principii* means assuming in the beginning that which was set forth to be proved, or, to put it more colloquially, begging the question.

was not simply inductive in the manner of naive positivism; but because it began with the concrete before it introduced those abstractions, it was even less like the speculative dialectic of the idealists. In Della Volpe's words,

We thus turn yet again to the same central point: the *reciprocal functionality* of induction and deduction, of matter and reason, of fact (or "accidental") and hypothesis (or "necessary"). It is the *twofold functionality*, required by the *scientific dialectic*, that produces *determinate* or historical abstractions and thereby laws in the materialist sense; it is symbolized by the methodological circle of concrete-abstract-concrete expounded by Marx in his 1857 introduction and applied with maximum rigor and success in *Capital.*[39]

Della Volpe's description of this method may seem reminiscent of those provided by certain other Western Marxists, for example the "progressive-regressive" method developed by Lefebvre and then extolled by Sartre in his *Search for a Method*. But Della Volpe drew epistemological implications from the C-A-C methodological circle that were all his own. The tension between hypothesis and fact that produced determinate rather than generic abstractions was grounded, he claimed, in a more fundamental disparity between thought and its object. Far more rigorously than Althusser, whose theoretical anti-empiricism, despite its unassimilated "materialist postulate," flirted with idealism, Della Volpe insisted on the ontologically materialist premise of Marxism. "The positivity and indispensability of matter itself as an element of knowledge," he contended, "follows from the very defectiveness and sterility of any (a prioristic) reasoning that takes no account of the material, of the extra-rational."[40]

Moreover, because all science depended on the logical law of contradiction, which forebade the pseudo-reconciliation of antinomies by dialectical mediation, a truly Marxist materialism was a far cry from orthodox Dialectical Materialism. The stubbornly heterogeneous nature of the world, in particular the irreducibility of objects to concepts, meant that a Hegelian "identity of identity and non-identity" was fraudulent metaphysics, not true science. Dialectical contradictions, which suspended the laws of formal logic, Della Volpe vigorously maintained, existed in thought alone; they should not be confused with the "real oppositions" that existed in the world where "A" was never equal to "non-A." Indeed, even Kant because of his phenomenalism had not gone far enough in extending the law of contradiction from thought to reality:

The principle of non-contradiction, which is the "logical" foundation of every

39. Della Volpe, *Logic as a Positive Science*, p. 200.
40. Ibid., p. 141.

judgment, coincides exactly with the "real" foundation, the "thinkable *given*." In other words, it coincides with *existence*, with its characteristic staticness-contemplativeness of "disinterested" feeling, the ultimate *foundation* of all judgments.[41]

Precisely how Della Volpe could be so certain that existence perfectly coincided with logical principle is not clear, especially as he insisted on the inevitable distance between thought and its object. To many of his critics, in fact, there was an implicit and undefended correspondence theory of truth in his argument that smacked of the positivism he claimed he had overcome. Nonetheless, by so arguing he tried to be true to both the interrelatedness of thought and object and their disjunction, that "circularity of the radical instances of discreteness and dialecticity, which is expressed in the logical-gnoseological structural principle of *tauto-heterological identity*."[42] Such an identity, he claimed, preserved the principle of non-contradiction, and was thus heterological, while at the same time recognizing the functional relatedness, the quasi-tautological unity, of matter and thought, object and subject, in the specific historical complex revealed by determinate abstractions.

Della Volpe thus did acknowledge a certain holistic impulse in Marxism, but it was by no means equivalent to the expressive variety espoused by the early Lukács. As he put it in words that could have been written by Adorno or Althusser,

The concept that there is an *original*, given unity (in other words, that oneness, the universal, lies at the absolute origin of things), a concept characteristic of Platonism, both ancient and modern, is the fundamental dogmatic criterion of Hegel's dialectic, for it amounts to the concept of a *pure* and therefore formalistic or abstract unity from which can arise only an equally formalistic multiplicity, a gratuitous multiplicity of pure concepts, with its characteristic wholly illusory and apparent negation-preservation in the negation of the negation (of the original unity).[43]

Not surprisingly, he was vehemently opposed to any type of anamnestic totalization, Platonic, Hegelian or Marcusean, that would use the power of memory to "re-member" the dismembered whole.[44] Vico's *verum–factum* principle, with its idealist assumption of a retrospective recognition by the makers of history of what they have made, was not more appropriate for understanding the historical than the natural world. There was only one universal scientific method, and that was the experimentalism of Galileo.[45]

41. Ibid., p. 36.   42. Ibid., p. 155.
43. Ibid., p. 133.   44. Ibid., pp. 106–9.
45. Because of his emphasis on experimentalism, Della Volpe thought he recognized a compatible point of view in the work of Ernst Bloch, whose *Subjekt-Objekt: Erläuterungen*

Accordingly, Della Volpe was hostile to any radical form of historicism in the Korschian or Gramscian sense.[46] In *Rousseau and Marx*, he attempted to find a formula to speak about history as a meaningful whole, without falling back into Hegelian notions of longitudinal totality. "Historical development," he wrote,

is decided by the continual revaluation and broadening of those past solutions of recurring human problems which it has *selected* as more general and closest to the universal, and hence also homogeneous with the solution of *its* real problems for the future. This selection is made so that among the chronological *precedents* (see the Hegelian historical "accidents") some, and only some, are seen to be logical and also *historical antecedents* of the present. These are thus both the *historical* present and its logical *conclusion*, or, better, it is the first because it is the second.[47]

A materialist view of history thus did recognize some logic to the whole, but not with the certainty of a priori dialectical metaphysics:

History, understood materialistically, i.e., as what it truly is, is indeed an *histoire raisonnée*. It is, though, very different from the Hegelian kind which is *too denuded* of historical "accidents"—"disturbances", certainly, of any preconceived rational order like that of the Hegelian dialectic which, however, claimed nonetheless to be the historical order as well. Note that Engels is often ensnared in this difficulty of Hegelianism, and that, for example, the article on *Dialectics* in the *Great Soviet Encyclopedia* is still inspired by this Engels, while Marx was seriously and fruitfully troubled by the problem of the relation of "logical" and "historical."[48]

That Della Volpe was himself troubled by this same relation was clear, as demonstrated by the significant shift in the title of his *Logic* from one edition to another. But the status of his own *histoire raisonnée* was never terribly clear; Western Marxism would have to wait until Habermas' more systematic attempt to "reconstruct historical materialism" before it would have a non-Hegelian concept of longitudinal totality worth considering seriously.

If Della Volpe rejected the expressive and longitudinal notions of totality that inspired the earlier Western Marxists, and scorned the accompa-

---

zu Hegel he praised in *Logic as a Positive Science*, pp. 183–84. Bloch's experimentalism, however, was a far cry from that of the Galilean tradition appropriated by Della Volpe for Marxism.

46. Althusser misleadingly included him in the historicist camp. See Louis Althusser and Etienne Balibar, *Reading Capital*, trans. Ben Brewster (New York, 1970), p. 314. Della Volpe, to be sure, rejected the strictly anti-historicist views of structuralist Marxism. See his critique of Althusser in "Una impostazione 'strutturale,'" *Rinascita* 11 (1968).

47. Della Volpe, *Rousseau and Marx*, p. 64–65.

48. Ibid., p. 65.

nying faith in anamnestic totalization, he was no less hostile to the normative versions many of them held as well. Not only did he denounce the
identity of subject and object as an idealist fantasy designed to annihilate
the inevitable otherness of matter, he also resisted the lure of that linguistically grounded theory of perfect intersubjective consensus which we've
seen attracted Gramsci in his less Crocean moods (and which we will
encounter in stronger form in Habermas). Although Della Volpe was interested in contemporary linguistics, he had no use for hermeneutics: language, he insisted with the faith of a positivist, was fully adequate to the
objects it attempted to describe. The result, as John Fraser has acutely
noted, was that Della Volpe sought "rigorous, rational, scientific *unity*
achieved by Marxist intellectuals in debate for the Party as collective *intellect* (as against Gramsci's sociologico-historical notion of the Party as collective *intellectual*)."[49] The goal of broader and non-hierarchically organized speech communities, which was a potential alternative to the
idealist notion of subject-object unity as the basis for a modified normative totalization, was thus anathema to Della Volpe, whose view of scientific method rejected the excessive anthropomorphism he saw in hermeneutic or consensus theories of truth.

Indeed, there was little indication in Della Volpe's work of what a normative totality would be like. The only speculation he seems to have attempted was in his political writings, which were devoted largely to the
reconciliation of Marx and Rousseau. Although conceding that Marx and
Engels were ambiguous in their published writings concerning Rousseau,
he claimed that they had never really understood their covert debt to his
political theory. Carefully distinguishing that theory from the writings of
Rousseau's contemporaries Mably and Morelly, whose versions of Communism suggested a universal levelling, Della Volpe argued that *The Social Contract* had called for a type of social equality that would also preserve certain forms of inequality based on personal merit. Socialist
equality would likewise nurture what Della Volpe called "egalitarian liberty": "the *right* of *all* to the *social* recognition of personal qualities and
abilities."[50] This right was the *libertas major* that was superior to the *libertas minor* defended by more liberal socialists like Mondolfo or Bobbio
as a legacy of bourgeois democracy worth preserving. The latter, which
uncritically accepted the necessity of representation, really meant the liberty of capitalists in the market place to be protected against the state.

In so arguing, Della Volpe was implicitly presenting a normative view

49. Fraser, *An Introduction to the Thought of Galvano Della Volpe*, p. 110.
50. Della Volpe, *Rousseau and Marx*, p. 58.

of totality that was directed not only against moderate social democrats like Mondolfo and Bobbio, but also against the more utopian Western Marxists who, extrapolating from Marx's controversial essay "On the Jewish Question," had hoped that Communism would usher in a realm of perfect harmony and wholeness in which the splits between man as bourgeois and man as citizen, economics and politics, would be entirely healed. Communism, Della Volpe warned, would need to preserve some form of legality, not reabsorb it into an antinomian kingdom of ends, an ethical paradise in which the coercive power of external laws would no longer be necessary. Although the socialist society of the future would "exist as a popular sovereign body, strongly unitary and authoritative, sufficiently so that it can prevent any centrifugal movement by individuals, groups, or parasitic classes,"[51] it would nonetheless permit legal redress against abuses from above. Marx himself, Della Volpe admitted, had been lax in spelling out just how important such legal guarantees would be after the revolution. Although rigorously exposing the fallacies of bourgeois justice, "he never concerned himself to the same degree with stressing the necessity of extending in the same socialist *state* the juridical, constitutional guarantees of each person-citizen."[52]

The "two souls" of modern liberty, civil and egalitarian, were thus not as completely opposed as many Marxists had assumed. Although Communist society "by definition is beyond classes, and beyond their corresponding antinomies and historical-intellectual deficiencies,"[53] its form would be very much like a tauto-heterological identity in which multiplicity and difference were preserved, if in a non-antagonistic manner, rather than spuriously overcome in a hypostatized pseudo-reconciliation. "So long as there is a state," he wrote, "even a proletarian state, Montesquieu's is still a true and compelling warning, inspired by the absolute monarchical government of his time, and one which can be extended . . . to any political power, even working-class power. He warned that 'it is of sovereign importance not to destroy or degrade human nature.'"[54]

Such caution from a stalwart of the PCI might be seen as covert criticism of its Stalinist residues, but unfortunately Della Volpe undercut its critical force by his absurd contention that it was in the contemporary Soviet Union that socialist legality was being fully realized. Basing his argument on the Soviet Constitution of 1936, as updated in 1960, and drawing on the learned commentaries of such "dispassionate" observers as A. Y. Vishinsky, he neglected to compare Soviet rhetoric with its actual

51. Ibid., p. 96.   52. Ibid., p. 108.
53. Ibid., p. 95.   54. Ibid., p. 121.

practice. Nowhere, in fact, did his methodological self-absorption and indifference to real historical investigation serve him as poorly as in his frequent paeans to the Soviet Union for safeguarding workers' rights through trade unions, honoring individual merit and generally avoiding the temptations of totalitarianism. The reproach of critics like Bobbio, that Della Volpe failed to link the preservation of any kind of genuine liberty, civil or egalitarian, major or minor, to the institutional structures of representative government that made it possible, was given credence by his fantasies about Soviet life.[55] Calling for the rule of law while denouncing its roots in parliamentary representation made Della Volpe's rhetoric about socialist legality ring hollow.

Still, by reminding his readers that even under Communism, no perfectly harmonious totality would be achieved in which the tension between politics and economics was completely overcome, he warned against ignoring the links between bourgeois democracy and its socialist successor, if at the same time he cautioned against seeing the latter as merely the completion or extension of the former. As Fraser put it, his importance lay "in breaking away from the ideological notion of totality which sees in socialism a polar opposite of capitalism, to be justified and analyzed in exclusive terms."[56]

If Della Volpe's wariness about perfectly expressive wholes, in which subjects would fully recognize themselves in their objects, had a fruitful influence on his political theory, it was no less important for that theory's aesthetic counterpart, which was presented most systematically in his *Critique of Taste*.[57] Here too he sought to undermine the prevailing Crocean or Gentilean orthodoxy in Italian thinking, to which he had himself originally adhered. Opposing the assumption that works of art should be understood as expressions of either their author's mind or of the age that nurtured them, he suggested an alternative based once again on the concept of a tauto-heterological identity. Art, he claimed, was neither a realm of higher values and ineffable intuitions nor a mere reflection of social

55. Norberto Bobbio, "Are There Alternatives to Representative Democracy?" *Telos* 35 (Spring 1978), p. 26. Bobbio's complaint is directed at Colletti, but it is a fortiori applicable to Della Volpe. Perhaps the reason for Della Volpe's failure to come to grips with Soviet reality was the peculiar anti-empirical bias of his methodologism. As Göran Therborn has observed, "'Method' in this tradition does not refer to research techniques but rather to explanatory logic, to the formal character of concepts and modes of explanation" (*Science, Class and Society: On the Formation of Sociology and Historical Materialism* [London, 1976], p. 43).
56. Fraser, p. 195.
57. For general considerations of his aesthetics, see Fraser, chap. 6, and David Forgács, "The Aesthetics of Galvano Della Volpe," *New Left Review* 117 (September–October 1979).

trends. It was also erroneous to equate it with pure images bereft of intellectual content, as Romantic aestheticians and supporters of art for art's sake had done. All art had a realistic, socially derived referent and thus, like science, had cognitive as well as affective value, but it differed from science in the way it produced knowledge.

To characterize the differences, Della Volpe turned to linguistics, in particular the glossematics of Louis Hjelmslev and the Copenhagen School.[58] In ways too technical to spell out now, he sought to use Hjelmslev's development of Saussurean linguistics in the service of a scientific semantics compatible with historical materialism. The result was not, however, equivalent to structuralism in the French sense of the term, because he refused to privilege *langue* over *parole*, or signifiers over signified.[59] In fact, he emphasized the necessity of recognizing their interpenetration, as he did the importance of understanding as the non-identical convergence of matter and thought. Science, to be sure, shared these characteristics with art, both being discourses with a common stake in concrete reason. But there was a crucial difference between them. As he put it in *Logic as a Positive Science,*

The work of art is an object endowed with a concrete rational structure (matter–reason, image–concept, etc.), exactly like the work of science or historiography. Nevertheless, it presents characteristics of its own, not gnoseologically abstract, but gnoseological–technical, i.e. *semantic* (inherent in its actual construction and therefore indispensable to its real, cognitive-practical value).[60]

In more specific terms, the basic distinction between science and art (or at least poetry) was not that the former was abstract and the latter concrete, but rather that the language of science was univocal and "omni-contextual," whereas that of art was polysemic and "organically contextual."[61] In other words, scientific concepts have fixed meanings that are applicable in any context, while the meanings of art are multiple and defined by their specific context. Poetry in particular is grounded in metaphor, which should be understood as a dialectic of heterogeneities, one of whose elements was intellect. Romantic aestheticians were thus wrong in defining metaphor as an immediate intuition of a unity. Both science and

58. What Della Volpe found attractive in Hjelmslev was his biplanar concept of language, which divided "glossemes" (or linguistic forms) into elements which form content (*plerematemes*) and elements which form expression (*cenematemes*). Insofar as language consisted of both of these kinds of elements, it was like a tauto-heterological identity.

59. Della Volpe, *Critique of Taste*, p. 101. Della Volpe's more general critique of structuralism can be found in his essays "Marxismo contro strutturalismo" and "Il caso Lévi-Strauss ovvero la grande vacanza che continue," both in *Opere 6*. See also his essay, "Settling Accounts with the Russian Formalists," *New Left Review* 113–114 (January–April 1979).

60. Della Volpe, *Logic as a Positive Science*, p. 207.

61. Della Volpe, *Critique of Taste*, p. 117.

art, Della Volpe contended, were ultimately translatable into everyday language, which was "omni-contextual" and polysemic. Paraphrase, that bugaboo of Romantic aesthetics, was thus an inherent part of any reception and criticism of art. In fact, such paraphrastic translation was the essence of aesthetic taste, which Della Volpe defined (with characteristic obscurity) as "the ability, once the semantic locus of the poem, the organic contextual, has been perceived, to register the passage from language–thought to style–thought—in other words the transition from the random and equivocal sense of the literal–material to the formal rigor of the polysemic."[62] Critical paraphrase is thus akin to scientific reasoning because it "represents that further—scientific— consciousness of the poetic process which classifies the poem as such by placing its polysemic concepts in a network of univocal concepts."[63]

To follow and analyze Della Volpe's elaboration of these principles and his application of them to specific examples of poetry and other arts would take us too far afield from our theme of totality, but insofar as it touches on that theme, the following observations are in order. First, there was an obvious parallel between his methodological critique of Hegelian dialectics in general and his distaste for idealist and Romantic aesthetics in particular. "A semantic dialectic," he insisted,

—inasmuch as it is a necessarily historical dialectic—cannot be the speculative dialectic of an idealistic *a priori* unity of opposites. Rather, it will be a real dialectic (=tauto-heterological identity), or dialectic of determinate abstractions, both polysemic and univocal; in short a systematic circle of heterogeneities, reason and matter. In this it follows the formula of a materialist, non-Kantian critique of the *a priori*, which infers the positivity and indispensability of matter as co-element of thought for knowledge (and action) in general.[64]

Second, all Marxist aestheticians who held to the idealist belief that art could achieve such a unity of opposites were wrong. Lukács, for example, was mistaken in his attempt to establish a realistic canon of art in contrast with naturalism or modernism because he grounded the former in an a priori telos of perfect wholeness,[65] which realistic art allegedly prefigured. Quoting Lukács, Della Volpe scornfully wrote:

62. Ibid., p. 132.   63. Ibid.   64. Ibid., p. 199.
65. Forgács thus seems in error in his otherwise very informative essay on Della Volpe's aesthetics when he attributes to him the belief that "what distinguishes the overall structure of a literary text from that of a scientific is its 'organic' quality, its closure" (p. 98). Instead, Della Volpe invokes what the deconstructionists will later call intertextuality when he writes in *Critique of Taste* that to understand the truth of a text,

The text-context has to be taken at the very least in a relation of *inter-dependence* with many other *text-contexts*—and not just "ideas"—which existed before it, and the respective historical experiences expressed in them. (p. 115)

"Art makes us intuit sensibly" the "dynamic unity" of the universal, particular and individual (the categories of Hegelian logic ever with us!), while science resolves this unity "into its abstract elements and seeks to conceptualize the interaction of these elements."[66]

Thus Erich Auerbach, according to Della Volpe, was right against Lukács and Engels to include Zola among the realists, because the Marxists' definition of realism was too narrow. It was also incorrect to seek too perfectly homologous a fit between a work of art and the social reality it reflected, as Goldmann was wont to do.[67] An idealist annihilation of heterogeneity was at work here. No less suspicious, Della Volpe contended, were attempts like that of Walter Benjamin to contrast a perfect *Ursprache* in which name and thing were one with their current allegorical disjunction; here too a "romantic mysticism"[68] could be detected.

The third implication of Della Volpe's aesthetics was, in fact, that no standard of implicit or potential wholeness could be introduced to differentiate "good" from "bad" art. For all art was inherently realistic and referred in some way to the world outside of it; all art combined ideas and concepts with forms and images; all art was a tauto-heterological identity of intellect and matter. Even music, Della Volpe contended, shared these qualities. Arguing for a musical grammar of note intervals, he wrote:

We cannot accept that "music does *not* constitute a system of signs." ... The theme–idea or series–idea, in other words what the music *says* (Adorno: *das gesagte*), *can* be *separated* from the music (contrary to the opinion of Adorno and others).[69]

Finally, Della Volpe's insistence that all art contained a social moment was related to his larger claim that language was also inevitably intertwined with society. This truth, he claimed, had been ignored in Stalin's celebrated critique of the reductionist linguistics of Marr,[70] who had made language part of the superstructure. Althusser, it will be recalled, had cited Stalin's critique to legitimize his defense of a decentered totality with relatively autonomous individual levels. For Della Volpe, language, art, and science, like all culture in general, had to be understood as less completely autonomous, as parts of a tauto-heterological unity that was neither entirely homogeneous and centered nor fragmented into entirely unrelated components magically tied together by a "last instance" that never came.

66. Della Volpe, *Critique of Taste*, p. 188.
67. Della Volpe, "Settling Accounts with Russian Formalists," p. 144.
68. Della Volpe, *Critique of Taste*, pp. 171–72.
69. Ibid., p. 219.
70. Ibid., p. 181.

In many ways, Della Volpe's aesthetics were refreshingly open-minded, especially because of his sympathy for non-organic works of art outside the canon of socialist or critical realism. But, as his detractors quickly pointed out, too much tolerance had its cost. For if *all* art works possessed the same essential characteristics, it was impossible to evaluate their specific critical content or social function. As one critic put it, "Della Volpe's method is incapable of handling artistic ideologies because it sees truth as omnipresent."[71] Indeed, Della Volpe's general theory of ideology was weak, because he seemed to equate it solely with the scientific sin of hypostatization, which made it more a problem of method than of politics.[72]

In fact, if one had to point to the most pervasive problem in Della Volpe's work, it would have to be his inclination to minimize difference and reduce virtually everything to the same pattern. Paradoxically, the great critic of hypostatization and a priori reasoning was himself prone to a dogmatic methodological monism; as we saw when examining his failure to compare Soviet rhetoric with the reality of Soviet life, he often avoided confronting evidence that undercut his preconceived assumptions. Not only was all art amenable to the same type of analysis, the method underlying that analysis was not very distinct from that used in the social or natural sciences. Marx had developed that method, his "moral Galileanism," in 1843, and never really diverged from it in his later work; nor was there any reason to do so today, even if it might be enriched by certain insights from newer disciplines like linguistics. For Della Volpe, far more a hedgehog than a fox, there was *one* logic and *one* experimental method, mechanical and dialectical materialism were not very distinct, and determinate abstractions were a universal quality of all valid cognition. Because of this homogenizing tendency, as critics like Vacca pointed out,[73] it was difficult to see how Della Volpe differentiated Marxist from bourgeois, or critical from affirmative, science, nor was there any real link between that science and the practice of the proletariat. For all his differences with Althusser, Della Volpe shared with him an inability to demonstrate the practical implications and effects of Marxist science.

And yet to compound the paradox, one of the sources of Della Volpe's attraction for the younger generation of anti-historicists was precisely his introduction of a method that seemed to allow them to go beyond the

71. Forgács, p. 105.
72. For a critique of Della Volpe's theory of ideology, see Amedeo Vigorelli, "Filosofia come scienza: Galvano della Volpe e l'autocritica dello storicismo marxista," *Aut Aut* 142–143 (July–Ocotober 1974), p. 108f.
73. Vacca, *Galvano Della Volpe e il marxismo*, p. 47.

apparent provinciality of Gramsci's (and Togliatti's) insistence on the uniqueness of the *via Italiana*. What has been called the "new orthodoxy"[74] resulting from Della Volpe's return to a universalist scientific method had explicit political ramifications in its rejection of Italian exceptionalism. Despite his own unswerving fidelity to PCI policy, his followers soon turned his ideas in a more militantly left direction, although as the central case of Colletti reveals, the turn was not always permanent.

Colletti was, in fact, the most important popularizer and politicizer of Della Volpe's ideas, including his concept of totality as a tauto-heterological identity. His ultimate disillusionment with many of the positions, both theoretical and political, that he had initially defended exemplifies once again the pattern in the careers of many Western Marxists: the vigorous dismantling of Lukács' problematic in the name of an alternative that itself soon turns out to be highly questionable.

Lucio Colletti was born in Rome, the son of a bank clerk, in 1924. Initially trained in the idealist philosophy that dominated postwar Italian culture, he wrote his doctoral dissertation in Rome on "The Logic of Benedetto Croce."[75] His dissertation director was Carlo Antoni, the distinguished author of two influential Crocean works, *From History to Sociology* and *The Struggle Against Reason*.[76] But Colletti seems quickly to have distanced himself from his mentor, in part because of a growing attraction to Marx. Unlike many other Italian intellectuals, however, he was not drawn to Marxism because of the links forged by Gramsci with Crocean idealism. Instead, he was converted by Lenin's work, especially that most anti-idealist of polemics, *Materialism and Empirio-Criticism*. Despite his studies with Antoni, he felt more sympathetic towards the "empirical realist" moment in Kant's critical philosophy, which he saw as compatible with Lenin's reflection theory of knowledge, than towards rationalist historicism.

When the Korean War began, Colletti decided to join the PCI because he concluded that it was necessary to take sides in the global confrontation then on the horizon. Reflecting on his Party experience many years

74. Vigorelli, p. 99.
75. In contrast to all of the other figures discussed in this study, Colletti has yet to be the object of a sustained analysis in English or Italian. The biographical data that follow come from scattered sources, most notably his 1974 interview in the *New Left Review*, and from my correspondence with Professor Colletti, in which he graciously responded to my questions.
76. Carlo Antoni, *From History to Sociology*, trans. Hayden V. White (Detroit, 1959) and *La lotta contro la ragione* (Florence, 1942).

later, Colletti claimed that he had had no illusions about who had attacked whom in the war, nor was he really attracted to Stalin and the type of party he sponsored. In fact, he seems to have experienced Stalin's death and Khrushchev's 1956 speech as "an authentic liberation,"[77] which would permit Communism to fulfill its long-denied promise. Nonetheless, like Althusser at approximately the same time, he was uncomfortable with the philosophical implications of de-Stalinization, which tended to reduce Marxism to a version of Hegelian humanism. Although never as dogmatically anti-humanist as Althusser, he returned to Marx's texts looking for a scientific version of socialism commensurate with Lenin's politics and philosophy.

The most convincing reading of those texts seemed that of Della Volpe, whose *Logic* he read in 1950. Impressed in particular by its appropriation of Kant's epistemology for Marxist purposes, he began identifying himself with Della Volpe's position in print in 1954.[78] Three years later, Colletti, along with Giulio Pietranera, joined Della Volpe on the editorial staff of *Società*. It was from this forum that he first began to attract widespread attention as a leader of a leftist faction within the PCI, more outspoken in its political views than Della Volpe himself. Although never identifying themselves with the Maoist opposition to Soviet leadership of the Communist movement,[79] the Della Volpeans shared many of the arguments advanced at a slightly later date by Althusser's Maoist followers in France. In a succession of debates in *Passato e presente*, *Rinascita*, *Società* and elsewhere,[80] Colletti extended Della Volpe's critique of Hegelian Marxism back to Soviet thinkers like E. V. Il'enkov and indeed to Lenin himself, at least the Lenin of the *Philosophical Notebooks*.[81]

The general hostility within the Party provoked by his abrasive chal-

77. Colletti, "A Political and Philosophical Interview," p. 136.
78. See his article "Il metodo dell'economica politica," *Critica economica* (June, 1954), in which he discusses Marx's 1857 introduction in Della Volpean terms.
79. Colletti, "A Political and Philosophical Interview," p. 332. In *Logic as a Positive Science*, Della Volpe does credit Mao with understanding the importance of the problem of tauto-heterological identity (p. 201), but he generally ignores his work.
80. In 1958, he had a debate with A. Giolitti in *Passato e presente* over the nature of labor in Marx, Giolitti arguing for an historicist understanding of it as a concrete reality, and Colletti responding that it should be understood as a determinate abstraction. In 1960, he debated Valentino Gerratana in *Società* over the issue of the constitutional state, which he felt had already been achieved in Italy and therefore ought not to be understood as an objective of PCI policy. In 1962, he had a confrontation with Cesare Luporini in *Rinascita* over the relationship between Hegel and Marx, in which he defended the Della Volpean position on this question.
81. See his introduction to E. V. Il'enkov, *La dialettica dell'astratto e del concreto nel Capitale di Marx* (Milan, 1961), and his introduction to Lenin, *Quaderni filosofici* in the first volume of *Il marxismo e Hegel* (Milan, 1958). Della Volpe, it should be noted, had already attacked Il'enkov; see *Logic as a Positive Science*, p. 196.

lenge to Togliattian orthodoxy led in 1964, the year Khrushchev fell from power, to Colletti's quiet departure from its ranks. As he recalled ten years later:

In one sense, the process of renovation for which I had hoped after the Twentieth Party Congress had failed to occur—but in another sense it had occurred, in a patently rightward direction. I slowly came to realize in the period from 1956 to 1964 that both the Soviet regime itself, and the Western Communist Parties, were incapable of accomplishing the profound transformation necessary for a return to revolutionary Marxism and Leninism. It had become structurally impossible for either the CPSU or the Western Parties to undergo a real democratization—in other words, not in the sense of a liberal or bourgeois democracy, but in the sense of revolutionary socialist democracy, of workers' councils.[82]

Colletti remained, however, an orthodox Della Volpean, at least until the late 1960s. With an eloquence that his mentor was never able to attain, he defended the view of Marx as the "Galileo of the historical-social world" in such essays as "Marxism as a Sociology," written in 1958 and republished a decade later in *From Rousseau to Lenin.*[83] But by 1967, a subtle new theme began to emerge in his work, which in retrospect allowed Colletti to speak of a "second period" in his intellectual development beginning at that time.[84] That new theme was the role of the concept of alienation in Marx's writings, which he first addressed in an essay on "Bernstein and the Marxism of the Second International," also included in *From Rousseau to Lenin.* Focussing on Marx's theory of value, Colletti realized its essential dependence on the concept of fetishism that classical economics lacked. What Marx had called the abstraction of labor in capitalism, he now understood, could only be grasped in relation to his theories of alienation and reification. In the second volume of *Marxism and Hegel* (his introduction to Lenin's *Philosophical Notebooks* had been published as the first), which appeared in 1969, and the extensive introduction he wrote for the Pelican Library edition of Marx's *Early Writings* in 1971,[85] Colletti emphasized the centrality of Marx's critique of alienation for all of his work.

In so doing, however, he still resisted the implication that this critique was in any way indebted to Marx's Hegelian provenance. Unlike Althusser, he claimed that there was no epistemological break in Marx, who was as much a scientist in 1844 as he was in 1867. Determined to stem the

82. Colletti, "A Political and Philosophical Interview," p. 319.
83. Colletti, *Ideologia e società* (Bari, 1969), in English as *From Rousseau to Lenin: Studies in Ideology and Society,* trans. John Merrington and Judith White (London, 1972).
84. Letter from Colletti to the author, Rome, May 23, 1982.
85. See note 36. Colletti reports that the introduction was written in 1971.

Hegelian Marxist tide in Italy, then cresting with the growing popularity of the Frankfurt School, Colletti doggedly insisted on the scientificity of Marxism, still in Della Volpean terms. Although he now permitted himself to chastise Della Volpe for failing to go far enough in his critique of value and of the state (both of which Della Volpe had maintained would endure even under socialism),[86] Colletti remained very much in the Della Volpean camp.

The only significant public indication of Colletti's incipient uneasiness with his mentor's position appeared in his political statements. While he defended Marx's scientific credentials, as Della Volpe had established them, he also strongly insisted that the revolutionary side of Marx's work, which Della Volpe rarely stressed, must not be forgotten.[87] However much he may have quarrelled with the Hegelian confusions in Lenin's *Philosophical Notebooks*, he looked to Lenin's politics, even after he left the PCI, as a guide to revolutionary practice. Arguing against the Togliattian attempt to represent Gramsci as a supporter of a gradualist popular front and demanding that Lenin's *State and Revolution* be taken seriously as an invocation not merely to seize state power, but also to destroy it,[88] Colletti directly challenged the PCI's policies, which he contended had never fully outgrown their Stalinist origins. Although like Della Volpe a professional philosopher, teaching at Rome and Salerno, Colletti was far more directly involved in political affairs than his mentor, even if his involvement was that of an outsider unattached to any party or sect.

By the mid-1970s, it became increasingly clear to Colletti that his attempt to square Marx's theory of alienation with his scientific pretensions was not working. Nor was he satisfied with his formulation of Marxism as both an analytic science and a revolutionary ideology. In 1973, he reread one of Kant's pre-critical works, his *Attempt to Introduce the Notion of Negative Qualities into Philosophy* of 1763, and realized that any theory claiming scientificity had to purge itself of all remnants of dialectical reasoning, most notably its concept of contradiction. Even more important, he now faced the unpleasant fact that Marx's theories of alienation and value were, alas, dependent on just such a dialectical foundation. The attempt to ignore this dependency had led to the troubling eclecticism of his

86. Colletti, *From Rousseau to Lenin*, p. 92. For Colletti, value, the objectification of human labor-power, was an example of the fetishism Marx thought would end with the revolution.
87. See, for example, his essay "Marxism: Science or Revolution?" in *From Rousseau to Lenin*, and his introduction to *Il marxismo e il' crollo' del capitalismo* (Rome, 1975).
88. Colletti, "Lenin's *State and Revolution*" in *From Rousseau to Lenin*, and "Antonio Gramsci and the Italian Revolution," *New Left Review* 65 (January–February 1971).

second period, which he now publicly repudiated. Like Althusser's self-criticism, although without its disingenuous and self-serving qualities, Colletti's disavowal of his earlier errors was an event of major importance in the history of Western Marxism for both theoretical and political reasons. What gave it special impact outside of Italy was that it took place in the pages of the *New Left Review*, which had only recently discovered his work as a replacement for the Althusserianism its editors were beginning to abandon as a legitimation for their belief in Marx's scientificity. Perry Anderson invited Colletti to sit for an interview in the spring of 1974. As Colletti remembers it,

The interview was not prepared. I did not know the questions; it was the result of four hours of conversation. I was not able to edit or control the text. The interview is naturally full of contradictions, because it caught me in a moment in which I was in full crisis.[89]

In a series of articles and short books that soon followed, Colletti attempted to work through his confusion. "Marxism and the Dialectic," written hurriedly in a week as a pendant to the Italian translation of the interview,[90] was still filled with hesitation and uncertainty.

He now conceded that Della Volpe's attempt to interpret Marx as a consistent scientist, which had been the inspiration of his own earlier work, had been based on a misreading of Marx's writings. A fresh look at them had led him to some new and disturbing conclusions:

It began to dawn on me that the theory of value was entirely at one with the theory of alienation and fetishism. "Abstract labor," or that creating "value," was alienated labor itself. Thus an intuition of mine many years earlier reasserted itself . . . that the processes of hypostatization, the substantiation of the abstract, the inversion of subject and predicate, far from being in Marx's eye modes of Hegel's logic that were defective in reflecting reality, were in fact processes that he located (or thought he located—the difference is unimportant for the moment) in the structure and mode of functioning of capitalist society.[91]

Admitting that Della Volpe had never been able to make sense of Marx's concept of fetishism because of his insistence that Marx was a Galilean, Colletti now acknowledged that those dialectical contradictions he and his mentor had consigned to the world of Hegel's mystifications were in fact "attributed by Marx—however embarrassing this viewpoint may be—to the *reality* of capital itself, not the *concept* of it formulated by the economists."[92] Engels, therefore, had not been the sole villain in distort-

89. Letter from Colletti to author, Rome, May 23, 1982.
90. Colletti, "Marxism and the Dialectic," *New Left Review* 93 (September–October 1975).
91. Ibid., p. 20.   92. Ibid., p. 21.

ing Marx's views and creating the illegitimate pseudo-science of Dialectical Materialism; Marx himself had to share some of the blame:

The contradictions of capitalism—from the contradiction between capital and
wage-labor to all the others—are not, for Marx, "real oppositions" (as I too, following Della Volpe, believed until yesterday), i.e. objective but "non-contradictory" oppositions, but are dialectical contradictions in the full sense of the word.[93]

The upshot of this discovery was that Colletti now regretfully acknowledged that Marx had two faces, that of the scientist and that of the
Hegelian philosopher. Such a recognition may have been an advance over
his earlier position in terms of historical accuracy,[94] but it left Colletti
both confused and dismayed. "I do not know whether the existence of
these two aspects is fatal or advantageous," he frankly admitted at the end
of his article. "What is not at issue is the fact that our task now is to find
out whether and how they can be reconciled. It is one we must take seriously. It is not to be solved with any verbal subterfuge."[95]

In the work he completed after 1974, most notably *Between Marxism
and No, The Twilight of Ideology* and *Divided Socialism* (a debate with
Alberto Asor Rosa, Massimo Salvadori and Paolo Spriano),[96] Colletti
came to a decisive conclusion about the implications of Marx's ambiguities. They were, he now acknowledged, fatal rather than advantageous.
Forced to choose between Marxism and science, as he understood it, he
chose the latter. Turning the arguments of anti-Hegelians like F. A. Trendelenburg, Hans Kelsen and Karl Popper against Marx,[97] he ruefully concluded that Marxism was a pseudo-science that had to be abandoned.

Along with Colletti's theoretical shift went a no less fundamental political one. As a still faithful Italian Marxist, Sebastiano Timpanaro, put it,

Once he finally realized that the dialectic was present in the work of Marx as well,
he drew the conclusion that communism was a utopian dream at best; any attempt

93. Ibid., p. 23.
94. For an extended defense of the internal contradictions in Marx, see Alvin W.
Gouldner, *The Two Marxisms: Contradictions and Anomalies in the Development of Theory* (New York, 1980). Gouldner refers to Colletti's *New Left Review* interview several
times with approval.
95. Colletti, "Marxism and Dialectic," p. 29. For an attempt to solve it by asserting that
dialectical contradictions do appear in reality, but only in specifically human reality, see Roy
Edgley, "Dialectic: The Contradiction of Colletti," *Critique* 7 (Winter 1976–1977). Colletti
specifically rejects this contention in *Tramonto dell'ideologia* (Bari, 1980), p. 94.
96. Colletti, *Tra marxismo e no* (Bari, 1977); *Il socialismo diviso*, ed. Paolo Mieli (Bari,
1978); *Del 1968 a oggi: Come siamo e come eravano* (Bari, 1980); and *Tramonto dell'i-
deologia*.
97. Trendelenburg and Popper are invoked in the essay "Contraddizione dialettica e
non-contraddizione" in *Tramonto*, which also contains a piece on "Kelsen e la critica del
marxismo." For Colletti's further reflections on Popper, in which he expresses concern about
the abuse of his ideas by his disciples, see "Popper tradito da Popper," *L'Espresso* 18, 20

actually to implement it would result in abominable tyranny. He has thus opted to live under the protection of bourgeois-democratic freedoms.[98]

The radical leftist critic of the PCI of the 1960s had indeed by the 1980s become the moderate social democrat concerned more about the links between Marxism and the Gulag Archipelago than between Marxism and the end of alienation. In fact, drawing on Kelsen's argument that Marxism's dream of an end to alienation was a form of anarchism, he repudiated his earlier defense of Lenin's *State and Revolution* and pointed to the contradiction inherent in its assumption that the maximization of state control could lead to the abolition of the state. He thus quietly returned to Della Volpe's less utopian political theory, even as he was repudiating his mentor's attempt to reconcile that theory with Marxism.

Colletti's third period, as he came to call it, was stimulated by more than theoretical considerations. He now read the lessons of history in a more sober and disillusioned way than before. Pessimistically contending that the proliferation of Marxist currents in the twentieth century meant the decomposition of its theoretical coherence rather than, as some have argued, its continued vitality, and connecting that decomposition with a more general crisis that began as early as 1923,[99] Colletti admitted that history had refuted Marx's predictions about the collapse of capitalism. Rather than insisting that Italy be understood in the general context of that putative collapse, as he had in his more Della Volpean phases, he conceded that Italy was, in fact, an exceptional case that needed to be treated solely in its own terms. Even Eurocommunism, he concluded, was a stillborn attempt to salvage the legacy of Leninism by trying to make it compatible with bourgeois democracy. Other efforts, like that of Perry Anderson in *Considerations on Western Marxism*, to forecast a new alliance of radical theory and revolutionary practice were equally ill-conceived and self-deluding.[100] In short, despite his continued hostility to the Frankfurt School,[101] his statements about the possibilities of radical transformation made Colletti sound more and more like an exponent of their politics of tempered despair. Talking of the "twilight of ideology," he fell

(May 23, 1982). The contemporary philosopher of science with whom Colletti most identifies is Mary B. Hesse.

98. Sebastiano Timpanaro, *On Materialism*, trans. Lawrence Garner (London, 1975), p. 257.

99. Colletti, *Il socialismo diviso*, p. 81.

100. Colletti, *Tra marxismo e no*, p. 144. When Anderson wrote *Considerations* he identified closely with many of Colletti's positions, but cautiously noted, "There is no reason to assume that he would assent to many of the particular arguments or judgments of this essay" (p. 42). Colletti's review, reprinted in *Tra marxismo e no*, shows the wisdom of this disclaimer.

101. Letter from Colletti to the author, Rome, June 18, 1982, in which he maintains that the Frankfurt School must be understood as an "episode in German romanticism."

back on a call for a renewed rationalism—although of the instrumental kind attacked by Critical Theory—that was designed to resist the invasion of post-structuralist and Nietzschean philosophies from France into Italy in the late 1970s.[102] Like Habermas, whose concept of reason was very different, as we will see, he was determined to uphold the tradition of the Enlightenment against its most recent detractors.

In so doing, he remained unremittingly hostile to those currents in Western Marxism that contributed, directly or indirectly, to the collapse of that tradition. Although grudgingly revising his estimation of Gramsci upwards for political rather than theoretical reasons,[103] he continued to excoriate all other Western Marxists for their anti-scientific sins. When, for example, Sartre died in 1980, he wrote a dismissive recollection of his "philosophy of the snack-bar" for *L'Espresso*,[104] the popular news magazine in which many of his more recent articles appeared. Even Habermas, whose balanced defense of science he judged preferable to that of most other Western Marxists, Colletti found wanting because of his attraction to hermeneutics.[105]

Colletti's disillusionment, in fact, went so far that he bitterly concluded that much of his own earlier philosophical work had been in vain. Renouncing what he called the "dogmatic triumphalism" with which he had defended every word in Marx's writings, he told the *New Left Review*:

If Marxists continue to remain arrested in epistemology and gnoseology, Marxism has effectively perished. The only way in which Marxism can be revived is if no more books like *Marxism and Hegel* are published, but instead books like Hilferding's *Finance Capital* and Luxemburg's *Accumulation of Capital*—or even Lenin's *Imperialism*, which was a popular brochure—are once again written. In short, either Marxism has the capacity—I certainly do not—to produce at that level, or it will survive merely as the foible of a few university professors.[106]

The work of Colletti's most recent period contributed, therefore, very little to the Marxist debate about totality; it was written from a self-consciously post-Marxist perspective. If we are to grasp the contribution he did make, we must return to the arguments of his more Della Volpean

102. For a discussion of this trend, see Amedeo Vigorelli, "Toward a Critique of the French Ideology," *Telos* 47 (Spring 1981). Colletti's critique of the new Nietzscheanism appears in *Tramonto*, p. 80f. See also his obituary notice on Heidegger in *Tra marxismo e no*. It is one of the small paradoxes of history that Colletti's hostility to dialectical reasoning was shared by Nietzsche, who once wrote: "There are no contradictions; we acquire the concept of contradictions only from logic, when it was erroneously transferred to things" (*Werke in drei Bänden*, ed. Karl Schlechta [Munich, 1956], vol. 3, p. 561).
103. Colletti, "A Political-Philosophical Interview," p. 345.
104. Colletti, "Una filosofia da snack-bar," *L'Espresso*, 26, 17 (April 27, 1980).
105. Letter from Colletti to the author, Rome, June 18, 1982, in which he writes, "Because I reject dialectics, I also reject hermeneutics."
106. Colletti, "A Political and Philosophical Interview," p. 350.

phases, in particular to *From Rousseau to Lenin* and *Marxism and Hegel.* In these works, he forcefully advanced Della Volpe's arguments against Hegelian Marxism, in particular against its concept (or concepts) of totality. He also called into question the alternative of its structuralist competitor. Although in certain instances the targets of his polemic were caricatured and his arguments tendentious, Colletti did introduce important considerations which inadvertently complemented several of those we have already traced in other contexts. Many of these derived from Della Volpe, but whereas the original formulations had been couched in what Anderson has accurately called Della Volpe's "impenetrable syntax and circular self-reference,"[107] Colletti was able to represent them in vigorous, straightforward and therefore more accessible prose.

Despite the differences between them during Colletti's second period—his greater emphasis on alienation, his impatience with his teacher's defense of the Soviet state, and his more outspoken hostility to Engels—the arguments of his work in the 1950s and 1960s were indeed largely those of his mentor. But by taking them to an extreme and expressing them with such polemical intensity, Colletti made their underlying premises (and underlying tensions) much clearer. Most notably, he exposed the strong affinity with Kantianism latent in the Della Volpean project, especially its view of science.

Colletti was not the first Italian Marxist to try to marry Kant and Marx. In the 1900s, Alfredo Poggi had followed the lead of Eduard Bernstein, Conrad Schmidt and Karl Vorländer in arguing for their compatibility.[108] Poggi's Kant, however, was the ethical theorist who provided a moral argument for socialism, whose victory could no longer be considered inevitable. Colletti staunchly rejected this view of Kant,[109] preferring instead to focus on the epistemological implications of his first *Critique* rather than the moral ones of his second. More specifically, it was Kant's defense of the analytical intellect (*Verstand*) against dialectical reason (*Vernunft*) that Colletti found especially attractive. Only a scientific methodology based on the primacy of the intellect, he insisted, could be truly compatible with materialism, for only a methodology recognizing the limits of reason and the existence of something (like Kant's things-in-

107. Anderson, *Considerations on Western Marxism,* p. 54.
108. For a discussion of Italian neo-Kantian Marxism and Poggi, see Santarelli, *La revisione del marxismo in Italia,* p. 265f. See also Giacomo Marramao, *Marxismo e revisionismo in Italia* (Bari, 1971).
109. Colletti, *Marxism and Hegel,* p. 189; and "A Political and Philosophical Interview," p. 325. The possibility of divorcing the scientific side of Kant from the moral is challenged from a more traditionally Dialectical Materialist perspective by the Trotskyist George Novack in his *Polemics in Marxist Philosophy* (New York, 1978), p. 203f.

themselves) outside of the mind could avoid the pitfalls of a priori hypostatization. Although Marx himself had never really clarified his debt to Kant (as he had also failed to do with Rousseau), he nonetheless was far more a Kantian than a Hegelian.[110]

Hegel, in fact, was the antithesis of Marx in virtually every respect. Except for his recognition of the importance of work and productive activity, which had eluded Kant,[111] Hegel represented more an obstacle to Marx than a model. Dialectical reason with its idealist concept of an all-inclusive totality was in fact the denial of true science, which was grounded in the intellect's insistence on the disparity between subject and object. No practical or intellectual mediation could fully transcend that distinction, which science had to register if it wanted to be true to reality.

To make his case against Hegel, Colletti, following Della Volpe, emphasized what he claimed were the roots of his thought in four non-scientific traditions. The earliest of these was ancient scepticism or Pyrrhonism, which was suspicious of the evidence given by our senses of an external, material world. Marxism, if it was sceptical at all, directed that scepticism towards reason, not the existence of a material world provided by the senses. Hegel, on the other hand, had begun the *Phenomenology* by demonstrating the falsity of immediate sense knowledge; like the sceptics of old, he annihilated the reality of matter.[112] The critical remarks he directed against scepticism in later sections of the *Phenomenology* were really aimed, so Colletti argued, against its modern versions, which denied the reality of thought, not of matter. The second tradition influential on Hegel was that of Christian mysticism, which Colletti detected in the concept of the Absolute Spirit. Arguing against the anthropomorphic reading of that concept in the work of Lukács, Marcuse and Kojève, he emphasized its roots in theology instead. Here too there was a hostile attitude towards matter and sensation, which drew on the neo-Platonic origins of Christian thought.

The third tradition to which Colletti pointed was Spinozism, which he called a form of "absolute immaterialism,"[113] in which finitude was dissolved into the infinite absolute. *Contra* Althusser, there was no way to

110. There is another alternative left unexplored by Colletti: that Marx was indebted more to eighteenth-century materialists like Diderot and Holbach than to either Kant or Hegel. This position is defended by Timpanaro against Colletti. See his *On Materialism*, p. 79. Colletti's general response to Timpanaro's naturalist materialism can be found in his "Political and Philosophical Interview," p. 327f.
111. Colletti, *Marxism and Hegel*, p. 219f.
112. Ibid., chapters 5 and 6.
113. Ibid., p. 30. For Colletti's more general critique of Althusser's attempt to marry Marx and Spinoza, see "A Political and Philosophical Interview," p. 332f., where he details his progressive disillusionment with Althusser's politics as well as theory.

reconcile Spinoza with Marxism or indeed with any science at all. Fourth and finally, Colletti contended that Hegel was profoundly indebted to Romanticism, including its philosophical exponents like Jacobi, who was the first to try to go beyond Kant's *Verstand* (if in the name of intuition rather than *Vernunft*). Hegel was at one with Jacobi, despite his superficial criticisms of him, in their common goal: "destruction of nature and, together with it, destruction of the intellect and of science."[114]

The result of all these influences, according to Colletti, was a concept of totality that was equated with the infinite, hostile to particular, finite matter, and a product of the imperialism of thought. Paradoxically, by trying to include everything, this concept left something essential out:

> The Hegelian "totality" is itself so *one-sided* and incomplete as to *exclude* and leave out the *principle of matter*, i.e. that other feature of identity which found expression, not in Parmenides, but in the Aristotelian principle of determination. The meaning of the latter is precisely that the finite is a real finite only when it lies *outside* the infinite; that being is real being only when it is *independent* of thought; that objects acquire their distinctive determinations only through the exclusion of the negative, of its opposite, i.e. of that logical universal which encompasses *everything* that the particular object itself *is not*.[115]

The profound sympathy that Colletti discerned between orthodox Dialectical Materialism and the earliest versions of Western Marxism was due to their common Hegelian heritage. Engels, Lenin in his more Hegelian moods, Lukács, Sartre, the Frankfurt School all expressed a common contempt for Kantian intellect that marked them as anti-scientific idealists. Colletti thus found trivial the distinction between following the Hegel of the *Phenomenology* and the Hegel of the *Logic*, which some commentators used to distinguish between Western Marxism and its orthodox predecessor.[116] Because all neo-Hegelians emphasized dialectical reason and denigrated intellect, they were inherently anti-scientific. Indeed, they betrayed a covert sympathy for irrationalism because of the similarities between *Vernunft* and sceptical intuition. A straight line could be drawn from the *Lebensphilosophie* of the late nineteenth century, most notably Bergson, to the critique of reification in Lukács, who, as Goldmann perceptively demonstrated, was saying the same thing (if in different form) as the frankly anti-scientific Heidegger.

114. Colletti, *Marxism and Hegel*, p. 147.
115. Ibid., p. 34.
116. See, for example, Russell Jacoby, "The Inception of Western Marxism: Karl Korsch and the Politics of Philosophy," *Canadian Journal of Political and Social Theory* 3, 3 (Fall 1979), p. 7. For another recent rejection of the distinction between the two Hegels, see Rüdiger Bubner, *Modern German Philosophy*, trans. Eric Matthews (Cambridge, 1981), p. 158f. Although Bubner's perspective is by no means like Colletti's, he shares his qualms concerning the division of Hegel's work into two distinct phases.

The most poisoned fruit of this corruption of Marxism was the Frankfurt School, against whom Colletti, like Della Volpe before him,[117] could not contain his wrath. Charging that its members attributed alienation and reification solely to the effects of science and technology rather than social relations, he damned them as reactionary Luddites, "the most conspicuous example of the extreme confusion that can be reached by mistaking the romantic critique of intellect and science for a socio-historical critique of capitalism."[118] *Dialectic of Enlightenment* in particular aroused his fury; its main virtue, he sarcastically claimed,

is that—since they lacked any real analysis, even of a purely philosophic kind, and reduced the relevant categories to mere empty sophistry or personal *bavardage*—they give us a sort of *Summa* of all the "horrors" and idiosyncracies which lie at the basis of philosophical production over many decades, without the effort of decipherment required to read Heidegger, or even Husserl's *Krisis*.[119]

With scarcely concealed contempt (and some confusion about their ages when they wrote the book), he condescendingly concluded, "These are the last 'flowers of evil' of the old spiritualism and of its impotent desire to destroy things: the swansong of two old gentlemen, slightly nihilistic and *démodés*, in conflict with history."[120]

Marcuse's *Reason and Revolution*, with its distinction between negative and positive thought, was no less of a scandal, expressing the same spiritualist and romantic distaste for the finite world that caused Sartre's existentialist "nausea." Marcuse's bankrupt politics of the "Great Refusal" followed from his inept philosophy; it was an ahistorical "*total negation* of the existing."[121] Rather than a true revolutionary, Marcuse was really "a fierce critic of Marx and of socialism"[122] whose "petty-bourgeois anarchism"[123] was little more than a resurrection of the ethical socialism of Bernstein.

Colletti conceded that the Frankfurt School, like Western Marxism in general, had been correct in calling for some theory of holism in opposition to positivist atomism, but they had gotten it all wrong. Marx's "whole is a totality, but a *determinate* totality; it is a synthesis of *distinct* elements, it is a unity, but a unity of heterogeneous parts."[124] Put more specifically, the key to Marx's holism was his concept of the social relations of production, which was first developed in the *1844 Manuscripts*.

117. See note 30.
118. Colletti, *Marxism and Hegel*, p. 175.
119. Ibid., p. 173.
120. Colletti, *From Rousseau to Lenin*, p. 137. Horkheimer was forty-nine and Adorno forty-one when they completed the book in 1944.
121. Ibid.   122. Ibid., p. 140.   123. Ibid., p. 233.   124. Ibid., p. 14.

In that work, Marx introduced the concept of man as a "generic natural being," which had two essential meanings:

First, that man is a "*natural* being," i.e. that he is a part of nature, and therefore that he is an objective being among other objective natural beings upon whom he depends and by whom he is conditioned; in short, he has his *raison d'être* (*causa essendi*) outside himself. . . . Second, that man is a *thinking* being, i.e. that what differentiates him from all other natural beings and constitutes his *specific* characteristics, is *not a thing*, i.e. a species of nature itself, but is *thought*, i.e. the universal, what is *general* or *common* in all things. This explains why man's specificity is not that of being a species, but that of being the *genus of all empirical genera*, i.e. the unity or overall *totality* of all natural species.[125]

Because Marx always held this dual concept of man, he never turned reason into a subject, as did Hegel and the Hegelian Marxists. Instead, he recognized that whereas man's specificity was to be generic (that is, the totalizer of all reality through his universalizing reason), his naturalness meant he was outside of the generic totalization produced by that reason. According to Colletti, Marx recognized two basic principles: the dialectical one that conceived man as a generic totalizer and

the anti-dialectical or materialist principle that contradiction does not eliminate *non*-contradiction (the principle of reason as a predicate rather than a subject)—in short, the principle of existence as an extra-logical element. Two principles which, if reconsidered in their organic connection, lead us back to the central theoretical postulate of this study, i.e. to tauto-heterological identity or "determinate abstraction."[126]

With this conclusion, it is clear how much the early Colletti was indebted to Della Volpe. His elaboration of his mentor's ideas had its force, especially in underlining the continuities between orthodox and earlier Western Marxism, in both its Hegelian and Spinozan forms. But in many ways it proved vulnerable to criticism. First, Colletti's attempt to reduce Hegel to a religious, romantic, anti-scientific irrationalist did not conform to the interpretation of him in most contemporary Hegel scholarship, Marxist or otherwise. Many commentators, for example, stress the importance of his critique of Jacobi, rather than their similarities as critics of Kant.[127] Nor do most other interpreters support Colletti's contention that

125. Colletti, *Marxism and Hegel*, p. 234. For a somewhat clearer version of the same ideas, see "A Political and Philosophical Interview," p. 328.

126. Colletti, *Marxism and Hegel*, p. 244.

127. See, for example, Charles Taylor, *Hegel* (Cambridge, 1975); Walter Kaufmann, *Hegel: A Reinterpretation* (Garden City, New York, 1965); and Maurice Mandelbaum, *History, Man and Reason: A Study in Nineteenth-Century Thought* (Baltimore, 1981). Insofar as Jacobi wanted to turn *Vernunft* into irrational intuition, it is arguable that he was closer to Kant with his desire to limit reason to make room for faith than to Hegel.

Hegel's negation of positive reality meant the "annilation" of finite matter in the name of some sort of infinite and homogeneous cosmic unity. For this was precisely the failing that Hegel had detected in Schelling and other premature reconcilers of all differences. The non-identity that was to be preserved in the "identity of identity and non-identity" was a barrier to such an annihilation, that "night in which all cows were black" against which Hegel fulminated. Nor was Colletti correct to claim that Hegelian Marxists inevitably cancelled out the otherness of the natural world in their eagerness to posit a dialectical totality encompassing everything; although Lukács may have excluded nature from the dialectical process, he did not deny its separate existence outside of human control.[128] And as we have seen, later Western Marxists were often critical of Lukács' failure to acknowledge the irreducibility of nature within even the most artificially generated dialectical totalization.

Still more questionable in Colletti's analysis of Western Marxism was his tendency to homogenize all its variants into an expression of the same irrationalist and anti-materialist attack on science. The most glaring example of his misreading was his caricatured appraisal of the Frankfurt School. Although there were certain passages in *Dialectic of Enlightenment* that could be construed as latter-day Luddism, the major animus of the book was directed against three targets: the domination of nature, the idealist rage against non-identical otherness, and the exchange principle of bourgeois society. What Colletti crudely saw as little more than anti-scientific romanticism, a regressive attack on the Enlightenment *tout court*,[129] was in fact a far more complicated dialectic with a definite social component. Intent as he was on defending the scientific method in Della Volpean terms, it was Colletti himself who factored out science from the larger social process and made it into an ahistorical method applicable in all circumstances and always with positive effects.

Nor was his contention that the Frankfurt School had advocated the annihilation of material otherness in the name of absolute constitutive subjectivity, either transcendental or anthropological, in accord with the facts. Questionable as this characterization was for Hegel himself, it was a fortiori so for the members of the Frankfurt School, who were no less hostile to idealist philosophies than Colletti. Adorno's *Negative Dialectics*

128. For a defense of Lukács against Colletti on this point, see Andrew Feenberg, *Lukács, Marx and the Sources of Critical Theory* (Towota, New Jersey, 1981), p. 209.
129. The Frankfurt School's ambivalence towards the Enlightenment is captured in Adorno's remark in *Prisms*, trans. Samuel and Shierry Weber (London, 1967), that "The reification of life results not from too much enlightenment but from too little, and ... the mutilation of man which is the result of the present particularistic rationality is the stigma of the total irrationality" (p. 24).

in particular warned against the dangers of conceptual imperialism, which it spurned in favor of what Adorno called the "preponderance of the object." In words that could easily have come from Colletti's pen, Adorno wrote,

Idealism, attesting the positive infinity of its principle at every one of its stages, turns the character of thought, the historic evolution of its independence, into metaphysics. It eliminates all heterogeneous being.[130]

Thus, despite his intentions, the argument of Colletti's work, as Ben Agger had correctly noted, "converges implicitly with the Frankfurt attack on Hegel's identity theory,"[131] and, it might be added, with its critique of expressive notions of totality as well.

Colletti generally ignored these similarities because of his inclination, very much like Della Volpe's, to homogenize discrete positions into uniform general tendencies.[132] Thus, for example, by yoking together idealism, irrationalism and intuitionism into one basic anti-scientific position, he lost sight of the internal dynamics of each. The result, as Paul Piccone has argued,[133] was reminiscent of Lukács' crude polemic in *The Destruction of Reason*, with the crucial difference that the destruction mourned by Colletti was that of *Verstand*, not *Vernunft*. Typical of Colletti's method was his assertion that all dialecticians were of the same positive, identitarian kind, which may have described certain Western Marxists, but was clearly inadequate for others. It was especially inappropriate for Adorno, who not only argued for a negative dialectics without closure, but also claimed that even within idealism there were certain tendencies leading in this direction. To take one example, whereas Colletti contended that infinity and totality were at one in idealism, Adorno claimed:

130. Adorno, *Negative Dialectics*, trans. E. B. Ashton (New York, 1973), p. 26.
131. Ben Agger, review of *Marxism and Hegel, Telos* 24 (Summer 1975), p. 191. In his letter of June 18, 1982, Colletti rejects this comparison, stressing the eclectic character of Adorno's work in which Hegelian *Vernunft* still plays a role. Adorno's distance from Colletti is captured in his insistence that "If one contaminates by association dialectics and irrationalism then one blinds oneself to the fact that criticism of the logic of non-contradiction does not suspend the latter but rather reflects upon it." Adorno, "Introduction," *The Positivist Dispute in German Sociology*, trans. Glyn Adey and David Frisby (London, 1976), p. 66.
132. In an interview Colletti gave to *Rinascita* entitled "Marx, Hegel e la Scuola di Francoforte," in May, 1971, he spoke admiringly of the recognition in the work of Alfred Schmidt and Jürgen Habermas of a certain similarity between Marx and Kant. But he neglected to perceive their debt on this issue to the older members of the Frankfurt School. The interview is reprinted in Cassano, ed., *Marxismo e Filosofia in Italia*, where his appreciation for Schmidt and Habermas appears on p. 294f.
133. Piccone, "The Future of Eurocommunism," *Theory and Society* 10, 5 (September 1981), p. 728.

The antinomy of totality and infinity—for the restless *ad infinitum* explodes the self-contained system, for all its being owed to infinity alone—is of the essence of idealism.

It imitates a central antinomy of bourgeois society. To preserve itself, to remain the same, to "be," that society too must expand, progress, advance its frontiers, not respect any limit, not remain the same.[134]

If Colletti could be insensitive to the internal complexities of the traditions he attacked, he sometimes was no less so to the one he tried to defend. There was, for example, an inherent tension in his own work between his Kantian epistemology, with its agnosticism about things-in-themselves, and his materialist ontology, which gave substantive content to those objects outside of human consciousness. As a recent defender of Lenin's reflection theory of epistemology has put it,

Lenin's remarks on Kant in his *Materialism and Empirio-Criticism* seem equally applicable to Colletti's Kantian interpretation of Marx. . . . In his imitation of Kant, Colletti's views have that same unresolved tension between materialist or realist ontology and idealist epistemology. Either we take his epistemology seriously, and go down the idealist road with Hegel and the latter-day Hegelians, or we take the materialist ontology seriously and travel the materialist road, replacing or supplementing Colletti's epistemology with something like the much despised *Wiederspiegelungstheorie*, suitably refined and made plausible.[135]

Ultimately, as we have seen, Colletti seems to have come to this same conclusion and, finding inspiration in one of Kant's pre-critical works, decided to travel down the materialist road. In so doing, he not only overcame some of the tensions of his own thought, but, ironically, abandoned his faith in Marxism as well. Included in that decision, it should be noted, was a rejection of Della Volpe's solution to the totality problem. As late as "Marxism and the Dialectic," Colletti was still stressing Marx's use of a tauto-heterological unity, even if he admitted that at times Marx was a covert Hegelian. But in an essay dedicated to Della Volpe's memory entitled "Dialectical Contradiction and Non-Contradiction,"[136] published in 1980, he withdrew his support for Della Volpe's formula, which he now considered itself tainted with dialectical residues. Claiming that it re-

134. Adorno, *Negative Dialectics*, p. 26.

135. David-Hillel Ruben, *Marxism and Materialism: A Study in Marxist Theory of Knowledge*, 2nd ed. (Atlantic Highlands, New Jersey, 1979), p. 154. From a non-Leninist perspective, Gary S. Orgel makes a similar criticism in his review essay "A Response to Professor Colletti: An Analysis and Critique of Marxism and Hegel," *Studies in Soviet Thought* 16, 1–2 (June 1976), p. 96. This issue is at the root of the quarrel between Colletti and Timpanaro. See note 110.

136. See note 97.

tained elements of Plato's dialectic of "diaresis," which Della Volpe had tried unsuccessfully to reconcile with Aristotle's notion of "primary substance," he wrote:

In the second paragraph of my "Marxism and the Dialectic," in the handling of "logical contradictions," I committed the error of still expounding it in the light of the dialectic: influenced by the thesis in Della Volpe's *Logic as a Positive Science* concerning the dialectical or tauto-heterological character of "reason" as "thinking of contradictions." In dialectics, logical opposites, that is, the contradictories—which should be the most irreconcilable and reciprocally exclusive extremes in that they do not allow a third which would recuperate and mediate them—are presented (and this is common both to the later Plato and to Hegel) as two opposites, each of which *implies* and *includes* the other. This derives from the attempt to transfer the characteristics of contrarity to contradiction and vice versa. What was said in the second paragraph of that essay remains valid, but only on the condition that one refers it not to the "logical contradiction" but to the real hybrid which is "dialectical opposition."[137]

Della Volpe's tauto-heterological unity, Colletti thus concluded, was such a dialectical hybrid, because he "had not drawn all the consequences of Kant's 1763 writing or of Trendelenburg. I would dare to say that he had not understood well the difference between 'real oppositions' or contrarities . . . [and] . . . logical contradictions."[138]

Colletti's insistence on the absolute importance of this difference meant that he repudiated any concept of totality, Della Volpean or otherwise, as incompatible with science. Whether or not this left him in what one observer called "a situation of objective theoretical impasse,"[139] it certainly prevented him from offering a defensible version of Marxist holism to replace the ones he and Della Volpe had rejected. What the Della Volpeans had achieved therefore was largely negative. Not only did they demonstrate some of the dangers in assimilating Marxism too quickly to romantic, idealist and anti-scientific traditions of thought, they also made clear some of the weaknesses in allegedly scientific correctives that were indebted more to Spinoza than Marx. That inordinate distrust of natural science, which we saw at its strongest in certain Western Marxists' hostility to sociology and psychology, had its price, which the Della Volpeans, if often in exaggerated and unnuanced ways, had helped to expose. Their own position suffered, to be sure, from an equally problematic reduction of philosophy to science, social science to natural science, social theory to sociology and politics to "correct" epistemology. The dissolution of the

137. Colletti, *Tramonto dell'ideologia* pp. 112–13.
138. Letter from Colletti to author, Rome, June 18, 1982.
139. Mariachiara Fugazza, "I due Marx di Colletti," *Aut Aut* 147 (May–June 1975), p. 118.

Della Volpean school in the late 1970s, most acutely registered in Colletti's apostasy, demonstrated the dangers latent in so restrictive a definition of Marxism. For once Colletti realized that Marx failed to conform to his increasingly narrow definition of legitimate science, he felt compelled to abandon the tradition entirely.

The reconstruction of Marxist holism would thus have to await someone who would avoid the pitfalls of neo-Hegelianism, drawing on the strengths of its various critics without, however, allowing their criticisms to undermine his allegiance to Marxism per se. It would need a theorist who was not hostile to natural science, but who would recognize its limited role in both creating and analyzing the social whole. It would likewise need someone who could appreciate the contributions bourgeois sociologists, psychologists, anthropologists and other social scientists could make to our understanding of a totality that was in part like a natural object. And concomitantly, it would require someone open to the insights that structuralist and systems-theoretic analyses might offer to Marxism, without, however, accepting unquestioningly their anti-subjectivist, anti-humanist bias.

But such a reconstruction would also require someone sensitive to the still latent possibilities for creating a normative totality that would overcome the pseudo-naturalist structure of contemporary society. Rather than seek those possibilities where the earlier Western Marxists had, in a meta-subject able to totalize society and recognize its totalization as a reflection of itself, it would have to focus on the intersubjective, dialogic linguistic communities whose promise we have already noted in the work of Gramsci and Merleau-Ponty. And finally, it would need a theorist who, for all of his holistic, synthesizing inclinations, would pay heed to the warnings against identity theory in the work of the Frankfurt School and their unexpected allies in the scientific Marxist camp.

The figure who embodied all of these characteristics, and thus provided the only potentially plausible salvation of Marxist holism to emerge from the wreckage of the Western Marxist tradition, was the German philosopher and sociologist Jürgen Habermas. If the narrative we have been emplotting in a tragic mode is to have a less somber end, we must turn to Habermas' Promethean effort to reconstruct Marxist holism on boldly new grounds.

CHAPTER FIFTEEN

Jürgen Habermas and the Reconstruction of Marxist Holism

The work of Jürgen Habermas, it has been widely recognized,[1] can be construed as both a continuation and critical reevaluation of the classical Critical Theory of the Frankfurt School's first generation. However much Habermas may have learned from Horkheimer, Adorno and Marcuse, he also sought to overcome what he perceived as the significant weaknesses in their legacy. To put it in its most general terms, Habermas attempted both to find a firmer normative foundation for Critical Theory and to lighten the darkly pessimistic vision of history to which it originally led.

Rejecting what he dubbed Adorno's politically defensive "strategy of hibernation,"[2] Habermas tried once more to find the links between theory and practice that animated the Frankfurt School during its earliest years. Rather than resting content with a micrological analysis of the ruins of a blasted totality, he boldly sought to reconceptualize its still discernable unity. Philosophy, he argued, must join once again with social, economic and political analysis, rather than remaining, as he once called Adorno's *Negative Dialectics,* "an empty exercise in self-reflection."[3] Critique must recapture its links with the concept of crisis, and in so doing,

---

1. For discussions of the links between Habermas and the older members of the Frankfurt School, see David Held, *Introduction to Critical Theory: Horkheimer to Habermas* (Berkeley, 1980); Paul Connerton, *The Tragedy of Enlightenment: An Essay on the Frankfurt School* (Cambridge, 1980); and Axel Honneth, "Communication and Reconciliation: Habermas' Critique of Adorno," *Telos* 39 (Spring 1979). For defenses of the older Frankfurt School against Habermas' revision, see James Schmidt, "Offensive Critical Theory? Reply to Honneth," *Telos* 39 (Spring 1979) and Gillian Rose, *The Melancholy Science: An Introduction to the Thought of Theodor W. Adorno* (New York, 1978), pp. 146–47.

2. Habermas, "Consciousness-Raising or Redemptive Criticism: The Contemporaneity of Walter Benjamin," *New German Critique* 17 (Spring 1979), p. 43.

3. Habermas, "Why More Philosophy?" *Social Research* 38, 4 (Winter 1971), p. 649.

uncover the yet unresolved crisis of late capitalism. What he termed the "left counterpart to the once-popular theory of totalitarian domination"[4] espoused by the older generation of Critical Theorists had to be replaced by a more differentiated analysis of the mixed possibilities for advance and regression in contemporary society. In short, the positive moment in Critical Theory should once again dominate, or at least vie for supremacy with, the negative.

There is a still broader context in which Habermas' work should be placed, for in addition to being a way out of the cul-de-sac of earlier Critical Theory, it also represents an extraordinarily ambitious attempt to reestablish the foundations of the Western Marxist tradition as a whole.[5] Although initially indebted to the paradigm introduced by Lukács and the other Hegelian Marxists of the interwar era, Habermas came increasingly to recognize the central inadequacies of their argument, many of which we have traced in previous chapters. But, unlike Adorno, Sartre, Althusser and Colleti, whose work registered in different ways the exhaustion of the Hegelian Marxist tradition without supplying a fully developed alternative, Habermas attempted to reground it in a more thorough-going and defensible fashion. To borrow the term he himself employed in reference to historical materialism, his has been a "reconstruction" of Western Marxism, defined as "taking a theory apart and putting it back together again in a new form in order to attain more fully the goal it has set for itself.[6]

Insofar as that theory was grounded, to quote Lukács' celebrated phrase once again, on the premise that "*the primacy of the category of totality is the bearer of the principle of revolution in the science*,"[7] Habermas' work has also been a "reconstruction" of Marxist holism. Acknowledging the force of many of the criticisms made against the original Hegelian Marxist paradigm, yet unwilling to accept a purely destructive analysis of its value, he turned to several non-Marxist theoretical systems in an effort to rescue the emancipatory potential he claimed remained latent in it.[8] In so doing, he demonstrated that Western Marxism, if no

4. Habermas, *Communication and the Evolution of Society*, trans. Thomas McCarthy (Boston, 1979), p. 72.
5. Habermas, in fact, was one of the few Western Marxists who actively responded to the work of his predecessors. As early as 1957 and his "Literaturbericht zur philosophischen Diskussion um Marx und den Marxismus," reprinted in *Theorie and Praxis* (Neuwied, 1963), he demonstrated his enormous grasp of virtually the entire tradition, with the possible exception of its Italian branch.
6. Habermas, *Communication and the Evolution of Society*, p. 95.
7. Georg Lukács, *History and Class Consciousness: Studies in Marxist Dialectics*, trans. Rodney Livingstone (Cambridge, Mass., 1971), p. 27.
8. Despite the charges of more orthodox Marxists that Habermas had left the fold completely, he vigorously protested that he was still within the Marxist tradition. See his inter-

longer viable in its original form, was not yet fully an historical phenomenon with little, if any, current efficacy. And he made equally clear the possibility of constructing a grand theoretical synthesis which would bravely try to accommodate the whole of human reality.

The context in which Habermas' reconstruction took place was radically different from that which spawned Western Marxism. Rather than growing out of an optimistic era when expectations of radical change seemed more realistic than utopian, Habermas' work emerged in the far more sober atmosphere of post-World War II Europe. Moreover, whereas in France and Italy of that period mass political parties of the Left drew on the Resistance experience to gain a foothold in the public life of their respective countries, Germany had neither a vigorous and unified Resistance movement nor a large-scale Communist Party. Leftist intellectuals were further isolated by the harsh Cold War climate of a divided Germany, where Marxism was understood by both its friends and enemies as equivalent to the Stalinist brand established in Ulbricht's German Democratic Republic. Not surprisingly, when Habermas came to grasp the existence of an alternative tradition of Critical Marxism, he did so with a great deal more circumspection than had his predecessors in the 1920s.

But if he did not share their apocalyptic hopes, neither was Habermas debilitated by the paralyzing despair that was often the outcome of their exaggerated expectations. Thus, when a New Left emerged in German universities during the 1960s, he was able to acknowledge in a cautious way the potential for radical change it represented.[9] And even when his relations soured with the more militant segments of the German movement, he retained an essentially positive impulse in his theoretical work. As a result, his ideas have remained powerful although the historical moment when they were first formulated has passed.

In more specific ways, Habermas was a product of a very different context from that which nurtured his predecessors. Born in 1929 in the small Rhenish town of Gummersbach, the son of a bureaucrat and the

---

view with Boris Frankel, "Habermas Talking: An Interview," *Theory and Society* 1, 1 (1974), p. 57. It is significant that Perry Anderson's attempt to draw up an "historical balance-sheet" of Western Marxism (*Considerations on Western Marxism* [London, 1976]) completely ignores Habermas' attempt to reconstruct it. Perhaps Göran Therborn's hostile article, "Jürgen Habermas: A New Eclecticism," *New Left Review* 67 (May–June 1971), persuaded Anderson that he was beyond the Marxist pale, although curiously, Therborn's piece was included in the *New Left Review*'s *Western Marxism: A Critical Reader* (London, 1977), for which Anderson's book was an intended introduction. In any event, by excluding Habermas, Anderson was able more easily to suggest the exhaustion of the Western Marxist tradition.

9. Habermas, *Toward a Rational Society: Student Protest, Science and Politics*, trans. Jeremy J. Shapiro (Boston, 1970).

grandson of a Lutheran minister,[10] Habermas came of political age with the collapse of the Third Reich and the beginning of the Allied occupation. The disturbing failures of postwar de-Nazification helped draw him to the Left. Unexamined continuities with the Nazi era in the newly founded Federal Republic, that "unmastered past" as the German Left came to call it, led him to question the political basis of the new regime. At the universities of Göttingen and then Bonn, where he completed his doctorate in philosophy with a thesis on Schelling in 1954,[11] he encountered professors whose denial of politics in general and the political ramifications of their work in particular repelled him. In 1953, when Heidegger republished his 1935 *Introduction to Metaphysics* without any attempt to come to grips with the intervening catastrophe and his own role in it, Habermas, who had been initially drawn to Heidegger's thought, lashed out at him in one of his first published essays.[12] At about the same time, he discovered *History and Class Consciousness* and was introduced to Marx's early writings by Karl Löwith. And then in 1955, he came across Horkheimer and Adorno's *Dialectic of Enlightenment*, whose impact, he later recalled, was enormous:

What fascinated me right away with those two was that they weren't engaging in a reception of Marx; they were utilizing him. It was a great experience for me to see that one could relate systematically to the Marxist tradition. . . . Of course I had been prepared for it on the basis of my reading of Lukács. At that point philosophical and political things began to come together for the first time.[13]

Habermas' enthusiasm for Critical Theory brought him in 1956 to Frankfurt, where he served as an Assistant at the Institute. It should be remembered, however, that by this time, the Frankfurt School had come to have serious reservations about its radical past. In fact, students were discouraged from reading the contents of the *Zeitschrift für Sozialforschung*, a complete copy of which, Habermas later recalled, "was kept in a crate in the Institute's cellar, nailed shut and out of our grasp."[14] Nonetheless, pirated copies of certain essays circulated among the increasingly radical student community at the Institute and Habermas was able to

10. For biographical information on Habermas, see his interview with Detlev Horster and Willem van Reijen in *New German Critique* 18 (Fall 1979).

11. Habermas, "Das Absolute und die Geschichte: von der Zwiespältigkeit in Schellings Denken" (Ph.D. diss., U. of Bonn, 1954).

12. Habermas, "Zur Veröffentlichung von Vorlesungen aus dem Jahre 1935," reprinted in *Philosophisch-politische Profile* (Frankfurt, 1971).

13. Habermas, interview with Horster and van Reijen, p. 32. See also his remarks in "The Dialectics of Rationalization: An Interview with Jürgen Habermas," conducted by Axel Honneth et al., *Telos* 49 (Fall 1981), pp. 5–8.

14. Habermas, "The Inimitable Zeitschrift für Sozialforschung: How Horkheimer Took Advantage of a Historically Oppressive Hour," *Telos* 45 (Fall 1980), p. 116.

understand how deeply indebted to Marxism his teachers had originally been. Indeed, he soon came to chastise them for harboring a "hidden orthodoxy"[15] because of their implicit acceptance of the labor theory of value, which he found cause to question. The example that was more potent for him was to be found in the early Frankfurt School's insistence on the links between theory and practice. Although Horkheimer and Adorno had suppressed the connection after their return to Germany, Marcuse had not. When he made his first visit back to Frankfurt after the war, to lecture at a conference in 1956 for the one hundredth anniversary of Freud's birth Habermas "first faced an embodiment and vivid expression of the political spirit of the Frankfurt School."[16]

In identifying with that spirit, Habermas also absorbed several traits of the Institute's repatriated leaders. He was for example, well schooled in the empirical techniques which they had brought back from America. Although he accepted their disdain for the exaggerated importance of empiricism in a non-dialectical social science, he valued its usefulness in confirming the insights of dialectical theory. When he later joined the Max Planck Institute for Research into the Life Conditions of the Scientific-Technical World in 1971, after a decade of teaching in Heidelberg and Frankfurt, he assembled a staff of young researchers who combined empirical and dialectical techniques in a number of collective projects.

Perhaps more significant, he also absorbed some of that tempered respect for bourgeois democracy brought back by the senior Critical Theorists from their American exile. Indeed, as a student growing up in a post-totalitarian Germany, he was even less suspicious than were his teachers with their memories of an earlier failed democratic experiment. As he later put it,

I myself am a product of "reeducation," and, I hope, not an all too negative one. By that I mean to say that we learned back then that the bourgeois constitutional state in its French or American form is a historical achievement. There is an important biographical difference between those who experienced what a half-hearted bourgeois republic like the Weimar Republic can lead to and those who formed their political consciousness later on.[17]

As a result, although he accepted certain aspects of the older Frankfurt School's analysis of the Culture Industry, he never adopted their belief in

15. Habermas, *Theory and Practice*, trans. John Viertel (London, 1974), p. 203.
16. Habermas, "Psychic Thermidor and the Rebirth of Rebellious Subjectivity," *Berkeley Journal of Sociology* 25 (1980), p. 3. In this memorial essay, Habermas identifies himself with the more affirmative moment in Marcuse's work in comparison with Adorno's more purely negative alternative.
17. Habermas interview with Horster and van Reijen, p. 31.

the virtually total manipulation of mass consciousness or the complete domination of an "administered society." Closer in fact to Antonio Gramsci with his faith in the possibility of popular education,[18] he rejected the elitist traces in his mentors' work and challenged the "privileged status which [they] must claim for their experience vis-à-vis the stunted contemporary subjectivity."[19]

Habermas, however, had no illusions about the reality of political life in the Federal Republic. The central argument of his *Habilitationsschrift*, written in 1962 on the *Structural Transformation of the Public Sphere*,[20] contrasted the earlier creation of a bourgeois public sphere, in which political issues were an object of communal discussion, with the present-day usurpation of that sphere by administrative and technical experts. True praxis, he insisted, must be distinguished from *techne*. Still, Habermas never lost his faith in the value of the bourgeois public sphere as a model for a socialist politics of the future. His attempt to find a new normative basis for totality rested in great measure on such a model.

Maturing in post-war Germany also seems to have instilled in Habermas a visceral horror of irrationality, which extended even beyond that of the earlier Critical Theorists. Whereas they damned instrumental reason for its tainted association with the domination of nature and thus at times seemed to be condemning science as such,[21] Habermas scrupulously restricted his critique to the inappropriate extension of instrumental reason beyond its proper sphere. More soberly than his predecessors, he questioned the possibility of a new, completely non-dominating science which would lead to the "resurrection of fallen nature."[22] Technical reason, he implied, was legitimate so long as it did not claim to embody reason per se.

Moreover, for all his early fascination with *Dialectic of Enlightenment*, Habermas remained far more positively inclined to the emancipatory claims of the Enlightenment than were Horkheimer and Adorno. Unlike the early Lukács, Bloch or Marcuse, there were no Romantic impulses in his Marxism. In all of his subsequent controversies, whether

18. For a comparison of the two, see Walter L. Adamson, "Beyond 'Reform or Revolution': Notes on Political Education in Gramsci, Habermas and Arendt," *Theory and Society* 6, 3 (November 1978).

19. Habermas, *Philosophisch-politische Profile*, p. 188.

20. Habermas, *Strukturwandel der Öffentlichkeit* (Neuwied, 1962). For an English synopsis of this argument, see "The Public Sphere," *New German Critique* 3 (Fall 1974), with an introductory essay by Peter Hohendahl.

21. For a discussion of how far they went in attacking science, see Eike Gebhardt's introduction to the "Critique of Methodology" section of *The Essential Frankfurt School Reader*, ed. Andrew Arato and Eike Gebhardt (New York, 1978), p. 512.

22. Habermas, *Toward a Rational Society*, p. 86.

with positivists, systems theorists, or hermeneuticists, he doggedly defended reason against tradition or arbitrary decisions as the ground of
both cognitive and normative judgments. And when the earlier Frankfurt
School defense of rationality on essentially Hegelian grounds seemed no
longer viable to him, Habermas resisted falling back on an instinctual
concept of reason, as did the later Marcuse, or an artistic one, as did the
later Adorno.[23] Instead, he proposed a new and original alternative that
drew on the linguistic turn in twentieth-century philosophy, whose implications so many other contemporary thinkers assumed were anti-ra-
tional. He then enriched it by grounding linguistic rationality in a socio-
logically based theory of communicative action, which insisted on the
rational dimension of the pre-theoretical *Lebenswelt*. In short, what Habermas called his "partiality for reason,"[24] was a central aspect of his entire project and as such was at the heart of his reconstruction of Western
Marxist holism.

To spell out that reconstruction in its full complexity would require a
detailed presentation of Habermas' still uncompleted *oeuvre*, which
George Lichtheim once compared with Hegel's in its encyclopedic
scope.[25] That comparison was made in 1969, before Habermas added
several new volumes to his encyclopedia, so it would be even more foolish
now than then to attempt a full-scale recapitulation in the space of one
chapter. Several recent full-length works have admirably performed this
courageous task.[26] What must suffice is a general consideration of the

23. For Habermas' rejection of these alternatives, see "Theory and Politics: A Discussion with Herbert Marcuse, Jürgen Habermas, Heinz Lubasz and Tilman Spengler," *Telos*
38 (Winter 1978–79).
    24. Habermas, *Legitimation Crisis*, trans. Thomas McCarthy (Boston, 1973), p. 142.
According to Joel Whitebook, "There is something compulsively modernistic about Habermas' project. It is as though he cannot seriously entertain any objections to the project of
modernity for fear of opening the Pandora's box of irrationalist regressivism" ("Saving the
Subject: Modernity and the Problem of the Autonomous Individual," *Telos* 50 [Winter
1981–82], p. 94). Habermas defends his "neglect" of the counter-enlightenment in "A Reply to my Critics" in John B. Thompson and David Held, eds., *Habermas: Critical Debates*
(Cambridge, Mass., 1982), p. 223f.
    25. George Lichtheim, *From Marx to Hegel* (New York, 1971), p. 175.
    26. Thomas McCarthy, *The Critical Theory of Jürgen Habermas* (Cambridge, Mass.,
1978); Julius Sensat, Jr., *Habermas and Marxism: An Appraisal* (Beverly Hills, 1979); Gar-
bis Kortian, *Metacritique: The Philosophical Argument of Jürgen Habermas*, trans. John
Raffan with intro. by Charles Taylor and Alan Montefiore (Cambridge, 1980); John B.
Thompson, *Critical Hermeneutics: A Study of the Thought of Paul Ricoeur and Jürgen
Habermas* (Cambridge, 1981); Held, *Introduction to Critical Theory*; and Connerton, *The
Tragedy of Enlightenment*. A still useful early account of Habermas' work can be found in
Trent Schroyer, *The Critique of Domination: The Origins and Development of Critical The-
ory* (New York, 1973). See also Russell Keat, *The Politics of Social Theory: Habermas,
Freud and the Critique of Positivism* (Chicago, 1981); Raymond Geuss, *The Idea of a Criti-
cal Theory: Habermas and the Frankfurt School* (Cambridge, 1981), and the excellent contributions to Thompson and Held, eds., *Habermas: Critical Debates*.

ways in which Habermas recast the terms of the Marxist discourse on totality to avoid the difficulties we have seen undermine the attempts of his predecessors.

Habermas, Boris Frankel has observed, "provides us with what is perhaps the most decisive critique of 'Hegelian Marxism' of which, ironically, he is regarded to be a leading exponent."[27] Although certainly arguable as a characterization of Habermas' work as a whole, Frankel's generalization underestimates the extent to which the early Habermas remained largely within the Western Marxist paradigm, in particular with regard to its concept of totality. Although he did acknowledge the idealist weaknesses in Lukács and Korsch,[28] he was initially very much in their debt. The limits of his apostasy are clearly demonstrated in one of his earliest essays, "Between Philosophy and Science: Marxism as Critique," composed in 1960 and published three years later in *Theory and Practice.*[29] One of its main targets was the attempt made by the celebrated economist Joseph Schumpeter to treat the components of Marx's theory in isolation from each other. Such an attempt, Habermas contended, "only ends up with the *disjecta membra,* torn out of the context of a dialectical understanding that comprehends the meaning of a theory envisaging society as a totality and related to praxis."[30] To sanction such a dismemberment, Habermas warned, was to underestimate Marx's indebtedness to Hegel's method:

The presupposition of Hegelian logic in Marxism is a widely pursued topic of the more recent critique of Marxism. Actually, Marx takes as his systematic point of departure the categories of the objective spirit; he premises the idea of morality, as the concept of society as a whole, in such a way that the realization of society must be measured by it, and thus recognized as the immoral condition of a world torn asunder.[31]

Not only did Habermas emphasize the Hegelian concept of totality as the root of Marxism, he also invoked Vico's *verum-factum* principle as a basic premise of a materialist philosophy of history. Vico, to be sure, still relied on providential intervention in the course of history and saw it in cyclical terms, but he was the first to recognize that mankind as a collec-

27. Frankel, intro. to "Habermas Talking," p. 40.
28. Habermas, "Literaturbericht zur philosophischen Diskussion um Marx und den Marxismus," p. 439f.
29. Habermas, *Theory and Practice,* chap. 6.
30. Ibid., p. 205.
31. Ibid., p. 217.

tivity was the author of that history. What was necessary to make the *verum-factum* principle more plausible was the Enlightenment's, in particular Kant's, belief in progress. Kant's dualism allowed him to take Vico's insight only so far, however, for:

The historical subjects are, as it were, split into their noumenal and their phenomenal aspects; they are the authors of their history, but still they have not yet constituted themselves as its subject—they are at once a causally determined species of nature and morally free individuals.[32]

Hegel's dialectical resolution of Kant's dualism, Habermas suggested, was needed to prepare the way for Marx, who "reconciles Vico, who is preserved [sublated] in Hegel, with Kant."[33]

The echoes of *History and Class Consciousness* were unmistakable in all of this; Habermas was clearly endorsing an essentially expressive view of totality as the objectification of a meta-subject. There was, however, one qualification which he introduced at the end of his essay. Josef Revai, it will be recalled, had questioned a central assumption of Lukács' argument in his 1924 review of the book.[34] If only the proletariat were the universal class, both subject and object of history, how was it possible, Revai asked, to speak of a unified historical subject in the past who "made" history and could know what it made? Merleau-Ponty in *Adventures of the Dialectic*, a work Habermas knew and respected, had approvingly invoked Revai's point about Lukács' "conceptual mythology"[35] in his own analysis of *History of Class Consciousness*. In his 1960 essay, Habermas drew a similar conclusion:

If the loose threads of the historical development can be tied together only at a relatively late stage, this network cannot then retrospectively be made to cover history as a whole; the fact that the global unity itself has only come to be historically contradicts an approach which makes the totality of history from the very beginning its premise. . . . The fact that the capacity for rationalization itself has only come to be historically, is in contradiction to a viewpoint which presumes a subject for history from the beginning.[36]

But having thus withdrawn his assent from the naive view that a creator-subject underlay the course of history from its origin, Habermas finished his essay by claiming that the practical implications of such a view might nonetheless be seen as healthy:

32. Ibid., p. 246.
33. Ibid., p. 248.
34. Revai, review of *History and Class Consciousness*, trans. with intro. by Ben Brewster, *Theoretical Practice* 1 (January 1971).
35. Merleau-Ponty, *Adventures of the Dialectic*, trans. Joseph Bien (Evanston, 1973), p. 54.
36. Habermas, *Theory and Practice*, p. 251.

From the lofty observation post of this fiction the situation is revealed in its ambiv-
alences, which are susceptible to practical intervention, so that an enlightened
mankind can elevate itself then to become what up to that point it was only fictitiously.[37]

In other words, although the concept of expressive totality was false as a
description of universal history, it was a model for a future socialist totalization in which subject and object were one.

Habermas remained within the Hegelian Marxist paradigm through
the early 1960s, although his position began gradually to shift away from
it. As he remembers it,[38] a major turning point came during the so-called
Positivism Dispute between Karl Popper and his followers and the Frankfurt School.[39] Habermas' first contribution to the controversy came in
1963 in an article entitled "The Analytic Theory of Science and Dialectics," which demonstrated his continued allegiance to his earlier position.
Adorno's opening salvo in the dispute, a critique of Popper's anti-holistic
logic of the social sciences,[40] had defended the dialectical concept of totality without that ambivalence we have seen expressed elsewhere in his
work. Against what he saw as Popper's positivism, he was apparently anxious to stress how much society should be understood as a total, if internally contradictory phenomenon. "Social totality," Adorno wrote,

37. Ibid., p. 252. It is interesting to compare these closing remarks with a similar conclusion in a later essay, where Habermas is more explicitly anti-Hegelian. In his 1972 piece
"Über das Subjekt der Geschichte; Diskussionsbemerkung zu falsch gestellten Alternativen," *Kulture und Kritik: Verstreute Aufsätze* (Frankfurt, 1973), he wrote:

The self-constituting subject of history was and is a fiction; in no way meaningless, however, is the intention, both expressed and hidden in it, to link the development of socio-cultural systems to the steering
mechanisms of self-reflection in the sense of a politically consequential institutionalization of discourses
(self-produced higher level intersubjective communities). (p. 398)

38. Conversation with Habermas, Starnberg, December, 1980. He also credits his reading in the later Wittgenstein for the change.

39. Adorno et al., *The Positivist Dispute in German Sociology*, trans. Glyn Adey and
David Frisby (London, 1976). Habermas also contributed to another celebrated dispute that
paralleled this one at the 1965 German Sociological Congress in Heidelberg. The subject
was Max Weber, whom Habermas accused of being an anticipator of the decisionist jurist
Carl Schmitt. The proceedings are in English in Otto Stammer, ed., *Max Weber and Sociology Today*, trans. Kathleen Morris (New York, 1971). For general discussions of the Positivist Dispute, see David Frisby's introduction to the English translation of Adorno et al., *The
Positivist Dispute*, and his earlier article "The Popper-Adorno Controversy: The Methodological Dispute in German Sociology," *Philosophy of the Social Sciences* 2 (June 1972), as
well as Agnes Heller, "The Positivism Dispute as a Turning Point in German Post-War Theory," *New German Critique* 15 (Fall 1978).

40. Adorno, "On the Logic of the Social Sciences" in *The Positivist Dispute*; this paper
followed Popper's at the Tübingen meeting of the German Sociological Association in 1961.
The final volume of essays contains a still earlier essay by Adorno from 1957. Popper's own
work on this question antedated the dispute by many years. In fact, it was part of a long-
running controversy among English philosophers (and their exiled continental counterparts
living in Britain) over the merits of methodological holism versus methodological individualism. For a useful selection of the relevant papers, see John O'Neill, ed., *Modes of Individualism and Collectivism* (London, 1973).

does not lead a life of its own over and above that which it unites and of which it, in its turn, is composed. It produces and reproduces itself through its individual moments. . . . This totality can no more be detached from life, from the cooperation and the antagonism of its elements than can an element be understood merely as it functions without insight into the whole which has its source [*Wesen*] in the motion of the individual himself. System and individual entity are reciprocal and can only be apprehended in their reciprocity.[41]

Habermas began his own essay by quoting these lines and then added:

Adorno conceives of society in categories which do not deny their origins in Hegel's logic. He conceptualizes society as totality in the strictly dialectical sense, which prohibits one from approaching the whole organically in accordance with the statement that it is more than the sum of its parts. Nor is totality a class which might be determined in its logical extension by a collection of all the elements which it comprises.[42]

Because the dialectical concept of totality recognized the reciprocity of whole and part, Habermas continued, it escaped the justifiable criticism directed by positivists like Ernest Nagel against a completely anti-analytic Gestaltist holism, which hypostatized the whole.[43] Nor should it be confused, he added, with the more empirical and analytic concept of the whole as a functional system:

The distinction between system and totality, in the sense mentioned, cannot be signified directly, for in the language of formal logic it would have to be dissolved, whilst in the language of dialectics it would have to be transcended.[44]

In addition to falling back on the distinction between formal and dialectical logic, which was a staple of Hegelian Marxism, Habermas also introduced a new defense based on a tradition that the Hegelian Marxists, as well as Adorno,[45] had ignored or rejected: phenomenological hermeneutics. The ultimate source of a dialectical holism, Habermas contended, could be located in the pre-scientific, pre-reflective experiences of what Husserl and Schutz had called the *Lebenswelt* (life-world):

41. Adorno, "On the Logic of the Social Sciences," p. 107.
42. Habermas, "The Analytical Theory of Science and Dialectics" in *The Positivist Dispute*, p. 131.
43. Ernest Nagel, *The Structure of Science* (London, 1961).
44. Habermas, "The Analytical Theory of Science and Dialectics," p. 132.
45. Adorno's criticism of Husserl appeared preeminently in *Against Epistemology: A Metacritique*, trans. Willis Domingo (Cambridge, Mass., 1982). For a critique of Critical Theory's neglect of phenomenology, see Paul Piccone, "Beyond Identity Theory" in John O'Neill, ed., *On Critical Theory* (New York, 1976). Adorno did, of course, express a certain interest in hermeneutics, at least of the kind developed in Benjamin's work. But to the extent that he privileged the isolated individual over the intersubjective community, his theory of truth lacked a truly hermeneutical dimension. For a discussion of his related critique of reflexive sociology, see Rose, *The Melancholy Science*, p. 143f.

The required coherence of the theoretical approach with the total societal process, to which sociological research itself belongs, similarly points towards experience. But insights of this sort stem, in the last instance, from the fund of pre-scientifically accumulated experience which has not yet excluded, as merely subjective elements, the basic resonance of a life-historically centered social environment, that is, the education acquired by the total human subject. This prior experience of society as totality shapes the outline of the theory in which it articulates itself and through whose constructions it is checked anew against experiences.[46]

The hermeneutic anticipation of totality must, however, prove itself in a dialectical interchange between theory and its object, whose relative congruence could be tested only through practice. Ultimately, and here Habermas was still very much the Hegelian Marxist, "this analysis would have to develop out of historical contexts the perspective of an action imputable to a total society as subject."[47]

Habermas' defense of Adorno's position thus drew on two distinct traditions: Hegelian dialectics and phenomenological hermeneutics. It was not a fully satisfactory mix. Although Habermas defended totality by opposing it to Gestaltist holism and functionalist systems theory, its positive content, as McCarthy has recognized,[48] is difficult to discern clearly.

In fact, in Habermas' next contribution to the Positivism Dispute, "A Positivistically Bisected Rationalism," which followed a critique of his first essay by the Popperian Hans Albert,[49] the concept of totality was far less prominent. One of Albert's complaints had been directed at Habermas' failure to develop that concept with enough rigor to escape Nagel's strictures against holism in general. His recourse to the distinction between formal and dialectical logic, Albert argued, was an "immmunization strategy"[50] designed to prevent close scrutiny of its value. In reply, Habermas said he preferred to call it a flanking maneuver, in which the unexamined assumptions of positivism were rendered problematic. He also addressed a series of other accusations, largely by drawing (even more than in the first essay) on the hermeneutic tradition, tempered to be sure by a stress on combining understanding with explanation.[51] But significantly, nowhere did he specifically defend the Hegelian-Marxist notion of totality against Albert's criticisms. In fact, as Agnes Heller has remarked, in

46. Habermas, "The Analytical Theory of Science and Dialectics," p. 135.
47. Ibid., p. 141.
48. McCarthy, The Critical Theory of Jürgen Habermas, p. 135.
49. Hans Albert, "The Myth of Total Reason: Dialectical Claims in the Light of Undialectical Criticism" in The Positivist Dispute.
50. Ibid., p. 168.
51. Habermas, "A Positivistically Bisected Rationalism" in The Positivist Dispute, p. 221. The necessity of combining understanding and explanation was also a major point in Habermas' debate with Gadamer.

this essay "the concept of totality disappears almost completely; the category of rational enlightenment is put in the center."[52] What was also deemphasized, although not yet totally abandoned, was the concomitant notion of a total social subject, the premise of an expressive holism.

Habermas' change of mind during the Positivism Dispute should not be understood as leading to a simple rejection of Marxist holism, but rather, as we have suggested, as an attempt at its reconstruction on firmer grounds. Although implicitly directed against Hegelian Marxism, it began by turning Hegel against himself. In an article written in 1967 for a *Festschrift* for Karl Löwith, entitled "Labor and Interaction: Remarks on Hegel's Jena *Philosophy of Mind*,"[53] Habermas argued that before developing his mature theory, Hegel had posited a suggestive explanation for the formation of the Spirit that he later abandoned. What Habermas found particularly worth rescuing in that early formulation was Hegel's insight into the intersubjective source of the Spirit's *Bildung*. Rather than conceiving it as a unified ego which objectifies itself and knows its objectifications through a monological process of self-reflection, as had Kant and Fichte, the young Hegel saw Spirit as a product of human interaction:

Spirit is not the fundament underlying the subjectivity of the self in self-consciousness, but rather the medium *within* which one "I" communicates with another "I," and *from* which, as an absolute mediation, the two mutually form each other into subjects.[54]

Moreover, Habermas argued, the young Hegel understood the formative process of the Spirit as occurring through three separate media, which could be distinguished for analytic purposes: symbolic representation or language, labor or the control of nature, and interaction or the struggle for recognition. Although Hegel posited the interpenetration of all three in the general *Bildungsprozess*, he resisted conceptualizing it in terms of any one. Attempts by subsequent thinkers to elevate one over the others were thus misinterpretations of Hegel's intentions. Ernst Cassirer, for example, had wrongly reduced the process to the dialectic of representation, whereas Theodor Litt had made it a function of the struggle for recogni-

52. Heller, "The Positivism Dispute as a Turning Point in German Post-War Theory," p. 54. Heller goes too far, however, in asserting in her later essay, "Habermas and Marxism" (Thompson and Held, eds., *Habermas: Critical Debates*, p. 22) that Habermas has entirely given up the category of totality. As this chapter tries to show, he only abandoned its Lukácsian version.
53. Habermas, reprinted in *Technik und Wissenschaft als Ideologie* (Frankfurt, 1969) and in the English translation of *Theory and Practice*, from which the following quotations are cited.
54. Ibid., p. 145.

tion. A third misinterpretation, Habermas contended, could be found among Hegelian Marxists:

Georg Lukács interprets the movement of intellectual development from Kant to Hegel along the guideline presented by the dialectic of labor, which at the same time guarantees the materialistic unity of subject and object in the world-historical formative process of the human species.[55]

Marx himself, Habermas concluded his essay, had also failed to maintain the distinction in all of his works. In *The German Ideology* in particular, "Marx does not actually explicate the interrelationship of interaction and labor, but instead, under the unspecific title of social praxis, reduces the one to the other, namely: communicative action to instrumental action."[56] Here began that later scientistic reading of Marx's work which ran through orthodox Marxism and led to the reduction of socialism to the socialization of the economy. This was a fundamental error because "*liberation from hunger and misery* does not necessarily converge with *liberation from servitude and degradation*, for there is no automatic developmental relation between labor and interaction."[57] To be sure, there was a relation between them of some sort, but Habermas, much to the chagrin of many of his critics,[58] chose not to spell it out. The main energy in his essay was directed towards emphasizing the heterogeneity of the formative process rather than finding a way to reintegrate it on a higher level.

In thus questioning the monological uniformity of the Absolute Spirit and its Hegelian Marxist surrogates, Habermas, it can be argued, was very much in the tradition of classical Critical Theory with its distrust of

---

55. Ibid., p. 157.
56. Ibid., pp. 168–169. This critique of Marx was expanded in *Knowledge and Human Interests*, trans. Jeremy J. Shapiro (Boston, 1971); and in Albrecht Wellmer, *Critical Theory of Society*, trans. John Cumming (New York, 1971).
57. Habermas, *Theory and Practice*, p. 169.
58. See, for example, Richard Winfield, "The Dilemma of Labor," *Telos* 24 (Summer 1975); John Keane, "Habermas on Work and Interaction," *New German Critique* 6 (Fall 1975); Ron Eyerman and David Shipway, "Habermas on Work and Culture," *Theory and Society* 10, 4 (July 1981); and Anthony Giddens, "Labour and Interaction" in Thompson and Held, eds., *Habermas: Critical Debates*. In his postscript to the revised edition of *Knowledge and Human Interests* (in English in *Philosophy and the Social Sciences* 3 [1973]), Habermas replied to the criticism that he overly separated work and interaction: "I do not mind at all *calling* both phenomena praxis. Nor do I deny that normally instrumental action is embedded communicative action (productive action is socially organized, in general). But I see no reason why we should not adequately *analyze* a complex, i.e., dissect it into its parts" (p. 186). But it was more the problem of how the complex would then be dialectically reunited that troubled many of his critics. See also the further clarification of the point in his reply in Thompson and Held, p. 263f.

first principles and philosophies of origin. And his pluralization of the *Bildungsprozess* might also be seen as echoing Adorno's stress on non-identity. But whereas the earlier Critical Theorists, at least Adorno, had generalized non-identity into a protest against positive dialectics of any kind, Habermas restored the possibility of such a dialectics within the sub-process of symbolically mediated interaction (which in his later work absorbed the Hegelian distinction between language and recognition). The basis for this positive turn was his belief, already expressed in his earlier analysis of the public sphere, in the possibility of meaningful intersubjective communication. Adorno had denounced such a hope as ideological in several places in his work,[59] and in adopting it, Habermas was going outside the Frankfurt School to draw on two alternative traditions. The first, which was within Western Marxism itself, had counterposed intersubjectivity to the monological, self-sufficient subject, whether individual or collective. Here Merleau-Ponty, whose example Habermas acknowledged, and Gramsci, whose he did not,[60] were the primary figures.

The second tradition was outside of Marxism and indeed was often self-consciously construed as anti-materialist. Paradoxically, Heidegger, for whose politics Habermas had little patience, was its unacknowledged source, thus providing yet another stimulus to Western Marxist holism beyond those mentioned in earlier chapters. It was, to be more precise, from two of Heidegger's most notable students, Hannah Arendt and Hans-Georg Gadamer, that Habermas drew his direct inspiration. Combined by him with Schutz's social interpretation of Husserl's *Lebenswelt*,[61] their work provided the foundation for that hermeneutical response to positivism which we have seen him employ in his entry in the Positivist Dispute. They also instilled in him an awareness of the old Aristotelian distinction between *techne* and *praxis*, which he invoked as early as his book on the public sphere.[62] Although Habermas had fundamental

59. See, for example, Adorno, *Minima Moralia: Reflections from Damaged Life*, trans. E. P. H. Jephcott (London, 1974), p. 101, where he refers to "the advocates of communicability as traitors to what they communicate." Habermas, however, claims that Adorno's use of Eichendorff's notion of "distant nearness" in *Minima Moralia* means "he returns to categories of intersubjectivity from which he philosophically abstains" ("The Dialectics of Rationalization: An Interview with Jürgen Habermas," p. 9, and *Theorie des kommunikativen Handelns*, vol. 1: *Handlungsrationalität und gesellschaftliche Rationalisierung* [Frankfurt, 1981], p. 523).

60. Conversation with Habermas, Starnberg, December, 1980.

61. Habermas discusses his debt to Schutz in "On the German-Jewish Heritage," *Telos* 44 (Summer 1980). For a useful summary of Schutz's work, see Richard J. Bernstein, *The Restructuring of Social and Political Theory* (Pennsylvania, 1978), part 3. Habermas' most extensive use of the concept of *Lebenswelt* comes in *Theorie des kommunikativen Handelns*, chapter 6.

62. Habermas, *Strukturwandel der Öffentlichkeit*, pp. 14 and 20. See also *Theory and Practice*, p. 286.

disagreements with both Arendt and Gadamer, largely centering on what he saw as the non-critical, even irrationalist implications of their theories,[63] he fully agreed with their refusal to reduce politics to technical administration or power to force. Instead, he followed their lead in embracing Aristotle's concept of *phronesis* as the proper model for the political realm, where a prudent consideration of alternatives should be carried out through an uncoerced process of discursive reasoning.

Habermas' integration of hermeneutics into his variant of Critical Theory might be seen as the first of a series of syncretic (or, if a less pejorative term is preferred, synthetic)[64] moves on his part in the cause of reconstructing Marxist holism. Heidegger, Schutz, Gadamer and Arendt were useful only up to a certain point. Although phenomenology and hermeneutics were holistic in their stress on the prior givenness of an already meaningfully constituted context for human action and thought—the famous hermeneutic circle in which parts illuminated wholes and vice versa—they provided no real criteria to move beyond an interpretive description of the whole to a critique of its oppressive dimensions.[65] What Habermas thus needed to remain a genuinely Critical Theorist was a way to escape the relativistic implications of a pure hermeneutics without, however, regressing to a discredited Hegelian rationalism. The initial attempt he made to find the answer came in the late 1960s, first in his inaugural address as Professor of Philosophy and Sociology in Frankfurt in

63. For Habermas' critique of Arendt, see "Hannah Arendt's Communications Concept of Power," *Social Research* 44, 1 (Spring 1977). He draws on her distinction between force (*Gewalt*) and power (*Macht*) in his contribution to Thompson and Held, p. 268. His more extensive criticism of Gadamer can be found in his review of *Truth and Method* in Fred Dallmayr and Thomas McCarthy, eds., *Understanding Social Inquiry* (South Bend, Ind., 1977) and the exchange between the two in *Continuum* 8, 1 and 2 (Spring–Summer 1970). For discussions of their dispute, see Dieter Misgeld, "Critical Theory: The Debate Between Habermas and Gadamer" in O'Neill, ed., *On Critical Theory*; Anthony Giddens, *Studies in Social and Political Theory* (London, 1977); David Couzens Hoy, *The Critical Circle: Literature and History in Contemporary Hermeneutics* (Berkeley, 1978); Jack Mendelson, "The Habermas–Gadamer Debate," *New German Critique* 18 (Fall 1979); the special issue of *Cultural Hermeneutics* 2, 4 (February 1975); and Martin Jay, "Should Intellectual History Take a Linguistic Turn? Reflections on the Habermas–Gadamer Debate" in Dominick LaCapra and Steven L. Kaplan, *Modern European Intellectual History: Reappraisals and New Perspectives* (Ithaca, 1982). There are also interesting observations on the debate in Richard Rorty, *Philosophy and the Mirror of Nature* (Princeton, 1979).

64. Therborn's article cited in note 8 uses the term "eclecticism," as does Held, *Introduction to Critical Theory*, p. 253. For Habermas' attempt to argue that he really is trying to synthesize a relatively small number of theories, see his interview with Horster and van Reijen in *New German Critique*, pp. 40–41.

65. In fact, one recent defender of a Heideggerian holism, Hubert L. Dreyfus, goes so far as to argue that beneath the theoretical whole of beliefs and presuppositions, there is an even more fundamental context of unexamined micro-practices, which are still less amenable to rational reflection. The result, faced unflinchingly by Dreyfus, is a kind of "practical nihilism." "Holism and Hermeneutics," *Review of Metaphysics* 34, 1 (September 1980), p. 19. For another treatment of holism in Gadamer, see Hoy, pp. 44–45.

1965 and then more extensively in *Knowledge and Human Interests,* published in 1968.[66] It was in these works that he spelled out his theory of three "anthropological"[67] interests which underlie all human cognition, interests which therefore could be used as constants against which the current status of human development might be measured.

Knowledge and Human Interest occasioned a very vigorous critical response,[68] whose intricacies need not concern us now, especially as Habermas' later position reflected movement away from the more vulnerable aspects of his position. But insofar as the book can be considered a way station on the road to his reconstruction of Marxist holism, the following points need to be made. Although the major burden of Habermas' argument was directed against positivism and the positivist residue in orthodox Marxism, it was also implicitly aimed at that cul-de-sac into which Adorno had taken Critical Theory. To the extent that the older generation of the Frankfurt School still held on to a watered-down Hegelian notion of reason, but no longer felt confident that history was the likely arena for its realization, they withdrew into that defensive posture Lukács had scornfully characterized as residence in the "Grand Hotel Abyss."[69] In order to relocate Critical Theory at a less melancholic address, Habermas attempted to rethink its epistemological foundation.

The groundwork for his argument had already been laid in his essay on the young Hegel, where he stressed the historical formation of the Spirit. In his 1965 inaugural address, he made a similar point against Kant's ahistorical notion of the subject: "*The achievements of the transcendental subject have their basis in the natural history of the human species.*"[70] But that history, he emphasized, was not randomly motivated. Instead, there were three basic cognitive interests that spurred human action: a technical interest in the instrumental control of nature, a practical interest in the maintenance of intersubjective communication, and an emancipatory in-

66. The inaugural address is included as an appendix to the English translation of *Knowledge and Human Interests.*

67. Anthropology is meant in the German sense of "philosophical anthropology." For a selection of Habermas' reflections on this subject, see the second section of *Kultur und Kritik.* See also Wolf Lepenies, "Anthropology and Social Criticism," *The Human Context* 3 (July 1971), for a comparison of the anthropologies of Habermas and Arnold Gehlen.

68. For a bibliography of the relevant articles and books, see the list appended to the English translation of the postscript to *Knowledge and Human Interests.* The main issues of the controversy are acutely summarized in Fred R. Dallmayr, "Critical Theory Criticized: Habermas's *Knowledge and Human Interests* and its Aftermath," *Philosophy of the Social Sciences* 2 (1972). See also Fred R. Dallmayr, ed., *Materielen zu Habermas' "Erkenntnis und Interesse"* (Frankfurt, 1971).

69. Lukács, 1962 preface to *The Theory of the Novel: A Historical-Philosophical Essay on the Forms of Great Epic Literature,* trans. Anna Bostock (Cambridge, Mass., 1971), p. 22.

70. Habermas, *Knowledge and Human Interests,* p. 312.

terest in the overthrow of exploitative relations of power and illegitimate social constraints. Whereas traditional theory, in Horkheimer's sense, had isolated knowledge as an end in itself, a truly critical theory recognized the intimate connection between cognition and interest, or to put it differently, theory and practice.

Habermas, however, had some difficulty formulating the precise status of the three interests. Although they derived from man's nature and were in this sense anthropological, they also were related to the increasing break with the purely natural, called culture. Although they were in part transcendental because they were an a priori presupposition of all knowledge, they were nonetheless also empirical because they developed only in the historical process of species formation.[71] Although in one sense equal in their relative autonomy, in another they were not, because the third interest in emancipation was ultimately derived from the other two.[72]

The emancipatory interest was in fact both the most problematical of the three and the most important. Without it, Habermas would have no real way out of the relativism of pure hermeneutics, but it covertly drew, as Habermas' critics were quick to point out,[73] on an undefended idealist identification of reason and will. Habermas, to be sure, had insisted that he had escaped idealism by emphasizing that the possibility for actual human emancipation was dependent on concrete material conditions in history, but his detractors were not silenced by the example he offered of an already established emancipatory practice, which he claimed could be found in Freudian psychoanalysis.

Habermas' use of Freud was enormously suggestive in many ways and marked a clear departure from earlier attempts to harness psychoanalysis for Marxist purposes, including those of the Frankfurt School. Instead of invoking it as a justification for the non-identity of the social and psychological, as had Adorno, or refashioning it into a theory of libidinal utopia, both remembered and potential, as had Marcuse, Habermas saw it essentially as a methodological model of personal ideology critique, which

71. The phrase Habermas used to cover over this ambiguity was "quasi-transcendental," which he later admitted was "a product of an embarrassment which points to more problems than it solves" (*Theory and Practice*, p. 14). Albrecht Wellmer has argued that the categories were more asymmetrical than Habermas first realized, instrumental action being transcendental in Kant's sense, but communicative action being more empirical. See his discussion in "Communications and Emancipation: Reflections on the Linguistic Turn in Critical Theory" in O'Neill, *On Critical Theory*, p. 252. From the point of view of hermeneutic critics of Habermas, he never successfully escaped his initial embarrassment, even after his linguistic turn. See, for example, David Couzens Hoy, "Taking History Seriously: Foucault, Gadamer, Habermas," *Union Seminary Quarterly Review* 34, 2 (Winter 1979).
72. Habermas conceded this point in his postscript to *Knowledge and Human Interests*, p. 176.
73. McCarthy, *The Critical Theory of Jürgen Habermas*, p. 95.

could then be extrapolated to the level of society. Less interested in the content of Freudian theory than in its role in therapeutic practice, he rejected the biologistic dimension of Freud's metapsychology as a scientistic misunderstanding of what really went on in the analyst's office. Neurotic symptom formation, he claimed, was due to internal communicative blockages—self-deceptions—which prevented the individual from knowing and being able to deal rationally with his unconscious feelings, impulses and desires. Psychoanalysis was a process of heightened insight on the part of the patient, whose self-reflection helped dissolve the pseudo-otherness of his symptoms, which controlled him as if they were externally determined.

But a purely hermeneutic process, Habermas cautioned, was not enough to relieve those symptoms. Instead, the added help of an explanatory theory or what Alfred Lorenzer had called a "depth hermeneutics"[74] had to be introduced by the analyst, who also served as the crucial focal point for a reenactment of the original conflict through the process of transference. "Analytic insight," Habermas argued, "complements a miscarried self-formative process, owing to a *compensatory learning process, which undoes processes of splitting-off.* ... The virtual totality that is sundered by splitting-off is represented by the model of pure communicative action."[75] In order to realize that model and thus dissolve the neurotic symptoms of the patient, both hermeneutic self-reflection and theoretical explanation had to be employed. The resulting knowledge had as its interest the patient's emancipation from his distress, a goal shared both by him and the analyst. The will to achieve rational understanding was thus a premise of the psychoanalytic process.

It was precisely the uncertain status of the will in social situations that caused Habermas' critics to question his move from psychoanalysis to "socioanalysis."[76] For whereas the patient and analyst shared an a priori interest in relieving the patient's neurotic symptoms, in society no such consensus could be assumed. Indeed, insofar as certain men or classes

74. Lorenzer, *Kritik des psychoanalytischen Symbolbegriffs* (Frankfurt, 1970) and *Sprachzerstörung und Rekonstruktion* (Frankfurt, 1970).
75. Habermas, *Knowledge and Human Interests,* p. 232.
76. This phrase is used by Therborn, "Jürgen Habermas: A New Eclecticism," p. 74, and Adamson, "Beyond 'Reform or Revolution,'" p. 443. For specific discussions of Habermas' use of psychoanalysis, see Christopher Nichols, "Science or Reflection: Habermas on Freud," *Philosophy of Social Sciences* 2 (September 1972); Donald McIntosh, "Habermas on Freud," *Social Research* 44, 3 (1972); and Keat, *The Politics of Social Theory.* The most frequent complaint against Habermas' use of Freud is that his overly intellectual reading of the psyche fails to consider the power of drives or instincts. This argument is congruent with the further complaint that Habermas underestimates the role of needs in motivating human action. See Agnes Heller, "Habermas and Marxism" in Thompson and Held, *Habermas: Critical Debates*; and Habermas' reply in the same volume.

benefited from the maintenance of ideological distortion and exploitative power relations, there was no reason to assume they would willingly enter the process of dialogic enlightenment suggested by the psychoanalytic model. Nor would their improved understanding of reality necessarily generate a desire to transform it. Symmetrical relations in a truly democratic public sphere could not be seen as a condition for social change, when in fact they were one of its goals.

In several restatements of his position,[77] Habermas admitted the force of his critics' arguments by introducing two new distinctions which in effect subdivided the emancipatory cognitive interest into three parts: rational reconstruction, self-reflection and strategic action. Self-reflection, he conceded to those who questioned his premature conflation of reason and will, was not equivalent either to politically necessary strategies of manipulation or the rational reconstruction of anonymous rule systems. The latter, for example Chomsky's notion of linguistic competence, were explications of intuitive capacities based on underlying structures. Because they were posterior reconstructions of those structures, they were neither purely a priori deductions nor a posteriori inductions. The quasi-transcendental embarrassment of the theory of interests could then be overcome without succumbing to hermeneutic relativism. Whereas self-reflection was intimately tied to practice, rational reconstruction, however, was not:

Self-reflection leads to insight due to the fact that what has previously been unconscious is made conscious in a manner rich in practical consequences: analytic insights intervene in life, if I may borrow this dramatic phrase from Wittgenstein. A successful reconstruction also raises an "unconsciously" functioning rule system to consciousness in a certain manner; it renders explicit the intuitive knowledge that is given with competence with respect to the rules in the form of "know how." But this theoretical knowledge has no practical consequences.[78]

Rational reconstruction, therefore, was closer to a traditional than to a critical theory in its admitted separation of reason from will, theory from practice. To the extent, however, that such rational reconstruction, like Freud's metapsychology, might enter into the process of self-reflection, they do have an "indirect relation to the emancipatory interest of knowledge."[79] But one inadvertent implication of Habermas' new distinction

---

77. In addition to the postscript of 1973, he also returned to the issues of the book in his foreword to the second edition of *Theorie und Praxis* in 1971.

78. Habermas, *Theory and Practice*, p. 23. For a discussion of problems in the notion of rational reconstruction, see Mary B. Hesse, "Science and Objectivity," in Thompson and Held.

79. Habermas, *Theory and Practice*, p. 24.

was a widening of the gap between theory and practice which unintentionally revived the dilemma of classical Critical Theory in its last years.

In response to the criticism of his social reading of psychoanalysis, Habermas introduced a second new distinction, which widened that gap still
further. Not only was emancipatory self-reflection to be separated from
rational reconstruction, it also had to be distinguished from strategic
action in which material interests objectively clashed. The latter had an
inescapably instrumental dimension, although its ultimate goal was to
foster expanded communicative interaction. The process of enlightenment was therefore not equivalent to political struggle in all its forms:

A reflexive theory can only be applied without contradiction under the conditions
of enlightenment and not those of strategic action. This difference is explicable as
a consequence of the retrospective posture of reflection. . . . The practical consequences of self-reflection are changes in attitude which result from insight into the
causalities *in the past*, and indeed result of themselves. In contrast, strategic action
oriented toward the future, which is prepared for in the internal discussion of
groups, who (as the avant-garde) presuppose for themselves already successfully
completed processes of enlightenment, cannot be justified in the same manner by
reflective knowledge.[80]

Habermas, however, was loath to turn this implicit defense of some
strategic instrumentalism into a justification for a Leninist avant-garde
party, which would claim a monopoly of both enlightening and strategic
practices. Indeed, against Oskar Negt's attempt to find an organizational
structure to include both,[81] Habermas argued that a certain tension between the two was healthy: "The autonomy of theory and enlightenment,
however, is required for the sake of the independence of political action."[82]
And he warned against assuming that those who engage in strategic
action can justify their superiority over their opponents with the same
validity that participants in a self-reflective process of consensus formation can claim for their decisions:

That the strategic action of those who have decided to engage in struggle, and that
means to take risks, can be interpreted hypothetically as a retrospection which is
possible only in anticipation, but at the same time not *compellingly justified* on
this level with the aid of a reflexive theory, has its good reason: the vindicating
superiority of those who do the enlightening over those who are to be enlightened
is theoretically unavoidable, but at the same time it is fictive and requires self-
correction: in a process of enlightenment there can only be participants.[83]

80. Ibid., p. 38–39.
81. Oskar Negt, *Politik als Protest* (Frankfurt, 1971).
82. Habermas, *Theory and Practice*, p. 36.
83. Ibid., p. 40.

This increased categorical complexity had several implications for Habermas' reconstitution of Marxist holism. By separating rational reconstruction from self-reflection and both from strategic action in the way that he now did, he further undermined the earlier Western Marxist reliance on Vico's *verum–factum* principle as the epistemological foundation of an expressive totality. Habermas did not, of course, deny the power of self-reflective knowledge, but he now more clearly than ever distinguished it from other cognitive modes. Secondly, his acknowledgement that reflexivity was basically past-oriented, which drew him closer than before to the classical Critical Theory emphasis on the liberating power of anamnesis,[84] meant that he needed a stronger source for the future-oriented emancipatory interest than he had developed. The normative dimension of his new concept of totality had to be grounded with greater acuity than he had managed in his work to date.

Knowledge and Human Interests can therefore be accounted as only a partially successful attempt to reconstruct Western Marxist holism along non-Lukácsian lines. In fact, Habermas' full emancipation from an expressive holism did not take place until he assimilated four more non-Marxist influences into his grand synthesis: sociological systems theory, which helped him reformulate his latitudinal notion of totality; psychological learning theory, which allowed him to recast his longitudinal concept of totality; the linguistic turn in Anglo-American philosophy, which helped him to develop a non-transcendental normative concept of totality; and the sociological tradition of modernization from Weber to Parsons, which provided him with more than a purely linguistic basis for his normative standards. Taking each in turn, we can grasp how extensive Habermas' reconstruction of Western Marxist holism actually came to be.

If the Positivist Dispute began to wean Habermas away from his earlier neo-Hegelian view of totality, a second debate, which some commentators have seen as a less acrimonious continuation of the first, furthered the process. Here even more obviously than in his confrontation with Popper and Albert, Habermas absorbed some of the arguments of his opponent. The debate in question took place between Habermas and the major German

84. John O'Neill's contrast between Marcuse and Habermas on their respective uses of memory seems to me overdrawn, if one takes into account Habermas' linkage of reflection and memory in the foreword to *Theory and Practice*. See O'Neill's remarks in "Critique and Remembrance," in *On Critical Theory*, pp. 3–4. Keat, in fact, taxes Habermas for relying too much on memory in his equation of psychoanalytic healing with freedom from idealized distortion (*The Politics of Social Theory*, p. 179).

spokesman for systems theory, Niklas Luhmann, from 1968 to 1973.[85] Coming to prominence at about the same time structuralism was popular in France, systems theory appeared as the most advanced expression of that long-standing desire to understand society scientifically, with the same tools used to make sense of nature. Combining cybernetics with informa- tion and organizational theory, its advocates promised a new paradigm that would be applicable to a wide range of problems in everything from biology to international relations. Habermas, in the Critical Theory tradition, was at first deeply opposed to such an approach in which the instrumental inter- est entirely overshadowed the communicative and emancipatory.

But, as we have seen in his qualified acceptance of hermeneutics, he was always critical of a purely action-theory, intersubjectivist view of so- ciety. In both his debates with the positivists and Gadamer, Habermas had argued against a purely *Verstehen* approach to social analysis for rea- sons he made clear in *On the Logic of the Social Sciences*[86] and his discus- sion of psychoanalysis in *Knowledge and Human Interests*. Luhmann, to be sure, had gone too far in the opposite direction and tried to dismiss the intersubjective dimension of society entirely. The result was that, like Talcott Parsons and other sociological functionalists before him, he tended to accept the current social whole as a given and focus only on questions of its increased technical manipulation. His tacit reliance on biological models of life and death also begged the question of how one might establish the identity of a social whole and thus judge whether it ended or was transformed. Only a social action theory that acknowl- edged the normative basis of societies, Habermas argued, could make such an understanding possible. Societies had to be understood as more than cybernetic information systems designed to decrease environmental complexity by an increase in their own differentiation. Turning Marxism into a variant of systems theory, as in fact was being urged by certain East German theorists at the time,[87] would be to reduce it to a pseudo-science of legitimation in which a managerial elite ruled undemocratically.

85. Habermas and Niklas Luhmann, *Theorie der Gesellschaft oder Sozialtechnolo- gie–Was leistet die Systemforschung?* (Frankfurt, 1971). The debate sparked three other collections of essays: Franz Maciejewski, ed., *Theorie der Gesellschaft oder Sozialtechnolo- gie: Supplement I* (Frankfurt, 1973); *Supplement II* (Frankfurt, 1974); and *Supplement III* (Frankfurt, 1975). For a summary of the debate, see Friedrich W. Sixel, "The Problem of Sense: Habermas v. Luhmann" in O'Neill, ed., *On Critical Theory*. For general summaries of systems theory, see Ludwig von Bertalanffy, *General Systems Theory* (London, 1968), and Walter Buckley, *Sociology and Systems Theory* (Englewood Cliffs, New Jersey, 1967). For more recent literature on the subject, see the annotated bibliographies in Scott G. McNall, ed., *Theoretical Perspectives in Sociology* (New York, 1979).
86. Habermas, *Zur Logik der Sozialwissenschaften* (Frankfurt, 1970).
87. For a discussion of the East German appropriation of systems theory, see Peter C. Ludz, "Marxism and Systems Theory in a Bureaucratic Society," *Social Research* 42, 4 (Win- ter 1975).

And yet, Habermas conceded, Luhmann was not altogether wrong in conceptualizing certain aspects of society in system-theoretic terms. In *Legitimation Crisis*,[88] published in 1973, Habermas distinguished between two forms of integration, which he called social and system:

We speak of social integration in relation to the systems of institutions in which speaking and acting subjects are socially related [*vergesellschaftet*]. Social systems are seen here as *life-worlds* that are symbolically structured. We speak of system integration with a view to the specific steering performances of a self-regulated *system*. Social systems are considered here from the point of view of their capacity to maintain their boundaries and their continued existence by mastering the complexity of an inconstant environment. Both paradigms, life-world and system, are important. The problem is to demonstrate their interconnection.[89]

The ultimate nature of that connection, Habermas contended, was hierarchical in the sense that the life-world exists before its transformation into an alienated system and persists even after that has occurred, in the same way that pre-reflective hermeneutic discourse precedes and underlies scientific discourse.

In so arguing, Habermas was restating the older Lukácsian notions of reification and society as "second nature" in contemporary language.[90] The systemic quality of much contemporary life was an expression of the alienation of the intersubjective life-world into seemingly natural objectifications, which appeared to be self-regulating processes. But unlike Lukács, he held back from suggesting that the complete reabsorption of system integration into social integration was a likely possibility. If, as he had contended in his earlier work, the dialectic of labor and the dialectic of symbolically mediated interaction were relatively autonomous, so too system and social integration resisted reduction to a common denominator. Although it was incorrect to follow Luhmann in turning the entire history of the species into the progressive mastery of environmental complexity, such a project was indeed part of human development. Another way to make this point, Habermas suggested, was to recognize that the species learns in two different dimensions, theoretical and practical. "The development of productive forces and the alteration of normative structures," he claimed, "follow, respectively, logics of growing theoretical and practical insight."[91]

88. See note 24. Some of Habermas' critics argued that he was much too uncritical in his appropriation of Luhmann's position. See, for example, Dick Howard, *The Marxian Legacy* (New York, 1977), p. 134, and Dominick LaCapra, "Habermas and the Grounding of Critical Theory," *History and Theory* 16, 3 (1977), p. 246.

89. Habermas, *Legitimation Crisis*, p. 4.

90. Habermas' continued adherence to this Lukácsian formula, at least insofar as it referred to the process of self-reflection, is made clear in his postscript to *Knowledge and Human Interests*, pp. 176 and 183.

91. Habermas, *Legitimation Crisis*, p. 14.

Legitimation Crisis was dedicated to demonstrating how unresolved crises in one mode of development influenced the other. Through a series of displacements, the crisis in the capitalist economy had been relocated in other levels of the social whole: first the level of politics, where a rationality or steering crisis ensued, then the level of social integration, where a motivational crisis followed, and finally, back in the political system, where a legitimation crisis resulted. Precisely how Habermas worked out this series of displacements or what his critics thought of his success need not concern us now. What is important for our purposes is that by incorporating Luhmann's systems theory into his own work he reformulated the latitudinal concept of totality for advanced capitalist society. Without acknowledging the parallel, he came close to replicating Althusser's notion of a decentered whole in which no one level was the basic determinant of the others. The difference, of course, was that he persisted in conceiving of one of the levels, that of social integration, in intersubjective terms, rather than reducing all of them to structural "practices" without any subjective determination. And insofar as this level was originally "superordinate"[92] to that of system integration, there was still some hope for the reversal of the present domination of instrumental rationality.

In addition to reformulating the latitudinal notion of totality, Habermas also reconstructed its longitudinal counterpart. Although earlier, essentially Hegelian notions of history as a universally coherent process of development were indefensible, it was nonetheless possible to construct an alternative that would avoid the equally disastrous mistake of seeing history as utterly without direction (or, perhaps worse, making it into a process of decline, as did Benjamin and Adorno in their more saturnine moods). Specifically rejecting what he saw as an anti-evolutionary view of history in the older Frankfurt School,[93] Habermas gingerly called for what he termed a "differential concept of progress" that "does not inhibit courage, but rather ensures that political action can hit its mark with greater accuracy."[94] To make his case that such a concept was possible, he had, in effect, to rewrite Kant's "Universal History from a Cosmopolitan Point of View" in terms that would convince survivors of Auschwitz, Hiroshima and the Gulag Archipelago.

As elsewhere in his work, his strategy was to pluralize rather than prematurely unify. "Among Hegelian Marxists like Lukács, Korsch, and Adorno," he complained, "the concept of social totality excludes a model

92. Ibid.
93. This is made most clear in "Consciousness-Raising or Redemptive Criticism: The Contemporaneity of Walter Benjamin."
94. Ibid., p. 59.

of levels,"[95] but it was only by appreciating the different levels of historical change that the concept of progress could be salvaged. It was incorrect, therefore, to see instrumental rationality, or in Luhmann's terms, the systemic reduction of environmental complexity, as the sole determinant of the historical process. However much it may have come to dominate the current social whole it never totally replaced other developmental tendencies. Similarly, it was wrong of orthodox Marxists to privilege the mode of production as the single motor of history. To equate the base or substructure of society always with the economy was mistaken, as Lukács had pointed out in *History and Class Consciousness*, even though the equation did characterize capitalism. In fact, Habermas argued, what originally distinguished man from his animal ancestors was less his ability to work on the world, which the transitional hominids had been able to do, than his creation of a kinship and familial system. Thus, both production and socialization, labor and communicative interaction, are fundamental to human development and should be understood as following related, but somewhat autonomous, historical patterns.

Because it no longer posited a unifying expressive origin for the historical process, a reconstructed historical materialism would avoid the problems besetting previous philosophies of history:

The *dogmatic version* of the concept of a history of the species shares a number of weaknesses with eighteenth-century designs for a philosophy of history. The course of previous world history, which evidences a sequence of five or six modes of production, sets down the *unilinear, necessary, uninterrupted, and progressive development of a macrosubject*. I should like to oppose to this model of species history a weaker version, which is not open to the familiar criticisms of the objectivism of philosophy of history.[96]

Habermas' "weaker version" demonstrated how much he had learned from Luhmann and from structuralist Marxists like Maurice Godelier, whose arguments he found fully compatible with Adorno's critique of a philosophy of origins:

Historical materialism does not need to assume a *species-subject* that undergoes evolution. The bearers of evolution are rather societies and the acting subjects

95. Habermas, *Communication and the Evolution of Society*, p. 143. Elsewhere, however, Habermas warned against too pluralized a concept of levels. In "Über das Subjekt der Geschichte: Diskussionsbemerkung zu falsch gestellten Alternativen," he wrote:

The collective singular of history cannot be eliminated through plural formation (*Bildung*). There are indicators that suggest that today the unity of history on this globe (and around it) is a reality, or to be sure—has *become* a reality. The unity of history is a result and not guaranteed from the beginning through a formative process of a self-producing subject. To be sure, this antagonistic world society, which is preparing itself, is the result of developments that follow the model of a hierarchical differentiation of basic structures. (p.396)

96. Habermas, *Communication and the Evolution of Society*, p. 139.

integrated into them: social evolution can be discerned in those structures that are replaced by more comprehensive structures in accord with a pattern that is to be rationally reconstructed.[97]

Moreover, the full achievement of a socialist society would not bring into existence an expressive meta-subject of the kind posited by Hegelian Marxism (and defended as a useful fiction by Habermas in his 1960 essay, "Between Philosophy and Science: Marxism as Critique"):

Even if social evolution should point in the direction of unified individuals consciously influencing the course of their own evolution, there would not arise any large-scale subjects, but at most self-established, higher-level, intersubjective commonalities.[98]

But however much Habermas may have accepted certain of the arguments of Luhmann and the Althusserians, he was still anxious to avoid their anti-normative, anti-humanist, anti-intersubjectivist bias. He discovered the antidote exactly where Lucien Goldmann had found it a generation before:

The stimulus that encouraged me to bring normative structures into a developmental-logical problematic came from the *genetic structuralism* of Jean Piaget as well, thus from a conception that has overcome the traditional structuralist front against evolution and that has assimilated motifs of the theory of knowledge from Kant to Pierce.[99]

Habermas, however, went beyond Goldmann in using Piaget to purge the decisionist residue in historical materialism, which Goldmann had seen as parallel to Pascal's wager on God. Bracketing the question of Piaget's possible bias as a psychologist of only Western development,[100] he contended that the process of individual cognitive maturation described in his work could be extrapolated to the species as a whole. Ontogenetic

97. Ibid., p. 140. Earlier, on p. 124, Habermas specifically credited Marxists like Godelier for teaching him something: "They have re-thought the base-superstructure relationship and conceptualized it in such a way that the proper contribution of normative structures can be saved from a reductionist short-circuiting."

98. Ibid., p. 140. For an argument that says Habermas never fully frees himself from the belief in a unified world history with mankind as its subject, see Connerton, *The Tragedy of Enlightenment*, p. 115. Connerton's main piece of evidence, however, comes from the 1965 inaugural address, before Habermas had fully worked through his early Hegelianism.

99. Habermas, *Communication and the Evolution of Society*, p. 124–25, where Habermas credited Goldmann for having seen the importance of Piaget first. What he did not choose to accept was the innatism he saw in Piaget's work. See the postscript to *Knowledge and Human Interests*, p. 184, where he compared Piaget and Chomsky on this point.

100. For discussions of these questions, see Susan Buck-Morss, "Socio-economic Bias in Piaget's Theory and its Implications for Cross-Cultural Studies," *Human Development* 18 (1975); and Thomas McCarthy, "Rationality and Relativism: Habermas's 'Overcoming' of Hermeneutics," in Thompson and Held, *Habermas: Critical Debates*, p. 68f.

development was thus a model for phylogenetic development, as Piaget himself had sometimes suggested.[101] There were homologies, Habermas argued, between the structure of the ego and collective world-views, just as there were between ego identity and group identity.

Cognitive development, moreover, took place not merely in instrumental terms, but in moral ones as well. "The species learns," Habermas suggested,

not only in the dimension of technically useful knowledge decisive for the development of productive forces but also in the dimension of moral-practical consciousness decisive for structures of interaction. The rules of communicative action do develop in reaction to changes in the domain of instrumental and strategic action; but in doing so they follow *their own logic.*[102]

To spell out just what this logic might be, Habermas relied not only on Piaget, but also on the work of the psychologists Lawrence Kohlberg and Jane Loevinger.[103] In so doing, he recognized that he was violating one of the essential taboos of classical Critical Theory:

Adorno, despite his Hegelianism, distrusted the concept of a developmental logic because he held the openness and the initiative of the historical process (of the species as well as the individual) to be incompatible with the closed nature of an evolutionary pattern.[104]

But although worth taking seriously, Adorno's warning could "grant no dispensation from the duty of justifying concepts with a critical intent."[105]

To fulfill that duty, Habermas spun out a highly abstract and complicated schema, often with the help of intricate charts, whose details cannot concern us now.[106] Because he insisted that a great deal of empirical work needed to be done to confirm its validity, it is clear that its status even in his mind was only provisional. Nor was Habermas trying to argue that the

101. Piaget, *Biology and Knowledge* (Chicago, 1971), pp. 359–60. For another recent attempt to use Piaget as a model for collective cognitive development, this time in artistic terms, see Suzi Gablik, *Progress in Art* (New York, 1977). The appropriateness of making ontogenesis into an independent variable has been questioned by Heller, "Habermas and Marxism," p. 38f.

102. Habermas, *Communication and the Evolution of Society*, p. 148.

103. For a bibliography of the various articles by Kohlberg and Loevinger, as well as by other developmental psychologists, drawn on by Habermas, see *Communication and the Evolution of Society*, pp. 220–21. For a comparison of Kohlberg and Habermas, see Herbert G. Reid and Ernest J. Yanarella, "Critical Political Theory and Moral Development: On Kohlberg, Hampden-Turner, and Habermas," *Theory and Society* 4, 4 (Winter 1977).

104. Habermas, *Communication and the Evolution of Society*, p. 72.

105. Ibid.

106. The relevant essays in *Communication and the Evolution of Society* are "Moral Development and Ego Identity" and "Historical Materialism and the Development of Normative Structures." For a comment on the charts, see Dick Howard, "Moral Development and Ego Identity: A Clarification," *Telos* 27 (Spring 1976). For a general critique see Michael Schmid, "Habermas's Theory of Social Evolution" in Thompson and Held.

logic of instrumental and moral development he posited was a necessary pattern for historical development, either of the species as a whole or its individual components.

Although there was an echo of Lukács' use of Weber's category of "objective possibility"[107] in his argument, Habermas refrained from turning it into a Hegelian exercise in the differences between the "essential" and "apparent" course of history. Nor did he share Bloch's prophetic utopian belief that the present contained prefigural traces of a future totalization:

We could probably fictionally assume the standpoint of future historians and from their now anticipated horizon of expectation understand our future as their (future) past. A corresponding history of future pasts would, however, be fictitious, not a historical but a futuristic novel. Then the idea of a history of all possible histories, i.e., the hypothetical anticipation of history as a whole or the assumption of a totality of history, is incompatible with the narrative structure of history. Universal history too must limit itself to the reconstruction of the past; it has no prognostic content.[108]

In fact, Habermas even cautioned against conflating his evolutionary scheme with any strictly narrative account of the past, which would then come to have more of a unified and determined character than was justifiable. Nonetheless, analytic separation (as in the earlier cases of labor and interaction or the three cognitive interests) did not mean for Habermas total isolation. Both the rigid structuralist distinction between deep structures and surface events and the premature dialectical unification of the two were mistaken:

It seems useful to me to start with the interdependence of two countervailing causalities. If we distinguish the plane of structural possibilities (learning-levels) from the plane of factual processes, then the two causalities can be clarified with a change of explanatory perspectives. The emergence of a new historical event can be explained by reference to contingent peripheral conditions and to the challenge of *structurally open possibilities*. On the other hand, the emergence of a new structure of consciousness can be explained with reference to the developmental logic of the pattern of previous structures and to an *impulse given by problem-generating events*.[109]

Habermas' emphasis here on possibilities included regression as well as progression, barbarism as well as socialism. "New learning levels," he wrote, "mean not only widened ranges of options, but also a structural

107. For a comparison of Lukács' and Habermas' use of Weber, see Francis Hearn, "The Dialectical Use of Ideal-Types," *Theory and Society* 2, 4 (Winter 1975).
108. Habermas, "History and Evolution," *Telos* 39 (Spring 1979), pp. 10–11. For Habermas' argument that historians do treat the past as if it culminated in a present universal history, see *Zur Logik der Sozialwissenschaften*, p. 273.
109. Habermas, "History and Evolution," p. 31.

shortage of respectively new resources and that means new categories of burdens. Horkheimer and Adorno's *Dialectic of Enlightenment* deals with this."[110] There could therefore be no guarantee that an evolutionary logic will be followed by the species. "It is not evolutionary processes that are *irreversible* but the structural sequences that a society must run through *if* and *to the extent* that it is involved in evolution."[111]

Because of the weakened status of Habermas' reconstructed historical materialism, it could never function in the manner of its orthodox Marxist predecessor, as a theodicy justifying a complacent political quietism. In fact, and here Habermas remained true to his earlier concerns,

The time-diagnostic application of evolutionary theories is meaningful only in the framework of discursive will formation, that is, in a practical argumentation in which the issue is to give reasons why in a determined situation certain strategies and norms of action rather than others will be chosen by certain actors.[112]

Thus, although as we have seen Habermas' work after *Knowledge and Human Interests* displayed a growing awareness of the attenuated relationship between certain kinds of theory and practice, he never abandoned his hope that the links would be maintained.

What did, however, grow increasingly problematic, especially after his estrangement from the German New Left, was the character of the practitioners implied by his theory. As many commentators have complained, Habermas' delocalizing of the agent of history into the species as a whole made the socially specific addressee of his work highly uncertain. Even putting aside the inaccessibility of his abstruse and difficult writing for the average reader (a problem, to be sure, shared by all Western Marxists), the precise audience for whom he wrote remained unclear. He staunchly resisted efforts like those of Oskar Negt and Alexander Kluge to call for a specifically proletarian public sphere.[113] Although at times he spoke highly of the programs of certain groups, such as the Young Social Democrats (Jusos) in Germany,[114] and argued for a kind of "radical reformism" that would work through the institutions of present-day capitalism to challenge it from within, Habermas remained in the Critical Theory tradition of intellectual isolation from specific political movements. While

110. Ibid., p. 35.

111. Habermas, *Communication and the Evolution of Society*, p. 141.

112. Habermas, "History and Evolution," p. 44.

113. Negt and Kluge, *Öffentlichkeit und Erfahrung. Zur Organisationsanalyse von bürgerlichen und proletarischen Öffentlichkeit* (Frankfurt, 1972). For a discussion of the debate over the "public sphere," see Peter Uwe Hohendahl, "Critical Theory, Public Sphere and Culture: Jürgen Habermas and his Critics," *New German Critique* 16 (Winter 1979).

114. Interview with Boris Frankel, p. 53f. Habermas has, in fact, frequently commented on current political questions. See his *Kleine politische Schriften I–IV* (Frankfurt, 1981).

continuing to speak out on political issues, especially in response to the outrageous accusation that the Frankfurt School was responsible for the West German terrorists of the mid and late 1970s, he retained a certain cautious distance even toward the "new social movements" of the early 1980s.

Perhaps, as Jean Cohen has argued, Habermas should not be faulted for failing to locate a revolutionary agent insofar as "the task of his political theory is not to find such an agent, but rather to initiate a process of reflection on norms and to analyze objective contradictions and possible areas of tension and struggle."[115] But assuming that this process cannot be carried out by everyone at once, it is important to ask *who* the actual participants are likely to be.

One candidate has been proposed by Cornelis Disco, who draws on Alvin Gouldner's notion of the intellectuals as a "new class,"[116] to argue that Habermas "clearly casts mature cultural intellectuals, with Critical Theory as their guide, in the role of emancipatory saviors."[117] Disco overstates his case by ignoring Habermas' frequent admonitions to the Critical Theory to assume only an "advocacy role," rather than that of political leader.[118] Moreover, as we have seen, he insisted that "in a process of enlightenment there can only be participants." Still, there is a certain plausibility in Disco's charge, at least insofar as the actual audience Habermas has attracted to date obviously consists of many more academics and intellectuals than any other social group. Nor should this connection be surprising if we recall the close ties between the general discourse of totality and the social role of intellectuals discussed in our introduction.

It would, however, be erroneous to argue that Habermas' appeal to intellectuals somehow set him apart from the Marxist tradition, and Western Marxism in particular. Gramsci, it will be remembered, had con-

115. Jean Cohen, "Why More Political Theory?" *Telos* 40 (Summer 1979), p. 74. It is clear that insofar as Habermas rejects an expressive or monologic view of history, the idea of an agent of history is incompatible with his viewpoint. See, for example, his critique of Marx's notions of class consciousness, class interest and class action as illegitimate extrapolations from individual consciousness, interests and actions: "Über das Subjekt der Geschichte; Diskussionsbemerkung zu falsch gestellten Alternativen," p. 398.

116. Alvin W. Gouldner, *The Future of Intellectuals and the Rise of the New Class* (New York, 1979). For Gouldner's own critique of Habermas, see *The Dialectic of Ideology and Technology: The Origins, Grammar and Future of Ideology* (New York, 1976). For a defense of Habermas against Gouldner, see the review of the book by Ray Morrow in *Telos* 32 (Summer 1977).

117. Cornelis Disco, "Critical Theory as Ideology of the New Class: Reading Jürgen Habermas," *Theory and Society* 8, 2 (September 1979), p. 196. For a similar critique, see the review of *Legitimation Crisis* by James Miller in *Telos* 25 (Fall 1975), which is answered by Jeremy J. Shapiro in *Telos* 27 (Spring 1976). Habermas himself treats it, with reference to an attack by R. K. Maurer, in his reply in Thompson and Held, p. 238.

118. Habermas, *Legitimation Crisis*, p. 117.

tended that all men were inherently intellectuals, although in capitalist society not all fulfilled a specialized intellectual function.[119] Like Gramsci, Habermas hoped that the current elite status of intellectuals would not be a permanent condition. Indeed, his refusal to conflate the current intellectual elite with the political vanguard, a mistake Gramsci had made in calling the Communist Party the "collective intellectual," demonstrates his wariness about turning the intelligentsia into "the emancipatory saviors" of mankind.

Of course, it might be argued in reply that despite Habermas' intentions, his theory, with its stress on rational reconstruction and discursive validity testing, objectively favored those who were best equipped to engage in such activities. If we accept the sociolinguist Basil Bernstein's well-known distinction between context-independent "elaborated linguistic codes," in which justifications are discursively evaluated, and more context-dependent "restricted linguistic codes,"[120] in which there is no reflexive justification for beliefs, and recognize, as does Bernstein, that they are closely related to class status in contemporary society, then Habermas' preference for the former may well suggest a tacit privileging of certain groups over others, even though his appeal is to mankind as a whole.

Habermas, in fact, did not really deal with the relationship between his universal pragmatics and sociolinguistics. In the Postscript to *Knowledge and Human Interests*, he posed the question:

Supposing transcendental consciousness is a hypostatization, what are the "empirical" units which we may put in its place? Should it be particular groups of scientists? The universal community of all scientists? "Society" in the sense of a self-constituting species subject? Or "society" in the sense of a species undergoing social evolution?[121]

The answer he gave was the last of these alternatives, but he never really offered a defense of its social plausibility. Instead, in "What is Universal Pragmatics?" he bracketed the question by arguing that "universal pragmatics is distinguished from empirical pragmatics, e.g., sociolinguistics, in that the meaning of linguistic expressions comes under consideration only insofar as it is determined by formal properties of speech situations in

---

119. Antonio Gramsci, *Selections from the Prison Notebooks*, ed. and trans. Quintin Hoare and Geoffrey Howell Smith (New York, 1971), p. 9. But Gramsci added that "The popular element 'feels' but does not always know or understand; the intellectual element 'knows' but does not always understand and in particular does not always feel" (p. 418). These are sentiments that Habermas seems not to have shared, having had a taste of what the "popular element's" feelings could be like during the Nazi era.
120. Basil Bernstein, *Class, Codes and Control*, 3 vols. (London, 1972, 1973 and 1975).
121. Habermas, postscript to *Knowledge and Human Interests*, p. 165.

general, and not by particular situations of use."[122] It was, however, the transition from general situations to particular ones that troubled his critics, who contended that he inadvertently opened the door to a new variety of elitism.

Whether or not this is the case can more clearly be determined by examining Habermas' attempt to recast the Western Marxist normative concept of totality. Here the basic innovation was the integration of contemporary linguistic philosophy into his system. Although Gramsci, Merleau-Ponty, Althusser, and Della Volpe were all, in different ways, interested in linguistics, it was only with Habermas that the celebrated linguistic turn of twentieth-century philosophy decisively entered the mainstream of Marxist thought. If it can be said that Habermas attempted to reconstruct the latitudinal concept of totality by juxtaposing systems theory against action theory, and reconstructed the longitudinal notion by extrapolating from psychological learning theory, his comparable reconstruction of the normative concept was deeply indebted to Anglo-American linguistic philosophy. Indeed, it was the growing centrality of language in his work that marked the final break with his Hegelian Marxist starting point. As he put it in a footnote to a later edition of *Theory and Practice,*

I myself have often made uncritical use of the idea of a human species which constitutes itself as the subject of world-history in this book as in subsequent writings. It was not until I began my preliminary work on a communication theory of society that the import and implications of the hypostatizing generation of subjectivity on the higher levels became clear to me.[123]

That preliminary work began during his debates with Gadamer and Luhmann and culminated in the theory of "universal pragmatics" outlined in a 1976 essay included in *Communication and the Evolution of Society.*[124] Although his initial interest in hermeneutics had focused his attention on linguistic issues, Habermas recognized that the hermeneutic circle with its dependence on the authority of received wisdom, those healthy "prejudices" that Gadamer had defiantly defended as prior to reason, could provide no vantage point from which ideologies or systematically distorted communication might be criticized. Insofar as the Idealist concept of reason no longer sufficed as a viable standard of such criticism, and the alternative defenses of reason as instinctual by Marcuse or as aesthetic by Adorno,[125] were no more persuasive, Habermas felt that it

122. Habermas, *Communication and the Evolution of Society,* p. 31.
123. Habermas, *Theory and Practice,* pp. 303–304.
124. See note 4.
125. According to Habermas, the artistic and instinctual defense of reason are related. In his 1978 discussion with Marcuse he argued that "because reason can no longer justify its

was only from within language itself that Gadamer's argument could be met.

Going beyond the work of Piaget, Kohlberg and Loevinger, Habermas suggested that alongside cognitive and moral development went an evolutionary progress in linguistic ability. Whereas Kohlberg's scheme had stopped at a sixth stage, which he called "the universal ethical principle orientation,"[126] Habermas added a seventh, in which a universal ethics of speech tied mankind together as members in a fictive world society. "Only at the level of a universal ethics of speech," he wrote, "can need interpretations themselves—that is, what each individual thinks he should understand and represent as his 'true' interests—also become the object of practical discourse."[127]

To describe this universal ethics, Habermas left German hermeneutics for contemporary Anglo-American linguistic philosophy, most notably the later Wittgenstein, Noam Chomsky, J. L. Austin and John Searle. The result, which resembled, but was not equivalent to, the "transcendental hermeneutics"[128] developed by Habermas' colleague Karl-Otto Apel, subjected the pragmatic dimension of language to a rigorous formal analysis, or in Habermas' terms, a rational reconstruction similar to the one he performed for historical materialism. Unlike the structuralist linguists who so strongly influenced French Marxism, Habermas contended that such a reconstruction could legitimately focus on the level of utterances, or what Austin called "speech acts" and Saussure "*parole*," rather than on the deep structures of "*langue*." Unlike the later Wittgenstein, he claimed that language games were not mutually incommensurable, but rather had common underlying characteristics, which allowed an analysis of the pragmatics of language to be universal in scope. Unlike Chomsky with his notion of an innate linguistic competence, which was mistakenly grounded in an a priori and monologic view of language,[129] he argued for

---

own normative concepts, such as justice, beauty, and humanity, it relies on evidence derived from a medium such as art, which is rooted not in theory but rather in the erotic or instinctive nature" ("Theory and Politics," p. 144).

126. Habermas, *Communication and the Evolution of Society*, p. 80. This stage defines right according to individual conscience on the basis of self-chosen ethical norms that are seen to be universal, consistent and logically comprehensive.

127. Ibid., p. 90.

128. Apel's major works are *Toward a Transformation of Philosophy*, trans. Glyn Adey and David Frisby (Boston, 1980), and *Analytical Philosophy of Language and the Geiteswissenschaften*, trans. Harald Hostelilie (Dodrecht, 1967); see also his contributions to *Hermeneutik und Ideologiekritik* (Frankfurt, 1971) and *Sprachpragmatik und Philosophie* (Frankfurt, 1973). For Habermas' reasons for rejecting the term "transcendental hermeneutics," see *Communication and the Evolution of Society*, pp. 22–25.

129. Habermas, "Toward a Theory of Communicative Competence" in Hans Peter Dreitzel, ed., *Recent Sociology, No. 2* (London, 1970), p. 130f.

a "communicative competence" that was developed over time through intersubjective interaction.

To put a complicated theory in its simplest terms, Habermas contended that every speech act inherently raises claims of validity and presupposes that such claims can be redeemed discursively. In engaging in dialogue, every speaker has the goal of an ultimate consensus that "terminates in the intersubjective mutuality of reciprocal understanding, shared knowledge, mutual trust, and accord with one another. Agreement is based on recognition of the corresponding validity claims of comprehensibility, truth, truthfulness, and rightness."[130] "Communicative competence" is the ability to achieve such an agreement in which all parties share a common view of the meaning of what is being said, of the referential content of propositions about the world, of the intentional, or what Austin would call "illocutionary," dimension of those propositions, and finally, of the authenticity and sincerity of the speakers in making them. What was particularly important for Habermas' purposes was the third of these dimensions, the illocutionary force of speech acts (the "I promise you that ..." or "I assert to you that ...", etc.) that gives language its ability to perform as well as describe. For it was here that the rationality of communicative competence was most manifest:

> In the final analysis, the speaker can illocutionarily influence the hearer and vice versa, because speech-act-typical commitments are connected with cognitively testable validity claims—that is because the reciprocal bonds have a rational basis.[131]

Because all non-instrumental speech acts have as their telos the achievement of perfect communicability, or what Habermas called an "undistorted speech situation," reason is grounded normatively in language itself. Although rarely achieved in its ideal state, such a situation functions counterfactually as the basis of all intersubjective interaction, as what might be called its non-transcendental, pragmatic, regulative idea. Because it is an immanent telos of every communicative act, and not merely the desire of the critical theorist, the perfect speech situation is not merely a *Sollen* (an ought) opposed to a *Sein* (what is). In tandem with Habermas' cautious appropriation of cognitive and moral evolutionary theory, it served as his surrogate for the crypto-Hegelian realism that had allowed earlier Western Marxists like Lukács to contrast their position

---

130. Habermas, *Communication and the Evolution of Society*, p. 3.
131. Ibid., p. 63. Habermas' appeal to "cognitively testable validity claims" betrays a residual correspondence truth theory in his work. For before incurring discursive redemption, statements of fact "contain the offer to recur if necessary to the *experiential source* from which the speaker draws the *certainty* that his statements are true" (pp. 63–64).

with the inadequate moralism of the Revisionists. In other words, one need not posit a dubious ontology of the "not-yet" like Bloch's in order to avoid the charge of wishful thinking unrelated to actual historical trends. The difficulty of Habermas' alternative, of course, was that it remained too general and formal for those who demanded a closer reading of those trends; if *all* speech has as its goal perfect communication, then history was in danger of being replaced by abstract philosophical anthropology. A more immanent theory, like that of the older Frankfurt School with its stress on contrasting specific cultural values with their actual betrayal, might have given Habermas' position a bit more historical weight.

Habermas may not have been as fully attuned to this problem as some of his critics wished,[132] but he was certainly aware of the necessity of going beyond language alone to specific social contexts. This awareness was especially apparent in his consideration of the concept of truth, which he claimed had to be understood discursively, like reason. In other words, truth is less a function of a perceptual congruence between a thought and its object than of a consensus within a community of speakers.[133] What prevented that consensus from being an ideological one based on coercion or authority was its institutional setting. That is, the ideal speech situation was only possible in a non-hierarchically organized, truly democratic public sphere in which the force of reasoned argument was the sole source of ultimate agreement.

Because Habermas stressed the extra-linguistic context in which discourse took place, it is incorrect to claim, as have some commentators,[134] that he reduced power to a purely communicative affair. As he put it in his debate with Gadamer, "This meta-institution of language as tradition is evidently dependent in turn on social processes that are not exhausted in

---

132. See, for example, Seyla Benhabib, "Modernity and the Aporias of Critical Theory," *Telos* 49 (Fall 1981). Habermas partly concedes the point in his reply in Thompson and Held, pp. 252–53.

133. Habermas spelled out his defense of a consensus theory of truth in the postscript to *Knowledge and Human Interests*, p. 166f, and in "Wahrheitstheorien" in *Wirklichkeit und Reflexion: Walter Schulz zum 60. Geburtstag* (Pfullingen, 1973). For a critical analysis of his argument, see McCarthy, *The Critical Theory of Jürgen Habermas*, p. 229f and Hesse, "Science and Objectivity." In response to the latter, Habermas admits that he has not taken the "evidential dimension" of truth sufficiently into account. See his essay in Thompson and Held, *Habermas: Critical Debates*, p. 274.

It might be noted that Habermas' theory of truth drew on the pragmatist tradition, particularly on C. S. Pierce, whose notion of a community of scientific investigators he discussed in *Knowledge and Human Interests*. Here as in so many other respects, he broke with classical Critical Theory, which vigorously rejected all forms of pragmatism. This is made especially clear in his 1981 interview, "The Dialectics of Rationalization," where he acknowledges that "I have for myself, in any case, said goodbye to an emphatic philosophical expectation of truth. This elitist concept of truth is a last remaining piece of myth" (p. 30).

134. Anthony Giddens, *Studies in Social and Political Theory* (London, 1977), p. 153.

normative relationships. Language is *also* a medium of domination and social power."[135] And as he emphasized in his critical appreciation of Arendt, "The concept of the political must extend to the strategic competition for political power and to the employment of power within the political system. Politics cannot, as with Arendt, be identified with the praxis of those who talk together in order to act in common."[136] Distorted communication is thus not merely a function of misunderstanding, but rather of constraining institutional situations as well. Or to put it in the terms of his reworked notion of latitudinal totality, the overcoming of crises in social integration is due in large measure to the resolution of other crises in system integration.

Because Habermas resisted the reduction of politics to discourse alone, however much he may have valued its importance, we can, I think, answer in the negative the question posed earlier about his alleged privileging of intellectuals as the saviors of mankind. For Habermas never saw the perfect speech situation as an end in itself or the surrogate for the Hegelian Marxist notion of normative totality as the identity of subject and object. It remained more a regulative ideal than a fully articulated form of life. Indeed, it was important "to differentiate between the symbolic structure of the *Lebenswelt* in general and the pluralism of life forms."[137] As he insisted in a recent interview:

One should not imagine the ideal speech situation as a utopian model for an emancipated society. I use it only to reconstruct the concept of rationality, that is, a concept of communicative rationality, which I would like to introduce as an opposition to Adorno and Horkheimer's *Dialectic of Enlightenment*.[138]

Although Habermas' modified notion of normative totality definitely depended on the attainment, or at least near-attainment, of truly democratic

135. Habermas, *Zur Logik der Sozialwissenschaften*, p. 287. Giddens cites this passage, but argues that "it cedes too much and too little to hermeneutics. Too much because, accepting the universality of language as the medium of being, it complements the mediation of traditions with an emphasis on power only at the cost of transmuting power into ideologically deformed communication; too little because it thereby fails to acknowledge the sense in which hermeneutics, in so far as it is concerned with all 'meaningful comprehension,' must be as basic to a critique of ideology as to any other human enterprise" (p. 153). My quarrel with this reading of Habermas is that it underplays the extent to which "ideologically deformed communication" is itself grounded in systemic, that is, extra-linguistic, constraints on the ideal speech situation. Power for Habermas, as the next quotation demonstrates, is more than just ideological. See his reply to Giddens' charge that he privileges norms over power in his contribution to Thompson and Held, p. 269.

136. Habermas, "Hannah Arendt's Communications Concept of Power," p. 21.

137. Letter from Habermas to the author, December 12, 1981. Habermas is then not as anti-pluralist as some of his critics assume, e.g., Keat, Chap. 6.

138. Habermas' interview with Horster and van Reijen, p. 42. He sharpens this point in his reply in Thompson and Held, p. 235, and in *Theorie des kommunikativen Handelns*, 1, p. 111f.

speech communities, it was grounded as well in a (somewhat vague) notion of the content of what was actually to be discussed. For if, as we have seen, Habermas opposed Kant's notion of cognition as disinterested, he also believed that interests were deeply involved in communicative interaction. That is, men had an emancipatory interest in more than just being able to engage in uncoerced discourse. There were, he argued in Rousseauist fashion,[139] certain concrete interests that could be understood as general—or, more precisely put, generalizable through discourse. "The advocacy role of the critical theory of society," he wrote in *Legitimation Crisis*, "would consist in ascertaining generalizable, though nevertheless suppressed, interests in a representatively simulated discourse between groups that are differentiated (or could be non-arbitrarily differentiated) from one another by articulated, or at least virtual, opposition of interests."[140] What precisely those general interests might be Habermas refused to say, because they could only be generated through the discursive process. Although at times he invoked the classical Frankfurt School defense of hedonism against asceticism and argued that needs were ultimately rooted in instinctual desires,[141] he never speculated about their specific content.

As a result, Habermas' revised normative concept of totality was considerably weaker than that of most earlier Western Marxists. Indeed, the frequent complaint that Habermas failed to supply a sufficient motiva-

139. Habermas' general appreciation of Rousseau can be found in the "Natural Law and Revolution" essay in *Theory and Practice*, as well as in *Communication and the Evolution of Society*, where Rousseau is credited for being the first to work out "the procedural type of legitimacy" (p. 185).

140. Habermas, *Legitimation Crisis*, p. 117. In the postscript to *Knowledge and Human Interests*, he argued against Rüdiger Bubner's definition of interest as necessarily partial and irrational:

The *presupposition* that interests are particular, although common in empiricist and decisionistic approaches to ethics, is highly debatable, if it is supposed to imply something more than a definition. As I have argued elsewhere, practical discourses are capable of testing which norms manifest generalizable interests and which are merely based on particular interests (these can at best be subjected to a compromise, provided power is distributed equally). Generalizable interests and norms which must be justified in discourses have a nonconventional core in that they are neither empirically *found to exist*, nor simply *posited* by a decision. Rather, they are at once *shaped* in a noncontingent manner and *discovered*. This must be so, if there is any meaning in saying that something like a *rational* human will exists at all. (p. 177)

For Bubner's reply, which argues that intersubjective dialogue does not necessarily produce universal interests, see his *Modern German Philosophy*, trans. Eric Matthews (Cambridge, 1981). Their debate goes through another round in Thompson and Held; see also Steven Lukes' contribution to the same volume for other questions about the generalizability of interests.

141. Habermas, *Communication and the Evolution of Society*, p. 91. The difference between needs and interests has never been thematically developed by Habermas, as it was by Agnes Heller and other students of Lukács. In *The Theory of Need in Marx* (London, 1974), Heller argues that

"Interest" is not for Marx a philosophical-social category of a general character. Interest as a motive of individual action is nothing but the expression of the reduction of needs to greed: in the philosophical generalization of the concept of interest, it is the "standpoint of bourgeois society" that is reflected. The

tional source for his emancipatory interest reflected the diminished status of his normative vision.[142] Although Kortian and Rose may be right in detecting a certain residue of idealist identity theory in the concept of an ideal speech situation,[143] Habermas clearly resisted allowing that residue to permeate his entire outlook. Some interests may be generalizable, but not all were. The fiction of a unified world community might be a regulative idea of discourse, but all that we might realistically hope for was "at most self-established, higher-level intersubjective commonalities." The unwarranted supremacy of instrumental reason might be challenged and the power of practical reason restored, but there was no guarantee that the dialectics of labor and symbolically mediated interaction would ever come together in a harmonious way. In short, for all his disdain for Adorno's negative dialectics and fetish of non-identity, Habermas remained at least in part a true inheritor of the Frankfurt School legacy. As he put it in the concluding paragraph of his essay on Walter Benjamin,

A theory of linguistic communication that wants to reclaim Benjamin's insights for a materialist theory of social evolution would have to consider together two Benjaminiam propositions. I am thinking of the assertion: "That there is a sphere of human agreement that is non-violent to the extent that it is wholly inaccessible to violence: the true sphere of 'mutual understanding,' language." And I am thinking of the warning that belongs here: "Pessimism all along the line. Absolutely . . . but above all, mistrust, mistrust and again mistrust in all mutual understanding reached between classes, nations, individuals. And unlimited trust only in I. G. Farben and the peaceful perfection of the *Luftwafe*."[144]

---

organic moment and the essential feature of the overcoming of alienation is precisely the disappearance of "interest" as a motive. (p. 58)

It is a mark of Habermas' movement away from Hegelian Marxism that he remains sceptical about the complete overcoming of alienation entailed in the replacement of interests by needs.

142. Richard Bernstein, *The Restructuring of Social and Political Theory*, p. 224; Schmidt, "Offensive Critical Theory?" p. 69; Giddens, *Studies in Social and Political Theory*, p. 156; Heller, "Habermas and Marxism," p. 25.

143. Kortian, *Metacritique*, p. 128; Rose, *The Melancholy Science*, p. 147. But see Habermas' protestation in his essay in Thompson and Held:

We cannot undertake to appraise forms of life centered on communicative action simply by applying the standards of procedural rationality. These forms of life comprise not only institutions that come under the aspect of justice, but "language-games," historical configurations of habitual practices, group memberships, cultural patterns of interpretation, forms of socialization, competencies, attitudes and so forth. It would make no sense to want to judge these syndromes as a whole, the totality of a form of life, from the standpoint of individual aspects of rationality. . . . Perhaps we should speak instead of a balance among moments incomplete in themselves, an equilibrated interplay of the cognitive with the moral and the aesthetic-expressive. (p. 262)

Habermas' interest in the aesthetic as a source of the substantive moment in the perfect speech situation is discussed in Martin Jay, "Habermas and Modernism," *Praxis International* 4, 1 (April 1984).

144. Habermas, "Consciousness-Raising or Redemptive Criticism: The Contemporaneity of Walter Benjamin," p. 59.

Indeed, in one very important sense, Habermas was even less utopian than certain senior Critical Theorists. From the very beginning of his work, he expressed scepticism towards any complete reconciliation with nature. His 1954 doctoral dissertation on Schelling had first touched on this theme, to which he returned in his 1960 essay on Bloch and his 1968 tribute to Marcuse.[145] In *Knowledge and Human Interests*, he made even more explicit his hostility, which was almost Della Volpean in its intensity:

The resurrection of nature cannot be logically conceived within materialism, no matter how much the early Marx and the speculative minds in the Marxist tradition (Walter Benjamin, Ernst Bloch, Herbert Marcuse, Theodor W. Adorno) find themselves attracted by this heritage of mysticism. Nature does not conform to the categories under which the subject apprehends it in the unresisting way in which a subject can conform to the understanding of another subject on the basis of reciprocal recognition under categories that are binding on both of them. The unity of the social subject and nature that comes into being "in industry" cannot eradicate the autonomy of nature and the remainder of complete otherness that is lodged in its facticity.[146]

Habermas' partiality for the Enlightenment, in fact, grew out of his close identification with its project to free man from his "embeddedness in nature" (*Naturwüchsigkeit*).[147] External nature would be mastered by a reduction of its complexity and concomitant increase in system complexity, as Luhmann had argued. Internal nature would be controlled by increased communicative competence. Language, therefore, was crucial for taming man's own naturalness:

When man reaches a certain stage of socio-cultural behavior, he reorganizes his animal behavior by subjecting it to the imperatives of truth claims. In this process, language operates like a transformer. When psychic processes like sensations, needs and feelings enter into the structures of linguistic intersubjectivity, they are transformed from inner states and episodes into intentional contents. Intentions can only be stabilized over time, if they become reflexive, i.e., if they are connected with one another through reciprocal expectations.[148]

.

145. Habermas, "Ernst Bloch—A Marxist Romantic," *Salmagundi* 10–11 (Fall 1969–Winter 1970); the original German title calls Bloch "a Marxist Schelling"; "Technology and Science as 'Ideology'" in *Toward a Rational Society*. For a defense of Marcuse, see William Leiss, *The Domination of Nature* (New York, 1972), p. 199f.
146. Habermas, *Knowledge and Human Interests*, p. 33. Including Adorno with the others ignores the extent to which his theory of non-identity conflicted with a simple hope in the complete resurrection of nature. It is also not completely true to Bloch to say he called for a resurrection; as we have seen, his philosophy stressed the emergence of a *new* subject of nature.
147. For a discussion of this concept and Habermas' use of it, see Jeremy J. Shapiro, "The Slime of History: Embeddedness in Nature and Critical Theory" in O'Neill, ed., *On Critical Theory*.
148. Habermas, Postscript to *Knowledge and Human Interests*, pp. 170–71.

In so arguing, Habermas seemingly returned to one of the initial premises of Western Marxist holism, the exclusion of nature from the totality, which was the fundamental premise of *History and Class Consciousness*. According to one observer,

> By introducing a dualistic framework to overcome the shortcomings of his prede-cessors, Habermas is following Lukács earlier in the century. Whereas Habermas introduces his dualistic framework to correct the monism of Horkheimer and Adorno, Lukács introduced his to correct the monism of Engels and the Second International. In both cases the goal is to "save the subject."[149]

The major difference, however, between the young Lukács and Habermas is that whereas the former excluded nature entirely from the social total-ity, the latter let it in through the back door. Or more precisely, he posited the dialectic of labor, the subject's mastery over the natural object, as the basic source of that system integration which was part of his reconstructed latitudinal notion of totality. Insofar as system integration resisted reab-sorption into social integration, *techne* into *praxis*, and the dialectic of labor into the dialectic of symbolically mediated interaction, nature would remain to haunt the human project. Unless Habermas could find a way to conceptualize a mediation of the distinctions he analytically pos-ited, a certain residue of non-identity theory remained in his work. And it is clear that for all the totalizing energy in his work, Habermas failed or refused to find such a mediation. As he put it in an interview where he pondered Schelling's answer to non-identity:

> I think that's a part of our conceptual heritage that we just can't reduce to a com-mon denominator. That is, if you wish, a bit of Kantianism in me. There's some-thing unresolved with Nature there.[150]

Habermas' sober attitude towards the resurrection of nature was no-where as evident as in his most recent work, the massive two-volume *The-ory of Communicative Action* published in 1981.[151] Rejecting the earlier Frankfurt School hope for a mimetic relationship between man and na-ture, Habermas argued that such a conceptualization was still rooted in a problematic subject-object consciousness philosophy. No less question-able was the traditional Frankfurt School assumption, grounded in the same philosophy, that instrumental rationality was the main source of man's current dilemma. Relying on a creative reappropriation of sociolog-

---

149. Joel Whitebook, "The Problem of Nature in Habermas," *Telos* 40 (Summer 1979), pp. 53–54. For similar critique of Habermas' view of nature, see Keat, *The Politics of Social Theory*, p. 87f, and Henning Ottmann, "Cognitive Interests and Self-Reflection," in Thompson and Held, p. 88f. Habermas' reply can be found in the same volume, p. 241f.
150. Habermas' interview with Horster and van Reijen, p. 42.
151. See note 59. Vol. 2 is subtitled *Zur Kritik der funktionalistischen Vernunft*.

ical modernization theory in Weber and Parsons, tempered by a recognition of its limitations, Habermas defended modernity as an "uncompleted project"[152] whose outcome was still uncertain. Increasing reification and other undesirable side effects of the process ought not to be seen as inevitable accompaniments of rationalization, as Weber with his notion of the "iron cage" and Adorno with his comparable concept of "the administered world" had feared. Rather, Habermas wrote, they

derived less from an absolutized purposive rationality in the service of self-preservation, an instrumental rationality gone wild, than from the unleashed functionalist rationality of system preservation, which treats lightly the rationality claim of communicative socialization and empties the rationality of the life-world.[153]

Or to put it differently, functionalist rationality designed to preserve the social system, which was a necessary part of the modernization process, spawned reification only if it overwhelmed—or to use Habermas' term, "colonized"—the life-world. What made this colonization particularly pernicious was the fact that the life-world itself had become increasingly rationalized in the modernization process. But its rationalization was of a very different kind, which Habermas called communicative rather than functional or instrumental.

The main addition of *Theory of Communicative Action* to Habermas' previous work was, in fact, his attempt to establish the idea of such a rationality embedded not merely in language or a universal communicative competence, but in social interaction itself. Rationality, he now contended, had less to do with the acquisition of true knowledge than the way in which knowledge was used in social relations. There were, he claimed, "forms of understanding" comparable to Lukács' "forms of objectification," some more emancipatory than others. These forms extended from the ritual practices of sacred cults to the symmetrical social interaction of the perfect speech situation. Insofar as modern society moved towards the latter, it was possible to talk of modernization as more than merely the growing pervasiveness of instrumental or functional rationality. In so arguing, Habermas hoped to escape the sterile alternative posed, on the one hand, by defenders of a modernization equated with only these latter forms of reason and, on the other, by their regressively anti-modernist opponents, who shared the same narrow conception of rationality.

Although a full-scale analysis of the intricacies of Habermas' sprawl-

152. Habermas, "Die Moderne: Ein unvollendetes Projekt," *Die Zeit* 39 (September 26, 1980); English version as "Modernity versus Postmodernity," *New German Critique* 22 (Winter 1981).
153. Habermas, *Theorie des kommunikativen Handelns*, vol. 1, p. 533.

ing argument, which contained discussions of a wide variety of issues in philosophy, sociology and anthropology, cannot be attempted here, certain of its implications for his reconstruction of a viable Marxist holism must be mentioned. In ways that were not designed to quiet his more orthodox Marxist critics' fears that he was an eclectic subverter of the purity of their theory, Habermas continued his reconceptualization of historical materialism by drawing on a wide variety of non-Marxist sources. Durkheim, Mead, Parsons, Schutz and especially Max Weber were read both "in the tradition of Western Marxism"[154] and "critically against" it.[155] Spurning a class-specific concept of reification, calling once again into question Marx's value theory, explicitly rejecting the philosophy of history that was still potent in the Frankfurt School, Habermas came perilously close to cutting virtually all of his ties to the Marxist tradition. And yet, the same basic impulse that underlay earlier versions of Critical Theory and indeed much of Western Marxism as well still motivated him. As he put it in a 1981 interview, his basic desire was for

the reconciliation of the decayed parts of modernity, the idea that without surrendering the differentiation that modernity has made possible in the social and economic spheres, one can find forms for living together in which real autonomy and dependency can appear in a satisfying relation, that one can move erect in a collectivity that does not have the dubious quality of backward-oriented forms of community.[156]

If, however, this implied a certain normative notion of totality, it would have to be conceptualized in strictly non-Hegelian Marxist terms. "Systems and action theory," he wrote, "are the *disjecta membra* of a dialectical concept of totality, which Marx and even Lukács had still used, without being able to reconstruct it in concepts that were the equivalent of the fundamental concepts of a logic that reverted back to Hegelian idealism."[157] Although it was not possible to reverse the dissolution of the dialectical concept of totality, it was nonetheless necessary to consider the possible relations among its fragments. Indeed, a reconstructed Marxist holism would have to reflect on the complicated interplay between the systemic and action-oriented dimensions of society in the past, the present and the possible future.

In *Theory of Communicative Action*, Habermas marshalled a wide variety of materials to do just that. In the simplest terms, his conclusions were as follows. In the pre-modern past, which Durkheim's concept of a

154. Ibid., vol. 1, p. 461.
155. Ibid., vol. 2, p. 448.
156. Habermas, "The Dialectics of Rationalization," p. 28.
157. Habermas, *Theorie des kommunikativen Handelns*, vol. 1, p. 460.

mechanical society ruled by a unified collective conscience helped us to understand, totalistic mythic thinking permeated a non-rationalized life-world of unexamined practices. In fact, the earliest community's unity was based on a pre-linguistic, if not pre-symbolic, normative consensus, which allowed no reflection on its legitimacy. Once the sacred founda-tions of this moral and cognitive order were challenged, however, say by contact with other societies, the need to ground world-views linguistically ensued and thus began a process of inevitable differentiation. "The disen-chantment and disempowerment of the sacred realm," Habermas wrote, "completes itself on the way to a *linguistic transformation (Versprachli-chung) of ritually secured normative fundamental agreements*: and with it comes the unleashing of the rationality potential in communicative action."[158] This potential is progressively actualized through what Piaget called the decentering of egocentrically held world-views. Now, for the first time, alternative world-views can be considered side by side in a pro-cess of communicative interaction. Emerging from within a still non-ra-tional life-world, which, *pace* Gadamer, is never *completely* available for rational reflection, a separate sphere of communicative rationality, which effects normative as well as cognitive decisions, comes into existence. This sphere, which includes the use of rational procedures in everyday life, increasingly (if unevenly) widens, as the species as a whole undergoes a collective learning process.

To demonstrate the concrete implications of this developmental scheme as it extended from the sacred realm to the profane, Habermas drew on Weber's analysis of the rationalization of religious world-views and the law, although without defining reason as narrowly as Weber was wont to do. Fleshing out the more abstract argument he had made in his earlier studies of Piaget and Kohlberg, he contended that "the rationalization of law mir-rors the same succession of pre-conventional, conventional and post-con-ventional fundamental concepts that developmental psychology had dem-onstrated for ontogenesis."[159] In other words, there was specific social evidence to confirm the historical viability of the evolutionary scheme that Habermas had so abstractly posited in his earlier work.

Such an evolution is not, however, without deep ambiguities; no tri-umphalist philosophy of history can guarantee the outcome. For para-doxically, the same impulse that led to the differentiation of the sphere of communicative rationality from the pre-rational life-world produced a differentiation *within* rationality itself. From within the communicatively

158. Ibid., vol. 2, p. 119.
159. Ibid., vol. 1, p. 350.

rational life-world, a more instrumental, functionalist, administrative rationality emerged, which gained increasing autonomy as a distinct subsphere of system integration. The uncoupling of this new sphere from the action-oriented context out of which it originally arose was facilitated by the widespread use of money and bureaucratic power as steering mechanisms in the specifically capitalist modernization process. In time, the domination of this new type of rationalization, its colonization of the life-world itself, led to the fallacious view that it was the only significant type of reason. Weber and Parsons had both mistakenly identified modernization with the totalizing power of bureaucratic systems rationality, although coming to very different conclusions about its implications for human freedom. So too had many Western Marxists, like the Frankfurt School, as indeed had Marx himself. According to Habermas, he had "not resisted the temptations of Hegelian totality thinking and construed the unity of system and life-world dialectically as an 'untrue whole'."[160]

It was time now, Habermas suggested, to cast aside the overly pessimistic implications of the earlier Western Marxist tradition and acknowledge both the legitimate achievements of modernization, even in its capitalist form, and the still potent resistance of the communicatively rationalized dimension of the life-world against its total colonization. Even the contemporary mass media, he argued, need not be understood solely in terms of the "culture industry" model, which was grounded too narrowly in a belief in the domination of instrumental reason. Neither Weber's charisma nor the later Frankfurt School's aesthetic dimension ought to be considered the only legitimate vantage points from which to criticize the administered world.

In fact, it was not so much the existence of systems rationalization that should be bemoaned as its unbalanced domination of its communicative progenitor. No perfectly harmonious normative totality, no utopian kingdom of ends in which the perfect speech situation was a fully realized universal form of life, was possible. But it was not too much to hope for a mediated rather than colonizing relationship between the two types of rationalization. Reification, understood as "*system-induced pathologies of the life-world*,"[161] rather than the alienation of a subjectively produced object from its creator, would thus be diminished, if not entirely overcome.

That this hope might not be entirely in vain, Habermas concluded, could be argued from the recent proliferation of what he called conflicts over the "grammar of forms of life."[162] Various neo-populist movements

160. Ibid., vol. 2, p. 501.
161. Ibid., vol. 2, p. 293.
162. Ibid., vol. 2, p. 576.

in Germany and elsewhere, such as those forming around ecological and peace issues, could be understood as protests of a communicatively rationalized life-world against its colonization by functional systems rationality and not merely a regressive attack on modernization *tout court*. As Habermas explained in a recent interview,

My real motive in beginning the book in 1977 was to understand how the critique of reification, the critique of rationalization, could be reformulated in a way that would offer a theoretical explanation of the crumbling of the welfare-state compromise and of the potential for the critique of growth in new movements without surrendering the project of modernity or descending into post- or anti-modernism, "tough" new conservatism or "wild" young conservatism.[163]

Whether or not such "new social movements" really offer an effective antidote to the domination of the life-world by systems rationality remains to be seen. But at least Habermas' attempt to rescue their critical potential for completing the project of modernization rather than merely negating it may offer a possible way out of the impasse into which Western Marxism has fallen. Concomitantly, it may suggest ways to revive the flagging fortunes of Marxist holism without merely resurrecting earlier, no longer viable, concepts of totality.

Habermas' attempt to reconstruct the Western Marxist concept of totality was, to be sure, limited. The latitudinal alternative he posited was based on a decentered, rather than expressive holism. System and social integration, functional and communicative rationalization, were related, but not reducible to a higher type of integrative unity. The differentiation produced by modernization could not be undone and indeed, in important ways, ought not to be. Longitudinal totality meant a reconstructed evolutionary process of learning skills in several areas, but one that could be validated only through a highly uncertain discursive process of will formation. Normative totality meant the achievement (or near achievement) of an ideal speech situation grounded in the institutional framework of a new public sphere where generalizable interests would be discursively articulated. But there would always be a residual antagonism between man and nature that would defy full totalization in discursive terms.

There are still a great number of unanswered questions in Habermas' extraordinary system, but perhaps none are as pressing as those raised by his theory of language. As we have seen, he emphasized its capacity to overcome communicative distortion through a process of discursive validity-testing. With psychoanalysis as his model, he argued that desires

163. Habermas, "The Dialectics of Rationalization," p. 15.

and needs, both subjective and objective, personal and social, could be brought into consciousness and discussed on rational grounds. In short, Habermas saw language—or more specifically, communicative action—as the fundamental human means of overcoming irrational internal nature in the service of enlightenment.

But the question must be asked, What if other dimensions of language are privileged over those Habermas has chosen to stress? What if language is conceived as having more than one telos, other than the goal of achieving undistorted speech? What if the metaphoric, polysemic, playful capacity of language is highlighted, rather than its discursive function?[164] What if the mimetic dimension of language, which Benjamin and Adorno praised for reducing the gap between man and nature,[165] is privileged over the reflective, which sets man apart from nature? What if the context-dependent, connotatively varied meanings of a restricted code are seen as preferable to the context-independent univocality of the intellectuals' elaborated code?[166] What if the capacity to lie or utter counter-factual statements is seen as more central to language than the capacity to tell or seek the truth?[167] What if linguistic consensus can be achieved by methods more akin to sophistic rhetoric than true rational discourse?[168]

What if language's deep structure, which Habermas has so far neglected to study,[169] can be understood to work against or even undermine the pragmatic utterances that strive for perfect communicability? What if the linguistic character of the personal unconscious—and perhaps, by extension, the social unconscious (or ideology)—is depicted in far bleaker terms than Habermas suggests? What if the id is conceived as the source of infinitely deferred desire on the model of the perpetual gap between signified and signifier? In short, *what if language is not seen as the antidote to nature and man's embeddedness in it, but rather as at least in part an expression of man's irrational "naturalness" itself?* If so, then Ha-

164. For a discussion of Habermas' general neglect of play, see Francis Hearn, "Toward a Critical Theory of Play," *Telos* 30 (Winter 1976–77).

165. See, in particular, Walter Benjamin, "On the Mimetic Faculty" in *Reflections, Essays, Aphorisms, Autobiographical Writings*, ed. with intro., Peter Demetz; trans., Edmund Jephcott (New York, 1978). For Habermas' critique of mimesis, see *Theorie des kommunikativen Handelns*, vol. 1, p. 512f.

166. Gouldner, *The Dialectic of Ideology and Technology*, p. 144f.

167. For an argument to this effect, see George Steiner, *After Babel: Aspects of Language and Translation* (London, 1975), p. 205f.

168. Bubner points to "the problem of sophistry" in his contribution to Thompson and Held, p. 50f.

169. One of the reasons Habermas rejected Apel's "transcendental hermeneutics" is that it would "have to be oriented around another model—not the epistemological model of the constitution of experience but perhaps the model of deep and surface structure" (*Communication and the Evolution of Society*, p. 24).

bermas' already weak and tentative reconstruction of the Western Marxist concept of totality would have to be accounted as weaker still.

It is precisely these questions and many more like them that have been raised by contemporary post-structuralist philosophy in France, particularly by Lyotard, Derrida, Foucault, Lacan and Deleuze. Not surprisingly, they have begun to be turned against Habermas by a new generation of critics.[170] Habermas has been willing in the past to confront his attackers, to refute them when he could and learn from them when he could not. In so doing, he has brilliantly exemplified the type of rational discourse demanded by his theory. Only if he continues that dialogue with those questioning his use of linguistic philosophy will the plausibility of his remarkable synthesis be maintained.[171] On that confrontation, I would contend in conclusion, rests the most likely possibility of a viable reconstitution of the Western Marxist tradition and, in particular, its much beleaguered concept of totality.

170. See, for example, LaCapra's Derridean critique in "Habermas and the Grounding of Critical Theory"; Hoy's partly Foucauldian and partly Gadamerian critique in "Taking History Seriously"; and the Lacanian critique in Rainer Nägele, "The Provocation of Jacques Lacan: Attempt at a Theoretical Topography apropos a Book about Lacan," *New German Critique* 16 (Winter 1979) and "Freud, Habermas and the Dialectic of Enlightenment," *New German Critique* 22 (Winter 1981). See also Michael Ryan's Derridean response to Nägele, "New French Theory in New German Critique," *New German Critique* 22 (Winter 1981); and his *Marxism and Deconstruction: A Critical Articulation* (Baltimore, 1982); Charles Lemert, *Sociology and the Twilight of Man: Homocentrism and Discourse in Sociological Theory* (Carbondale, Ill., 1979), chapter 8; and Jonathan Arac, "The Function of Foucault at the Present Time," *Humanities in Society* 3, 1 (Winter 1980). To the extent that post-structuralist thought is indebted to Nietzsche, Habermas' anti-Nietzscheanism, most clearly shown in the discussion of him in *Knowledge and Human Interests,* has come in for criticism. See, for example, James Miller "Some Implications of Nietzsche's Thought for Marxism," *Telos* 37 (Fall, 1978), p. 40. Radical feminists have also used post-structuralist arguments against Habermas. See, for example, Gayatri Chakravorty Spivak, "Three Feminist Readings: McCullers, Drabble, Habermas," *Union Seminary Quarterly Review* 35, 1–2 (Fall 1979–Winter 1980). Even the original French progenitors of these writers have taken on Habermas. See, for example, Jean-François Lyotard, "Réponse à la Question: Qu'est-ce que le postmoderne?" *Critique* 419 (April 1982).

171. In a 1978 interview with Angelo Bolaffi, *Telos* 39 (Spring 1979), Habermas did comment on Foucault. Although admitting that he considered his work "an important contribution to the analysis of bourgeois forms of domination," he warned against Foucault's non-dialectical negation of reason:

It is characterized by the fact that it universalizes just one fundamental form, specifically that of an instrumental economic or administrative rationality. However, we must be careful not to throw out the baby with the bathwater and to avoid a new irrationalism; in Foucault's case, I see a certain danger. (p. 170)

In his more recent essay, "Modernity versus Postmodernity," Habermas categorized the deconstructionists as "the Young Conservatives" (p. 13). In a letter of December 12, 1981 to the author, Habermas writes, "I myself find the question that you pose extraordinarily interesting. I actually intend now to argue more in more detail with poststructuralism."

Epilogue:
The Challenge of Post-Structuralism

Like a flock chased by an infinite shepherd, we, the bleating wave,
would flee, endlessly flee from the horror of reducing being to totality.

GEORGES BATAILLE

Drawing our attention to the peculiar placement of the discussion of Nietzsche in *Knowledge and Human Interests*, Dominick LaCapra recently remarked,

It is situated as an oddly dangling supplement to the section on Freud which ends the principal body of the text and comes immediately before the Appendix. This somewhat "castrated" position is symptomatic of Habermas' treatment of Nietzsche, in which Habermas often seems at a loss to know what to do with Nietzsche. His analysis, in which Nietzsche emerges as a paradoxical "virtuoso of reflection that denies itself," tends to obscure the nature of Nietzsche's critique of both positivism and the metaphysical tradition—a critique which recent French thinkers have emphasized.[1]

LaCapra is indeed correct in noting Habermas' uneasiness with the implications of Nietzsche's thought, which had a far more potent influence on the first generation of Frankfurt School thinkers, especially Adorno.[2] But he exaggerates when he claims that Habermas often seems confused in his response. For it is clear that Habermas explicitly rejects Nietzsche's challenge to the universalist and rationalist aspirations of the Enlightenment.

1. Dominick LaCapra, "Habermas and the Grounding of Critical Theory," *History and Theory* 16, 3 (1977), p. 252. LaCapra's use of "castration" here is not fully clear. French Freudians often employ the castration complex to suggest the anxiety produced by the loss of wholeness experienced when meaning is too elusive and ambiguous to be incorporated in a totalized way. But since Habermas is the father figure here, the one who is doing the castrating by putting Nietzsche outside of his main text, it is hard to see how he is being made anxious by this loss. Rather, it may be more likely that LaCapra, who insists on including Nietzsche as a pivotal figure in the Western cultural tradition, is the one feeling the anxiety produced by Habermas' exclusion of him.
For another Derridean critique of Habermas on Nietzsche, see James Ogilvy, *Many Dimensional Man: Decentralizing Self, Society and the Sacred* (New York, 1979), pp. 348–49.
2. See Peter Pütz, "Nietzsche and Critical Theory," *Telos* 50 (Winter 1981–82).

While Nietzsche was right in recognizing the connection between knowledge and interests, and thus superior to the naive positivists, he trivialized the link by psychologizing it and turning it into a radical scepticism about all knowledge. Thus, according to Habermas, "Nietzsche carried to its end the self-abolition of epistemology inaugurated by Hegel and continued by Marx, arriving at the self-denial of reflection."[3] In so doing, he expressed "the cynicism of a, as it were, self-denying bourgeois consciousness" by assimilating the "historical loss of force of normative validity claims as well as the Darwinian impulses to a naturalistic self-destruction of reason."[4]

Habermas did not deny Nietzsche's courage in destroying bourgeois reason. "His heroic style," he writes, "also reveals the pain that cutting the umbilical cord to the universalism of the Enlightenment caused him after all."[5] But in the new Nietzscheans of today, "the pain has either been reduced to nostalgia or given way to a new innocence—if not precisely to the innocence that Nietzsche once postulated—for which positivism and existentialism have prepared the foundations."[6]

Indeed, rather than registering that pain, many of the contemporary devotees of Nietzsche have found it possible to rejoice in the crisis of Enlightenment values whose loss they refuse to mourn. This affirmative reaction has been nowhere as keenly apparent as in the recent philosophical phenomenon, originating in France but now widely influential elsewhere, that has come to be known as post-structuralism or deconstructionism.[7] Although certain of its representatives shared a number of attitudes with Adorno, they tended to spurn his "melancholy science" in favor of Nietzsche's "gay" alternative. They may be looking into the same abyss as he

3. Jürgen Habermas, *Knowledge and Human Interests*, trans. Jeremy J. Shapiro (Boston, 1971), p. 290. More recently, Habermas has returned to Nietzsche, whose impact on post-structuralism he explicitly acknowledges. See his "The Entwinement of Myth and Enlightenment: Re-reading *Dialectic of Enlightenment*," *New German Critique* 26 (Spring–Summer 1982).

4. Jürgen Habermas, *Legitimation Crisis*, trans. Thomas McCarthy (Boston, 1973), p. 122.

5. Ibid.

6. Ibid.

7. For introductory surveys of post-structuralism, see John Sturrock, ed., *Structuralism and Since: From Lévi-Strauss to Derrida* (Oxford, 1979) and Vincent Descombes, *Modern French Philosophy*, trans. L. Scott-Fox and J. M. Harding (Cambridge, 1980). The "invasion of the mind-snatchers from the Continent," as one of the snatched, Geoffrey Hartmann, once put it, has had its greatest impact among literary critics. For general treatments of the results, see Frank Lentricchia, *After the New Criticism* (Chicago, 1980) and Vincent B. Leitch, *Deconstructive Criticism: An Advanced Introduction* (New York, 1983). A less hospitable response can be found in Gerald Graff, *Literature Against Itself: Literary Ideas in Modern Society* (Chicago, 1979). For a selection of the post-structuralist appropriations of Nietzsche, see David B. Allison, ed., *The New Nietzsche: Contemporary Styles of Interpretation* (New York, 1977) and the "Nietzsche's Return" issue of *Semiotexte* 3, 1 (1978).

did from the safe vantage point of a "Grand Hotel," but the view from
their room has proven to be far more agreeable than it ever was from
Adorno's. Attracted neither by the nostalgia for a lost order they detect in
Lévi-Strauss nor by the hopes for a future one they see in the Western
Marxists, the post-structuralists affirm instead the infinite play of desire,
non-identity, difference, repetition and displacement that earlier thinkers
had decried as an expression of alienation and estrangement. Manic explosions of laughter rather than the tortured anguish of an Adorno or
Sartre are their response to the frustration of utopian hopes.[8] That "unhappy consciousness" which Hegelians and Hegelian Marxists had found
so repellent turns out to be not so morose after all.

Although certain anticipations of post-structuralism can be found in
the later work of Merleau-Ponty, its adherents are unremittingly hostile to
the traditions that nurtured his thought: phenomenology, existentialism,
Hegelianism, and structuralism, at least insofar as all of those movements
shared a yearning for some sort of plenitude. They are no less hostile to
the other variants of Western Marxism that drew on these traditions.
Even Althusser—who in certain respects, including a positive attitude
towards Nietzsche, was close to post-structuralist positions—has come in
for his share of criticism. Loosely connected in complicated ways with the
so-called "New Philosophers" who were often disillusioned Althusserians, the post-structuralists are the main reason for what one observer has
called "the stagnation of Marxism, followed by its complete disappearance from the French scene"[9] in the 1970s.

In the English-speaking world, post-structuralist arguments have also
recently been aimed at Western Marxism in general and Habermas'
attempt to revive it in particular. For example, Andreas Huyssen complained that

Habermas ignores the fact that the very idea of a wholistic [sic] modernity and of
a totalizing view of history has become anathema in the 1970s, and precisely not
on the conservative right. The critical deconstruction of enlightenment, rationalism and logocentrism by theoreticians of culture, the decentering of traditional
notions of identity, the fight of women and gays for a legitimate social and sexual
identity outside of the parameters of male, heterosexual vision, the search for

8. Gilles Deleuze, "Nomad Thought" in *The New Nietzsche*, p. 147. The explosive, Dio-
nysian laughter with which they identify often has, however, something grim about it. It is
the kind of laughter captured by Baudelaire in the concluding lines of his famous poem
"L'Héautontimorouménos":

> Je suis de mon coeur le vampire
> —Un de ces grands abandonnés
> Au rire éternel condamnés,
> Et qui ne peuvent plus sourire!

9. Descombes, p. 129.

alternatives in our relationship with nature, including the nature of our own bodies—all these phenomena, which are key to the culture of the 1970s, make Habermas' proposition to complete the project of modernity questionable, if not undesirable.[10]

It is thus precisely because of Habermas' desire to reconstitute the Western Marxist discourse of totality that he has become suspect, even by thinkers like Huyssen who consider themselves still to be on the Left. There has, in fact, been a general move away from the totalistic emphasis that marked the earlier Anglo-American reception of continental Marxism, as some former New Leftists scramble to accommodate the arguments of post-structuralism. Thus, for example, Stanley Aronowitz, who recently, in a critique of Wallerstein's *Modern World System* published in 1981, blithely defended "the" Marxist notion of totality against systems theory,[11] could then argue in a book that appeared in the same year, *The Crisis in Historical Materialism*,

Theory must comprehend that Marxism's economic *logocentricity* has constituted its major weakness, both theoretically and politically. I do not argue from the premise of either the famous expressive totality of Lukács or the structuralist concept of totality to support this perspective. In both cases, the aim is to overcome differences in order to achieve proletarian unity.[12]

Invoking Gramsci's concept of an historical bloc and turning it in an avowedly anti-holistic direction, he concludes, "The new historic bloc would have to become anti-hegemonic as a political and social principle, recognizing the *permanence* of difference, which Marxism believes, at least implicitly, can be overcome by socialist transformation."[13]

Aronowitz's new direction is exemplary of a general trend both here and in Europe. Although there are certain counter-examples—Russell Jacoby ends his recent book on Western Marxism with a *profession de foi* in the possibility of expressive totality, and Fredric Jameson struggles to make a totalistic discourse compatible with post-structuralism in his 1981 critique of *The Political Unconscious*[14]—the move "from Marx

---

10. Andreas Huyssen, "The Search for Tradition: Avant-Garde and Postmodernism in the 1970s," *New German Critique* 22 (Winter 1981), p. 38. In a later essay, "Critical Theory and Modernity," *New German Critique* 26 (Spring–Summer 1982), Huyssen seems to back away somewhat from this position.

11. Stanley Aronowitz, "A Metatheoretical Critique of Immanuel Wallerstein's *The Modern World System*," *Theory and Society* 10, 4 (July 1981), p. 505.

12. Stanley Aronowitz, *The Crisis in Historical Materialism: Class, Politics and Culture in Marxist Theory* (New York, 1981), p. 127. For a similar argument, see André Gorz, *Farewell to the Working Class: An Essay on Post-Industrial Socialism*, trans. Michael Sonenscher (London, 1982).

13. Ibid., p. 128.

14. Russell Jacoby, *Dialectic of Defeat: Contours of Western Marxism* (Cambridge, 1981), p. 126; Fredric Jameson, *The Political Unconscious: Narrative as Socially Symbolic

to Hegel" in the 1960s has turned in the 1970s and 1980s into a recapitulation of an earlier shift "from Hegel to Nietzsche."[15] And at the center of this new Nietzscheanism is a pointed attack on the concept of totality in any and all of the forms we have encountered.

It is thus fitting that we close our discussion of Western Marxist holism by lingering for a while with the reasons why the concept has suddenly come into such strong disrepute among Anglo-American commentators. Some of these rehearse the various theoretical criticisms made by many Western Marxists themselves against most kinds of holism. Others are unique to the discourse of post-structuralism. Still others may be indirectly adduced from recent developments which, while outside theoretical life itself, nonetheless have found their echo within it.

It would be misleading to try to turn a series of thinkers who insist on the importance of difference, as much as the post-structuralists do, into a uniform movement. As the label itself indicates, they have been defined largely in terms of what they followed rather than what they espoused, always a sign of a still inchoate cultural phenomenon, as the comparable case of post-modernism also demonstrates. There has, in fact, been no shortage of disputes among them, some for theoretical, some for political and some, no doubt, for personal reasons.[16] And yet if one had to find one

---

Act (Ithaca, 1981), *passim.*

Like Aronowitz, Jameson contends that "the privileged form in which the American Left can develop today must therefore necessarily be that of an *alliance politics,*" but then he adds in direct opposition to his co-editor of *Social Text,* "and such a politics is the strict practical equivalent of the concept of totalization on the theoretical level" (p. 54). Jameson's insistence on the relevance of the category of totality to American leftist politics takes note of the differences between the French and American scenes. In the former, anti-totalization goes hand in hand with the revolt against the historical centralization of the French state, which affected even those elements of society arrayed against it. In America, however, ethnic, racial and regional fragmentation has been a major obstacle to centralization of any kind; it may therefore play into the hands of conservative forces to suggest more of the same as a political strategy. One might add that a theoretical critique of totality fits comfortably with traditional American intellectual inclinations as well. See, for example, the classic defense of pluralism against monism in William James, *Pragmatism* (New York, 1907), chapter 4. For a penetrating critique of the difficulties Jameson has in reconciling post-structuralism with Western Marxism, see Dominick LaCapra, "Marxism in the Textual Maelstrom: Fredric Jameson's *The Political Unconscious,*" *History and Theory* 21, 1 (1982).

In Europe as well, the attempt to salvage totality has not been completely abandoned. See, for example, Furio Cerutti, *Totalità, bisogni, organizzazione: Ridiscutendo "Storia e coscienza di classe"* (Florence, 1980).

15. These are the titles of two well-known books by George Lichtheim and Karl Löwith.

16. Perhaps the best known of these is the dispute between Foucault and Derrida. See the latter's "Cogito and the History of Madness" in *Writing and Difference,* trans. Alan Bass (Chicago, 1978); and the former's reply in the second edition of *Folie et déraison: Histoire de la folie à l'âge classique* (Paris, 1972).

common denominator among the major figures normally included in the post-structuralist category—Jacques Derrida, Michel Foucault, Jacques Lacan, Roland Barthes, Gilles Deleuze, Jean-François Lyotard, Julia Kristeva, Philippe Sollers and their comrades *avant la lettre*, Georges Bataille,[17] Maurice Blanchot and Pierre Klossowski—it would have to be their unremitting hostility towards totality.

Lacan, as we noted earlier, identified the individual's sense of totality with the illusory wholeness of the "mirror" stage of development before entrance into the "symbolic" stage of language. His scorn for the ego psychology that informed Habermas' appropriation of Freud was shared by virtually all those after 1968 who suddenly discovered the virtues of psychoanalysis. Barthes' like-minded critique of the ideology of a unified literary text, which he applied *inter alia* to the concept of realistic fiction so dear to Lukács and official Communist aestheticians, was no less influential. Stressing the materiality of language and exposing the fiction of authorial intentionality as the origin of a text, he helped undermine the narrative integrity of the allegedly organic work of art. Along with Althusserian critics like Macherey, whose attack on Lukácsian principles was launched from a more explicitly Marxist vantage point, he made it extremely difficult to return to the neo-Hegelian aesthetics that had inspired many earlier Western Marxists.

Deleuze, heavily indebted to Nietzsche, defended a "nomadic" rather than "sedentary" philosophizing and radically repudiated closure in any kind of philosophy. With Felix Guattari, he praised schizophrenia for revealing the reality of man as a desiring machine subversive of any fixed order, personal or social. Lyotard, who began as a member of the Socialism or Barbarism group, came to celebrate the disintegrative power of capitalism for liberating man from the illusion of a unified and stable truth. Agreeing with Adorno's emphasis on non-identity, he nonetheless rejected the still-Hegelian "nostalgia" for totality he saw latent in *Negative Dialectics*.[18] Kristeva and Sollers, the major powers on the journal *Tel Quel*, adopted themes from semiology to radicalize the analysis of Barthes in a more explicitly political direction. Attacking totalizing centrism and substituting intertextuality for intersubjectivity, they linked the sins of linguistic false consciousness directly to bourgeois ideology. Or at least they did so before *Tel Quel*, like much else in French intellectual life in the 1970s, turned its back on Marxism.

17. Bataille, to be sure, evinces considerable nostalgia for community, but his "general economy" based on transgression, expenditure (*dépense*) and waste explodes the closure of what he calls a "restricted economy." For an account of this thought, see Michelle H. Richman, *Reading Georges Bataille: Beyond the Gift* (Baltimore, 1982).

18. Jean-François Lyotard, "Adorno as the Devil," *Telos* 19 (Spring 1974).

Never really engaged with Marxism and therefore more sweeping in his denunciation of totality as far more than merely a bourgeois fantasy, Derrida radically deconstructed the entire "ontotheological," "logocentric" and "phonocentric" tradition of Western metaphysics.[19] Attacking the fallacy that unmediated speech was prior to mediated writing, he proposed a "grammatological" analysis of culture that recognized the impossibility of ever recapturing some original perfect presence. Ruthlessly denouncing the yearning for origins and transcendental signifieds, while at the same time acknowledging the inevitability of that yearning, he introduced a series of evocative and deliberately equivocal terms—*différance* (suggesting both difference and deferring), supplementarity (the addition of something missing and the addition of a surplus), the trace (the residual presence of an absence), etc.—in order to capture the infinite play of an untotalized reality, a reality, as he put it, of "holes" rather than "wholes."[20]

Equally contemptuous of holistic thinking, Foucault directed his fire against the totalizing assumptions of conventional historiography and in so doing called into question the possibility of future totalizations as well. In ways that we will soon explore, he tried to escape from the predominantly linguistic preoccupations of many post-structuralists into an analysis of power that exposed the dangers of totalism in political as well as intellectual terms.

The political implications of post-structuralism were themselves not very clear. Although the *Tel Quel* group and others, including their followers in the English-speaking world like Rosalind Coward and John Ellis,[21] initially may have tried to find a Marxist message in post-structuralism, its nihilistic or anarchistic impulses soon came to the fore. Criticizing the search for origins (*arches*) implied, anarchically, the impossibility of plenitude in the future as well. Rather than hoping for the restitution of the "festival" in the sense of Lefebvre or the Situationist Guy Debord, who

19. "Ontotheology," a term Derrida borrowed from Heidegger, suggests the strong religious residue in ontological efforts to represent plenitude and presence. "Logocentrism" implies the belief that language can be perfectly expressive of a thought, instead of always being decentered in relation to it. "Phonocentrism" suggests the belief that the essence of language is speech rather than writing, which is seen as derivative. Derrida's defense of a "grammatology" does not privilege writing over speech as itself more essential, but rather insists on the impossibility of giving priority to either.

20. Jacques Derrida, "La parole soufflée," in *Writing and Difference*, p. 178.

21. Rosalind Coward and John Ellis, *Language and Materialism: Developments in Semiology and the Theory of the Subject* (London, 1977). Fredric Jameson has been the most prominent American defender of the radical implications of certain aspects of post-structuralism. In addition to the book cited above, see his major essay on Lacan, "Imaginary and Symbolic in Lacan," *Yale French Studies* 55–56 (1977). A still more recent, but not very successful, attempt to establish Derrida's Marxist credentials is made by Michael Ryan in *Marxism and Deconstruction: A Critical Articulation* (Baltimore, 1982).

idealized the May, 1968, events as a communitarian overcoming of alienation, they argued that the incessant play of non-identity and difference
was a superior state of being. Rather than trying to contain and master
(or, to use a favorite term, "recuperate") heterogeneity and contradiction
in a theodicy-like *Aufhebung*, they followed Nietzsche in linking life with
the inevitability of a certain amount of discord and even violence.[22] The
pacification of existence desired by so many Western Marxists to them
smacked of death and the suppression of healthy difference. Holding out
no hope for the restoration or creation of the centered, unalienated subject, collective or individual, they were also critical of any intersubjective
alternative, Habermasian or otherwise. Like Foucault in the famous part-
ing words of *The Order of Things*, they rejoiced in the prospect that "man
would be erased, like a face drawn in sand at the edge of the sea."[23]

But if post-structuralism revealed a nihilist or anarchist potential, as
well as a neo-Marxist one, it also paradoxically contained the seeds of a
quietistic politics as well. For in a night in which all cows were piebald, the
possibility of meaningful change seemed very limited indeed. Their critics
on the left were quick to point out these implications. To take one recent
example, Marshall Berman writes that Foucault

offers a generation of refugees from the 1960s a world-historical alibi for the sense
of passivity and helplessness that gripped so many of us in the 1970s. There is no
point in trying to resist the oppressions and injustices of modern life, since even
our dreams of freedom only add more links to our chains; however, once we grasp
the total futility of it all, at least we can relax.[24]

In his few comments on post-structuralism, Habermas has argued essentially the same point. Calling them the "young conservatives," he warns:

They claim as their own the revelations of a decentered subjectivity, emancipated
from the imperatives of work and usefulness, and with this experience they step

22. See, in particular, Derrida's essays on Emmanuel Levinas and Antonin Artaud in
Writing and Difference. The shattering of the subject celebrated by post-structuralism has
had its effect on many of its American followers, who acknowledge its violent implications.
See, for example, the work of Leo Bersani, in particular *A Future for Astyanax: Character
and Desire in Literature* (Boston, 1976) and *Baudelaire and Freud* (Berkeley, 1977).
23. Michel Foucault, *The Order of Things: An Archaeology of the Human Sciences*,
trans. Alan Sheridan (New York, 1973), p. 387.
24. Marshall Berman, *All That is Solid Melts into Air: The Experience of Modernity*
(New York, 1982), p. 35. For a more sweeping attack on the political implications of deconstructionism by the English Trotskyist, Terry Eagleton, see his *Walter Benjamin, or Towards
a Revolutionary Criticism* (London, 1981). Not only does he claim that the Anglo-Saxon
reception of Foucault "provides a glamorous rationale for erstwhile revolutionaries unnerved into pessimism by the current problems of class struggle in the advanced capitalist
societies" (p. 58), he also argues that deconstruction manages to be both liberal reformist
and ultra-leftist at the same time (p. 134).

outside the modern world. . . . To instrumental reason, they juxtapose in mani-
chean fashion a principle only accessible through evocation, be it the will to power
or sovereignty, Being or the dionysiac force of the poetical. In France this line leads
from Bataille through Foucault to Derrida.[25]

One source of the contention that post-structuralism is inherently conservative or at least unable to offer any hope for overcoming the imperfec-
tions of contemporary society is the charge that its advocates are, as
Hayden White has said of Derrida, "imprisoned in structuralism's hypostatized labyrinth of language."[26] To the extent that Foucault has deliberately sought to break free from language's "prisonhouse," as Nietzsche
liked to call it, his critique of Marxist holism is perhaps the most interesting to follow in some detail. For of all the post-structuralists, he has been
most determined to extend that critique beyond language, philosophy,
psychology and culture to society and politics. In so doing, Foucault has
presented the most direct challenge to the Western Marxist tradition, out
of which in fact he himself originally came. He is in a sense the post-
structuralist equivalent of Habermas in that both take language very seriously, but refuse to confine their considerations to it alone. It may be an
exaggeration, but only a small one, to say that the cutting edge of the
current debate over holism is the confrontation now looming between
these two figures. One way to characterize it is to say that Foucault has
combined many of the arguments we have traced in the Western Marxist
critics of Lukácsian holism, most notably Althusser, Adorno and Merleau-Ponty, and turned them in a radically anti-Marxist direction, while
Habermas, taking the same arguments to heart, has tried to reconstruct
Marxist holism on essentially new grounds. Insofar as the contest is still in
its initial stages, it would be imprudent for an intellectual historian to
speculate on the outcome. But at least we can begin to clarify the questions at issue. Although this is not the place to attempt a sustained analysis of Foucault's remarkable *oeuvre*,[27] certain of its essential features must
be understood to make clear his arguments against holism, Habermasian
or otherwise.

25. Jürgen Habermas, "Modernity versus Postmodernity," *New German Critique* 22
(Winter 1981), p. 13.
26. Hayden White, *Tropics of Discourse: Essays in Cultural Criticism* (Baltimore,
1978), p. 280.
27. The secondary literature on Foucault is only beginning to accumulate. See Alan
Sheridan, *Michel Foucault: The Will to Truth* (London, 1980); Hubert L. Dreyfus and Paul
Rabinow, *Michel Foucault: Beyond Structuralism and Hermeneutics* (Chicago, 1982);
Charles Lemert and Garth Gillan, *Michel Foucault: Social Order and Transgression* (New
York, 1982); and Pamela Major-Poetzl, *Michel Foucault's Archaeology of Western Culture:
Toward a New Science of History* (Chapel Hill, 1983).

What must be grasped first is the extent of Foucault's initial indebtedness to Western Marxism and the concomitant intensity of his struggle to free himself from its coils. Although he cannot be understood without reference to a host of other intellectual influences—ranging from Blanchot, Bataille and Klossowski to Binswanger and even Heidegger—Foucault, like most French thinkers of his era, was immersed in a Marxist universe of discourse. He was briefly a member of the PCF after the war, and he subsequently studied or engaged in fruitful interactions with three figures we have met before: Hyppolite, Canguilhem and Althusser. From Hyppolite, he learned the same lesson that had so impressed Merleau-Ponty in the 1940s: that Hegel did not betoken the end of philosophy, but rather its beginning. As he put it in his inaugural lecture at the Collège de France in 1970,

Instead of conceiving philosophy as a totality ultimately capable of dispersing and regrouping itself in the movement of the concept, Jean Hyppolite transformed it into an endless task, against the background of an infinite horizon. . . . For Hyppolite, philosophy, as the thought of the inaccessible totality, was that which could be rejected in the extreme irregularity of experience; it was that which presents and reveals itself as the continually recurring question in life, death and memory. Thus he transformed the Hegelian theme of the end of self-consciousness into one of repeated interrogation.[28]

From Canguilhem, Foucault deepened his knowledge of the brilliantly idiosyncratic French tradition of the philosophy of science, whose impact on Western Marxism we have already remarked. With Canguilhem's help, he produced his first works on madness and the clinic,[29] which drew on the anti-historicist concept of scientific development initially proposed by Bachelard. His account of the constitution of the discourse of biology in *The Order of Things* also owed much to Canguilhem's insights. Although what he called his archaeological history of knowledge differed somewhat from Canguilhem's more straightforward epistemological history of science,[30] Foucault shared his suspicion of continuity and cumulative progress.

And in exchanges with Althusser, Foucault deepened his appreciation

28. Foucault, "The Discourse on Language" appended to *The Archaeology of Knowledge*, trans. A. M. Sheridan Smith (New York, 1972), p. 236.
29. Foucault, *Maladie mentale et personnalité* (Paris, 1954); retitled *Maladie mentale et psychologie* for the second edition in 1962; trans. by Alan Sheridan as *Mental Illness and Psychology* (New York, 1976); and *Folie et déraison: Histoire de la folie à l'âge classique* (Paris, 1961), trans. by Richard Howard as *Madness and Civilization* (New York, 1965). For his views on Canguilhem, see his "Georges Canguilhem: Philosopher of Error," *I & C: Technologies of the Human Sciences* 7 (Autumn 1980).
30. Foucault, *The Archaeology of Knowledge*, p. 190.

of Marx as something other than a humanist whose critique of capitalism was grounded in a philosophical anthropology.[31] Although he soon broke with Althusser's attempt to establish the scientificity of Marxism in opposition to its allegedly ideological alternatives, and never accepted his teacher's belief that the totality was determined in the last instance by the economy, he could still acknowledge as late as 1975 that:

> It is impossible at the present time to write history without using a whole range of concepts directly or indirectly linked to Marx's thought and situating oneself within a horizon of thought which has been defined and described by Marx. One might even wonder what difference there could ultimately be between being a historian and being a Marxist.[32]

Foucault's radicalism was not confined to pious expressions of his debt to Marx's methods. In the 1960s and 1970s, he actively participated in a number of political causes, most notably prison and mental health reform and the emancipation of homosexuals. Although never espousing any simple unity of theory and practice, he nonetheless clearly found ways to combine his scholarly work with his deeply felt political convictions.

And yet, the major animus of that work came to be directed against many of the central tenets of Western Marxism, in particular the need for a viable concept of totality. Sartre was not far off the mark in 1966 when he warned that "Behind history, of course, the target is Marxism. This is an attempt to constitute a new ideology, the last bulwark which the bourgeoisie can still erect against Marx."[33] Indeed, it is arguable that Foucault should be seen as much as a post-Western Marxist as a post-structuralist. For when he allowed Nietzsche to rouse him from what he called "the confused sleep of dialectics and of anthropology,"[34] Foucault also awakened from his Marxist dreams. And unlike Althusser or the Della Volpeans, he refused to hold on to the hope that a non-dialectical Marxism could be salvaged from the wreckage. Here his hostility to holism seems to have played a key role. Insofar as Marxism of whatever variety still insisted on the category of totality it was complicitous with the very system it claimed to oppose. As he put it in a 1971 interview, the idea of the "whole of society"

31. Ibid., pp. 12–13. Louis Althusser acknowledged a reciprocal debt to Foucault in *Reading Capital*, trans. Ben Brewster (New York, 1970), p. 16.

32. Foucault, *Power/Knowledge: Selected Interviews and Other Writings 1972–1977*, ed. Colin Gordon, trans. Colin Gordon et al. (New York, 1980), p. 53. Later, however, he would deny that he was ever actually a Marxist. See Gérard Raulet, "Structuralism and Post-Structuralism: An Interview with Michel Foucault," *Telos* 55 (Spring, 1983), p. 198.

33. Sartre, "Jean-Paul Sartre répond," *L'Arc* 30 (October 1966), p. 88.

34. Foucault, *Language, Counter-Memory, Practice: Selected Essays and Interviews*, ed. with intro. Donald F. Bouchard, trans. Donald F. Bouchard and Sherry Simon (Ithaca, 1977), p. 38.

arose in the Western world, within this highly individualized historical development that culminates in capitalism. To speak of the "whole of society" apart from
the only form it has ever taken is to transform our past into a dream. We readily
believe that the least we can expect of experiences, actions, and strategies is that
they take into account the "whole of society." This seems absolutely essential for
their existence. But I believe that this is asking a great deal, that it means imposing
impossible conditions on our actions because this notion functions in a manner
that prohibits the actualization, success, and perpetuation of these projects. "The
whole of society" is precisely that which should not be considered except as something to be destroyed.[35]

To aid in that destruction, Foucault systematically considered and rejected all of the varieties of holism we have encountered in this study. In his
work as an historian of ideas, he deliberately challenged the possibility of
conceiving history as a longitudinal totality. There could be no closure at
the end of time that would render coherent the whole of history. "The
nineteenth century is commonly thought to have discovered the historical
dimension," he wrote, "but it did so only on the basis of the *circle*, the
spatial form which negates time, the form in which the gods manifest
their arrival and flight and men manifest their return to their native
ground of finitude."[36] Instead of a "total history" which "draws all phenomena around a single center," he called for a "general history" which
would "deploy the space of a dispersion."[37] Although coming to deny the
charge that he saw only discontinuities in history,[38] Foucault, especially in
earlier works like *The Order of Things*, refused to speculate on the ways
in which one historical era was transformed into another. Even when
he shifted his emphasis from archaeology to genealogy to describe the
method he used in his more recent work, he still identified with Nietzsche's criticism of a history

that reintroduces (and always assumes) a suprahistorical perspective: a history
whose function is to compose the finally reduced diversity of time into a totality
fully closed upon itself; a history that always encourages subjective recognitions
and attributes a form of reconciliation to all the displacements of the past; a
history whose perspective on all that precedes it implies the end of time, a completed development.[39]

Nor did Foucault accept the assumption that specific eras could themselves be understood as latitudinal wholes. Although acknowledging a

35. Ibid., p. 233.   36. Ibid., p. 85.
37. Foucault, *The Archaeology of Knowledge*, p. 10.
38. Foucault, *Power/Knowledge*, p. 111. It is useful, however, to compare this disclaimer with Foucault's earlier remark in his essay on "Nietzsche, Genealogy, History," in
Language, Counter-Memory, Practice that "History becomes 'effective' to the degree that it
introduces discontinuity into our very being" (p. 154).
39. Foucault, *Language, Counter-Memory, Practice*, p. 152.

522   Epilogue: The Challenge of Post-Structuralism

certain debt to the structuralist historian Georges Dumézil's concept of periods as unified "combinatories,"[40] he insisted that the particular "discursive" unities he studied were never homogeneously grouped around a common center. In *The Archaeology of Knowledge*, he wrote:

My aim is most decidedly not to use the categories of cultural totalities (whether world-views, ideal types, the particular spirit of the age) in order to impose on history, despite itself, the forms of structural analysis. The series described, the limits fixed, the comparisons and correlations made are based not on the old philosophies of history, but are intended to question teleologies and totalizations.[41]

Rather than expressing a constitutive genesis or a sharing of a common telos, the discursive formations, or *epistèmes*, that he chose to study were dispersed, decentered force-fields of statements (*énoncés*) that lacked the mediated integration of dialectical totalities. Neither sentences nor propositions, statements are linguistic formulations, materially embodied signs or speech acts, that emanate from the discourse itself rather than from speaking subjects. Within specific discursive formations, they exist in a condition of what Foucault calls "rarity" because they are expressions of the limited possibilities of what can be enunciated in each *epistème*. Rather than a "closed, plethoric totality of meaning," they form "an incomplete fragmented figure"[42] whose surface the historian can only describe, never penetrate.

Anticipating the inevitable charge that this was a form of ascetic positivism, Foucault defiantly wrote:

If, by substituting the analysis of rarity for the search for totalities, the description of relations of exteriority for the theme of the transcendental foundation, the analysis of accumulations for the quest of the origin, one is a positivist, then I am quite happy to be one.[43]

His was a positivism, to be sure, shorn of its scientistic claims, a Nietzschean positivism of perspectival rather than neutral cognition. But it was still closer to positivism than to dialectical thought in its disdain for essential levels of reality beneath apparent ones and its hostility towards the possibility of mediation and sublation. From Foucault's perspective, both Hegelian and scientific Marxists were wrong to search for some principle of coherence, however decentered, beneath the plurality of appearances.

40. Foucault acknowledges his debt to Dumézil in the preface to the first edition of *Histoire de la folie*. Dumézil's debt to structuralism may have been one of the reasons that Foucault was also initially assimilated to that position by many commentators.
41. Foucault, *The Archaeology of Knowledge*, pp. 15–16. Foucault's complete escape from a totalizing discourse has, to be sure, itself been a matter of some dispute.
42. Ibid., p. 125.
43. Ibid.

If such coherence could be found, it was only on the "surface" itself, a surface which hid no dialectical depths.

Hegelian Marxists were particularly misguided in searching for some collective or meta-subject genetically responsible for the whole. Rather than wasting their time trying to recover this subject through some sort of anamnestic totalization, the historian should emulate Nietzsche's principle of "active forgetting" and rely on his "counter-memory"[44] to make sense of the haphazard and random conflicts that make up historical change. Rather than trying to commemorate monuments in the past or to restore an alleged plenitude before alienation, the historian should approach the past as a "concerted carnival,"[45] an opportunity to lose oneself in the multiple identities presented by the historical record.

In the writings of Foucault's middle period, which can perhaps be said to have lasted from *The Order of Things* in 1966 until *Discipline and Punish* in 1975,[46] the main source of his critique of holism was linguistic. Although he never deliberately extrapolated from the model of structuralist linguistics that had been bequeathed to French thought by Saussure and Jakobson, he nonetheless absorbed the major lesson of their work: that language was a system anterior and therefore resistant to the intentionality of men as subjects. It was for this reason that he used the term "discourse" in a way diametrically opposed to the way it was employed by Habermas, who, as we have seen, was indebted to the very different linguistic tradition of hermeneutics. For Foucault, discourse had nothing to do with intersubjective dialogue; it implied instead the inertial and impenetrable materiality of language which always undercut what he saw as the fiction of intended meaning. Hoping for some perfect speech situation was as deluded as positing a constitutive subject at the origin of a discourse. The hermeneutic desire to regain the alleged immediacy of speech between two subjects, which was the dream of classical rhetoric, was doomed to failure:

The space of language today is not defined by Rhetoric, but by the Library: by the ranging to infinity of fragmentary languages, substituting for the double chain of

44. Foucault, *Language, Counter-Memory, Practice*, p. 160. Hostility towards anamnestic totalization was shared by all the post-structuralists. See, for example, Derrida's comments on the inevitability of *differance* in memory traces in *Speech and Phenomena and Other Essays on Husserl's Theory of Signs*, trans. with intro. David B. Allison, preface by Newton Garver (Evanston, 1973), p. xv.

45. Foucault, *Language, Counter-Memory, Practice*, p. 161. Recapturing the carnivalesque was also a major preoccupation of the Russian critic Mikhail Bakhtin. For a good introduction to his work and its relationship with deconstructionism and the Left, see Dominick LaCapra, "Bakhtin, Marxism, and the Carnivalesque" in *Rethinking Intellectual History: Texts, Contexts, Language* (Ithaca, forthcoming).

46. Foucault, *Discipline and Punish: The Birth of the Prison*, trans. Alan Sheridan (New York, 1978).

Rhetoric the simple, continuous, and monotonous line of language left to its own devices, a language fated to be infinite because it can no longer support itself upon the speech of infinity. . . . A language which repeats no other speech, no other Promise, but postpones death indefinitely by ceaselessly opening a space where it is always the analogue of itself.[47]

To believe that one could escape from the infinite hall of mirrors that was language, Foucault warned, was to succumb to the temptation of "transcendental narcissism,"[48] the illusion that there was an Archimedean point outside the flux.

In the work he completed after the mid-seventies, Foucault's critique of holism gained a new stimulus. Or rather it returned to the extra-linguistic focus of his earlier works on institutions like the clinic. Although he never abandoned his bleak view of the limitations of linguistic totalization, he came to see that discourse was itself merely a special case of a more pervasive reality. As he put it in an interview in 1977,

What I should like to do now is to try and show that what I call an apparatus is a much more general case of the *epistème*; or rathe:, that the *epistème* is a specifically *discursive* apparatus, whereas the apparatus in its general form is both discursive and non-discursive, its elements being much more heterogeneous.[49]

In *Discipline and Punish* and the ambitious six-part study of sexuality launched with *The History of Sexuality: The Will to Know* in 1976,[50] Foucault sounded a new Nietzschean theme: the ubiquity of power. Knowledge, he now argued in a manner that bore superficial resemblance to Habermas' analysis of *Erkenntnisinteressen*, was always grounded in power relationships. What separated Habermas from Foucault was their very different interpretationsf of power itself. Whereas the former followed Hannah Arendt in distinguishing communicative, consensual power from coercive violence or force,[51] the latter scorned "the longing for a form of power innocent of all coercion, discipline and normaliza-

47. Foucault, *Language, Counter-Memory, Practice*, p. 67.
48. Foucault, *The Archaeology of Knowledge*, p. 203. This term has been used by David Couzens Hoy to criticize Habermas. See Hoy, "Taking History Seriously: Foucault, Gadamer, Habermas," *Union Seminary Quarterly Review* 34, 2 (Winter 1979).
49. Foucault, *Power/Knowledge*, p. 197.
50. Foucault, *The History of Sexuality* volume 1: *An Introduction*, trans. Robert Hurley (New York, 1980).
51. For Habermas' debt to Arendt, see in particular his essay "Hannah Arendt's Communications Concept of Power," *Social Research* 44, 1 (Spring 1977). For Arendt's view of power as people acting "in concert," see especially *The Human Condition: A Study of the Central Dilemmas Facing Modern Man* (Chicago, 1958). For a recent argument based on anthropological evidence that power can have a non-coercive as well as coercive dimension, see Pierre Clastres, *Society Against the State*, trans. Robert Hurley and Abe Stein (New York, 1977).

tion."[52] Although there were certainly differences between one mode of power apparatus and another, power like language was prior to the subject and could never be overcome in the name of perfect intersubjectivity. Foucault was careful to insist, however, that his view of power ought not to be seen solely as a negative one. Power did not suppress something healthy and natural that could be liberated for mankind's betterment. Those Western Marxists like Marcuse or Reich who had tried to harness Freud in the name of a Marxism that would end sexual as well as other forms of alienation were in error. There was no primal sexuality that had been repressed by the power relations of capitalism or patriarchy. Power, in fact, was what created the very notion that something called "sexuality" existed at all. The "knowledge" of such an entity was a construct of power in the service of disciplining the human body. What he liked to call "bio-power" was also subtly reinforced by such constituting practices as the confessional, which helped create the sense of subjectivity in Western culture. In this sense, power could be seen as positive as well as negative, even though what it generally created were new forms of control rather than liberation. There were, to be sure, pockets of inchoate resistance that opposed the absolute power of power, but they never could prevent its reappearance in new and equally sinister forms.

There was no way to overcome power, Foucault argued, because it did not emanate from a central source which could be challenged and overthrown. The traditional concept of sovereignty was fallacious in assuming that a single locus of power could be identified. A microphysics of power, probing its multiple and diverse manifestations, would show otherwise. Marxism, therefore, was deluded in believing that a revolutionary seizure of power or a change in the mode of production would radically alter the nature of society. The fashionable preoccupation of French Althusserians with the state, in which ideology was transformed into Ideological State Apparatuses,[53] masked the extent to which power operated in a much more dispersed and localized manner. The domination that should be studied, Foucault insisted, was not that "of the King in his central position, therefore, but that of his subjects in their mutual relations: not the uniform edifice of sovereignty, but the multiple forms of subjugation that have a place and function within the social organism."[54]

52. Foucault, *Power/Knowledge*, p. 117.
53. Althusser developed this concept in *Lenin and Philosophy and Other Essays*, trans. Ben Brewster (New York, 1971). For an attempt to use some aspects of Foucault's analysis within a still essentially Althusserian framework, see Nicos Poulantzas, *State, Power, Socialism*, trans. Patrick Camiller (London, 1978); and Göran Therborn, *The Ideology of Power and the Power of Ideology* (London, 1980). The latter reports that Althusser was beginning to abandon the rigid ISA formula shortly before his final breakdown (p. 85).
54. Foucault, *Power/Knowledge*, p. 96.

Foucault's interest in the "polymorphous techniques of subjugation,"[55] as he liked to call them, and his conviction that they were part of a complex network of power, invites comparison with the classical Frankfurt School's analysis of the "administered society." Indeed, there were a number of obvious parallels between his work and theirs, although Foucault was unaware of them until the mid-1970s.[56] In *Discipline and Punish*, he presented a picture of increasingly pervasive domination that complemented that provided by Horkheimer and Adorno in *Dialectic of Enlightenment*; in both cases, instrumental rationality was accused of complicity in the process (although Foucault tended to equate it with reason *tout court* in ways that the Frankfurt School never did).[57] His keen sensitivity to the micro-techniques of power was reminiscent of a similar awareness in the work of Benjamin, whose research into nineteenth-century Parisian life anticipated some of Foucault's findings.[58] For all his playful embrace of a Nietzschean positivism, he recognized, as they did, that the positivist dream of knowing man scientifically grew out of and reinforced the techniques of surveillance and manipulation developed by power to "normalize" and discipline men. He was no less attuned to the link between the

---

55. Ibid.

56. Author's conversation with Foucault, October 27, 1980. See also "Structuralism and Post-Structuralism: An Interview with Michel Foucault," p. 200. The parallels between Critical Theory and post-structuralism have now become widely remarked. Eagleton, for example, claims that "there is hardly a theme in contemporary deconstruction that is not richly elaborated" in Adorno's work (*Walter Benjamin*, p. 141). The figure for whom post-structuralists seem to have most affection is Benjamin, about whom Derrida has written with admiration. See his "Ein Porträt Benjamins" in Burkhardt Lindner, ed., "*Links hatte noch alles sich zu enträtseln . . .*" *Walter Benjamin im Kontext* (Frankfurt, 1978). Carol Jacobs also tries to capture him for deconstruction in her *The Dissimulating Harmony* (Baltimore, 1978); for a rebuttal, see Irving Wohlfahrt, "Walter Benjamin's Image of Interpretation," *New German Critique* 17 (Spring 1979). Both Paul de Man and Geoffrey Hartmann, among prominent American deconstructionists, have also written approvingly of Benjamin. For another comparison of Critical Theory and post-structuralism, see David Gross, "Lowenthal, Adorno, Barthes: Three Perspectives on Popular Culture," *Telos* 45 (Fall 1980).

57. In a recent interview with Paul Rabinow, which appeared in *Skyline* (March, 1982), Foucault tries to distance himself from the accusation that he is simply an irrationalist:

There is the problem raised by Habermas: if one abandons the work of Kant or Weber, for example, one runs the risk of lapsing into irrationality.
    I am completely in agreement with this, but at the same time, our question is quite different: I think that the central issue of philosophy and critical thought since the eighteenth century has always been, still is, and will, I hope, remain the question, *What* is this reason that we use? What are its historical effects? What are its limits, and what are its dangers? How can we exist as rational beings, fortunately committed to practicing a rationality unfortunately crisscrossed by intrinsic dangers? . . . In addition, if it is extremely dangerous to say that Reason is the enemy that should be eliminated, it is just as dangerous to say that any critical questioning of this rationality risks sending us into irrationality. (pp. 18–19)

What is still lacking, however, in his work is an attempt to discriminate among aspects (or versions) of rationality in order to locate more clearly its beneficial and pernicious dimensions.

58. See, for example, Walter Benjamin, *Charles Baudelaire: A Lyric Poet in the Era of High Capitalism*, trans. Harry Zohn (London, 1973), p. 47, where the repressive implications of the numbering of houses in Paris is discussed.

conceptual suppression of difference (or in Adorno's terms, non-identity) and the social suppression of unorthodoxy.

The desire to see the whole of society as a transparent unity, which Foucault saw behind both Rousseau's image of the social contract and Bentham's idea for a model prison, the Panopticon, was thus a blueprint for totalitarianism. Indeed, the very assumption that history had a unified coherent meaning was, Foucault contended, a tool of disciplinary power:

> The disciplinary methods reveal a linear time whose moments are integrated, one upon another, and which is orientated towards a terminal, stable point; in short, an "evolutive" time. But it must be recalled that at the same moment, the administrative and economic techniques of control reveal a social time of a serial, orientated type: the discovery of an evolution in terms of "progress.". . . These two great "discoveries" of the eighteenth century—the progress of societies and the geneses of individuals—were perhaps correlative with the new techniques of power, and more specifically, with a new way of administering time and making it useful, by segmentation, seriation, synthesis and totalization.[59]

Critical Theory's deep suspicion of evolutionary temporalization, suspended only with Habermas' reconstruction of historical materialism, thus found in Foucault an obvious echo. So too did its dislike of the fetishization of labor and productivity, which he saw as symptomatic of the discipline of the body, a form of subtle dressage in which docility was corporeally inscribed. And finally, although the Frankfurt School maintained an ambivalent attitude towards the value of the bourgeois individual, it shared with Foucault a deep distrust of the varieties of pseudo-individualism that marked subservience in the modern world.

Foucault's image of that world, in fact, resembled at times the fully realized disciplinary society that Marcuse, from his more Hegelian perspective, had called completely one-dimensional. But like the senior members of the Frankfurt School, Foucault always claimed that total discipline could never be achieved. Power created its contrary, resistance, even if only partial and isolated. Thus, at the end of *Discipline and Punish*, he could write:

> In this central and centralized humanity, the effect and instrument of complex power relations, bodies and forces subjected by multiple mechanisms of "incarceration", objects for discourses that are in themselves elements for this strategy, we must hear the distant roar of battle.[60]

And in the first volume of his history of sexuality, he could, in equally military terms, claim that "the rallying point for the counterattack

59. Foucault, *Discipline and Punish*, p. 160.
60. Ibid., p. 308.

against the deployment of sexuality ought not to be sex-desire, but bodies and pleasures."[61]

The nature, however, of the battle for bodies and pleasures was not immediately apparent in Foucault's writings. His insistence on the inevitability of power in the coercive sense suggested that resistance could never hope to diminish in very significant ways the grip of domination. Foucault was clearly outraged at certain forms of that domination, but it was never very clear from what normative vantage point, aside from his own personal preferences. If the humanist notion of a subject whose true needs could be repressed was merely a myth,[62] in whose name did Foucault so heatedly criticize the blight of increasing panoptic normalization? If there were no truth, but only "truth effects" expressing certain power relations, then how could one be confident that his call for a "general economy of pleasure not based on sexual norms"[63] would not lead to a new form of oppressive power, of the kind, say, attacked by Marcuse as "repressive desublimation"? If rationality in all its forms led to the exclusion of marginality and difference, why would irrationality (or less pejoratively put, *a*rationality) avoid a new exclusionary politics—one aimed at those dedicated to realizing a universal rational discourse in Habermas' sense?

Nor was the self-reflective epistemological vantage point from which Foucault himself proceeded very clear. If truth was merely an effect of power, what was the place within the network of power relations that allowed him to see through the illusions of his age? If Habermas could be attacked, as we saw he was by Disco, for expressing the ideology of the humanist wing of Gouldner's "new class," whose ideology or power interests did Foucault's work express? Moreover, if intersubjectivity were a fraud and rational discourse impossible, who was the intended audience for Foucault's books? Who were to be the collaborators in his localized attacks on specific instances of discipline and normalization?

In short, what Habermas said about Nietzsche in *Knowledge and Human Interests* might also be applied a fortiori to Foucault and the new Nietzscheanism in general:

61. Foucault, *The History of Sexuality*, p. 157.
62. Foucault, to be sure, does recognize the existence of the subject at certain places in his work, for example, in *Language, Counter-Memory, Practice*, where he writes: "The subject should not be entirely abandoned. It should be reconsidered, not to restore the theme of an originating subject, but to seize its functions, its intervention in discourse, and its system of dependencies" (p. 137). But it is clear that he generally considers the idea of a centered subject a myth.
63. Foucault, *Power/Knowledge*, p. 191.

Nietzsche—and this puts him above all others—denies the critical power of reflection with and only with the *means of reflection itself*. . . . Yet Nietzsche is so rooted in basic positivist beliefs that he cannot systematically take cognizance of the cognitive function of self-reflection from which he lives as a philosophical writer. The ironic contradiction of a self-denial of reflection, however, is so stubborn that it cannot be dissolved by arguments but only appeased by invocations. Reflection that annihilates itself cannot rely on the aid of beneficent regression. It requires auto-suggestion to conceal from itself what it unceasingly accomplishes, namely critique.[64]

Should Foucault decide to examine more systematically and self-critically the sources of that critique which his work certainly expresses, then it is possible that some of the distance between his current position and that of Habermas may narrow. For although it is unlikely that he will abandon a coercive for a communicative concept of power, or replace his view of language as an impersonal archive with one stressing its intersubjective dimension, reflection on the conditions and intentions of his own work may lead him away from his radically anti-humanist Nietzscheanism. There are indications that Foucault, like Habermas, is willing to grow beyond his initial positions partly on the basis of dialogue with his critics,[65] so it is possible that an exchange between the two, either directly or indirectly, may produce light as well as the inevitable heat.

Such speculation, of course, may reflect my own hopes rather than any likely outcome, so it is perhaps best to return to the issue of totality and consider in conclusion why Foucault and the post-structuralists have found so ready a hearing among its critics. If, to begin with a general point, totalistic claims have often been made by intellectuals who arrogate to themselves the capacity to know society as a whole, then the recent loss of faith in that capacity may reflect a new modesty on the part of many intellectuals. One sign of the weakening of this hubris may be seen in the virtual disappearance in recent years of the inflated notion of a modernist avant-garde representing the cutting edge of the cultural future. Artistically inclined intellectuals are less prone than they were in the years when Western Marxism was also at its height to consider themselves spokesmen for the species or at least the privileged bearers of its potential

64. Habermas, *Knowledge and Human Interests*, p. 299.
65. This observation is based on Foucault's participation in the conference devoted to his work at the University of Southern California in October, 1981. In the workshop run by Robert d'Amico and myself at the conference, Foucault engaged in a very stimulating exchange over the points of difference between his approach and that of Habermas.

consciousness. Not only did their attempts to join with the political avant-garde miscarry, as the case of Surrealism most obviously shows, but they also lost most of their confidence that modernism was destined to triumph universally. The muddled cultural politics of post-modernism today expresses this loss in ever clearer terms.

If the cultural avant-garde is now increasingly called into question, the concept of a political vanguard, which was composed primarily of radical bourgeois intellectuals, has experienced no less of a crisis. Even in its non-Leninist forms, intellectual vanguardism has lost much of its allure. Foucault's popularity draws, at least in part, from his registering of this fact. As he put it in 1977,

For a long period, the "left" intellectual spoke and was acknowledged the right of speaking in the capacity of master of truth and justice. He was heard or purported to make himself heard, as the spokesman of the universal. To be an intellectual meant something like being the consciousness/conscience of us all. I think we have here an idea transposed from Marxism, from a faded Marxism indeed. . . . Some years have now passed since the intellectual was called upon to play this role. A new mode of the "connection between theory and practice" has been established. Intellectuals have got used to working, not in the modality of the "universal", the "exemplary", the "just-and-true-for-all", but within specific sectors, at precise points where their own conditions of life or work situate them. . . . This is what I would call the "specific" intellectual as opposed to the "universal" intellectual.[66]

Foucault's suspicion about universalist intellectuals also motivates two recent books that, paradoxically, try to demonstrate how intellectuals are beginning to establish themselves as a distinct class in society with aggrandizing designs: George Konrád and Ivan Szelényi's *The Intellectuals on the Road to Class Power*, and Alvin Gouldner's *The Future of Intellectuals and the Rise of the New Class*.[67] In the former, written clandestinely in the early 1970s, two Hungarian sociologists describe the increased power gained by intellectuals as the directors of economic "rational redistribution" in Eastern Europe. The right to exercise that control is claimed by intellectuals because of their alleged technical and managerial superiority. According to Konrád and Szelényi, rational redistribution has not been so rational after all, and a new class structure has arisen to replace the traditional one socialism tried to abolish. They also argue that the way

66. Foucault, *Power/Knowledge*, p. 126.
67. George Konrád and Ivan Szelényi, *The Intellectuals on the Road to Class Power: A Sociological Study of the Role of the Intelligentsia in Socialism*, trans. Andrew Arato and Richard E. Allen (New York, 1979); Alvin W. Gouldner, *The Future of Intellectuals and the Rise of the New Class* (New York, 1979). For more recent and often more disillusioned expressions of similar sentiments, see the symposium on "The Role of the Intellectual in the 1980s," *Telos* 50 (Winter 1981–82).

to combat the new inequality that has resulted is not to revert to a teleological style of thinking which once again draws on "the category of a
goal-oriented human totality."[68] However innocent in intent, such a reversion would play into the hands of a new kind of Leninism:

> If the New Left cannot go beyond insisting that intellectuals should enunciate
> universal social goals and lead broad opposition movements, rather than give ex-
> pression to their own particular interests, then there will be nothing in its thinking
> to distinguish it from traditional Bolshevism. . . . Leftism ceases to be leftist if it
> only serves the ethos of redistribution.[69]

Gouldner's faith in the universalistic claims of the "New Class" of intellectuals, as he likes to call it, is no less ambivalent. Although assigning
it the role of "the most progressive force in modern society" and calling it
"the center of whatever human emancipation is possible in the foreseea-
ble future,"[70] he recognizes its sinister potential as "the nucleus of a *new*
hierarchy and the elite of a new form of cultural capital."[71] Its dependence
on what he calls a "culture of critical discourse," which, *contra* Habermas, is limited to a socially defined mandarinate of those educated in
privileged ways, means that for all its claims to represent the whole, the
New Class is really restricted to "the knowing, the knowledgeable, the
reflexive and the insightful."[72] Thus, "the New Class is the universal class
in embryo, but badly flawed."[73] Like Konrád and Szelényi, Gouldner acknowledges a potentially dangerous link between intellectuals with their
self-aggrandizing totalistic claims and authoritarian forms of state socialism. "It is precisely because control of the means of production by the
state is a mechanism advantaging the New Class," he writes, "that this is
supported by them rather than democratizing the means of production.
Socialism, then, is a way of extending the New Class's cultural capital."[74]
Accordingly, the holistic claims of Marxists, Western or otherwise, ought
not to be taken at face value as the expression of selfless identification
with the good of humanity; Marxism, he concludes, is in fact "the false
consciousness of cultural bourgeoisie who have been radicalized."[75]

Resistance to those claims in recent years has not come, however, from
the place from which it traditionally emanates, the working class itself.
Either intellectuals with bad consciences like the authors mentioned
above or, more frequently, the groups mentioned by Huyssen and Aronowitz earlier in this discussion have been the more vocal source. The groups
in question were those traditionally excluded from the dominant Marxist

68. Konrád and Szelényi, p. 242.   69. Ibid., p. 251.
70. Gouldner, p. 83.   71. Ibid.   72. Ibid., p. 85.
73. Ibid.   74. Ibid., p. 61.   75. Ibid., p. 75.

concept of the historical subject: women, racial minorities and homosexuals. To many of them, the fiction of a unified meta-subject of history has been far worse than a theoretical error, for it has also expressed the tacit hegemony of white, heterosexual, patriarchal males in the history of the Left. Although one might argue that the move away from expressive totality and the absolute domination of the male proletariat began as early as Lukács' *Lenin* in 1924, the totalizing impulse in the tradition remained too strong for those conceived of as junior partners in the common struggle to feel comfortable with their roles.[76] The Western Marxist discourse on totality has thus been in part a casualty of the rise to prominence of new groups on the Left who are suspicious of both the proletariat as the ascribed subject of history and the intellectuals who claim to speak on behalf of the totalizing subject. Although on occasion this suspicion can be taken too far, as in the case of those feminists who see discursive rationalism of the kind promulgated by Habermas as a male ideology,[77] it is difficult on the basis of past experience to deny its validity entirely.

An even more potent stimulus to the undermining of Marxist holism can arguably be detected in the deeply troubling history of socialism in power in this century. If the capacity of remembrance to totalize history as a coherent and meaningful whole was frequently evoked by certain Western Marxists to justify their hopes for the future, it has become increasingly difficult to blot out the disturbing memory of socialism's practical failures. Although it is true that anamnestic totalization can be a weapon of the Left against the Right—Critical Theory's version of it seems to have played a role in helping postwar Germany come to terms with its "unmastered past"[78]—it can also serve the opposite function. The extraordinary impact of Alexander Solzhenitsyn's *The Gulag Archipelago* in France during the 1970s, when the so-called New Philosophers cited it again and again in the struggle to free themselves from the remnants of their earlier Althusserianism,[79] bears witness to the anti-leftist potential in remem-

76. Some feminist discourse has, to be sure, developed its own totalistic impulses. See the critique of these in Jean Bethke Elshtain, *Public Man, Private Woman: Women in Social and Political Thought* (Princeton, 1981), p. 224.

77. See, for example, Michael Ryan, *Marxism and Deconstruction*, p. 145. As the unidentified "intellectual historian" who failed to take Ryan's question with the appropriate gravity at the conference he mentions, I would still reply that his view of women, third world or otherwise, as somehow incapable of engaging in communicative rationality, is simply demeaning to the women who can and do just that. Derrida's essay "The White Mythology: Metaphor in the Text of Philosophy" in *Margins of Philosophy*, trans. Alan Bass (Chicago, 1981) is the source of his contention.

78. Paul Connerton makes this point in *The Tragedy of Enlightenment: An Essay on the Frankfurt School* (Cambridge, 1980), p. 10.

79. See, for example, Bernard-Henri Lévy, *Barbarism with a Human Face*, trans. George Holoch (New York, 1979), p. 153f.

brance. Not even Bloch's alternative concept of *anagnorisis*, the recognition of anticipatory traces of future plenitude in the past, seems to have prevented many observers from finding traces of a future hell instead.

And when the distant memory of the Gulag is combined with fresher memories of new horrors in the name of socialism, most notably the Cambodian disaster, it has become even more problematic to excuse unfortunate methods in the name of a positive outcome. There has, in other words, been no new version of *Humanism and Terror* to appear in answer to Solzhenitsyn in the way Merleau-Ponty's book defiantly arose to refute the similar arguments in Koestler's *Darkness at Noon*. The appeal to the longitudinal totality of history as the court of ultimate judgment has lost much of its allure, as indeed it had for Merleau-Ponty himself after the Korean War.

Concomitantly, there has been a growing fear in certain quarters on the Left that the old argument linking the Marxist aspiration for normative totality and totalitarian politics made by earlier critics like Camus may have a certain legitimacy after all. As a former member of Lukács' Budapest School, Mihály Vajda, has cautiously admitted,

The attempts to put the blame for the totalitarian forms of domination of "existing socialism" on the totalizing principle of the Marxist theory of society suffer from one serious shortcoming: they attribute to ideologies a power they have never had. Yet it is impossible to attempt to analyze the structures of society and the forms of domination in Eastern Europe, the system of "existing socialism," separately from the ideology of Marxism, as if this totalitarian form of domination had nothing to do with the ideas of Marx, as if the legacy of Russian conditions and traditions had only distorted and had not in any way put into practice the conception of socialism.[80]

For Vajda, the enthusiasm that certain early Western Marxists, especially Bloch and Lukács, had for Russia was not unrelated to their stress on totality. Hoping that normative wholeness might be achieved in the antibourgeois and anti-rationalist culture of Dostoevskyan Russia, they lived instead to see its perverted realization in the Russia that emerged after the revolution.

Agreeing with his fellow Hungarians Konrád and Szelényi that antiparticularist experiments in rational redistribution have a totalitarian potential, Vajda nonetheless modifies their argument that it was the intellectual class per se that spawned the problem. He emphasizes the importance of transplanting Hegelian ideas of rational holism from the West to the East, where attempts to put it into effect could more easily succeed:

80. Mihály Vajda, *The State and Socialism: Political Essays* (London, 1981), p. 107.

In Russia one could realize "true" rationality and humanity precisely because it was not yet corrupted by bourgeois rationality. But it was not only the relatively minor role of the empirical working class, but (in connection with this, although not identical) the absence of individual rational modes of behavior that made Russia so susceptible to the terror of the general.[81]

Thus, the lesson of the Russian and Eastern European examples is that the Hegelian concept of normative totality is most likely to be realized in countries where bourgeois modernization failed to occur. This linkage, which of course is the opposite of Marx's expectation, means that socialism *and* barbarism rather than socialism *or* barbarism is the formula to describe much twentieth-century history. And most significantly, the Hegelian Marxist discourse on totality may possibly shoulder some of the responsibility for this undesired turn of events.

It is not by accident that Hungarians like Vajda, Konrád and Szelényi (and one might add others like Ferenc Feher, Agnes Heller and György Márkus) have come to this conclusion. Initially the defenders of Western Marxism in Eastern Europe, they have ironically become the bearers of bad news from that part of the world to the West, where most of them have been forced to emigrate. The particular bad news that they have brought is not merely that Eastern Marxism is a disastrous failure, which is no real news at all, but rather that the Western Marxism to which they originally adhered is itself deeply flawed as an antidote to the horrors of its Eastern counterpart. Ample evidence of the shift can be seen in the contrast between their reactions to the Prague Spring in 1968 and the Polish Autumn twelve years later. Whereas many Critical Marxists both in the East and the West interpreted the Czechs' "Marxism with a Human Face" as an attempt to realize Marxist humanism and its promise of a non-alienated socialist community, the Polish case has been understood in different terms. As Andrew Arato put it,

No one in Poland seeks to remythologize the workers as a universal subject. Even in this radical interpretation [of Jacek Kuron], Solidarity's aim is not to establish unity but autonomous heterogeneity, i.e., its political function should be to defend the establishment of a whole host of associations that in the future would make the union one institution among equals.[82]

Solidarity's goal, in other words, was the rejuvenation of civil society—understood in more communitarian than competitive, individualist terms—against the state with its rational redistributive ethos. Ever since

81. Ibid., p. 122.
82. Arato, "Civil Society Against the State: Poland 1980–1981," *Telos* 47 (Spring 1981), p. 34.

Marx's "On the Jewish Question," the existence of a civil society split off from the state has been taken by Marxists as a prime example of aliena- tion, which would be overcome by what Marx called "human emancipa- tion." Now, however, the *Aufhebung* of this split seems to promise instead the suppression of differences in the name of an allegedly unified whole. What Gouldner once called "nightmare Marxism"[83] now appears latent in its most utopian dreams.

But even among those leftists who hold out hope that socialism will be able to awaken from its nightmares, confidence in the concept of totality often seems on the wane. Here too historical rather than merely theoreti- cal considerations have been paramount. When the Western Marxist par- adigm was initiated it was possible to conceptualize capitalism as a world system that would be supplanted in time by a completely new system known as socialism in the same way that feudalism gave way to capital- ism. Indeed, much of the animus of Lukács and his radical colleagues against the Revisionists was directed against their muddying of the differ- ences between the two systems. But beginning with Stalin's fateful deci- sion to salvage the results of 1917 by falling back on a defense of "social- ism in one country," it has become clear that capitalism's capacity to survive and transform itself was greater than originally anticipated and, even more disheartening, that socialism in a non-global context could quickly betray its promise. Western Marxism, of course, developed in re- sponse to this dilemma, but initially at least it held on to the belief that the new order convulsively emerging in the twentieth century could be grasped as a coherent, if contradictory, whole. The recovery of Western Marxism by the New Left in the 1960s and early 1970s in the English- speaking world corresponded, at least to a certain degree, with the cau- tious revival of those hopes.

But one need only allude to certain subsequent events—the debacle of Maoism in China, the explosion of Islamic anti-modernism in the Middle East, the souring of emancipatory hopes in Indochina, the collapse of Eurocommunism, the repressive Soviet actions in Afghanistan and Po- land, and the growing realization that neither capitalist nor socialist gov- ernments seem to have the ability to stave off economic disaster—to real- ize how difficult it is today to conceptualize the world as a meaningful whole, let alone one heading in a positive direction. Even within the nar- rower confines of one country, the task of mounting a holistic critique of

83. Alvin W. Gouldner, *The Two Marxisms: Contradictions and Anomalies in the De- velopment of Theory* (New York, 1980), p. 380f.

society has come to seem insuperable, as the recent growth of the so-called "new populism" on the American Left demonstrates.[84]

And yet paradoxically, even after one acknowledges all of these reasons why the discourse of totality is now so much in disfavor, it is precisely because of one of contemporary history's most frightening realities that it is both impossible and unwise to abandon it entirely.[85] That reality is captured in the chilling remark from Adorno's *Negative Dialectics* that we have had occasion to cite before:

> No universal history leads from savagery to humanitarianism, but there is one leading from the slingshot to the megaton bomb. It ends in the total menace which organized mankind poses to organized men, in the epitome of discontinuity. It is the horror that verifies Hegel and stands him on his head.[86]

If, as many of its critics claim, totality means closure and death, the end of difference, desire and non-identity, then the threat of global holocaust compels us to take it very seriously indeed. The escape into an anti-holistic particularism by "specific" as opposed to "universal" intellectuals, which Foucault and others advise, fails to confront this incontrovertible reality. That infinite carnivalesque play of which the post-structuralists are so fond may well turn out to be much more suddenly and decisively finite than they or anyone else would desire unless some means of thwarting nuclear totalization is found. And without acknowledging the complex interrelatedness of our planetary existence, no such solution is likely to be forthcoming.

The search for a viable concept of totality, which we have seen animating Western Marxism, should not therefore be written off as no more than

84. For defenses of the New Populism, which stress its decentralized vision of social change, see Martin Carnoy and Derek Shearer, *Economic Democracy* (White Plains, N.Y., 1980); Lawrence Goodwyn, *The Populist Movement* (New York, 1978); Harry C. Boyte, *The Backyard Revolution* (Philadelphia, 1980); and Tom Hayden, *The American Future: New Visions Beyond Old Frontiers* (Boston, 1980).

85. Another reason why it may be impossible to abandon it entirely is suggested by Jameson when he notes that deconstructionist positions may be "second-degree or critical philosophies, which reconfirm the status of the concept of totality by their very reaction against it." (*The Political Unconscious*, p. 53). Derrida himself seems to confirm the inevitability of the unresolved dialectic between totality and anti-totality in his response to a question put to him at the 1966 conference on structuralism at Johns Hopkins:

I didn't say that there was no center, that we could get along without the center. I believe that the center is a function, not a being—a reality, but a function. And this function is absolutely indispensable. The subject is absolutely indispensable. I don't destroy the subject; I situate it. That is to say, I believe that at a certain level both of experience and of philosophical and scientific discourse, one cannot get along without the notion of subject.

(*The Structuralist Controversy: The Languages of Criticism and the Sciences of Man*, eds. Richard Macksey and Eugenio Donato [Baltimore, 1970], p. 271.)

If the subject and the center are indispensable functions on a certain level of experience and discourse, is it not equally possible to argue that totality is as well?

86. Theodor Adorno, *Negative Dialectics*, trans. E. B. Ashton (New York, 1973), p. 320.

a benighted exercise in nostalgia for a past plenitude or the ideology of intellectuals bent on legitimating their domination of the rest of mankind. For if the human race is to avoid the negative totality of nuclear catastrophe, we may well need to find some positive alternative. As the philosopher who has so often been used against the concept of totality once observed, decadence means "that life no longer dwells in the whole."[87] Nietzche may indeed have been an unsurpassed analyst of the varieties of that decadence, as his post-structuralist admirers never tire of reminding us, but he was no less anxious to overcome its lure in the name of a new wholeness he called life.[88] It is, I would argue in conclusion, very much in the spirit of this Nietzsche rather than the one celebrated by his recent French defenders that Adorno once wrote:

In a world of brutal and oppressed life, decadence becomes the refuge of a potentially better life by renouncing its allegiance to this one and to its culture, its crudeness, and its sublimity. . . . What can oppose the decline of the west is not a resurrected culture but the utopia that is silently contained in the image of its decline.[89]

If the Western Marxist discourse on totality can be said, Habermas aside, to have undergone such a decline, is it too much to hope that amidst the debris there lurks, silent but still potent, the germ of a truly defensible concept of totality—and even more important, the potential for a liberating totalization that will not turn into its opposite? If not, then we are likely to suffer that terminal closure which will demonstrate what a serious rather than merely playful deconstruction of human culture really can mean. Should this latter outcome be avoided, it will perhaps be in some measure due to the legacy left by the agonizingly flawed, yet admirably heroic, efforts made by the Western Marxists to see things whole. The questions they asked continue to be the right ones, even if the answers they offered were not. There is little reason to expect that better ones will be forthcoming in the immediate future, but to give up the search is to resign ourselves to a destiny against which everything that makes us human should compel us to resist.

87. Friedrich Nietzsche, *The Birth of Tragedy and the Case of Wagner*, trans. Walter Kaufmann (New York, 1967), p. 170. Nietzsche refers here specifically to the literary style of decadence, but his remark can be extrapolated to decadence in a more general sense.
88. For an example of Nietzsche's positive view of totalization, at least on an individual level, see his admiring description of Goethe in *The Twilight of Idols*:

What he wanted was *totality*; he fought the mutual extraneousness of reason, senses, feeling and will (preached with the most abhorrent scholasticism by *Kant*, the antipode of Goethe); he disciplined himself to wholeness, he created himself.

(*The Portable Nietzsche*, ed. Walter Kaufman [New York, 1968], p. 554.)
89. Theodor Adorno, *Prisms: Cultural Criticism and Society*, trans. Samuel and Shierry Weber (London, 1967), p. 72.

Selected Bibliography

Rather than listing all of the works, primary and secondary, cited in the text, I have provided a more modest guide for the reader who is interested in probing the issues and figures treated in this study. The following books and articles, therefore, have been chosen with two goals in mind. The first is to present the secondary sources I have found most profitable to consult. The second is to direct the reader towards those works in which very extensive bibliographies of both primary and secondary texts can be found. The titles preceded by an asterisk contain such bibliographies and should be consulted, along with the footnotes of the present study, by anyone seeking a greater command of the literature on Western Marxism and the issue of totality.

The bibliography is arranged according to the chapters in the book; following a general section on Western Marxism, which corresponds to the Introduction, there are sixteen sections corresponding to the fifteen chapters and epilogue.

General Works on Western Marxism

Agger, Ben, ed. *Western Marxism, an Introduction: Classical and Contemporary Sources.* Santa Monica, Calif., 1979.

Anderson, Perry. *Considerations on Western Marxism.* London, 1976.

Aronowitz, Stanley. *The Crisis in Historical Materialism: Class, Politics, and Culture in Marxist Theory.* New York, 1981.

Bubner, Rüdiger. *Modern German Philosophy.* Translated by Eric Matthews. Cambridge, 1981.

Dallmayr, Fred R. *Twilight of Subjectivity: Contributions to a Post-Individualist Theory of Politics.* Amherst, Mass., 1981.

Gombin, Richard. *The Radical Tradition: A Study in Modern Revolutionary Thought.* Translated by Rupert Dwyer. New York, 1979.

Gouldner, Alvin W. *The Two Marxisms: Contradictions and Anomalies in the Development of Theory.* New York, 1980.

Grahl, Bart, and Piccone, Paul, eds. *Towards a New Marxism.* St. Louis, 1973.

Hirsh, Arthur. *The French New Left: An Intellectual History from Sartre to Gorz.* Boston, 1981.

Howard, Dick, and Klare, Karl, eds. *The Unknown Dimension: European Marxism Since Lenin.* New York, 1972.

Jacoby, Russell. *Dialectic of Defeat: Contours of Western Marxism.* Cambridge, 1981.

Jameson, Fredric. *Marxism and Form: Twentieth-Century Dialectical Theories of Literature.* Princeton, 1971.

(*) Kelly, Michael. *Modern French Marxism.* Baltimore, 1982.

Kilminster, Richard. *Praxis and Method: A Sociological Dialogue with Lukács, Gramsci and the Early Frankfurt School.* London, 1979.

Kolakowski, Leszek. *Main Currents of Marxism.* Vol. 3: *The Breakdown.* Translated by P. S. Falla. Oxford, 1978.

(*) Lunn, Eugene. *Marxism and Modernism: An Historical Study of Lukács, Brecht, Benjamin, and Adorno.* Berkeley, 1982.

(*) McClellan, David. *Marxism after Marx.* London, 1979.

Miller, James. *History and Human Existence: From Marx to Merleau-Ponty.* Berkeley, 1979.

New Left Review, ed. *Western Marxism: A Critical Reader.* London, 1977.

Piccone, Paul. *Italian Marxism.* Berkeley, 1983.

(*) Poster, Mark. *Existential Marxism in Postwar France: From Sartre to Althusser.* Princeton, 1975.

1. Totality and Holism

(*) O'Neill, John, ed. *Modes of Individualism and Collectivism.* London, 1973.

(*) Phillips, D. C. *Holistic Thought in Social Science.* Standford, 1976.

(*) Rousseau, G. S., ed. *Organic Form: The Life of an Idea.* London, 1972.

Wilden, Anthony. *System and Structure: Essays in Communication and Exchange.* London, 1972.

2. Georg Lukács

Arato, Andrew, and Breines, Paul. *The Young Lukács and the Origins of Western Marxism.* New York, 1979.

Congdon, Lee. *The Young Lukács.* Chapel Hill, 1983.

Feenberg, Andrew. *Lukács, Marx, and the Sources of Critical Theory.* Totowa, New Jersey, 1981.

(*)Lapoint, François H. *Georg Lukács and His Critics: An International Bibliography with Annotations* (1910–1982). Westport, Conn., 1983.

Löwy, Michael. *Georg Lukács: From Romanticism to Bolshevism.* Translated by Patrick Camiller. London, 1979.

(*) Mészáros, István. *Lukács' Concept of Dialectic.* London, 1972.

Parkinson, G. H. R., ed. *Georg Lukács: The Man, His Work, and His Ideas.* New York, 1970.

———. *Georg Lukács.* London, 1977.

3. Karl Korsch

Buckmiller, Michael, ed. *Zur Aktualität von Karl Korsch.* Frankfurt, 1981.

(*) Goode, Patrick. *Karl Korsch: A Study in Western Marxism.* London, 1979.

Kellner, Douglas, ed. *Karl Korsch: Revolutionary Theory.* Austin, 1977.

Pozzoli, Claudio, ed. "Über Karl Korsch," *Jahrbuch Arbeiterbewegung 1* (special issue 1973).

4. Antonio Gramsci

(*) Adamson, Walter L. *Hegemony and Revolution: A Study of Antonio Gramsci's Political and Cultural Theory.* Berkeley, 1980.

Boggs, Carl. *Gramsci's Marxism.* London, 1976.

Buci-Glucksmann, Christine. *Gramsci and the State.* Translated by David Fernbach. New York, 1980.

Cammett, John. *Antonio Gramsci and the Origins of Italian Communism.* Stanford, 1971.

(*) Clark, Martin. *Antonio Gramsci and the Revolution that Failed.* New Haven, 1977.

(*) Davidson, Alastair. *Antonio Gramsci: Towards an Intellectual Biography.* London, 1977.

Entwistle, Harold. *Antonio Gramsci: Conservative Schooling for Radical Politics.* Boston, 1979.

Femia, Joseph V. *Gramsci's Political Thought: Hegemony, Consciousness and the Revolutionary Process.* Oxford, 1981.

Fiori, Giuseppe. *Antonio Gramsci: Life of a Revolutionary.* Translated by Tom Nairn. New York, 1971.

Joll, James. *Antonio Gramsci.* London, 1977.

Mouffe, Chantal, ed. *Gramsci and Marxist Theory.* London, 1979.

Nemeth, Thomas. *Gramsci's Epistemology: A Critical Study.* Atlantic Highlands, N.J. 1980.

Sassoon, Ann Showstock. *Gramsci's Politics.* New York, 1980.

Spriano, Paolo. *Antonio Gramsci and the Party: The Prison Years.* Translated by John Fraser. London, 1979.

5. Ernst Bloch

Bahr, Erhard. *Ernst Bloch.* Berlin, 1974.

(*) Hudson, Wayne. *The Marxist Philosophy of Ernst Bloch.* London, 1982.

Schmidt, Burghart. *Ernst Blochs Wirkung: Ein Arbeitsbuch zum 90. Geburtstag.* Frankfurt, 1975.

Unseld, Siegfried, ed. *Festschrift, Ernst Bloch zu Ehren: Beiträge zu seinem Werk.* Frankfurt, 1965.

6. Max Horkheimer

Arato, Andrew, and Gebhardt, Eike, eds. *The Essential Frankfurt School Reader.* Introduction by Paul Piccone. New York, 1978.

(*) Connerton, Paul. *The Tragedy of Enlightenment: An Essay on the Frankfurt School.* Cambridge, 1980.

Dubiel, Helmut. *Wissenschaftsorganisation und politische Erfahrung: Studien zur frühen Kritischen Theorie.* Frankfurt, 1978.

(*) Friedman, George. *The Political Philosophy of the Frankfurt School.* Ithaca, 1981.

Gumnior, Helmut, and Ringguth, Rolf. *Max Horkheimer in Selbstzeugnissen und Bilddokumenten.* Reinbek bei Hamburg, 1974.

(*) Held, David. *Introduction to Critical Theory: Horkheimer to Habermas.* Berkeley, 1980.

(*) Jay, Martin. *The Dialectical Imagination: A History of the Frankfurt School and the Institute of Social Research, 1923–1950.* Boston, 1973.

Lienert, Franz. *Theorie und Tradition: Zum Menschenbild in Werke Horkheimers.* Bern, 1977.

O'Neill, John, ed. *On Critical Theory.* New York, 1976.

Skuhra, Anselm. *Max Horkheimer: Eine Einführung in sein Denken.* Stuttgart, 1974.

(*) Slater, Phil. *Origin and Significance of the Frankfurt School: A Marxist Perspective.* London, 1977.

Söllner, Alfons. *Geschichte und Herrschaft: Studien zur Materialistischen Sozialwissenschaft, 1929–1942.* Frankfurt, 1979.

(*) Tar, Zoltan. *The Frankfurt School: The Critical Theories of Max Horkheimer and Theodor W. Adorno.* New York, 1977.

7. Herbert Marcuse

(*) Kātz, Barry. *Herbert Marcuse and the Art of Liberation: An Intellectual Biography.* London, 1982.

(*) Schoolman, Morton. *The Imaginary Witness: The Critical Theory of Herbert Marcuse.* New York, 1980.

8. Theodor W. Adorno

(*) Buck-Morss, Susan. *The Origin of Negative Dialectics: Theodor W. Adorno, Walter Benjamin, and the Frankfurt Institute.* New York, 1977.

Grenz, Friedemann. *Adornos Philosophie in Grundbegriffen: Auflösung einiger Deutungsprobleme.* Frankfurt, 1974.

(*) Lindner, Burkhardt, and Lüdke, W. Martin, eds. *Materialien zur ästhetischen Theorie Theodor W. Adornos: Konstruktion der Moderne.* Frankfurt, 1979.

Oppens, Kurt, et al. *Über Theodor W. Adorno.* Frankfurt, 1968.

Pettazzi, Carlo. *Theodor Wiesengrund Adorno: Linee di origine e di sviluppo del pensiero (1903–1949).* Florence, 1979.

(*) Rose, Gillian. *The Melancholy Science: An Introduction to the Thought of Theodor W. Adorno.* New York, 1978.

Wolin, Richard. *Walter Benjamin: An Aesthetic of Redemption.* New York, 1982.

9. Henri Lefebvre

Caute, David. *Communism and the French Intellectuals, 1914–1960.* London, 1964.

Hirsh, Arthur. *The French New Left: An Intellectual History from Sartre to Gorz.* Boston, 1981.

(*) Kurzweil, Edith. *The Age of Structuralism: Lévi-Strauss to Foucault.* New York, 1980.

Lichtheim, George. *Marxism in Modern France.* New York, 1966.

Schmidt, Alfred. "Henri Lefebvre and Contemporary Interpretations of Marx." In *The Unknown Dimension: European Marxism Since Lenin*, edited by Dick Howard and Karl E. Klare. New York, 1972.

Sève, Lucien. *La Différence. Deux essais: Lénine, philosophe communiste. Sur "La somme et le reste" d'Henri Lefebvre*. Paris, 1960.

Soubise, Louis. *Le Marxisme après Marx*. Paris, 1967.

10. Lucien Goldmann

Baum, Hermann. *Lucien Goldmann: Marxismus contra vision tragique?* Stuttgart, 1974.

Evans, Mary. *Lucien Goldmann*. Brighton, 1981.

(*) Goldmann, Lucien. *Cultural Creation in Modern Society*. Translated by Bart Grahl; Introduction by William Mayrl; Bibliography compiled by Ileana Rodriguez and Marc Zimmerman. St. Louis, 1976.

Naïr, Sami, and Lowy, Michael. *Goldmann ou la dialectique de la totalité*. Paris, 1973.

Zima, Pierre V. *Goldmann: Dialectique de l'immanence*. Paris, 1973.

11. Jean-Paul Sartre

Aron, Raymond. *History and the Dialectic of Violence: An Analysis of Sartre's "Critique de la Raison Dialectique."* Translated by Barry Cooper. New York, 1976.

Aronson, Ronald. *Jean-Paul Sartre: Philosophy in the World*. London, 1980.

(*) Belkind, Allen. *Jean-Paul Sartre: Sartre and Existentialism in English: A Bibliographical Guide*. Kent, Ohio, 1970.

Chiodi, Pietro. *Sartre and Marxism*. Translated by Kate Soper. New York, 1976.

(*) Contat, Michel, and Rybalka, Michel. *The Writings of Jean-Paul Sartre*. 2 vols. Evanston, 1974.

Fell, Joseph P. *Heidegger and Sartre: An Essay on Being and Place*. New York, 1979.

LaCapra, Dominick. *A Preface to Sartre: A Critical Introduction to Sartre's Literary and Philosophical Writings*. Ithaca, 1978.

(*) Lapointe, François. *Jean-Paul Sartre and his Critics: An International Bibliography, 1938–1980*. Bowling Green, Ohio, 1981.

Mészáros, István. *The Work of Sartre*, Vol. 1: *Search for Freedom*. Atlantic Highlands, N.J., 1979.

Poster, Mark. *Sartre's Marxism*. London, 1979.

(*) Silverman, Hugh J., and Elliston, Frederick A., eds. *Jean-Paul Sartre: Contemporary Approaches to His Philosophy*. Pittsburgh, 1980.

(*) Wilcocks, Robert. *Jean-Paul Sartre: A Bibliography of International Criticism*. Alberta, 1975.

12. Maurice Merleau-Ponty

Bannan, John F. *The Philosophy of Merleau-Ponty*. New York, 1967.

(*)Cooper, Barry. *Merleau-Ponty and Marxism: From Terror to Reform*. Toronto, 1979.

544   Selected Bibliography

Geraets, Theodore F. *Vers une nouvelle philosophie transcendentale: La genèse de la philosophie de Maurice Merleau-Ponty jusqu'à la Phénoménologie de la perception.* The Hague, 1971.

Gillan, Garth, ed. *The Horizons of the Flesh: Critical Perspectives on the Thought of Merleau-Ponty.* Carbondale, Ill., 1973.

(*)Kruks, Sonia. *The Political Philosophy of Merleau-Ponty.* Atlantic Highlands, N.J., 1981.

Langan, Thomas. *Merleau-Ponty's Critique of Reason.* New Haven and London, 1966.

Mallin, Samuel B. *Merleau-Ponty's Philosophy.* New Haven and London, 1979.

Rabil, Albert, Jr. *Merleau-Ponty: Existentialist of the Social World.* New York and London, 1967.

Spurling, Laurie. *Phenomenology and the Social World: The Philosophy of Merleau-Ponty and its Relation to the Social Sciences.* London, 1977.

Tilliette, Xavier. *Merleau-Ponty ou la mesure de l'homme.* Paris, 1970.

13. Louis Althusser

(*) Althusser, Louis. *Essays in Self-Criticism.* Translated, Introduction and Bibliography, by Grahame Lock. London, 1976.

Anderson, Perry. *Arguments Within English Marxism.* London, 1980.

(*)Callinicos, Alex. *Althusser's Marxism.* London, 1976.

Clarke, Simon, et al. *One-Dimensional Marxism: Althusser and the Politics of Culture.* London, 1980.

Cotton, Jean-Pierre. *La Pensée de Louis Althusser.* Toulouse, 1979.

Schmidt, Alfred. *History and Structure.* Translated by Jeffrey Herf. Cambridge, 1981.

Thompson, E. P. *The Poverty of Theory and Other Essays.* New York, 1978.

14. Galvano Della Volpe and Lucio Colletti

Fraser, John. *An Introduction to the Thought of Galvano Della Volpe.* London, 1977.

Montano, Mario. "The 'Scientific Dialectics' of Galvano Della Volpe." In *The Unknown Dimension: European Marxism Since Lenin.* Edited by Dick Howard and Karl E. Klare. New York, 1972.

Vacca, Giuseppe. *Scienza stato e critica di classe: Galvano Della Volpe e il marxismo.* Bari, 1970.

15. Jürgen Habermas

Dallmayr, Fred R., ed. *Materielen zu Habermas' "Erkenntnis und Interesse."* Frankfurt, 1971.

Geuss, Raymond. *The Idea of a Critical Theory: Habermas and the Frankfurt School.* Cambridge, 1981.

(*)Görtzen, René. *Jürgen Habermas: Eine Bibliographie seiner Schriften und der Sekundärliteratur, 1952–1981.* Frankfurt, 1982.

Held, David. *Introduction to Critical Theory: Horkheimer to Habermas.* Berkeley, 1980.

Keat, Russell. *The Politics of Social Theory: Habermas, Freud and the Critique of Positivism*. Chicago, 1981.

Kortian, Garbis. *Metacritique: The Philosophical Argument of Jürgen Habermas*. Translated by John Raffan with an introduction by Charles Taylor and Alan Montefiore. Cambridge, 1980.

McCarthy, Thomas. *The Critical Theory of Jürgen Habermas*. Cambridge, Mass., 1978.

Sensat, Julius, Jr. *Habermas and Marxism: An Appraisal*. Beverly Hills, 1979.

Schroyer, Trent. *The Critique of Domination: The Origins and Development of Critical Theory*. New York, 1973.

Thompson, John B. *Critical Hermeneutics: A Study of the Thought of Paul Ricoeur and Jürgen Habermas*. Cambridge, 1981.

(*)Thompson, John B., and Held, David, eds. *Habermas: Critical Debates*. Cambridge, Mass., 1982.

E. Post-Structuralism

Allison, David B., ed. *The New Nietzsche: Contemporary Styles of Interpretation*. New York, 1977.

Coward, Rosalind, and Ellis, John. *Language and Materialism: Developments in Semiology and the Theory of the Subject*. London, 1977.

Descombes, Vincent. *Modern French Philosophy*. Translated by L. Scott-Fox and J. M. Harding. Cambridge, 1980.

Dreyfus, Hubert L., and Rabinow, Paul. *Michel Foucault: Beyond Structuralism and Hermeneutics*. Chicago, 1982.

Graff, Gerald. *Literature Against Itself: Literary Ideas in Modern Society*. Chicago, 1979.

Leitch, Vincent B. *Deconstructive Criticism: An Advanced Introduction*. New York, 1983.

Lemert, Charles, and Gillan, Garth. *Michel Foucault: Social Order and Transgression*. New York, 1982.

Lentricchia, Frank. *After the New Criticism*. Chicago, 1980.

Macksay, Richard, and Donato, Eugenio, eds. *The Structuralist Controversy: The Languages of Criticism and the Sciences of Man*. Baltimore and London, 1972.

Major-Poetzl, Pamela. *Michel Foucault's Archaeology of Western Culture: Toward a New Science of History*. Chapel Hill, 1983.

Ryan, Michael. *Marxism and Deconstruction: A Critical Articulation*. Baltimore, 1982.

Sheridan, Alan. *Michel Foucault: The Will to Truth*. London, 1980.

Sturrock, John, ed. *Structuralism and Since: From Lévi-Strauss to Derrida*. Oxford, 1979.

White, Hayden. *Tropics of Discourse: Essays in Cultural Criticism*. Baltimore, 1978.

Index

Abrams, M. H., 15, 50n, 57n, 230n, 433n
Action, 345
Action Française, 79, 158n, 291
Activists, 277
Adamson, Walter L., 19, 154n, 155n,
    159n, 164n, 169n, 170n, 172n,
    467n, 480n
Addis, Laird, 61n
Adler, Frank, 19, 172n
Adler, Max, 33n, 124, 305, 309
Adorno, Theodor W., 3, 6, 8, 52n, 75n,
    149n, 157, 168, 171n, 177, 188,
    197–198, 200, 202–204, 208–209,
    211, 215, 219–221, 224n, 229, 234,
    238–275, 280, 288–292, 299, 303,
    312, 317n, 326, 330, 333, 355,
    359–360, 374–375, 381n, 413–415,
    431, 435, 442, 455, 457–458,
    462–463, 465–468, 471–473, 476,
    478–479, 486–487, 489, 491, 494,
    498, 500–503, 508, 510–512, 515,
    518, 526–527, 536–537;
    "The Actuality of Philosophy," 244,
    255–259;
    on aesthetics, 272–273, 326;
    Aesthetic Theory, 52n, 242, 272–273;
    Against Epistemology, 245n;
    on alienation, 267;
    and Benjamin, 246–247, 251–252,
    254–255, 259–261, 264, 270,
    288–289;
    breaks with Western Marxist tradition,
    257–259, 261, 274–275;
    Dialectic of Enlightenment, 171n, 210,
    215, 218, 220–221, 229–230, 242,
    261–264, 269, 273, 414, 455, 457,
    465, 467, 491, 498, 526;

on Durkheim, 280;
role of exchange value in modern
    society, 260–261, 268–271;
critique of fascism, 262;
"On the Fetish Character of Music,"
    254;
on history, 261–264, 273–274, 536;
and Horkheimer, 215, 255;
critique of humanism, 243;
immanent critique, 266;
conception of individual, 260–261,
    266–267, 269–272;
The Jargon of Authenticity, 242, 271,
    333;
and Kracauer, 245–246, 254–255,
    266n;
criticism of communicative language,
    253, 272, 274;
on the possibility of liberation,
    260–261, 263–267, 273;
and Lukács, 254–255, 257, 268–270,
    478, 512;
critique of Mannheim, 208–209;
on Marx, 267–269;
"melancholy science," 241, 511;
on memory, 229, 234, 238, 241–242,
    256, 273;
Minima Moralia, 241n–242, 265,
    272n, 425n, 476n;
on nature, 149, 241, 261–262, 269,
    273–274;
Negative Dialectics, 241–244, 255,
    259n–260, 263, 265, 267–271, 273,
    457, 462, 515, 536;
on negative dialectic, 241–242,
    253–254, 256, 258, 260–261,
    265–267, 271, 274, 458–459, 515;

relationship between negative and
   positive dialectics, 242;
and Nietzsche, 510, 537;
Philosophy of Modern Music, 242,
   252n, 289n;
and politics, 264–265, 271, 274;
The Positivist Dispute, 75n, 265n,
   267n–268, 458n, 471n;
praxis, 8, 253, 258, 261, 271;
Prisms, 20n, 242, 289n, 457n, 537;
and psychoanalysis, 204n, 479;
limits of rationality, 258–259, 262,
   274;
and reification, 229, 255, 267–270,
   280, 457n;
and Schoenberg, 252–255, 259, 289;
on science, 256, 467n;
parallels with Scientific Marxism, 240,
   270, 299;
"On the Social Situation of Music,"
   254;
"The Sociology of Knowledge and its
   Consciousness," 208–209n;
on Surrealism, 289, 292;
on totality, 202, 208, 240–242,
   246n–248, 254–275, 413,
   471–472;
comparison of totality and death, 271,
   333;
conception of truth, 257–259,
   269–270, 312
Ady, Endre, 5, 82
Aeschylus, 53n, 92
Aesthetic modernism, 10, 187–188,
   278–293, 302, 322–325, 416, 430,
   530
Aesthetics, 48–53, 57, 87–98, 300–303,
   328, 439–443;
aesthetic dimension, 52, 220, 223, 416,
   506;
aestheticization of totality, 48–49,
   52–53;
Marxist aesthetics, 8–9, 127, 132,
   302–303. *See also individual authors*
Agger, Ben, 458
Albert, Hans, 473, 483
Alexander, Ian W., 333n
Alicata, Mario, 428
Alienation, 3, 9, 15n, 21, 43, 50, 55, 63,
   76–78, 95–96, 98, 110, 114n, 126,
   141, 188, 195, 266, 273, 293, 298,
   301, 328, 393, 397, 446–447,
   449–450, 452, 455, 500n, 506, 512,
   517, 523, 525
Allison, David B., 511n
Alquié, Ferdinand, 286n, 362n
Alt, John, 19
Althaus, Horst, 93n

Althusser, Hélène, 391n, 397, 421
Althusser, Louis, 3, 5–9, 12, 28–29,
   38–39, 41n, 56n, 70–71, 146, 152,
   158, 163, 164n, 183, 190, 240, 276n,
   280–281, 283, 299, 303, 324–325,
   328, 330, 333, 355, 384–422, 425,
   429–430, 432, 434–436n, 442–443,
   445–446, 448, 453, 463, 486, 494,
   512, 518–520, 525
and aesthetic modernism, 416;
on alienation, 328, 397;
and Bachelard, 393, 398–399, 401,
   417;
and class struggle, 418–419;
and Comte, 390, 398;
and Della Volpe, 443;
and Durkheim, 280–281, 398, 409;
economic determinacy in "last
   instance," 407–409, 419–420, 442;
epistemological break, 394, 446;
on epistemology, 398–401, 404–405,
   415, 419;
Essays in Self-Criticism, 400, 417, 419;
For Marx, 9n, 71n, 394–396, 405, 417;
parallels with Frankfurt School,
   413–415, 422;
and Gramsci, 404, 408n, 413;
critique of Hegel, 38–39, 56n,
   405–406, 419–420;
critique of humanism, 394–396, 398,
   411, 418;
"Ideological State Apparatuses," 397,
   404–405n, 525;
on ideology, 394, 401–405, 411–412,
   415;
and Korsch, 146, 419;
Lenin and Philosophy, 71n, 397;
and Lukács, 398, 401, 405, 413;
on Marx, 394, 396–398, 400,
   406–407, 418;
conception of materialism, 400–401,
   417;
on Montesquieu, 38;
overdetermination, 38, 407;
relationship to PCF, 392–394, 412,
   420–421;
and politics, 395–396, 412, 420–421;
and the problematic, 314, 391;
and psychoanalysis, 401–403;
Reading Capital, 394n–396, 408–410,
   414;
and reification, 397;
Response to John Lewis, 397;
science-ideology distinction, 401,
   417–418;
and Spinoza, 28, 39, 399–401;
Stalinist implications of his philosophy,
   388, 390, 405;

conception of structure, 406–408,
410–411, 419;
structure in dominance, 281, 406–407,
412;
rejection of subjectivity, 399, 403,
410–411;
techne–praxis distinction, 411;
theoretical practice, 396–397,
399n–400, 412, 416–418;
on time, 190, 324, 409–410, 414–415;
on totality, 190, 389–390, 405–408,
417;
rejection of *verum-factum* principle,
399, 404;
and Western Marxist tradition, 299,
486–490, 405, 412–416, 422
Alvarez, A., 284n
Anagnorisis (Recognition), 190,
237–238, 413, 533
Anamnesis (Recollection). *See* Memory
Anderson, Perry, 1, 3–4, 6, 15, 36, 69,
151n–152n, 163n, 165n, 250n, 283,
357n, 387n–388n, 394n–395n,
413n, 416, 428n, 430n, 448, 450,
452, 464n
Andler, Charles, 286
Angevins, 26
Année Sociologique, 282
Annenkov, Paul, 11
Anspacher, H. L., 24n
Antal, Frigyes, 99
Anti-Semitism, 62, 262
Antoni, Carlo, 444
Apel, Karl-Otto, 495, 508n
Aquinas, Saint Thomas, 26
Arac, Jonathan, 509n
Aragon, Louis, 285, 287–288, 293
Arato, Andrew, 1n, 19, 76n–78n, 81n,
84n, 89n, 94n, 106n, 109n, 112n,
115–116n, 118n, 128n–131n,
196n–197n, 209, 216n, 219n, 274,
304n, 306n, 308n, 534
Arendt, Hannah, 476–477, 498, 524
Arguments Group, 3, 147n, 297, 304n,
333, 402
Aristotle, 25–28, 30, 186, 225, 300, 303,
325, 433, 454, 460, 476–477
Arnold, Matthew, 68
Aron, Raymond, 2n, 327, 334, 336, 344n,
348, 356n, 363n
Aronowitz, Stanley, 1n, 19, 513–514n,
531
Aronson, Ronald, 19, 336n, 344n, 354n
Art, 41, 50–51, 90, 94, 117, 415. *See also*
Aesthetic modernism, Aesthetics
Artaud, Antonin, 517n
Arvon, Henri, 302n
Astruc, Alexander, 342n

"Attentismus," 67
Auerbach, Erich, 93, 442
Augustine, Saint, 26, 31, 40n, 225
Auschwitz, 243
Austin, J. L., 495
Aut-Aut, 332, 425
Authenticity, 40n–41
Avanti!, 100n, 151
Averroës, 186
Avicenna, 186
Avineri, Shlomo, 57n–58n, 413n
Axelos, Kostas, 297n, 333

Bachelard, Gaston, 299n, 393–394,
398–399, 401–402, 417, 519
Badaloni, Nicola, 426
Bahr, Erhard, 174n, 176n–177n
Bahti, Timothy, 17
Baillie, J. B., 286
Bakhtin, Mikhail, 523n
Bakunin, Mikhail, 147
Balakian, Anna, 284n
Balázs, Béla, 99
Balibar, Etienne, 387, 390n, 394n–395,
397n, 408, 410, 436n
Balzac, Honoré de, 302
Bammel, G. K., 129n
Banfi, Antonio, 425
Bannan, John F., 361n
Barkin, Kenneth D., 75n
Baron, Samuel H., 66n
Barthes, Roland, 288n, 327, 386, 515
Bartoli, Matteo, 160
Basso, Lelio, 426
Bataille, Georges, 370n, 510, 515,
518–519
Bates, Thomas R., 165n, 172n
Bathrick, David, 19
Baudelaire, Charles, 358, 512n
Bauer, Bruno, 64, 125, 326
Bauer, Edgar, 64
Bauer, Otto, 4
Baum, Hermann, 304n, 328n
Baumgarten, Alexander, 49
Bayle, Pierre, 29
Beaufret, Jean, 335
Beaujour, Michel, 291n
Beauty, 49–51, 94
Beckett, Samuel, 272–273
Beer-Hofmann, Richard, 87, 89
Beethoven, Ludwig van, 255
Beimel, Walter, 349
Bell, Daniel, 327
Benda, Julien, 170n–171n
Benhabib, Seyla, 19, 497n
Benjamin, Jessica, 19
Benjamin, Walter, 3, 5–6, 8, 12, 149n,

157, 171n, 177, 185, 188–190, 200,
216–217, 224, 228n–229, 234–235,
237–238, 242, 245–257n,259–264,
270–272, 287–289, 291, 355, 415,
442, 472n, 486, 500–501, 508, 526;
"The Author as Producer," 260;
"Edward Fuchs," 189n, 217n, 228n,
234–235, 237;
on the communicative function of
language, 246, 253, 272, 442;
and Lukács, 247;
and memory, 224n, 228n–229,
234–235, 237–238;
The Origin of German Tragic Drama,
247–252, 260;
and origin of negative dialectics,
251–252;
parallel with Post-Structuralism, 526;
critique of progress, 217n, 262–263,
415;
and "redemption," 248–249, 251;
"On Some Motifs in Baudelaire," 229;
denigration of subjectivity, 248–249,
251, 260;
on Surrealism, 288–290;
Theses on the Philosophy of History,
189n, 217n;
on totality, 246n–252;
conception of truth, 248–249, 251
Bentham, Jeremy, 69, 527
Bentley, James, 175n
Berg, Alban, 253
Berger, John, 284
Bergin, Thomas Goddard, 33n
Bergson, Henri, 96, 109, 154, 191, 225,
277–278, 363, 366, 368, 454
Berlin, Isaiah, 33n, 35, 37n, 59n
Berman, Marshall, 40n, 53n, 517
Berman, Russell, 19, 119n–120n, 263n
Bernanos, Georges, 343
Bernstein, Basil, 493
Bernstein, Eduard, 44, 67, 104, 133, 309,
452, 455
Bernstein, Richard J., 500n
Bersani, Leo, 287n, 517n
Bertalanffy, Ludwig von, 484n
Besitzbürgertum, 72
Best, Michael H., 411n
Bettelheim, Charles, 417n
Bible, 29, 93
Bildung, 43, 46, 55, 88, 91, 101, 159, 474
Bildungsbürgertum, 13, 72
Binswanger, Ludwig, 341n, 519
Birnbaum, Norman, 27n
Bismarck, Otto von, 73
Bisztray, George, 302n
Blackburn, Robin, 122n, 413n
Blanchot, Maurice, 515, 519

Bloch, Ernst, 2–4, 6, 8, 10, 26, 79, 82,
117, 127–128, 149, 157n, 171,
173–195, 198, 202–203, 211,
214–215, 220, 237–238, 249,
251–252, 273–274, 288–289, 295,
303–304n, 313, 316, 324, 350, 353,
355, 376, 413–415, 430n,
435n–436n, 467, 490, 497, 501,
533;
and *anagnorisis*, 190, 238;
role of economy, 184, 191–192;
on history, 182–183, 185–189, 195;
and identity theory, 182;
Inheritance of Our Times, 178n, 188;
and intensive totality, 189;
and Korsch, 192;
and Lukács, 178–187, 195, 303;
comparison with Marcuse, 237–238;
and memory, 237–238;
on modernist art, 187–188, 194,
288–289;
and mysticism, 180;
on nature, 182, 184–187, 190, 195;
non-synchronicity, 176, 188–189, 324,
415;
as philosopher of October Revolution,
176, 195;
philosophy of hope, 26, 176, 180,
182–184, 187–189, 192–194, 238,
497;
The Principle of Hope, 178n, 183, 187,
193;
debt to process philosophy, 191,
194–195;
critique of progress, 189–190;
on socialism, 176;
Spirit of Utopia, 178n, 180–182;
Subject-Object, 178n, 184;
on totality, 174–175, 180–183, 185,
187–192, 195, 202, 413;
"traces," 187, 190, 194, 238, 251;
*Tübingen Introduction to
Philosophy*, 178n, 189–190n;
utopian/religious aspects, 174, 180,
183, 192, 195
Bloch, Josef, 66n, 407
Bloch, Marc, 343n, 409
Blondel, Eric, 233
Blum Theses. *See* Lukács
Bobbio, Norberto, 426, 437–439
Böcklin, Arnold, 177
Boehme, Jacob, 184–185, 308
Boelhower, William Q., 304n, 319
Boggs, Carl, 19, 152n, 154n, 166n
Bolaffi, Angelo, 509n
Bologna, Sergio, 172
Bongiovanni, Bruno, 278n
Bonss, Wolfgang, 200n

Bordiga, Amadeo, 130, 152, 162–166, 172
Borkenau, Franz, 315n
Bosanquet, Bernard, 68
Bourgeois, Léon, 279
Bourgeois culture, 68–69, 73, 81–84,
    86–87, 91–92, 97–98, 100,
    108–110, 112, 122, 132–133, 148,
    154, 177, 188, 214, 257, 274, 284,
    386;
  antinomies in, 78, 87, 91n, 108–109,
    112, 114, 122, 177, 183, 188, 200,
    214, 257, 274
Bourgeois social thought, 68–80, 85–98,
    103, 108–110;
  in England, 68–69;
  in France, 70–71;
  in Germany, 73–80;
  in the young Lukács, 85–98. See also
    Sociology
Bouwsma, William, 40n
Bowles, Samuel, 19
Boyte, Harry C., 536n
Bradley, Francis Herbert, 68
Brasillach, Robert, 343
Braudel, Fernand, 409
Brecht, Bertolt, 3, 6, 8, 12, 132, 189, 213,
    303, 416
Bredel, Willi, 303
Breines, Paul, 19, 81n, 84n, 89n, 100n,
    106n, 115n, 118n, 127–133n, 178n,
    197n, 223n, 304n, 306, 308n
Breton, André, 284–287, 289–291,
    293–294
Brewster, Ben, 398n, 402n
Bricanier, Serge, 7n
Brick, Barbara, 216n
Bronner, Stephen Eric, 19, 135n
Brown, Alison Pogrebin, 224n, 226
Brown, Marshall, 230n
Brown, Norman O., 222n, 239
Brüggemann, Heinz, 132n
Bruno, Giordano, 186
Brunschvicg, Léon, 277, 334, 358
Brzozowski, Stanislaw, 102
Buber, Martin, 246, 339n
Bubner, Rüdiger, 454n, 499n, 508n
Büchner, Ludwig, 73
Buci-Glucksmann, Christine, 152n, 390
Buckley, Walter, 484n
Buckmiller, Michael, 129n–130n
Buck-Morss, Susan, 19, 149n, 196n,
    204n, 211n, 241n, 244, 246n–247n,
    251n–252n, 268, 274, 288n, 488n
Budapest School, 5n, 304n, 533
Bukharin, Nikolai, 4, 11, 120, 123–124,
    127, 136, 156, 158, 431
Bulthaup, Peter, 224n
Bürger, Peter, 263n

Burke, Edmund, 68
Burnier, Michel-Antoine, 345n
Burns, Elizabeth, 323n
Burns, Rob, 302n
Burns, Tom, 323n
Bury, J. B., 34
Butler, E. M., 57n

Callinicos, Alex, 387n, 409n, 417n
Calvinism, 40
Cammett, John, 154n
Camus, Albert, 21, 60, 286–287, 297,
    323, 335, 338n, 348, 367, 383,
    391n, 533
Canguilhem, Georges, 393, 398–399,
    401, 409, 417, 519
Capetians, 26
Capitalism, 8–9, 23, 37, 68, 95, 100, 108,
    118, 133–134, 137, 140, 143, 172,
    192–194, 210, 216, 268–269, 290,
    296, 323–324, 328, 348, 433, 446,
    449–450, 455, 487, 491, 515, 520,
    525, 535
Carlyle, Thomas, 95n
Carnoy, Martin, 536n
Carr, E. H., 131
Carroll, David, 96n
Cases, Cesare, 426
Cassano, Franco, 425n
Cassirer, Ernst, 30–31, 39, 309, 334, 474
Castoriadis, Cornelius, 366, 383
Castroism, 395n
Caudwell, Christopher, 4n
Caute, David, 276n, 294n–295n, 314,
    329, 345n, 393n, 401n
Cavaillès, Jean, 399–400, 417
Caws, Mary Ann, 299n
Céline, Louis–Ferdinand, 343
Ceppa, Leonardo, 140
Cerroni, Umberto, 426
Cerutti, Furio, 132, 135n, 425, 514n
Césaire, Aimé, 292n
Charlton, D. G., 70n
Chatelet, François, 297
Chesneaux, Jean, 410n
Chestov, Léon, 335
Chiaramonte, Miriam, 338n
Chiaramonte, Nicola, 338n
Chinese Revolution, 6
Chiodi, Pietro, 336n, 344n, 347n–349,
    351n
Chomsky, Noam, 481, 488n, 495
Christian thought, 26, 45, 54, 57–58,
    95, 453
Cieszkowski, August von, 125
Città Futura, 429

Civil society, 58, 62–64, 163, 165, 432, 534–535
Clark, Martin, 170n, 172n
Clark, Terry Nichols, 393n
Clarke, Simon, 283n, 387n, 389n, 407n, 411n, 418n
Clarté, 297n
Class consciousness, 101, 112–113, 121, 123, 136, 141–142, 166, 202–203, 296, 492n. See also Trade union consciousness
Class struggle, 47, 98, 120–121, 135, 138, 144, 159, 162, 192–193, 207, 222, 279–280, 418–420;
as motor of history, 47, 418–419
Clastres, Pierre, 524n
Cliff, Tony, 417n
Clifford, James, 299n
Cobbett, William, 69
Cohen, Jean, 19, 492
Cohen, Stephen, 123–124
Cohn-Bendit, Daniel, 384n
Coleridge, Samuel Taylor, 68–69, 231, 300
Collective subject. See Meta-subject
Collège de France, 366, 375, 519
Colletti, Lucio, 3, 6–7, 10n, 29n, 42n–44, 66n, 71, 79, 81n, 102, 130n, 164, 333, 419n, 422, 426–431, 433, 439n, 444–461, 463;
on alienation, 43, 446–448, 450, 452, 455;
and Althusser, 445–446, 453;
choice between Marxism and materialism, 449–450, 459;
critique of dialectic, 29n, 448–449, 454–460;
"Dialectical Contradiction and Non-Contradiction," 449n, 459–460;
critique of Frankfurt School, 447, 450, 455, 457–458;
From Rousseau to Lenin, 446, 452;
critique of Hegel, 433, 453–454, 456–458, 460;
and Kant, 447, 452–453;
"Marxism and the Dialectic," 448–449, 459–460;
Marxism and Hegel, 3n, 66n, 71n, 430n, 446, 451–452, 458n;
on materialism, 452–457, 459;
and the PCI, 428, 444–447;
on subject–object disparity, 453;
on totality, 450–460;
and Western Marxist tradition, 448, 450–451, 454–458
Collins, Douglas, 358n
Comintern, 12, 103, 118–119, 129–130, 139, 143, 151n, 164–165n, 172

Communication. See Gramsci; Habermas; Language
Communism, 23, 35, 65, 84, 101, 110, 145n, 164, 168, 173, 184, 186, 192, 194, 239, 277–278, 296, 348, 369, 405, 410, 421, 437–439, 445, 450
Communist Party. See KPD; Leninism; PCF; PCI; Stalinism
Communist Party (Hungary), 119, 196
Community, 21, 28, 30, 39, 45, 62, 69, 76, 78, 98, 308, 316, 339, 504–505
Comte, Auguste, 27, 69–71, 75n, 278, 280–281, 286, 390, 398
Condorcet, Marquis de, 31
Congdon, Lee, 81n, 89n, 99n
Connell, R. W., 418n
Connerton, Paul, 196n, 212n, 218n, 263, 272n, 462n, 468n, 488n, 532n
Connolly, William E., 411n
Conservatism, 27
Contat, Michel, 342n
Contemporaneo, Il, 425
Cooper, Barry, 361n, 365n, 371n
Cooper, D. G., 343n
Copenhagen School, 440
Corbin, Henri, 335
Cornelius, Hans, 203n–204n, 211, 245, 247
Cornforth, Maurice, 4n
Cornu, August, 276n
Council Communists, 2, 7n, 122, 154, 172
Cousin, Victor, 286
Coward, Rosalind, 402n, 516
Critical Theory, 18, 152, 197–198, 200–202, 204–205, 209–211, 215–218, 220, 232, 234, 236, 264, 266–267, 270n, 272, 274–275, 325–326, 414, 416, 425, 451, 462–463, 465–467, 472, 475–478, 482–484, 489, 491–492, 501, 526n–527, 532. See also Adorno; Frankfurt School; Habermas; Horkheimer; Marcuse
Croce, Benedetto, 73, 150, 152, 154–160, 167, 169, 424, 437, 439, 444
Crow, Dennis, 81n
Cubism, 284
Culler, Jonathan, 328n, 386n
Cultural hegemony. See Gramsci
Cybernetics, 411, 484

Dadaism, 284, 293
D'Alembert, 31
Dallmayr, Fred P., 19, 116n, 214, 362n, 379n, 478n
D'Amico, Robert, 19, 529n

Dante, 26, 91, 96
Darwin, Charles, 10, 148
Davidson, Alastair B., 150n–151n, 154n–155n, 166n
Dawson, Carl, 230n
Déat, Marcel, 296
de Beauvoir, Simone, 336, 346n, 374
de Bonald, Louis, 70
Debord, Buy, 298n–299n, 516
Deborin, Abram, 102n, 129n–130
Debray, Régis, 395–396
de Certeau, Michel, 402n
Deconstruction, 15n, 287n, 511, 517, 537
de Gandillac, Maurice, 334
De Gasperi, Alcide, 423
de Gaulle, Charles, 359, 394n
De Leon, Daniel, 154n
Deleuze, Gilles, 399n, 509, 512n, 514
Della Volpe, Galvano, 3, 6–8, 43, 131, 146, 240, 303, 333, 388, 409n, 414, 422, 426–453, 455–456, 458–461, 494, 520;
    parallels with Adorno, 431, 435;
    on aesthetics, 439–443;
    and Bloch, 435n–436n;
    hostility towards Critical Marxism, 431;
    Critique of Taste, 409n, 429, 439–443;
    determinate abstraction, 431–435, 441, 443;
    disparity between thought and its object, 431, 434–435, 440;
    on experimentalism, 435–436n, 439n, 443;
    and the Frankfurt School, 431–432;
    critique of Hegel, 432–435, 441;
    on history, 436;
    and humanism 430;
    on ideology, 443;
    on language, 430, 437, 440–443;
    Logic as a Positive Science, 428–429, 432–436, 440, 445, 460;
    on Marx's concept of totality, 433–434;
    and political involvement, 428, 444;
    and praxis, 430, 443;
    Rousseau and Marx, 429, 436–438;
    on totality, 432–444;
    rejection of verum–factum principle, 435, 437;
    and Western Marxist tradition, 429–431, 434, 444
del Noce, Augusto, 153n, 426n
Delzell, Charles F., 423n
de Maistre, Joseph, 70
de Man, Paul, 90n–91n, 526n
Derrida, Jacques, 1n, 24, 161, 283, 297n, 359n, 391n, 419, 509, 514–516, 518n, 523n, 526n, 532, 536n
de Ruggiero, Guido, 73

Desan, Wilfred, 338n
Descartes, René, 34–35, 38, 71, 286, 306, 310, 315, 338, 341, 352, 355, 362, 376, 380, 400
Descombes, Vincent, 343n, 362n, 366n–367n, 370n, 398n, 419n, 511n–512
Desnos, Robert, 284
de Waelhens, Alphonse, 366
Dialectic, 14, 29, 35, 44–45, 49, 53–54, 61, 65, 69, 71, 75–76, 103–105, 115–118, 120, 123–125, 127, 134–135, 144, 146, 148–149, 158, 165n, 184, 201, 221–222, 253, 260–261, 265–267, 276, 289, 292, 352, 374, 380, 434, 436, 440–441, 447–449, 451n, 453–454, 458, 460, 476, 522;
    dialectic of defeat, 8, 19;
    dialectic of labor, 114;
    dialectic of nature, 66, 115, 128, 148, 158, 185, 190, 318, 349, 414n. See also individual authors; Dialectical materialism; Historical materialism
Dialectical Materialism, 66, 68, 107n, 127, 133, 141, 156, 191, 194–195n, 197, 294, 305, 312, 317–318, 364, 386, 388, 398, 422, 427, 430–431, 434, 443, 449, 452n, 454
Diamat. See Dialectical materialism
Diderot, Denis, 28, 31, 40, 59–60, 453n
Diederichs, Eugen, 133
Dietzgen, Joseph, 7n
di Girolemi, Remigio, 26
Dilthey, Wilhelm, 74, 77–79, 82, 88, 91, 106, 115, 203, 249, 256, 311
Disco, Cornelis, 492, 528
Dobb, Maurice, 4n
Dostoevsky, Feodor, 83, 91, 96n–98, 179, 189, 194
Doubrovsky, Serge, 323n, 328
Drews, Jörg, 177n
Dreyfus, Hubert L., 477n, 518n
Driesch, Hans, 75
Drieu la Rochelle, Pierre, 343
Droysen, Johann Gustav, 74
Dubiel, Helmut, 199, 206n, 216n
Dufrenne, Mikel, 366, 374n
Duhem, Pierre, 393
Dühring, Eugen Karl, 138
Dumézil, Georges, 522
Dumont, Louis, 61n
Dunayevskaya, Raya, 67n, 134n
Duncker, Hermann, 129n
Durkheim, Emile, 22, 70–71, 75n, 278–283, 290, 299, 379, 389, 398, 409, 504;
    on totality, 22, 279–282
Duvignaud, Jean, 295, 297n

Eagleton, Terry, 9n, 322n, 329n, 416,
    517n, 526n
Ebbinghaus, Hermann, 232
Eckhart, Meister, 432n
Ecole Normale Supérieure, 276, 334, 336,
    387, 392, 395, 402
Ecole Pratique des Hautes Etudes, 294,
    306
Economy, 2–3, 7–8, 28n, 32, 38, 47,
    66n–67, 75, 85, 100, 108–110, 121,
    128, 133, 139, 152, 154–155, 166,
    201, 281, 295, 367, 386, 390, 418,
    486, 520;
    primacy of economy (economism), 2–3,
    7–8, 28n, 38, 66n–67, 85, 100, 110,
    123, 128, 133, 139, 154, 201, 281
Edgley, Roy, 449n
Edie, James M., 382n
Ehrenfels, Christian von, 75n
Eichendorff, Joseph von, 272n, 476n
Eisenstein, Sergei, 284
Eliade, Mircea, 25
Eliot, T. S., 69
Elites, 10–13, 101. See also Intellectuals
Elleinstein, Jean, 421
Ellis, John, 402n, 516
Elshtain, Jean Bethke, 532n
Eluard, Paul, 285, 287, 293
Empiricism, 30, 45, 69
Encyclopedia, 31
Engels, Friedrich, 7, 9, 13, 60n, 66, 102,
    115–117, 136–138, 141, 148–149,
    158, 167, 185, 190, 302, 318, 407,
    430, 436–437, 442, 448, 452, 454,
    502
Enlightenment, 29n, 30–33, 39, 47–48,
    52, 70, 79, 88n, 148, 175, 184, 263,
    316, 324, 389, 393, 398, 451, 457,
    467, 470, 501, 510–511;
    and totality, 30–32. See also Adorno,
    Dialectic of Enlightenment;
    Horkheimer, Dialectic of
    Enlightenment
Entwistle, Harold, 169n
Erfurt Program, 67
Erikson, Erik, 22
Ernst, Paul, 82–83
Esperanto, 161–162
Establet, Roger, 395
Eurocommunism, 150, 162, 450, 535
Evans, Mary, 304n
Evans, Richard I., 306n
Existentialism, 6, 10, 14, 40, 89, 244, 256,
    292, 294, 298–299, 305, 315, 318,
    331–361, 368–369, 372–373, 378,
    385–386, 411, 425, 427, 511–512.
    See also Marxism, Existential;
    Merleau-Ponty; Sartre

Existenzphilosophie, 78
Exploitation, 9, 100, 217, 397
Expressionism, 133, 177, 187, 284,
    288–289n
Eyerman, Ron, 475n

Fabians, 69, 133, 136
Fackenheim, Emil, 57n
False consciousness, 203–204, 207
Family, 205
Fascism, 6, 9, 119, 130, 143, 188–189,
    193–194, 215, 217, 262, 332,
    343–344n, 370–371, 428n
Faust, 51, 53n, 65
Febvre, Lucien, 409
Federici, Silvia, 333n
Feenberg, Andrew, 19, 84n, 99n,
    107n–109n, 116n, 414n, 457n
Feher, Ferenc, 5n, 81n–83n, 88n–89n,
    95n, 118n, 254n, 302, 315n, 534
Feher, Zoltan, 83n
Fekete, John, 19
Fell, Joseph, 336n, 358
Femia, Joseph, 165n, 169n
Ferguson, Adam, 52
Fetishism of commodities, 109, 180
Fetscher, Iring, 112n, 129n–130n, 134n,
    184n, 191n
Feudalism, 37, 145
Feuer, Lewis S., 65n
Feuerbach, Ludwig, 6, 107, 125, 298, 394
Fichte, J. G., 39, 53, 56, 91, 104–109, 115,
    125, 139, 165, 171, 183, 202, 326,
    474
Filloux, Jean–Claude, 279n
Finocchiaro, Maurice A., 123n, 154n
Fiori, Giuseppe, 151n, 154n, 163n
Fisch, Max Harold, 33n
Fischer, Ernst, 65
Fischer, Friedrich Theodor, 93
Fischer, Kuno, 76
Flaubert, Gustave, 96n, 228, 358
Fleischer, Helmut, 31n, 194n
Foa, Victor, 8, 307
Fogarasi, Béla, 99, 130n
Forgács, David, 439n, 441n, 443
Forgetting. See Memory
Fortini, Franco, 425–426
Foucault, Michel, 1n, 18, 20n, 385–386,
    393, 409n, 414, 417, 509, 514–530,
    536;
    The Archaeology of Knowledge, 386n,
    522;
    counter-memory, 523;
    Discipline and Punish, 523–524,
    526–527;

on discourse, 522–523;
and Frankfurt School, 526–527;
and Habermas, 507–511, 517–518,
  523–524, 528–529;
on history, 521, 527;
The History of Sexuality, 524;
and Hyppolite, 385n, 519;
on the individual, 528;
on language, 522–524, 529;
and Marx, 386, 520;
The Order of Things, 386n, 517, 519,
  521, 523;
on power-knowledge relationship, 516,
  524–529;
concept of rationality, 526n;
on sexuality, 525, 527–528;
critique of totality, 518, 520–529
Fougeyrollas, Pierre, 297n
Fourier, François Marie Charles, 184, 192,
  223, 289
Fowlie, Wallace, 284n, 287
Frankel, Boris, 464n, 469, 491n
Frankel, Serge, 304n
Frankfurt School, 3, 8, 10n, 18, 20n, 124,
  149, 171, 187, 193, 195–198, 200,
  205–206, 208–210, 213, 216,
  218–220, 223–224n, 230, 238–239,
  242, 244, 307, 325–328, 350, 359,
  376, 413–415, 425, 431, 447, 450,
  454–455, 457–458, 461–462,
  465–466, 468, 471, 476, 478–479,
  486, 492, 497, 499–500, 502, 504,
  506, 510, 526–527;
parallels with Althusser, 413–415, 422;
and Bloch, 187;
parallels with Foucault, 526–527;
and Goldmann, 325–326;
and Italian Marxism, 431–432, 447,
  450, 455, 457–458;
and Korsch, 149, 259;
critique of Mannheim, 206–207;
on memory, 238–239;
on domination of nature, 170–171,
  187, 229–230, 414;
origins of, 196–197;
neglect of phenomenology, 472n;
and politics, 142n, 197, 213, 307, 327;
and praxis, 205–206, 208, 213, 466;
on totality, 195, 198.
See also Adorno; Critical Theory;
  Horkheimer; Institute of Social
  Research; Marcuse
Frankfurt Parliament, 72
Fraser, John, 426n, 428–429, 437, 439
Freedom, 59, 64–66, 93, 98, 101,
  110–111, 118, 157, 173, 339–342,
  345
French Revolution, 27, 39, 42–43, 45,

47–48, 52, 58, 70, 103, 143, 194,
  213
Frenzel, Ivo, 177n
Freud, Sigmund, 9–10, 18, 22, 88n, 186,
  203–205, 215, 223n–224, 232–233,
  235–236, 238–239, 243, 245, 285,
  290–291, 299, 326, 341, 400n, 402,
  404, 407, 430n, 466, 479–481, 510,
  515, 525;
on totality, 22.
See also Psychoanalysis
Friedman, George, 196n
Friedmann, Georges, 277
Frisby, David, 75n, 471n
Frohschammer, Jakob, 191
Fromm, Erich, 3, 197, 200, 204–205,
  215, 430n;
Marcuse's criticism of, 204n
Fugazza, Mariachiara, 460n
Functionalism, 75n
Funk Rainer, 204n
Furlong, E. J., 225
Fustel de Coulanges, Numa Denis, 76
Futurism, 284

Gabel, Joseph, 304n, 329n, 401
Gablik, Suzi, 489n
Gadamer, Hans-Georg, 18, 161, 208n,
  473n, 476–477, 494–495, 497, 505
Gagnebin, Jeanne M., 224n
Galileo, 431, 435, 446, 448
Galileo Circle, 98n–99, 115n
Gallagher, Catherine, 9n
Gallas, Helga, 302n
Galston, William A., 39n, 44n
Garaudy, Roger, 277n, 295, 328, 347,
  393–395
Garosci, A., 169n
Gassen, Kurt, 79n
Gay, Peter, 30, 44n
Gebhardt, Eike, 196n, 467n
Gehlen, Arnold, 478n
Geisteswissenschaften, 82, 88, 91, 115,
  158, 203, 398
Gelb, Adhemar, 203, 363n
Gemeinschaft. See Community
Genet, Jean, 322, 324, 358
Genetic Structuralism, 9, 320, 326,
  329–330, 488.
See also Goldmann; Piaget
Gentile, Giovanni, 73, 79, 171, 427, 439
George, Stefan, 89
Geraets, Theodore F., 334n, 336n, 361n
Geras, Norman, 113n, 142n, 413n
Gerlach, Erich, 131n, 147n
Gerratana, Valentino, 151, 388n, 429, 445
Gershman, Herbert S., 284n–285n, 292n
Gesellschaft, 76, 78, 98

Gestalt Psychology, 9, 14, 22n, 75, 203n–204, 208, 282, 363, 378, 389, 472–473
Geuss, Raymond, 468n
Geymonat, Ludovico, 426
Gibbon, Edward, 32
Giddens, Anthony, 475n, 477n, 497n–498n, 500n
Gide, André, 277, 345
Gierke, Otto von, 76
Gillan, Garth, 361n, 518n
Gintis, Herb, 19
Giolitti, A., 455n
Girard, René, 322
Giroux, Henry A., 169n
Gitlin, Todd, 19
Glucksmann, André, 387, 396–397n, 409n, 411n
Glucksmann, Miriam, 283n, 322n, 324n, 386n
Godard, Jean-Luc, 395
Godelier, Maurice, 387, 411, 487
Goethe, Johann Wolfgang von, 29, 51, 53n, 60, 96, 146, 186, 227, 230, 247, 252, 255, 537n
Goldmann, Annie, 304n, 315n, 329n
Goldmann, Lucien, 3–6, 8, 11, 23, 44–45, 68, 71, 81n, 89, 98n, 109n, 127, 137, 168, 278, 299, 304–333, 335n, 337, 346, 348, 353, 367n, 370, 377, 414, 416, 425, 430n, 442, 454, 488;
  critique of Adorno, 325–327;
  on aesthetics, 322, 442;
  and Althusser, 324, 328, 414, 416;
  detotalization, 321;
  on Heidegger, 331–332, 454;
  The Hidden God, 71n, 306, 314–315, 318–323, 328n, 353n;
  on history, 317, 329;
  on "homologies," 322–325, 329;
  The Human Sciences and Philosophy, 306, 311–313, 318;
  critique of identity theory, 310, 321, 327, 414;
  Immanuel Kant, 44–45, 306, 309n, 315, 331;
  on Kant, 44–45, 307–309;
  and Korsch, 137;
  relation to Lukács, 305, 307, 311, 313, 318, 325, 327, 329–330;
  Lukács and Heidegger, 307n, 331;
  on Marxism and Pascal's wager, 98n, 316–319, 329, 353–354;
  on nature, 318;
  relation to Piaget, 319–320, 325;
  and politics, 305n, 307, 312, 327;
  on praxis, 137, 312, 329;

on proletariat, 307, 312, 327;
  Racine, 307;
  Recherches dialectiques, 306, 319;
  and reification, 328;
  sociology of literature, 304, 306–307, 322, 325–326;
  on totality, 23, 308–326, 329–330;
  conception of totalizing subject, 312–314, 317, 320–322, 328–329;
  and "tragic vision," 71, 310–311, 314–315, 318
Gombin, Richard, 172n
Gombrowicz, Witold, 322
Goode, Patrick, 129n
Goodwyn, Lawrence, 536n
Gordon, Colin, 520
Gorman, Robert A., 427n
Görtzen, René, 468
Gorz, André, 8, 167n, 307, 513n
Gotha Congress, 67, 271
Gouhier, Henri, 306
Gouldner, Alvin W., 2n, 11n, 13, 23, 61n, 66n, 84n, 103n, 124n, 170n, 185n, 279n, 449, 492, 508n, 528, 530–531, 535
Grabenko, Yelena Andreyevna, 97
Graff, Gerald, 511n
Gramsci, Antonio, 1–3, 6–7, 9, 12, 67, 72n–73, 80, 100, 103, 116n–117n, 124, 127–129, 149–174, 183, 185, 187, 194–195, 198, 203, 209, 214, 221, 257, 261, 274, 295–296n, 311, 336, 350, 354, 371, 388, 390, 404, 408n, 413–414, 418, 423–424, 426–427, 431, 436–437, 444, 447, 451, 461, 467, 476, 492–494, 513;
  absolute historicism, 156–158, 170, 183, 261;
  activist impulse in his thought, 154–155, 157;
  and Althusser, 158, 163;
  and Croce, 152, 154–155, 169;
  on education, 168–170;
  on freedom, 157, 173;
  on hegemony, 150, 162, 164–170, 404;
  on history, 155–157, 169;
  and idealist tradition, 157–158, 166, 171;
  on intellectuals, 12, 153, 166–169, 209;
  intersubjective concept of rationality, 156–162, 165–166, 170–171, 194;
  legacy, 150–152, 424–425;
  "The Modern Prince," 168, 171;
  emphasis on national differences, 162–165;
  on nature, 158–159, 170–171, 185;
  "organicism," 153, 155, 167;

conception of party, 168–171;
on praxis, 153–156, 160, 166, 169n,
171;
Prison Notebooks, 72n, 150–151, 158,
169, 173, 413, 427;
on proletariat, 156, 159n, 161,
165–168, 171–172;
and psychology, 159n, 203;
"revolution against *Capital*," 2, 4, 100,
155, 388;
relation between state and society, 163;
"The Study of Philosophy," 153;
and Taylorization, 166, 170;
totalitarian implications of his thought,
166, 168–169;
on totality, 157–158, 160, 162–166,
168, 171, 173, 413;
on workers' councils, 154n, 171–173
Gramsci, Gennaro, 151n
Grassi, Ernesto, 160
Graziadei, Antonio, 129
Greeks (ancient), 25–27, 30, 34, 40, 42,
48–49, 51n, 57, 92–97, 100, 230,
301;
on history, 26;
on totality, 25–27
Green, Thomas Hill, 68
Grenz, Friedemann, 241n
Grido del Popola, Il, 151
Groethuysen, Bernard, 311n
Groh, Dieter, 67n
Gropp, Rugard Otto, 191n
Gross, David, 174n, 526n
Gruber, Helmut, 277n
Grünberg, Carl, 197–199, 211
Grünberg Archiv, 123
Guala, Chito, 70n, 282n
Guattari, Felix, 515
Guesde, Jules, 279
Guevara, Che, 395n
Guild socialism, 69
Gulag Archipelago, 532–533
Gumnior, Helmut, 197n, 211n
Gurvitch, Georges, 334, 336, 352
Gurwitsch, Aron, 363
Guterman, Norbert, 276n–277, 364

Habermas, Jürgen, 3–4, 6, 10n, 20, 49,
161, 167n, 170, 177, 188, 191, 194,
198, 219, 223–224n, 257n, 262,
272, 274, 291, 317, 358, 367n, 383,
411n, 414, 436–437, 451, 458n,
461–513, 517–518, 523–524,
526n–528, 531–532, 537;
and Althusser, 486;
theory of anthropological interests,
478–480;

*Communication and the Evolution of
Society*, 463, 487–491, 494, 508n;
theory of communicative action,
502–506;
communicative interaction, 358, 468,
475–476, 478–480, 482, 484, 487,
493–497, 507–508;
"Consciousness-Raising or Redemptive
Criticism," 257n, 262n, 462n,
486n, 500;
and traditional Critical Theory, 219,
272, 274, 462–463, 465–466,
475–476, 478–479, 483, 489, 491,
500–501, 503, 510;
and Gadamer, 473n, 476–477, 494,
497, 505;
and Gramsci, 161, 461, 467, 476, 493;
and Hegel, 469–474, 494, 511;
and hermeneutics, 472–473, 476–477,
479–481, 484–485, 494–495, 523;
on history, 470–471, 473, 486–487,
490–492n, 497, 505, 507;
"History and Evolution," 490–491;
and instrumental reason, 467, 475, 477,
479n, 482, 484, 486–487, 489, 500,
502, 506;
on intellectuals, 492–493, 498;
Knowledge and Human Interests, 475n,
478, 483–485n, 491, 493, 497n,
501, 510, 528;
and learning theory (Piaget), 483,
488–490, 494–495, 505;
Legitimation Crisis, 291n, 484–486,
499, 511n;
linguistic intersubjectivity, 194, 468,
474, 478–479n, 483, 493–500, 507;
and Lukács, 465, 470, 475, 485,
490, 502;
critique of Marcuse, 223, 466n, 468;
and Marx's labor theory of value, 466,
475, 504;
and memory, 483;
on modernity, 468n, 503–504,
506–507, 511–513;
"Modernity versus Post-Modernity,"
291n, 509n, 519n;
and modernization theory, 483,
503–507;
on nature, 478, 500–502, 507;
and Nietzsche, 510–511, 528–529;
development of a positive dialectic,
463, 476;
and the Positivist Dispute, 471–474,
476, 483;
and Post-Structuralism, 507–511,
517–518, 523–524, 528–529;
concept of power, 497–498, 524;
and praxis, 469, 475n, 481–482, 491;

and psychoanalysis, 479–482,
    484, 507;
on the public sphere, 467, 476,
    481, 507;
reconstruction of historical materialism,
    463–464, 468, 478, 483, 487, 491,
    495, 504, 509;
on reification, 485, 503, 506–507;
replacement of meta-subject by
    intersubjectivity, 461;
"A Reply to My Critics," 468n, 475n,
    477n, 480n, 492n, 497n–500n,
    502n;
*Structural Transformation of the Public
    Sphere*, 467, 476n;
on Surrealism, 291;
and systems theory (Luhmann),
    483–488, 494, 501, 504;
techne-praxis distinction, 411n, 467,
    476, 479, 502;
Theory of Communicative Action,
    476n, 502–506;
Theory and Praxis, 463n, 469,
    474–475, 481n, 494;
on totality, 462–463, 468–476, 483,
    486–487, 494, 498–499, 504,
    506–507, 509, 515;
concept of truth, 497–498, 503;
"undistorted speech situation," 383,
    496–500, 506–507, 523;
"universal pragmatics," 493–499, 508;
and *verum-factum* principle, 469–470,
    483;
on Weber, 471n;
and Western Marxist tradition,
    461–462, 469, 476, 483, 494,
    502, 506;
"What is Universal Pragmatics?"
    493–494
Hamann, Johann Georg, 32
Hampshire, Stuart, 29
Hardenberg, Friedrich von [pseud.
    Novalis], 87, 92
Harich, Wolfgang, 193
Harkness, Margaret, 302
Harris, H. S., 73n
Hartmann, Eduard von, 191
Hartmann, Geoffrey, 511n, 526n
Hartsock, Nancy, 400n
Hauser, Arnold, 98n–99, 289n
Hawkes, Terrence, 386n
Hayden, Tom, 536n
Hearn, Francis, 112n, 490n, 508n
Hebrew Philosophy, 26, 29, 93, 177, 246
Heckman, John, 285n–286n, 333n
Hegedüs, Andras, 5n, 304
Hegel, G. W. F., 2, 4, 27–29, 31, 34, 36,
    38–39, 43, 47, 52–61, 63–65, 67,
    70–73, 78–79, 87, 90–93, 95–96,

99n, 102–106, 108–110, 115, 121,
    125–126, 129, 131, 133–136, 138,
    141, 143, 147, 149, 157–158, 160,
    164, 180, 182–184, 186, 189, 191,
    201–202, 208, 211, 213, 217,
    220–224, 226–227, 235, 239, 244,
    254–255, 261, 263, 265, 267n, 272,
    276, 285–287, 292–295, 297n,
    299–300, 305, 307, 309–310, 314,
    325–326, 339–340, 343, 347, 350,
    356, 362–364, 368–372, 377n,
    379–380, 382, 385, 399–400,
    405–406, 413–414, 419–420, 427,
    431–433, 435, 445n, 448, 453–454,
    456–460, 469–471, 474–475, 478,
    511, 514, 519, 536;
Absolute Spirit, 54–57, 59–60, 64–65,
    158, 191, 369, 474–475;
Aesthetics, 53, 300, 314;
"Beautiful Soul," 60, 213, 370;
concrete totality, 58;
cunning of reason, 53n;
determinate negation, 55, 221, 254;
on dialectic, 47, 53–55, 221–222;
distinction between system and method,
    60–61;
on freedom, 58–59;
on ancient Greece, 57;
on history, 55, 59–60, 105;
identity theory as ontological
    assumption, 54–56, 59–60;
on Kant, 53–54;
role of labor, 347;
Logic, 56–57, 209, 226, 293–294,
    454;
master-slave relationship, 343;
on nature, 54;
"ought" versus "is," 54;
Phenomenology, 54–55n, 60n, 109n,
    209, 223n, 286, 294, 315, 339, 347,
    368, 453–454, 474;
religious aspects of, 57–58, 184–185;
Hegel Renaissance, 71, 79, 244,
    285–286, 294, 335, 348;
speculative reason, 49, 53–54, 76;
and Spinoza, 29, 54–56, 60;
state versus civil society, 58–59;
subject's ability to know totality,
    56–57;
on time, 54–56, 59;
on totality, 54–60, 222;
good versus bad totality (infinity), 56,
    58–59, 64, 96, 202, 382;
criticism of personal totality, 59–60;
unhappy consciousness, 58, 339, 512;
on *Verstand* and *Vernuft*, 54;
and Vico, 54, 57, 160.
    See also individual authors
Hegelianism: in Germany, 72–73;

in Italy, 72–73;
Left Hegelianism, 64, 125–127, 281n;
Neo-Hegelianism, 44, 73, 152, 164;
Right Hegelianism, 66, 73
Hegemony. See Gramsci
Heidegger, Martin, 192–194, 225–266,
235, 239, 242n, 244–245, 256, 271,
297n, 308, 315, 317, 323, 326,
331–341, 343, 346–349, 352–353,
355, 357, 360, 362, 372, 375n,
377–379, 385n, 451n, 454–455,
465, 476–477, 516n, 519;
concept of Being, 331–334, 349;
Being and Time, 225, 244, 309, 331,
337, 346, 377;
French misunderstanding of, 335–336,
343, 347–348;
"Letter on Humanism," 335, 346, 348
Heine, Heinrich, 47
Helander, Sven, 102–103n
Held, David, 196n, 462n, 468n,
477n, 488n
Heller, Agnes, 5n, 115, 303n–304, 308n,
312n, 317n, 329, 411n, 471n,
473–474, 480n, 489n, 499n–
500n, 534
Hellman, Stephen, 424n
Helvétius, Claude–Adrien, 28
Heraclitus, 298
Herbenick, Raymond, 382n
Herder, Johann Gottfried, 32, 43
Herf, Jeffrey, 1n, 19
Hermeneutics, 17–18, 161–162, 171,
194, 238, 249, 437, 451, 468,
472–473, 477, 479–480, 484–485,
494–495, 523;
hermeneutics of suspicion, 238.
See also Gadamer
Herr, Lucien, 286
Hertweg, Manfred, 193
Hesiod, 26
Hess, Moses, 120, 125–127
Hesse, Mary B., 449n, 481n, 497n
Hilferding, Rudolf, 4, 323n, 451
Hill, Christopher, 4n
Hiller, Kurt, 133, 207, 277
Hindemith, Paul, 254
Hindess, Barry, 409
Hirsh, Arthur, 293n, 295n, 384n,
387n–388n, 412n
Hirst, Paul Q., 280–281n
Historical materialism, 36, 121–122, 137,
141n, 148, 156, 181, 204, 262, 281n,
308, 364, 370, 389, 440, 463,
487–488, 491, 495, 527
Historicism, 32, 74–75, 77, 427, 444;
absolute historicism, see Gramsci;
revolutionary historicism, see Korsch
History. See individual authors on;

universal history, 105, 262–263, 265,
281, 471
Hitler, Adolf, 119n, 193
Hjelmslev, Louis, 430, 440
Hobbes, Thomas, 27, 356
Hobsbawm, Eric J., 4n, 121n, 147, 178
Hohendahl, Peter Uwe, 272n, 304n,
467n, 491n
Holbach, Paul-Henri Thiry, Baron d', 28,
453n
Holborn, Hajo, 78n
Hölderlin, Friedrich, 51, 242
Holism. See Totality
Hollier, Denis, 335n
Holocaust, 243
Hólon, 25
Homer, 91–97, 111
Honigsheim, Paul, 179n, 212
Honneth, Axel, 272n, 462n, 465n
Hooker, Richard, 27
Horkheimer, Max, 3, 6, 8, 33n, 36n,
171n, 196–221, 224n, 238–239,
242, 245, 252, 255–256, 258,
261–263, 270n, 274, 355, 363n,
414, 455, 462, 465–467, 479, 491,
498, 502, 526;
administered society, 216–219, 503;
and Adorno, 215, 255;
"The Authoritarian State," 216–219,
242, 263;
Dialectic of Enlightenment, 171n, 210,
215, 218, 220–221, 229–230, 242,
261–264, 269, 273, 414, 454, 457,
465, 467, 491, 526;
distinction between dialectic and
development, 217;
Eclipse of Reason, 215, 218;
need to take empirical data into
account, 202;
"existential judgment," 210, 216, 218;
on history, 209–210, 216–217;
immanent critique, 218;
irreducibility of individual to
collectivity, 204, 211–212, 214, 218;
and Kant, 211–212;
on labor, 212;
and Lukács, 197, 199, 201–202, 205,
211, 214–215;
critique of Mannheim, 207–208;
and memory, 224n, 229, 238–239;
on nature, 214–215;
non–identity of concept and reality,
213–215;
and praxis, 8, 205–206, 208, 213, 218;
integration of psychology, 203–205,
211;
rejection of asceticism, 212;
on totality, 199–202, 206–208,
210–211, 214, 216–217, 219;

totality and empiricial research,
    199–202, 256, 258;
"Traditional and Critical Theory," 201,
    210, 214n;
conception of truth, 206,208–209;
and *verum-factum* principle, 213
Horster, Detlev, 465n–466n, 477n, 498n,
    502n
Horthy, Miklós, 83n
Howard, Dick, 19, 167n, 181n, 192n,
    329n, 362n, 366n, 383n, 485n, 489n
Hoy, David Couzens, 477n, 479n, 509n,
    524n
Hudson, Wayne, 174n, 177n, 179n, 191
Hughes, H. Stuart, 68n, 169n, 281n,
    344n, 362n
Hughes, Serge, 73n
Huizinga, Johan, 432n
Hulliung, Mark, 37n
Humanism, 4, 243, 394–396, 398, 411,
    418, 430, 445;
Marxist humanism, 3, 5, 107, 152, 191,
    194, 205, 215, 220, 267, 269, 281,
    290, 294–295, 297, 353, 387, 395,
    397, 420, 430, 534.
See also individual authors
Humanité, L', 421
Humboldt, Wilhelm von, 74
Hume, David, 21, 30, 45, 225, 428, 431
Husserl, Edmund, 38, 78, 203, 245,
    333–336, 347, 360, 362n–363, 366,
    369, 372, 377, 379, 382, 455, 472,
    476.
See also Phenomenology
Huszadik Szagad (The Twentieth
    Century), 83
Huyssen, Andreas, 19, 512–513, 531
Hymes, Dell, 283n
Hyppolite, Jean, 71, 286, 294, 335, 368,
    385, 393, 519

Idealism: English, 68n–69;
German, 2, 4, 15n, 39–41, 43–44n, 49,
    53, 63, 87, 107, 214, 225, 248, 286;
Italian, *See* Croce.
See also Fichte; Hegel; Kant
Identity theory, 23n, 50–51, 54–60, 111,
    117, 126, 139, 149, 171, 182,
    211–212, 222–223, 239, 251, 256,
    268, 271, 310, 312, 349, 369, 375,
    399, 414, 434, 437, 457–458, 475,
    498;
as aspect of expressivism, 139,
    211–212, 222, 251, 310, 352, 458,
    471, 473, 483.
See also individual authors

Ideology, 101, 140–141, 207, 394,
    401–405, 411–412, 415, 443
Iggers, Georg G., 27n, 74n
Il'enkov, E. V., 445
Independent Socialist Party, 133
Individual, 24, 26n, 28, 30, 40–43, 46,
    57–59, 60–61n, 63, 68–70, 72, 94,
    101, 108, 111, 142, 153, 156, 199,
    212, 218, 246, 279, 281–282,
    308–310, 316, 332, 339, 350, 352,
    358, 527;
possessive individualism, 40.
See also individual authors
Industrial Revolution, 27, 70
Institute of Social Research, 149n,
    196–201, 203–205, 213n, 215, 226,
    229, 232, 239, 243–244, 255, 258,
    266, 465–466;
Aspects of Sociology, 266n;
Studien über Autorität und Familie,
    205n;
Studies on Prejudice, 200;
totalizing impulse in, 199–201
Intellectuals, 10–14, 30, 68–69, 72, 74,
    82, 98–99, 126, 153, 206–207,
    312n, 405, 492–493, 498,
    528–534, 537;
and origin of concept of totality, 10–14,
    99, 207, 312n, 492, 528–532, 537.
See also Gramsci; Mannheim
Internationale, 100, 133
Intersubjectivity. *See* Gramsci; Habermas;
    Language; Meta-subject; Totality
Ishaghpour, Youssef, 307n
Israel, Joachim, 61n
Izenberg, Gerald N., 341n

Jacobi, Friedrich Heinrich, 53, 454, 456
Jacobins, 13, 142, 152, 160, 168
Jacobitti, Edmund E., 73n
Jacobs, Carol, 526n
Jacoby, Russell, 7n–8n, 19, 102n, 131n,
    134n, 213n, 224n, 454n, 513
Jakobson, Roman, 288n, 408, 523
Jakubowsky, Franz, 3
James, William, 514n
Jameson, Fredric, 19, 52n, 81n, 98n, 107,
    185, 224, 235, 287, 344n, 357n, 359,
    388n, 402n, 409n, 416n, 513–514n,
    516, 536n
Jankélévitch, Vladimir, 367n, 393
Jansenism, 315
Jaspers, Karl, 44n, 335, 372n, 432n
Jaurès, Jean, 66, 277, 279, 286
Jay, Martin E., 2n, 16, 18n, 36n, 52n,
    176n, 196n, 199n–201n,
    203n–204n, 206n, 214n, 216n,

224n, 243n–244n, 246n, 262n,
    264n, 413n, 477n, 500n
Jeunesse Etudiante Chrétienne, 391
Joachim of Fiore, 26
John of Salisbury, 26
Johnson, Richard, 393n, 395n–396n
Joll, James, 154n
Jones, Gareth Stedman, 81n, 84n, 108n,
    115, 122n, 413n
Jordan, Z. A., 66n, 70n
Joyce, James, 288
July Revolution, 234
Jung, Carl, 203, 237, 251

Kafka, Franz, 323
Kamenka, Eugene, 33, 35
Kammler, Jörg, 81n
Kanapa, Jean, 347
Kant, Immanuel, 1, 10, 31–32, 39–40,
    43–51, 53–56, 60, 75n–79, 90–91,
    93, 103, 106, 109n, 116, 133, 146,
    204, 212, 214, 244–245, 261,
    272–273, 300, 305–310, 326, 331,
    334, 345–346, 352, 367, 389, 398,
    431, 434, 444–445, 447, 452–454,
    456, 458–460, 470, 474–475,
    478–479n, 486, 488, 499, 526n,
    537n;
  aestheticization of totality, 48–49;
  on aesthetics, 48–49;
  "Back to Kant" movement, 76–77;
  rejection of dialectics, 44–45, 54;
  and French Revolution, 25, 47–48;
  on history, 46–48;
  on nature, 46, 48, 54;
  on totality, 44–49;
  on Vernuft, 54.
  See also Neo-Kantianism
Karabel, Jerome, 166n
Kardiner, Abraham, 350
Karol, K. S., 391n, 397n, 421n
Karsz, Saül, 391n, 394n
Kätz, Barry, 220n
Kaufmann, Walter, 57n, 456n
Kautsky, Karl, 7, 10–11, 66, 129,
    134–135, 142, 166
Keane, John, 475n
Keat, Russell, 394n, 468n, 480n, 483n,
    498n, 502n
Kelley, Donald R., 62n
Kellner, Douglas, 19, 129n, 131n,
    134n–136, 142n, 193n
Kelly, George Armstrong, 39n–40n,
    53n–54n, 56n–57n, 309n
Kelly, Michael, 71n, 286n
Kelsen, Hans, 449–450
Kettler, David, 81n, 98n–99, 206n

Khruschev, Nikita, 314, 393–394, 424,
    445–446
Kierkegaard, Søren, 83, 86–87, 95, 179,
    247, 335, 338, 340, 350, 352, 358,
    362, 368
Királyfalvi, Béla, 304n
Kirchheimer, Otto, 200, 219n
Klare, Karl, 19
Klee, Paul, 263
Kline, George L., 333n
Klossowski, Pierre, 233n, 370n, 515, 519
Kluge, Alexander, 491
Kluke, Paul, 198n
Kockelmans, Joseph J., 357n, 362n
Koestler, Arthur, 365, 533
Koffka, Kurt, 204
Kofler, Leo, 3, 33n, 304n
Kohlberg, Lawrence, 489, 495, 505
Koigen, David, 102–103n
Kojève, Alexandre, 71, 282, 286, 294,
    335–336, 340–341, 343, 362, 368,
    370, 376, 453
Kolakowski, Leszek, 5, 25n, 39n, 66n–67,
    73n, 102n, 142n, 145, 159, 178, 192,
    266, 391n, 400n
Kommunismus, 100
Konrád, George, 13, 168n, 530–531,
    533–534
Köpeczi, Béla, 101n
Kornilov, L. G., 113
Korsch, Hedda, 129n–130n, 133, 142n,
    147n, 196–197n
Korsch, Karl, 1n, 3, 6–7, 9, 11n–12, 67,
    80, 102–103, 116n–117n, 119, 122,
    124, 127–151, 156, 158–159, 163,
    166, 168, 172, 183, 185, 192,
    195–203, 208, 215, 259, 274, 295,
    311, 336, 343, 350, 371, 388, 393,
    413–414, 419, 425, 436, 469, 486;
  ambiguity of his formulation of
    expressivism, 139–140, 143,
    147, 149;
  "Anti-Critique," 130, 132, 138, 142,
    144, 148;
  anti-Hegelian turn, 144–147;
  comparison with Bloch, 192;
  on dialectic, 144, 146;
  on essence–appearance distinction,
    143;
  and Frankfurt School, 149;
  "Fundamentals of Socialization," 134,
    139;
  hostility to psychology, 9, 203;
  idealization of working class, 143,
    147, 166;
  Karl Marx, 11n, 145–147, 425;
  and Lukács, 128–130, 141, 144,
    148–149;

Marxism and Philosophy, 1n, 102, 129,
    131–132, 135–137, 139n–140, 142,
    146, 148–149, 158, 197, 221, 425;
    "The Marxist Dialectic," 135–136;
    on nature, 141, 145–149, 185;
    and politics, 142–143;
    "practical socialism," 133;
    on praxis, 128–129, 131n–132,
    136–138, 140–142, 147, 149n;
    on proletariat, 131n, 135–139, 413;
    on reification, 141–142n, 149;
    "revolutionary historicism," 136–138,
    140, 142, 144–145, 147, 183, 208,
    259;
    scientific inclinations, 131–132,
    135–139, 143–149, 158;
    "Ten Theses," 147;
    on totality, 132, 134–135, 138–142n,
    145–149, 413;
    on worker aristocracy, 131n;
    on workers' councils, 134
Kortian, Garbis, 468n, 500
Kosík, Karel, 5, 333
Kostov, T., 392
Kovel, Joel, 19
Koyré, Alexandre, 334, 393
KPD, 119, 133, 196
Kracauer, Siegfried, 16, 176, 188, 190,
    224n, 245–246, 252, 254–256,
    259, 264
Krahl, Hans–Jürgen, 213
Kristeva, Julia, 328, 515
Kronstadt Rebellion, 113
Kruks, Sonia, 362n, 367n–368n, 379n
Kübler, Renate, 177n
Kuhn, Thomas, 394n
Ku Klux Klan, 187
Külpe, Oswald, 179
Kultur, 83
Kun, Béla, 100–101, 119
Kunfi, Zsigmond, 101n
Künzli, Arnold, 243n
Kuron, Jacek, 534
Kurzweil, Edith, 293n, 386n, 391n

Labor, 52, 95, 100–101, 108, 114, 118,
    180, 212, 228, 270–271, 347, 351,
    410, 432, 445n–446, 448–449, 466,
    474–475, 485, 487, 490, 502, 527;
    division of, 52, 100.
    See also Vico, *verum-factum* principle
Labriola, Antonio, 33, 73, 102, 154
Labrousse, Ernest, 409
Lacan, Jacques, 20, 22, 161, 299n,
    378–379n, 385–386, 402–403,
    408n, 416, 509, 514, 516n
LaCapra, Dominick, 18, 292n, 336n,
    344n, 359n, 485n, 509n–510,

    514n, 523n
Lafargue, Paul, 33
Laing, R. D., 343n
Lakatos, Imre, 15
Lalande, André, 367n
Landauer, Gustav, 80
Landler, Jenö, 119
Landmann, Michael, 79n, 186n,
    190n–191n, 194n, 238n
Langan, Thomas, 361n
Langbaum, Robert, 230n
Lange, Friedrich Albert, 76
Language, 22, 156, 159–162, 170,
    290–291, 293, 298–299, 357–358,
    378–380, 383, 389, 402–403, 408,
    430, 437, 440–443, 461, 468, 474,
    476, 481, 483, 493–499, 501, 503,
    505, 507–508, 515–516, 518,
    523–525
Lask, Emil, 78–79, 82–83, 106, 308, 331
Lassalle, Ferdinand, 66–67, 120,
    124–125, 138, 182, 271
Laurenson, Diana, 313
Lautréamont, Comte de, 287
Leach, Edmund, 386
Lebensphilosophie, 77–78, 84, 86, 176,
    246, 454
Lecourt, Dominique, 386n, 392n–393n
Lee, Edward N., 362n
Lefebvre, Henri, 3, 6–7, 23, 124,
    277–278, 293–299, 305, 315n,
    328–329, 337, 343, 347, 350, 352,
    359, 364, 369, 382, 390, 434, 516;
    on alienation, 293, 296, 298;
    closed versus open totality, 296;
    on dialectic, 295, 297–298;
    Dialectical Materialism, 294–296n;
    Everyday Life in the Modern World,
    294n;
    on language, 298;
    on nature, 297–298;
    on praxis, 294;
    The Sociology of Marx, 296n, 298;
    La Somme et la reste, 277n, 293n;
    on totality, 23, 295–298
Lefort, Claude, 3, 366, 383
Leibniz, Gottfried Wilhelm, 29–30, 225n,
    406
Leiss, William, 19, 501n
Leitch, Vincent B., 511n
Lemert, Charles, 509n, 518n
Lenhardt, Christian, 224n, 228
Lenin, Vladimir I., 4, 11, 56n, 67, 80, 85,
    101, 103, 112, 118, 120, 123, 129,
    139, 142–143, 155, 162–163,
    165–166, 170n, 176, 218, 276, 318,
    390, 413, 429, 444–447, 450–451,
    454, 459;
    Materialism and Empirio–Criticism,

121, 390, 444, 459
Leninism (Bolshevism), 7, 10–11, 98, 103,
  110, 112–113, 123–124, 130–131n,
  137, 147, 150, 152, 155–156, 162,
  165, 168–172, 176, 179–180, 191,
  193–195n, 208–209, 278, 284, 314,
  329, 359, 365, 373–374, 388, 392,
  395–396n, 398, 412, 417, 421, 424,
  427, 431, 446, 482, 493, 530–531
Lentricchia, Frank, 511n
Lenzer, Gertrud, 70
Leopardi, Giacomo, 156
Lepenies, Wolf, 478n
LeSenne, R., 367n
Lessing, Gotthold Epraim, 29
Lesznai, Anna, 98n
Levinas, Emmanuel, 297, 334, 336, 517n
Levine, Donald N., 77n
Levine, Norman, 103n
Lévi–Strauss, Claude, 282–283, 320,
  324, 327, 367n, 379–380, 385–386,
  389, 391, 410, 512;
  on totality, 389
Lévy, Benny, 353n
Lévy, Bernard–Henri, 367n, 532n
Levy, Heinrich, 79n
Lewin, Kurt, 350
Lewin, Michael, 61n
Lewis, John, 392, 397, 417, 419
Leyden, W. von, 225
Liberalism, 72–73, 76, 207
Lichtheim, George, 44n, 82n, 84n, 169n,
  276n, 315n, 329, 357n, 392, 395,
  468, 514n
Lienert, Franz, 197n
Lindenfeld, David F., 68n, 75n, 203n
Lindner, Burkhardt, 241n
Lingis, Alphonso, 233n
Linguistics. See Language
Link–Salinger, Ruth, 80n
Lipps, Theodor, 179
Lisa, Athos, 168
Lissetsky, El, 284
Litt, Theodor, 474
Littré, Emile, 70
Litván, György, 99n
Lock, Grahame, 387, 393n
Locke, John, 30, 34
Loevinger, Jane, 489, 495
Long, Tom, 1n
Lo Piparo, Franco, 160
Lorenzer, Alfred, 480
Loria, Achille, 154
Lotze, Rudolf Hermann, 76
Lovejoy, Arthur, 16, 21, 41n, 47n, 51n
Lovell, Terry, 416n
Lowenthal, Leo, 3, 6, 83n, 197, 200, 325n
Löwith, Karl, 53n, 465, 474, 514n
Löwy, Michael, 81n–83n, 118n, 120,

127, 178n, 184, 231n, 304n–305n,
  329
Lubasz, Heinz, 223n
Lüdke, W. Martin, 241n–242n, 273
Ludz, Peter C., 484n
Luhmann, Niklas, 484–488, 494
Lukács, Georg, 1–10, 12, 14, 23,
  27–28n, 35–36, 39n, 43–47,
  52–53, 57, 60n–61n, 67–68, 71,
  75n–132, 135, 138–139n, 141–144,
  148–149, 151, 153–159, 163, 168,
  170–171, 176–185, 187–188, 191,
  195–203, 205–209, 212–215, 219,
  221–222, 228, 240, 245–247,
  249–251, 254–255, 257, 259, 261,
  267–268, 270, 274–275, 278n, 288,
  295–297, 299, 301–307, 310–314,
  317–318, 320–322, 325–326,
  328–331, 335–336, 340–341, 343,
  347, 349, 352–353, 356, 358–359,
  369, 371–373, 383n, 387–388,
  390–393, 398, 401, 405, 412,
  414–416, 419n, 425, 427,
  430–431n, 435, 441–442, 444,
  453–454, 457–458, 463, 465, 467,
  469–470, 475, 478, 485–487, 490,
  496, 499n, 502–504, 513, 515,
  532–533, 535;
  and Adorno, 254–255, 257, 268–270,
  478, 512;
  critique of aesthetic modernism,
  187–188, 195, 255n, 288, 302–303,
  322, 441;
  on aesthetics, 85–98, 301–304, 250,
  383n, 441–442, 515;
  on alienation, 95–96, 98, 110, 114n,
  126, 401;
  appearance–essence distinction, 92,
  112, 141, 183;
  and Bloch, 181–185, 303;
  Blum Theses, 119–120n, 124, 163,
  302;
  "Bolshevism as a Moral Problem," 98,
  110;
  critique of bourgeois culture, 81–84,
  86–89, 91, 97, 100, 108–110, 112;
  and class consciousness, 101;
  imputed class consciousness, 112–113,
  121, 123, 141–142, 311;
  conflation of reification and
  objectification, 114, 148;
  conversion to Marxism, 98–99, 317n;
  The Destruction of Reason, 86n, 317,
  332, 458;
  on importance of economy, 97–98,
  100–103;
  Essays on Thomas Mann, 83n;
  Existentialism or Marxism, 347n,
  371n;

extensive versus intensive totality, 92,
   95, 303;
conception of freedom, 93, 98, 101,
   110–111, 118;
and Goldmann, 305, 307, 311, 313,
   318, 325, 327, 329–330;
on Hegel, 57n, 61n, 87, 92n, 125–126,
   184;
and Heidegger, 331–332;
conception of historical subject, 94,
   106–109, 115–116, 122, 212;
on history, 90–91, 105–106, 108, 111,
   122, 356, 470;
History and Class Consciousness, 1, 10,
   12, 14, 44, 61n, 81n–82n, 84–85,
   87, 99n, 102–118, 120–123,
   125–128, 132, 141n, 143–144,
   148–149, 158, 171, 177, 181–183,
   185, 187–188, 191–192n, 197, 208,
   212–213, 228, 246, 257, 267, 296,
   303–305, 307, 309n–311, 318, 321,
   331, 335, 349, 356, 358, 367,
   372–373, 413, 415, 425, 430, 463n,
   465, 470, 487, 502;
repudiation of History and Class
   Consciousness, 12, 84–85, 120, 123;
identification of Marxism with method,
   60n–61n, 144, 153, 430;
on identity theory, 111, 117, 126,
   182–183;
critique of Kant, 44;
and Korsch, 128–130, 141, 148–149;
importance of labor, 35, 101, 114, 118;
Lenin, 120–123, 141n, 143, 532;
and Thomas Mann, 83, 99;
"Mein Weg zu Marx," 82n;
on memory, 106, 228;
and Merleau-Ponty, 371n–373, 383n,
   470;
on nature, 87, 108, 114–118, 127, 148,
   158, 185, 318, 341, 414, 457;
"objective possibility," 112, 123, 141,
   490;
"The Old Culture and the New
   Culture," 100–101;
The Ontology of Social Being, 117;
conception of the Party, 112–113, 118,
   120;
and politics, 118–120, 332;
on praxis, 85, 101–102, 104, 106–109,
   114, 116, 122–123, 127, 129, 141n;
on proletariat, 100–101, 107–113,
   115, 118, 121–122, 161, 183,
   207–208, 213, 313, 329;
idealization of proletariat, 112;
hostility to psychology, 9, 88n, 115,
   117, 203;
on reconciliation, 85, 118n, 125, 134n,
   142;

and reification, 95, 101, 109–112,
   114–117, 126, 141, 148, 170–171,
   181, 183, 228, 268–270, 454;
"revolutionary culturalism," 99–102,
   120, 155;
as "romantic anti–capitalist," 84–85,
   95n, 101;
and Simmel, 78n;
Soul and Form, 82, 85–90, 92, 97, 117,
   177, 305, 310, 314, 335, 358;
The Theory of the Novel, 46, 81n–83n,
   86, 90–98, 100, 105–107, 180n,
   183, 228, 246n, 249, 261, 301, 303,
   305, 322, 335n, 358;
on totality, 23, 52–53, 84–97,
   101–127, 148, 183, 187, 195, 211,
   213, 301–302, 349–350, 414;
on concrete totality, 95, 104–105, 112,
   121;
move away from expressive totality,
   120, 122, 127;
on primacy of totality, 14, 85, 103–105,
   144, 153, 430, 463;
and verum–factum principle, 107–108,
   111, 116, 122, 257;
"What Is Orthodox Marxism?"
   104–105, 121;
The Young Hegel, 52n, 57n, 125–126,
   184
Lukes, Steven, 70n, 279n, 499n
Lunn, Eugene, 19, 80n, 241n, 246n,
   251n–252n, 288n, 302n
Luporini, Cesare, 425, 445
Luppol, I. K., 129n
Luxemburg, Rosa, 4, 7, 66n, 113, 120,
   142–143, 162, 166, 210, 451
Lyotard, Jean-François, 49n, 509n, 515
Lysenko, Trofim, 392, 416, 420

Mably, Gabriel Bonnot de, 437
McBriar, A. M., 69n
McCagg, William O., 82n
McCarthy, Thomas, 19, 468n, 473, 479n,
   488, 497
Macciocchi, Maria Antonietta, 152n,
   396n, 399n, 424n–425
McDonnell, Kevin, 416n, 422n
McDougall, William, 69
Mach, Ernst, 305
Macherey, Pierre, 328, 387, 415–416
Machiavelli, Niccolo, 168
Maciejewski, Franz, 484n
McInnes, Neil, 3n, 134n, 169n
McIntosh, Donald, 480n
McLellan, David, 11n, 28n

MacPherson, C. B., 40, 59n
Magri, Lucio, 426–427
Maier, Joseph, 213n
Maine de Birain, François–Pierre, 71, 76
Major–Poetzl, Pamela, 518n
Makkreel, Rudolf A., 77n
Malcolm, Norman, 225
Mallet, Serge, 8, 167n, 307, 329
Mallin, Samuel B., 361, 377n
Malraux, André, 284, 322, 324, 383n
Mandelbaum, Maurice, 27n, 32n, 68n, 70n, 74n, 362n, 456n
Manifesto, Il, 356, 426–427
Mann, Thomas, 83, 90, 99, 213, 324
Mann, Tom, 69
Mannheim, Karl, 12, 14, 27n, 74–75, 99, 126, 145, 206–208, 256n, 258; *Ideology and Utopia,* 206–208
Mansbach, Steven A., 284n
Manuel, Frank E., 26n
Maoism, 4, 358, 394–395, 417n, 445, 535
Mao Tse–Tung, 394, 407, 418
Marburg School (Neo–Kantianism), 76, 398
Marcel, Gabriel, 335, 363
"March Action," 119, 164
Marchais, Georges, 421
Marck, Siegfried, 129n
Marcuse, Herbert, 3, 6, 8, 11, 44, 52, 73, 106, 185, 197–198, 204n, 208–209n, 212, 219–243, 245, 255, 257n–258, 260, 264, 270n, 273, 290–291, 326–327, 329, 332, 340, 343–344n, 347n, 355, 402, 406, 416, 430n, 435, 453, 455, 462, 466–468, 479, 483n, 494, 501, 525, 527–528;
aesthetic dimension, 52, 220, 223, 416, 506;
The Aesthetic Dimension, 52n, 224, 230–231;
on aesthetics, 220, 223–224, 230–232, 239;
"The Affirmative Character in Culture," 232, 255n;
comparison with Bloch, 237–238;
Counterrevolution and Revolt, 224, 227, 230–231, 235, 239;
Eros and Civilization, 52, 204n, 223n–224, 227, 234, 236–237, 239;
criticism of Fromm, 204n;
on Hegel, 221–223, 226–227, 235, 239;
Hegels Ontologie, 224, 226, 232;
and Heidegger, 225–226, 235, 239;
and identity theory, 222;
on memory, 106, 223–236, 340, 355;
memory as Archimedean point for

critical theory, 234;
memory and dereification, 227–229;
revolutionary potential of memory, 224, 226–228, 234–235, 406;
domination of nature, 229–230;
and negative dialectic, 220–222, 226;
and New Left, 221, 223;
One-Dimensional Man, 220, 224, 234;
on praxis, 229, 234, 237;
critique of progress, 234;
and psychology, 225, 232–234, 479;
conception of rationality, 223;
Reason and Revolution, 44, 208, 221–222, 326, 455;
on reification, 222;
and Romanticism, 52, 229–230;
on Sartre, 344n, 347;
on sexuality, 220, 223, 232;
on Surrealism, 290–291;
on totality, 220–224, 236, 239–240;
oppressive totalization of modern society, 221–222;
concept of truth, 208;
faithfulness to Marxism's utopian potential, 220, 223, 227–228, 231, 233–234, 236, 264
Marek, Franz, 65
Markus, György, 5n, 81n, 86n, 89n–90n, 92n, 304, 534
Márkus, Maria, 5n
Marr, Nikolay Y., 442
Marramao, Giacomo, 130n–131n, 142n, 216n, 425, 452n
Martin, Daniel, 304n
Martin, Jacques, 391
Martin du Gard, Roger, 324
Marx, Heinrich, 62n
Marx, Karl, 1–4, 9–11n, 13, 27–30, 33–36, 38–39, 43, 47, 53, 60–69, 75n, 80, 84–85, 95, 99n, 101–102, 104–110, 114, 118, 120, 125–127, 129n, 135–138, 140–142, 144–149, 156, 167, 174, 178, 180–181, 184, 186, 190, 199, 204–205, 215–217, 220–222, 227–229, 238–239, 263, 267–271, 276, 278, 281n, 283, 285, 293–294, 297n–298, 302, 307–309, 312, 318, 320, 333, 347, 349, 351–352, 364, 366, 369–371, 373, 381n, 391, 394, 396–397n, 400, 402, 404–405, 407, 410–411, 413, 416, 418, 420, 425, 430–434, 437–438, 442–450, 452–453, 455–456, 458n–461, 465, 469–470, 475, 499n, 501, 504, 506, 511, 513, 520, 533–535;
and aesthetics, 301;
on alienation, 43, 63, 65, 301, 351;
Capital, 2, 4, 27n, 101, 108–109, 140,

146–148, 209, 267–268, 320, 388,
      394, 418, 433–434;
critique of classical political economy,
      61–62, 125–126;
on class struggle, 47;
The Communist Manifesto, 13,
      136n–137;
and dialectic, 29;
Economic and Philosophical
      Manuscripts of 1844 (Paris
      Manuscripts), 61n–62, 84, 101–102,
      114, 142n, 186, 229, 276n, 294, 364,
      394, 455;
Eighteenth Brumaire, 35, 65n,
      227–228;
on freedom, 65–66, 101;
The German Ideology, 62–63, 475;
Grundrisse, 3, 27n, 63, 95n, 136n, 301;
and Hegel, 61, 63–65, 222, 433n;
critique of Hegel's Philosophy of Right,
      137, 432;
on history, 35–36, 61n–63, 105, 222;
The Holy Family, 61n, 64;
Introduction to a Critique of Political
      Economy, 432–433;
labor theory of value, 228, 270, 351,
      446, 448, 466;
conception of materialism, 30, 65;
as methodological individualist, 61n,
      65;
On the Jewish Question, 43, 62, 64,
      438, 535;
and organicism, 27–28;
and praxis, 64;
and Romanticism, 61, 63;
conception of society, 61n–62, 64;
and Spinoza, 28–29;
on totality, 23n, 27–28, 61–66, 125,
      222;
Vico's influence on, 33–36
Marx-Engels Institute, 198
Marxism. See also individual authors;
      Budapest School; Council
      Communists; Dialectical
      Materialism; Frankfurt School;
      Historical materialism; Leninism
      (Bolshevism); Maoism; Second
      International; Stalinism; Trotskyism
—Anglo–Marxism, 4, 397
—Anti–Hegelian Marxism, 3–4, 14, 38,
      44, 131, 145–146, 198
—Austro–Marxism, 4, 44, 124, 305, 308
—Critical Marxism, 2n, 10, 13, 66n, 144,
      190, 224, 306, 314, 431–432, 464,
      534
—Eastern Marxism, 2, 19, 66n, 127, 198,
      301, 534. See also Leninism
      (Bolshevism); Stalinism

—Existential Marxism, 8, 10, 328,
      330–361. See also Merleau-Ponty;
      Sartre
—Hegelian Marxism, 3, 14, 38, 84, 103,
      123, 128, 134, 136–137, 146, 186,
      190, 195, 197–198, 202–203, 211,
      222, 245, 247, 257, 267, 270n, 303,
      305, 320, 329, 382, 384, 430, 445,
      452, 455–457, 463, 469, 471–475,
      488, 494, 500, 512, 522–523, 534
—Orthodox Marxism, 2, 8, 37, 67, 80,
      100, 107, 129n, 133, 173, 194, 204,
      263, 277, 305, 314, 347, 382, 390,
      399, 454, 475, 478, 487, 491, 504
—Phenomenological Marxism, 10, 333
—Schopenhauerian Marxism, 10
—Scientific Marxism, 2n, 9–10, 13, 38,
      66n, 123, 128, 131–132, 147, 190,
      240, 277, 427, 452, 522. See also
      Althusser; Colletti; Della Volpe
—Structuralist Marxism, 10, 70, 128,
      270, 330, 384, 386–388, 397, 487.
      See also Althusser
—Vulgar Marxism, 7n, 11, 28n, 104, 398
—Western Marxism, age as common
      denominator, 4, 6;
break with Eastern Marxism over labor
      camps, 278, 372, 392;
and the crisis of bourgeois culture, 80;
and the crisis of capitalism, 324;
emphasis on cultural criticism, 3, 8–9,
      301;
as a reaction to dialectical materialism,
      2, 67, 295;
disillusionment and the breakdown of
      Western Marxism, 8, 19, 215–216,
      274, 387, 464, 530, 533–534;
versus Eastern Marxism, 2;
emancipatory claims of, 2, 9;
Eurocentrism of, 5;
Gramsci as first self–conscious Western
      Marxist, 163;
attitudes towards Hegel as defining
      characteristic, 2–4, 454;
impact of History and Class
      Consciousness, 1–2, 101–102;
recognition of Idealist heritage, 2;
insufficiency of Scientific/Critical and
      Hegelian/Anti-Hegelian dichotomies,
      2–4, 190–191;
as an integration of Utopian and
      Scientific Marxism, 173;
increasing isolation from politics, 12,
      307;
and Kant, 44, 309, 454;
repudiation of longitudinal totality,
      106, 157, 274, 317, 355, 372;
as a critique of the Lukácsian synthesis,

116–117, 123, 299, 303, 330,
358–359, 416, 436;
Merleau–Ponty and origins of concept,
1–2, 4, 278;
and domination of nature as theme, 36,
170–171, 274;
and the New Left, 5, 422, 535;
openness to other intellectual currents,
6, 9–10, 15, 25, 391, 468, 478, 483,
492;
origin of concept, 1–23, 144;
concern with praxis, 6–8, 64, 123;
attitudes towards psychology, 203;
and recovery of Marx's early writings,
3;
resistance to the sociologization of
Marxism, 124;
repudiation of Second International, 7;
attitudes towards social revolution,
6–7, 11;
as a critique of subject–nature
relationship in Lukács, 116–117,
274, 297, 318, 414, 457, 502;
attitudes towards time, 414–415;
totality as unifying concern, 14–15,
23–24, 84, 109;
and varieties of totality, 413–414;
Vico's importance for, 36–37
Marxist Perspectives, 19
Mass society, 59
Materialism, 3, 28, 30, 36, 39, 65, 67, 73,
76, 121–123, 144, 154, 161,
212–213, 247, 253, 265, 293,
346–347, 452, 501. *See also*
Dialectical materialism; Economy;
Historical materialism
Mattick, Paul, 143, 149
Maurer, Charles B., 80n
Maurer, R. K., 492n
Maurron, Charles, 328
Mauss, Marcel, 70, 282–283, 379, 389
May, Karl, 187
Mayakovsky, Vladimir, 284
Mayer, Gustav, 124
"May 1968," 287, 298, 324, 359,
395–396n, 517
Mayrl, William, 327n
Mead, Margaret, 504
Mehlman, Jeffrey, 65n
Mehring, Franz, 9, 146
Meinecke, Friedrich, 52, 74
Meinong, Alexius, 68n
Memory, 96n, 106, 183, 190, 223–230,
332, 406, 435, 437, 483, 523, 532.
See also individual authors
Mendelson, Jack, 477n
Mendès–France, Pierre, 366
Menger, Carl, 75

Merker, Nicola, 426
Merleau–Ponty, Maurice, 1–4, 6, 110,
122n, 130n, 278, 282, 287, 299,
304n, 318n, 336–338n, 343,
348–350, 358, 360–386, 391–392,
413, 425, 429, 461, 470, 476, 494,
512, 518–519, 533;
comparison with Adorno, 374–375;
Adventures of the Dialectic, 1, 110n,
122n, 130n, 278, 304n, 338n,
349–350, 366–367n, 372–375,
382–383n, 470, 533;
on aesthetics, 383n;
philosophy of ambiguity, 362n, 374n,
382;
on dialectic, 374, 380–381;
and Gestalt psychology, 363;
and Hegel, 362–363, 368–369, 372,
377n–378;
and Heidegger, 362, 372, 377–379;
on history, 364, 368–372, 374–375,
377, 470;
on humanism, 370, 373, 375–377, 380;
Humanism and Terror, 365, 370, 375;
and Husserl, 363, 366, 369, 372, 377,
382;
critique of identity theory, 375;
philosophy of inclusion, 363;
and language, 358, 366, 378, 380,
382–383;
on Lukács, 122n, 350, 367n,
371n–373, 470;
on nature, 363, 376–377;
Phenomenology of Perception, 364,
367–368, 382;
The Primacy of Perception, 362n, 366;
on proletariat, 122n, 370–375;
conception of rationality, 368–369,
372, 382;
and Sartre, 361, 366, 373–374, 380,
383;
Sense and Nonsense, 365, 371;
Signs, 366, 375, 382;
and Structuralism, 282, 366–367n,
378–380, 382;
The Structure of Behavior, 364, 378;
on nature of subjective consciousness,
363, 376–378;
on totality, 287, 362–364, 367–382;
attitudes towards USSR, 365, 371–372,
381;
on violence, 370–371;
wager on Marxism, 366, 370–372;
on origins of Western Marxism, 1–2, 4,
278;
and the Western Marxist tradition, 367,
373, 376, 378, 382
Merrington, John, 163n, 169n

Mészáros, István, 81n–82n, 84n, 93,
    304n, 336n, 342n
Metaphor, 146, 161–162, 171, 288n,
    440–441, 508
Meta-subject, 2, 8, 42, 48, 60, 65, 74, 94,
    107–113, 115, 121, 157, 159–160,
    171, 182–183, 190, 212, 214,
    259–261, 269, 271–272, 274, 295,
    302, 317, 339–340, 352, 371, 410,
    413, 461, 470, 488, 523, 532. *See
    also* Hegel, Absolute Spirit;
    Proletariat
Metonymy, 288n
Michelet, Jules, 32–33
Miliband, Ralph, 405n
Mill, John Stuart, 69
Miller, D. A., 96n
Miller, J. Hillis, 15n
Miller, Jacques–Alain, 408
Miller, James, 19, 362n, 492n, 509n
Milne, A. J. M., 68n
Mimesis, 90, 93, 302, 383n, 442, 502,
    508
Misgeld, Dieter, 477n
Mitterand, François, 395n
Mitzman, Arthur, 76n
MLN, 344n
Mode of production, 140, 187, 281, 391,
    410–411, 487
Modernism. *See* Aesthetic modernism
Modernization theory, 483, 508–507
Moleschott, Jakob, 74
Monde, Le, 421
Mondolfo, Rodolfo, 102, 427, 437–438
Money, 77, 295, 506
Monism, 28
Montano, Mario, 426n–427n
Montesquieu, Baron Charles de Secondat
    de, 32, 37–40, 42, 399, 438
Moore, G. E., 69
Morawski, Stefan, 9, 301n
Morelly, 437
Morhange, Pierre, 277, 293
Morin, Edgar, 295, 297
Mornet, Daniel, 39
Morrall, John B., 26n
Morris, William, 69
Morrow, Raymond, 152n, 492n
Mosca, Gaetano, 167
Mosse, George, 52
Mouffe, Chantal, 152n, 154n
Mougin, Henri, 347
Mounier, Emmanuel, 335
Mueller, Iris W., 69n
Münzer, Thomas, 181n
Musil, Robert, 323
Mussolini, Benito, 71, 151, 155, 157, 164,
    166, 423
Myth, 71

Nadeau, Maurice, 284n–285n
Nagel, Ernest, 472–473
Nägele, Rainer, 20n, 509n
Nagy, Peter, 82n
Nair, Sami, 304n–305n, 307n, 327n
Nationalism, 52, 73, 76, 80, 137, 164
Natorp, Paul, 79
Naturalism, 36
Natural law, 30, 37–38, 194
Nature. *See individual authors*
Naturwissenschaften, 158
Naville, Pierre, 291, 368, 385
Nazism, 86n, 130, 192–193, 292, 396n,
    465. *See also* Fascism
Negative dialectics. *See* Adorno
Negri, Antonio, 426
Negt, Oskar, 145n, 176, 192n–193n,
    482, 491
Nelson, Leonard, 207
Neo-Kantianism, 14, 68, 76–79, 82, 90,
    110–112, 124, 129n, 133, 148, 177,
    211, 244, 246, 277, 308, 327, 334,
    398
Neo-Platonism, 25, 78, 177, 453
Nettl, J. P., 67n
Neue Sachlichkeit, 254
Neumann, Franz, 200, 219n
New German Critique, 19
New Left, 8, 11, 18–19, 131, 147, 167,
    175n, 213, 221, 223, 324, 359, 367,
    422, 425, 464, 491, 513, 531, 535
New Left Review, 3n, 5, 9n, 19, 387, 448,
    451
New Philosophers, 8, 19, 367, 512, 532
"New Populism," 536
Newton, Isaac, 46, 186
New Working Class, 8, 167, 327. *See also*
    Mallet
Nicholas of Cusa, 189
Nichols, Christopher, 480n
Nietzsche, Friedrich, 13, 74–75n, 77, 92,
    161, 189, 212, 233–235, 238, 241n,
    268, 362, 370n, 379, 399n–400n,
    451, 509n–512, 517–518, 520–523,
    528–529, 537
Nisbet, Robert A., 27n, 76
Nizan, Paul, 277–278, 344, 399n;
    The Watchdogs, 278
Nizolio, Mario, 160
Non-synchronicity. *See* Bloch
Nouvelle Critique, La, 328, 402
Novack, George, 452n
Novalis. *See* Hardenberg
Novelli, 286
Nyugat (The West), 83

Objectification, 3, 77, 114, 122, 148. *See
    also* Alienation; Reification

O'Brien, Ken, 204n
October Revolution. *See* Russian
    Revolution
Ogilvy, James, 510n
O'Hara, Harry, 193n
Olafson, Frederick A., 346n
Olivetti, Gino, 172
Ollmann, Bertell, 63n
O'Neill, John, 224n, 471n, 483n
Oppens, Kurt, 240n
Ordine Nuovo, L', 151, 171, 173
Organicism, 25–29, 38, 43, 65, 69–70,
    91n, 95, 300–301n, 303, 350;
    and conservatism, 27
Orgel, Gary S., 459n
Orsini, Claude, 131n
Orsini, G. N. Giordano, 25n
Ortega y Gassett, José, 289n, 432n
Ottmann, Henning, 502n
Ottwalt, Ernst, 303

Pachter, Henry, 131n
Paci, Enzo, 332, 425
Pannekoek, Anton, 7n
Panzieri, Raniero, 426
Paracelsus, 185
Parain, Brice, 367n
Pareto, Vilfredo, 167
Parkinson, G. H. R., 81n
Parmenides, 25, 454
Parsons, Talcott, 14, 75n, 124, 483–484,
    503–504, 506
Partos, Paul, 141n–142n
Pascal, Blaise, 27, 44n, 71, 98n, 278, 283,
    310, 315–318, 370, 488
Paserini, Giambattista, 72
Passato e presente, 445
Pastore, Annibale, 169n
Paulhan, Jean, 290
PCF (Parti Communiste Français),
    277–278, 285, 293–294, 345,
    347–348, 359, 364–365, 371,
    386–388, 391, 393–398, 402, 412,
    416, 420, 424, 519
PCI (Partito Comunista Italiano),
    150–152, 155, 162, 172, 422–429,
    438, 444–445, 447, 450
Péguy, Charles, 278
Perlini, Tito, 424n, 426
Permanent Revolution, 143
Perse, Saint–John, 322
Peters, F. E., 25n
Petrović, Gajo, 333
Phelan, Tony, 188n
Phenomenology, 55, 78, 225, 244–245,
    256, 294, 333–336, 347, 362–366,
    368, 374, 377, 379, 382, 384–386,
    425, 477, 512

Phenomenon-Noumenon distinction, 45,
    54, 110–111
Phillips, D. C., 75n
Philosophes, 28–31, 40
Philosophies, 277–278n, 293
Phronesis, 477
Physiocrats, 32
Piaget, Jean, 9, 306, 314, 319–321,
    325–326, 330, 367n, 488–489, 495,
    505. *See also* Genetic Structuralism
Piccone, Paul, 1n, 19, 72n–73n, 84n,
    121n, 137n, 152n, 164, 166n, 170n,
    196n, 263n, 333n, 458, 472n
Pierce, C. S., 161, 488, 497n
Pieri, Sergio, 425n
Pierrot, Jean, 285n
Pietism, 40
Pietranera, Giulio, 426, 429, 445
Plato, 25, 59, 92, 183, 225, 248, 300, 325,
    433, 435, 460
Plekhanov, Georgii Valentinovich, 7,
    9–10, 29n, 66
Plenge, Johann, 102–103n
Poggi, Alfredo, 452
Poincaré, Jules Henri, 393
Polin, Raymond, 367n
Polis, 42, 57
Politzer, Georges, 277, 293, 401
Pollock, Friedrich, 196–197, 200, 211,
    216–219, 245, 274
Polycentrism, 162
Popper, Karl, 74, 144n, 221, 266, 449,
    479, 483
Popper, Leo, 86
Popular Front, 143, 164, 424
Port-Royal, 310, 315
Positivism, 16, 27, 68n–71, 102, 116,
    144, 154, 176, 201, 216, 471–474,
    476, 478, 522, 526
Positivism Dispute, 16, 471–474, 476,
    483
Poster, Mark, 19–20n, 71n, 276n, 278n,
    286n, 293n, 297n–298n, 304, 308n,
    333n, 344n–345n, 347n, 351, 357n,
    359, 362n, 393n, 397n, 402n
Postone, Moishe, 19, 216n, 267
Post–Structuralism, 19, 49, 161–162,
    290, 370n, 379, 383, 386, 441n, 451,
    509–529, 536–537. *See also*
    Foucault
Poulantzas, Nicos, 75n, 387, 390n,
    396n–397n, 412, 525n
Poulet, Georges, 230n–231n
Pozzoli, Claudio, 129n, 132n
Prague Spring, 534
Prawer, S. S., 301n
Praxis, 2, 6–8, 14, 27n, 36, 64, 71, 101,
    106–111, 114, 116, 121–123,
    128–129, 136–137, 140–142, 147,

149n, 153–156, 166, 169n, 171, 193, 205–206, 208, 213, 218, 229, 234, 253, 258, 261, 271, 290, 312, 329, 332, 349, 351, 356, 359, 396–397, 399n–400, 412, 416–418, 430, 443, 469, 475n, 481–482, 491, 520. *See also individual authors*
Praxis, 5, 304n, 325, 333n, 416n, 430n
Process philosophy, 140, 191, 194–195
Progress, 26, 31, 34, 42, 45–46, 55–56, 70, 157, 171, 189, 217, 234, 262–263, 355. *See also individual authors*
Proletariat, 13, 100–101, 107–113, 115, 118, 120–122, 126–127, 131n, 135–140, 143, 148, 155–156, 157–159n, 161, 163, 165, 167–168, 171, 183, 189–190, 192, 194, 207–208, 212, 220, 228, 234, 255, 259, 267n, 284, 296, 298, 302, 307, 312–313, 327n, 329–330, 356, 370–375, 381, 413, 443, 470, 491, 532;
dictatorship of, 100, 113, 119, 420;
as universal class (meta-subject), 107–108, 110, 113, 115, 121–122, 148, 157–158, 161, 165, 183, 190, 194, 207, 212, 228, 259, 284, 302, 313, 330, 356, 371–372, 375n, 470, 532. *See also individual authors*
Prometheus, 65
Protestantism, 40
Proudhon, Pierre–Joseph, 352
Proust, Marcel, 229–230, 340
PSI (Partito Socialista Italiano), 426
Psychoanalysis, 6, 9, 204–205, 232–233, 235, 245, 293, 326, 341–342, 358, 401–403, 479–482, 484, 507, 515;
existential psychoanalysis, 341–342, 358. *See also* Freud
Psychology, 22, 30, 88–89, 115, 117, 159n, 203–205, 225, 232–234, 237, 280, 460, 483, 488–490, 494–495, 505, 515, 518;
and totality, 22. *See also* Gestalt Psychology; Piaget; Psychoanalysis
Puech, Henri–Charles, 334
Pugin, Welby, 68
Pütz, Peter, 510n
Pyrrhonism, 453

Quaderni Rossi, 425
Quesnay, François, 32

Rabassiere, Henri. *See* Pachter
Rabil, Albert, Jr. 276n, 361n, 364n, 377n, 381

Rabinbach, Anson, 19, 176n
Rabinow, Paul, 518n, 526n
Racine, Jean, 310, 315, 328
Rader, Melvin, 27n, 63n
Radnoti, Sandor, 178n, 247n
Radvanyi, Laszlo, 140
Rajk, László, 392
Rancière, Jacques, 395–396
Ranke, Leopold von, 17, 74, 144, 244
Rassemblement Démocratique Révolutionnaire, 348, 365
Räte. *See* Workers' Councils
Raulet, Gérard, 520n
Reason (Rationality). *See individual authors*
Recherches Philosophiques, 334
Recognition. *See* Anagnorisis
Redfern, W. F., 277n–278n, 399n, 401n
Reflection theory, 121, 140, 324, 390, 439–440, 444
Reformation, 40
Reich, Wilhelm, 3–4, 6, 12, 203, 205, 525
Reid, Herbert G., 489n
Reification, 3, 95, 109–111, 114–117, 126, 141, 148–149, 170–171, 181, 195, 203, 228–230, 255, 267–270, 280, 287, 289, 323, 328, 331, 397, 404, 446, 454–455, 485, 503, 506;
dereification, 183, 228–230n, 404. *See also individual authors*
Relativism, 77, 110
Religion, 22, 25, 28, 57, 63, 97, 102, 181, 192, 195, 214, 219, 238, 262–263;
primitive, 25;
and totality, 22, 25, 175
Renaissance, 40, 72, 100–101, 160, 169, 185
Renan, Ernest, 70, 286
Resistance Movement, 6, 8, 150, 278, 295, 360, 364, 391–392, 396n, 464
Revai, Josef, 122, 130n, 149, 372, 413, 470
Revisionism, 10, 44, 67, 104, 110, 112, 133, 535. *See also* Second International
Revolution of the Saints, 13
Revue Marxiste, La, 277
Richman, Michelle, 515n
Richter, Melvin, 68n
Rickert, Heinrich, 77, 79n, 110, 179n, 246
Rickman, H. P., 76n
Ricoeur, Paul, 18, 238, 374–375, 389;
hermeneutics of suspicion, 238
Riechers, Christian, 152n
Riemann, G. F. B., 189
Rimbaud, Arthur, 285, 287, 290
Rinascita, 425, 445, 458n
Ringer, Fritz K., 14, 76n, 207

Ringguth, Rolf, 197n
Riquelme, John Paul, 381n
Risorgimento, 72–73
Robbe-Grillet, Alain, 322–324
Robespierre, Maximilien, 42, 47, 213
Robins, Kevin, 416n, 422n
Rochet, Waldeck, 394n
Rochlitz, Rainer, 332n
Rohrmoser, Gunter, 242n
Romanticism, 15, 27, 29, 32, 39, 51–52,
    56, 59–61, 63, 65, 84, 87, 95n, 97,
    133, 184, 230–231, 285, 300–301,
    431–433, 440–441n, 454, 467
Ropischin (Boris Savinkov), 98n
Rorty, Richard, 477n
Rosa, Alberto Asor, 89n, 162n, 425, 449n
Rose, Gillian, 109n, 240n, 265, 267–270,
    280n, 381n, 398n, 462n, 472n, 500
Rosen, Stanley, 25n, 54n
Rosenzweig, Franz, 244, 297n
Rossanda, Rosanna, 426
Rossi, Mario, 426
Roth, Guenther, 67n
Rousseau, G. S., 301n
Rousseau, Jean–Jacques, 32, 34, 39–43,
    45, 47, 58–59, 64, 186n, 309–310,
    393, 415n, 428, 437, 453, 499, 527;
    individual totality and the origin of
    expressivism, 40–43;
    general will, 42, 58, 309;
    will of all, 42, 45
Rousset, David, 348, 365
Rovatti, Pier Aldo, 332, 425
Rubel, Maximilien, 27n, 278, 430n
Ruben, David–Hillel, 400n, 459n
Rücker, Silvie, 81n
Ruge, Arnold, 62
Rühle, Jürgen, 191n, 193n, 424n
Runciman, W. G., 75n
Rusconi, Gian Enrico, 143n, 425
Ruskin, John, 69, 231
Russell, Bertrand, 69, 225
Russian Revolution, 6, 13, 44, 80–81,
    100, 103, 122, 129, 131n, 165,
    176–177, 179, 195, 197, 421
Rutigliano, Enzo, 170n, 425n
Ryan, Michael, 509n, 516n, 532n
Ryazanov, David, 198
Rybalka, Michel, 342n, 359n
Ryle, Gilbert, 225

Saint–Simon, Claude Henri, 27, 70, 184
Salvadori, Massimo, 426
Salvadori, Roberto, 285n, 426, 449
Salvemini, Gaetano, 163–164
Sammons, Jeffrey L., 188n, 190–191n
Santarelli, Enzo, 427n, 452n
Sapir, Edward, 22

Sapronow, T. W., 130
Sarraute, Nathalie, 323
Sartre, Jean–Paul, 3, 6, 8, 60, 162, 168,
    213, 260, 276, 287, 291–292, 297,
    299, 303, 318n, 321, 323–324, 326,
    328, 330, 333n–362, 364–367,
    373–374, 376–380, 383–385,
    389–390, 392, 403, 406, 410, 413,
    415, 425, 434, 451, 454–455, 463,
    512, 520;
    on alienation, 337;
    Being and Nothingness, 337–348,
        350–351, 353, 355–356, 358, 361,
        373–374n;
    parallel with Bloch, 353;
    The Communists and the Peace, 365;
    Critique of Dialectical Reason, 297,
        343n, 348–355, 357–361, 374, 385;
    and Descartes, 338, 352, 362;
    on dialectical reason, 352;
    "dirty hands" and "clean hands," 60,
        213, 348, 364;
    "Existentialism is a Humanism,"
        345–346, 353n;
    and existential psychoanalysis,
        341–342, 358;
    relationship between for–itself and
        in–itself, 338–341;
    on freedom, 339–342, 345;
    and Heidegger, 333n, 337–341,
        348–349, 353;
    on history, 340, 352–356, 360;
    on humanism, 345–346, 353;
    The Idiot of the Family, 358–359;
    Imagination, 336n;
    conception of the individual, 339, 350,
        352, 354, 358;
    parallel with Lacan, 403;
    and language, 357–358;
    on Lukács, 349, 352;
    "Materialism and Revolution," 346,
        364;
    and Merleau-Ponty, 348, 361,
        365–366, 373–374, 380, 383;
    denial of meta-subject, 339–340,
        352–353;
    on nature, 340–341, 357, 376;
    Nausea, 337, 340, 343, 345;
    and objectification–alienation
        relationship, 351, 356;
    and ontological materialism, 346–347;
    and practico–inert, 351, 356;
    and praxis, 349, 351, 356, 359;
    on scarcity, 357;
    Search for a Method, 348–349, 353,
        358, 415, 434;
    on Surrealism, 291–292, 348;
    on terror, 356–357;
    on totality, 287, 297, 337–344,

348–360, 413, 415;
and detotalization, 321, 352, 355–360;
The Transcendence of the Ego, 336;
and "us–object," 339–340;
and *verum–factum* principle, 341, 356;
and Western Marxist tradition, 350,
    355, 358–359;
and "we–subject," 260, 353;
What is Literature?, 291, 348;
The Words, 342–343
Sassoon, Anne S., 152n
Saussure, Ferdinand de, 282, 367n,
    378–380, 389, 440, 495, 523
Sayre, Robert, 325n
Schacht, Richard, 43n, 59n, 351n
Schachtel, Ernst, 232–233n
Scheler, Max, 256, 334
Schelling, Friedrich, 53n, 55, 185, 250,
    457, 465, 502
Schiller, Friedrich, 39, 49–54, 56, 87n,
    95–96, 157, 177, 186n, 223, 235,
    300–301, 432–433n;
aestheticization of totality, 49–53, 87n
Schlegel, Friedrich, 51, 230, 300
Schleiermacher, Friedrich, 249, 256
Schmid, Michael, 489n
Schmidt, Alfred, 3, 116n, 185n, 211n,
    293n, 297n, 387n, 458
Schmidt, Burghart, 175n, 186n
Schmidt, Conrad, 452
Schmidt, James, 19, 78n, 81n, 88, 206n,
    333n, 462n, 500n
Schmitt, Carl, 471n
Schmitt, Hans–Jürgen, 187n, 288n
Schmoller, Gustav, 75–76
Schoenberg, Arnold, 252–255, 258, 272,
    289
Scholasticism, 26
Scholem, Gershom, 177, 246–247n, 288n
Schoolman, Morton, 19, 220n
Schopenhauer, Arthur, 10, 179–180, 212,
    239
Schroyer, Trent, 19, 224n, 468n
Schucht, Tatiana, 151n
Schumpeter, Joseph, 469
Schuster, Sir Ernest, 133
Schutz, Alfred, 472, 476–477, 504
Schweitzer, Charles, 342
Science, 117, 230, 256, 457, 460–461
Scientific Method, 27, 66, 75, 117, 148,
    398, 431, 435, 437, 441
Screen, 387, 416n
Searle, John, 495
Second International, 2, 6–8, 10, 29n,
    36–37, 60, 66–67, 80, 82, 102, 110,
    129, 138–139, 154, 179, 195n, 197,
    276, 388, 390, 398, 418, 427, 430,
    446, 502;

conception of dialectic and totality, 66.
    See also Bernstein, Eduard; Dialectical
    materialism; Engels; Kautsky;
    Reflection theory
Second Nature, 43, 78, 95, 109–111,
    116, 228, 255, 261, 267, 269, 414n,
    485. *See also* Reification
Second Reich, 73
Seghers, Anna, 303
Seidler, Irma, 86, 89n
Semiotics, 328, 515. *See also* Language
Sensat, Julius, 468n
Serrati, Giacinto Menotti, 164
Sexuality, 220, 223, 232
Shaftesbury, Anthony Ashley, third Earl
    of, 27
Shakespeare, William, 53n, 301
Shapiro, Jeremy J., 19, 236n, 492n, 501n
Shearer, Derek, 536n
Sher, Gerson S., 5n, 304n, 333n
Sheridan, Alan, 409, 518n
Shipway, David, 475n
Shklar, Judith N., 42n, 57n
Shmueli, Efraim, 333n
Short, Roger, 285n
Shue, Henry G., 84n
Siebert, Rudolf, 214n
Silone, Ignazio, 423
Silverman, David, 405n
Silverman, Hugh J., 379n, 383n
Simmel, Georg, 77–80, 82, 86, 107–110,
    179, 244–245
Simonds, A. P., 206n, 208n
Singer, Brian, 387n
Situationists, 292, 298n
Sixel, Friedrich W., 484n
Skuhra, Anselm, 197n
Slater, Phil, 196n, 205n, 213n
Slavery, 28, 37
Smart, D. A., 7n
Smith, Brian, 225, 236
Smith, Colin, 367n, 369n
Smith, Gary, 246
Smith, Neil, 400n
Smuts, Jan C., 24
Social Action Theory, 75n
Social contract, 30, 35, 37, 39–43, 58, 64,
    398, 406, 437, 527
Social Darwinism, 28, 118
Social Democratic Party of Germany
    (SPD), 4, 7, 66–67, 119, 129–130,
    133n, 137, 143, 179
"Social Fascism," 119, 143, 164
Socialism, 27, 37, 99, 134–135, 141, 150,
    154, 165–167, 170–171, 173–174,
    176, 190, 205, 222, 447, 455,
    530–535;
scientific versus utopian, 173

Socialisme ou Barbarie, 383, 515, 534
Socialist Realism, 288, 294n
Società, 425, 428–429, 445
Sociology, 27, 33n, 69–70, 75–77, 115, 117, 124, 461
Socrates, 92
Soffer, Reba N., 69n
Sohn–Rethel, Alfred, 3, 412n
Solidarism, 279, 281
Solidarity, 534
Soll, Ivan, 56n
Sollers, Philippe, 328, 515
Söllner, Alfons, 200n–201n
Solmi, Renato, 425n
Solzhenitsyn, Alexander, 532
Sombart, Werner, 199
Sophocles, 92
Sorbonne, 306
Sorel, Georges, 33, 71, 99, 104, 133n, 154, 160, 166, 278, 284, 286
Soupault, Philippe, 285
"Southern Question" (Italy), 154n
Southwest German School (Neo-Kantianism), 77, 398
Spaier, Albert, 334
Spann, Othmar, 14, 372n
Spaventa, Bertrando, 72–73, 150, 164, 424
Spengler, Tilman, 223n
Spiegelberg, Herbert, 333n, 362n–363n, 366n
Spinella, Mario, 130n, 425
Spinoza, Baruch, 10, 28–30, 34, 38–39, 45, 55–56, 60, 309, 316, 328, 394n, 399–401, 407, 409, 416, 419–420, 431, 453–454, 460;
belief that "all determination is negation," 29;
on nature, 29;
pantheism, 45, 309;
on totality, 28–30. *See also individual authors*
Spirito, Ugo, 426n
Spivak, Gayatri Chakravorty, 509n
Spriano, Paolo, 151n, 449
Spurling, Laurie, 361n, 363n, 379n
Stalin, Joseph, 119–120, 163, 318, 354, 392, 409, 423, 442, 445, 535
Stalinism, 4, 119–120, 130–131n, 134n, 143, 151, 172n, 184, 193–194, 294, 297, 314, 347, 354, 372, 388, 391, 394, 405, 409, 412, 417n–418n, 421, 424, 426, 429, 438, 445, 447, 464
Stanley, John L., 71n
Stark, Werner, 27n
State, 25–26, 28, 38, 47, 58, 63–64, 66–67, 73–74, 80, 120, 131, 142, 163, 301, 447;

organic theory of, 25–27
State socialism, 23
Steiner, George, 17, 85n, 177n, 247n, 332, 508n
Sten, Jan, 129n
Stendhal (Henri Beyle), 255
Stern, Fritz, 73
Stirner, Max, 74, 326
Storm, Theodor, 89–90
Stravinsky, Igor, 252, 254
Structuralism, 6, 14, 70, 282–283, 290, 299, 319–321, 328, 378–379, 382, 384–386, 389, 391, 396, 408–409, 417, 440, 452, 461, 484, 512, 518, 522n–523, 536n.
See also Althusser; Genetic Structuralism; Goldmann; Lévi–Strauss; Marxism, Structuralist; Piaget
Struve, Walter, 207n
Sturm und Drang, 39, 41
Sturrock, John, 386n, 511n
Subjectivity, 14, 66–67, 71, 94, 106–111, 113–115, 125, 127, 133, 399.
See also individual authors
Surrealism, 278–279, 283–294, 298–299, 348, 368, 530;
and language, 290–291;
and totality, 283–288, 292
Swart, Koenraad W., 344n
Swingewood, Alan, 124n, 313n
Syndicalism, 69
Systems Theory, 14, 16, 124, 411, 461, 468, 483–487, 513
Szabó, Ervin, 5, 71, 99
Szelényi, Ivan, 13, 168n, 530–531, 533–534

Taine, Hyppolite, 70, 286, 322–323
Talmon, J. L., 42n
Tar, Judith Marcus, 83n, 98n
Tar, Zoltan, 193n, 196n, 210
Tasca, Angelo, 165, 171, 423
Tat, Die, 133
Taylor, Charles, 41n, 53n, 56n–57n, 456n
Taylor, Frederick Winslow, 170
Taylorization, 166, 170
techne, 411, 467, 502
Technology, 35, 99, 123, 187, 333, 347, 455
Telos, 19, 333n
Tel Quel, 328, 515–516
Temps Modernes, Les, 346, 365, 368, 383
Terracini, Umberto, 171
Terror. *See* Merleau–Ponty; Sartre
The Terror (French Revolution), 58
Terry, Emmanuel, 387

Tertulian, Nicolas, 305n
Tran Duc Thao, 333n
Theoretical Practice, 387
Therborn, Göran, 10n, 270n, 281n, 394n,
    401, 405n, 439n, 464n, 477n, 480n,
    525n
Third International, 2, 129–130, 133,
    197, 424
Third Reich, 52, 73, 465
Third Republic, 279, 281–283, 343
Third World, 6, 13
Thomas, Paul, 19
Thompson, E. P., 4n, 387n–388n,
    391n–392, 411n
Thompson, John B., 468n
Thorez, Maurice, 391, 394n
Tiersky, Ronald, 277n
Tilliette, Xavier, 361n
Time, 50, 54, 56, 94, 96n, 105–106, 186,
    189–191, 288, 409, 414–415.
    See also Memory
Timpanaro, Sebastiano, 397n, 412n,
    419n, 426, 449–450, 453n, 459n
Tito, Marshall Josip Broz, 392
Togliatti, Palmiro, 150, 152, 162, 164,
    171, 423–424, 444, 446–447
Tökés, Rudolf L., 100n, 119n
Tolstoy, Leo, 91, 96–97
Tönnies, Ferdinand, 76, 98
Torode, Brian, 405n
Totalitarianism, 21, 42, 153, 169, 192,
    219, 221, 261, 297, 332, 348, 367,
    370, 383, 426, 439, 463, 527, 533
Totality: aestheticization of, 48–53, 73,
    220, 223, 416, 506;
    as antidote to economic determinism,
        201, 295, 367, 390;
    and the work of art, 15;
    and conception of culture, 21;
    compared with Gestalt, 22n;
    holistic aspects of late 19th century
        non–Marxist social thought, 68–80;
    intellectuals and origins of concept,
        10–14, 99, 207, 312n, 492,
        528–532, 537;
    Marxist holism in Second International,
        66–67;
    Marxist versus non–Marxist versions of
        holism, 24–25, 27–28, 175;
    meta–totality, 59, 317;
    psychological origins of concept,
        21–22;
    identified with totalitarianism, 21, 153,
        221, 261, 266, 292, 297, 348–349,
        354, 370–371, 383, 405, 450, 527,
        533;
    as unifying concern of Western
        Marxism, 14–15, 23–24, 84, 109.
    See also individual authors

—Concrete Totality, 58, 95, 104–105,
    112, 121, 295, 400. *See also* Hegel;
    Lukács
—Decentered (non-genetic) Totality,
    108n–109n, 122, 146, 161–163,
    171, 183, 188, 283, 406, 442, 486,
    507, 522.
    See also Althusser; Colletti; Della Volpe
—Descriptive Totality, 23–24
—Detotalization, 95, 162, 220, 321, 352,
    355–360. *See also* Sartre
—Expressive (genetic) Totality, 38–39,
    41, 43, 47, 59–60, 107n, 114, 118,
    120, 122, 127, 139–140, 143, 147,
    149, 158–159, 163, 183, 190, 195,
    214, 222, 251, 259, 274, 295, 310,
    352–353, 374, 410, 413–414, 416,
    419, 435–436, 439, 458, 470–471,
    473, 483, 487, 507, 513, 522, 532;
    Hegel and origins of, 50–60;
    and identity theory, 139, 211–212, 222,
        251, 310, 352, 458, 471, 473, 483;
    Kant and origins of, 47;
    and longitudinal totality, 47, 59,
        64–65, 121–122, 138–139, 183,
        353, 374–375, 409, 470–471, 487,
        507;
    Lukács' move away from, 120, 122,
        127;
    Rousseau and origins of, 41, 43;
    as solution to antinomies of bourgeois
        culture, 114, 118, 183, 214
—Extensive Totality, 92, 95, 303n
—Individual (personal) Totality, 40–41,
    59–60, 87, 106
—Intensive Totality, 92, 95, 189, 303n
—Latitudinal Totality, 32, 59, 65, 145,
    149, 183, 187, 222, 266, 483, 486,
    494, 498, 502, 507, 521
—Longitudinal Totality (History), 26, 31,
    47, 59, 64–66, 70, 105, 121,
    138–139, 145, 156, 182–183, 189,
    216–217, 222, 262–263, 265–266,
    281, 288, 317, 353, 369, 374, 409,
    436, 486, 494, 507, 521, 533. *See
    also* History, Memory *under
    individual authors*
—Natural Totality, 27–28, 65, 163. *See
    also* Organicism
—Normative Totality, 23, 25, 28, 42–43,
    45–48, 63, 65, 70, 87, 91, 93–94,
    97, 105, 111, 115, 117, 142, 157,
    161, 171, 173, 182, 195, 201, 208,
    216–219, 239, 242, 255, 259, 263,
    266, 271, 283, 296, 298, 301, 308,
    315, 351, 356, 369, 375, 383, 411,
    437–438, 461, 467, 483, 494,
    498–499, 504, 506–507, 511,
    533–534

—Personal Totality, 59–60
—Totalization, 15, 45, 48, 63, 125, 159,
    162, 168–169, 228, 239, 250, 253,
    255, 261, 271, 287, 332, 340–341,
    344, 406, 413;
  objective versus subjective, 125;
  versus totalities, 48.
  See also Economy; Memory;
  Meta-subject; Proletariat
Trade union consciousness, 11, 112–113,
    142
Trauerspiel, 249–250
Trendelenburg, F. A., 449, 460
Trentin, Bruno, 8, 307
Trilling, Lionel, 40n
Troeltsch, Ernst, 74
Tronti, Mario, 131n, 426
Trotsky, Leon, 4, 33, 113, 143, 163, 285,
    425
Trotskyism, 4, 277n, 291, 383, 425–426
Trozzi, Mario, 154n
Tucker, Robert C., 301n
Turgot, Anne Robert Jacques, 31
Turkle, Sherry, 401n, 408n
Tzara, Tristan, 293

Ulbricht, Walter, 176, 193, 464
Ulmen, G. L., 116n, 197n
Unger, Roberto Mangabeira, 21
Unitá, L', 164
Universal Subject. See Meta-subject;
  Proletariat
Unseld, Siegfried, 175
Urry, John, 394n

Vacatello, Mario, 425
Vacca, Giuseppe, 131, 425–426n, 443
Vailati, Giovanni, 160
Vajda, Mihály, 5n, 88n, 107n, 115, 132,
    141, 304, 533–534
Valéry, Paul, 383n
Valla, Lorenzo, 160
van Breda, H. L., 363n
van Dooren, W., 54n
Vanguard party, 11, 113, 118, 120, 152,
    168, 172, 209, 284, 412, 493, 530
van Reijen, Willem, 465n–466n, 477n,
    498n, 502n
Vasoli, Cesare, 424n
Vera, Augusto, 72, 164, 293
Verene, Donald Philip, 32n, 58n
Verene, Molly Black, 32n
Verret, Michel, 395n–396n, 416n
Verstraeten, Pierre, 348n
Verum–factum principle. See Vico
Vichy, 306
Vico, Giambattista, 32–39, 43, 45, 57,

60, 72, 107–108, 113, 116, 122,
    160, 213, 257–259, 341, 356, 399,
    404, 414, 435, 469–470, 483;
  and Hegel, 54, 57, 160;
  on history, 34–37;
  influence on Marx, 33–36;
  verum–factum principle, 34–35, 54,
    60, 107–108, 116, 122, 213,
    257–259, 341, 356, 399–400, 414,
    435, 469–470, 483
Vienna Circle, 256
Vigorelli, Amedeo, 443n–444n, 451n
Vilar, Pierre, 410n
Vishinsky, A. Y., 438
Vitalism, 75
Vittorini, Elio, 424
Vogt, Karl, 73
Völkisch movement, 52–53, 73, 80, 212,
    254
Voltaire (François-Marie Arouet), 32
"Voluntarism," 2, 152, 154
Vörlander, Karl, 452

Wade, Ira O., 29n
Wagner, Adolph, 75–76
Wagner, Richard, 253
Wahl, Jean, 335, 368
Waldberg, Patrick, 284n
Wallerstein, Emmanuel, 513
Walzel, Oskar, 51n
War, 58, 133
Weber, Alfred, 99
Weber, Marianne, 83
Weber, Max, 75, 78, 82, 109–110, 112,
    141, 179–180, 206, 366, 375, 471n,
    483, 490, 503–506, 526n
Weber, Samuel, 20n
Weber, Shierry, 19
Weil, Felix, 149n, 196–199
Weimann, Robert, 322n
Weimar Republic, 119n, 203, 207, 244,
    255, 466
Weingartner, Rudolph H., 77n–78n
Weitling, William, 11
Wellmer, Albrecht, 475n, 479n
Wertheimer, Max, 75, 204
Wessell, Leonard P., 61n
White, Hayden, 18, 23, 34, 518
Whitebrook, Joel, 19, 502n, 568n
Whitehead, A. N., 24, 69, 376
Wilcocks, Robert, 336n
Wilden, Anthony, 385n
Wilkinson, David, 284n
Wilkinson, James D., 364n
Will, 29, 39, 46, 110, 133, 218, 412
Willey, Thomas E., 76n, 79n
Williams, Gwyn A., 152n

Williams, Raymond, 4n, 9, 69, 167, 322n, 329
Wilson, Edmund, 33
Winckelman, J. J., 48–49, 52, 57, 93
Windelband, Wilhelm, 77, 79
Winfield, Richard, 475n
Winkler, Heinrich August, 323
Witte, Bernd, 247n
Wittfogel, Karl August, 76, 116, 123, 196–197n
Wittgenstein, Ludwig, 4, 161, 471n, 481, 495
Wohl, Robert, 19, 79n, 277n
Wohlfart, Irving, 224n, 526n
Wolfe, Bertram D., 153n
Wolff, Richard D., 1n, 4n
Wolin, Richard, 19, 246n–247n, 260n, 272n–273n, 287n, 327n
Wordsworth, William, 15n, 231
"Workerism," 11, 126, 164, 166, 423
Workers' Councils, 7, 113, 118, 120–121, 130–131n, 134, 168, 170n–173, 218, 446
World War I, 6–8, 67, 83, 220, 323, 387, 425
World War II, 6, 176, 198, 215, 276, 304, 323, 364–365, 367, 381, 423, 464
Wright, Eric Olin, 19

Wundt, Wilhelm, 108
Wyschograd, Michael, 225n

Xenos, Nick, 135n, 139n

Yanarella, Ernest J., 489n
Yates, Frances A., 225n

Zehm, Günther, 193
Zehrer, Hans, 207n
Zeitgeist, 32
Zeitschrift für Sozialforschung, 200, 203–204, 208, 210–212, 216, 253n–254, 465
Zeldin, Theodore, 279n, 327n
Zeller, Eduard, 76
Zhdanov, Andrei, 294n, 401, 416, 424, 431
Zima, Pierre V., 304n, 329
Zimmerman, Marc, 325n
Zinoviev, Grigory, 129, 145n, 165n
Zipes, Jack, 19
Zitta, Victor, 82n
Zola, Emile, 302, 442
Zuidervaart, Lambert, 272n
Zukin, Sharon, 19

Designer: In-house
Compositor: Innovative Media
Printer: Vail-Ballou Press
Binder: Vail-Ballou Press
Text: 10/13 Sabon
Display: Sabon &
Garamond Old Style